Liberal Parties in Western Europe

This book is a comparative study of liberal parties in Western Europe, examining the role and development of liberal parties within individual countries, the internal party structure and organisation, electoral audiences, coalitions and government participation, party programmes and strategies, and international and cross-national links. It not only tries to fill a gap in the study of political parties cross-nationally, but also to highlight the important role liberal parties play in the political systems of Western Europe. Whilst it is undeniable that most liberal parties in Western Europe are small and that they are as a result not able to dominate any government in which they participate, they have sometimes been in a position to exert influence which bears little relation either to their voting base within the electorate as a whole or their parliamentary strength. This is most obviously true in the case of the Free Democrats (FDP) in the Federal Republic of Germany, with the party long being able to play a crucial 'pivotal' role.

Emil J. Kirchner is a Lecturer in the Department of Government, University of Essex.

Liberal Parties in Western Europe

Edited by
Emil J. Kirchner

The right of the University of Cambridge to print and sell all manner of books was granted by Henry VIII in 1534. The University has printed and published continuously since 1584.

CAMBRIDGE UNIVERSITY PRESS
Cambridge
New York New Rochelle Melbourne Sydney

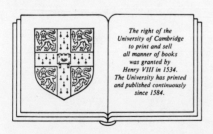

Published by the Press Syndicate of the University of Cambridge
The Pitt Building, Trumpington Street, Cambridge CB2 1RP
32 East 57th Street, New York, NY 10022, USA
10 Stamford Road, Oakleigh, Melbourne 3166, Australia

First published 1988

Printed in Great Britain at The Bath Press, Avon

British Library cataloguing in publication data

Kirchner, Emil Joseph
Liberal parties in Western Europe.
1. Western Europe. Liberal parties, to
1988.
I. Title
324.24'06'09

Library of Congress cataloguing in publication data

Liberal parties in Western Europe / edited by Emil J. Kirchner.
Includes index
ISBN 0-521-32394-0
1. Political parties – Europe. 2. Liberalism – Europe.
I. Kirchner, Emil Joseph.
JN94.A979L53 1988
324.24'06 – dc 19 87-38183

ISBN 0 521 32394 0

VN

Contents

Tables

Diagrams

Maps

Notes on the contributors

David Arter is a Senior Lecturer in European Politics at Leeds Polytechnic. He is author of *The Emergence of a Green Movement in Finnish Politics* (1977).

David Broughton is completing his doctorate at Essex University and at the time of writing was a Research Assistant in the Department of Politics, University of Glasgow. His main research interests are in electoral behaviour, on which he has written a number of articles.

John Curtice is a Lecturer in Politics at the University of Liverpool. He is co-author (with A. Heath and R. Jowell) of *How Britain Votes* and has written widely on the Liberal Party and electoral politics in Britain.

Hans Daalder is a Professor of Political Science at the University of Leiden. He is co-author of *Western European Party Systems: Continuity and Change* (1983) and has published widely on Dutch and comparative politics.

John Frears is a Senior Lecturer in European Studies at Loughborough University. He is author of *France in the Giscard Presidency* (1981) and has published many articles on French politics.

Derek Hearl is a Research Assistant in the Department of Government at Essex University. He is co-author of *Idealogy, Strategy and Party Movement: A Comparative Analysis of Election Programmes in Nineteen Democracies* (1986).

Rudolf Hrbek is a Professor of Political Science at the University of Tübingen. He is co-author of *The European Parliament on the Eve of the Second Direct Election* (1984) of *Community Bureaucracy at the Crossroads* (1983), and of many articles on political parties and interest groups.

Peter Humphreys is a Lecturer in the Department of Government at the University of Manchester.

Emil Kirchner is a Lecturer in the Department of Government at the

University of Essex. He is author of *The European Parliament: Performance and Prospects* (1984) and co-author of *The Role of Interest Groups in the European Community* (1981).

Ruud Koole is Director of the Documentation Centre of the Dutch political parties Nederlandse Politieke at the University of Groningen and a part-time member of the Department of Political Science at the University of Leiden.

Jørn Leiphart works for the Norwegian Social Science Data Services and has published articles on political parties and electoral behaviour.

Ulf Lindström holds a research position with the University of Umeå, Sweden. He is author of *Fascism in Scandinavia 1920–1940* and has written several articles on the Scandinavian party systems.

Richard Luther is a Lecturer in Politics at Lancashire Polytechnic and his main area of research is Austrian politics.

Geoffrey Pridham is a Reader in European Politics at the University of Bristol. He is editor of *Coalition Behaviour in Theory and Practice: an inductive model for Western Europe* (1986) and of *The New Mediterreanean Democracies: regime transition in Spain, Greece and Portugal* (1984).

Christopher Rudd is a Lecturer in the Department of Political Studies at the University of Otago, New Zealand. He has published various articles on Belgian electoral politics.

Daniel Seiler is a Professor in the Faculty of Social and Politcal Sciences at the University of Lausanne, Switzerland. He is author of *Compôtement Politique Comparé* (1985) and of *Les Partis Politiques: Analyse Comparative* (1986), and has published widely on Belgian and Swiss politics.

Gordon Smith is a Professor in the Department of Government at the London School of Economics. He is author of *Politics in Western Europe* (1984) and co-editor of *Party Government and Political Culture in Western Germany* (1982), and has published numerous articles on German politics and West European party systems.

Michael Steed is a Senior Lecturer in the Department of Government at the University of Manchester. He is author of 'France' in S. Henig (ed.), *Political Parties in the European Community* (1979), the Foreword to A. Cyr *Liberal Party Politics in Britain* (1977), 'The Liberal Party' in H. Drucker (ed.), *Multi-Party Britain* (1979), 'The Liberal Parties of France, Germany, Italy and the U.K.' in R. Morgan and M. Silvestri (eds.), *Moderates and Conservatives in Europe* (1981) and the pamphlet 'Who's a Liberal in Europe?' (1975).

Lars Svåsand is a Professor at the Institute of Comparative Politics, University of Bergen, Norway. He is author of *Politiske Partier* (1985) and has written many articles on political parties.

Alastair Thomas is Head of Division of Political Science at Lancashire Polytechnic. He is co-author of *Social Democratic Parties of Western Europe* (1977) and of *The Consensual Democracies? The Government and Politics of the Scandinavian States* (1982).

Ingemar Wörlund is working on a doctoral dissertation at the Department of Political Science, University of Umeå, Sweden. His main fields are party organisation and political geography.

Preface

The purpose of this book is to provide a comparative analysis of liberal parties in Western Europe. It not only tries to fill a gap in the study of political parties cross-nationally, but also to highlight the important role liberal parties play in the political systems, especially in governing coalitions of Western Europe. Whilst many liberal parties are small, they have sometimes been in positions where they can exert an influence which bears little relation either to their voting base within the electorate as a whole, or their parliamentary strength. Why this is so and whether liberal parties will retain this influence in the light of changes in voting patterns and the party system, are important questions for political scientists to which this book seeks to provide answers.

The stimulus to write this book came from work David Broughton and I undertook on the German Liberal Party (FDP) in 1983. I was fortunate to attract three scholars who, under the leadership of Michael Steed, had met in December 1981 in Marburg, West Germany, as part of a large group, for the purpose of compiling a book on liberal parties. In a meeting at Essex University, in March 1985, fourteen of the twenty-one contributors to the book met to finalise a common framework for research of the thirteen country studies. The country chapters are designed to produce descriptive analyses of liberal parties in national settings: past-, present- and future-oriented. Though the country analyses give the appearance of case studies, adherence to the common framework allows for comparability on, for example, liberal parties' policies and strategies, complemented by a number of specifically written comparative chapters. Most of the individual manuscripts were written and finalised throughout 1986.

I would like to thank the authors of the individual chapters for their forebearance. Hopefully, my 'nomadic' lifestyle (from Essex, England to Florence, Italy and on to Connecticut, USA) did not inflict too many problems on contributors.

I am indebted to David Broughton, who helped in getting the project off the ground and who assisted in editorial activities. A word of thanks also to Alfonso Nunez for his help on the data collection of electoral and ministerial statistics and to Pamela Keech for her fast and efficient typing.

Last but not least, I would like to thank the Friedrich Naumann Foundation, especially Dr Gerhard Raichle, for their generosity in sponsoring the meeting in March 1985 and the Commission of the European Communities for financial support.

1

Introduction

Emil J. Kirchner

The study of political parties has long attracted the attention of social scientists with widely divergent interests and aims. Whether they have concentrated, for example, upon questions of internal party structure and organisation, the tasks of electoral mobilisation and interest aggregation or the overall effects of system change, it has invariably been assumed that parties have played and will continue to play indispensable roles in the political systems of Western democracies. This remains the case despite recent claims that parties are in 'decline' as a result of increasing bureaucratisation of the political process and the development of the 'corporate' state, doubts about the existence of genuine policy differences between parties and the increase in electoral volatility amongst the mass public.

Yet, whilst acknowledging the prominent place political parties have generally held in academic studies, liberal parties have been largely neglected as objects of such studies. Though liberal parties of four Western European countries are dealt with in the book by Morgan and Silvestri (1982), their analysis also contains conservative parties and they do not employ a systematic framework for comparing either type of liberal party. Similarly, though describing general features of liberal parties in terms of ideology, history and organisational features, the books by Stammen (1978) and von Beyme (1985) do not attempt a systematic comparison between liberal parties. There are no apparent reasons for the neglect of liberal party analysis although there are frequent references to liberal parties as 'minor' parties,[1] presumably purely on the basis of size rather than influence or attraction over time. This book seeks to fill this long-standing gap by providing an analysis of the significance of liberal parties in the context of developments and changes within each national party system as well as internal and structural alterations within the parties themselves.

Concentrating upon liberal parties in Western Europe is also valuable for a greater understanding of the factors affecting party continuity and discontinuity. Liberal parties were among the first political parties to form, and their long-serving and influential records, as participants in parliaments and governments, raise important questions not only about their capabilities and impact but also about the contextual factors (party systems, electoral systems and political environment) in which they operate. Contextual factors, for example, enable some liberal parties to perform 'pivotal' or crucial roles in coalition formation. An analysis of these roles might well, therefore, throw some light on coalition theory and coalition behaviour as well as on the process of party organisational change and innovation. The latter relates to the saliency of liberal party policy, in both the long and short term, and how accommodating liberal parties are in policy terms *vis-à-vis* their coalition partners. How relevant is the belief that many liberal parties fulfil a functional role by exercising a 'modernising' or 'correcting' policy influence on their coalition partners and thereby contribute to the stability and continuity of different political systems?

Clearly, specific aspects of policy content and partisan accommodation involve more detailed reference to the content of liberalism and liberal ideology, in particular, how they were originally conceived and developed and the ways in which they have changed over time.

WHAT IS LIBERALISM?

Whilst lengthy historical surveys of liberal traditions exist (Laski (1936), de Ruggiero (1927), Manning (1976), Salvadori (1977)), no clear definition has emerged as to what liberalism is or what liberal ideology consists of. This is not a critical observation on the perceptive and penetrating accounts the above scholars have provided on the subject but it merely underlines that the absence of a widely accepted working definition is the result of the different national traditions under which liberalism has developed. These different traditions manifest themselves in the form of different political parties, each bearing the name of liberalism or related labels with more than one such party in a number of countries. The two roads of Italian liberalism as represented by the Republican Party (PRI) and the Liberal Party (PLI), are a case in point.

Though the origins of liberalism date back to the seventeenth century and are an important component of the 'Enlightenment' period in Europe, the term 'liberalism' first came into use in English in 1815 and it only acquired real significance through the attitude taken by different political groupings to the French Revolution (von Beyme (1985) 31–2). In challenging both absolutism and obscurantism, political liberalism, according to Salvadori (1977) focused on four main themes: religious tolerance, free inquiry, self-government, and the market economy. Liberal values and ideas relate to conscience, justice in politics, the rights of racial and religious minorities, civil liberties, and the right of the ordinary individual to be effectively consulted in decisions which directly affect him (Alan Bullock (1977) 347).[2]

Liberalism, as Bogdanor argues, is an essentially political philosophy, not a view about the structure of social and economic life, which is the concern of its ideological competitors. He states:

> The organisation of society and the economy is but a means to the enjoyment of liberal values; and so a liberal society is compatible, in principle, with a range of different economic and social systems. *(1983) 176–7*

Following Salvadori (1977) we can identify two historic roots/trees of liberalism in Western Europe: the English-speaking version and the continental (primarily French) version. The former was identified with an expansion of democratic values and constitutional forms, as well as with the notion of free trade and internationalism, whilst the latter was seen as rejecting economic as much as political and intellectual authoritarianism and it was often linked to the process of nation-building. However, liberalism's continental version, deeply divided as it was between moderates and progressives, was – finally – almost completely taken over by the moderate group. What were the principal disagreements between the two main groups which lay at the heart of this division?

Whilst both agreed on basic principles and values, they disagreed, as Salvadori (1977) 34 points out,

> on the range of institutions (moderates tending to elitism, and progressives being committed to the universalisation of fundamental institutions – suffrage for all, education for all, property in one form or another for all) and on policies, particularly those concerning the economy and international relations. Moderates and progressives usually cooperated when drafting constitutions. When the centrifugal pull was strong each wing went its own way, to merge again when threatened by powerful authoritarian enemies.

Moderates can mostly be identified with liberalism or liberal-conservatism, whereas progressivism appeared under the label of liberalism as well as under that of radicalism, republicanism and social democracy. However, rather than seeing these groups as mutually exclusive, there is considerable overlap between them. Radical parties emerged mostly in countries which had a republican tradition, a large Catholic population and in which the socialist movement developed later into a powerful political force (France and Italy). Radicalism, as von Beyme (1983) 43 argues, proved less of a threat to liberalism in those countries in northern Europe where competition came from radical peasants' movements, where small farmers were in opposition to the major landowners, who largely remained loyal to the conservatives.

The division between moderates and progressives has continued and it is often reflected in the two wings of modern liberal parties in Western Europe. Two examples are the German FDP with its 'national liberal' and 'social liberal' factions and Norway where the division is between 'conservative liberals' and 'moderately social democratic liberals'.

Moreover, whilst individual countries' political history and culture has contributed substantially to liberal parties developing often sharply differing attitudes, it can also be seen that liberalism, as conceived and developed in the nineteenth century, differs from its counterpart in the twentieth century. This difference had its roots in the creation of the Welfare State in the period immediately after the Second World War. As early as 1904 Hobhouse argued that

> the old liberalism has done its work. It had been all very well in its time, but political democracy and the rest are now well established facts. What is needed is to build a social democracy on the basis so prepared, and for that we need new formulae, new inspirations.[3]

It is therefore difficult, if not impossible, to arrive at a definition of liberalism which can be expected to have validity in several different countries at the same time. Given these difficulties concerning the establishment of exactly what a liberal party is in reasonably objective terms, how can a comparative analysis of liberal parties in Western Europe best be attempted?

THE FRAMEWORK OF ANALYSIS

Two main approaches to the analysis of political parties can be distinguished. First, a broadly based approach which examines the structures, functions and activities of parties and party systems which are then illustrated with specific examples from particular countries. Examples of this type of study are Duverger (1954) and Sartori (1976). Secondly, a cross-national descriptive approach, which considers parties on the basis of adherence to different ideological 'families'. Examples of this approach are Paterson and Thomas

(1977), Irving (1979), Layton-Henry (1982), McInnes (1975) and Middlemas (1980).

In making a choice between the two and in applying our decision, a number of different issues have first to be dealt with in a comparative analysis. First, whilst there are reasons to compare parties of the same ideological 'family' (enabling a clearer picture of similarities and differences to emerge), it must also be remembered that political parties affect and compete with each other, and this impact should not be neglected.

Secondly, the geographic scope of the analysis has to be determined. A concentration on Western Europe, which this study attempts, means the exclusion of parties bearing liberal labels in Australia, Canada and Japan, and we are thus denied interesting comparisons between different types of liberalism in a wider geographic context. On the other hand, by restricting the analysis to Western Europe we hope to produce more common themes amidst more comparable developments than would otherwise be the case.

Thirdly, within the chosen geographic region decisions have to be taken on the basis of certain criteria as to the inclusion or exclusion of different parties as candidates for analysis. For example, should the main emphasis be on the historic settings of liberal parties rather than looking at them as contemporary phenomena? If the first criterion is applied, it might lead to a voluminous account of many divergent historical specimens and would certainly involve difficulties in reaching a workable definition of liberalism over time. Consequently we decided to use a party's contemporary as opposed to its historic liberalism as the main criterion for selection. This is in line with Gordon Smith's distinction, made elsewhere in this book, between *de jure* liberalism which is composed of ideological, historical, organisational and electoral elements, and a *de facto* one, the nature of which has to be ascertained by looking at the parties involved and which can be described as 'hypothetical', 'synthetic', 'reconstructed', 'behavioural', or even 'potential' liberalism.

Thus, instead of beginning with so-called 'objective' criteria of liberalism, the parties were selected by each individual country contributor according to common guidelines and compared according to a common framework. 1. If parties call themselves liberal in their manifestos and propaganda and they present and invoke liberalism or liberal ideas and principles as key elements in their conception of their political roles. 2. Leading political commentators, journalists and national specialists would classify the parties in question as 'liberal'. 3. The parties are members of cross-national organisations or groups which regard themselves as liberal and which can carry a 'liberal' label without serious dispute. 4. After establishing significant elements of a basic liberal identity, the parties are clearly not members of any other ideological *famille spirituelle*.

Fourthly, we need to ask which components of liberal parties will be compared and how? In order to ensure comparability between chapters, six main themes, with a number of sub-categories, made up the framework of analysis. Accordingly, liberal parties will be analysed systematically on the basis of:

origin and historical development;
organisation and structure;
electoral performance and electoral base;
participation in government;
policies and programmes;
strategies (mostly in coalition terms).

These themes are not necessarily mutually exclusive and might overlap but it is analytically meaningful to separate them.

It is important to stress that whilst the selection of liberal parties is based on the contemporary European setting, the six proposed themes try to strike a balance between the past, present and future perspectives of liberal parties. This attempt will help to avoid the analysis becoming too 'time-bound' and restricted in its perspective.

A total of thirteen Western European countries were chosen for this analysis. These include all the Scandinavian countries, except Iceland, the Benelux countries, Austria, Germany, Switzerland, France, Italy and the United Kingdom. Ireland was omitted because it appeared that little, or not sufficient, evidence of an explicitly 'liberal' party existed. Similarly, the absence of a 'liberal' party in Greece (virtually since the late 1970s) and in Spain (in the post-Franco period) were reasons for exclusion. Finally, the arrival of a liberal party in Portugal by 1985 coincided with the conclusion of our research project and could therefore not be incorporated.

Furthermore, four general chapters are included in this book dealing with classifications of liberal parties in a comparative sense. These chapters attempt to classify different strands of liberalism, assess the extent to which liberal parties are similar or different in their party programmes, and examine the relevance and significance of existing liberal parties. The concluding chapter will attempt to draw together the common strands of the different national analyses.

In the following a brief outline of each of the six themes is given with reference to the guidelines and questions which country contributors used in their respective analyses.

THE DEVELOPMENT OF LIBERAL PARTIES

Although some of the liberal parties to be dealt with in this book are of more 'recent' origin, like D'66 in the Netherlands or the FPÖ in Austria, most of them have either long traditions or important historical antecedents. It is important, therefore, to examine liberal party development and to try to bring out similarities and differences between countries. Such an examination must include the development of liberal parties in the context of different party system evolution over time, especially with regard to relevant institutional or constitutional factors. A further concern relates to factors affecting continuity or leading to the fragmentation of liberal parties. This aspect is dealt with below.

Once initial goals such as party establishment, confronting conservative parties (or aristocratic/church powers) either from within or outside the country, and success in nation-building, had been achieved, the diversity and heterogeneity of interests of liberal parties surfaced and often led to splits and fragmentation. By representing broad coalitions on specific issues, essentially disparate elements rather than an ideology, liberal parties could not easily deal with the cleavages, which led to the formation of other parties capable of articulating more 'progressive' policies or the interests of more clearly defined groups, such as farmers in Scandinavia and industrial workers everywhere.

The division between 'moderates' and 'progressives' centred primarily on the degree and speed with which republican, parliamentary or democratic means should be introduced, although they also focused at times on issues such as free trade versus protectionism. These divisions were primarily the result of indigenous factors, emanating from within liberal parties themselves. Liberal parties, however, faced other important challenges which were exogenous (socio-structural and contextual factors) and it is the latter which had the greatest impact on the continuity of liberal parties. The exogenous factor became so important partly because of the neglect by liberal parties of changing with the times. Salvadori (1977) 135 refers to this neglect as 'the sin of pride' and goes on to argue that

> liberal institutional structures were undermined by four major forces born from the emancipation that liberal success had brought. They were represented by the dogmatic sectors of the intelligentsia, by capitalist

exploiters, by frenzied revolutionaries, by nationalists quickly sliding towards racism and imperialism.

Among the most prominent exogenous factors were the following:

a) The introduction of male universal suffrage and the formation of socialist or labour parties. This meant that liberal parties received a smaller percentage of votes than they had received in pre-1914 elections from larger electorates. However, the introduction of proportional representation can be seen as a positive factor for the continuation or limited success of liberal parties, as the absence of it, in the British case, so aptly demonstrates (Bogdanor (1983) 58).

b) The adoption by other parties of policy programmes similar to those of liberal parties. This made it more difficult for the latter to retain a distinct identity, with the middle-class support base of liberal parties being particularly affected by this development. In addition, the complexion of the middle class changed from a predominance of small- and medium-sized business owners and liberal professions to one in which white-collar workers and civil servants became significant elements. This had repercussions for the traditional base of liberal party support.

The decline of liberal parties is a disputed subject in many Western European countries. In some countries, like Finland and Norway, there appears to be a long-term and continuous decline. In other countries, like the United Kingdom, there has been a marked revival in the 1970s and 1980s after the drastic fall in voting strength experienced in the early part of this century. Whether liberal parties will survive and continue to be successful will depend on a number of different factors, relating to challenges posed by other parties, to coalition behaviour and strategies, and to the electorate and policy programmes. One potentially important factor will be party organisation and structure. It is the apparent general organisational 'weakness' of liberal parties which we will consider next.

PARTY ORGANISATION AND STRUCTURE

The organisational potential of liberal parties (membership, finance, interest-group support) can be regarded as low in comparison with other parties. Although they were among the first to emerge, liberal parties never built up the solid party organisations or membership support which is characteristic of their main competitors – the conservatives/Christian democrats and the socialist/labour parties. In some countries, liberal parties were aided in their formation and development by such groups as trade unions, freemasonry (Belgium) and equivalent national associations (Switzerland). These organisations served as an infrastructure to help establish a relatively effective system of communication and mobilisation. However, these parties had no tightly controlled structure, using instead contacts with some of the organisations mentioned to compensate for the lack of internal organisation.

Moreover, liberal parties formerly rallied voters around broad national interests that were not associated with particular groups. Indeed, their lack of identification with group interests were their strength. In most countries, therefore, liberal parties either neglected to develop supporting organisations among leading interest groups, as the other parties had done, or, once they tried to do so, lost out to their main competitors.

The following will be of particular interest in the country chapter analyses to follow. Have liberal parties retained a 'cadre' status or have they adopted the 'mass' party characteristic of their main competitors? What is the degree of decentralisation or power distribution within each liberal party? Is there 'elite'/leadership decision-making at the expense of widespread party consultation? What is the relationship between the national leadership and the parliamentary party of each and the rank and file? What is the nature of relations between major interest-group organisations and liberal parties, and to what extent can such groups be identified as active supporters of liberal parties? How are liberal parties financed? To what extent do they depend on public subsidies as a source of party income? Is their share of public subsidies higher than that of other parties?

What other means do liberal parties have to compensate for relatively low membership density and organisational capacity? Some liberal parties have been able to use their participation in government as compensating factors and have effectively developed much more along the lines of *Wählerpartei* (voters' party) than as a *Mitgliederpartei* (members' party). It is to the attraction of the liberal parties to the mass electorate that we turn next.

ELECTIONS AND ELECTORAL BASE

Before the First World War, liberal parties played a considerable role in parliaments and governments, usually alternating with conservatives for the main share of the spoils of offices. In several countries the fortunes of liberal parties changed, some with stark and even dishonourable results, in the period between the two World Wars. In the post-Second World War period the election results for liberal parties in Western Europe have been mixed. Some seem to be gathering strength, whilst others seem still beset by a chronic decline. As the case of the Swedish Liberal Party demonstrates, however, a party which experienced the greatest loss of votes between 1966 and 1982 had one of the greatest turn-arounds in electoral fortunes in 1985.

Elections and electoral performances inevitably raise the question as to who votes for liberal parties? Can such votes be classified according to commonly used social background variables such as class, religion, ethnicity and region? Support for liberal parties has often been associated with an electorate of either a middle-class origin or with an anti-clerical outlook. Individual country chapters will shed some more light on the 'middle-class' and religious factor as a basis for liberal party support and this point will be taken up once more in the concluding chapter of the book.

Additional questions to be tackled by country contributors will involve the following themes. How stable is support for liberal parties over time? Can a 'core' electoral base for liberal parties be identified? Evidence seems to suggest that most liberal parties are not able to rely on the strong loyalties and affective ties of their voters in terms of regular voting support. If that is so, such a situation might have negative implications for the future of liberal parties but equally it might be positively associated with being able to attract voters with a loosely held partisanship or with being more flexible in highlighting topical issues than competing parties.

It will also be interesting to note whether liberal support is widely spread throughout each country or whether it is regionally or locally concentrated. Is there a marked urban–rural distinction or a 'younger' rather than 'older' electorate supporting liberal parties?

Events within other parties and the electorate's perception of liberal parties are important determinants for liberal party support. This can also be said about prevailing electoral systems. In Germany, for example, the operation of an electoral system of 'personalised proportional representation' permits voters to engage in 'ticket splitting' from which the FDP seems to benefit substantially. Another factor of considerable importance in electoral terms is whether or not liberal parties hold government posts or possess experience in government.

GOVERNMENT PARTICIPATION

This section in each of the country chapters will be concerned with the extent to which liberal parties co-operate and form coalitions with other parties in each political system. On what basis do they act in this way? What is the relative importance of portfolios, policies and other kinds of benefits? How often have liberal parties participated in national governments and who have been their partners? To what extent do liberal parties stick with the same coalition partner and to what extent do they alternate partners? Are liberal parties essential to the formation of a coalition? How does coalition formation at local level compare with national level? The involvement of liberal parties in government goes back in many countries to the inception of parliamentary regimes in the nineteenth century and was a prominent feature in many Western European countries in the period between the two World Wars. This trend of regular participation continued in the post-Second World War period in countries like Belgium, Finland, France, Germany, Italy, Luxemburg and Switzerland. Whilst there are also a number of countries where this participation took place occasionally, it is only in Britain that the Liberal Party was kept out of office,[4] largely as a result of the prevailing electoral system.

It will be important to consider to what extent structural and contextual factors permit liberal parties to play such instrumental roles in coalition formation, in government participation and in holding key ministerial posts. The German FDP, for example, has been seen as benefiting from the regular failure of the other parties to win an overall majority. Similarly, in the Italian political context, the permanent exclusion of the PCI from government can be seen as enhancing the coalition roles of parties in the centre, such as the PRI and the PLI.

Government incumbency has provided some liberal parties, like the German FDP, with the opportunity to project themselves into the limelight to claim some of the credit for sustained economic success and affluence and to use the mass media to good effect in terms of stressing the achievements of the governments in which they have participated. Government participation has, however, also meant a certain trade-off between the specific and general policy content of liberal parties.

POLICY PROGRAMMES

The extent to which liberalism or liberal ideas and principles are significant in terms of the strategies developed by the liberal parties in each country is an important question in this section. Can a precise liberal ideology be derived from such principles and do they play key roles with regard to policies promoted by liberal parties and with which the various parties are identified? To what extent are the roles of the liberal parties within each party system derived from a clear 'ideological input' or are they essentially dependent on other factors like coalition policy agreements?

Difficulties arise in placing the policy content of liberal parties either in a two-dimensional (left to right) analysis, or in relation to the other parties in a given system. The positioning of liberal parties on the relevant dimensions is crucially dependent on the component elements making up each one as well as the time period under scrutiny and the saliency of each dimension at the time.

Recognising the elusive character of liberal parties in ideological and policy content, and the difficulty in placing liberal parties on a left–right continuum, Gordon Smith suggests two dimensions for evaluating contemporary liberal parties. These two dimensions are economic and social liberalism and they are contrasted with the degree to which the rights of individuals are stressed or the rights of the state to intervene in society are emphasised. In this way Smith develops four types of liberal parties in which the liberal-conservative and the liberal-radical are the dominant ones.[5] Furthermore, by stressing the ambivalence of liberal parties he offers a perspective for examining how liberal parties are, on occasion, able to switch between coalitions of quite different complexions. Liberal parties project a blurred image which makes it difficult to retain a stable electoral base but this image also provides flexibility in coalition formation and in capturing 'floating voters'. Derek Hearl, in his analysis of liberal party manifestos, sheds some more light on the way liberal parties present themselves to the public and their party activists.

Because of their size and inability to expand their appeal beyond a temporary attraction to 'floating' voters, liberal parties' influence can often be maximised with a much larger coalition partner. But on occasions, coalitions can also entail dangers for the survival of liberal parties in terms of becoming too identified with the loss of popularity experienced by the major coalition partner. It is the aspect of coalition strategy to which we will turn next.

STRATEGY

Among the points to be explored in this section will be: When are coalition partners chosen (before or after elections)? What flexibility do liberal parties have in changing coalition partners? Are liberal parties essential members of particular coalitions? Are there traditions of co-operation at national level which are opposed or contradicted at either regional or local level? What is the form and nature of the bargaining process between liberal parties and others? Are the electoral co-operative arrangements which are practised by the French liberal and centre parties (UDF) or by the British Liberal Party and the SDP between 1981 and 1982 models for similar arrangements in other countries?

Being small parties, the problems which liberal parties face are similar in many countries and made more acute by the need to defend small partisan bases and weak affective ties amongst the electorate as a whole. In this section it is therefore interesting to examine how liberal parties face up to new challenges or challengers in areas involving both 'old' and 'new' politics. For example, how do liberal parties respond to the challenge from ecological groups, the young, well-educated and urban voters? Liberal parties, like other centre parties, have been 'squeezed' by other parties. In the 1970s and 1980s it appeared that liberal parties became particularly vulnerable to the manoeuvres of other parties, encompassing in some instances, like Finland and Norway, questions of party survival, whilst in other instances, like Germany, affecting the 'pivotal' role in coalition formation, at least at state (*Land*) level.

On the other hand, there is much talk of electoral dealignment and realignment[6] with regard to party identity which seems to increase the pool of 'floating' voters or 'vote switchers' and thus might benefit the liberal parties with their centrist appeal. With such increasing electoral volatility, a substantial number of liberal party voters appear to use the party as a temporary stop on their way between other parties. The implications of this phenomenon might well reinforce ambivalent tendencies in liberal party policies and programmes, but it might also assure survival or at least limited success. We will return to this point in the concluding chapter of the book.

CONCLUSION

The foregoing discussion has tried to show the relevance and significance of liberal parties in the political systems of Western Europe and it has indicated the valuable contribution a comparison of liberal parties could make for a greater understanding of political parties, coalition theories and party system development. Besides seeking to fill a long-standing gap in the current literature on political parties, this book should also shed greater light on the role, development and activities of liberal parties than has been attempted before.

Questions raised in the six sections outlined might not find detailed answers in the country chapter contributions, but they will provide suggestions of the most important areas to be focused upon and, importantly, they will also help to ensure that a cross-national comparison can be made. In this way we hope to be able both to compare and to contrast the development of the liberal parties involved in sufficient detail to enable us to reach more general conclusions about their likely roles and impact in the future.

NOTES

I would like to acknowledge the collaboration of David Broughton in the research proposal of the project on *Liberal Parties in Western Europe* on which this Introduction is based.

1 See, for example, K. Strom and L. Svåsand, 'Political parties in decline: dilemmas and strategies', paper presented at the Fifth International Conference of Europeanists, Washington, DC, October 1985, p. 6.
2 Cited by Vernon Bogdanor, *Liberal Party Politics* (1983) 187.
3 Bogdanor, *Liberal Party Politics* (1983) 179.
4 The British Liberal Party was, of course, part of the Lib–Lab Pact between 1977 and 1978 without, however, holding any cabinet posts.
5 This classification corresponds roughly to the main types of liberal parties proposed by K. von Beyme as liberal-conservative and liberal-radical (1985) 45.
6 See, for example, R. Dalton, S. Flanagan and P. Beck (eds.), *Electoral Change in Advanced Industrial Democracies: Realignment or Dealignment?* (1984).

REFERENCES

Beyme, K.v. (1985) *Political Parties in Western Democracies* (Aldershot: Gower).
Bogdanor, V. (1983) *Liberal Party Politics* (Oxford: Oxford University Press).
Browne, E. and J. Dreijmanis (eds.) (1983) *Government Coalitions in Western Democracies* (London: Longman).
Daalder, H. and Peter Mair (eds.) (1983) *Western European Party Systems: Continuity and Changes* (London: Sage).
Dalton, R.J., S.C. Flanagan and P.A. Beck (eds.) (1984) *Electoral Change in Advanced Industrial Democracies* (Princeton: Princeton University Press).
Duverger, M. (1954) *Political Parties* (London: Methuen).
Epstein, L.D. (1967) *Political Parties in Western Democracies* (New York: Praeger).
Henig, S. (ed.) (1979) *Political Parties in the European Community* (London: Allen & Unwin).
Henig, S. and John Pinder (eds.) (1969) *European Political Parties* (London: PEP/Allen & Unwin).
Irving, R.E.M. (1979) *The Christian Democratic Parties of Western Europe* (London: Allen & Unwin).
Janda, K. (1980) *Political Parties: A Cross-National Survey* (New York: Free Press).
Laski, H. (1936) *The Rise of European Liberalism* (London: Allen & Unwin).
Lawson, K. (1982) *The Comparative Study of Political Parties* (New York: St Martin's Press).
Layton-Henry, Z. (1982) *Conservative Politics in Western Europe* (London: Macmillan).
Manning, D.J. (1976) *Liberalism* (London: J.M. Dent & Sons).

McInnes, N. (1975) *The Communist Parties of Western Europe* (Oxford: Oxford University Press).
Middlemas, K. (1980) *Power and the Party: Changing Faces of Communism in Western Europe* (London: André Deutsch).
Morgan, R. and S. Silvestri (eds.) (1982) *Moderates and Conservatives in Western Europe*, (London: Croom Helm).
Paterson, W. and A.H. Thomas (eds.) (1977) *Social Democratic Parties in Western Europe* (London: Croom Helm).
Raschke, J. (1977) *Organisierter Konflikt in westeuropäischen Parteien: Eine vergleichende Analyse parteiinterner Oppositionsgruppen* (Opladen: Westdeutscher Verlag).
Rose, R. (1980) *Do Parties Make a Difference?* (London: Macmillan, 2nd edn).
Ruggiero, G. de (1927) *The History of European Liberalism*, trans. R.C. Collingwood (London: Oxford University Press).
Salvadori, M. (1977) *The Liberal Heresy: Origins and Historical Development* (London: Macmillan).
Sartori, G. (1976) *Parties and Party Systems: A Framework for Analysis* (Cambridge: Cambridge University Press).
Stammen, T. (1978) *Political Parties in Europe* (London: John Martin Publishing Ltd).
Strom, K. and L. Svåsand (1985) 'Political parties in decline: dilemmas and strategies', paper presented at the Fifth International Conference of Europeanists, Washington DC, October 18–20, 1985.

2

Between left and right: the ambivalence of European liberalism

Gordon Smith

THE LEGACY OF HISTORICAL LIBERALISM

Political scientists have some difficulty in dealing with the nature of liberalism and the role played by liberal parties. The problems are not new. In *The Rise of European Liberalism*, Harold Laski drew attention to the latent conflict between two fundamental liberal principles:

> What, then, is the liberalism we have here to discuss? It is not easy to describe, much less to define, for it is hardly less a habit of mind than a body of doctrine. As the latter, no doubt, it is directly related to freedom; for it came as the foe of privilege conferred upon any class in the community by virtue of birth or creed. But the freedom it sought had no title to universality, since its practice was limited to men who had property to defend.[1]

It is not that freedom and property necessarily stand in conflict, but in the context of modern European political development, with the rise of mass democracy, the contradictions became evident, soon to be expressed as property versus freedom.

One consequence is that there is a streak of ambiguity running through European liberalism which is seen in the varied character of liberal parties: some are regarded as belonging to the left, some are more at home on the right, while others hover uneasily between the two. Other political traditions, it is true, also give rise to uncertainties, but not to the same extent. The major families – conservative, Christian democrats, social democrats, and communist – all have a greater ideological coherence. If there are doubts, they relate more to the status of individual parties rather than to the tradition itself; the parties within a family group have sufficient affinity so as to supply a secure point of reference. For liberal parties that security is absent.

In most party systems, liberal parties now occupy a minor place, and there is the temptation to treat liberalism as just of marginal significance, an interesting historical survival. But its lasting contribution in the making of modern Europe is not to be ignored: arguably, the West European democracies owe more to the liberal tradition than to any other. What is also evident is that despite its weaknesses liberalism has not entirely lost its relevance at the party level; liberal parties have not only shown a tenacious will to survive, they have also experienced a strong revival in several countries. That resurgence has to be explained.

Liberalism enjoyed its hey-day during the nineteenth century, and the strong influence of once-dominant liberal parties persisted for the first few decades of the twentieth century. Their successes were for the most part bound up with the interests of the rising bourgeoisie, the middle classes, who sought personal liberties and freedom for economic enterprise. Liberalism was in the vanguard of movements for constitutional reform and for the enlargement and the protection of civil liberties. As an expression of radical dissent, liberalism came into conflict with the authoritarian state and the elites who benefited from its power. Liberalism also came to be opposed to the interests and authority of the churches, especially where organised religion and the state acted in alliance against enlightened progress. Battles against the privileges and power of the church gave liberal parties an indelible anti-clerical colouring.

The extent of these conflicts varied from one country to another, so that individual liberal parties differed in their emphasis – economic freedom, constitutional reform, or the secularisation of the state – although the issues were also linked. An additional ingredient was supplied by the force of nationalism, with its effect varying according to the extent to which national aspirations still had to be satisfied. For those countries where the nation-building process was incomplete when the modern party system was still in its formative stage, liberalism became the natural mobilising force to forge the new nation state. That national identification did not, however, automatically reinforce the radical image of liberalism; on the contrary, the appeal of nationalism could just as easily work against other liberal ideals, and those tensions sometimes had the consequence of fragmenting a previously unified liberal party.

Whatever the strength of their particular appeals and despite their notable achievements, liberal parties subsequently went into a steep decline, a process of party decay that appeared irreversible. Although we can put forward a number of reasons for their failure in the twentieth century, it may nonetheless be puzzling that precisely liberalism should have been so adversely affected.

It is clear that once the primary demands for constitutional advance had been met, some of the impetus of radical liberalism waned. The same is true for national liberalism to the extent that the nation state had become a secure reality. Anti-clericalism also lost much of its drive once the churches had been forced to come to terms with the secular state. All those developments meant that the liberal parties had become identified with the liberal democracies which they had principally been instrumental in creating. In a sense, liberal parties had become superfluous: they were radical parties whose major aims had been realised; henceforth their task was more to conserve. Yet that function was better suited to conservatism which, in proving able to absorb fundamental constitutional and other changes without entirely sacrificing its traditional values, was more adept at maintaining a new *status quo*. Nor, except for the differences in the interests of particular economic sectors, did liberalism show any fundamental divergence from conservatism with regard to economic philosophy or the defence of the rights of property.

It was not only the satisfaction of its chief demands that blunted liberalism but also the changing social composition of European electorates. As long as voting rights were severely restricted, liberal parties had an important, sometimes dominant, voice in parliaments, but as the electorate was widened and universal adult suffrage became the norm, so they were found unable to win over the newly enfranchised social groups. That was scarcely surprising, since the new voters were largely those with little material stake in society, not the propertied or professional middle classes. The principal beneficiary was social democracy and its different brand of radicalism. Its new radicalism entailed an emphasis on the conflictual nature of class interests in society, and the increasing sense of class polarisation – heightened by the arrival of communist parties – had a further effect in leading many of those who had previously supported a liberal party to move to a party firmly of the right. The full arrival of class politics – that is, as the leading feature of European party systems – meant that liberalism, caught between left and right, had no special contribution to make. It was ironic that the radical demands of liberalism, once met, led to its seeming redundancy and eclipse.

A CHOICE OF PERSPECTIVES

If we are to evaluate the present-day fortunes of liberalism, the choice is between tracing its historical legacy and concentrating on its present-day features. Neither way by itself is likely to prove entirely satisfactory: much of historical liberalism has little relevance for the present time, and a purely contemporary focus on liberal parties would leave the discussion in a curious void.

Almost without exception, liberal parties of today can trace their antecedents well back into the nineteenth century. Liberal parties still look back to their roots and their original ideals; even though they have been prone to split on occasion and may have changed their titles, the party traditions themselves are largely unbroken. Causes for which a party stood long ago may have lost their salience, but the effects and traditions can persist indefinitely. One such lingering legacy is anti-clericalism. Direct confrontation with the churches is nowhere of importance, but conflict over particular issues of religious morality and teaching – such as abortion, divorce and church schools – can rekindle old passions, and liberal parties can be counted on to be in the forefront of any controversy. Such occasional reminders of past hostility also draw attention to the social bases of liberal support – a consistent skew towards those whose religious ties are minimal, a pattern contrasting with the kind of support received by a Christian democratic party. In a more attenuated form, the national emphasis of some liberal parties is still evident even though the time for a rampant nationalism has long since passed. Above all else, however, liberal parties maintain their connections with the two original tenets of liberal ideology, the two freedoms: economic freedom and the liberties of the individual.

On all these counts, historical liberalism is still relevant for its contemporary counterpart. But there are important differences. Not only have most of the old battles been won, there is a constant stream of new issues on which parties have to take a stand, and new social groups have to be attracted if voting support is to be assured. Those problems affect all parties, but the liberals have inevitably felt the strains more than most because the liberal creed, consistent in the nineteenth century, has since had to live with its central ambiguity exposed, the problem of reconciling the two freedoms. They themselves have continually to be reinterpreted as the context of economic activity and social life alters.

It may be that an overconcentration on the continuities of the liberal tradition is misplaced, and instead we should switch attention to the contemporary era entirely. Such a complete divorce, however, would be totally unrealistic, since a party's ideology, stemming from its tradition, is an essential yardstick for comparative evaluation. The only alternative would be to base judgements completely on the behaviour and policies of existing liberal parties: 'Liberalism is what liberal parties do.' The contrast between the two perspectives can easily be made too sharp, since certain basic themes have maintained their importance, but there are also significant differences, and they especially relate to the context in which liberal parties operate. That context is largely determined by the structure of the party system which sets the constraints and governs the competitive space of liberal parties operating from a minority position. In other words, 'behaviour' is a factor in its own right – and coalition behaviour is likely to be a leading indicator for a contemporary evaluation.

There is no pressing need to make a stark choice between a *de jure* liberalism on the one hand and a *de facto* kind on the other.[2] Indeed, any one-sided insistence is likely to be misleading. The former would require constant reference to a party's pedigree and to 'first principles', while the latter would just take into account the actions of a party over a relatively short period. Rather than seek to combine both approaches, in the first instance we can best take them separately. What will become apparent is that the ambivalence of European liberalism emerges as a common factor. Whether that is necessarily a handicap is quite another question.

LIBERALISM, THE ECONOMY AND THE STATE

At the heart of liberal ideology is the creed of individualism and, as a complement, a mistrust of the power of the state. Both were evident in an economic philosophy which demanded maximum freedom for the individual entrepreneur and a minimum of state intervention. More generally, for the relationship between the individual and society, liberalism shied away from collective action, and especially from state collectivism. Carried to an extreme, this version of 'old liberalism' is bound to be a caricature of any liberal party. Nonetheless, the concept of the 'night-watchman state' – one restricted to a minimum range of functions – does capture the spirit of the liberal *Weltanschauung*.

Old liberalism could not hope to survive as a relevant doctrine for liberal parties in the twentieth century. Its major components, unbridled economic individualism and anti-collectivism, both became anachronisms. In the first place, massive and permanent state intervention in the economy was forced on governments regardless of their political complexion: they were obliged to assume a responsibility for national economic performance and for the level of employment. As the role of the state and its commitments have grown, so also has the state itself become an important economic actor and is thus likely to swamp market forces through its actions. Secondly, the commitments assumed by the state also refer to its social responsibilities, in other words to the growth of state collectivism, and the concept of the 'Welfare State' epitomises the character of state collectivism in Western Europe. Through the network of social provisions – health, education, social security – as well as by means of transfer payments and redistributive taxation, the state has the obligation of meeting minimum standards and of improving the life-chances of the mass of the population – which also happens to be the bulk of the electorate.

Against that back-cloth the ideology of old liberalism appears remote, and its practical expression is more likely to be found in the small 'anti-tax' protest parties than in mainstream liberal ones, and they have had to come to terms with the expanded role of the state in the twentieth century. However, that process of accommodation has been uneven, so much so that two types of liberalism have emerged, one which still draws on original liberal inspiration and another which has gone much further in absorbing the norms of state intervention and collectivism. Labels are bound to be somewhat arbitrary, but it is useful to describe the former as 'liberal-conservative' and the latter as 'liberal-radical'.[3]

For the liberal-conservative party, the affinity with aspects of old liberalism is evident; in that sense it is 'conservative', although the term also draws attention to the kind of relationship the party will have within the party system. The gravitational pull of old liberal ideology should not be exaggerated; we have to bear in mind that the two forms of liberalism relate to two quite different eras in European history. The liberal-conservative party operates in the context of a high level of state involvement, and – leaving party rhetoric aside – terms such as neo-liberalism imply marginal adjustments in favour of market forces, not the wholesale withdrawal of the state nor the total dismantling of state welfare systems. That is not to say that the distinction between the liberal-conservative and the liberal-radical forms is only a difference in emphasis, for the liberal-radical type in many respects has much more in common with social democracy which, with its collectivist/interventionist orientation, stands as the polar opposite of the *laisser-faire* individualism associated with old liberalism.[4]

Yet even if the distinction between the two forms of liberalism is accepted as accurate, the question is why the liberal-radical element should have taken its particular direction and thus have been made susceptible to the 'pull' of social democracy. One answer is that it was precisely the tradition of radical dissent in liberalism which forged the essential link with the political left. That connection is of obvious importance, but it also leaves much unexplained. Most significantly, it does not account for the apparent reconciliation taking place between individualism and collectivism which, after all, should be deeply opposed.

Sir Ernest Barker supplied one answer to this problem in refusing to accept that individualism and collectivism are necessarily irreconcilable. He argued that instead of a dichotomy, individualism and collectivism formed part of a 'single and harmonious process'. They were integral to 'a process of the extension of personal rights which may be called individualism, but a process entailing, at the same time, an extension which may be called by the name of collectivism'.[5] Barker's formulation helps in understanding why the liberal-radicals could 'come to terms with' collectivism: it provided a framework within which individual rights were subsumed. Yet the picture of harmonisation can be overdrawn, and the extension of the collectivist state generates tensions which demarcates the liberal-radicals from social democracy, while for the liberal-conservatives any extension of state involvement only serves to confirm their opposition.

LIBERALISM IN EUROPEAN PARTY SYSTEMS

The distinction between two expressions of liberalism, its 'conservative' and 'radical' wings, goes some way in showing the complex quality of liberalism on an ideological plane. That complexity is reflected in the nature of liberal parties in Western Europe: they belong in one or other of two recognisable 'camps', liberal-radical and liberal-conservative. With that apparently straightforward division, it may seem that, although there is a liberal split, it is simple rather than complex. Yet there are complications. One stems from the basis on which parties are allocated to one or the other groupings, and relatedly, another arises because a party can on occasion change camps or even seemingly swing back and forth between them.

Deciding whether a party should be counted as liberal-radical or liberal-conservative involves weighing various factors: its history, the programme of the party, and the position it takes on particular issues. Above all else, however, we have to look at the kind of alliance it is prepared to enter, particularly the nature of coalitions in which a liberal party participates. While coalition behaviour is not always an unequivocal guide, for instance where a party is willing to make an 'unholy alliance' for purely tactical reasons, in longer-term arrangements there will be strong indications of a party's priorities with regard to its programme and policies.[6]

For liberal parties, the whole question of coalitions is of the utmost importance. The fact that they normally have a far smaller share of the vote than the conservatives, Christian democrats and social democrats means that they can only assert themselves in government by allying themselves with one or more of the larger parties. That minority status is, however, more than counterbalanced by the position they occupy in a party system: they have a greater eligibility than parties firmly located on the right or left. This potential allows them to wield an influence on government formation disproportionate to their electoral strength. Liberal parties with a consistently small share of the vote can have a decisive voice in the composition of a coalition, whereas a party on the right or left may have to emerge as the strongest party in order to assure its place in government. The capability of a liberal party is greatest in a three-party system, where it, as the small third party, holds the balance, and its decisive influence, as opposed to participation, declines appreciably as the number of parties increases.[7]

The pivotal place that liberal parties occupy and the consequent choice of coalition strategies that is open to them gives liberal parties undoubted *positional* advantage which makes up for their electoral weakness, and their fairly high participation in government also gives them a prominence that is lacking for a minor opposition party. But the advantages should not be exaggerated: it is precisely the positional benefits which lead to *definitional* problems – in other words, how a liberal party should define itself in the party system.

In one sense the problem is resolved by the breakdown as between the liberal-radical and the liberal-conservative types. But that distinction is hardly likely to appeal to the parties themselves, since they will be inclined to stress their liberal credentials above all else. Moreover, the distinction implies that there is a fundamental dividing line between the conservative and radical forms, and yet – in the context of the party system – is that really the case? While it is true that some liberal parties are consistent in the line they follow, the leading role they can play means that a liberal party can belong consecutively to coalitions of the left and right. Does such switching mean a sudden transformation of, say, a liberal-radical party into a liberal-conservative one?

That is a highly unlikely outcome, so that the ambivalence of liberal parties acting within party systems has to be accounted for on other grounds. One explanation takes the line of saddling liberal parties with the reputation of ingrained opportunism; that may apply on occasion to the behaviour of some parties but it is not a charge that can generally be brought. A second and more promising line is to examine the motivation that leads a liberal party to enter a governing partnership with a party with which it has little in common. In such cases there may be good negative reasons, such as to keep another party out or to act as a brake on the major governing party. This latter strategy of using a liberal 'corrective' implies a kind of 'opposition from within', and it can be more efficacious than external forms of opposition.

Liberal ambivalence can also be promoted by the ideological make-up of the other parties. Consider the not unusual case where liberals have to contend with the presence of a large and 'centre-leaning' Christian democratic party. The latter, unlike a typical conservative party, has a broad ideological straddle and an electoral following which is equally wide. Both factors make it difficult for a liberal party to find adequate competitive space. The choice it therefore faces is between siding with the left and making a liberal-radical stance the basis of its appeal or else to join with the Christian democrats, but in that case it has to stress other aspects, the liberal-conservative ones. If it follows that course, however, then it will immediately appear to be on the 'right' of the Christian democrats as a result of its leap-frogging manoeuvre.

The twists and turns of liberal parties seeking to maintain themselves in the party system confirm the ambivalence that is inherent in their ideological roots. Yet there is a different light in which they can be shown: the ambiguities of European liberalism derive in large measure from the overarching strength of the traditions of 'left' and 'right'.

LIBERALISM BETWEEN LEFT AND RIGHT?

Imprecise as the connotations of left and right may be, they reflect the course of European economic and social development over the past two centuries and the terms on which European electorates were mobilised. Their entrenchment is such that historical experience is encapsulated in the way that parties are conventionally ordered, how parties see themselves, and how voters perceive them as well.

All these factors come together to dictate the terms of party competition. Few parties are able to escape these influences, since they are forced to take positions on the issues and the agenda set by the major parties of left and right, and that applies to the electoral contest as well as to parliamentary activity and the formation of coalitions. Least affected are those parties which press claims that have no relationship at all with the ingredients of the left/right axis – for instance, the demands of regional or national minority parties – but liberal parties do not have that immunity, for their ideology is closely intertwined with those of left and right.

With a unilinear ordering, it is natural to treat liberal parties, whether conservative or radical, as related to the centre of the party spectrum. Yet, lacking in distinctive qualities, the concept of 'centre' is scarcely satisfactory. Thus for Duverger the centre was 'nothing more than the artificial grouping of the right wing of the left and the left wing of the right'.[8] In terms of party *competition* alone, that judgement may not be inaccurate, since parties necessarily respond according to the mould in which they are set. But if liberalism is just given a centre label it is reduced to being a kind of bland average and that surely is an underestimation.

What works against liberalism in particular is the one-dimensional view of political attitudes and ideology which the actual functioning of party systems has encouraged. Once a wider perspective is taken, however, the temptation to allocate liberal parties to a hypothetical centre is removed. There is no shortage of alternative multi-dimensional orderings, and they can either incorporate left/right as one dimension or abandon them entirely. Thus the axes taken can expand the understanding of left and right by distinguishing between the economic and political components of both.[9] An alternative is to introduce a different concept, for instance new/old politics or establishment/anti-establishment. Whichever course is adopted, liberal parties gain a distinctiveness that is otherwise lacking.

Broad schematic renderings have their uses, but they may fail to bring out the particular situation of a liberal party. One way of taking a more specific approach is indicated by Pappi's model of the West German party system.[10] Pappi, in arguing that 'one should give up the simple framework of a left–right dimension underlying the German party system' sets out in its place a triangular relationship based on a three-party system.[11] This model shows the positive basis for alignment between any two of the parties, and it emphasises the significance of certain fundamental issues that help to explain coalition linkages. Instead of portraying the liberals as an 'opportunistic' centre party on the left–right axis, Pappi's alternative presentation puts all three parties on an equal footing. Neither the nature of the issues nor the structure of the West German party system is exactly reproduced elsewhere, but a similar kind of analysis is applicable to other systems. Moreover, the model has a general relevance, since the three West German parties represent the three major West European traditions – Christian democracy, social democracy and liberalism – and the pivotal role of the liberals in coalition formation highlights the potential of liberal parties in other countries.

The question of liberalism 'between' left and right can be answered in two ways. On the level of party competition the left–right axis is dominant, but the underlying relationships are far more complex, and the idea of parties being 'between others' is misleading. A further question arises, however, in considering the competitive dominance of the left–right axis: how far is it likely to be affected by changes in West European party systems, and what are the possible consequences for liberal parties?

LIBERAL PARTIES AND SYSTEM CHANGE

Evidence of a growth in electoral volatility and a decline of partisan attachments points to a weakening of the structuring power of left and right and of the parties that make them the basis of a general appeal.[12] The rise of new issues, issue-based voting, and the 'new politics' all point to a loss in the power of the traditional polarity. That does not at all mean a corresponding failure of the associated parties, although their fortunes will fluctuate, but it does imply that they will find it increasingly difficult to dictate the terms of party competition. Also to be taken into account is their ability to absorb new issues; since the concepts of left and right are themselves rather elastic, it follows that parties can embark on refashioning their programmes and redefining their ideologies without at the same time relinquishing their claims to belong to the left or right. Nevertheless, their traditional appeals were based, explicitly or implicitly, on identifiable class interests which for long helped to give a 'frozen' appearnace to West European party systems. It is this electoral base which has weakened, so that their ability to redefine left and right is only a partial compensation.

Like all others, liberal parties are affected by the impact of electoral change. Unlike the other traditional parties, they showed their vulnerability at a much earlier stage in being unable to retain the allegiance of the middle classes, and the lack of a secure core vote meant that they lost the status of a major party. The picture may now be changing, since other parties are becoming just as susceptible; relatively at least, liberal parties are in a less disadvantageous position.

They may also benefit from their proven flexibility, and liberal parties could be in a better position to attach themselves to new issues that arise. It is also true that the liberal values, especially those relating to the freedom of the individual, will become more relevant, and that is particularly so for voters, who have lost their party loyalties and who no longer see voting as an expression of group identity.

The changes in European party systems and the process of

dealignment are all favourable developments for liberal parties, since they are freer from the pressures exercised by left and right. Any revival of their fortunes will not come about automatically, and for some rescue is too late, but the survival of liberalism as a political force appears better assured now than seemed likely a few decades ago.

NOTES

1 H. Laski, *The Rise of European Liberalism*, Allen & Unwin, 1936, p. 15. See also K. von Beyme, *Political Parties in Western Democracies*, Gower, 1985. He writes: 'The principles of freedom were supplemented by a conviction of the need for equality. As long as the battle was against the privileges of the aristocracy Liberalism was egalitarian, and it remained so with regard to equality before the law, in its attitude towards legal discrimination and in the battle for political rights for minorities' (p. 32).

2 There are important consequences in choosing between *de jure* and *de facto* liberalism. In the former case, the emphasis will be on parties calling themselves 'liberal', but in the latter, there will be no such restriction; in other words, parties can be described as 'liberal' even though they are of recent origin and do not use the title, perhaps not specifically regarding themselves as such. Terms such as 'behavioural', 'synthetic' or 'reconstructed' liberalism should then be used.

3 The varieties of liberalism are categorised by writers in different ways. The usage adopted here follows that previously employed in my wider treatment of party traditions in *Politics in Western Europe*, 4th edn, Heinemann/Gower, 1983. Klaus von Beyme, however, tends to make the primary distinction between 'liberals' and 'radicals', *Political Parties*, p. 33.

4 The distinction between the two types of liberalism can be shown in diagram form according to the different emphasis they place on its economic and social aspects:

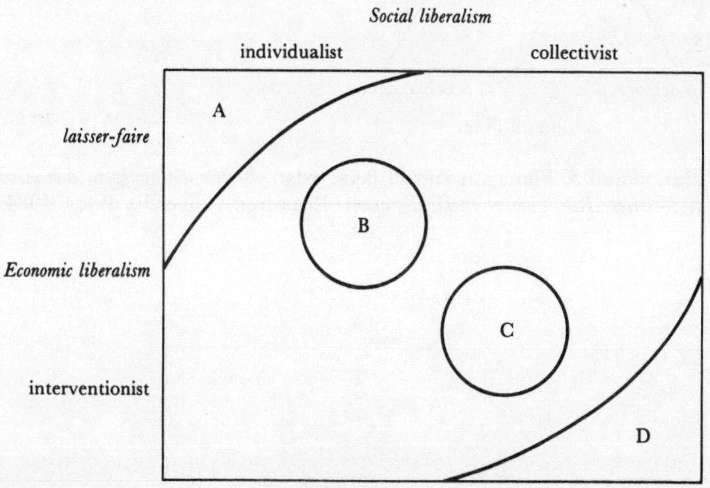

A = old liberalism B = liberal-conservative
C = liberal-radical D = social democratic

5 Ernest Barker, *Principles of Social and Political Theory*, Clarendon Press, Oxford, 1951, p. 268.

6 See *Politics in Western Europe*, pp. 104–6, for a listing of parties according to a liberal-conservative/liberal-radical breakdown. Thus of the 23 parties counted as 'liberal', 11 are described as liberal-radical and 12 as liberal-conservative. A large weight has been given to the kind of coalition a party joins. By no means all of those listed would formally be described as liberal – the *de facto* or 'behavioural' approach has been adopted (see n. 2 above).

7 The outstanding example of the decisive role of a liberal party – and by the same token the corresponding 'weakness' of the major parties – is in West Germany where the Free Democrats (with never more than 12.6 per cent of the vote since 1949) have been in office far longer than either of the two major parties, even though they have taken up to 90 per cent of the vote between them. The arrival of the Greens (in 1983) to give a four-party system may point to a weakening of the FDP's position.

8 Maurice Duverger, *Political Parties*, 4th edn, Methuen, 1964, p. 215.

9 See S. Finer, 'Left and right' in V. Bogdanor (ed.), *The Dictionary of Political Institutions*, Blackwell, 1987.

10 Franz Urban Pappi, 'The West German party system', *West European Politics*, October 1984, pp. 7–26.

11 Pappi shows the triangular relationship of the parties in the following form (p. 12):

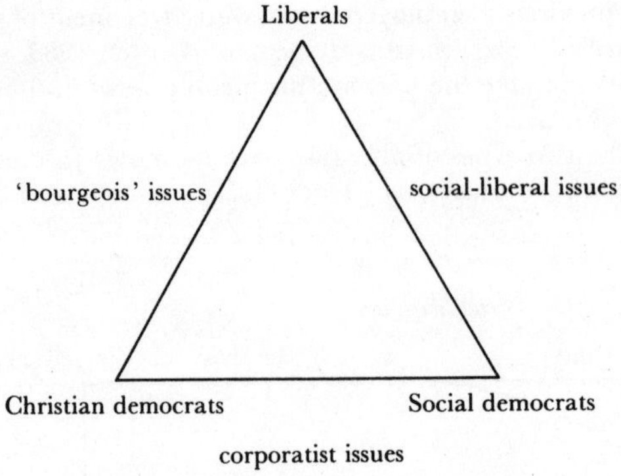

12 See R. Dalton and S. Flanagan and P. Beck (eds.), *Electoral Change in Advanced Industrial Societies: Realignment or Dealignment?* Princeton University Press, 1984.

3

Two roads of Italian liberalism: the Partito Repubblicano Italiano (PRI) and the Partito Liberale Italiano (PLI)

Geoffrey Pridham

INTRODUCTION; WHO ARE THE ITALIAN LIBERALS?

When identifying liberalism in Italy after the Second World War, familiar comparative distinctions between types of liberalism are indeed relevant. Such distinctions as between 'radical' and 'moderate' – or between 'social' and 'economic' or simply 'progressive' and 'conservative' forms of liberalism are all directly applicable to the Italian Republican and Liberal Parties respectively, as a broad description of their basic and somewhat divergent programmatic outlooks over time. As to that other set of distinctions between liberal parties, namely whether they are 'historical' or *de jure* as against *de facto* or 'behavioural' forms of liberalism, the PLI and PRI fall respectively into the two different categories. This is first and foremost because the former calls itself 'liberal' and the latter does not, although this is not to deny that the Republicans represent a 'historical' party in Italy of their own variety.

In other words, the PRI and the PLI express different versions of the same ideological tendency as seen in comparative terms. So far as this Italian example is concerned, any diachronic assessment of the two parties in question will show that however much they have converged strategically and programmatically in recent years they nevertheless boast separate traditions, have usually followed different paths in government and have for most of their histories possessed rather distinct social and electoral bases. Acknowledging therefore the truism that political parties are hardly static entities, such mutual movement on the part of the PRI and PLI may well be viewed as pursuing 'two roads of Italian liberalism'. There are certainly obvious attractions in comparing two separate party-political exponents of a common ideological tendency within the same national system.

It is necessary at this point to clarify the basis of selecting the political parties in this survey of liberalism in Italy. While the inclusion of the PLI is self-evident, that of the PRI as *de facto* liberal is based on both expert opinion and self-definition although not on party history, a basis that is discussed further below. The exclusion on the other hand of the Radical Party (PR) is less clear-cut, since this originated as a split on the left of the Liberal Party itself in 1956, and there is some case for arguing that, at least in the past, it has represented 'liberal values'. But the main reason for excluding it lies with the radicals' basic self-reconstruction in the later 1960s, after being virtually forgotten in the intervening decade as a continuing 'liberal' fringe party. That is, they moved sharply to the left proclaiming their essential task as 'that of a reforming and revolutionary alternative based on secular and libertarian methods, structures and objectives'.[1] Consequently, there has since the 1960s been a significant gap on the ideological spectrum between the Radicals and the Republicans who have commonly been viewed as 'moderate left'.[2] In short, the PR started as a radical liberal party but transformed itself into a party of the 'New Politics', and it is this that essentially demarcates it from mainstream liberalism in Italy.

APPROACHING ITALIAN LIBERALISM: THE PRI AND PLI IN COMPARATIVE PERSPECTIVE

We begin with the conventional left–right spectrum, as this is especially important because the left–right divide has remained uppermost in Italian political attitudes after the Second World War, at both elite and popular levels, notwithstanding political and social change and more specifically evidence of some decline in the intensity of ideological divisions among the party elites – though not so much the public – since the 1960s.

The Italian Republican and Liberal Parties have invariably been described in both comparative literature on political parties and in specialist studies on Italian politics as respectively 'left-wing Liberals' and 'right-wing Liberals' or alternatively as 'left-inclined' and 'right-inclined' Liberal Parties. There is ample survey evidence bearing out

Table 3.1 *Mean self-location of different party supporters on the left–right continuum for 1973, 1975, 1979, 1980, 1981*

	1973	1975	1979	1980	1981
PCI	1.8	2.5	2.2	2.0	2.3
PSI	3.2	3.7	3.8	3.0	3.5
PSDI	4.2	4.7	4.3	4.5	5.1
PRI	4.8	4.8	4.2	4.4	4.9
DC	5.6	5.9	5.5	5.6	5.7
PLI	6.6	6.5	6.8	6.7	6.6
MSI	8.7	8.3	8.9	8.9	7.9
Polarisation Index	0.77	0.64	0.74	0.77	0.62

Source: Ivo H. Daalder, 'The Italian party system in transition' in *West European Politics*, July 1983, p. 227.

this broad classification of their ideological leanings, as in Table 3.1. This illustrates the strong consistency in the mean self-location of both parties over time; and this is for a period (1973–81) which witnessed some important political and strategic changes, i.e. the end of the centre-left, the experiment with communist support for governments (1976–9) and then the five-party coalition involving the move of the PCI back into opposition.

Whatever ideological distance between these two parties, the PRI and PLI have commonly been seen as sharing the same subculture, i.e. liberal, sometimes called 'lay'. According to Zariski, although linked to anti-clericalism, this subculture has been marked by programmatic incohesion: 'with no real agreement on social or economic policy, the only bases for political consensus are a certain attitude of suspicion *vis-à-vis* the Catholic church and an affirmation of the virtues of the capitalist system (in its *laissez-faire* or Keynesian version, as the case may be)'.[3] While there is no question about the PRI and PLI both being 'historical' parties with traditions dating back to the Risorgimento, many post-war experts on Italian politics have chosen to emphasise the predominance of just two subcultures – the Marxist and the Catholic. The main difference between the two main subcultures and the liberal one is that the former have been institutionalised through associational and collateral networks linked to the PCI and DC, and that the lay one by and large has not.

Whatever classifications have been used – their main difference is to question the contours of the lay or liberal subculture – the PRI and PLI have generally been located on the same side of the principal cleavage divisions of Italian politics after the Second World War. For instance, Farneti placed them consistently close together in his identification of party positions at different points of time in the period 1945–80: the PRI and PLI were pro-market rather than pro-state on the economic cleavage, pro-USA rather than pro-USSR on the international cleavage, pro-constitution rather than for another institutional arrangement on the institutional cleavage, for reform rather than revolution (or reaction) on the social cleavage and pro-state rather than pro-church on the state/church cleavage.[4] What this indicates is that there has existed very broadly speaking a potential for general policy convergence between the PLI and PRI, as distinct from actual agreement or otherwise on policy issues at given times. Moreover, such spatial cleavage patterns usually do not take full account of the influence of party traditions and identity.

As to party self-definition and the question of the *de facto* liberal status of the Republicans, the differences between the two parties are well summarised by Giovanni Ferrara (a PRI senator):

> The two historical parties are different in many senses. The urge for political reform, now long-standing, of the PRI carries the name of Ugo La Malfa, that is a political, economic and institutional culture with a fundamentally democratic stamp and predominantly Anglo-Saxon origins (the thirties, Roosevelt and a certain English Labourism), but rooted in the ideas of Nitti and Amendola, of Southernness and of the Action Party about the new problems of Italy and post-Fascist industrial democracy . . . The Liberals are associated with another mould of thinking, not distant from the Republican but certainly different – that of Einaudi. And for political forces which are not large and are very selected in their composition, their derivations and political–cultural modes of language count for much. That which may appear as affinity can become competition . . .[5]

One other approach to party self-definition is through transnational party links. While the PLI and PRI have belonged together in the Liberal group in the European Parliament and in the 'extra-parliamentary' ELD, the PRI has not joined the older Liberal International which, because of its stronger association with liberal traditions, again underlines the PRI's *de facto* rather than *de jure* liberalism. One other possibility is to identify bilateral cases of transnational party closeness, which are not always confined to members of the same transnational organisation. For instance, the PLI has usually been seen as close to the British Conservatives and the PRI to the British Liberals (who feature as progressive liberals in the European context).[6] While such transnational links have limited domestic political importance, it is interesting to note that the PLI–PRI alliance for European elections in 1984 produced some

Table 3.2 *Support for liberal parties in pre-fascist national elections in Italy, 1913–24*

	Liberals, National Bloc and liberal movements, %	Republicans, Constitutionals, Democrats and Radicals, %
1913	47.6	23.0
1919	8.6	37.0
1921	26.2	19.0
1924	3.3	6.0

Source: Paolo Farneti, *The Italian Party System, 1945–1980* (1985) 76, 78.

alienation among committed party voters so that the combined vote of these parties fell. Thus, whatever *de facto* closeness exists between them, their separate identities still count.

The imprint of these two parties' histories on their own relationship is such that the historical background of these parties, so far as this has a bearing on party development since the Second World War, has to be considered. Most obvious here is the liberals' dominance in the Italian political system from unification in 1870 until the rise of fascism in the 1920s. As Table 3.2 shows, the ruling lists were dominant electorally, although the adoption of universal suffrage with a proportional system by 1919 considerably weakened the liberals, who only established a party machine in 1922. During the rise and consolidation of fascism, the liberals sought at first to exploit 'fascist dynamism' against the challenge from the socialists, then attempted to compromise with the new regime before being suppressed along with the other parties. The majority of liberals remained somewhat critical towards Mussolini without going as far as organised opposition,[7] although individual groups of liberals went in different directions – several into active support of the regime, some into exile and a few eventually joined the Resistance. Somewhat by contrast, the PRI was founded as an organised party as early as 1895, as a small radical force which was both anti-clerical and anti-monarchy (as its name emphasised), and from the later 1920s it emerged as uncompromisingly anti-fascist.

Fascism was above all significant for this present study as it brought into relief the conflict between the progressive and conservative schools of Italian liberalism.[8] This happened in a way that made it more difficult for the PLI to overcome this traumatic period because of the collaboration of high bourgeois circles with fascism. This divergence in the background and political tendencies of the PLI and

PRI was demonstrated immediately after the Second World War in their respective attitudes towards the role of the CLN (Committe of National Liberation) cross-party alliance based on the Resistance. While the PRI (together with those of its future leaders like La Malfa who were then in the Action Party) strongly supported its continuation and its policies for political and social change, the PLI soon decided to break with the CLN and embarked on a reconstructionist course, e.g. by favouring the return of the monarchy, opposition to reform of the southern economy based on landed interests, by generally presenting itself as spokesman for the conservative classes who feared radical change and political purges.[9] Nevertheless, the anti-fascist tradition as such became absorbed into the post-war Italian political consensus having ultimately the effect of demonising the political right and discrediting the term 'conservative' (as analagous to 'reactionary').[10] In this respect, the position of the PLI has been ambiguous, for it could also be seen as *de facto* conservative in many of its policy lines; and that was especially true during Malagodi's secretaryship.[11]

Finally, this formative stage of the party system after the Second World War was crucial in the history of Italian liberalism as it saw its political space substantially reduced. This occurred mainly because the newly-founded DC rapidly succeeded in monopolising the broad centre-right, given its strong inter-class appeal helped by its Catholic roots, its organisational superiority over the PLI (including its support by the church and Catholic associations) and the fact that, unlike the liberals, it was not tainted by association with fascism. The fascist period proved to be a fundamental turning-point in the nature of the Italian party system as a whole. This is not merely because structurally it paved the way for the combined dominance in that system of the Catholic and Marxist tendencies (the latter represented by both the PCI and PSI), which had been marginal in the pre-fascist liberal system; but also as qualitatively that dominance drew on their intensive organisational penetration of society and respective sub-cultural roots. This was all the more possible because of these parties' prominence in Resistance activity. This fundamental change in the relative strength of the parties compared with pre-fascist Italy was soon evident in the local elections of March 1946 and those to the Constituent Assembly later that year,[12] with much loss of former liberal voting groups to the DC in particular, including the professional intelligentsia at the activist level. The liberals were unable to prevent this; and it is significant that many monarchists joined them following their own defeat in the 1946 referendum on the monarchy, thus strengthening the PLI's position now on the right of the spectrum. As we know, these developments of 1945–6 were consolidated on the right by the DC's electoral victory in 1948 and furthermore by the PCI's and PSI's combined dominance on the left.

This is not to take a determinist line on party development in post-war Italy, for this obviously depended also on the performance of the various parties in question. Indeed, this latter theme really forms the background to the rest of this chapter, so far as the Liberals and Republicans are concerned.

REPUBLICAN AND LIBERAL PARTY STRATEGIES: FROM MUTUAL CONFLICT TO CONVERGENCE

The broad strategic dictates of the PRI and PLI have already been identified in terms of their ideological placement and limited room for manoeuvre given their small status and the situation of multi-party competition. It is thus possible to speak of a 'crowding of the centre' in Italian politics mainly because it has been monopolised by the DC, with the PRI and PLI on opposite sides of that dominant party on the left–right spectrum for most of the period after the Second World War. But the ideological spectrum, useful though it is in pointing directions in party strategy, is one-dimensional and rather simplistic; hence, we have also to consider both the actual intensity of ideological divisions and the very dynamics of the party system.

For most of the period after the Second World War, from the cold war onwards, the 'centre' in Italy has been not so much an elusive entity as in some other countries but rather bounded by the deep left–right divide. That is, the 'centre' has in effect been located on the right of that divide in what Galli saw in the 1960s as a case of 'imperfect bipartyism' and Sartori as a 'multipolar polarised system' in his theory of 'polarised pluralism'.[13] The outcome of this was to make the PRI and PLI dependent on the dominant DC in their strategies; or, as Allum puts it, 'their highest aspiration, both individually and collectively, could only be the conditioning of the Christian Democrats towards either conservative or reformist policies'.[14] This is a fair summary of the PLI's and PRI's respective positions as coalition partners of the DC for most of the period after the Second World War. For instance, the PRI was for at least the first half of that period constrained over any 'opening to the left' by the latter's lack of legitimacy. Any such 'opening' was most of all conditional on basic political as well as strategic changes on the part of the left rather than on initiatives from the PRI, as may be seen with the move of the socialists towards the centre-left formula in the early 1960s and the 'historic compromise' strategy of the communists in the

1970s. Equally, the PLI has for most of this post-war period been constrained in any 'opening to the right' by the lack of legitimacy of the extreme right, deriving from historical experience reinforced by the anti-fascist consensus. Indeed, once the axis of Italian politics shifted more to the left in the 1970s – essentially because of the growing (though as yet incomplete) legitimation of the PCI – the PLI found its room for manoeuvre to the right of the DC eroded so that from 1976 under new leadership the PLI itself attempted a move to the left. It should be added that this move, made out of desperation, seemed viable because the DC showed serious signs of decline. Hence, in the last decade, the 'centre' has remained 'crowded' less exclusively because of DC dominance and more because of the number of party actors locating themselves there, while the left–right divide has slackened with Farneti offering us the model of 'centripetal pluralism', as an updated version on Sartori.[15] As a result, the 'elusiveness' of the centre has become more apparent because it has become more mobile.

This significant change in the dynamics of the Italian party system has presented both new opportunities but also new uncertainties for the small parties, including the PRI and PLI. This leads us to consider how much their respective strategies have adapted successfully to this change, and taken advantage of it. But, first of all, it is necessary to establish the general reasons behind the strategic survival of these small parties in order to place their more recent movement in context. These may be summarised as institutional, cleavage-determined, traditional/territorial and personalistic.

Institutionally, it is simply that the pure proportional representation electoral system has encouraged and made possible the survival of small parties *per se*, which is further facilitated by flexible rules for the formation of parliamentary groups. But this alone is hardly sufficient as an explanation, seeing that some small parties in Italy have been temporary actors on the parliamentary stage, e.g. the left socialist PSIUP 1964–72, and the Monarchists who eventually disappeared in 1972. The obvious difference between these examples and parties like the PRI and PLI is the latters' importance in coalition politics and hence role in the system. The relevance here, too, of the various cleavages is that their overlapping has made it difficult for the party system to crystallise into two cohesive blocs to the disadvantage of small parties. If one takes Farneti's scheme of different cleavages (see above, note 4), the Republicans and Liberals appear on the same side as and close to the DC on the economic, international and social cleavages in opposition to the PCI (although since the mid-1970s the PCI is seen as straddling the international cleavage). While these two parties have been on the same side of the state–church cleavage as the Communists (intermittent in terms of being issue-salient) throughout the 1945–80 period, they have together also moved closer to the PCI on the institutional cleavage (as more insistent on institutional reform, bearing in mind that the PCI has become increasingly system-supportive). One may add that since Farneti's schema (up to 1980) such overlapping has increased, in line with the loosening-up of the left–right divide. The traditional or territorial determinant simply refers to the fact that both small parties have depended greatly on localised strongholds of popular support, lending them a certain stability. This arises from local traditions of republicanism and liberalism (one might say a localised form of these two parties as 'historical'), linked to localised sectoral patterns of electoral behaviour.

Finally, as secondary to these various determinants, these two parties have enjoyed the prestige and visibility associated with leaders of some stature – notably, Malagodi in the case of the PLI and Ugo La Malfa and Spadolini in the case of the PRI. Equally, their lack at times of strong or charismatic figures – as with some PLI secretaries – has reduced their strategic visibility. But, given the minimal importance of charisma in the parties' electoral strength (it only became first apparent in the PRI's case with the 'Spadolini effect' in the 1983 election), one must really explain the strategic survival of the Republicans and Liberals in terms of the above-mentioned 'structural' determinants. It is these that have guaranteed them their role in the coalitional game – hence policy determination and access to patronage – subject, of course, to the strategy requirements of the ruling Christian Democrats.

For this reason, studies of Italian politics have commonly differentiated among the small parties between 'minimal' or fringe parties and 'small' parties proper (notably the PRI and PLI);[16] alternatively, by giving the latter the status of 'intermediary' parties. For example, the PLI for a long time played a 'blackmail function' (to use Sartori's term) on the right of the DC, such as in exploiting conservative opposition to the new centre-left alliance in the 1963 election. Similarly, a decade later in 1972, the DC formed a coalition with the PLI primarily to cover itself to the right at the time when support for the MSI was on the rise. Such an intermediary function is different from a pivotal role in alliance strategy, which numerically can only be performed by a third party, namely the PSI in Italy. This function has become more possible with the weakening of DC dominance. It is significant here that within the five-party alliance (*pentapartito*) since the early 1980s both the Republicans and the

Liberals have attempted to make their relationship with the PSI more 'organic' in order to create more political space for themselves *vis-à-vis* the DC. This convergence has nevertheless retained elements of past conflict between the parties concerned, and it is therefore to their individual strategies that we now turn.

Any direct comparison of the PRI and PLI strategies diachronically can easily identify their main differences, in accordance with their respective roles as reformist or conservative 'correctives' to the DC. This was most in evidence when the PRI helped to promote and participated in the centre-left alliance based on a policy of reforms in the 1960s, and the PLI opposed it. The PLI argued at the time that the centre-left would eventually open the way to Communist participation in the state. Clearly, the anti-communist motive has been uppermost in PLI strategy considerations, even after the legitimation of the PCI had progressed some way. One member of the PLI's national directorate underlined that the ideological space between his party and the PCI was unbridgeable and even included local politics in this argument, for the two parties had 'a different conception of urban life',[17] a view confirmed by the head of the PLI's national office in Rome for regional and local government on the grounds that the PCI had totalitarian pretensions in local politics.[18]

The PRI's anti-communism is different in being less absolute in its strategic behaviour towards the PCI. In line with La Malfa's definition of his party as a non-Marxist, moderate party of the left, the PRI is 'culturally' rather than dogmatically anti-communist, recognising the important integrative role of the PCI with respect to social change in Italy after the Second World War. This position of relative 'openness' towards the PCI, which was conditional on the continuing 'Westernisation' of that party, was highlighted most of all late in 1977 when La Malfa advocated a closer involvement of the PCI in government (following Berlinguer's speech at Moscow criticising the Soviet model on the occasion of the sixtieth anniversary of the Russian Revolution). This initiative was firmly opposed by the PLI, which withdrew its support for the Andreotti government a few months later when the PCI 'entered the majority', i.e. formed a legislative coalition with the DC, PSI, PSDI and PRI.

Since this experiment with the 'National Solidarity' formula ended in 1979, the general strategic situation has changed substantially with the return of the PCI to opposition, a further weakening of the DC (notably, its electoral loss in 1983) and a *rapprochement* between the PLI and the PSI, which twenty years before had been political enemies. This last movement in the direction of a stronger 'third force' has been commonly called the 'lay-socialist pole', sometimes bifurcated into the 'socialist pole' (PSI and PSDI) and the 'lay pole' (PRI and PLI). It may be viewed as a case of strategic convergence, though not an 'organic' alliance, for the mutual behaviour of parties within the 'lay-socialist pole' has illustrated that left–right considerations are by no means the only factor in its operation.

Conflict between the PRI and PSI because of the former's own ambitions for a pivotal role, acerbated by political rivalry between Spadolini and Craxi, has prevented this pole from becoming cohesive. As we have seen, strong personalities count for much in determining and dominating the strategies of small parties and especially changes in them. Furthermore, the electoral fortunes of the parties obviously help to determine how far they are in a position to press their strategic options, e.g. his party's electoral success in 1983 gave Spadolini political weight as a bargaining counter in the coalitional game. Finally, such convergence between these smaller parties has once again shown that, whatever rational common motives they might have (above all, to reduce the power of the DC), their individual historical identities always surface with all the implications these have for electoral impact and political rivalry.

IDEOLOGY MADE REAL: PRI AND PLI POLICY POSITIONS COMPARED

From the preceding discussion of ideology and strategy, our confirmation of the PRI and the PLI as respectively 'left-inclined' and 'right-inclined' versions of the liberal tendency together with their common position on cleavage divisions would initially suggest their differences have been circumscribed, however much they have been in conflict or converged over the period since the Second World War. Given, however, the limitations of the left–right spectrum, even with Italy's highly polarised post-war politics, and recalling that this spectrum has not remained static, we really have to differentiate between policy areas.

One useful starting-point is to construct a picture of the parties' positions on key given issue areas, as typical of their broad policy lines.[19]

PRI and PLI policy lines

PRI

Economic policy: for a degree of state intervention and economic planning (e.g. state corporations); for incomes policy; for policy of economic rigour in the recession; in favour of strengthening the co-operative movement; generally, a strong emphasis on 'rational' approaches as assuring 'freedom from sectoral interests', and the historical influence of Keynes and the 'New Deal'.

Social policy: welfare capitalism, for an extensive welfare state; an emphasis on civil liberties and individual rights, but also a sense of the collective whole; self-identity as 'socialists' but 'non-Marxist', of *democrazia sociale* or 'democracy with social obligations'.

Institutions: traditionally pro-decentralisation (for the introduction of the regions), and more recently strongly for institutional reform.

Church/state: anti-clerical by tradition, i.e. against special church privileges and discrimination against religious minorities.

External policy: staunchly pro-NATO and for European integration.

PLI

Economic policy: traditionally for the free-market economy, *laissez-faire* in outlook; a limited view of economic planning (e.g. in relation to a policy of retrenchment, overhaul of the swollen bureaucracy), essentially opposed to government regulation of the private sector.

Social policy: limited government expenditure, preferably confined to necessary public works and improving the existing social security system; generally, against the concept of the *stato assistenziale* or Welfare State and a strong emphasis on individual rights.

Institutions: against the introduction of the regions (preferred to strengthen the existing provincial governments); more recently, open to institutional reform as part of cross-party convergence here, but in an adaptive rather than transformative sense.

Church/state and external policy: essentially the same approach as the PRI.

What this does is to identify continuities in policy line, and also differences and similarities between the two parties. Thus, the PRI and PLI have been most apart on socio-economic affairs and close, if not identified, on church/state relations and foreign and defence policy. One can, of course, see historical and ideological influences present in both respects, but particularly indicative of position on the left–right spectrum must be social and economic policy in the first instance. In this respect, the above supports the distinction between the PRI and PLI as representing respectively 'social' and 'economic' liberalism. But what it does not really do is to take account of movement in policy lines, not to mention specific policy stands at given points of time, as dictated by alliance considerations or environmental demands. Some brief examination of their policy lines at different stages of the post-war period should throw some light on this problem.

In the aftermath of the Second World War, the two parties were far apart as noted above in discussing their historical development. The PLI's restorative line and the PRI's advocacy of radical change were expressed in their diametrically opposed positions on the monarchy and agrarian reform. While the first issue was settled in the 1946 referendum, the latter remained on the agenda until the early 1950s and divided the two parties sharply with the PRI insisting on agrarian reform as a condition for government participation and the PLI going into opposition over the issue.[20] On economic affairs, the two parties were less far apart than later – when the PRI began to support state corporations strongly come the 1950s – although the PRI's firm position on southern development in Italy (a personal concern of La Malfa) and favourable view of the planning element in Marshall Aid marked it off from the Liberals. The gap on economic policy opened up distinctly following the election to the PLI secretaryship in 1954 of Malagodi, who allied his party with entrepreneurial and business interests. In the following decade, the general policy movement of the two parties diverged further to the extent of the PRI promoting reformist policies in the centre-left alliance and the PLI decidedly opposing these. Specifically, this was evident over the centre-left's nationalisation policies, decentralisation of the state structure (the regions were at last introduced across the country) and emphasis on full employment. Particularly prominent in the PRI policy line was La Malfa's technocratic and modernising approach over the political economy, linking this with the problems of state management.[21]

Towards the end of the centre-left alliance, the PRI began to advocate a policy of austerity to cope with the worsening economic condition including an incomes policy, opposition to the *scale mobile* indexing system as inflationist and demand for control of public expenditure. While this led to conflicts with the trade unions and differences of view with government partners, the PRI's disillusionment with the centre-left alliance and failure to carry through some reforms did not result in any shift back towards the PLI. On the contrary, La Malfa's assessment of government ineffectiveness only encouraged his eventual interest in a further 'opening to the left'. Come the early 1980s, with the adoption of the *pentapartito* alliance formula, there has been convergence between the PRI and PLI but mainly as a result of movement on the part of the latter. This has been particularly seen in their common emphasis on fighting inflation, while they have also shared the same position on installing medium-range US missiles on Italian soil; though the PRI has been more emphatic on institutional reform and 'moral recovery' (i.e. rooting out corruption).

In effect, this recent stage has seen the two parties at their closest compared with any previous stage of the post-war period. This is confirmed by the findings of the ECPR project on party manifestos, according to a two-dimensional scale.[22] On the left–right scale (economic policy), the PRI has remained in roughly the same position on the centre-left for both pre-1960 and post-1960 averages, while the PLI moved distinctly from centre-right towards the centre in the latter half of the post-war period. On the 'social fabric' scale (e.g. individual freedom, law and order, moral values), it has been the PRI that has shown the most movement from a radical progressive position in its pre-1960 average to one almost right of centre in the post-1960 period, overtaking the PLI which moved mildly from centre-left to centre. The salient issue in question, so far as the PRI is concerned, is its hard line in fighting terrorism which has been a constant problem since the end of the 1960s. Obviously, such movement must be attributed in part to issue problems arising in the social and international environment, and clearly this point above all carries for the recession in the later period.

But parties also adopt policy stands with some reference to their previous lines, e.g. it is possible to see some continuity between the PRI's austerity policy from the late 1960s (maintained under Spadolini's leadership) with its earlier economic thinking. At the same time, small parties in particular may undergo some policy redirection with a change of leadership, well illustrated by the rise of Malagodi and his movement of the PLI further to the right. Similarly, the PRI owed much of its policy line – above all, on economic affairs – to the strong and persistent influence of its leader Ugo La Malfa, an economist by profession and also a Sicilian (which explained his commitment to the condition of southern Italy). One final variable in defining policy lines relates to the common constraints of alliance politics in influencing the respective positions of the Republicans and the Liberals.

GOVERNMENT PARTICIPATION AND COALITION POLITICS

In so far as there is a logical connection between parties' strategies, their general policy lines and actual alliances with other parties, one would expect parallel developments between our discussion so far of the PRI and PLI and their participation in government and coalition politics. This is broadly the case, for while these two parties were together in some of the post-war cabinets under De Gasperi and not again until the *pentapartito* coalitions from the early 1980s they tended to follow different paths in the intervening thirty years. In other words, for most of the period after the Second World War, they have usually not shared government participation.

One should, of course, bear in mind that Italian coalition politics has habitually embraced variations of legislative coalitions, where some government-supporting parties do not join the cabinet. On this basis, one can identify cases of both parties together offering external support or abstention to DC(-led) governments, i.e. 1953–4, 1960–2, 1972 and 1976–8; and also cases when the one party promised external support or abstention to governments in which the other was a participant, i.e. 1954–5, 1955–7, 1972–3 and 1979–80. It is possible to argue in general that these intermittent cases illustrated greater policy closeness than when the PLI opposed outright the PRI in government and vice versa. But – without going into the particularities of each example of external support – it should also be said that such legislative coalitions may simply involve *ad hoc* or short-term policy convergence (remembering that Italian coalitions are invariably short-lived), quite apart from individual considerations of power and personal ambition. In short, coalition politics in Italy has to be viewed in multidimensional perspective, and this is bound to qualify the logical relationship hypothesised at the start of this section.

As to longevity of formal government participation, there is a stark difference between the two parties with the PRI serving much longer in office than the PLI. Taking the period of over 40 years from the end of the Second World War to the end of 1985, the total for the PRI is 256 months (more than 21 years) and 158 months (more than 13 years) in the case of the PLI. In fact, the PLI was absent from the cabinet table for exactly 25 years from the centrist Segni government of 1955–7 until the centre-right government under Andreotti of 1972–3. Such a record leads one to consider whether the PRI can be called a 'party of power' in the way the PLI cannot, seeing too that national office (especially continuity in it) presents not only opportunities for policy implementation but also, in the Italian system, patronage on an extensive scale. The PRI's placement more towards the centre of the spectrum than the PLI might well suggest one basic reason why it has been in government more often, but first of all it is important to consider the general role of small parties in Italian coalition politics.

The polarised left–right divide in Italian politics after the Second

World War combined with the problem of the PCI's legitimacy has accorded the small parties in the centre – and especially the PSI once it became *koalitionsfähig* in the 1960s – what Farneti has seen as a 'pivotal' or at least 'relevant' role in coalition politics in that country.[23] That is, they have benefited from the fact that one of the two major parties (the PCI) has been permanently excluded from power, thus enhancing the political position of parties like the PRI and PLI. It is schematically possible to see the DC performing a dominant-pivotal role – so long as it remained as dominant, i.e. until the 1970s – moving leftwards to favour the PRI and rightwards to favour the PLI, depending on circumstances (e.g. electoral trends, the balance of power among the factions in the DC). The existence of institutionalised factionalism, above all in the DC, is relevant to our discussion of the small parties. Internal DC factions or alliances between them have often looked to partner-parties to strengthen their own candidates for government leadership, a behavioural pattern that has also sometimes been used by DC prime ministers to counter policy challenges from internal party rivals. The consequent heterogeneity of Italian coalitions has itself encouraged the inclusion of small parties even when not mathematically necessary for formal majorities. This tendency in Italy to think more of a 'working majority' or a 'political majority' to assure the passage of legislation has been reinforced in recent years by the increasing habit among government back-benchers (known as 'snipers') of voting against individual government policies. But this practice of forming 'over-large' coalitions (to use the coalition theory term), favouring the inclusion of small parties in government, was evident already in the years immediately after the Second World War. For instance, De Gasperi formed a four-party coalition (DC and PSDI and PRI and PLI) after the 1948 election, even though the DC had won an absolute majority of seats, both to strengthen solidarity behind the new Italian republic but also with the lay parties to counter the influence of Catholic fundamentalist pressures within his own party.[24] Given this favourable position of small parties in Italian coalition politics, one may ask how this has been exploited by the PRI and PLI.

In the first stage of the post-war period, the PRI became known as the most loyal ally of the DC in the centrist alliance – it remained in government without interruption during 1947–53 – both to prevent (with the PSDI) government policy from moving to the right and to avoid being isolated in this highly polarised situation between left and right.[25] Apart from external policy, the PRI was, however, not so very influential in view of the DC's numerical and political dominance in those coalitions, although its influence in domestic policy increased somewhat in the early 1950s when the PRI alone remained with the DC in government, e.g. over land reform. Subsequently, the PRI's electoral decline in the 1950s and early 1960s undercut its political position, so that for a decade it remained distant from government, alternating between *ad hoc* external support and opposition. The centre-left from the early 1960s saw the re-entry of the PRI into government, committed strongly to the policy of reforms, although the DC's stalling over some reforms led to the Republicans becoming disillusioned. The *pentapartito* coalitions have, on the other hand, seen PRI influence at its greatest, simply because DC dominance had declined as highlighted by Spadolini, the PRI leader, becoming the first non-DC prime minister since 1945, in 1981–2 (in fact, the first non-DC leader to be invited to form a government, though he failed, was La Malfa shortly before his death in 1979). Spadolini used his role to push strongly for the austerity policy and to boost his own popularity to the advantage of his own party. The main problem for the PRI in this more favourable coalition alignment has been the ambitious PSI strategy under Craxi, for the latter's chances for exploiting the weakened DC position have been greater.

The PLI's long absence from government during most of the post-war period obviously reduced its opportunities for political influence considerably. Its intermittent participation in centrist coalitions after the Second World War and *ad hoc* external support for some governments in the 1950s does not really qualify this point (apart from Einaudi's contribution to financial policy), as it played a fringe role in the coalitional balance. Malagodi sought to overcome this problem by political and organisational revival of his party from the mid-1950s, but although he eventually achieved some electoral success in opposition to the centre-left (notably in the 1963 election) his party remained politically isolated. The PLI's re-entry into government in 1972, when Malagodi acquired the important portfolio of the Treasury, was all too brief; while the PLI's continuous presence in *pentapartito* governments from 1981 has not led to any dramatic reversal of this unfavourable position. Certainly less isolated than ever before, the PLI has nevertheless remained subordinate to both the PSI and also the PRI, which politically and electorally has come to dominate among the small parties.

As indicated above, these two parties have owed much of their governmental presence and visibility to certain major leaders, e.g. Sforza as Foreign Minister under De Gasperi, La Malfa in various economic ministries during the centre-left alliance (e.g. Budget, Treasury) as well as Deputy Prime Minister, Malagodi at the

Table 3.3 *PRI and PLI participation in coalitions. Composition of Italian cabinets, 1945–88*

Period of office (Number of months)	Prime Minister	Parties in the cabinet
1. 6–11/45 (5)	Parri	Action party, DC, PCI, PLI, PSI, PDL (Democratic Labour)
2. 12/45–7/46 (6)	De Gasperi	DC, PCI, PSI, Action Party, PDL, PLI
3. 7/46–2/47 (6)	De Gasperi	DC, PCI, PSI, PLI, PRI
4. 2–4/47 (3)	De Gasperi	DC, PCI, PSI
5. 5/47–5/48 (11)	De Gasperi	DC, PSDI, PLI, PRI
6. 5/48–1/50 (20)	De Gasperi	DC, PSDI, PRI, PLI
7. 1/50–7/51 (17)	De Gasperi	DC, PSDI, PRI
8. 7/51–6/53 (23)	De Gasperi	DC, PRI
9. 7/53 (½)	De Gasperi	DC (external support of PRI)
10. 8/53–1/54 (5)	Pella	DC (external support of PRI, PLI and Monarchists)
11. 1/54 (½)	Fanfani	DC
12. 2/54–6/55 (16)	Scelba	DC, PSDI, PLI (external support of PRI)
13. 7/55–5/57 (22)	Segni	DC, PSDI, PLI (external support of PRI)
14. 5/57–6/58 (13)	Zoli	DC (external support of Monarchists and MSI)
15. 7/58–1/59 (7)	Fanfani	DC, PSDI (external support of PRI)
16. 2/59–2/60 (12)	Segni	DC
17. 3–7/60 (4)	Tambroni	DC
18. 7/60–2/62 (18)	Fanfani	DC (external support from PSDI, PRI, PLI)
19. 2/62–6/63 (16)	Fanfani	DC, PSDI, PRI (external support of PSI)
20. 6–11/63 (6)	Leone	DC
21. 12/63–6/64 (7)	Moro	DC, PSI, PSDI, PRI
22. 7/64–1/66 (18)	Moro	DC, PSI, PSDI, PRI
23. 2/66–6/68 (27)	Moro	DC, PSI, PSDI, PRI
24. 6–11/68 (5)	Leone	DC
25. 12/68–7/69 (6)	Rumor	DC, PSI, PRI
26. 8/69–2/70 (6)	Rumor	DC (external support from PSI and PSDI)
27. 3–7/70 (3)	Rumor	DC, PSI, PSDI, PRI
28. 8/70–1/72 (17)	Colombo	DC, PSI, PSDI, PRI
29. 2–6/72 (4)	Andreotti	DC (external support from PRI, PSDI and PLI)
30. 6/72–6/73 (12)	Andreotti	DC, PSDI, PLI (external support from PRI)
31. 7/73–3/74 (8)	Rumor	DC, PSI, PSDI, PRI
32. 3–10/74 (7)	Rumor	DC, PSI, PSDI
33. 11/74–2/76 (15)	Moro	DC, PRI (external support from PSI and PSDI)
34. 2–7/76 (5)	Moro	DC (external support from PSDI)
35. 8/76–3/78 (19)	Andreotti	DC (abstention from PCI, PSI, PSDI, PRI, PLI)
36. 3/78–3/79 (12)	Andreotti	DC (external support from PCI, PSI, PSDI, PRI)
37. 3–8/79 (4)	Andreotti	DC, PSDI, PRI
38. 8/79–4/80 (8)	Cossiga	DC, PSDI, PLI (abstention of PSI and PRI)
39. 4–10/80 (6)	Cossiga	DC, PSI, PRI
40. 10/80–6/81 (8)	Forlani	DC, PSI, PSDI, PRI
41. 6/81–8/82 (13)	Spadolini	PRI, DC, PSI, PSDI, PLI
42. 8–11/82 (3)	Spadolini	PRI, DC, PSI, PSDI, PLI
43. 12/82–8/83 (8)	Fanfani	DC, PSI, PSDI, PLI
44. 8/83–8/86 (36)	Craxi	PSI, DC, PRI, PSDI, PLI
45. 8/86–3/87 (7)	Craxi	PSI, DC, PRI, PSDI, PLI

Table 3.3 (*cont.*)

Period of office (Number of months)	Prime Minister	Parties in the cabinet
46. 3/87–7/87 (4)	Fanfani	DC, PSI, PRI, PSDI, PLI
47. 7/87–3/88 (7)	Goria	DC, PSI, PRI, PSDI, PLI

(The party of the Prime Minister is given first among the list of cabinet participants).
Source: Vernon Bogdanor (ed.), *Coalition Government in Western Europe* (1983) pp. 214–15, updated.

Treasury and recently Spadolini as Prime Minister (subsequently Minister of Defence under Craxi). The tendency of the PRI to hold economic and financial policy portfolios, particularly with La Malfa and also under the *pentapartito* with Visentini, is of course in line with that party's priority given to that area, just as its early post-war and recent tenure of external policy portfolios has expressed the party's traditional Atlanticist position. Except for Einaudi's importance as Minister for Finance and the Treasury (also Deputy Prime Minister) after the Second World War, briefly also holding the Foreign Ministry in the mid-1950s and Treasury in 1972–3, the PLI has been less present in the high offices of state than the PRI. Under the *pentapartito*, Liberals have occupied secondary posts like Health under Spadolini and Industry and Commerce under Craxi. In total, the PRI has benefited more than any of the small parties through its participation in government (see Table 3.3). According to one estimate up to the early 1980s, it had enjoyed an average of 3.3 times the ministerial posts it was entitled to on proportional grounds, with 2.4 in the case of the PLI and 2.1 for the PSDI.[26] Despite this, the PRI has not exploited its position to any considerable extent for patronage purposes.[27] This is partly because of its smallness when compared with the DC and PSI (i.e. literally numbers of portfolios), but more particularly because of its principled view of power as personified by its long-time leader La Malfa.[28] Similarly, Spadolini has been an exponent of a moralistic approach to national office. The Liberals, though less principled in such matters, have not been in government long enough to exploit its privileges much.

The greater role of the PRI compared with the PLI has been replicated in regional and local government. This may be illustrated by the number of mayors, administrators and municipal councillors held by these parties in local government. For instance, one survey in 1984 put the figures as follows.

Table 3.4 *PRI and PLI in local government*

	Mayors	Administrators	Councillors	TOTAL
PRI	51	580	1,249	1,880
PLI	53	229	732	1,014

Source: Arturo Parisi (ed.), *Luoghi e Misure della Politica* (1984) 134.

There has been a similar preference as at the national level in favour of including small parties in local administrations even when numerically not necessary, more often than not benefiting the PRI rather than the PLI.

This is because of the PRI's advantageous placement closer to the centre of the spectrum, all the more as the PCI has not been excluded from office locally and alternation has occurred in many cases. For instance, the PCI has sought 'broad alliances' of the left in local government, including alliances with the PRI. The PLI has coalesced locally almost entirely with the DC or PSI as well as the PRI and PSDI, with only a handful of communes (mainly small and insignificant) where it has participated alongside the PCI. The basic difference here between the PLI and PRI is that the PLI has refused co-operation with the PCI out of principle, while the latter has chosen to coalesce with the Communists on an *ad hoc* basis rather than for 'strategic' reasons. The PRI's strategic advantage was visibly in evidence in the early 1960s when it helped to initiate the centre-left alliance in local politics in certain northern cities, a move that was strongly opposed by the Liberals. More recently, there has been a gradual increase in *pentapartito* coalitions locally allowing the PRI to play something of a pivotal role, depending on the local balance in party strength. In fact, it has been easier for the Republicans to pursue a less subordinate position locally and regionally than in national politics because the DC has been less dominant in the former, especially in the big cities, while the PCI has sometimes been willing to cede the mayor's post for the sake of a broad alliance. The *pentapartito* has also benefited the PLI, albeit less considerably than the PRI, for while the Liberals were absent from regional governments during the 1970s they have recently entered several from the early 1980s.

THE PRI AND PLI AS ORGANISATIONAL STRUCTURES: LOOSE-ASSOCIATIONAL AND TOP-HEAVY?

We need to consider the operation of party structures both horizontally and vertically, e.g. the role of the parliamentary groups and the

Table 3.5 Membership of PRI

1964	54,871
1977	108,859
1980	106,536
1983	108,201

Source: Arturo Parisi and Angelo Varni (eds.), *Organizzazione e Politica nel PRI: 1946–1984* (1985 Bologna) 95.

Table 3.6 *Membership of PLI*

1973	150,000
1975	140,000
1985	39,200

From miscellaneous PLI sources.

power position of party secretaries, hierarchical decision-making processes and the role of the membership as well as possible links with interest groups. A differentiation between party statutes and actual practice is appropriate especially when examining small parties. Formally, the PRI and PLI have structures which in pure outline are very similar to those of the major Italian parties: national congress and council, national directorate and the political (in the PLI, general) secretary, followed by regional and provincial units and local sections, not to mention collateral organisations (youth and culture) though these last are much less articulated than with the PCI, DC and PSI. But what marks the Republicans and Liberals off from these three other parties is, quantitatively, the extent to which these structures are replicated across the country (there is in fact very much local and also regional variation in the presence of their lower-level units); and, qualitatively in the regularity and intensity of party activity.

One important explanatory factor must be the two parties' organisational histories. That is, the PRI can boast a longer organisational history compared with the PLI in the first instance, while their common emergence after 1945 as small parties with threadbare organisations underlined their weak starting positions. Consequently, they have essentially depended on voluntarism rather than a body of functionaries not least because their small membership (see Tables 3.5 and 3.6) has also meant restricted financial resources depending on the presence or absence of external finance from special interests; moreover, state financing of parties was not instituted until three decades after the Second World War. This reliance on voluntarism has furthermore been buttressed by prevailing norms within these parties. In the case of the PRI, they have been characterised by a traditional attachment to ideas and freedom of conscience rather than party activism as such.[29] As to the PLI, it has until quite recently been described as 'a party of gentlemen more inclined towards Rotary conferences than the corridors of the Montecitorio' (the national Parliament),[30] a remark that suggested negative effects from the PLI's long absence from power. Altogether, the term most usually applied to the PRI and PLI is 'parties of opinion', namely as lacking any capillary organisation and dependent on middle-class votes as their base.

Historical explanations would suggest a vicious circle in these two parties' organisational development after the Second World War: their political role as small parties in a crowded multi-party system and the dominance of the political spectrum by the major parties has inhibited their organisational expansion; equally, their organisational weakness has hardly been a good basis for a more assertive political role. But how far can organisational development be autonomous from political variables, thus breaking this vicious circle? In the case of these two parties, several attempts have been made precisely to stimulate organisational revival. It is perhaps significant that these have been related to a change of leadership and strategic redirection, underlining the importance of strong personalities in small parties. With the PLI, the best example is Malagodi's attempt at organisational reform after he assumed the secretaryship in 1954, strengthening the middle level of party organisers and helped here by external finance from business interests.[31] Ultimately, this contributed to the PLI's election success in 1963 (rising from 3.5 to 7 per cent), but it was at the cost of political isolation, and subsequent elections showed only too clearly that this result was never consolidated. Zanone's plans for organisational reform of the PLI from the mid-1970s failed to materialise, partly because he was not a strong figure but more especially because his strategic move towards the centre yielded no lasting results.

Similarly, the example of the PRI has underlined the close link between the organisational and the political. The first serious policy for organisational reform arose with La Malfa's assumption of the party secretaryship in 1965 and the confirmation of his centre-left strategy. While earlier post-war efforts at reform had encountered internal party apathy,[32] the latter was now undercut by the PRI's decline in voting support (down to 1.4 per cent in both 1958 and 1963 elections) by the time La Malfa became leader. Statutory changes were made at the 1965 and 1968 congresses to improve the functioning of the national executive organs and regulate more effectively internal party activity, replacing what has been called the PRI's traditional 'artisan' style of organisation.[33] These changes in the operation of the PRI structure facilitated a subsequent increase in membership (see Table 3.5) and the number of local sections of the PRI. Yet, it is necessary to emphasise their limited importance, for the PRI still remained a rather weakly institutionalised party; indeed, this case only showed how difficult it is for small parties above all to overcome their organisational past.[34] In fact, these changes had only minimal political impact in terms of electoral support for the PRI (which rose cautiously to 2.0, 2.9 and 3.1 per cent in the subsequent three elections). The new Spadolini leadership of the PRI from 1979 also embarked on a programme of organisational expansion.[35] It has been more successful primarily because of the electoral momentum achieved by the party (rising to the unprecedented level of 5.1 per cent in 1983), especially its ability to capitalise on the growing floating vote at the expense of the DC. Social and political change has, therefore, indirectly helped open the way for some organisational growth on the part of the PRI. Following its election success in 1983, the Republicans sought to strengthen further their organisation in an attempt to consolidate their new position.[36]

Examining the internal operation of these two parties lends corporeal form to their constitutional structures outlined above. Although the parliamentary groups have remained rather small (e.g. PRI, 14 and 29; PLI, 5 and 16 – in the Chamber of Deputies, in 1976 and 1983 respectively), they have tended to remain dominant over their organisations, thus fitting the model of political parties which are both loose-associational and top-heavy.[37] Their collective national leaderships have been generally identified with their parliamentarians,[38] even if the latter have not always coincided strictly with the composition of the main executive organs of the parties, i.e. their national directorates.[39] An important aspect of their horizontal-level structures is the central role played by the party secretaries, both in party strategy and in representing the party externally. In the case of the PRI, the constitutional position of the political secretary was upgraded in organisational reforms of 1968 and 1978, in turn strengthening his role as the symbol of party unity.[40] Similarly, in the case of the PLI, Zanone once remarked that 'for the small parties image identification with the secretary is almost inevitable, above all because of television'.[41] This may suggest that the role of party secretary has offered charismatic rather than bureaucratic leadership, given also the lack of bureaucratisation within the PRI and PLI, but in fact performance here has depended much on the individual incumbent. At the same time, the party secretary might well be constrained internally in two respects. First, he has to carry with him his executive in policy and strategy decisions, and it is relevant to note that the organisational reforms of the 1960s increased the size of the various national organs of the PRI. Secondly, overlapping with this, the secretary's internal base depends invariably on the balance of factions within his own party. Like most of the other Italian parties, the PRI and PLI have shown evidence of factionalism though usually in a less institutionalised form than the major ones have. Both parties over time have consisted of some three or four factions whose changing strength between congresses has provided precise measures of the internal support for the incumbent secretary.

Factional allegiance has also dominated vertical relations within the party structures. Such vertical linkages have been essentially informal, despite organisational reforms as in the PRI, since they have focused on contacts between parliamentarians and their constituencies.[42] Furthermore, participation in these small parties has tended to be minimal except – most of all – where their grass-roots have a subcultural basis and have been articulated through auxiliary organisations. The only significant example has been with the PRI in Romagna which has long historical roots, drawing on a tradition of Republican co-operatives and associational life.[43] Other smaller examples, usually among Republicans rather than Liberals, may be found elsewhere, though less institutionalised as forms of subcultural infrastructure. In Tuscany, for example, this is true of certain localities in the province of Massa Carrara (with its libertarian and anarchist tradition, strengthened by Republican anti-fascist Resistance activity) as well as in the province of Grosseto. In the latter, several instances of local PRI activism can be attributed to traditions going back to Garibaldi reinforced subsequently by a Resistance record among some PRI local notables or particularly active individuals in more recent times. A classic instance of this has been Susanna Agnelli (sister of the head of Fiat), mayoress of Monte Argentario in Grosseto province since 1974 and simultaneously national deputy at Rome.[44] Apart from such local factors, the growth in PRI membership as a whole from the early 1980s opens up the possibility of a mild improvement in its low rate of participation, although this is too recent a phenomenon to generalise about yet.

Otherwise, one has to look to external interest groups as performing an ersatz organisational and especially financial role for these parties. One may note some difference between the PRI and PLI here, for the latter has been more ready to ally itself with special interests most notably with business and industry under Malagodi (the employers' organisation Confindustria transferred support from the DC to the PLI from the early 1960s because of its hostility towards the centre-left alliance). The PRI has been much more reluctant to have such firm links with special interests for reasons of party identity, although it has enjoyed some loose and temporary links with certain state corporations as in the 1950s; also at times in the 1970s with entrepreneurial figures like Gianni Agnelli and Guido Carli, the banker.[45] However, since state finance was introduced in 1974 these two parties have predominantly depended on this for their income. The PRI's link with the trade-union movement through Republican membership in the moderate left Union of Italian Labour (UIL – together with the Social Democrats) has provided some further collateral organisational support of the party structure.

In conclusion, it may be said that indeed the PRI and PLI are together loose-associational and top-heavy in the operation of their structures, even taking account of periodic cases of organisational reform. Furthermore, this discussion of their structures has emphasised the close interplay between organisational and political dynamics with a tendency to confirm their role as small parties. Nevertheless, despite these important similarities, the PRI and PLI have to some extent followed distinct as well as separate organisational roads. This has been most of all evident in the PRI's greater readiness to embrace organisational values albeit to a limited degree, in some awareness of having a mass base (even though in reality this has been extremely localised), in a stronger sense of party autonomy *vis-à-vis* interest groups and, of course, it must also relate to the different social bases of the two parties.

THE ELECTORAL BASES OF THE PRI AND PLI: HARD-CORE SUPPORT OR 'OPINION VOTING'?

The most important electoral parameter of all in Italy since the Second World War has been the high level of stability in voting behaviour for much of this period. This does help much in explaining the constancy in the two parties' level of support, subject to the impingement of political variables – most notably, in the PLI's clear opposition to the centre-left in the 1963 election. The gradual increase in opinion voting and volatility together with a certain loosening of the dominant subcultures as from the divorce referendum of 1974 have presented new opportunities for the small parties, even though the extent of this change should not be overrated. As to the size of the two parties' electoral bases, that is simply demonstrated in the accompanying Table 3.7. Taking individual results, this support has ranged from a high point of 7.0 (the PLI in 1963) to a low point of 1.3 per cent (the same party in 1976), with an average for the national elections from 1946 to 1987 inclusive of 2.83 per cent for the PRI and 3.82 per cent for the PLI. By the standards of Italy's multi-party system, that once again places them in the category of 'small' rather than 'minimal' parties, all the more because of a general renaissance of small-party support during the 1980s.

There are various ways of explaining Republican and Liberal electoral support before focusing on its social composition and answering the introductory question. First, competition in this multi-party system has influenced the scope of Republican and Liberal support, and ideological space between individual parties. Particularly interesting in this respect is vote exchanging between those parties close on the spectrum, including the PRI and PLI. Both of them have often exchanged votes with the DC, schematically seen as placed between them, though in reality their relative positions are hardly so simple. The DC, for instance, benefited from former voters of both these parties at times of high anti-communist mobilisation on its part, as in the 1948 and 1976 elections; just as in 1979 the PRI made gains at the expense of the DC, a tendency magnified in the election of 1983.[46] At times, too, there has been a direct exchange between the PRI and PLI such as in 1979 to the latter's advantage,[47] this invariably occurring when they have been seen as close on the spectrum.

What is also significant is these two parties' vote exchanging 'outwards' on the ideological spectrum. Over the first half of the period after the Second World War, the PLI succeeded in absorbing almost all the former monarchist electorate,[48] although here we are in fact talking about a 'structural' or consolidated exchange. There has also been some exchanging between the PLI and the neo-fascist MSI, while the PRI has hardly ever exchanged votes with the latter. As a survey of the 1979 and 1983 results has shown, the PRI's main exchange partners were the DC, the 'socialist-radical area' and to some lesser extent the PLI.[49] So, the above evidence does indicate some cyclical closeness between the PRI and PLI, but more often than not their separateness as electoral forces. For instance, this has been illustrated by the fact that vote exchanging between them has been less direct than indirect, usually via the DC.[50]

Secondly, any diachronic assessment of the electoral development

Table 3.7 *National elections in Italy, 1946–87*
(for Chamber of Deputies)

	PRI		PLI	
	%	seats	%	seats
1946	4.4	23	6.8	41
1948	2.5	9	3.8	19
1953	1.6	5	3.0	13
1958	1.4	6	3.5	17
1963	1.4	6	7.0	39
1968	2.0	9	5.8	31
1972	2.9	15	3.9	20
1976	3.1	14	1.3	5
1979	3.0	16	1.9	9
1983	5.1	29	2.9	16
1987	3.7	21	2.1	11

of the PRI and PLI will confirm this general picture of separateness. Taking broad patterns, the PLI gained and was at its high point during the 1950s and especially 1960s, with the opposite in the case of the PRI. In the 1970s, however, and especially since Spadolini assumed the PRI leadership, the trend has been the other way round with the PLI falling to its low point and the PRI achieving new heights in electoral favour. In other words, the electoral development of the PRI in the period after the Second World War has been in the form of a 'U' curve with maximum support in 1946 and 1983 and the bottom of that curve in 1958–63 (although the PRI again lost support in 1987). This does lead us to consider the question of the stability of their electorates over time. Apart from the exceptional circumstances of the formative stage of the party system up to the 1948 election, there have been no dramatic turns in their electoral support save for the PLI's rise in 1963 and possibly its drop in 1972, since when its decline has been gradual. The PRI's electoral development downwards and then upwards has in fact been rather steady, save for its escalation in support in 1983.

This picture would concur overall with the long-term stability of the Italian electorate since the Second World War, but recent elections show a qualitative change in the nature of support for these two parties and the PRI in particular. From having a well-defined but geographically restricted base (especially strong traditionally in central Italy), the PRI has begun to break out of this and spread its support more evenly across the country. As a survey of its 1983 election result has demonstrated, the base of the PRI has become less

Table 3.8 *Social composition of the electorates of the PRI and PLI*

	PRI, %			PLI, %			Whole Electorate, %
	1968	1972	1976	1968	1972	1976	1968
Farmers	0.0	0.3	0.2	0.2	0.5	0.6	0.7
Workers	1.1	0.0	0.2	0.8	0.9	11.9	28.9
Artisans	3.5	4.9	12.3	0.5	0.6	14.8	19.4
Subordinate tertiary	10.2	8.8	9.6	0.3	0.3	1.2	10.4
Tradespeople	2.7	7.6	5.3	19.2	10.3	16.3	6.9
White-collar workers	54.0	55.1	55.7	33.0	41.3	30.1	24.7
Professional and managerial classes (*ceti superiori*)	28.5	23.2	16.6	45.9	46.1	25.2	9.0
Total	100.0	100.0	100.0	100.0	100.0	100.0	100.0

Source: M. Barbagli et al., *Fluidità Elettorale e Classi Sociali in Italia* (1979), 127, 139, 140.

static and more heterogeneous than before, increasing support outside its traditional strongholds and generally becoming more and more urban-based.[51] Especially dramatic was the rise in the vote for the PRI in the city of Milan (from 5.4 to 12.3 per cent), pushing the PSI into third place. This same survey also showed that only a third of the PRI's support in the 1983 election had voted for it in the immediate past.[52] However, the risks as well as the opportunities entailed by the loosening-up of traditional party attachment were illustrated subsequently by the combined losses of the PRI/PLI alliance in the European elections of 1984 and by PRI losses in the local elections of 1985 and the national elections of 1987.

That social change lies behind this qualitative change in Italian voting behaviour is underlined by a restructuring of the social composition of the two parties' electoral bases producing some convergence between them here (as shown in the accompanying Table 3.8). Traditionally, the PLI had been especially attractive to the high bourgeoisie, especially that in the fashionable residential districts of the large cities, as well as industrialists and landowners (in the south). The overall result, however, of the PLI's strong haemorrhage in votes from 1968 to 1976 was not only that it lost most of its electorate *per se* but furthermore that it changed the nature of its social base, from largely the higher classes (*ceti superiori*) in 1968 to a more balanced spread of support and particularly from white-collar workers (*impiegati*) in 1976.[53] The PRI has similarly seen a growth in support among *impiegati* and the professional middle class as a whole, notably in 1983, as part of the 'urbanisation' of its electoral base.[54] There has now emerged a strong correlation between voting by *impiegati* and support for both the PRI and PLI.[55] On the other hand, working-class support for these two parties has remained minimal over time. Only worthy of mention here is some industrial working-class support for the PRI in selected localised strongholds like Romagna, which may be described as 'historical'. The other interesting feature of this restructuring of the electoral bases of these parties has been in terms of regional balance (see Table 3.9). While the PLI used to have its main strength in the south, its chief gains have come from the north in recent times, just as we have seen the PRI has become more of a 'national' party in this respect.

In short, the PRI and PLI have converged in the social composition of their electoral bases in so far as they have both increasingly become 'opinion parties', though the PRI has achieved more substantial success here than the PLI. This is somewhat in contrast with the past when their largely different electorates had derived from 'historical' republicanism or liberalism or differences in traditional class or occupational affiliation. These areas of hard-core support have somewhat weakened although, in the PRI's case mainly, they still remain important. The latter's chances for electoral growth and a more important political role have risen with the increase in 'opinion voting', but this has also made its electorate more unstable; while the instability of the PLI's electorate had been earlier demonstrated by its collapse of support in the 1970s. At the same time, whatever basic changes have taken place in their respective electoral bases, the PRI and the PLI still merit the label of middle-class parties.

CONCLUSION

Our examination of the Republican and Liberal Parties in Italy broadly confirms the introductory thesis about two roads of liberalism in that country, the one distinctly 'historical' and the other *de facto* (though 'historical' in its own right as republican). In a sense, there should be no surprise that this thesis applies, considering the importance of the historical dimension in both cases. As types of parties, the PRI and PLI have shown many distinct differences such as in their respective placements in the left–right spectrum, their strategies and participation in government and also the nature of their electoral support, not to mention some differences in policy lines while showing more similarity in their common organisational

Table 3.9 *Percentage distribution of PRI and PLI votes by geographical area*
(for Chamber of Deputies, 1972, 1976 and 1979)

	PRI, %			PLI, %		
	1972	1976	1979	1972	1976	1979
N.W.	32.6	33.1	31.1	45.1	42.6	48.1
N.E.	20.0	22.8	21.7	18.3	15.8	16.1
Centre	21.6	20.1	20.8	15.7	13.1	14.1
Deep south	15.7	14.8	14.9	12.0	16.2	12.6
Islands	10.2	9.3	11.5	8.9	12.3	9.1
ITALY	100.0	100.0	100.0	100.0	100.0	100.0

Source: Arturo Parisi (ed.), *Mobilità senza movimento: le elezioni del 3 giugno 1979* (Bologna, 1980) 158.

Table 3.10 *Percentage distribution of PRI votes by geographical area, 1946–83*

	1946	1948	1953	1958	1963	1968	1972	1976	1979	1983
Industrial areas	10.3	11.0	15.3	19.8	16.0	18.4	32.5	33.0	31.1	38.4
'White' areas	5.0	3.6	3.9	7.7	4.9	5.6	9.2	11.9	10.6	11.9
'Red' areas	37.8	42.1	42.7	41.5	33.5	25.2	22.0	21.3	22.0	19.4
Whole south	46.9	43.3	38.1	31.0	45.6	50.8	36.3	33.8	36.3	30.3
ITALY	100.0	100.0	100.0	100.0	100.0	100.0	100.0	100.0	100.0	100.0

Source: P. Corbetta and A. Parisi (eds.), *Il Voto Repubblicano: alle origini del 26 giugno* (Bologna, 1984) 12.
(NB: In comparing these two tables, there is a difference in the territorial definition of the regions of Italy.)

weakness. One can, of course, see their convergence in party development on several places over the past decade – strategic, policy-wise, electoral – and certainly there is less ideological space between them than ever before.

But will these two roads of Italian liberalism actually meet as distinct from converge? In the light of this study, one should perhaps remain cautious, given all the evidence about the continuing influence of party history and tradition on the identity and behaviour of the PRI and PLI; although certain circumstances, most evidently a major electoral reform in Italy, might well help to counter this influence. It is useful at this point to assess this problem in terms of three basic relationships when examining the general role of political parties. On all three counts, it may reasonably be concluded that the two parties have become closer: with regard to the state, because their sharing of government responsibility has for the first time since the period immediately after the Second World War become continuous; with regard to the community, because their electorates have become more similar; and obviously, too, because their own alliance within the *pentapartito* formula has replaced previous alliances which have usually divided them. It is also possible to pursue this argument in terms of the mutual dynamics of these three relationships. This is likely to suggest that, depending on future political events, the basis for a more institutionalised link between the PRI and PLI or even a merger would not be so artificial as it might have been earlier in the post-war period.

NOTES

1 James Hanning, 'The Italian Radical Party and the "New Politics"' in *West European Politics*, October 1981, p. 268.
2 The PR and the PRI were apparently close after the former first split from the Liberals, e.g. they formed an alliance for the local elections in 1958; but there has been little to suggest any closeness since.
3 Raphael Zariski, *Italy: the Politics of Uneven Development* (Dryden Press: Hinsdale, Illinois, 1972) 111.
4 Paolo Farneti, *The Italian Party System, 1945–1980* (Frances Pinter: London, 1985) 14–15.
5 Giovanni Ferrara, 'La sfida liberale' in *La Repubblica*, 25.11.81. Francesco Nitti was Prime Minister of Italy, 1919–20, an economist and later an anti-fascist figure. Giovanni Amendola was a major anti-fascist figure and earlier known for his writings in liberal journals. The Action Party, a part of intellectuals of the radical democratic tradition, played a prominent role in the Resistance and in providing political leadership during 1943–5, but it subsequently failed to maintain a political role in post-war Italy. Luigi Einaudi, a major exponent of liberal economic theories, later became a minister under De Gasperi and President of the Italian Republic, 1948–55.
6 Interview with Massimo Scioscioli, Istituto di Studi per La Storia del Movimento Repubblicano, Rome, 22.10.85.
7 Giuseppe Mammarella, *Italy after Fascism: a political history 1943–65* (University of Notre Dame Press, Indiana, 1966) 40.
8 Mammarella, *Italy after Fascism*, p. 40.
9 F. Catalano, 'The rebirth of the party system, 1944–48' in S.J. Woolf (ed.), *The Rebirth of Italy, 1943–50* (Longman: London, 1972) 62–3, 80–1.
10 See interview with the historian Roberto Chiarini in *Panorama*, 2.4.84, pp. 72–81.
11 In an interview with the author, Rome, 15.11.77, concerned with the specifics of politics in Tuscany, Giovanni Malagodi, unprompted, launched into a defence of his party as not 'fascist', as some people claimed. Cf. interview with Egidio Sterpa, member of the PLI national directorate and a leader of his party's right-wing, Rome, 23.7.83, his comment that in the PLI there is a 'moderate' form of

liberalism that 'at its limits can stretch as far as being conservative in its more extreme right form'.

12 In the Constituent Assembly elections, 1946, the DC gained 35.1%, the Socialists 20.7%, the Communists 18.9%, the Liberals 6.8% and the Republicans, 4.4%.

13 Giorgio Galli, *Il Bipartitismo Imperfetto: Comunisti e Democristiani in Italia* (Il Mulino: Bologna, 1966), Giovanni Sartori, 'European political parties: the case of polarised pluralism' in J. LaPalombara and M. Weiner (eds.), *Political Parties and Political Development* (Princeton University Press: Princeton, 1966).

14 Percy Allum, *Italy–Republic without Government?* (Weidenfeld & Nicolson, London, 1973), 63.

15 Farneti, *The Italian Party System*, esp. ch. 4.

16 Farneti, *The Italian Party System*, p. 54.

17 Interview with Egidio Sterpa, 23.7.83.

18 Interview with Sergio Trauner, head of PLI's national office for regional and local government, Rome, 16.12.81.

19 The list of PRI and PLI policy lines is constructed on the basis of representative party policy documents, the author's interviews and portraits of the parties' policy stands in R. Zariski, *Italy: The Politics of Uneven Development*, pp. 174–8.

20 G. Mammarella, *Italy after Fascism*, p. 202; Sergio Telmon, *Ugo La Malfa* (Rusconi: Milan 1983) 41, 82.

21 S. Telmon, pp. 120, 136.

22 Based on material provided by Derek Hearl at the preparatory meeting on this project, Essex University, March 1985.

23 Farneti, *The Italian Party System*, pp. 29–30.

24 Mammarella, *Italy after Fascism*, pp. 196–7.

25 Mammarella, *Italy after Fascism*, p. 155.

26 A. Marradi, 'Italy from "centrism" to crisis of the centre-left' in Eric C. Browne and John Dreijmanis (eds.), *Government Coalitions in Western Democracies* (Longman: New York, 1982) 62.

27 A. Parisi and A. Varni, *Organizzazione e Politica nel PRI: 1946–84* (Bologna, 1985) 111; Norman Kogan, *A Political History of Postwar Italy* (Praeger: New York, 1981) 21.

28 Obituary of La Malfa in *The Economist*, 31.3.79.

29 Parisi and Varni, *Organizzazione e Politica nel PRI*, pp. 13–14, esp. the comment by Pacciardi, the PRI leader, that 'for all of us politics has always been a matter for after work hours'.

30 Quoted in *La Repubblica*, 19.11.81.

31 Interview with Paolo Piccio Crepas, PLI, Rome, 22.10.85.

32 Parisi and Varni, *Organizzazione e Politica nel PRI*, pp. 29, 32.

33 Parisi and Varni, *Organizzazione e Politica nel PRI*, pp. 67–9 and 81 ff.

34 Parisi and Varni, *Organizzazione e Politica nel PRI*, pp. 104–5, 114.

35 Parisi and Varni, *Organizzazione e Politica nel PRI*, pp. 60, 63.

36 Report in *Panorama*, 21.11.83, pp. 46–8.

37 E.g. S. Passigli, 'Le tre componenti del gruppo dirigente repubblicano' in *Città e Regione*, December 1981, p. 94.

38 Parisi and Varni, *Organizzazione e Politica nel PRI*, pp. 158–9.

39 Parisi and Varni, *Organizzazione e Politica nel PRI*, p. 129.

40 Parisi and Varni, *Organizzazione e Politica nel PRI*, pp. 83, 114.

41 Interview with *La Repubblica*, 11.11.81.

42 Parisi and Varni, *Organizzazione e Politica nel PRI*, p. 111.

43 Parisi and Varni, *Organizzazione e Politica nel PRI*, pp. 13, 15, 109–10.

44 This information on Tuscany draws on various interviews there in 1977 with political leaders in the province of Grosseto.
45 Interview with Massimo Scioscioli, Rome, 22.10.85.
46 A. Parisi (ed.), *Mobilità senza movimento: le elezioni del 3 giugno 1979* (Il Mulino: Bologna, 1980) 76; P. Corbetta and A. Parisi, *Il Voto Repubblicano: alle origini del 26 giugno* (Bologna, 1984) 50–1.
47 R. Leonardi in H.R. Penniman (ed.), *Italy at the Polls, 1979* (American Enterprise Institution for Public Policy Research: Washington, 1981) 189–90.
48 P. Farneti, *The Italian Party System*, p. 27.
49 Corbetta and Parisi, *Il Voto Repubblicano*, pp. 49–51.
50 M. Barbagli et al. (eds.), *Fluidità Elettorale e Classi Sociali in Italia* (Il Mulino: Bologna, 1979) 71, 84 and 103.
51 Corbetta and Parisi, *Il voto Repubblicano*, pp. 15–16, 55, 57.
52 Corbetta and Parisi, *Il Voto Repubblicano*, p. 55.
53 Barbagli et al., *Fluidità Elettorale*, pp. 140–1.
54 Corbetta and Parisi, *Il Voto Repubblicano*, pp. 25–9.
55 Barbagli et al., *Fluidità Elettorale*, pp. 126–7, 132, 136.

4

The FDP in the Federal Republic of Germany: the requirements of survival and success

Emil Kirchner and David Broughton

INTRODUCTION

On the face of it, it may seem obvious that the Free Democratic Party (FDP) has acted as the standard bearer of liberalism in the Federal Republic of Germany since 1949. Certainly, the party is invariably classified by observers both inside and outside the country as being 'liberal'. There is also considerable evidence, in the FDP's manifestos and other documents as well as in the fact that the party's candidates usually bear 'liberal' labels, to suggest that such a designation is widely accepted without question. In addition, the party has long been a leading member of the Liberal International.

Yet when we begin to look beyond the label at the actual principles which the FDP professes to champion and which it wants to see implemented and protected, any apparent clarity of purpose and distinctiveness immediately becomes blurred and ambiguous.

Whilst this can be partly explained by reference to the difficulties involved in defining 'liberalism' as a whole, the FDP's problems in establishing an identity for itself based on 'liberal' ideas have been accentuated by the party's enforced role within the post Second World War German party system as a 'corrective' or 'pivot' between the two major parties, the Christian Democrats (CDU/CSU) and the Social Democrats (SPD).[1]

This means that the FDP is often able to exploit its structural position as a usually indispensable coalition partner in order to base its electoral appeal on its ability to prevent either main party achieving an absolute majority in the Bundestag. The party also claims that 'moderation' in the conduct of the federal government results from its fulfilling of such a role.

The FDP has often emphasised a strategy proven over time which plays down any substantive ideological content in favour of generalities and emphasis on stability and continuity. Yet it also needs to suggest that the party has a unique identity and profile capable of producing specific ideas worthy of mass support.

This inherent conflict at the very heart of the FDP's political role has sometimes acted as an important source of tension between the different sections of the party. On many occasions, however, the general adherence to a vaguely worded set of 'liberal' precepts has proved invaluable as a means of keeping the party united in times of internal disputes over both policy and coalition formation.

However, it would be wrong to imply that such conflicts are a new phenomenon within German liberalism. Disagreements of this kind can be traced in an institutionalised form back to the Weimar Republic, with clear roots apparent even in the failed German Revolution of 1848.

THE DEVELOPMENT OF LIBERALISM IN GERMANY

As in many other European countries, modern liberalism in Germany surfaced in the aftermath of the French Revolution. In particular, it had to come to terms with new and radical ideas concerning popular democracy designed to challenge the widespread authoritarian basis of political power which prevailed at the time.[2]

Two specific questions were to prove especially difficult for the liberal movement to answer. First, what was their attitude to the problem of creating lasting German national unity, a source of long-standing conflict across the whole political spectrum and one with direct and unavoidable salience where a number of principalities and states rather than a nation existed.

Secondly, to what extent could the liberals support the concept of parliamentary democracy whilst the mysticism of the German romantic movement (*Volksgeist*) and the philosophy of Hegel emphasising the essential separation of state and society were increasingly influential? The painting of the 'objective' state as the legitimate protector of stability as opposed to the 'subjective' and partial interests in society beneath was important in undermining the intellectual credibility of proposals for major reforms. The idea was also important in limiting the spread of the perception that fundamental change was necessary at all.

The late industrialisation of Germany and the delayed rise of a working class until near the end of the nineteenth century meant that any sustained push for reform had to come from the middle classes but the lack of any organised and independent resistance to the old leadership elites ensured the failure of the 1848 Revolution. There was, in any case, no 'crisis' to precipitate radical changes in the system, with the passivity of the populace resulting from the Reformation and the Thirty Years War combining with Prussian military hegemony having the effect of consigning any proposals for constitutional reform to oblivion.

It was clearly impossible for the liberal movement to avoid grappling with these problems, especially when the development of Germany as an industrial power saw the sharpening of interest conflicts between the mass of the workers and the traditional power elites. The ambivalence and uncertainty of liberals on topics of such significance were certain to feed through into their overall political strategy, particularly affecting their relationship with conservative and nationalist groups on one side was well as radical forces on the other. However, the control of the decision-making structure by bureaucratic rather than party politicians meant that the presentation of clear alternatives was irrelevant, with co-operation between different groups neither encouraged nor necessary.

We can date the development of two distinct strands of German liberalism from the time of the failed 1848 Revolution, although the formation of separate political parties articulating the differences that existed only took place in the mid-1860s. The main groups were the 'national' liberals, whose principal aim was the creation of German unity rather than the construction of a responsible parliamentary system, whereas the 'progressive' liberals emphasised internationalism and the need to build a constitutional framework within which liberal democratic values could take root and flourish.

These different approaches re-emerged in the Weimar Republic after the débâcle of the First World War, with the formation of two parties, the DDP (German Democratic Party) and the DVP (German People's Party). It has to be said, though, that neither party was particularly adept at playing its part in the running of an effective government, despite the participation of both in most of the coalitions that were formed. The accentuation of sectional interests at the expense of wider concerns and the promotion of a rigidly defined *Weltanschauung* were second nature to parties used to a system of government where willingness to compromise and respect for any 'rules of the game' were not required. There was also little incentive for any party to recruit capable leaders since the workings of the system offered only uncertain rewards and prospects for advancement.

The disposition of most parties between 1918 and 1933 towards non-co-operation with each other meant that none were in a position to resist effectively the appeal of national socialism as it swept through the country after 1930. Many of the supporters of the two liberal parties defected to more right-wing and conservative groupings and all the remaining liberal members of the Reichstag after the last free elections in March 1933 voted for Hitler's Enabling Act.

It could certainly be pointed out that an electoral system of proportional representation and a blurring of clear lines of responsibility between a popularly elected president, the Reichstag and the chancellor of the day were significant elements in the eventual demise of the Weimar system of government. Nevertheless, the inability of the parties to run a political structure based on parliamentary democracy was of prime importance in instilling in ordinary people a generally negative reaction towards parties and their behaviour. This paved the way for the mass mobilisation undertaken by the National Socialists on the basis of promises to end the bitter conflicts and endless divisions which had come to characterise the Weimar years in the eyes of many.[3]

With all parties free from any sense of real responsibility, the liberals in particular were highly prone to splintering since unity on more than a temporary basis proved impossible to fashion. Unity was, in any case, hardly a pre-requisite for exercising power in such a fragmented system, with thirty-eight parties taking part in the election of July 1932.

Despite the Nazi aim of 'modernising' German society through the policy of *Gleichschaltung* and the introduction of a command economy, the collapse of the National Socialist regime in 1945 permitted some of the major political forces of the Weimar Republic, mainly the SPD and the Catholics, to re-emerge relatively intact. The victorious allies were mainly interested in rebuilding a free market economic structure in the Federal Republic but they were also determined to lay down new ground rules for the conduct of partisan conflict. Whilst pledging themselves to the restoration of a liberal democratic system, the occupying powers maintained a tight grip on all political activity, including the licensing of parties as one element in a gradual return to competitive politics. This was probably helpful in terms of mass identification with the new structure since extremist and potentially anti-system parties were not initially allowed to stand at elections.

Of equal significance was the role which political parties were now expected to play. According to article 21 of the *Grundgesetz* (Basic

Law), the parties 'shall take part in the forming of the political will of the people'.[4] For the first time, therefore, the parties were given an explicit function to perform and they were also allowed the responsibility and power to fulfil it. This was an important factor in the gradual but unmistakable process of social integration which eventually came to affect many aspects of life in the Federal Republic, in stark contrast to the deeply embedded divisions of the Weimar years.

The liberal movement obviously could not stand still in the face of such developments. As both the CDU/CSU and SPD began to establish organisational bases across the whole country and to formulate broad-based appeals to the German electorate, the pressure on the liberals to come together in one party became irresistible. The rapid absorption of the other small regional and sectional parties into the Christian/conservative camp in the 1950s demonstrated the indispensability of greater unity and cohesion than in the past if liberal ideas were to maintain an independent voice and expression.

It also soon became clear that the FDP, founded in 1948 from liberal groups of various kinds, would be in a position to have an important say with regard to federal government policy if it proved itself able to fulfil a functional role as a *Mehrheitsbeschaffer* (majority provider/creator) in a 'balanced' party state. Whilst this has sometimes appeared unlikely, particularly when disputes over coalition options have sown the seeds for bouts of long-running internal dissension, the possibility of exerting disproportionate influence and claiming key ministerial portfolios in the process has usually acted as adequate 'cement' to keep such conflicts within bounds.

The FDP's attempt to become recognised as the *dritte Kraft* between the two major parties was, however, limited to coalition formation with one or the other. Its inability to expand its electoral base markedly or to retain the loyalty of its voters for very long meant that the opportunities thrown up by its position had to be exercised with caution, even given opinion-poll evidence which suggests that the party playing such a 'braking' role is approved of by German voters.[5]

Another important reason for a newly fashioned organisational unity between the different strands of liberal thought lay in the introduction of the 5 per cent electoral exclusion barrier, below which no party is represented in the Bundestag. The FDP has sometimes hovered dangerously close to this level of support (most obviously in 1969) but it has always managed to survive by stressing the party's value as a 'pivot' as well as an ability to ensure the creation of a government with majority support.

Party unity was also easier to achieve in the period after 1945, since it was clear that the FDP would be able to exert power over policy within a system of responsible parliamentary government. Such a radically different situation from the Weimar era can partly be accounted for by the constitutional and institutional provisions underpinning the Bonn Republic. However, it is at least equally important not to overlook the role which political leaders played in reshaping mass expectations regarding the legitimacy of partisan conflict and the role of political parties in making the system widely acceptable in terms of both socio-economic and political outputs.[6]

For the FDP, it was also important to be involved in the federal government on practical grounds. The party is the smallest in the Federal Republic in terms of membership[7] and with a limited budget to sustain its presence, it is clearly highly restricted in what it can be expected to achieve in opposition to much bigger parties. Incumbency, in contrast, has provided the FDP with the opportunity to project itself into the limelight, to claim some of the credit for sustained economic affluence and to use the mass media to good effect in terms of stressing the achievements of the governments in which the party has participated.[8]

This also meant that some of the more prominent members of the party became well known, something which later permitted the FDP to emphasise the competence and ability of 'their' ministers in future electoral appeals, downgrading in the process the ideological content of their policies. Such an emphasis on its leadership elite might seem inevitable in such a small if influential party, one with constant worries concerning parliamentary survival after the next federal election. In such a situation, running the party will almost certainly be largely placed on the shoulders of such people. The consequences of this for the FDP's decision-making procedures and its internal organisation are considered in the next section.

PARTY STRUCTURE AND ORGANISATION

We have already dealt with the FDP's internal structure and decision-making processes in detail elsewhere,[9] yet we cannot ignore such factors in any examination of the party's behaviour since both provide important clues as to the nature of the FDP and the role it has come to play.

Clearly, the Free Democrats are not a mass party in any sense, in contrast to both the Christian Democrats and the Social Democrats.[10] Whilst this might mean that the party is easier to keep together as a coherent and united entity, the federal structure of the Republic has forced all the parties to form and maintain area and regional organisations, a necessity which contains the seeds for potential conflicts of all kinds between national and sub-national levels.

This might not be particularly significant, of course, if each section of the party is fully cognisant of its own responsibilities and duties and, equally importantly, each accepts its share of influence as being equitable. Problems begin to arise when the decision-making procedures themselves and the inter-relationships between the different groups within the party are uncertain in theory and inconsistently applied in practice.

On the surface at least, the FDP's internal structure is similar to that of many other parties. It has established the usual panoply of committees, congresses and an executive, but the almost constant involvement in government has given the parliamentary party, and the leadership elite in particular, an overwhelming degree of authority to take even crucial decisions, without invoking the formal consultative process implied by the party's structure.

More often, most notably in the coalition change to the Christian Democrats in the autumn of 1982, vital decisions are taken and implemented and they are then justified and legitimated *afterwards* at party congresses called, in effect, to acknowledge a *fait accompli*.[11]

Such actions suggest an almost complete lack of influence by the ordinary members on the party's overall direction, an impression reinforced by the fact that coalition changes in 1969 and 1982 were accompanied by substantial numbers of members leaving the FDP (about 29,000 and 9,000 respectively) rather than staying and arguing for their particular coalition preference.

The need to participate in government has ensured that the Free Democrats have developed much more along the lines of a *Wählerpartei* (voters' party) than a *Mitgliederpartie* (members' party), probably an important factor in the relatively low membership total of around 80,000.

Nevertheless, the FDP is still able to attract financial support from some of the biggest business conglomerates in the country. Although the party is heavily dependent on the reimbursement of election costs by the state,[12] they have also received considerable funds from firms such as Horten as a result of their unambiguously free-market economic policies and fiscal policies designed to encourage steady growth and prosperity.

Even though the Christian Democrats are also credible in claiming belief in the value of such ideas, they are essentially a party of interest aggregation, where general policy principles are sometimes not realised in terms of specific policy implementation.

The FDP is reliant to an important degree on such contributions from industry since it has never been able, unlike the two major parties, to call on and retain the long-term backing of organised interest and pressure groups. Whilst the SPD is supported by the industrial trade unions federated in the DGB, and the CDU/CSI receives both moral and financial aid from the Catholic church, the Free Democrats are only able to rely on some help from the BDI (which also backs the Christian Democrats) and an assortment of white-collar and professional groups in teaching and the civil service such as the DBB, DAG and the ULA.[13] The party also receives support from some farming organisations in the north of the country.

The functional attraction of the FDP to certain middle-class groups as one result of the specific policies it espouses has recently been under sustained attack through the increasing appeal of various green and ecological organisations, both at an institutional level and at the level of the mass electorate. The latter clearly constitute a serious threat to the FDP's long-term position since the party's ability to succeed on its own terms turns crucially on its retention of a role which has enabled it to exert disproportionate influence over many of the coalitions formed in the Federal Republic.

If that capability was undermined or even overtaken by 'alternative' groups, the future for the FDP, given its development so far as a party defined by its position within the overall political system, would be perilous indeed. Even though the Free Democrats have become adept at escaping just when the trap-door appears to be opening, such an unpredictable future can hardly be regarded as reassuring for the morale of the party faithful or the ability of the FDP to attract notoriously fickle voters to its cause.

This latter group are clearly essential to the FDP in terms of its present function, yet the party is not in a position to rely on regular support at successive elections. The electoral base of the Free Democrats has undergone several quite distinct changes since 1949, changes which are closely related both to the party's coalitional options and behaviour and its appeal at different times to disaffected voters who normally choose one of the major parties.

THE ELECTORAL BASE OF THE FDP

Of all the aspects of the FDP which have been analysed in the past, the party's attraction to voters at different elections and its support within particular social groups have received most attention. The conclusion has generally been that the mass base of the Free Democrats is small and unstable over time, with a tiny percentage of

Table 4.1 *The highest, lowest and mean vote shares of the main liberal parties, 1871–1912*

	Highest, %	Lowest, %	Mean, %
German People's Party	2.2 (1893)	0.4 (1874)	1.3
National Liberals	30.2 (1871)	12.5 (1898)	19.5

Stammwähler and a reliance on 'capturing' floating voters and those with weak or no partisan ties to the major parties.[14]

As a result, the party does not draw especially strong support from any subdivisions of the most commonly employed socio-structural variables, although it does usually receive greater backing from groups such as Protestants and the new middle class than from industrial workers or Catholics.

We will consider these points later on in this section but we first want to extend our perspective by looking at the electoral performance of the various liberal groupings in the First Reich as well as during the Weimar Republic.

Table 4.1 sets out the highest, lowest and mean vote shares of the main liberal parties between 1871 and 1912.

The National Liberals were obviously the stronger political force over the whole period, although both parties suffered declines in their vote shares towards the end.

When we examine Table 4.2 which details the vote shares of the DDP and DVP between 1919 and 1933, a clear pattern is discernible – a strong start (23 per cent of the vote altogether), followed by a sharp decline, particularly between 1920 and the first election of 1924 and at the three polls in 1928, 1930 and July 1932, a sequence ending with a paltry combined total of 1.9 per cent in 1933.

Both periods demonstrate, therefore, substantial and almost monotonic decreases in vote and seat shares which very nearly forced the liberal parties to the point of extinction. The parties' attraction to voters does seem to have been unstable, with a divided liberal movement unable to convince people that they held the answers to economic crisis and societal turbulence.

Any comparison of these results with the FDP's track record in the Federal Republic is not, of course, straightforward, given the development of a highly integrated political culture since 1949 and the operation of an electoral system of 'personalised proportional representation' which permits voters to engage in 'ticket splitting'.

Nevertheless, the main contrast which can be drawn out centres on

Table 4.2 *The seat and vote shares of the liberal parties, Reichstag elections, 1919–33*

	German Democratic Party (DDP)		German People's Party (DVP)		Total	
	Seats, %	Votes, %	Seats, %	Votes, %	Seats, %	Votes, %
1919	17.8	18.6	4.5	4.4	22.3	23.0
1920	8.5	8.3	14.2	13.9	22.7	22.2
1924 (May)	5.9	5.7	9.5	9.2	15.4	14.9
1924 (Dec.)	6.5	6.3	10.3	10.1	16.8	16.4
1928	5.1	4.9	9.2	8.7	14.3	13.6
1930	3.5	3.8	5.2	4.5	8.7	8.3
1932 (July)	0.7	1.0	1.2	1.2	1.9	2.2
1932 (Nov.)	0.3	0.9	1.9	1.9	2.2	2.8
1933	0.8	0.8	0.3	1.1	1.1	1.9

Source: Mackie and Rose (1982) ch. 8, pp. 140–61.

the tendency of the FDP's vote share both to rise *and* fall rather than undergo an almost continual decline as with its predecessors' before the Second World War. This conclusion applies to the second vote (*Zweitstimme*) which the party has received and it has always been able to persuade enough voters to support it to ensure the party's rise above the 5 per cent electoral exclusion barrier (*Sperrklausel*).

Whether this indicates the effectiveness of the FDP's propaganda or ignorance of how the electoral system actually works (probably a mixture of both),[15] the party's survival has been secured through an emphasis on attracting second votes from people who supported either the Christian Democrats or the Social Democrats with their first.

The FDP has not won a direct mandate (first vote) since 1957 and if we therefore assume that people who give it their first vote are its 'stalwart' supporters, it becomes clear that this segment of the party's electoral base is very small indeed (see Table 4.3). For the Free Democrats to look to parliamentary longevity even in the medium term, an emphasis on the value of the party in fulfilling its ascribed function within the overall system has been essential rather than focusing upon the attractiveness of specific policies or the principles on which they are based.

Considerable care has to be taken to ensure that electors can always be attracted to the FDP in sufficient numbers when required and this becomes a particularly delicate task if a switch in coalition partners is

Table 4.3 *The electoral performance of the FDP, 1949–87*

Election year	First vote, %	Second vote, %	Difference, %	No. of seats
1949[a]	—	11.9	—	52
1953	10.8	9.5	+1.3	48
1957	7.5	7.7	−0.2	41
1961	12.1	12.8	−0.7	67
1965	7.9	9.5	−1.6	49
1969	4.8	5.8	−1.0	30
1972	4.8	8.4	−3.6	41
1976	6.4	7.9	−1.5	39
1980	7.2	10.6	−3.4	53
1983	2.8	7.0	−4.2	34
1987	4.7	9.1	−4.4	46

[a] Each elector only had one vote in 1949.
Source: Pulzer (1982); Forschungsgruppe Wahlen, Mannheim (1983 and 1987).

implemented as in 1982 or the party is threatened with 'contamination' by the unpopularity of its major partner of the time.

At national elections, the Free Democrats have shown themselves to be very adept at confronting and overcoming such difficulties, when all the party's skill and experience can be directed at ensuring the continuation of the FDP in its time-honoured role as a 'brake'.

The main problem for the FDP at regional level in the ten *Länder* necessitates a different kind of emphasis. Most states only allow electors one vote which means that they must make a clear choice between competing parties in the absence of any possibility to 'split their tickets'. The FDP continues to run campaigns which stress the party's importance as a 'corrective' but these tactics, if successful, will inevitably draw votes from one or both of the major parties, perhaps ensuring as a result that post-election coalition formation will be less straightforward.

When we consider the FDP's electoral performance at state level, a number of interesting similarities with the national level emerge. Table 4.4 sets out the mean Free Democratic vote share in each of the *Länder* at both levels of the system over the entire period since Second World War. The states are ranked according to the size of the FDP's electoral support at regional level although the order would not change radically if the party's federal results were used instead.

It is clearly possible to divide the different states into three groups. First, the FDP performs best at both national and state level in Baden-Württemberg and Hesse. The former was the heartland of the DVP in the Weimar Republic and the latter's social structure is ideally suited

Table 4.4 *The average FDP national and state vote share in each* Land, *1946–87*

Land	FDP average vote state elections %	FDP average vote Federal elections %	No. of state elections	No. of federal elections	Period covered
Baden-Württemberg	13.9	12.2	12	11	1946–87
Hesse	11.8	12.4	12	11	1946–87
Bremen	10.8	9.8	12	11	1946–87
Saarland	10.0	8.9	8	9	1947–87
Berlin	9.9	—	12	—	1946–87
Rhineland Palatinate	8.7	9.9	11	11	1947–87
Hamburg	7.7	10.8	11	11	1946–87
North Rhine-Westphalia	7.4	8.1	10	11	1947–87
Lower Saxony	6.6	8.5	10	11	1947–87
Schleswig-Holstein	5.7	8.3	11	11	1947–87
Bavaria	6.1	6.7	11	11	1946–87

to the party's appeal, with its high proportion of socially mobile and well-educated white-collar and public-sector workers.[16]

The second group is made up of Bremen, Saarland, Berlin, Rhineland Palatinate and Hamburg. These are small states in terms of both area and population and the FDP has had to face up to the reality of entrenched support for the main parties in all of them. The SPD is particularly strong in Bremen and Hamburg and until recently in Berlin, whilst the agriculturally-based and Catholic rural communites of the Saar area and the Rhineland Palatinate have proven to be fruitful areas for the Christian Democrats.

The third and final group of states comprises North Rhine-Westphalia, Lower Saxony, Schleswig-Holstein and Bavaria, with the FDP recording its lowest average share of the vote at state level in those four *Länder*. The Free Democrats have never been able to mount any kind of effective challenge to the CSU in Bavaria at either level of the system, and they have also not been able to sustain their electoral appeal in the other three states in the face of the much bigger organisations of the two main parties.

This might not, however, matter much if the FDP proves itself capable of surmounting the 5 per cent barrier, since in fulfilling a 'balancing' role, the party will often be able to exert considerable

Table 4.5 *The average FDP state election vote share, 1946–87*

Period	Number of state elections	Average FDP vote share %
1946–9	14	12.6
1950–3	10	15.7
1954–7	11	13.8
1958–61	11	8.4
1962–5	10	8.9
1966–9	10	8.3
1970–3	11	6.5
1974–7	11	7.9
1978–81	11	6.6
1982–5	14	5.2
1986–7	8	6.4
1946–87	121	9.1

influence on the basis of a much lower average vote share than either the SPD or the CDU/CSU.

The electoral performance of the Free Democrats has therefore been variable in the different *Länder* at both national and state level but it is also important to note that the party's average support in regional elections has changed over time.

This does appear to indicate a decline at *Land* level which was not replicated at national level (see Table 4.5), until the party is now, on average, hovering very near the 5 per cent barrier in the last seventeen state elections between 1982 and 1987. This figure was boosted, in addition, by the FDP's relatively good performance in the three regional polls in the Saarland, North Rhine-Westphalia and Berlin in 1985. In the five state elections in 1987, the party's performance showed some improvements.

As Table 4.5 shows, however, the party was averaging 15.7 per cent in the ten state polls between 1950 and 1953 and 13.8 per cent in the next eleven which took place between 1954 and 1957. We can therefore divide the post-war period into different sections – successful years between 1946 and 1957, a sharp drop between 1958 and 1961, but then relatively stable at the lower level until 1969, followed by another noticeable decline between 1970 and 1973. A slight recovery was then achieved in the years until 1977, and then yet another drop until 1981, followed by a potentially disastrous support loss at state level after the change in federal coalition partners to the CDU/CSU in 1982, a trend which has now stabilised somewhat but which obviously leaves no margin for error whatsoever. Over the whole period between 1946 and 1987, the FDP's average vote share has been 9.1 per cent in the 121 state elections to have taken place.

It would appear from the above that the FDP suffers vote losses at state level for a number of different reasons, but they all seem to be related to the party's actions and political events at federal level.

The dip in support between 1958 and 1961 coincided with the exclusion of the Free Democrats from the Christian Democratic majority government of the time, and the losses after 1970 and 1982 can both be largely placed at the door of the *Wende* to the SPD in 1969 and the return to the CDU/CSU in 1982. The drop in support at state level in the late 1970s can be put down to the FDP's 'contamination' by the unpopularity of the SPD, its major federal coalition partner during that period.

Nevertheless, the most recent decline since 1982 suggests renewed problems for the Free Democrats in establishing and maintaining an appeal and a presence at state level. Up to 1970, the FDP had nearly always been represented in all of the ten regional assemblies, [17] with the party's first failure to climb thc 5 pcr cent barrier after the *Wende* of 1969 occurring in Lower Saxony and the Saarland the next year, followed by a vote share of 3.8 per cent in Schleswig-Holstein in 1971.

Between 1982 and 1983, however, at seven state elections, the Free Democrats failed to win 5 per cent of the votes at any, although the three polls held in 1985, the one in Lower Saxony in 1986 and the five held in 1987 suggest that this decline is far from irreversible. It may well be that the party is increasingly focusing its attention on the national level, even though state governments have important decision-making powers both in their own respective areas and through the Bundesrat.[18]

One other reason for the FDP's most recent electoral difficulties is the rise of the Greens, particularly at *Land* level, with their ability to attract electors who had previously formed key 'target groups' for the Free Democrats. Since about 1978, the two parties have been struggling against one another to win over young, well-educated voters who mostly live in urban areas and whose partisan ties are less deeply embedded and more fickle than older, less educated people.

Table 4.6 contains the results of an analysis of the FDP vote at the last two federal elections in 1980 and 1983 on the basis of certain categories of the most commonly employed social background variables deemed to structure voting choice. These elections illustrate neatly both the variability of support for the Free Democrats and its evenness across the different sub-divisions of the chosen groups.

In 1980 the FDP polled 10.6 per cent of the second votes (the party's third-best result since the end of the Second World War) and this is reflected in its support amongst the selected social groups. We can conclude from this analysis that the FDP draws its main support from the middle class, Protestants and those with no religious

Table 4.6 *The socio-structural bases of the FDP vote, federal elections 1980 and 1983*

Overall category	Selected groups	National mean %	FDP vote 1980 %	FDP vote 1983 %	Difference 1983–1980 %
Class	Working class	39.4	4.4	1.7	−2.7
	Middle class	57.7	14.5	4.7	−9.8
	Farmers	2.9	5.9	4.8	−1.1
Religious denomination	Catholic	45.8	8.0	4.0	−4.0
	Protestant	48.0	11.9	4.3	−7.6
	None	5.0	15.7	3.0	−12.7
Religious practice	Practising	22.7	6.0	2.9	−3.1
	Non-practising	77.5	11.1	3.8	−7.3
Age	Under 25	14.0	9.0	3.2	−5.8
	26–39	23.5	12.6	5.2	−7.4
	40–59	37.1	10.7	4.3	−6.4
	Over 60	25.5	8.2	3.3	−4.9
Sex	Male	46.8	10.8	4.1	−6.7
Urban/rural	Urban	84.4	10.6	3.7	−6.9
Union members	Members	21.0	8.9	1.3	−7.6
	Non-members	79.0	10.7	4.8	−5.9

Source: Own analysis of data from 'Wahlstudie 1980' and 'Wahlstudie 1983'.
Note: The data from the 'Wahlstudie 1987' were not available for secondary analysis at the time of writing.

affiliation, as well as those aged between 26 and 39, whilst its appeal is clearly weak amongst the working class, Catholics and people over 60 years old.

The 1983 data demonstrate the decline in support for the Free Democrats across the board as well as the narrow range within which the party operates in terms of its attraction to particular groups. It also suggests that reliance upon an examination of the social base of the FDP leaves much of the story untold since the figures imply a strong likelihood that the party would fail to climb the 5 per cent hurdle, yet we know that the party actually received 7 per cent of the second votes in 1983.

We therefore have to try and assess where those 'extra' votes came from and to surmise why they were given. It is a long-standing dispute within political science as to whether vote transfers between parties in absolute figures can be regarded as reliable in the absence of large and extended panel surveys.[19]

Nevertheless, it is possible, given the Federal Republic's electoral

Table 4.7 *The extent of 'ticket splitting' amongst FDP list voters, 1957–83*

Party supported on first vote	Second (list) votes for the FDP %							
	1957	1961	1965	1969	1972	1976	1980	1983
FDP	85.0	86.5	70.3	62.0	38.2	60.7	48.5	29.1
SPD	3.8	3.1	6.7	24.8	52.9	29.9	35.5	10.1
CDU/CSU	7.5	8.1	20.8	10.6	7.9	8.0	13.3	58.3
Greens	—	—	—	—	—	—	2.0	1.7
Others or not valid	3.7	2.3	2.2	2.6	1.0	1.4	0.8	0.9

Source: Soe (1985) Table 6.3, p. 145.

system, to see where the FDP's second votes came from when available information concerning the extent of 'ticket splitting' is gathered since it shows who gained the first votes of those who supported the Free Democrats with their second (see Table 4.7).

These figures show that the FDP has been able to attract support over time from 'first' voters of both major parties, most notably SPD sympathisers in 1972 and 1980 and CDU sympathisers in 1983. Such 'coalition voters' were probably favouring the continuation of a particular coalition administration, with the electoral system allowing them to express such a preference clearly. This also implies that such people can be alienated as well as attracted, with the FDP having to be careful that its appeal can be reshaped and refocused as necessary in time for the next election.

Its consistent success in this area combined with the ability to play the role of a 'majority former' has meant that the FDP has been able to win a big say in the decision-making of coalitions at both federal and state level. The party's regular participation in government on such a slender electoral base has clearly been a major success, with the FDP enjoying the benefits of incumbency whilst simultaneously reinforcing its claim to office as a 'brake' within the system as a whole.

THE FDP'S PARTICIPATION IN GOVERNMENT

The involvement of the Free Democrats in the national government of the Federal Republic has become a given in any analysis of the country's electoral politics. The FDP has participated in coalition for nearly 30 of the 38 years since 1949, entering 13 separate governments with the major parties in the process.

Whilst both the DDP and the DVP were also virtually always members of most of the coalitions of the Weimar Republic, the FDP has been able to exert more influence and extract more concessions as the price for its participation, given its 'pivotal' position between the SPD and the CDU/CSU.

This is most clearly reflected in the party's ability to assume more ministerial portfolios than it would normally be due on the basis of the seats which it contributes to the coalition as a whole. Its position also means that the formation of a majority government has nearly always been dependent on the FDP's favour since neither major party appears able to win an overall majority on its own (the one exception being the Christian Democratic government between 1957 and 1961).

Table 4.9 sets out the number of parliamentary seats held by the FDP and the number of cabinet seats which the party gained when the subsequent administration was formed. The party did particularly well in 1972 when the SPD gave it five seats out of a total of eighteen, on the basis of only 8.4 per cent of the vote, a share nevertheless indispensable to the continuation of the coalition first formed in 1969.

The Free Democrats have played essentially the same 'bridging' role at state level although different coalition formations have often existed in the *Länder* compared with the political composition of the federal government of the time. This might be a reflection of the lack of authority of the FDP national leadership in the states, but equally it can be a useful situation to be in, since *Land* governments can be used as 'test beds' for potential future coalitions at national level. It has to be said, in addition, that changes at federal level have usually been followed by appropriate changes, if necessary, in the states, although the time taken to implement such switches has varied between different regions.

The FDP has also held important ministerial portfolios. Table 4.10 details the ministries which the FDP has controlled in the period since the Second World War, the number of times they held each post in partnership with which major party and the total length of time involved.

This information produces a number of interesting contrasts. When in coalition with the Social Democrats, the FDP has always been in a position to control Foreign Affairs, Interior and Agriculture and for most of the time, Economics. In stark contrast, it has only been able to run Foreign Affairs and Economics with the Christian Democrats since 1982, and the FDP has never been in charge of the Interior Ministry or Agriculture in such a coalition.

Table 4.8 *The participation of the FDP in the federal government, 1949–87*

Date	Chancellor	Parties in government
20.9.1949	Adenauer (CDU)	CDU–CSU–FDP–DP
20.10.1953	Adenauer II	CDU–CSU–FDP–BHE–DP
24.10.1957	Adenauer III	CDU–CSU–DP
14.11.1961	Adenauer IV	CDU–CSU–FDP
17.10.1963	Erhard (CDU)	CDU–CSU–FDP
26.10.1965	Erhard II	CDU–CSU–FDP
1.12.1966	Kiesinger (CDU)	CDU–CSU–SPD
21.10.1969	Brandt (SPD)	SPD–FDP
15.12.1972	Brandt II	SPD–FDP
16.5.1974	Schmidt (SPD)	SPD–FDP
15.12.1976	Schmidt II	SPD–FDP
5.11.1980	Schmidt III	SPD–FDP
1.10.1982	Kohl (CDU)	CDU–CSU–FDP
6.3.1983	Kohl II	CDU–CSU–FDP
25.1.1987	Kohl III	CDU–CSU–FDP

Source: Abridged from von Beyme (1983) 18, and updated from *Keesing's Contemporary Archives* (1987).

Table 4.9 *The parliamentary and cabinet seats of the FDP, 1949–87*

Period covered	No. of Bundestag seats	Seat contribution to coalition %	No. of cabinet seats	Cabinet seats %
1949–53	52	24.5	3	21.4
1953–7	48	13.9	4	20.0
1961–5	67	21.1	5	23.8
1965–6	50	16.6	4	18.2
1969–72	30	11.2	3	18.8
1972–4	42	14.8	5	27.8
1974–6	42	14.8	4	25.0
1976–80	40	15.2	4	25.0
1980–2	54	19.1	4	23.5
1982–3	54	18.6	4	23.5
1983–7	34	12.2	3	17.7
1987–	46	17.1	4	21.1

Source: Keesing's Contemporary Archives (1970–84).

Table 4.10 *National ministries held by the FDP, 1949–87*

	Main coalition partners					
Ministry	CDU/CSU	Period	SPD	Period	Total number	Length of time
Chancellor	0	—	0	—	0	—
Foreign Affairs	3	1982–	5	1969–82	8	18 years
Interior	0	—	5	1969–82	5	13 years
Finance	4	1961–6	0	—	4	5 years
Economics	3	1982–	4	1972–82	7	15 years
Labour/Social Policy	0	—	0	—	0	—
Defence	0	—	0	—	0	—
Agriculture and Food	1	1982–3	5	1969–82	6	13 years
Justice	8	1949–57, 1961–5, 1982–	0	—	8	17 years
Transport	0	—	0	—	0	—
Posts	0	—	0	—	0	—
Housing/Urban Affairs	3	1949–57, 1965–6	0	—	3	9 years
Refugees	2	1961–3	0	—	2	2 years
Intra-German relations	2	1963–6	0	—	2	3 years
Research and Technology	3	1962–6	0	—	3	4 years
Education	1	1987–	0	—	1	6 months
Economic Co-operation	5	1949–57, 1961–5	0	—	5	12 years
Health	0	—	0	—	0	—
Federal Property	1	1961–2	0	—	1	1 year
					55	

Source: Adapted from Norpoth (1982) Table 1.3, p. 25 and updated from *Keesing's Contemporary Archives.*

This reflects, of course, the competing claims of the CSU (the Bavarian sister party of the CDU) for adequate ministerial representation, given its usually greater contribution of seats to the three-party coalition than the FDP's. It is also a way of attempting to limit intra-governmental conflicts over each partner's share of the spoils, although this often proves insufficient to still policy disputes and personal tensions, particularly between the CSU and the FDP.

We can see that the FDP was only allotted relatively minor ministries in the early coalitions with the Christian Democrats in the

1950s and 1960s such as Housing, Research and Technology and Economic Co-operation, but the party was able to lay claim to very important offices with the formation of the first coalition with the SPD.

This might suggest that the Social Democrats were desperate to win federal power after such a long period out in the cold, but it should also have proved a very powerful incentive for the Free Democrats to remain loyal to such a coalition, although the failure to do so in the autumn of 1982 might well lead the SPD to be less generous in any future coalition with the FDP.

In contrast to 1982, however, the FDP has normally wanted the coalition of which it was presently a member to continue and it has stressed its own value within such a formation in terms of 'good' government. The question obviously arises, though, about how explicit the FDP should be in stating its preference.

The party is usually content merely to let voters assume that it wants a continuation (always the case since 1972) and this is reinforced by the nature of the FDP's elections campaigns with their emphasis on stability and proven competence. Nevertheless, this can be toned down in favour of a more ambiguous approach, although when the party adopted such a tactic at the 1969 federal election, it came very close to being excluded from the Bundestag when it received only 5.8 per cent of the second votes. At that election the party had not been in government for three years and its moves towards the SPD meant the loss of some pro-CDU/CSU voters.

Campaigns which stress generalities and 'valence' issues as well as the fulfilling of 'brake' functions – rather than highlighting the attractiveness of FDP attitudes and policy stands – do, however, mean that potential conflict between the Free Democrats and their likely major post-election partner is minimised. Nevertheless, personality clashes are always likely to provide an undercurrent of disagreement which could surface in disputes over decisions of all kinds.

It might appear from the emphasis of this chapter so far that the specific policies which the FDP advances are largely irrelevant and essentially tactical concerns for a party whose *raison d'être* has developed so strongly along functional lines. Such an assumption would seriously underestimate the potency of policy agreement or disagreement for the formation of coalitions and in particular, their maintenance. The necessary trade-offs and compromises between parties will clearly be greatly influenced by each partner's priorities and the extent to which each government is 'open' or 'closed' in terms of policy distance on key issues.[20]

Concentrating too heavily on the FDP's role within the political system as a whole would also imply an acceptance of a clear dichotomy between 'power' and 'policy' although, in reality, both are intertwined and interdependent to a degree which makes it difficult to analyse their impact separately.

Even though opinion-poll evidence suggests that the FDP is not perceived by the wider electorate in terms of its specific policies,[21] election manifestos and policy statements serve a number of different purposes, some of which relate more to internal party disputes than the construction of a wide-ranging appeal to the country as a whole.

THE POLICIES OF THE FDP

When the FDP was first formed in the years immediately after the Second World War, the bringing together of the different strands of liberal thought appeared organisationally essential in the face of the development of broadly based major parties as the main competitors for votes. This was a crucial element in the development of the strategy of the Christian Democrats but the SPD also slowly followed suit, particularly after their Bad Godesberg conference in 1959. This did mean, however, that the distinct emphases with regard to policy priorities which set the 'national' and the 'progressive' liberals within the FDP apart were allowed to coexist without any sustained attempt being made to integrate them into a coherent long-term programme.

Given the size of the FDP and its weak organisational structure, each state party tended to have its own ideas about what should constitute liberal policy and how it should be implemented, with the main divisions being closely associated with the 'national/economic' and 'progressive/social' classification mentioned before.

In the early coalitions with the Christian Democrats in the 1950s, the need to rebuild the shattered German economy was clearly paramount. This ensured that any conflicts with the CDU/CSU centred on foreign policy in general and the return of the Saar to Germany and the terms of entry into the EC in particular.[22]

Even though the CDU possessed an influential labour wing during this period (now much diminished in influence), there was widespread agreement between the coalition partners on the need to maintain the central tenets of a free economy in order to ensure steady growth and increasing affluence.

Nevertheless, the FDP had to be careful that its independence and identity were retained if it was not to appear as a mere appendage of the Christian Democrats. As a result, distinct policies were increasingly developed by the party – policies which left no doubt, however, that the need for 'opposition within the coalition' was more a question of priorities and emphases than fundamental disagreements.

Yet, it was also important, if the Free Democrats were to keep open the option of an eventual coalition with the SPD and to develop their own status as the *dritte Kraft* within the system, that the party possessed a unique profile in terms of policy. It was to these ends that younger members of the party turned after the accession of Ludwig Erhard to the chancellorship in 1963 in succession to Adenauer.

The ejection of the party into opposition with the formation of the 'Grand Coalition' in 1966 and the election of Walter Scheel as party leader in 1968 were key events in changing the image of the FDP from a party content to promote continuity and stability to a party actively professing a need for a more reformist social and education policy. The party also recognised the need to confront the *de facto* division of Europe.

The development of *Ostpolitik* and the general emphasis on reform simultaneously gave credibility to the two aims mentioned above. A coalition with the SPD was now a real possibility and the FDP had found an issue which it could 'claim' for itself, even though some members of the Christian Democrats had also been thinking along similar lines.[23]

With the departure of many 'national' liberals from the party after the formation of the first federal coalition with the SPD in 1969, the ascendancy of the 'social' liberals within the FDP was reflected in the *Freiburger Thesen* passed at the party congress in 1971. Whilst the importance of economic growth could obviously not be ignored, the time had arrived for setting out a coherent and progressive policy for the party.

Even though such an emphasis was vital to a relatively harmonious coalition relationship with the SPD, the economic difficulties of the 1970s following the oil crises early in the decade ensured that the party's orthodoxy in questions of economic management came to the fore once more, most notably in the *Kieler Thesen* of 1977. Internal party conflicts over the approach to adopt towards recession were reinforced by coalition disagreements and an increasing inability to arrive at compromises which left both parties reasonably satisfied.

The seemingly inexorable rise in unemployment to 1.7 million at the end of 1981 (the worst figure since 1953) gradually brought the underlying conflict over economic affairs between the SPD and the FDP to a head. The Free Democrats believed the way to combat the growing total of jobless lay in tax cuts and reducing welfare spending, whilst the Social Democrats remained adamant in their refusal to sanction the implementation of such ideas.

Disputes over the economy were not the only source of tension between the two parties. The question of Helmut Schmidt's ability to keep the SPD behind his leadership on the siting of cruise missiles and the growing uncertainty in the Republic's relationship with NATO and the EC caused increasing concern amongst FDP leaders. They gradually came to the view that the party as a whole had more in common with the Christian Democrats on key issues relating to both the economy and foreign affairs.

This perception is widely believed to have been strengthened by the influx of more 'economic' liberals to the FDP parliamentary party after the 1980 federal election[24] and combined with the problems of taking *Ostpolitik* any further after the initial treaties had been signed in the early 1970s, the papering-over of disagreements on the economy proved insufficient to sustain the essential basis of any social democratic–liberal coalition.

Whilst it is certainly true that economic success and prosperity have an overhwhelming significance for most West German voters[25] – and this is reflected in the positions the parties take up – the uncertainty with regard to the overall development of foreign policy was also important in the decision of the FDP to switch sides to the Christian Democrats in 1982. Policy conflict has been a regular occurrence within the ranks of the FDP and the outcome of such disputes is clearly likely to be highly significant for coalition formation and maintenance. Yet the ability to change the emphasis of policy priorities so as to keep different coalition options alive has been vital to the ability of the Free Democrats to fulfil a 'bridging' role within the system to date.

Whilst it is obviously possible to track the changes which the FDP has made in terms of policy over the post-war period, it is important both to distinguish between long-term principles and specific election manifestos as well as between theoretical commitments and political practice. Social reforms are likely to be limited in times of economic difficulty, and whilst the general belief in greater educational opportunities, more participation in decision-making and the protection of civil rights are likely to remain unimpaired by the pressures exerted in such a situation, the hard choices that have to be made inevitably force good intentions to the side of the political stage.

It is this need to choose between policy priorities as well as coalition partners that has ensured the FDP's appearance of considerable flexibility with regard to both programmes and principles. Whilst flexibility might suggest an ability and willingness to seek out compromise whenever possible, it might also imply an essential interchangeability of programmatic commitments not found in parties belonging to other ideological families. However, it is only when we attempt to stand back a little and examine the party's overall strategy that we can really make sense of the need for this kind of approach.

THE STRATEGY OF THE FDP

In this section we want to draw together the strands of the analysis contained in the preceding parts of the chapter in an attempt to evaluate the impact of the most salient features we have considered in terms of the FDP's overall strategy. This will clearly necessitate an assessment of what the party is trying to achieve and the methods and tactics it employs to do so.

The fulfilling of the role of a 'pivot' or a 'majority former' is clearly crucially dependent on the regular failure of the other parties to win an overall majority, and the Free Democrats have usually been able to play shrewdly on the aspects of the reconstructed German political culture which legitimate coalition rather than single-party governments. This is also to be seen in terms of the party's propaganda which highlights the indispensability of the FDP as a 'protector' of continuity and stability.[26]

On this basis, the party has been able to exert a disproportionate amount of influence on the governments of the Federal Republic despite a tiny 'core' support base and a constant need to win over 'coalition voters' and others with weak partisan ties at each election. It might seem paradoxical, therefore, that a party which is often hovering just above the 5 per cent electoral exclusion barrier can credibly portray itself as a stable element in the country's party system. Nevertheless, the considerable flexibility at the very centre of the FDP's approach to electoral politics in its development as a *Wählerpartei* heavily dependent on leadership decisions and cues has given it room for manoeuvre denied to other parties with more rigidly structured organisations and stronger ties to particular social groups.

This adaptability has been vital to the party's success over the post-war period. The ability to win more than 5 per cent of the second votes at every national election contrasts sharply with the rapid demise of other small parties in the 1950s. This is something made even more remarkable by the history of the liberal movement earlier in the century which can be summed up as chequered at best and politically irrelevant at worst. Fulfilling a 'bridging' role has enabled the FDP to participate in government for a longer period in total than either the Christian Democrats or the Social Democrats as well as to assume important ministerial portfolios. The party also contributed to the creation and protection of the principles of the *Rechtsstaat* as well as the construction of a political system and culture which, despite occasional bouts of nervousness, appears both successful and stable to most outside observers.

If we want to consider the prospects for the FDP continuing to play such a role in the future, the recent challenge of the Greens provides important evidence as to the tactics the Free Democrats are likely to adopt to ensure that they are able to remain the 'pivot' of the party system.

After the electoral disasters at state level which befell the FDP after the *Wende* to the CDU/CSU in the autumn of 1982, the eventual – if perhaps slow – political death of the FDP was once again being predicted. The last six state election results in 1985–6 have indeed been unspectacular, and the election of Martin Bangemann as the new party leader to replace Hans-Dietrich Genscher has done little to revive the enthusiasm of the party faithful battered by the events surrounding the coalition switch of 1982.

Yet it would be unfair to describe the FDP as anything other than seasoned and adroit survivors through thick and thin. It is also too soon to predict the end of the Greens as a political movement. In the same sense as the FDP, they are likely to gain or suffer on the swings and roundabouts of political fortune as a result of events and actions in which they are not directly involved but in which they are the potential beneficiaries or losers. For that reason alone, the party appears unlikely to disappear from view altogether, even given its self-inflicted wounds and tendency towards self-destruction which only provides further material for those in competing political parties and the media who wish to portray the Greens as 'extremists' and as 'irresponsible'.

The outcome of the January 1987 federal election clearly illustrated the role the FDP has claimed as its own for most of the post-war period. Once more, the FDP appealed for second votes as a reward for its 'braking' on the Christian Democrats, especially the CSU and Franz-Josef Strauss in particular. This claim was given greater credibility during the campaign by Strauss's attacks on the FDP and the foreign policy pursued by Genscher within the ruling coalition. The FDP's slogan of 'vote for performance' appeared effective, since 70 per cent of the electorate wanted the FDP to remain represented in the Bundestag (Forschungsgruppe Wahlen (1987) p. 53) even though Bangemann was making little impact as a national political figure.

The FDP gained 2.1 per cent of the second votes compared to 1983, with the CDU/CSU recording its worst result since 1949. The FDP is generally reckoned to have benefited considerably from 'ticket splitting' by 'coalition voters'. In the subsequent coalition, the FDP were given four cabinet portfolios (Foreign Affairs, Economics, Justice and Education and Science) – that is one more than in 1983.

Whilst the general buoyancy of the economy and the stark weaknesses of a divided opposition certainly contributed to the coalition's overall success, it also seems clear that the FDP were yet again able to exploit the long-standing aversion within the German electorate towards one-party government. The ability of the FDP also to occupy the 'moderate centre' on socio-economic matters was of some importance for the party's image but the party has little left to distinguish it from the Christian Democrats, with the exception of Genscher's dogged but undogmatic foreign policy.

In reality, the FDP's functional role has received even greater emphasis since 1982, given the fact that it has no credible alternative to the present federal coalition. The party is represented in nine of the ten state parliaments but it is a member of only three state governments. Where the FDP could be 'useful' as a member of a majority government, it usually receives more than 5 per cent of the votes (at federal level and in the Lower Saxony state election of 1986, for example). Where this is not widely perceived to be the case, the party often falls below the 5 per cent hurdle as in the 1986 Hamburg and Bavaria state elections.

CONCLUSION

It would certainly be tempting to summarise our analysis by saying that the FDP has been one of the most successful liberal parties in Western Europe on the basis of the influence which it has exerted on decision-making at both main levels of the German polity. This influence remains closely linked to the party's ability to carve out and maintain a niche for itself as a 'corrective' or 'balancing' political force. However, we need to anchor this conclusion firmly in an altogether broader perspective which takes into account the structural and contextual factors permitting the party to play this role with such a slender and variable electoral base.[27]

We have only briefly mentioned a number of important features of the political culture in the Federal Republic of Germany after the Second World War. Yet it is undeniable that the FDP's position has been much strengthened by its ability to portray itself as a guarantor of stability and continuity to an electorate with an endemic fear of social polarisation and severe partisan conflict.

Although the party has always been small in relation to its main competitors, this has allowed the FDP to develop along lines ideally suited to exploit the opportunities provided by the inability of either the Christian Democrats or the Social Democrats to win overall majorities in the Bundestag. The flexibility and adaptability inherent in the party's approach has given them more room to change tack without a fatal loss of credibility. It has also allowed the party to avoid endless internal disputes over the direction the FDP should be moving in.[28]

Whilst this has admittedly largely been achieved by elite decision-making at the expense of widespread party consultation, the success of this approach has had the effect of blunting the cutting edge of criticism concerning the lack of internal party democracy.

Indeed, it could be argued that if the FDP were to become a bigger party, with more members and a larger *Stammwählerschaft*, it would have to set about competing on equal terms with the CDU/CSU and the SPD, a task to which it is likely to be both ill-suited and unprepared. At the moment, much of the rhetoric providing the overall framework of partisan debate leaves the FDP relatively unscathed.

In a very real sense, the FDP has become the prisoner of its own electoral success. It has gained influence in government and made a clear appeal to German voters on the basis of playing a purely functional role which has forced the party to downgrade ideological principles, policy commitments and close ties to particular social groups. Whilst this situation might not appear to hold a potent threat to the FDP's future – given the experiences of the post-war period – the rise of the Greens since 1978 provides an example of the likely source of such a danger and its nature.

The conclusion of stability and little overall change has long permeated analyses of partisan politics in the Federal Republic of Germany. If either the CDU/CSU or the SPD lose their ability to integrate large segments of the electorate behind them, the structure of the party system could change in unpredictable ways and by an uncertain degree. The possibility of great 'dealignment' would provide a new label for a situation which the FDP has faced since 1949. For the Free Democrats, electoral opportunity and electoral danger have always been the two sides of the same coin.

NOTES

1 Until recently, it was true that little had been written on the FDP, particularly in English. We have tried to rectify this omission with four papers (see references for details). This chapter concentrates on the Free Democrats but it is also important to take post-war political developments as a whole into account. For such

background see, for example, the relevant sections of the following: David Conradt (1986) *The German Polity* (3rd edn, New York: Longman); Gordon Smith (1986) *Democracy in Western Germany. Parties and Politics in the Federal Republic* (Aldershot: Gower); Gordon Smith and Herbert Döring (eds.) (1982) *Party Government and Political Culture in Western Germany* (London: Macmillan); Kendall L. Baker, Russell J. Dalton and Kai Hildebrandt (1981) *Germany Transformed. Political Culture and the New Politics* (London: Harvard University Press).

2 There are a number of works on the history of German liberalism available, many of them published under the auspices of the Friedrich-Naumann-Stiftung. Two examples are: Barthold C. Witte, Hans Reif, Friedrich Henning and Werner Stephan (1966) *Geschichte de deutschen Liberalismus* (Opladen: West-deutscher Verlag) and Friedrich C. Sell (1981) *Die Tragödie des deutschen Liberalismus* (Baden-Baden: Nomos, 2nd edn). Also of interest is the book by Paul Rothmund and Erhard R. Wiehn (1979) *Die FDP/DVP in Baden-Württemberg und ihre Geschichte. Liberalismus als politische Gestaltungskraft im deutschen Südwesten* (Stuttgart: Kohlhammer).

3 The Weimar Republic has been studied in considerable depth in several works. A recent addition to the literature is Ernst Rudolf Huber (1984) *Ausbau, Schutz und Untergang der Weimarer Republik* (Stuttgart: Kohlhammer). In English, the following have relevant sections: Karl Dietrich Bracher (1970) *The German Dictatorship* (New York: Praeger); Gordon A. Craig (1978) *Germany, 1866–1945* (New York: Oxford University Press) and Ralf Dahrendorf (1967) *Society and Democracy in Germany* (New York: Doubleday).

4 *Grundgesetz für die Bundesrepublik Deutschland* (1976) (Bonn: Bundeszentrale für politische Bildung) 29.

5 Allensbach Institute polls in 1977 and 1980 asked people whether they agreed with the statement: 'As a third party, the FDP is still important nowadays. As a government party, it can keep the big parties, i.e. the CDU/CSU and the SPD from establishing their policies completely'. 49% of a sample of 1,000 people aged 16 and over in the Federal Republic and West Berlin did agree with it in July 1977; 33% didn't think it was necessary to have the FDP fulfilling such a function and 18% were undecided. In August 1980, the figures were 57% agreeing, 23% disagreeing and 20% undecided. Elisabeth Noelle-Neumann (ed.) (1981) *The Germans. Public Opinion Polls, 1967–1980* (London: Greenwood Press) 200.

6 The idea that economic prosperity and affluence have been vital to widespread acceptance of the legitimacy of the political system in the Federal Republic after the Second World War is used as a starting point for many analyses. For a recent look at the inter-relationships involved, see H.G. Peter Wallach, 'Political Economics' in H.G. Peter Wallach and George K. Romoser (eds.) (1985) *West German Politics in the Mid-Eighties. Crisis and Continuity* (New York: Praeger) 235–56. Also part two entitled 'Wahlen und Ökonomie' in Max Kaase and Hans-Dieter Klingemann (eds.) (1983) *Wahlen und politisches System. Analysen aus Anlass der Bundestagswahl 1980* (Opladen: Westdeutscher Verlag) 173–317.

7 At the end of 1981, the FDP had 86,747 members, whereas the CSU alone had more than 175,000. (FDP figures supplied by the *Bundesgeschäftsstelle* in Bonn. CSU figures by the *Süddeutsche Zeitung*, 25.5.82, p. 15.) According to Søe (1985) 171, the switch in coalition partners to the Christian Democrats in 1982 sparked off a membership loss to an extent that by early 1984 the FDP had only about 70,000 members.

8 These are some of the advantages of incumbency. For a cross-national consideration of whether incumbency is generally advantageous or disadvantageous, see Richard Rose and Thomas T. Mackie (1980) 'Incumbency in

government: asset or liability?' *Studies in Public Policy*, no. 54 (Glasgow: Centre for the Study of Public Policy, University of Strathclyde). Their conclusion suggests that incumbency does not give an electoral advantage to governing parties but equally, it is not a liability.

9 See Broughton and Kirchner (1983) 9–15, (1984b) 10–14, (1986).

10 The FDP is much more of a 'cadre' than a 'mass' party to use Duverger's distinction between the two. Maurice Duverger (1964) *Political Parties. Their Organization and Activity in the Modern State* (London: Methuen) 62–71. Both the CDU/CSU and the SPD can be described as 'mass' parties on the basis of the criteria he uses.

11 Although, as Søe (1985) 160 points out, the FDP's party congress in Freiburg at the end of January 1983 passed a motion by a two-thirds majority requiring that conference agreement must be obtained in future *before* any coalition changes or agreements are entered into.

12 In 1982, the FDP's total income of DM 22.7 million was made up as follows: 35.0% from dues and subscriptions, 19.0% from other contributions, 28.7% from the state, and 17.3% from other miscellaneous sources. In contrast, the SPD received 56.1% of its income from subscriptions, whilst the CDU/CSU took in 50.3% of its total funds in this way (*Offenbach Post*, 2. 12. 83, p. 3).

13 DGB = Deutscher Gewerkschaftsbund (equivalent of the British TUC).
BDI = Bundesverband der deutschen Industrie (equivalent of the British CBI).
DBB = Deutscher Beamtenbund (civil service federation).
DAG = Deutsche Angestellten Gewerkschaft (white-collar employees' union).
ULA = Union der leitenden Angestellten (senior white-collar employees' union).

14 See, in particular, Heino Kaack, 'The FDP in the German party system' in Karl H. Cerny (ed.) (1978), *Germany at the Polls. The Bundestag Election of 1976* (Washington DC: American Enterprise Institute) 77–110, especially pp. 80–2 as well as Forschungsgruppe Wahlen (1980) 38–40; (1983) 38–9; (1987) 52–5.

15 Before the 1972 federal election, as many as 53% of the respondents in an INFAS poll thought that the first vote was more important than the second for the distribution of seats in the Bundestag. Before the 1983 federal election, only 11% believed this, although 25% thought both votes were equally important. *Politiogramm. INFAS-Report. Bundestagswahl 1983. Wahl zum 10. Deutschen Bundestag am 6. März 1983: Analysen und Dokumente* (Bonn–Bad Godesberg) 96. For a general discussion of the present electoral system, see the article by Eckhard Jesse, *Frankfurter Allgemeine Zeitung*, 25.2.83, p. 8.

16 More than half (51.3%) of Hesse's population were categorised as *Angestelle und Beamte* (white-collar workers and civil servants) in 1982, with 37.9% being *Arbeiter* (workers) and 10.7% being self-employed or independent. In 1950, the proportion of white-collar workers was only 21.1%. Forschungsgruppe Wahlen (1983) *Wahl in Hessen. Eine Analyse der Landtagswahl am 25. September 1983.* Report no. 35, p. A9.

17 The two exceptions to this occurred in Schlewswig-Holstein between April 1947 and September 1950 and in West Berlin between December 1958 and March 1963.

18 The Bundesrat has considerable influence in areas such as the federal budget, fiscal policy and constitutional amendments, and in matters directly affecting the *Länder*, the consent of the upper chamber is required.

19 For example, the reports from INFAS in Bonn-Bad Godesberg cite absolute figures with regard to vote transfers, whereas Forschungsgruppe Wahlen in Mannheim base their analyses on cross-sectional and aggregate data.

20 The idea of an 'open' coalition is based on a hypothetical policy dimension on which the parties forming the coalition are not next to one another, i.e. another party not in the coalition could be placed between them on that particular dimension. A 'closed' coalition is where the coalition partners are contiguous on the relevant dimensions. See Norpoth (1982) and Schmidt (1983) 44–56.

21 The FDP is perceived much more in terms of its overall role within the system. In the 1980 *Wahlstudie*, twenty-four different responses were given to the question 'why did the FDP win votes?' at the 1980 election. None of the answers had much to do with 'liberal' ideas or principles, with more emphasis being placed on the party's 'corrective' role. *Zentralarchiv für empirische Sozialforschung der Universität zu Köln*, study no. 1053.

22 The 'national' liberals were keen to prevent any developments which could hinder eventual German re-unification and Steed suggests that the anti-clerical stance of the FDP made it wary of joining the original six countries in the EEC. Michael Steed, 'The liberal parties in Italy, France, Germany and the UK' in Roger Morgan and Stefano Silvestri (eds.) (1982) *Moderates and Conservatives in Western Europe. Political Parties, the European Community and the Atlantic Alliance* (London: Heinemann Educational) 162–92, esp. 170.

23 Most notably, the CDU Foreign Minister Gerhard Schröder, as well as Ludwig Erhard when he was chancellor. There was strong resistance from the CSU to any changes which moved away from the 'Hallstein Doctrine' which stated that the Federal Republic would not establish diplomatic relations with any country which recognised the DDR.

24 Soe (1985) 149. Even though the right or 'economic' wing of the FDP was in a clear majority within the parliamentary party after 1980, the party's executive was still fairly evenly divided between 'economic' and 'social' liberals after this date.

25 This is apparent in virtually every opinion poll and survey conducted in the Federal Republic. Questions dealing with the importance of price stability, incomes and economic growth always show these themes to be very highly rated by the German voters. Examples for the period 1975–82 are contained in the INFAS report on the 1983 federal election (see note 15).

26 The idea of 'balance' and the stress on *Vernunft* (reasonableness) have always pervaded much of the FDP's election material. The party has also regularly attempted to contrast its own image with the 'extremists' in the main parties and the need for a 'brake' or moderating influence as a result.

27 The Allensbach Institute has regularly asked the following question: 'Do you think that it is better for a country to have only the one political party so that there is as much unanimity as possible or would it be better to have several parties so that different opinions may be freely expressed?' In November 1978, 68% of the respondents chose the option of several parties, with the lowest percentage doing this being 45% in June 1956. Elisabeth Noelle-Neumann (ed.) (1981) *The Germans 1967–1980*, p. 132.

28 Even so, Professor P. Seibt has suggested, the FDP can sometimes appear to be a party with little independent propulsion and an unstable steering capacity – with the constant risk of losing all momentum! We are grateful to Professor Seibt for this incisive characterisation of the FDP, provided at the conference on West European liberal parties at the University of Essex in February 1985.

REFERENCES

Albertin, Lothar (ed.) (1980) *Politischer Liberalismus in der Bundesrepublik* (Göttingen: Vandenhoek and Ruprecht).

Beyme, Klaus von (1983) 'Coalition government in Western Germany' in Vernon Bogdanor (ed.), *Coalition Government in Western Europe* (London: Heinemann Educational) 16–37.

Broughton, David and Kirchner, Emil (1983) 'The FDP in transition – again?', paper presented at the Annual Conference of the Political Studies Association of the United Kingdom, University of Newcastle upon Tyne, 12–14 April 1983.

Broughton, David and Kirchner, Emil (1984a) 'The FDP in transition – again?', *Parliamentary Affairs*, 37:2, Spring 1984, pp. 183–98. (Shortened version of Broughton and Kirchner (1983).)

Broughton, David and Kirchner, Emil (1984b) 'The FDP and coalition formation in the Federal Republic of Germany: "ideological input", party structure and party strategy', paper presented at the ECPR Joint Sessions of Workshops, University of Salzburg, 13–18 April 1984.

Broughton, David and Kirchner, Emil (1986) 'The FDP and coalition behaviour in the Federal Republic of Germany: multi-dimensional perspectives on the role of a pivotal party' in Geoffrey Pridham (ed.) *Coalition Behaviour in Theory and Practice: An Inductive Model for Western Europe* (Cambridge: Cambridge University Press).

Wahlen, Forschungsgruppe (1980) *Bundestagswahl 1980. Eine Analyse der Wahl zum 9. Deutschen Bundestag am 5. Oktober 1980*, Bericht no. 25, 9 October (Mannheim: Forschungsgruppe Wahlen).

Wahlen, Forschungsgruppe (1983) *Bundestagswahl 1983. Eine Analyse der Wahl zum 10. Deutschen Bundestag am 6. März 1983*, Bericht no. 32, 9 March (Mannheim: Forschungsgruppe Wahlen).

Wahlen, Forschungsgruppe (1987) *Bundestagswahl 1987. Eine Analyse der Wahl zum 11. Deutschen Bundestag am 25. Januar 1987*, Bericht no. 45, 28 January 1987 (Mannheim: Forschungsgruppe Wahlen).

Henning, Friedrich (1982) *FDP Die Liberalen – Porträt einer Partei* (Munich: Günter Olzog).

Irving, R.E.M. and Paterson, W.E. (1987) 'The West German general election of 1987', *Parliamentary Affairs*, July 1987, 40:3, pp. 333–56.

Mackie, Thomas T. and Rose, Richard (1982) *The International Almanac of Electoral History* (2nd edn, London: Macmillan).

Norpoth, Helmut (1982) 'The German Federal Republic: coalition government at the brink of majority rule' in Eric C. Browne and John Dreijmanis (eds.), *Government Coalitions in Western Democracies* (London: Longman) 7–32.

Pulzer, Peter (1982) 'The politics of electoral law in Germany', seminar paper, Department of Government, University of Essex, 16 March 1982.

Pulzer, Peter (1987) 'The West German federal election of 25 January 1987', *Electoral Studies*, 6:2, August 1987, pp. 149–54.

Schmidt, Manfred G. (1983) 'Two logics of coalition policy: the West German case' in Vernon Bogdanor (ed.) *Coalition Government in Western Europe* (London: Heinemann Educational) 38–58.

Schuchardt, Helga and Verheugen, Gunter (eds.) (1982) *Das liberale Gewissen* (Hamburg: Rowohlt Taschenbuch).

Søe, Christian (1985) 'The Free Democratic Party' in H.G. Peter Wallach and George K. Romoser (eds.), *West German Politics in the Mid-Eighties. Crisis and Continuity* (New York: Praeger) 112–86.

5

Great Britain – social liberalism reborn?

John Curtice

INTRODUCTION

Organised liberalism has survived in Britain in the face of a number of formidable obstacles. Although once one of two great parties of state, the principal social cleavage it helped articulate, religion, has long since lost its electoral significance. After the First World War British politics came to be dominated by class, and in the process the Liberal Party not only lost electoral support but also split on more than one occasion and saw one wing of the party joining the Conservatives. Since 1945 none of its members has held ministerial office and by 1951 its electoral support had fallen to 2.5 per cent of the vote. These difficulties have been compounded by the operation of the single-member plurality system which has ensured that its geographically evenly spread vote has never been able to secure more than a handful of seats.

Yet despite this unfavourable combination of circumstances, organised liberalism has not only survived but now flourishes. There is but one Liberal Party able to command a level of support which would in any other West European country accord it major party status. True, it has given up some of its independence by entering into an electoral alliance with the Social Democratic Party, formed in 1981 after a split within the Labour Party. But the formation of that party was encouraged by the leader of the Liberal Party himself as a means of pursuing the party's long-term strategy and now the SDP–Liberal Alliance is seen by some as the rekindling of a progressive ideological tradition which originated within the Liberal Party at the turn of the century. The British Liberal Party is clearly one of the most important forces in West European liberalism.

HISTORY

The Liberal Party emerged as one of the two main parties of state following the confused and complex manoeuvrings of mid-Victorian politics. Its formation is sometimes dated precisely to June 1859 when a meeting of opposition leaders agreed to unite in order to oust the incumbent minority Conservative administration and form a new government under Palmerston. But in reality the new political grouping composed of Whig aristocrats, Peelites (former members of the Tory Party who favoured free trade) and Radicals emerged gradually, and it was only in 1868 when a Liberal government was elected under the premiership of Gladstone that the party was clearly established as a major electoral force.

The Liberal Party of the second half of the nineteenth century was a broad and evolving church. In its early years it both represented the new middle class who favoured *laissez-faire* economics and such measures of political reform as the extension of the franchise, together with the Whig portion of the landed aristocracy. Many of the latter left the party in 1886 over the issue of Irish Home Rule, but the former group remained important all through the late Victorian and Edwardian period, despite a gradual drift of middle-class electoral support to the Conservatives. Meanwhile the extension of the franchise in 1867 and again in 1884 saw the beginnings of the enfranchisement of the working class which gave much of its support to the Liberals. But central to the party's electoral support and identity was its position as the promoter of the cause of nonconformity (and of Catholicism) against the interests of the established Anglican church. For example, it favoured the disestablishment of the Anglican church in Wales and the reduction of the church's influence upon the education system.

Thus, in common with other European liberal parties at this time, the British Liberal Party represented the forces of progress and change against those of the status quo. In contrast to conservatism it took a largely hopeful view about the human condition.[1] It constituted one of the two major parties in the two-party system which operated in Great Britain (though not in Ireland) between 1867 and the First World War, holding office for about half the time during that period.

But the gradual enfranchisement of the working class (which was completed in 1918) and its growing political consciousness raised important problems for the Liberal Party. The party had historically favoured free trade and minimal governmental interference in the economy. Amongst its working-class electorate, however, there were growing demands for governmental action to alleviate the excesses of the unfettered operation of capitalism.

The party responded in a number of ways. Intellectually, a philosophy of 'social' or 'new' liberalism was developed by writers such as Hobhouse and Hobson.[2] They recognised that liberalism needed to turn its attention away from the pursuit of political liberty which was largely being achieved and towards the demands for social justice. Furthermore, they accepted that the unfettered operation of market forces did not produce social justice and that positive action by the state was required. They distinguished themselves from socialists, however, by rejecting the collective ownership of the means of production and accepting the ability of the market to promote the creation of wealth if not its equitable distribution. The development of this non-socialist response to the problem of class inequality was important in both providing the British Liberal Party with an intellectual tradition which has put it on the 'social' or 'left' end of the family of liberal parties and because it gave it a philosophy which was close to that espoused by many social democrats in the emerging Labour Party.[3]

This intellectual development had political consequences. The Liberal government which was elected to office in 1906 set about implementing a series of measures, such as the introduction of old age pensions, designed to redistribute income and wealth. Indeed, the introduction by Lloyd George of the 'People's Budget' of 1909, which amongst other things proposed a set of land taxes and a supertax on those with high incomes, led to a constitutional crisis between the Commons and the Lords which, after two elections, resulted in the diminution of the latters' legislative powers. The Liberal Party also responded tactically to the formation of the Labour Party in 1900 by agreeing a secret electoral pact whereby Labour and Liberal candidates largely succeeded in avoiding contesting the same constituencies.

But the Liberal Party's response to the rise of the working class proved to be inadequate. Even before the First World War the social distance between Labour and Liberal manifested itself in the failure of many Liberal associations to put forward candidates from working-class backgrounds. But during the war the first of a series of disastrous splits occurred in the party, which left it in no state to respond to the final enfranchisement of all of the working class in 1918, the change in the social fabric of the country and the end of electoral co-operation with the Labour Party.

Events were precipitated by the Liberal government's conduct of the First World War. Many of the measures required for its successful promotion, especially the introduction of conscription, were an anathema to many Liberals, including Asquith, the prime minister; but to its critics the government was dilatory and weak. In 1915 Asquith was forced to form a coalition with the Conservatives, and then in December of the following year he was ousted as prime minister and replaced by another leading Liberal, Lloyd George. The party split between those who remained loyal to Asquith and stayed out of the government and those who supported Lloyd George and the coalition government he headed. Although the split was fuelled more by personality differences than by ideological ones, its reverberations affected the party throughout the post-First World War period. Most seriously, the decision of Lloyd George to continue the coalition after the cessation of wartime hostilities meant that the party fought the 1918 election split into its Asquith and Lloyd George wings. This gave a newly confident Labour Party the opportunity to win over the working-class vote, overtake the Liberals in terms of votes and seats, and claim the title of His Majesty's Opposition. Labour's ranks were further swelled by a significant drift of social liberals into its social democratic wing.

Lloyd George's coalition government collapsed in 1922 following a revolt by Conservative backbenchers and in 1923 the Lloyd George and Asquithian wings of the party were reunited. In the election of that year the party appeared to recover its major party status. Although still only the third-largest party, no one party held a majority of seats. But the party failed to exploit its position. It refused to grasp the possible opportunity of forming a minority administration itself, and lent support from the backbenches to a Labour government without extracting any agreement as to the policies the government should pursue. Yet ten months later it combined with the Conservatives to bring the government down over a domestic political scandal. The party's actions only served to enhance the credibility of the Labour Party as a party of government while antagonising both those of its supporters who felt closer to the Conservatives and those who felt closer to Labour. Indeed, the 1924 election saw the termination of most of the local electoral pacts the party had with the Conservatives and Labour, and the loss of one-third of its electoral support the previous year resulted in the loss of over two-thirds of its seats. The Liberal Party faced for the first time the full consequences under the single-member plurality electoral system of having a geographically evenly spread vote, and it entered upon the minority status in the House of Commons from which it has yet to re-emerge successfully.

But minority status did not bring the party immediate relief from the difficulties of choosing government partners. At the 1929 election

Table 5.1 *Electoral performance since 1918*

	Liberal Party		Liberal National		Lloyd George Liberals	
	Votes, %	Seats	Votes, %	Seats	Votes, %	Seats
1918	13.0	36			12.6	127
1922	18.9	62			9.9	53
1923	29.7	158				
1924	18.4	44				
1929	23.6	59				
1931	6.5	32	3.7	35	0.5	4
1935	6.8	21	3.7	33		
1945	9.0	12	2.8	11		
1950	9.1	9				
1951	2.6	6				
1955	2.7	6				
1959	5.9	6				
1964	11.2	9				
1966	8.5	12				
1970	7.5	6				
1974 (Feb.)	19.3	14				
1974 (Oct.)	18.3	14				
1979	13.8	13				
1983	25.4	23				
1987[a]	22.6	22				

[a] Figures for these elections include votes cast for the Social Democratic Party which was fighting in alliance with the Liberal Party. Liberal Party candidates alone won 13.7% of the vote in 1983 and 12.8% in 1987, securing 17 seats on both occasions.

Sources: F.W. Craig, *British Electoral Facts 1832–1980* (Chichester, Parliamentary Reference Services, 1981); F.W. Craig, *Britain Votes 3: British Parliamentary Election Results 1983* (Chichester, Parliamentary Reference Services, 1983).

Table 5.2 *Liberal participation in government since 1916*

Period	Liberal Parties involved	Coalition partner(s)
December 1916–October 1922	Lloyd George Liberals	Conservative, Labour (until January 1919)
August 1931–September 1932	Liberal party	Conservative, National, Labour
October 1931–May 1940	Liberal National	Conservative, National, Labour
May 1940–May 1945	Liberal Party, Liberal National	Conservative, Labour
May 1945–July 1945	Liberal National	Conservative

The Liberal Party provided support from the backbenches for the Labour administrations of January to November 1924 and January 1929 to August 1931. The Liberal Party had a formal pact with the Labour government between March 1977 and September 1978.

Labour emerged as the largest party but without an overall majority. The Liberals, now led by Lloyd George, decided – as in 1924 – to give support to a minority Labour administration from the backbenches, but serious divisions opened up within the party with one section, headed by Sir John Simon, preferring a switch of support to the Conservatives. Then, following the collapse of the Labour government in the financial crisis of August 1931, the party agreed to enter the National government, only to find itself in a government which broke the principle of free trade and precipitated into fighting a general election in collaboration with the Conservatives. Eventually, in September 1932, the official party under Samuel decided to leave the government while the Liberal Nationals under Simon stayed. Although subsequent attempts were made to reunite the two wings of the party, the Liberal Nationals (renamed National Liberals in 1948) continued to ally themselves with the Conservatives, and in 1947 agreed to integrate their party organisation with the Conservatives. National Liberals no longer distinguished themselves from other Conservative candidates after the 1966 general election. Their defection helps to explain why in the modern British Liberal Party 'social' rather than 'national' liberalism predominates.

The Second World War saw the last taste of governmental office that the Liberal Party has ever secured. The party agreed to accept office in Churchill's coalition government in 1940 and remained there until the conclusion of the war with Germany in May 1945. Although no Liberal was included in the inner war cabinet, one leading party member made a significant contribution to the government's planning for the post-war period. William Beveridge, who became a Liberal MP in 1944, was the author of a report which led to the post-war introduction of the Welfare State in its modern form. In addition, the ideas of the Liberal economist J.M. Keynes gained acceptance and were to dominate post-war management of the economy, emphasising in particular the pursuit of full employment.

But while the ideas of social liberals might be influencing government policy, after the 1945 election the party itself appeared headed for extinction – it won only 12, mostly rural peripheral, seats. In 1951 the party reached its nadir – six seats and $2\frac{1}{2}$ per cent of the vote. After this result Clement Davies, the Liberal leader, held talks with Winston Churchill about the possibility of the Liberals joining the Conservative administration. If Davies had not eventually decided to say no, the British Liberal Party may well not have survived. As it was, it continued to suffer a continued loss of membership and organisational resources.

The turning point came in 1954–5.[4] At the Inverness by-election of

1954 the party's candidate succeeded in winning 36.0 per cent of the vote in a seat which had been uncontested in 1951. There was a smattering of good results in the subsequent general election in 1955, but the first sign that the party might re-emerge from its rural and peripheral base was the Torquay by-election of December 1955 when the party's vote increased by 9 per cent. The following year saw the first signs of an attempt to breathe new life and purpose into the party organisation while Jo Grimond succeeded Clement Davies as leader.[5]

Under Grimond the party underwent an intellectual and electoral revival. He not only attempted in his own writing and speeches to provide a new purpose and strategic direction for the party, but also succeeded in attracting a number of academics and policy advisers who provided it with a whole range of new policy ideas. Grimond outlined a role for the party as a non-socialist alternative to the Conservative Party which was aiming to replace the Labour Party through a realignment of the left. The party evolved new policies, for example, in favour of industrial co-partnership, the devolution of power to local government, opposition to an independent nuclear deterrent and entry into the Common Market, while a long-ranging internal battle eventually saw the party abandon the principle of free trade.[6]

The party's electoral revival was seen not so much in general elections as in by-elections, which have become central in its periodic post-war revivals. The party succeeded in winning its first post-war by-election in Torrington, a rural seat in Devon, in 1958. More spectacular was the capture of Orpington, a London suburban seat, from the Conservatives. The Liberal candidate won 53 per cent of the vote while the Conservative vote fell by 22 per cent compared with the 1959 general election. The result appeared to be a vindication of Grimond's strategy. The party was supposedly appealing to a new section of society, the new socially and geographically mobile middle class, for whom the traditional class-based appeal of the Conservative and Labour Parties held little interest. This group, which was believed to be disproportionately present in Orpington, had enabled the party to defeat the Conservatives while reducing Labour to a mere 9 per cent of the vote.

Although the party's result in the 1964 general election was clearly its best post-Second World War achievement – 11 per cent of the vote (although still only nine seats) which with only half of the seats contested implied an overall level of support of 16 per cent – the narrow election of a Labour government and its subsequent re-election in 1966 by a commanding majority cast considerable doubt over Grimond's hopes of eclipsing the Labour Party. Grimond resigned in 1967 and the party entered a further period of retrenchment until in 1972 and 1973 a sequence of four by-election victories was followed in February 1974 by the party's most successful general election campaign to date. It succeeded in fighting on a broad front for the first time since 1950, contesting five-sixths of the seats and winning one-fifth of the vote.

Although the electoral system only gave the party a meagre reward of 14 seats, neither the Conservatives nor Labour secured an overall majority. The defeated Conservative prime minister, Edward Heath, asked the Liberal leader, Jeremy Thorpe, to consider forming a coalition government. It was the Liberals' first opportunity to enter government for 23 years. But it soon emerged that there was considerable opposition within the party to such a coalition and a minority Labour administration took office.

But only three years later a government was once more looking to the Liberal Party for support. By March 1977 the incumbent Labour administration had lost the narrow overall majority it had secured in the general election of October 1974 and was in danger of defeat in the House of Commons. The recently elected leader, David Steel, was keen to enhance the credibility of the Liberal Party and agreed to give the government support in return for a formal system of consultation with the Liberal Party on the government's legislative programme. The Lib–Lab pact was, however, a bumpy experience for the party which suffered internal divisions about its wisdom and value, and electoral unpopularity at by-elections. It was ended in autumn 1978, twelve months before an election was due.

In truth, the party was still deeply uncertain about its long-term strategic aims. But in 1981 the original Grimond strategy of a realignment of the left suddenly seemed a much more realistic prospect when the Labour Party suffered a serious split. Four former cabinet ministers led a group of defectors from the social democratic wing of the Labour Party who were concerned about what they believed was a move by that party to the left on a number of issues including nuclear disarmament and opposition to the Common Market. Their defection appeared to represent an opportunity for the Liberal Party to become a non-socialist left-wing alternative to the Conservative Party. The progressive tradition, which had been the ideological bedrock of the Edwardian Liberal Party and which had divided after the First World War into the social liberal wing of the Liberal Party and the social democratic wing of the Labour Party, seemed to be reuniting once more.

The defectors did not, however, join the Liberal Party but created their own new party organisation – the Social Democratic Party (SDP). Indeed this manoeuvre was encouraged by David Steel himself, recognising that many of its leading figures were not prepared to join the Liberals and in the belief that such a party would draw more support away from Labour than a defection to his own party.[7] But from the beginning the SDP and the Liberal Party have been committed to an alliance in which the parties do not contest the same constituencies, fight on a common manifesto and agree to operate together, should they form a government. The relationship has had its tensions, most notably over defence and on the allocation of which parliamentary constituencies each party should fight, but the fortunes of the two parties now seem inextricably linked and they are widely regarded as one single competitive force at elections, known as the Alliance. The SDP is not, however, a member of the Liberal International nor, despite the fact that it fought the 1984 elections to the European Parliament in tandem with the Liberals, of ELD. In the event of a formal merger of the two parties, the international affiliations of any new party will be one of the issues to be settled.

The foundation of the SDP and of the Alliance was closely followed by the third post-war Liberal revival. Once again a sequence of by-election victories raised hopes of a breakthrough. Opinion polls in the second half of 1981 put the Alliance in a clear lead, something never achieved on any continuous basis by the Liberals before. But although in 1982 the Alliance gained over a quarter of the vote, a higher proportion than that achieved by the Liberals since 1923, the electoral system gave the Alliance only 23 seats, 17 Liberal and 6 SDP, the most disproportional result produced in any British election. Although between 1983 and 1987 it won a majority of the votes cast in all parliamentary by-elections, breakthrough again eluded it at the 1987 election. A little over one-fifth of the vote gave it just 22 seats.

The last thirty years have undoubtedly seen a revival of organised liberalism in Britain. Although it has not yet broken the Conservative/Labour domination of government and parliament, it is, in collaboration with the SDP, close to the level of electoral support where it has at least a realistic prospect of holding the balance of power. What is the modern nature of this party which aims to return to the central stage of British politics after sixty years of playing no more than a minor part?

ORGANISATION AND STRUCTURE

The Liberal Party's structure has historically had two distinctive characteristics. The first is that although it was the first party in Britain to respond to the widening of the franchise in the late nineteenth century by creating a mass party organisation, it has retained many of the characteristics of a cadre party. The second is that the party's constitution does not clearly establish either the sovereignty of the mass party over the parliamentary leadership or give the parliamentary leadership clear control over the mass party. But in both respects there have been important changes in recent years.

The most significant changes have come in the extent to which the party is a mass or cadre party. The pressures and demands which have been made upon the party as a consequence of its greater electoral success have resulted in a number of important modifications to a traditionally diffuse and decentralised structure. Some of the clearest changes have come in the area of membership and finance.

Membership has never been unimportant to the party. Indeed, the party has regarded the expansion of its membership as one of its important objectives as it has re-emerged from the doldrums of the 1950s, for at least two reasons. First, the party has been unable to secure large financial contributions from industry, trade unions or other organisations and is thus constantly short of financial resources. The expansion of its membership was a way of improving its financial position. Secondly, because of its lack of financial resources, the party became dependent upon a volunteer activist base in order to conduct the nuts and bolts of campaigning. It was encouraged in this endeavour by evidence from both parliamentary and local government elections that intensive local campaigning could help to increase the party's vote to an extent that did not appear true for the Conservative and Labour Parties. But it was not until the late 1970s that the party reached the position of being a national party in the sense of having at least a rudimentary local party organisation in every parliamentary constituency.

But Liberal Party membership has until recently been strictly a local affair. The party had no central record of its members or the size of its membership. National party membership was accorded to all those whose constituency party paid the due affiliation fee. Further, although party members played a central role in raising money for their local parties, they made relatively little contribution to the financial support of the national party which was heavily dependent upon financial contributions from certain wealthy individuals and the Joseph Rowntree Social Service Trust, a trust established by a Quaker businessman, which funds a number of non-charitable political and social causes.

However, in 1983 the party introduced a system of national

membership cards. The system still respected the party's decentralist sympathies and no national register of members was set up as a result of it, but it did permit the party to ascertain its total membership reasonably accurately. In the two years that it has been in operation, the party's national membership has stuck at just over 100,000 members, nearly twice that of its SDP allies during the same period. But the system has also enabled the party for the first time to increase significantly the proportion of its central expenditure which is financed by income from its local party organisations. Thus, in 1982, the last non-election year before the introduction of the new system, just 22 per cent of the Liberal Party organisation's central income came through the constituencies, while another 18 per cent came from the financial appeal at its annual assembly, much of which is contributed by local parties and individuals. In 1985, in contrast, nearly one-half of the headquarters' income came from the constituencies, while the assembly appeal contributed a further 15 per cent. For the first time, the party is achieving the situation where a majority of its regular headquarters income comes through the contributions and activities of its mass membership.[8] Even so the central party's financial resources are still pitifully small. Its turnover was still less than half a million pounds in 1985, half that of the SDP headquarters whose membership contributed nearly two and a half times more to their income than the Liberal membership did to its headquarters, despite its much smaller number of members.

This transition from being more akin to a cadre party to being more akin to a mass party has also occurred in a number of other areas. The parliamentary party has often looked like a small collection of local notables. Every member owes little of his election to the national popularity of the party and a lot to his own local effort to secure election, often building upon a local Liberal base in the Celtic fringe or some other part of the rural periphery. Consequently, neither the party leader nor the mass party has had any effective disciplinary sanctions. The weekly meetings of the party are often relatively casual affairs.

But in recent years there has been increasing pressure upon the parliamentary party to act in a more formal and disciplined manner. One significant influence was the Lib–Lab pact of 1977–8; for the first time the parliamentary party had some responsibility to help maintain a government in office. More recently the increased electoral strength of the Alliance has meant that both their opponents and the public have paid far greater attention to the activities of the party in parliament, and major splits are potentially embarrassing. Thus Norton found that in the 1979–83 parliament the parliamentary Liberal Party was no more likely to go into opposite division lobbies than either the Conservative or Labour Parties.[9] Most recently a well-publicised division within the party over the future of British nuclear weapons has resulted in moves to invoke the doctrine of collective responsibility upon official party spokesmen for the first time.

Similar developments have also occurred within the mass party. The party has a federal structure with separate parties in Scotland and Wales and a strong regional structure within the English party. This was reflected in the composition of its national executive committee, the body responsible for all aspects of the party other than policy-making, which was dominated by regional representatives. In consequence, it acted as a sounding board for local interests rather than as a body capable of giving strategic direction. Such direction was usually only possible when a group of party notables emerged whose authority was based upon their standing with the parliamentary leadership and the mass party, rather than any constitutional offices they might hold. But in 1984 the composition of the national executive committee was revamped and its powers more precisely defined. It now consists primarily of the principal party officers together with members elected by the party's council on a nationwide basis, and it has proved to be much more effective at co-ordinating the work of the party. A second important change has been a decision to employ centrally-paid agents in each region. Although this change was widely regarded within the party as a manifestation of its decentralist principles in its direction of resources away from the London headquarters, it gives headquarters control over the key-professional employee in each region and thus influence upon the activities of regional and local parties.[10]

However, the party is still far from having the highly-disciplined and centralised structure of a mass party. The limited power and resources of the centre is clearly demonstrated by two examples. The first is the gradual development of a second party headquarters under the auspices of the Association of Liberal Councillors. This body was created in the 1960s in order to co-ordinate and foster the work of the party's local government councillors. But after 1970 the party could no longer afford the services of a local government officer at headquarters and the response to the increased demand for services and support which followed a substantial increase in the party's representation on local authorities in the early 1970s was met by the independent action of the ALC rather than from party headquarters. A small professional staff headquarters was established – symbolically at Hebden Bridge in Yorkshire rather than in London. Its range of services has grown substantially and includes many that would have normally been expected to have been provided by party headquarters.

The second example is the party's candidate selection procedures. Candidate selection is the responsibility of local associations. The national party does have a vetting procedure to ensure that its candidates reach a minimum standard, but because until recently the party has been searching for candidates to fight its less winnable seats, that power has in practice been a limited one. The leadership has little influence over whether a seat should be fought, and if so, by whom. Its limited powers were no more clearly demonstrated than in the negotiations with the SDP over which seat should be fought by each party. These were conducted at regional level and below, and on the Liberal side the leadership's wishes were sometimes ignored or overturned, in contrast to the position within the SDP.

The relationship between the parliamentary leadership and the mass party also combines the features of two alternative models. The party does not subscribe simply to a delegate model in which the mass party has the right to overrule and direct the parliamentary leadership, or to a leadership-dominated model in which the leader has strong control over the mass party. The mass party has the autonomous right to appoint its principal office-holders. Further, since 1976 the leader has been elected by the mass party membership and in a recent, but as yet unused change, is subject to re-election at least once in a parliament. The party's annual assembly makes authoritative pronouncements on party policy. But the decisions of that assembly cannot bind the parliamentary party; its decisions are sovereign only so far as the mass party is concerned. In addition, the chairmanship of two important committees – the Policy (formerly Standing) Committee and the Candidates Committee – are reserved to parliamentarians. In other words, power in the Liberal Party is shared between the parliamentary party and the mass party.

In practice the constitutional position appears to give the parliamentary leadership short-term flexibility and the opportunity to take initiatives, but it is difficult for the leader to sustain a position in the long run in direct opposition to his party. The parliamentary leadership has sustained a number of significant defeats, for example on incomes policy (1976), on attitude to economic growth (1979), on the siting of cruise missiles (1981) and on the future of Britain's non-nuclear capability (1986). But the leadership has not been obliged to take immediate cognisance of these decisions in the position it has adopted in parliament and elsewhere and has tried, where possible, to seek a compromise or a reversal of the policy decisions. In any case, on all such occasions the assembly has not defied the united position of the parliamentary party, but has sided with a publically expressed view held by a minority of MPs.[11] Its actions have helped to influence debate occurring within the parliamentary party and have not been a simple case of conflict between the mass and parliamentary party. The debate is usually resolved through the adoption of a position agreed by both the mass party and the parliamentary leadership.

But if the Liberal leader undoubtedly shares power, he does hold the power of initiative. Much of his freedom for manoeuvre has come from the diffuse distribution of power at the centre and the lack of an effective co-ordinating mechanism. The leader has been able to take it upon himself to fill the gap. Thus, under Thorpe, for example, the party's general election campaign was directed by a committee entirely of his own appointment. Similarly, under both Grimond's leadership and his own, Thorpe had responsibility for directing financial and other resources towards target seats without being accountable for his actions to any organ of the mass party.

Although the power-sharing relationship between leadership and mass party has not fundamentally changed in recent years, there have been a number of subtle changes. Many of them would superficially appear to strengthen the hand of the mass party. As already noted, the leader has since 1976 been elected by the mass party membership. Prior to 1979 the preparation of the party's general election manifesto was entirely the prerogative of the party leader, but at the 1979 election, the last occasion on which the party produced its own manifesto, the main programme was prepared by a subcommittee of the party's Standing Committee, with only the preface being written by the leader on his own.[12] Finally, there has been a clear reduction during Steel's leadership in the extent to which *ad hoc* structures have been created without the agreement and participation of the mass party. Thus, the general election committee in 1979 and 1983 was established jointly by the leader and the mass party.

However, these changes have not, in practice, served to diminish the leader's power. Indeed, they have demonstrated that the active support of the mass party provides the leader with legitimacy and authority for his actions and views, which he would not otherwise have. Thus, on a number of occasions when Steel has faced opposition within his mass party he has argued that because he was duly elected leader of the mass party it has the duty to support him and his objectives. This proved particularly powerful in his efforts to persuade the party to sustain the Lib-Lab pact. By working through the constitutional structures of the party, Steel has been better able to manage opposition than his predecessors.

While the internal affairs of the Liberal Party have been put on a firmer constitutional basis in recent years, this has been counteracted by its relations with the SDP. Although the Alliance is widely regarded by the electorate as one electoral force, it so far lacks any clear constitutional status in either party. The Liberal Party's constitution neither recognises the Alliance nor does it provide for any structure for conducting relations with the SDP. There is no official mass body linking the members of both parties. Many of the major committees which have been created for this purpose have been done so on the sole authority of the leaders, although more recently, committees responsible for agreeing policy have mainly been created on the authority of the Policy Committee. Indeed, the maintenance of relations between the two parties at national level has been heavily dependent on informal personal contact between notables from both parties. The strains caused by this process – they were revealed in the attempt to secure an agreed Alliance defence policy in preparation for the 1987 election – suggested, however, that this position is not tenable. As the pressures of electoral popularity have encouraged greater formality in the Liberal Party's own internal proceedings, so can they be expected to require similar steps in its external relations with the SDP. Indeed, a heated debate over the future of the Alliance was provoked immediately after the 1987 general election following a public call for a merger of the two parties by David Steel.

While external relations with another party are central to the Liberal Party's current electoral strategy, relationships with interest groups play an unimportant role in the party's life. Although external pressure groups played a fundamental role in the party's early life in bringing together and maintaining the party's electoral coalition, the modern party has long prided itself on its freedom from organised interests. This claim is central to the image it projects as a classless party which is able to govern in the interests of the nation as a whole. It has, however, been noted that the revival of the Liberal Party in the late 1950s and early 1960s coincided with a considerable increase in the number of pressure groups concerned with a range of social issues and that both may have sprung from the same impetus of social concern.[13] But this link, if it does exist, does not extend to there being any clear formal links between Liberal activists and such pressure groups.

ELECTORAL SUPPORT

As we have already discovered, the Liberal Party has gained substantial electoral strength in recent years. But what is the basis of this increase? What is the character of Liberal electoral support?

There are some methodological difficulties in dealing with this question. Because of the electoral pact between the Liberals and the SDP at the 1983 and 1987 general elections, it is not possible to analyse the electoral support for the Liberals at those elections separately from that for the SDP. The elector effectively had the decision whether to vote for a Liberal or an SDP candidate made for him. Further, full data on the social composition of the Alliance vote at the 1987 election is not available at the time of writing. What we do here is to examine how far Alliance support is different from that for the Liberal Party alone, both by comparing its pattern of support in 1983 with that for the Liberal Party in 1979 and also by considering any differences in the pattern of party identification for the two parties. Such preliminary indications as there are about Alliance support in 1987 suggests that the picture painted here remains broadly correct.[14]

It has widely been accepted that the growth of the Liberal vote has largely been built upon sand. Its vote has appeared to lack any strong sociological, psychological or attitudinal roots. Thus its vote lacked any clear concentration of strength in any socio-economic group. Liberal voters appeared not so much to be endorsing the policies of the Liberal Party as protesting against those of its opponents, and were attracted to the party only by general notions of image. But two weaknesses were identified as providing the greatest impediment to the party's long-term electoral prospects. First, its vote was extremely fickle. The party found it difficult to retain the support at subsequent elections of the recruits it gained at previous ones. Secondly, its vote was geographically evenly spread. Under the single-member plurality electoral system this was a substantial handicap unless the party could win over a third of the vote.

Tables 5.3 and 5.4 suggest that 1983 Alliance support was merely a larger version of the old Liberal vote. The advent of the Alliance appears to have had little impact upon the character of Liberal support. The party's support was only a little stronger in the middle class than in the working class. While the party was generally somewhat weaker in urban than in rural areas, the differences were not large. Its support in most regions of the country was within a few per cent of the overall national level. Although in 1983 its support was more stable than Labour's, this reflected the fact that Labour's overall level of support fell by ten percentage points. More instructive is a comparison with the Conservatives; although the overall level of Conservative support was falling, while Alliance support was rising,

Table 5.3 *Electoral base*

		1979 %	1983 %
Class	Working class	13	22
	Middle class	17	28
	Farmers[a]	8	11
Religion[b]	Catholic	8	21
	Church of England	14	25
	Other Protestant	21	28
	None/other	12	25
Age	Under 25	19	23
	25 to 29	16	29
	40 to 59	13	25
	Over 60	10	20
Sex	Male	15	23
	Female	13	26
Urban/rural	Urban	10	23
	Mixed	13	25
	Rural	17	28

[a] These figures should be treated with caution because of small numbers. The percentage are based on Ns of 24 (1979) and 25 (1983).
[b] Religion is 'declared' religion, not 'practising'.
Source: British Election Study 1979 and 1983, except for urban/rural which is calculated from election results. Non-voters are excluded from all calculations.

1979 Liberal voters were less loyal to the Alliance than 1979 Conservative voters were to their party.

Why then, given the volatile nature of its support, has the Liberal Party been able to increase its support at all? It is frequently argued that it has benefited from a weakening of the electoral basis of the Conservative and Labour Parties produced by partisan dealignment and class dealignment. The former refers to a weakening in the strength of Conservative and Labour Party identification. In part this is often explained as a consequence of class dealignment but can also be accounted for by independent factors such as the poor performance, particularly with regard to the economy, of both the Conservative and Labour Parties in office, which has weakened the commitment of their adherents to their party. But whatever the reason for the change, the weakening of party identification has reduced the loyalty of Conservative and Labour supporters and made them more willing to consider a third party alternative.

According to the class dealignment thesis, Conservative and Labour support has declined because of a weakening of the importance of class and of the class cleavage in social and political life. Just as

Table 5.4 *Geographical distribution of vote*

	Under 10%	11–15%	16–20%	21–5%	26–30%	31–5%	36–40%	Over 40%
1979	Inner London West Midlands Metropolitan County Industrial South Wales Clydeside conurbation Rest of Scotland industrial belt	Outer London East Midlands South Yorkshire West Yorkshire Greater Manchester Merseyside Rest of North- West Tyne and Wear Rest of North Rest of Scotland	South East East Anglia Rest of West Midlands Rest of Yorkshire Rural Wales	Rest of South- West Scottish Highlands	Devon and Cornwall			
1983				Inner London East Midlands West Midlands Metropolitan County South Yorkshire Greater Manchester Merseyside Rest of North- West Tyne and Wear Industrial South Wales	Outer London South East East Anglia Rest of West Midlands West Yorkshire Rest of Yorkshire Rest of North Rest of Scotland	Rest of South- West	Devon and Cornwall Scottish Highlands	

			Rural Wales Clydeside Conurbation Rest of Scotland Industrial Belt				
1987	Industrial Wales	Inner London West Midlands Metropolitan County South Yorkshire Greater Manchester Rest of North- West Tyne and Wear Clydeside Conurbation Rest of Scotland industrial belt	Outer London East Midlands Rest of West Midlands West Yorkshire Rest of Yorkshire Merseyside Rest of North Rural Wales Rest of Scotland	South-East East Anglia	Rest of South- West	Devon and Cornwall	Scottish Highlands

Table 5.5 *Class basis of Liberal vote*

	1979	1983
Salariat	17	31
Routine non-manual	15	27
Petty Bourgeoisie	10	17
Foreman and technicians	13	25
Working class	13	20

Source: Heath et al. (1985).

religion declined as a cleavage at the turn of the century – producing in its wake the decline of the Liberal Party – so now the decline of the class cleavage is encouraging the decline of Conservative and (more especially) Labour support. This thesis is, however, much more controversial than the partisan dealignment thesis. It has been challenged on the grounds that although it is true that the proportion of middle-class voters voting Conservative and the proportion of working-class voters voting Labour has declined, it is not clear that this has been a consequence rather than a cause of the rise in Liberal and Alliance support.[15] If the class cleavage had declined independently of the rise of Alliance support, one would anticipate that the remaining Conservative and Labour support would have been less strongly structured by class, but there is no evidence of a consistent secular trend in that direction.

In any case both these theses imply that the rise in Liberal support reflects the weakness of Conservative and Labour support rather than positive regard for the Liberal Party. But a closer look at the evidence does reveal that the traditional interpretation of the weak character of the Liberal vote is in need of some modification. A more subtle fivefold class schema reveals that the Liberal and Alliance vote is noticeably stronger amongst those in salaried occupations in the professions and in management, but noticeably weaker amongst the *petite bourgeoisie* (see Table 5.5). There is perhaps no stronger indication of the unimportance of classical economic liberalism in the modern Liberal Party than its weaknesses amongst small entrepreneurs, including (despite its greater strength generally in rural areas) farmers.

Why are the Liberal Party and the Alliance stronger among the salariat?[16] We can, in fact, identify a core group of Alliance supporters. Amongst those who hold a university degree, work in the public sector and are members of a trade union, Alliance support reached 52 per cent in 1983. This core group is a very small section of the total population – those with a degree, for example, constitute only 4 per cent of voters, but it does indicate that the Alliance does have a specific appeal to a certain section of society.

Indeed, it is amongst this group that social liberal attitudes are most prevalent. Analysis of the 1983 post-election survey revealed that the better educated were more likely to adopt liberal positions on such issues as law and order, immigrants and the death penalty, and were also particularly supportive of at least some form of Welfare State spending, most notably in non-means tested areas such as education and the health service. The liberal arts tradition within British education appears to help produce a group of people with a distinctive set of social liberal values, values which often lead them to seek employment in one of the unionised caring professions within the public sector. It is important to note, however, that on issues central to the class divide such as nationalisation and the redistribution of income and wealth, this group does not adopt a particularly left-wing position.

Indeed, if we look at the electorate as a whole, we discover that this particular combination of attitudes – of liberalism on social issues and right-wing or centrist attitudes on economic issues – proves to be particularly favourable towards Alliance voting. The Alliance vote appears no longer to be wholly uninfluenced by electors' attitudes or values, but has become somewhat more concentrated amongst a section of the electorate with a distinctive set of attitudes. The degree of concentration should not be overemphasised – Alliance support was of the order of 35–40 per cent amongst this group compared with 26 per cent generally – but it is important for two reasons. First, those with right or centre liberal views have been a growing proportion of the electorate in recent years, and secondly, Alliance support amongst this group was very stable. There does, then, appear to be an opportunity for the Liberal Party and the Alliance to secure a stable basis of support amongst a growing section of the electorate.

Although this concentration of the Alliance vote amongst a certain section of the electorate is new, it does not appear to be a direct consequence of the formation of the SDP. A concentration of Liberal support amongst centre and right liberals was evident in 1979 before the formation of the SDP. Indeed, analysis of the social and attitudinal characteristics of Liberal and SDP identifiers reveals mostly marginal differences between them. The only striking feature was that more SDP identifiers were very likely to have had a previous history of voting for Labour than Liberal identifiers. But their attitudes were only marginally to the left of liberal identifiers while they were actually slightly more likely to be middle class.

There is thus some evidence of an emerging new electoral base to

Liberal and Alliance support. But equally, the remnants of the old bases have not disappeared either. Table 5.3 shows that Alliance support amongst 'other Protestants' was higher than amongst other religious groups. This reflects a clear tendency for Methodist and other non-conformists, particularly those who were practising, to vote for the Alliance and identify with the Liberal Party (though not the SDP).[17] Similarly, as Table 5.4 demonstrates, Alliance support is still somewhat higher in parts of the periphery than elsewhere – its support was highest in the Scottish Highlands and in Devon and Cornwall in the far South-West of England.

GOVERNMENT PARTICIPATION

Although the Liberal Party has been excluded from national office since 1945, the attitude it should adopt towards participation in future has become an increasingly important issue for the party as the prospect of a parliament in which no party holds an overall majority apparently becomes greater. Chastened by its unhappy experience in the inter-war period the party had become extremely wary of agreeing to participate in any coalition government; but in the last ten years it has begun to grapple with the questions that would be raised for it by the existence of a 'hung' parliament at national level and has considerable experience at local level of collaboration with other political parties.

The party has long been committed to the introduction of proportional representation, a reform that would almost undoubtedly result in coalition government. But for a long time it did not think through its attitude towards participation in a coalition government. In consequence the party was wholly unprepared when the February 1974 election produced a hung parliament and the incumbent Conservative prime minister, Edward Heath, invited Jeremy Thorpe to talks at 10 Downing Street over the possibility of forming a coalition government. Although the offer was swiftly refused, Thorpe's decision to agree to talk at all led to considerable controversy within the party. The row rumbled on throughout the remainder of that year and the 1974 assembly showed considerable reluctance to endorse participation in a coalition, although it avoided ruling it out entirely.

But with the election of David Steel in 1976 the party acquired a leader with a commitment to achieving a Liberal role in government and a willingness to enter into coalition or other deals if he felt they would aid the party's long-term advancement. Within months of his accession to the leadership that opportunity came when the incumbent Labour government lost its overall majority and faced a decisive vote of confidence in the House of Commons. The Liberal Party agreed to support the Labour government in return for a number of specific commitments, of which the most important so far as the party was concerned was that the government should use its best endeavours to secure the introduction of a system of proportional representation in the election of Britain's delegation to the European Parliament and the establishment of a formal system of consultation between Labour ministers and their shadow spokesmen in the Liberal Party. The pact which commenced in March 1977 remained in existence until September 1978, despite the failure in December 1977 of the House of Commons to support the use of proportional representation in the European elections. Although there were reservations within his party over the benefits it was deriving from the pact, Steel was determined to maintain it for as long as possible. He was concerned not so much with winning particular policy concessions in the short term as to demonstrate the ability of the Liberal Party to participate responsibly in government.[18]

By 1979 the Liberal Party was able to agree a coherent attitude towards its future participation in government. It aimed to share the balance of power in the House of Commons, and indicated that in the event it would be prepared to negotiate with either party and that the introduction of proportional representation would be its central aim. This position is still pursued within the Alliance, except that it has focused somewhat less explicitly on aiming only for the balance of power rather than the opportunity to govern in its own right.

This substantial change in the party's position was also promoted by its growing strength in local government since the early 1970s. Liberal councillors not infrequently found themselves as the third party holding the balance of power between two larger groups. Their choice of which party to co-operate with has varied from place to place and from time to time, but few councillors have shown any reluctance to make a deal with another party, and some local parties have attempted to change the working practices of their councils to make them more attuned to a situation where no one party has control.[19] Until recently, however, it was rare for the Liberal Party to supply either a minority or a majority administration for a large council. Only in Liverpool did it achieve that position before 1985. Recent electoral success has, however, seen Liberal dominated Alliance majority or minority administrations formed in three London boroughs and on six county councils. In all these cases Liberal councillors have shown no reluctance to form minority administrations and to conduct the negotiations with other parties needed to make them work.

POLICY

One of the central planks of nineteenth-century liberalism was the achievement of political liberty. But once many of the proposed reforms had been implemented, social and economic rather than political issues came to the fore. But for the modern British Liberal Party political issues are still of the greatest importance. As its 1979 manifesto put it: 'Political reform is the starting point.'[20] Constitutional change is once more at the centre of the Liberal Party's programme because it believes that if Britain is to solve its economic problems of slow economic growth and high unemployment, it needs to change its political system. The party wishes to end the adversarial style of politics epitomised by the ritual banter between government and opposition in the House of Commons and replace it with an emphasis on collaboration between parties and stability of governmental policy.

The chief jewel in the crown of the Liberals' constitutional programme is electoral reform – the introduction of a system of proportional representation which would, given the failure of any party to win over 50 per cent of the vote since 1945, almost ensure that the post-war tradition of single-party government would be replaced by coalitions, with the Alliance as the hinge between Conservative and Labour.

But the Liberal Party's constitutional proposals do not simply represent a pragmatic preference for the presumed economic benefits of an alternative system of government. It is also strongly imbued with a traditional liberal concern for the individual. Thus its preferred electoral reform is the single transferable vote system with its emphasis upon voting for individual candidates rather than parties. More generally, it wishes to decentralise government as far as possible both by strengthening local government and by creating a system of regional government (although it is uncertain how far regional government can be established within England). Individuals are to be encouraged to participate in the political system by taking decisions at the lowest possible tier of government. Finally, it proposes the introduction of a Bill of Rights to provide a written guarantee of civil liberties, something wholly lacking in Britain's unwritten constitution.

The British Liberal Party thus very clearly continues the liberal tradition of seeing the economic as subordinate to the political. But in the economic sphere its adherence to social rather than classical liberalism is clear. The party does retain a general faith in the role of the market as a wealth creator. But it is not in any sense wedded to the doctrine of classical liberalism. The party emphasises the liberal tradition of Keynes and Beveridge rather than of Hayek and Friedman. State intervention is judged pragmatically according to how far it promotes individual liberty and the threat that inequality poses to individual liberty:

> We seek to spread wealth and power, believing that liberty is best promoted through the responsible actions of men and women working together within diverse communities. We therefore see equality, or rather a diminution of gross inequalities, as a consequence of such a liberal society rather than an end in itself. We judge state intervention, not as itself good or bad, but by its contribution to the development of a liberal society.[21]

Thus, since the Second World War the party has generally adopted a pragmatic attitude towards nationalisation. It has usually only called for changes at the margins, favouring for example the denationalisation of the steel industry in the 1950s, but recognising that state control could be preferable to private monopoly in such areas as electricity and gas supply. It has shown strong support for the Welfare State, with a particular concern for the capacity of education to enable the individual to realise his or her potential, and has proposals for the integration of the system of taxes and welfare benefits in order to improve the ability of the fiscal system to redistribute income and wealth fairly.

Indeed, the post-war period has seen the end of free trade and *laissez-faire* as an important strand of thought within the party. In the 1950s the party included a number of leading advocates such as Arthur Seldon, Edward Martell and Oliver Smedley who fought for their views with some limited success. The debate centred on such issues as the attitude the party should adopt towards state intervention in agricultural markets and towards possible British membership of the EC which – although it operated a free-trade market amongst its member countries – imposed a high-tariff barrier against the goods of non-members. By the early 1960s, however, the Liberal Party had clearly decided to abandon this part of its intellectual inheritance. Given the concentration of its vote in rural areas, the preference of farmers for a system of agricultural support was influential. Many of the party's leading free traders subsequently resigned, and some of them were to become leading figures in the new monetarist right whose ideas were accepted by the Conservative Party in the late 1970s.

The party has indeed largely retained its faith in Keynesian fine tuning as an instrument for controlling the economy in the wake of the monetarist backlash of the late 1970s and early 1980s. It has, in consequence, accepted a significant role for public expenditure. In this it has placed itself closer to the Labour Party than to the Conservative Party but is rather more cautious than Labour in the size of the increase in public expenditure which it is prepared to countenance in order to reduce the existing high level of unemployment.

A further consequence of its continued faith in Keynesian economics has been an acceptance of the value of pursuing economic growth. Indeed the pursuit of growth and modernisation, in part by means of centralised planning, was a central feature of the vision Grimond established for the party.[22] But this aspect of the party's Keynesian inheritance has been challenged in recent years. Influenced by a growing concern for the environment, the party has begun to question some of the premises of its earlier stance. In 1979 a motion asserting that 'substantial economic growth as conventially measured is neither achievable nor desirable' was passed against the wishes of the party's leadership. Although the full implications of that statement have not been followed through, the party's environmentalist concern has expressed itself in, for example, a call for an immediate halt to the expansion of Britain's nuclear power industry and its eventual phasing out.

The party not only has a significant green streak to it but also a doveish one. This reveals itself in its attitude towards nuclear weapons. The party has, like liberal parties on the European continent, consistently favoured NATO and has accepted the American nuclear umbrella. It has, furthermore, wished to strengthen defence co-operation between the West European allies. But, at the behest of the party leadership, it decided as early as 1958 to oppose Britain's continued retention of its own nuclear independent capability, Polaris, and more recently its proposed replacement by Trident. The party assembly further voted in 1981 (against the advice of its leadership) to oppose the deployment of American cruise missiles on British soil. This anti-nuclear stance and a wish to reduce the nuclear stakes has proved to be the biggest obstacle in finding agreement on policy with the SDP, who both favours the deployment of cruise and a replacement for Polaris, albeit one less powerful than Trident. While the party leadership was successful in 1985 at persuading the party assembly to accept the retention of Polaris so that it could be included in arms negotiations talks, it proved unable – in a narrow but spectacular defeat – in 1986 to persuade it to accept the possibility of a replacement for Polaris which involved close collaboration with both France and the non-nuclear West European powers. But recent defence debates within the party have been notable not only for the decisions that have been reached but for the divisions it has revealed. The party found itself torn between, on the one hand, a dislike of Soviet-style communism and a wish to promote and defend European collaboration and, on the other, a concern for the risks that the deployment of nuclear weapons holds for the future of mankind. As with conscription in the First World War, Liberals find decisions on defence amongst the most difficult they have to make.

STRATEGY

The aim of the Liberal Party ever since the electoral disasters of the early 1950s has been to regain its major party status. Three principal strategies have been pursued during this period in order to achieve that aim. Two have been national ones, the third is more local.

The period of Grimond's leadership produced not only a policy direction for the party but also a strategic one. Grimond put forward the view that the party should aim to achieve a realignment of the left in which the Liberal Party would replace the Labour Party as a major party of state. This strategy required the party to present itself as a more effective left-of-centre challenger to the Conservative Party than Labour was. It was born out of Labour's failure to win three consecutive elections between 1951 and 1959, at a time when the Liberal Party had made some progress. Labour's narrow electoral victory in 1964 and its substantial one in 1966 largely destroyed the credibility of this strategy, as it no longer could be argued that Labour was incapable of defeating the Conservatives.

Between Grimond's resignation in 1967 and Steel's election to the leadership in 1976 the party lacked any clear national strategy. But under Steel the party has had a clear strategic direction – the achievement of credibility through a preparedness to co-operate with others both inside and outside government – thus Steel's eager willingness to participate in the Lib–Lab pact of 1977–8 and to form an electoral and policy pact with the SDP since 1981. The strategy has both its similarities and differences with Grimond's strategy. Both acts of co-operation that have actually occurred have been with Labour or predominantly former Labour politicians; the party has thus pursued co-operation with those to its left rather than the right. But the SDP's founders were from the right rather than the left of the Labour Party and both the Liberals and the SDP have made clear their hope of winning the balance of power in parliament in order to produce less ideologically extreme and more stable government – in these respects the Alliance has appeared to be aiming for the role of a centre political party in a multi-party system rather than that of the left-of-centre party in a two-party system.

Both these strategies share the aim of providing a nationwide electoral credibility for the party. But given the geographical evenness of its vote, this has appeared to be insufficient on its own. The 1983 election demonstrated that even a quarter of the vote could result in little more than a handful of seats. Thus, the party has seen a number of efforts to concentrate its resources into achieving local credibility and building up its strength in particular places.

In truth this has not been one strategy but several. In part it was reflected in the policy adopted by the party in the 1950s and 1960s of only putting forward candidates where it had a reasonable local organisation and could fight more than a paper campaign. Debate occasionally surfaced during this period as to whether the party should fight on a broad or a narrow front, although – given the considerable independence of local constituency parties – the decision whether or not to fight a seat was in reality not in the national party's control. The eventual emergence of a broad front in February 1974 with 517 candidates reflected a grass-roots upsurge of optimism rather than a preordained policy. But since then, the party has made deliberate efforts to ensure it fought most constituencies. Such a strategy was felt to have two advantages. It enabled the party to maximise its national vote and thereby bolster its case for proportional representation and it meant it could present itself as an alternative government, should its electoral support ever take off.

Another strand of the local strategy was the effort of Jeremy Thorpe to stimulate Liberal voting in certain target seats where the prospects of a good Liberal performance were thought to be strong. Thorpe's efforts were designed to identify not only future general election success but also to promote good performances at by-elections. Ever since the party's successes at Torrington in 1958 and Orpington in 1962, parliamentary by-elections have been looked upon by the party as an opportunity not only to win seats that with varying degrees of success were retained at general elections, but also to provide a stimulus to the party's national electoral popularity. The party's constituency campaigns were, however, often strongly tailored to what was thought to be electorally advantageous locally, and together contained inconsistencies that could not have been fitted into a coherent national electoral appeal.[23] The party was essentially relying upon its ability to attract protest votes which did not require the presentation to the electorate of an image of a party of government.

But the most distinctive 'local' electoral strategy pursued by the Liberal Party has been community politics.[24] Both a political philosophy and an electoral strategy, community politics was endorsed by the party assembly in 1970. Although never fully taken up by the party leadership, in many ways it built upon the decision taken ten years previously deliberately to build up the party's organisation through concentrating on local elections. According to community politicians, the party had to be more than a traditional vote-getting machine. Rather, it should campaign actively in the community in order to help people overcome the insensitivity and injustice perpetuated by modern bureaucracy and thereby regain some control over their life. In practical terms this often meant that the party concentrated on certain target wards and its prospective local or parliamentary candidate played an enhanced role as a social worker, helping people sort out their problems with the local council (such as the local street lighting, litter or broken pavement); by means of this activity and intensive campaigning a local Liberal credibility was achieved.

Community politics had a number of successes. The party made significant gains in local elections in some inner city areas where the party had traditionally been weak, such as Liverpool, Birmingham and Leeds. One of the successful by-election campaigns of 1972 and 1973 (Sutton and Cheam) used community politics techniques. More generally, it helped popularise a set of campaigning and electoral techniques within the party, particularly through the medium of the Association of Liberal Councillors, and it enabled Liberals to build up pockets of strength in individual wards. But it has been by no means clear that a local council vote for the Liberals will necessarily be translated into a parliamentary vote at a general election. Some of the party's more disappointing parliamentary election performances have occurred in places where it has been successful in local elections.

These local and national strategies have come together in one particular area – the stimulation of tactical voting. This involves an attempt by the party to turn the constraints of the single-member plurality system to its electoral advantage. The party has attempted to persuade the supporters of a locally third-placed Conservative or Labour candidate to switch to the Liberal candidate in order to defeat the incumbent candidate of the other major party. This tactic has been more successful in appealing to Labour rather than Conservative supporters and has helped to contribute to a significant number of the party's successes.[25] The party's national claim to be a left-wing alternative to Labour, more capable of defeating the Conservatives, is clearly consistent with an appeal to locally third-placed Labour supporters. But it is also clear that new tactical votes are only won on a relatively small scale and only when the local Liberal candidate is perceived to be in very serious contention with his principal opponent. It is unlikely that tactical voting can deliver a large parliamentary bridgehead for the party.[26]

None of these strategies have, however, attempted to tackle what might be regarded as the fundamental long-term weakness in the party's electoral position, its lack of a stable vote and the lack of a stable image in the minds of the electorate as to what the party stands for. The party has concentrated on the most immediate means it believes it has to hand of maximising its role in the short term, even if that support is built upon a protest vote and is otherwise rather fickle. It has still not wholly answered for itself the question that has been asked of it since the 1920s – where does it stand in a polity where class is an important electoral cleavage? Its ability to regain a long-term position as a party of government must be in doubt for so long as there is a widespread ignorance amongst the electorate of just what the British Liberal Party and the Alliance believe in.

NOTES

1 M. Brock, 'The liberal tradition' in V. Bogdanor (ed.) *Liberal Party Politics* (Oxford: Clarendon, 1983). On the early Liberal Party, more generally, see J. Vincent, *The Formation of the British Liberal Party* (Hassocks: Harvester, 1976).
2 H.V. Emy, *Liberals, Radicals and Social Politics* (Cambridge: Cambridge University Press, 1973); P.F. Clarke, *Liberals and Social Democrats* (Cambridge: Cambridge University Press, 1978); M. Freeden, *The New Liberalism* (Oxford: Clarendon, 1978).
3 Clarke (1978).
4 M. Steed, 'The electoral strategy of the Liberal Party' in Bogdanor (1983).
5 W. Wallace, 'Survival and revival' in Bogdanor (1983).
6 J. Rasmussen, *The Liberal Party* (London: Constable, 1965) ch. 6; A. Cyr, *Liberal Party Politics in Britain* (Brunswick, N.J.: Transaction, 1977).
7 I. Bradley, *Breaking the Mould?* (Oxford: Martin Robertson, 1981) 79–80.
8 This development is being further encouraged by the agreement between the Liberal Party and the SDP that corporate donations should be used to finance the joint 'Alliance fund' rather than either of the two individual parties. Figures are calculated from the *Liberal Party Annual Report and Accounts*.
9 P. Norton, 'The Liberal Party in parliament' in Bogdanor (1983).
10 See also the argument in D.J. Wilson, *Power and Party Bureaucracy in Britain* (Farnborough; Saxon, 1975).
11 The importance of this is demonstrated in R. Rose, 'The political ideas of English party activists', *American Political Science Review*, 56 (1962) 360–71.
12 The party constitution does, however, give the party leader a veto over the contents of the party's general election manifesto.
13 See Cyr (1977) 285–9.
14 Opinion-poll evidence suggests indeed that Alliance support became even more concentrated in the middle class than it had been in 1983, particularly the public-sector university-educated middle class. See, for example, I. Crewe, 'A new class of politics', *The Guardian*, 15 June 1987.
15 See A. Heath, R. Jowell and J. Curtice, *How Britain Votes* (Oxford: Pergamon, 1985): A. Heath, R. Jowell and J. Curtice, 'Understanding electoral change in Britain', *Parliamentary Affairs* 39, (1986), 150–64; I. Crewe, 'On the death and resurrection of class voting; some comments on "How Britain Votes"', *Political*

Studies 34, (1986) 620–38; A. Heath, R. Jowell and J. Curtice, 'Trendless fluctuation: a reply to Crewe', *Political Studies* (forthcoming).

16 The following passage is based upon Heath et al., (1985) *passim*.

17 Amongst all Methodists, 20% had a Liberal Party identification in 1983, compared with 12½% of the electorate as a whole. Only 6% identified with the SDP, the same proportion as amongst the electorate as a whole. Amongst Methodists who attended a service at least once a week, 29% identified with the Liberal Party.

18 For a full account of the Lib–Lab pact see A. Michie and S. Hoggart, *The Pact* (London: Quartet, 1978).

19 One notable example of such a development has been on Cheshire County Council where rules have been established to ensure that all parties have access to the professional advice of the council's officers rather than just the governing party. Cheshire's practice has subsequently been imitated by other councils.

20 *The Real Fight is for Britain* (London: Liberal Publication Department, 1979) 2.

21 *Foundations for the Future* (London: Liberal Publication Department, 1982) 3.

22 A. Gamble, 'Liberals and the economy' in Bogdanor (1983).

23 R. Rose, *Influencing Voters* (London: Faber, 1967).

24 P. Hain, *Community Politics* (London: Platform, 1976).

25 Steed (1979).

26 M. Steed and J. Curtice, *One in Four* (Hebden Bridge: Association of Liberal Councillors, 1983).

REFERENCES

Essential reading

A. Beith, *The Case for the Liberal Party and the Alliance* (London: Longman, 1983).

V. Bogdanor, *Liberal Party Politics* (Oxford: Clarendon, 1983).

C. Cook, *A Short History of the Liberal Party* (London: Macmillan, 1976).

A. Cyr, *Liberal Party Politics in Britain* (Brunswick, N.J.: Transaction, 1977).

J. Grimond, *The Liberal Challenge* (London: Hollis & Carter, 1963).

A. Heath, R. Jowell and J. Curtice, *How Britain Votes* (Oxford: Pergamon, 1985).

J. Rasmussen, *The Liberal Party* (London: Constable, 1965).

M. Steed, 'The Liberal Party' in H. Drucker, *Multi-Party Britain* (London: Macmillan, 1979).

Further reading

J. Alt, I. Crewe and B. Sarlvik, 'Angels in plastic: Liberal support in 1974', *Political Studies* 25, (1977) 343–68.

P.F. Clarke, *Liberals and Social Democrats* (Cambridge: Cambridge University Press, 1978).

C. Cook, *The Age of Alignment: Electoral Politics in Britain 1922–29* (London: Macmillan, 1975).

P. Lemieux, 'Political issues and Liberal support in the February 1974 British general election', *Political Studies* 25 (1977) 323–42.

J. Vincent, *The Formation of the British Liberal Party* (Hassocks: Harvester, 1976).

T. Wilson, *The Downfall of The Liberal Party 1914–35* (London: Collins, 1966).

6

Liberalism in France

John Frears

INTRODUCTION

France has never had a great liberal party in the way that Canada or Great Britain have. Furthermore the word 'liberal' in France does not mean the same as it does in English. In France, its principal meaning is opposition to state intervention in economic or social life. For the French, Thatcherism is a kind of liberalism. In identifying liberalism in France, therefore, we shall not be looking for a great party with a long tradition but we shall be seeking to identify political forces belonging to Gordon Smith's 'liberal-conservative' classification rather than to a 'liberal-radical' one.

The chapter chooses to identify the UDF (Union pour la Démocratie Française), a federation of parties which were known as the *Giscardiens* when Valéry Giscard d'Estaing was president, as the political force that is best described as liberal. There are two reasons for this. One is that the *Giscardiens* have always used the word liberal in their appeal to the electorate and in their attempt to distinguish themselves from their coalition partners, the Gaullist RPR. The second is that Giscard d'Estaing as a political leader has been an authentic liberal in the English as well as the French sense of the word. In his speeches and writings before and during his presidency he has argued for tolerance, civil liberties, social reform, a less authoritarian and centralist style of government, and more recently for *moins d'état* – rolling back the state.

Choosing the *Giscardiens* as the French liberal party is nevertheless risky. First of all, they are not a party but a collection of three parties (plus several other smaller fragments). Secondly, the three parties, as we shall see, have very diverse origins. The Republican Party (PR) is the descendant of the old independent conservatives and *modérés*. The CDS (Centre des Démocrates Sociaux) is the descendant of the

Christian Democrat MRP. These two elements, therefore, belong historically and in terms of electoral sociology to the Catholic right. The third element, the Radical Party, has historically been a party of the republican and anti-clerical left. However, it is important to stress at the outset that the old cleavages over the church and the republic are now so far back in the past as to be irrelevant – and in any case they never stopped radicals and *modérés* governing in coalition even then. The third difficulty about choosing the UDF to represent liberalism is that it is not a member of the Liberal International. That distinction belongs to a party that does not exist: the democratic left group from the French senate, which includes members of the Radical Party and also the left-radicals (MRG), a very small, separate party allied to the Socialists and to the socialist government of 1981–6. Nor is the UDF as a whole a member of the Liberal group in the European Parliament. The PR, regarded as unacceptably right-wing by British liberals, is a member, but CDS Members of the European Parliament sit with the Christian Democrat group (see Table 6.8 on p. 142).

The final and most risky part of choosing the UDF to represent liberalism is that it may not last. The star of Giscard d'Estaing has faded since his presidency and without a leader in power with whom it can identify it might easily break up. In the 1978 election, when Giscard was president and the three parties that supported him formed the UDF, the French electorate divided neatly into two sets of two: on the left the Communist Party 21 per cent and the Socialists (including their MRG appendage) 25 per cent, and on the right and centre the government coalition of Gaullist RPR 23 per cent and UDF 21 per cent. That fourfold division is still there, though the numbers are slightly different, and I believe we can classify it as authoritarian left and democratic left, authoritarian right and liberal right.

THE STRANDS OF LIBERALISM IN FRANCE

The UDF is a loose federation of the non-Gaullist parties of the liberal centre and right that supported Giscard d'Estaing when he was president – indeed it takes its name from the book *Démocratie Française*[1] in which he set out his liberal political philosophy.

The largest component of the UDF is the Republican Party. Up till 1977 they were called the *Républicains Indépendants* (RI) and had been the original supporters of Giscard d'Estaing when, in 1962, he called on the electorate to support de Gaulle in the referendum on direct presidential elections. The other conservatives and moderates, not to mention the Radicals, the MRP, and the whole of the left, opposed his constitutional innovation in the name of hallowed parliamentary tradition and went down to heavy defeat both in the referendum and in the election that immediately followed. Giscard's little group survived and became a distinctive part of the Gaullist-dominated government coalition.

Analysis of the right and centre in France has been dominated by the approach of René Rémond and François Goguel. The former classified three historic strands in the French right,[2] the counter-revolutionary supporters of a legitimist monarchy, the 'Bonapartists' who are more democratic but favour authoritarian leadership in the hands of one man, and thirdly the 'Orleanists', the moderate, bourgeois, and liberal right. It is the Orleanists who, according to this classification, are the ancestors of today's Republican Party – against absolutism, against crude or doctrinaire anti-clericalism in the early years of this century, in favour of balanced budgets and sound money – the kind of government represented by Poincaré in the 1920s or Pinay in the 1950s. François Goguel, in his famous book on the Third Republic,[3] makes the historic distinction between what he calls the 'party of the established order' and 'the party of movement', preferring these terms to 'right' and 'left'. The conservatives and *modérés*, who were never organised into political parties until the MRP appeared after the Second World War, he classifies as belonging to the 'party of the established order', supported above all by the Catholic faithful with the electoral strongholds in the regions where the church was strongest.

Descendants of the 'Orleanist' part of the 'party of established order', if you will, the *Giscardiens* at all events found themselves in 1962 grouped round the brilliantly rising star of the young minister of Finance, who was the grandson of a Third Republic minister and inheritor of his parliamentary seat in the Puy de Dôme. They adapted themselves very skilfully to what was in 1962 the new politics of stable majority government. They were a reliable part of the parliamentary majority that supported the presidential leadership of General de Gaulle. However, particularly after Giscard himself left the government in 1966, they proved themselves to be effective critics whenever de Gaulle or the government appeared to act in an authoritarian manner or to abuse their powers. This was the period which Giscard described as *'oui . . . mais'*-support for stable government but not unconditional support for everything de Gaulle did and particularly not for the 'solitary exercise of power'. Indeed, Giscard played a big part in the eventual defeat of de Gaulle when he announced that he would not be voting yes in the 1969 referendum, de Gaulle's last appeal for the confidence of the French people over the rather odd pretext of senate reform. Giscard and the Independent Republicans supported Georges Pompidou at the presidential election that followed the resignation of de Gaulle, while most of the other elements of today's UDF remained in the opposition. It was not until Giscard himself was a candidate for the presidency, after the death of Pompidou in 1974, that he was joined by the Centre Democrats and Radicals and offered to bring them into his presidential majority. It was from then on that the whole of the non-Gaullist part of the majority were collectively known as the *Giscardiens*.

The second most important component of the UDF is the descendant of the Christian democratic MRP. It took a very long time for Catholics to accept a democratic republic and they were regarded by their political opponents right up to the Second World War as reactionaries whose real desire was the restoration of a 'hierarchical authoritarian state modelled on their church'. There was, however, a progressive Catholic tradition in France in the liberal Catholicism of Sangnier's 'Sillon' and the short-lived political party Action Libérale Populaire in the early years of this century, the small Parti Démocrate Populaire (of which the founder of the European Community Robert Schuman was a leading member) in the 1920s and 1930s. It was the Catholic leaders of the Resistance in the Second World War, who had demonstrated their commitment to democracy and the republic, who at the liberation formed the MRP. For a time it was the leading party of France and it participated in most of the governments of the Fourth Republic (1946–58). Its progressive social and economic policies place it to the left of the Radical Party at the time. Its voters, however, tended to be less progressive than its leaders and many of them deserted the MRP for Gaullism in the Fifth Republic.

In the 1960s as – under the impact of rapid industrial modernisation – French society became more secular, the MRP transformed itself into the Centre Démocrate and the old Catholic trade union CFTC into the non-confessional CFDT. The MRP had joined the opposition in 1962 after de Gaulle made some disparaging remarks about European union, though some former leading figures like Maurice Schumann later broke away and were absorbed back into Gaullism. The leader of the Centre Démocrate was Jean Lecanuet who had made a favourable impact on the public as a presidential candidate against de Gaulle in 1965. Under his leadership most of the Centre Démocrate remained in the opposition under Pompidou as well as under de Gaulle. In 1973 they formed an alliance with the Radical Party called the Reform Movement. In 1974 they backed

Giscard for president and entered the government coalition. In 1976 they reformed themselves into the CDS so that some of the pro-Pompidou centrists (known as the CDP and present in government under Pompidou from 1969 to 1974) could rejoin their ranks. Since 1978 the CDS has been a central element in the *Giscardien* UDF, ideologically slightly less favourable to economic liberalism than its partners.

The third party of the UDF is the Radical Party or Parti républican radical et radical-socialiste, to give its full historic title. Formed in 1901, it is the oldest party in France. Historically it has always been regarded as a party of the left, as belonging to Goguel's 'party of movement'. Radicalism in the Third Republic was the inheritor of the traditions of the French revolution: for the republic, for the enlightenment, for science, for reason, for individualism, for private property, for patriotism, for parliament, above all for the separation of church and state. It was against aristocracy, the church, absolutism, excessive state power. Most of the great names of the Third Republic are associated with radicalism: Gambetta, Clémenceau, Herriot. Never socialist, it sometimes joined forces at elections or in government during the Third Republic with the Socialists as in 1924 or in the 1936 Popular Front. Never Catholic, it or parts of it were frequently to be found in alliance with conservatives and *modérés* – 1919, 1926, 1934.

After the Second World War the Radical Party has experienced a series of disastrous splits so that what remains is a tiny fragment. It was always diverse. Some of its members, like Pierre Cot, were fellow-travellers of the Communist Party, some were quite far to the right and quit the party in the mid 1950s over the issue of keeping Algeria French, some – like Michel Debré or Jacques Chaban-Delmas – were ardent Gaullists. The first big split came in 1955 between the supporters of Edgar Faure, who wanted the Radical Party to continue as an adroit and pragmatic government party with no particular ideological constraints, and the supporters of Pierre Mendés-France, who wanted the party to be a dynamic and progressive force for social reform. Mendés-France was a vigorous reforming prime minister in 1954–5 who successfully extracted France from its disastrous war in Indo-China. A lot of people who today are prominent in the Socialist Party, such as François Mitterrand or Charles Hernu, would have liked to see a great *rassemblement* of the democratic left under the leadership of Mendés-France. However, Mendés lost control of the party in 1957, and he and his friends left it in 1959. He remained a man of the left, and eventually, with Michel Rocard, became a leading figure in a small and rather revolutionary fragment of French socialism called the PSU.

Most radicals – the most notable exception was Mendés-France – did not oppose the return to power of de Gaulle in 1958. However, though ex-radicals like Edgar Faure found their way into government from 1966 on, the party was part of the opposition from the end of the Algerian war in 1962 to the death of Pompidou in 1974. In the later 1960s they joined the Federation of the Democratic and Socialist Left (FGDS) under the leadership of François Mitterrand in electoral alliance with the Communist Party. After the electoral débâcle of 1968 and the Soviet invasion of Prague had reawakened anti-communist instincts, the FGDS broke up. Under the leadership of a modernising newspaper publisher, Jean Jacques Servan-Schreiber, the party formed an alliance with the Centre Démocrate, called, as we have already seen, the Reform Movement. This caused yet another split. Those radicals whose electoral strongholds were in the traditional bastions of the republican left, basically in the southern half of France and particularly the South-West, preferred to ally themselves for electoral or ideological reasons to the Socialists and Communists. In 1972 they formed their own separate party, the MRG (Mouvement des Radicaux de Gauche) which is closely allied to, indeed dependent upon, the Socialist Party, and, as part of the union of the left, signed the *Programme Commun* with the Socialists and Communists. In 1978 thirty MRG candidates were given Socialist endorsement and in 1981 a mere thirteen. In the Fabius government (1984–6) three of the 41 ministers and secretaries of state were MRG. In 1986 seven MRG *députés* were elected on socialist lists.

There are a few other small elements in the UDF – a few dissident ex-socialists called the PSD, a few independents, and a few notables who just use the appellation UDF – but the PR, CDS, and Radical Party are the main organised parts of what today constitutes liberalism in France. They have in common an antipathy to the authoritarian style of Gaullism with its cult of the leader and to the collectivist policies of socialism. They also share a recent past in which they supported the liberal reformism of President Giscard d'Estaing and they support the new liberal rallying cry of *moins d'état*. However, the UDF is still too diverse and too divided to be a great French Liberal Party. That has never existed.

STRUCTURE AND ORGANISATION

Each of the parties of the UDF has its own organisation, headquarters, leadership, local branches, and national congresses. How-

Table 6.1 *Structure of UDF Parties*

PR (Parti Républicain)	CDS (Centre des Démocrates Sociaux)	Rad (Parti Radical)
Local level	*Local level*	*Local level*
Federation at *département* (county) level; members elect a president, a federal bureau, and a federal council. Federation can organise local committees and sections	*Centre départemental* elects a president and a *département* secretary subject to approval by political bureau; holds a convention every two years	*Comité de base* usually at parliamentary constituency level *Federation* at *département* level; elects its bureau at a departmental general assembly *Regional federation*
National level	*National level*	*National level*
Convention: sovereign body for major political decisions; convened by *comité directeur*; composition: all party members *National council:* meets twice a year under chairmanship of secretary-general; determines party line; can censure political bureau; elects secretary-general and political bureau Composition: delegates elected by federation general meetings (2-ballot system, 2-year term) – at least 60% of council national and European members of parliament regional, county, and Paris councillors, and mayors presidents of *département* federations national personalities designated by political bureau (not more than 10% of council)	*National congress* (at least every 2 years; extraordinary sessions called by political bureau or political council) – decides 'political orientation' of party; elects party president and secretary-general (2-year terms) by 2-ballot system Composition: members of political council 2 delegates from each *département* centre plus 2 for every 50 members *Political council:* guardian of congress decisions; decides agreements with other parties. Composition: members of political bureau national and European Members of Parliament	*Annual congress* (provision for calling extraordinary additional congresses by executive committee or 30 federations) – decides party's fundamental principles and programme; elects party president Composition: executive committee members secretary-general and treasurer of every federation mayors and councillors parliamentary candidates delegates from *département* federations (1 per 50 members) delegates from party committees editors of party journals

Comité directeur: meets quarterly or at request of half its members under chairmanship of secretary-general; discusses party policy on national and international issues

Composition:

- members of political bureau
- Group leaders from national assembly and senate
- 10 *députés*, 10 senators, 2 MEPs
- former secretaries-general
- 30 federal presidents elected by national council
- 30 federation delegates to national council elected by national council
- party treasurer and legal adviser

Political bureau: elected for 2 years by national council on a list system; head of winning list becomes secretary-general and the remainder of his list composes the bureau; meets twice a month

Secretary-general directs all party organisation and appoints, from political bureau, national secretaries for different aspects of policy or organisation; appoints federation secretaries and constituency representatives

Parliamentary candidatures

decided by secretary-general and political bureau

- 2 representatives from each region (elected in regional electoral units)
- 1 from each *département* centre (plus 1 per 50 members)
- presidents of regional and *département* councils, mayors of large cities, 5 other mayors and a Paris councillor appointed by political bureau up to 20 national councillors elected by political council
- representatives affiliated bodies and Young CDS
- up to 30 coopted party members

Political bureau: directs the party

Composition:

- former party presidents
- president (elected by congress)
- secretary-general (elected by congress)
- 6 vice-presidents (elected by political council)
- treasurer and assistant secretaries-general (elected by political council)
- up to 10 national secretaries (elected by political council)
- 6 *députés*, 6 senators, 2 MEPs
- CDS ministers
- 10 non-parliamentarians elected by political council
- 1 from each affiliated body and Young CDS up to 3 co-opted personalities

Parliamentary candidatures

endorsed by political bureau on proposal of *département* centres

Executive committee: responsible for party organisation, appoints party committees for aspects of policy and organisation; 2-year term

Composition:

- bureau members
- national and European members of parliament
- former party presidents and prime ministers
- presidents of regional and *département* federations
- presidents of party committees
- 100–110 delegates from regional federations

Bureau: directs the party; 2-year term

Composition:

- party president (elected by annual congress)
- secretary-general (elected by executive committee)
- 30 members elected by executive committee (proportional representation lists but absolute majority for list with most votes)

Parliamentary candidatures

endorsed by executive committee on the proposal of, or after consultation with, federations ever, they are all small parties in which a parliamentary elite and municipal or regional notables play a predominant part. Duverger's famous category – cadre parties – lives on in the component parties of the UDF. Their organisations are summarised in Table 6.1. The only significant difference between the three is that the largest of them, the PR, gives much greater powers to its secretary-general who has his own team to form the political bureau. Today the secretary-general of the PR is the presidentially ambitious Minister of Culture, François Léotard.

The UDF itself scarcely has a structure. Its first secretary-general, Michael Pinton, who had been one of the organisers of Giscard's successful presidential election campaign of 1974, wanted the UDF and its leadership to have a high profile, to make policies and to be a *Giscardien* liberal party. The component parties, however, were not prepared after the defeat of Giscard in 1981 to support anything like this. The UDF continued to exist but its next secretary-general, Jean-Philippe Lachenaud saw himself as a co-ordinator and administrator, not as a political leader. The UDF has its headquarters in Paris, a small staff, and is directed by the *Bureau de l'UDF* on which the component elements are represented – the three political parties mentioned above, the dissident ex-socialists (PSD) and the *adhérents directs* (a group of individuals who do not belong to any of the affiliated parties but determinedly constitute a separate entity). Also represented on the *Bureau* are the *Perspectives et Réalités* clubs. *Perspectives et Réalités* is the most authentically *Giscardien* of all the components of the UDF. The clubs were set up by Giscard in 1966 as think-tanks for new ideas and political discussion, and as nurseries of pro-Giscard political talent. They have their own elegant headquarters in Paris and an organiser, Alain Lamassoure, who was a civil servant on Giscard's presidential staff. Finally, there are also seats on the *Bureau* for certain prominent individuals like Giscard himself and Simone Veil, former minister and President of the European Parliament, leader of the joint UDF–RPR list at the 1984 European elections, and for the leaders of the UDF group in the national assembly and the UDF 'Intergroupe' in the senate – so called because UDF supporters are scattered across three groups in the senate (see Table 6.8).

The functions of the UDF as an organisation in relation to its component parts have still not been decided. Rather like the SDP–Liberal Alliance before 1987 in Great Britain, there has not yet been agreement on a joint organisation for communications, on a joint party conference, on joint training for candidates, on a joint network for local councillors, on joint finance. What has been accepted, again rather like the SDP–Liberal Alliance, is joint preparation of major campaigns, some co-ordination of public statements, and above all *investitures*, that is to say the arrangements for designating and endorsing election candidates with the UDF label and for conducting negotiations with the RPR on the composition of lists. The *investiture* function is by far the most important of the UDF's organisational activities. The proportional representation system adopted for the 1986 elections involved the presentation of lists of candidates in each *département*. A UDF commission, chaired by Jean-Claude Gaudin, President of the UDF group in the national assembly, and representing all the elements of the UDF including *Perspectives et Réalités*, first had to arbitrate between the competing bids from UDF component parties for good places on lists, then negotiate with the RPR on whether to have joint lists or separate lists, and finally to seek as many list leaderships and 'electable' places for the UDF on joint lists as possible. All this involved a great deal of acrimony, rivalry, and delicate calculation.

There is no reliable information available about the finance or membership of French political parties. Sources of finance are kept concealed and membership figures always inflated. In government the parties of the UDF benefited from subsidies in various forms, such as the secondment of ministerial or parliamentary staff for party work. In opposition, the main sources of finance were presumably wealthy backers and the individual members who, for all the components of the UDF together, probably total around 60,000.

ELECTIONS AND LIBERALISM

It is virtually impossible to write the electoral history of liberalism in France for three main reasons. The first is that the antecedents of today's UDF parties were frequently adversaries – the Catholics and moderates being part of Goguel's 'party of the established order', the radicals belonging to the 'party of movement'. The second is that alliances between parties in France are constantly changing and sometimes parts of a party are in different alliances from other parts. Some of the radicals in 1919 teamed up with the conservative *Bloc national*. Some did not. In 1956 some of the Mendesist radicals were in the Republican Front with the socialists, others were in the opposite camp. The third and greatest difficulty, however, is that in the Fifth Republic the *Giscardiens* have been in alliance with Gaullism and this means that the *Giscardien* vote in most of the elections has depended more on the outcome of negotiations with the Gaullists over allocation of constituencies than on the 'liberal' appeal of the

Table 6.2 *Liberals in elections since 1900*

Date	*Electoral system*	*Main issue*	*Moderate Conservatives vote %*	*Radicals vote %*	*Christian/ Centrists vote %*
Third Republic 1871–1940					
1902	2 ballot	anti-clericalism	Con 28.3	26.9	
			Lib 4.6		
1906	,,		Con 29.4	34.7	
			Lib 14.0	36.4	
1910	,,		Con 19.0	38.5	
			Lib 1.8		
1914	,,	military service	28.5	34.7	
1919	PR – departmental lists	national unity, fear of Bolshevism	*Bloc national* (inc. some Radicals) 33.4	17.4	
1924	,,		Right 35.5	*Cartel des gauches* (Radicals and Socialists) 38.1	
1928	2 ballot		22.9 (inc. pro-Poincaré Radicals)	17.7	
1932	,,	economic crisis	23.4	19.2	
1936	,,	Popular Front	25.0	14.6	
Fourth Republic 1946–58					
1945	PR – departmental lists		15.6	10.5	MRP 23.9
1946 (June)	,,	rejection of Constitution	12.8	RGR 11.6	MRP 28.2
1946 (Nov)	,, (modified)		12.9	RGR 11.1	MRP 25.9
1951	PR – lists with 'apparentement'		14.1	10.0	MRP 12.6

1956	,,		15.3	Republican Front (Mendés-France Radicals plus Socialists): 11.3 Edgar Faure Radicals: 3.9	MRP 11.1
Fifth Republic 1958–					
1958	2 ballot	support for de Gaulle	Independents 22.9	8.3	MRP 11.1
1962	,,	support for de Gaulle and referendum on presidential elections	pro-de Gaulle Independents (*Giscardiens*) 5.9 anti-de Gaulle Independents: 7.7	7.1	MRP 9.1
1967	,,		Independent Republicans (RI) (*Giscardiens*)[a] 5.5	(in FGDS with Socialists)	CD 13.4
1968	,,	Events of May	RI[a] 7.7	,,	PDM 10.3
1973	,,		RI[a] 6.6	Reform Movement (Rad + CD) 13.1	
1978	,,	Socialist/Communist alliance	UDF[a] (Republicans + Radicals + Centrists) 21.4		
1981	,,	Mitterrand President	UDF[a] 19.1		
1986	PR – departmental lists	Socialist record	RPR/UDF 43.1[b]		

[a] In electoral alliance with Gaullists.

[a] Some joint RPR/UDF lists, some separate lists. Separate UDF lists averaged 20.3%.

Giscardiens themselves. The electoral history of the three strands of liberalism that have led to today's UDF and the evolution of the UDF in the Fifth Republic are given in Table 6.2. It is simplified, even over-simplified, and the figures must be interpreted with great caution.

The party system in the Fifth Republic has undergone profound changes from the days of the Fourth Republic for two main reasons. The first was the emergence of Gaullism as a dominant political force and in the 1960s virtually a majority party – something France has never seen before. The original *Giscardiens* – Independent Republicans – attached themselves to Gaullism as coalition partners and electoral allies from 1962 on. The opposition parties were affected, too. It was the dominance of Gaullism that forced the communist and non-communist left into an alliance. With a two-ballot electoral system it was vital for them at least to make an electoral pact for second ballot withdrawals, or risk being slaughtered by the Gaullist candidates in virtually every constituency. The second main influence on the party system in the Fifth Republic has been the introduction of direct presidential elections. The presidency has emerged as the dominant branch of the executive – provided it can count on a 'presidental majority' in parliament, which up to 1986 was always achieved. Each of de Gaulle's first two successors, Pompidou and Giscard d'Estaing, tried to widen the 'presidential majority'. Pompidou won support for his candidature not merely from the Gaullists, the Independent Republicans, but from part of the opposition centre as well. Giscard in 1974 gathered into his majority the whole of what remained of the opposition centre – the *Centre Démocrate* and the Radicals – and paved the way for the *Giscardien* UDF to be formed in 1978.

Let us now analyse the elections of the Fifth Republic to see what are the size and characteristics of the *Giscardien* or liberal vote. As far as the original *Giscardiens* (Independent Republicans) are concerned, the elections from 1962 on were fought as allies of the Gaullists. In 1962 and 1967 a single candidate in each constituency received the official endorsement of the government majority, so the *Giscardiens* who stood as candidates were the beneficiaries of all the support for de Gaulle and the government available in their allocated constituencies. In 1968 and 1973 the practice of 'primaries' began to spread (see Table 6.3). A 'primary' is a first ballot contest between a *Giscardien* and a Gaullist. The one who does least well withdraws from the second ballot in favour of his partner. In 1978, the only parliamentary election when Giscard was president, there were primaries between UDF and RPR in 80 per cent of all constituencies. In

Table 6.3 *Electoral pacts – 1967–86*

1967	Gaullist/RI (Independent Republican) alliance (UDVe); one UDVe candidate per constituency	Socialist/Radical alliance (FGDS); one FGDS candidate per constituency; second ballot pact with Communists (PC)
1968	Gaullist/RI alliance; 50 'primaries' (first ballot contests between RI and Gaullist candidates)	as 1967
1973	Gaullist/RI/CDP alliance; 61 primaries	Radical/CD alliance (Reform Movement) one Reform candidate per constituency; Left Radicals (MRG) in alliance with Socialists (UGSD) and second ballot pact with PCF
1978	Gaullist (RPR)/UDF alliance; 387 primaries; UDF candidates: 194 PR, 98 CDS, 56 Rad., 39 other	Socialist/MRG/PCF as 1973
1981	RPR/UDF alliance (UNM); one UNM candidate per constituency; UDF candidates: 113 PR, 76 CDS, 24 Rad., 67 other	as 1978
1986	RPR/UDF alliance; joint lists in 61 *départements* (41 led by RPR, 20 led by UDF) separate lists in 35 *départements*; UDF list leaders: PR 11 joint RPR–U DF, 17 separate UDF CDS 6 ,, 10 ,, ,, Rad 2 ,, 1 ,, ,, Other 3 ,, 7 ,, ,,	Socialist/MRG joint lists

1981, to defend themselves against the feared socialist landslide, the partners were back to single candidatures again. Table 6.4 shows the numbers of UDF candidates and winners from each component party. Since the 1981 candidates were endorsed by the whole RPR/UDF alliance, their share of the vote is no indication of a separate UDF vote.

The best two parliamentary elections from which to gauge liberal strength in the Fifth Republic are, given caution in interpretation, 1973 and 1978. In 1973 the liberal or non-Gaullist parts of the government coalition (Independent Republicans and former opposition centrists called the CDP) obtained, on the basis of a limited number of primaries and a limited number of allocated candidatures elsewhere, mainly in their areas of strength, 10.3 per cent of the first ballot vote. At the same election the liberal opposition (*Centre Démocrate* and Radicals continued in the Reform Movement)

Table 6.4 *UDF parties – parliamentary elections 1978 and 1981*

	1978			1981		
	candidates[a]	vote %	winners	candidates	vote %	winners
PR	194	10.7	66	113	9.2	32
CDS	98	5.3	31	76	5.3	19
Rad.	56	2.1	8	24	1.0	2
Other	39	3.7	18	67	3.6	8
UDF total		21.8	123		19.1	61

[a] first ballot 'primaries' between RPR and UDF in 1978

obtained 13.1 per cent. The four best regions for the Reform Movement were Alsace, Upper Normandy, Lower Normandy, and Lorraine – all in the traditionally Catholic North-West and North-East. The *Giscardiens* were most successful in Rhône-Alps and Lorraine.

In 1978 with primaries virtually everywhere one can get a proper assessment of the *Giscardien* or liberal vote and it came out at 21.8 per cent nation-wide. It is still necessary to be cautious, however, because studies show that in any constituency the choice made by electors between the RPR and UDF candidates usually fell upon the one that was the best established local *notable* – either the incumbent *député* or an important local mayor.[4]

In 1986, when the electoral system was changed to proportional representation by lists, with each *département* (county) a separate multi-member constituency, the RPR/UDF presented joint lists in some *départements* and separate ones in others. In 35 out of the 96 *départements* where they presented separate lists the UDF averaged 20.3 per cent (21.9 per cent outside the Paris region, only 12.3 per cent in the eight *départements* of the Paris region where the RPR is very strong). The separate UDF lists outscored the RPR in a number of regions – notably Brittany, Alsace, Provence, and Midi-Pyrenées. The nationwide RPR–UDF score was 43.1 per cent, so 1986 confirms the position of 1978 with UDF electoral strength slightly, but not much, below that of the RPR, each with the support of about one fifth of voters. Once again, however, it is the identification of the UDF in many areas with a prominent regional leader (Lecanuet in Upper Normandy, Baudis in Toulouse, Gaudin in Marseille, Léotard in Var, Méhaignerie in Ille-et-Vilaine, Giscard d'Estaing in the Auvergne) which is the key to its electoral success rather than the occupation of a 'liberal' constituency.

Table 6.5 *Presidential elections – Fifth Republic: liberal candidates*

			1st ballot %	2nd ballot %
1965	Jean Lecanuet	President of MRP (1986 president of UDF)	15.8	
1969	Alain Poher	President of senate (centrist – MRP background)	23.4	42.4
1974	Valéry Giscard d'Estaing	Minister of Finance under de Gaulle and Pompidou; RI	32.9	50.7
1981	Valéry Giscard d'Estaing	President of the Republic	27.8	47.8

In presidential elections the success of 'liberal' candidates is presented in Table 6.5.

The vote for Lecanuet in 1965 represents the limit of opposition centrism in a party system gradually polarising into two camps, the Gaullist coalition and the left. Nevertheless his was a thoroughly liberal campaign stressing European union, civil liberties, and democracy. So, too, was the campaign of Alain Poher in 1969, though his success was the result of exceptional circumstances. He had attracted favourable public attention in his constitutional role as interim president after de Gaulle's abrupt resignation. Furthermore, the socialists were very divided and a lot of left-wing voters supported Poher tactically on the grounds that he was the best placed to beat Pompidou in a second ballot.

In 1974, Giscard d'Estaing also based his campaign on liberal themes – a more open and democratic style of government, greater civil liberties, social reform. Consequently his 32.9 per cent at the first ballot is in a way the greatest success achieved by a 'liberal' candidate in the Fifth Republic. However, he had considerable support from sections of the Gaullist party, including Jacques Chirac who considered he was the only candidate who could stop the left from winning the election. Furthermore, he had been a member of de Gaulle's and Pompidou's governments so that many electors could express their Gaullism by voting for Giscard. In 1981 Giscard stood for re-election and achieved 27.8 per cent at the first ballot. He was supported by the UDF and opposed by the RPR whose candidate was Jacques Chirac. Nevertheless, the 1981 Giscard vote was not just a 'liberal' vote, it was also a 'legitimist' vote for an incumbent president.

The years of the Giscard presidency gave us one other instance of a

Table 6.6 *European Parliament elections – liberal lists*

1979	Simone Veil list (Union for France in Europe)	27.9%
	Servan-Schreiber list (Emploi–Egalité–Europe)	1.8%
1984	Joint UDF–RPR list (Union of the Opposition) – leader Simone Veil	43.0%
	Olivier Stirn list (Entente radicale écologiste) (dissident radicals and MRG and ecologists)	3.3%

large 'liberal' vote separate from the RPR: the European election of 1979. The list led by the liberal and reforming Minister of Health Simone Veil, and seen as the presidential list, came top with 27.4 per cent – easily beating the more nationalistic appeal of the Chirac list (16 per cent). Liberal strength could not be tested in the 1984 European elections because there was a joint UDF–RPR list, also led by Simone Veil.

In local elections in the 1970s and 1980s the UDF and RPR have normally fought on joint lists – the only spectacular exception being when Jacques Chirac decided to seize the mayoralty of Paris for the RPR against the wishes of President Giscard d'Estaing in 1977. The cantonal elections (for *département* or county councils) have been contested by the RPR and UDF as allies – with primaries in some wards and single candidatures in others. For what they are worth, the figures for the cantonal elections of 1979, 1982, and 1985 show scores for the UDF of 21.1 per cent, 18.8 per cent, and 19.3 per cent respectively.

These election results, local and national, taken as a whole over the last twenty years, with all the problems of interpretation involved in disentangling alliances, indicate that the 'liberal' family is, along with Gaullism and communism, one of the four families of the French party system and that its national level of support is somewhere between 18 and 25 per cent of the electorate.

Table 6.7 shows the social groups that voted UDF in 1978 (when there were 'primaries' in most constituences) and for Giscard d'Estaing in the presidential election of 1981. The points to note are that in the earlier election the electorates of the two government coalition partners, in contrast to the socialist and communist electorates, was very similar. One could not argue that the UDF had more appeal to the young or to workers than the RPR, for example. The coalition partners had a strongly middle-class and Catholic vote. In 1981 Chirac (RPR) actually did relatively much better than Giscard d'Estaing amongst middle-class occupations and farming

Table 6.7 *Voting by social category – 1978 and 1981*

	1978 Election (1st ballot)				1981 Presidential election (1st ballot)			
	PC	PS	UDF	RPR	Marchais	Mitterrand	Giscard	Chirac
Total electorate	21	25	21	22	16	26	28	18
Men	24	25	21	22	17	29	23	19
Women	19	25	22	24	14	24	32	18
Occupation (Head of family)								
Farmers	9	17	33	31	4	22	31	34
Self-employed	14	23	25	26	8	15	32	31
Professions, management	9	17	33	31	5	16	29	35
Clerical workers	18	29	14	20	15	29	21	16
Manual workers	36	27	16	14	28	30	20	12
Retired etc.	17	26	25	26	10	28	41	13
Religion								
Regular church-going Roman Catholics	2	13	39	31	2	12	50	26
Occasional church-going Roman Catholics	11	20	28	33	6	24	37	23
Non church-going Roman Catholics	24	30	17	20	18	31	22	17
No religion	49	29	4	66	39	29	6	7
Age								
18–24	28	25	17	15	24	22	23	11
25–34	26	24	18	17	23	27	16	18
35–49	19	25	20	24	15	27	27	20
50–64	20	24	22	23	11	26	28	24
65+	15	25	27	28	7	28	48	11

with Giscard – at the end of a somewhat unsuccessful presidential term – getting a 'legitimist' vote mainly from the elderly and from the devout.

The tables that conclude this section show the presence of the UDF among regional and parliamentary *notables* and its regional strengths. Table 6.8 shows that UDF elites are considerable in number even after the setback of the 1981 parliamentary elections but very diverse. In the senate and the European Parliament UDF members sit in a variety of different groups. Table 6.9 shows the best regions for the UDF in terms of the popular vote and in terms of *notables*. It is

Table 6.8 *UDF elites – June 1986*

	PR	CDS	Rad.	PSD	UDF	Other	Total
National assembly députés	62	39	6	1	22		130
Senators							148
Centrist Union Group	—	61	2	1	1	6	71
Union of Republicans and independents	44	—	—	—	2	4	50
Democratic Left Group	—	2	19	1	5	—	27
European Parliament members							21
Christian Democrat-Group	—	2	—	—	7	—	9
Liberal Group	4	—	3	—	5	—	12
Presidents of conseils généraux	13	17	4	1	7	—	42
Mayors of cities over 30,000 pop.	12	11	5	6	8	—	42
including	PR – Caen, Orleans, Toulon, Tourcoing						
	CDS – Rouen, Strasburg, Metz, St Etienne, Versailles						
	Rad. – Nancy, Aix-en-Provence						
	Other UDF – Lyon, Toulouse, Perpignan						
Presidents of regional councils	6	4	1	1	2	—	14

noticeable that the greatest areas of strength are in the Catholic East and the Catholic West where the tradition of voting 'moderate' or centrist/conservative goes back to the beginning of universal suffrage. The old republican bastions of radicalism – as in the South-West for example – have not been retained for the UDF, although Toulouse is a UDF city and the UDF mayor of Toulouse did become president of the Midi-Pyrénées regional council after the March 1986 election.

PARTICIPATION IN GOVERNMENT

In the Third Republic (1870–1940) radicals and moderates, though adversaries, were often coalition partners. In the Fourth Republic (1946–58) Radicals, moderates, and MRP were in practically every coalition. Indeed six Radicals, four MRP, and two moderates served

Table 6.9 *(a) UDF – best regions*

	25% + vote UDF 1978	30% + vote Giscard 1981	25% + *députés* 1981	50% + *conseil général* presidencies 1985	60% + senators 1985	Regional Council presidency 1986
Alsace	*	*	*	*(2/2)	*	*
Brittany	*	*	*	*(3/4)	*	
Pays de Loire	*	*	*	*(5/5)	*	
Lower Normandy	*	*			*	*
Lorraine	*	*				*
Auvergne	*	*	*	*(2/4)		*
Rhône-Alps	*		*		*	*
Champagne			*	*(3/4)		*
Centre			*	*(3/6)	*	*

(b) UDF – worst regions

	under 17% vote UDF 1978	under 25% vote Giscard 1981	No *députés* 1978 or 1981	under 15% *conseil général* presidencies 1985
Limousin	*	*	*	*(0/3)
Midi-Pyrénées	*	*		*(1/8)
Aquitaine	*	*	*	
Nord-Pas-de-Calais	*			*(0/2)

as prime minister. In the Fifth Republic most of them (with significant exceptions like Mendés-France) were part of the coalition that supported de Gaulle during the Algerian crisis and the establishment of the new Republic. From 1962, however, partly because of de Gaulle's attitude to European union, partly because of opposition to the referendum or direct Presidential elections, the Radicals, MRG, and most of the moderates except Giscard's Independent Republicans found themselves in opposition.

From 1962 to the Socialist victory in 1981 coalition formation followed the pattern described above in the section on 'Elections and liberalism', pp. 133–42. That is to say, it followed the widening of the presidential majority achieved first by Pompidou, who brought in some of the opposition-centre parliamentarians (who became, in the 1973 elections, the CDP) and finally by Giscard d'Estaing who brought in Lecanuet's *Centre Démocrate* and Servan-Schreiber's Radical Party, while the left-wing Radicals attached themselves to the Union of the Left in opposition.

When de Gaulle and Pompidou were president the *Giscardiens* were a small minority in the government but occupied some of the most important ministries. Giscard himself, for example, was Minister of Finance from 1962 to 1966 and under Pompidou from 1969 to 1973, and Raymond Marcellin was Minister of the Interior (though not in the least a liberal one) from 1968 to 1974. When Giscard became president the UDF became the senior coalition partner to the chagrin of the Gaullists.

In the period 1966–9 when Giscard d'Estaing was out of office, the *Giscardiens*, as we noted above, practised the coalition strategy of '*oui . . . mais*' – loyal but occasionally critical support. They acted as a ginger group inside the government majority, exerting influence on behalf of back-bench parliamentarians, warning the government if it was abusing its powers, acting much more independently than the Gaullist *députés* were allowed to do. A similar tactic of '*oui . . . mais*' was used, but with more rancour, by Chirac and the RPR in the latter years of the Giscard presidency, even to the point of refusing to vote for the budget in 1979, though falling into line at the vote of confidence that ensued. In 1986 the UDF came back into government but Prime Minister Chirac ensured that all the most powerful ministries went to the RPR. Excluded leaders like Giscard d'Estaing and Raymond Barre have showed signs of a return to '*oui . . . mais*'.

The 'official' leaders of the UDF were given jobs in the Chirac government – but in the cultural and technical ministries. The Secretary-general of the PR, François Léotard (of whom more in the concluding section) was Minister of Culture and Communication. The president of the CDS Pierre Méhaignerie was Minister of Housing, Transport and Regional Development. The president of the Radical Party André Rossinot was Minister for Relations with Parliament. There was UDF Ministers for Industry and for Education. For Defence, President Mitterrand insisted that a 'non-political' technician be appointed. The choice fell on civil servant André Giraud, former head of the Atomic Energy Commission, who in fact joined the UDF.

Voting discipline in parliament has not been a strong point among the diverse group of *notables* that constitute the UDF group. However, the governments they sustained always got the legislation they wanted. It is worth noting, though, that one of Giscard's main social reforms as president – the law permitting abortion – was achieved only with the support of the left. 45 UDF and 24 Gaullists voted for it, 73 UDF and 116 Gaullists against. Since March 1986 the Chirac government has been able to count on the full support of UDF *députés*, even the 'Barrists' who had strong reservations about 'cohabitation' (see concluding section) and even if it meant giving the government enabling powers to enact by decree measures they do not particularly like – such as the opportunity given to the Ministry of the Interior to gerrymander the return to a single-member electoral system in favour of the RPR.

THE POLICIES OF THE UDF

During the period of socialist government (1981–6) they key word of the political debate in which the opposition groups – RPR and UDF – were engaged was Liberalism. Liberty, responsibility, and enterprise were being crushed by the tentacular state, bureaucratic controls, and excessive taxation. When the opposition came back to power it was, like Ronald Reagan and Margaret Thatcher, going to roll back the state, reduce its interference in education, cut down regulations, and privatise nationalised corporations. This debate was not confined to the UDF. The RPR tried to out-liberal the liberals in the amount of deregulation and privatisation it could promise.

The fullest statement we have of the policies of the UDF–RPR alliance in opposition is their *Propositions pour l'Alterance* presented at the *Convention Libérale* in June 1985. This document was drawn up by Giscard's two think-tanks and a Gaullist one called 'Club 89'. Giscard's two are *Perspectives et Réalités* (see the section on 'structure and organisation', pp. 129–33 above), the most authentically *Giscardien* element in the UDF, and a personal group convened by the

Table 6.10 *Liberal participation in governments in the Fifth Republic*

		Percentage of government	In five top jobs[a]
de Gaulle presidency 1958–69			
Debré 1958	5 Ind., 4 MRP, 1 Rad.	37	Pinay (Ind.) F Berthoin (Rad.) I
Pompidou I April 1962	3 Ind., 5 MRP, 1 Rad.	31	Giscard (Ind.) F
Pompidou II Oct. 1962	3 RI	12	Giscard (RI) F
Pompidou III 1966	3 RI	11	—
Pompidou IV 1967	3 RI	10	—
Couve de Murville 1968	4 RI	13	Marcellin (RI) I
Pompidou presidency 1969–74			
Chaban-Delmas 1969	7 RI, 3 CDP	26	Giscard (RI) F Marcellin (RI) I
Messmer I 1972	5 RI, 3 CDP	27	Giscard (RI) F Marcellin (RI) I
Messmer II 1973	7 RI, 3 CDP	26	Giscard (RI) F Marcellin (RI) I
Messmer III 1974	5 RI, 2 CDP	24	Giscard (RI) F
Giscard d'Estaing presidency 1974–81			
Chirac 1974	9 RI, 5 CDS, 2 Rad., 8 other[b]	70	Poniatowski (RI) I Fourcade (RI) F Lecanuet (CDS) J
Barre I 1976	10 RI, 3 CDS, 4 Rad, 10 other	75	Barre (UDF) PM and F Poniatowski (RI) I
Barre II 1977	12 RI, 5 CDS, 3 Rad, 10 other	75	Barre (UDF) PM and F Bonnet (RI) I
Barre III 1978	12 PR, 3 CDS, 2 Rad, 8 other	66	Barre (UDF) PM Bonnet (PR) I
Mitterrand presidency 1981–			
Chirac 1986	6 PR, 6 CDS, 2 Rad., 2 other	42	—

[a] Prime Minister (PM), Foreign Affairs (FO), Finance (F), Interior (I), Justice (J)
[b] non-party 'presidential majority'

former president and rather grandly, not to say pompously, called 'The council for the future of France'.

It begins with a phrase taken straight from Giscard's book *Démocratie Française*: 'real liberalism . . . recognises the individual as the sole source and exclusive end of all social and political organisation'.[5] He must, therefore, freely enjoy the fruits of his efforts. What follows is very different in tone, however, from the generous ideas on social justice, civil liberties, more open democracy and reservations about blind market forces, contained in the earlier presidential writings. The themes emphasised are the reduction of public expenditure, the reduction of the highest marginal tax rate on individuals to 50 per cent, the abolition of the wealth tax, and the denationalisation of the information and banking sectors and as much of the industrial sector as possible. In social services and health there would be a greater attempt to concentrate help where it was needed. In education there would be greater freedom of choice for parents, more control over schools for local authorities, more rigorous assessment of teachers, and the creation of private universities. There would be greater freedom for and competition in television and radio, immigration would be more strictly controlled, law and order would be more effectively enforced. This programme, slightly more moderate in tone and content, was confirmed in the RPR/UDF election platform *Pour gouverner ensemble* which appeared in January 1986.

Two further questions remain briefly to be considered. What, if any, are the differences between Gaullists and the UDF? To what extent is the programme, briefly presented above, credible? One of the central ideas of Gaullism has been the old Jacobin and Napoleonic idea of using the power of the state to secure national objectives. France in the Fifth Republic has been the most *dirigiste* state in the Western World. National independence, the keystone of Gaullist doctrine, meant having an internationally viable French firm in every key economic sector. At the end of 1985 it was clear from the statements of some leading Gaullists that they were having second thoughts about what was for them a new ideology of economic liberalism. Even now that 'privatisation' has been launched by the Chirac government, it is doubtful whether there has been a conversion to non-intervention. It is important to stress that Giscard d'Estaing, as president, was just as *dirigiste* as his Gaullist predecessors and that the other leading figure in the UDF, former Prime Minister Raymond Barre, is an interventionist, too. The answer to the first question, then, is that the differences between RPR and UDF are differences of style much more than differences of policy. The style of the UDF and its leaders is less aggressive, less nationalistic, more European. The RPR is more hectoring on themes such as communism, law and order, or national pride, is a more authoritarian machine with a strong cult of the leader. The differences of actual policy, however, are minimal: after all Gaullists and *Giscardiens* governed together for over twenty years and are doing so again.

Is the policy programme credible? The past record in government of *Giscardiens* and Gaullists does not suggest that the state will be rolled back. In the area of civil liberties the record of President Mitterrand has been, with the deplorable exception of the Greenpeace affair, much better than that of Giscard: less intervention in television news reporting, less executive intervention in the judicial process, better protection for accused persons, the abolition of the death penalty. In the economic sphere Giscard has, since his defeat in 1981, written about the need to liberate the French economy from the *étatiste* tradition of Colbert, through the reconstruction philosophy of the Resistance and post-Second World War planning, culminating in the 'appetite for action and economic intervention of *la haute administration*, the epitome of a centralising structure, cut off from direct knowledge of the life of industry, but avid to command and direct'.[6] This cannot be serious. Giscard is the supreme Fifth Republic example of the interventionist technocrat from the *grandes écoles*. In Great Britain in early 1986 there was a furious controversy over the survival of the British helicopter industry. Margaret Thatcher's view was that the shareholders should decide in a free market. Can anyone imagine the French state, with Giscard d'Estaing or Raymond Barre at the helm, carrying non-interventionist liberalism to that point?

THE STRATEGY OF THE UDF

The central strategic problems for the UDF are the continued existence of a distinct 'liberal' family and the search for a leader who can win the presidency. This chapter has stressed the diversity of the UDF's components – historical diversity, ideological diversity. Calling them all – from radicals to Christian democrats – 'Orleanists' Alain Duhamel writes that within the Orleanist ranks

> one finds sincere reformists and acknowledged conservatives, militant christians and confirmed secularists, liberals smitten by modernism and reactionaries sometimes originating from the extreme right. They have, however, solid convictions in common. They are European, moderately Atlanticist, mildly regionalist, wanting to establish a centre-right, concerned for moderation, consensus, toleration, and, for some of them, social justice.[7]

Maintaining a separate and liberal centre-right is not going to be easy. Each of the UDF's three parties stresses continually its separate existence and tries to launch its own leader. This is particularly true of the PR with its secretary-general, François Léotard, trying to emerge as a youthful national figure, a sort of French Gary Hart (1983 model). He is the only UDF personality to have been given a politically important and prominent 'non-technical' ministry in the Chirac government: Culture and Communications (including control of television and privatisation of parts of it). Léotard has already announced his presidential ambitions. The UDF strategy in early 1986, at all events, was to stay together and fight the March elections in partnership with the RPR.

The 1986 election was a reasonably successful one for the UDF. Under the system of proportional representation introduced by the Socialist government, the UDF could have presented separate lists in every *département* and tested its electoral appeal to the full. In the end this was done mainly in the larger *départements* with ten or more seats. In most of the smaller ones it was considered more advantageous for the RPR–UDF alliance to present joint lists on which a share-out of 'electable' places had been negotiated. In 61 of the 96 *départements* there were joint lists. The RPR obtained list leadership in 41, the UDF in 20. In the regional council elections held the same day, however, (and very important to a federation of local *notables* like the UDF, especially under the 1982 decentralisation laws which give regional council presidents much greater powers), the UDF had 42 joint-list leaderships and the RPR 20. The UDF emerged (see Table 6.8) with 14 regional council presidencies out of 22 (RPR 6, PS 2). The number of UDF *députés* elected more than doubled to 130 (see Table 6.8 for party composition).

Before the election there was an interminable debate within the RPR and UDF about 'cohabitation'. Should one consent to lead or even to serve in government while a Socialist president of the republic remained in office. The most prominent refuser of 'cohabitation' was Raymond Barre, strongly supported by the CDS and its leader Pierre Méhaignerie (now Minister of Housing, Transport, and Regional Development). In the event Raymond Barre did not personally have a very successful election – his list in Lyons did not do particularly well – and the narrow victory for the RPR–UDF alliance meant that Mitterrand could not possibly be expected to resign and that all RPR and UDF *députés* would have to rally round and sustain the governments's narrow majority in motions of confidence and legislative proposals. The UDF's most prominent leaders – Giscard d'Estaing, UDF President Jean Lecanuet, leader of the European election list Simone Veil, and of course former Prime Minister Raymond Barre – were all excluded from the Chirac government. François Léotard, the secretary-general of the Republican Party, was – as has already been noted – the only personality to be given a ministry in which to make a political mark.

The strategic problem for the UDF is to find a leader behind whom it can unite and win back the Presidency. Giscard d'Estaing has gradually faded from sight and Raymond Barre emerged as the strongest candidate for the UDF to support at the 1988 Presidential election – but he is more of a Conservative than a Giscard-style liberal. President Mitterrand reigned during the period of 'cohabitation' in a position of magnificent detachment, faithfully appointing the government wanted by the electors, constitutionally signing its acts into law, gravely if sadly expressing his reservations about some of its measures. The Socialists, and in particular Mitterrand who can personally determine the date of the next presidential election in 1988 or before, have rapidly recovered popularity. The Socialist Party is trying to consolidate its role as a modernising social-democratic consensus party, a 'liberal' party one might almost say. This is what it was when Laurent Fabius was prime minister (1984–6) and that is how it fought the 1986 election, gaining its highest score in any election in its history except the euphoric one in June 1981 just after the presidential victory of François Mitterrand. The UDF remains a significant electoral force in France but it will be very hard to find a winning strategy.

Giscard d'Estaing always hoped to be the focus of a great liberal and modernising *rassemblement*, of a centrist *élan* rejecting the extremisms of right and left in favour of national unity, of 'two Frenchmen out of three' (to quote the title of his most recent book) as moderate reformists in a harmonious consensus. There is no liberal party in France yet to give expression to this aspiration.

NOTES

The author gratefully acknowledges the support of the Nuffield Foundation, London, in the research for this chapter.

1 V. Giscard d'Estaing, *Démocratie Française*, Paris, Fayard, 1986.
2 R. Rémond, *The Right Wing in France from 1815 to de Gaulle*, Philadelphia, University of Pennsylvania Press, 2nd edn, 1966.
3 F. Goguel, *La Politique des Partis sous La IIIe République*, Paris, Seuil, 1948.
4 J.R. Frears and J.-L. Parodi: *War will not take place – the French Parliamentary elections of March 1978*, London, C. Hurst, 1979, p. 72.
5 V. Giscard d'Estaing, *Démocratie Française*, p. 44.
6 V. Giscard d'Estaing, *Deux Français sur Trois*, Paris, Flammarion, 1984, p. 182.
7 A. Duhamel, *Les Prétendants*, Paris, Gallimard, 1983, p. 51.

7

Liberal parties in the Netherlands

Hans Daalder and Ruud Koole

LIBERAL PARTIES IN THE NETHERLANDS DEFINED

Two Dutch parties can legitimately claim to be part of the liberal *famille spirituelle*, the *Volkspartij voor Vrijheid en Democratie* (People's Party for Freedom and Democracy, or VVD in the Dutch acronym) which adopted its present name in 1948 and which has been a member of the Liberal International since 1960, and *Democraten '66* (or D'66 – recently renamed D66 without apostrophe), which, established in 1966 as a party of radical reform, consciously sought to break the hold of traditional class and religious alignments in Dutch politics in favour of a far going programme of institutional reform.

Of these two parties, the VVD undoubtedly has the older and better title.[1] The 1948 party grew from the *Partij van de Vrijheid* (Freedom Party) which was established in 1946 as a new incarnation of the pre-Second World War *Liberale Staatspartij De Vrijheidsbond*. That party in turn had been formed in 1921 to collect a number of different liberal and other parties which had developed side by side in a period of limited franchise and a district system before the First World War, and in the aftermath of that war. In the nineteenth and early twentieth centuries the liberals had regarded themselves (and had been regarded by others) as very much a dominant force in Dutch politics. They had represented the cause of constitutional reform – which had led in 1848 to a comparatively early breakthrough of responsible parliamentary government in the Netherlands, under a constitutional revision which was very much the work of a liberal Professor of Constitutional Law, Johan Rudolf Thorbecke. They gave voice to a mainly secular bourgeoisie and intelligentsia and thought of themselves as 'the thinking part of the nation'. Their position in Dutch society (e.g., in commerce and government, in the universities and the media) seemed sufficiently secure not to demand special organisational effort. In fact, a liberal party had been only organised in 1885, and then mainly as a defensive measure against the growing competition from religious opponents: notably the Calvinists and increasingly also the Catholics, who had eventually combined in a massive onslaught on the secular forces in Dutch society. For a time it had looked as if the major division of Dutch politics would be between a left (consisting of liberals of many persuasions) and a right (consisting of Calvinists and Catholics). But this potential symmetry had been broken from the end of the nineteenth century by the addition of the socialists, who initially seemed to join the liberals on the left side of politics, but who in the first two decades of the twentieth century became very much competitors to liberal and religious groupings alike. Liberals had thus increasingly been forced to live and work in a political environment determined by two fault lines: one of religion and one of class – if they were on the 'left' side on the first of these two cleavages, they were more and more to land on the 'right' side on the other of these two dimensions.

The tri-partite division of liberals, religious groupings and socialists eventually led to a major political reform, agreed by the major political movements during the First World War in 1917. A new constitutional revision provided for universal suffrage, proportional representation and complete equality of finance for public and religious schools. The 1917 reforms tended to stabilise the relations of power between the different groups in Dutch society: they confirmed a majority position in parliament for the coalition of Calvinists and Catholics, each of whom, however, increasingly went their separate ways; they revealed a comparatively modest position for the socialists (who had difficulty to gain and retain even a quarter of the vote in the period between the two World Wars); and they ushered in a substantial decline for the remainder, notably the explicit liberals among them.

The need to fight elections nation-wide had been one factor for the consolidation of a number of disparate liberal groups to unite in 1921. But one distinct group, the radical *Vrijzinnig-Democratische Bond* (VDB, originally established in 1901 as a radical alternative to other liberal groups) did not join the new union, and in fact did electorally do somewhat better than the new amalgamated Liberal Party. Proportional representation, combined with an exceedingly low threshold, exposed the liberals to considerable competition from smaller interest parties, authoritarian splinters, conservative Calvinists, and eventually a national-socialist party. In the 1937 national elections – the last held before the German occupation in 1940 – the liberals fell to only 4 out of 100 seats in the lower house of parliament, the radical VDB retaining another six. A combined vote of less than 10 per cent of the nation stood in stark contrast indeed to the dominant position that liberals had been wont to have in Dutch society in the nineteenth century – a position then so self-evident that they had spurned the timely use of the weapon of political organisation. Liberals could hardly conceive of themselves as a minority force, even though the very process of democratisation and mass mobilisation of religious and socialist parties had made them just that.

The situation after the liberation of 1945 did not look very much better. The radical VDB amalgamated, not with the new Liberal Party, but with the socialists and a number of progressive elites from some of the religious groupings in the new *Partij van de Arbeid* (which in adopting the title 'Labour Party' consciously sought to divest itself from an earlier socialist ghetto position). The new *Partij van de Arbeid* won only 6 out of 100 parliamentary seats in 1946. In 1947 it entered into negotiations with a number of disillusioned former leaders of the pre-Second World War VDB who had left the new Labour Party (partly over disagreement with the government's handling of the Indonesian issue, partly from a desire to resist too much government planning and control, partly from a sense of personal spite and isolation). This led to the establishment of the People's Party for Freedom and Democracy (VVD) in 1948. In that same year one of its major leaders, D.U. Stikker, joined a new broad-based coalition cabinet as Minister for Foreign Affairs. His relations with the VVD-leader in parliament, P.J. Oud (a pre-Second World War Minister of Finance, then belonging to the radical VDB), became increasingly embittered. Disagreement between Stikker and Oud over the political status of New Guinea (which had not been transferred to Indonesia in 1949 and remained under Dutch rule) eventually led to the fall of the cabinet in 1951, and the ouster of liberals from the succeeding cabinet one year later. For the next twenty years the VVD was not to rise above a vote of 12.2 per cent. But a break between socialists and Catholics, which occurred in December 1958, led to a renewed entry of liberals into government in May 1959.

Clearly, then, once the role of other political groups had become dominant in a system of social segmentation, known now even beyond Dutch borders as the system of *verzuiling*,[2] the liberals became one of the lesser players in Dutch politics. On the same logic, their relative importance could only grow when the *verzuiling*-system broke up, notably through the hemorrhage suffered by the Catholic subculture in the 1960s and 1970s.[3] From the early 1970s, the strength of the liberals began to rise. In 1966 a new radical party was formed, *Democraten '66*.

If the major liberal party, the VVD, could trace its ancestry back to a hundred years ago or more, D'66 was very much a new political phenomenon. It was formed by a number of young intellectuals, of somewhat different political background, and often not even politically active before.[4] The new party proclaimed the need to do away with past political divisions, whether of class or religion. It emphasised the need to recast the Dutch political system, so as to make it more 'open' and 'democratic'. To this end voters, who in the existing multi-party system were powerless in affecting the choice of cabinets, should be given the right to vote for a prime minister. As a prime minister so chosen would have a clear electoral mandate of his own, this implied giving up one of the fundamental characteristics of a parliamentary system of government. The new party did not deem this a defect. For exactly the need to sustain a cabinet – divided as parliament was between a large number of political parties – tended to condemn parliament to a position of impotence, so D'66 leaders argued. Did not the American constitution – where a directly elected President faced an equally directly elected, but vigorous Congress – indeed prove that giving different state organs an independent mandate might go far in ensuring a strong democratic political system?[5]

D'66 initially seemed, if anything, a radical anti-system party. Why then include it in a chapter on liberal parties? One reason is a negative one: neither originating from, nor appealing especially to, any one of the more important Dutch subcultures of the time (Catholics, Calvinists or socialists), the new party seemed at a minimum liberal by default: rejecting both religion and class as a legitimate basis of party organisation, it gave voice to demands heard mainly in the circle of a secular intelligentsia. The party proclaimed the need for 'pragmatism' over what it termed 'antiquated ideologies'. This resembled a stand which historically had been identified with the non-religious left. Within that left, it tended to take a more radical position than the VVD, reminiscent of the radical VDB in the first forty years of the twentieth century.

Entering parliament in 1967 with an unprecedented gain of seven seats, the new party found itself in opposition side by side with the socialists, facing a cabinet formed by the religious parties and the liberal VVD. Rubbing shoulders with the socialists on opposition benches led to a *rapprochement*. In 1971 socialists, D'66 leaders and a new left-wing splinter which had broken away from the larger religious parties (the self-styled radical PPR) formed a political cartel, which presented a common programme and a joint list of *ministeriables* to the electorate. Ideas for the formation of a new Progressive Party were actively canvassed at the time, not least in D'66 circles. Yet, the socialist embrace threatened to become a death-knell to the new D'66 party. It therefore began to remove itself somewhat from a position of vicinity to the major socialist party. One way of doing so was to emphasise its opposition to traditional socialist tenets, including strong state interference in the economy. A major element in D'66 policy posturing was and remained the need to meet a new technological era with confidence and an open mind for scientific progress. At the same time, the new party gave also voice to some post-material values, including concern with ecological issues and the need to emancipate individuals of any sex or sexual disposition. Being deliberately 'democrat' and 'libertarian', the party could not help reminding observers of an older liberal strand, which – although far from dead in the larger and more official liberal VVD – did not always represent a dominant element in it.

TYPES OF PARTIES

Neither the liberal VVD nor the new D'66 party could properly be described as mass parties in the sense given to this term by Maurice Duverger.[6] Other parties, notably the protestant Anti-Revolutionary Party (which was the oldest political party in the Netherlands) and the socialists, undoubtedly had a stronger mass base, and a more elaborate party organisation. One factor why in the period between the two World Wars the official liberal party had done so badly was a lack of efficient organisation (the radical VDB at that time doing somewhat better both organisationally and electorally). Attempts at institutional reform undertaken after the 1937 electoral débâcle came too late. Even in 1946 the newly established liberal party (*Partij van de Vrijheid*), and its successor (the VVD), seemed initially to seek recourse more in professional campaigning techniques than in building up a large political organisation. Political meetings of the VVD reminded observers of social events, with members of upper-class families getting together in a somewhat unwonted climate of political oratory, rather than participating in a meeting of a genuine political organisation.

However, such a tradition gave way to more serious organisational efforts especially from the early 1970s onwards. No longer a minority party condemned to operate in a political market where other political parties (i.e. the major religious parties and the socialists) nurtured their own secure clienteles, the liberal VVD set out to capture an increasing share of an increasingly volatile electorate. As we shall see, the liberals proved indeed able to change from what had tended to be for long a rather stable, mainly elitist party to a party which attracted a greatly expanded membership and vote.

The development of D'66 offers a rather different perspective. The new party had from the outset something of the character of a *club* in the French sense of that word. Rather than relying on the trappings of a large-scale, formal organisation, it threw open membership to all and sundry, seeking to maintain as much of a tradition of direct democracy as possible. As an amateur organisation, and a movement overly-dependent on media attention, D'66 was highly vulnerable. Both as an electoral force and as an organisation, it showed something of a yo-yo movement: enjoying a period of grace in the first five years after its establishment, but then falling behind so much that it seemed moribund, at one time falling to as low as only 300 members. The party was revived in the mid-1970s by a new political leader, Jan Terlouw, who used a typical gimmick to test the ability of the party to survive: Terlouw declared that he would only lead the party into a new election, if political activists could muster 66,666 signatures pleading for it to go on, while signing up at least 1,666 new members. The party showed a new *élan* and scored a remarkable electoral success in 1981, to crash down with an equally resounding defeat only one year later.[7] Then again, the party seemed almost dead for a time. It was revived once more, this time largely by its original leader, H.A.F.M.O. van Mierlo, who staged a rather personal campaign in 1986 as he had done in 1967, and saw his efforts rewarded by an increase in seats and votes in an election in which the official liberals lost substantially.

ORGANISATION AND STRUCTURE: THE VVD

What then was the organisational structure of the VVD and what organisational developments took place in the 1970s and 1980s?

The most important feature of the VVD is undoubtedly the very substantial increase in its membership. The number of members rose rapidly in the 1970s, from an initial 40,000 to about 100,000 in 1978 and again in 1982 (with figures about 10 per cent less in following years, see Table 7.1). This figure is rather substantial, compared with other major parties: the socialists, for instance, had in 1985 only marginally higher absolute membership figures, for an electorate which in 1986 was about double that of the liberals, while for a similar

Table 7.1 *Membership of Dutch liberal parties 1946–86*

Year	Volkspartij voor Vrijheid en Democratie	Democraten '66
1948	22,175	
1954	30,000	
1959	35,000	
1964	30,000	
1966	35,000	1,500
1967		3,700
1968	35,000	3,850
1969		5,057
1970	38,000	6,400
1971		5,620
1972	41,536	6,000
1973	68,414	6,000
1974	78,759	300
1975	82,831	
1976	87,571	2,000
1977	97,376	4,410
1978	100,510	8,424
1979	92,314	11,676
1980	85,881	14,638
1981	92,830	17,765
1982	102,888	14,500
1983	95,528	12,000
1984	89,120	8,774
1985	86,821	
1986	89,570	8,500

Note: Membership registration was somewhat haphazard for the VVD until 1972; D'66 membership figures are for some years approximations only.
Source: R.A. Koole and G. Voerman, 'Het lidmaatschap van politieke partijen na 1945' in: *Jaarboek Documentatiecentrum Nederlandse Politieke Partijen 1985*, Groningen, 1986, pp. 115–76.

number of votes as the socialists in 1986, the Christian democrats had about 130,000 members in 1985. The comparatively high membership figure of the liberal VVD might be explained by two factors: a deliberate organisational drive on the part of the VVD, which under a new young leader, Hans Wiegel, chosen in 1971, consciously aimed at changing the earlier, somewhat elitist character of the party into a more populist one; and relatively low membership dues, taking into account the generally rather prosperous parts of the population which tend to provide the core of active VVD sympathisers.

For the rest, the organisational structure of the VVD tends to be standard. Based on some 600 local branches, the party has intermediate organisational levels, according to the various district boundaries within which they must enter candidates, in provincial or national elections. Lower bodies send representatives to both these intermediate levels and national party organs. The party congress is formally the highest governing structure, being composed of delegates from the local branches, with representatives having a weighted vote according to the number of members they represent. The party congress must vote on the general party programme, and on any more specific electoral programme. It also chooses the party chairman, the deputy chairman, and the party treasurer, and at most six other members who jointly form the standing committee of the national executive. The national executive itself includes those directly elected members, plus the 19 chairmen of the intermediate party organs at the district level for national elections. In addition, five persons attend meetings of the national executive in a consultative role: the chairmen of the parliamentary groups in the upper and lower house, a representative from the members elected to the European Parliament, the chairman of the association of liberal local government representatives, and a representative of the youth organisation of the party. The national executive meets at least every two months, the party congress once a year. During the year there are several meetings of the *Partijraad*, an intermediate body which includes the full membership of the national executive, all liberal members of the two houses of parliament and the European Parliament, a number of representatives from each of the 19 district councils weighted according to the share of members each of these districts has as a proportion of the national membership, four representatives of the organisation of liberal women, plus 15 members chosen in their individual capacity by the national executive, these members having an advisory status only. The *Partijraad* can decide matters which have been delegated to it and take provisional decisions to be ratified later by the party congress.

Decisions on the nomination of party candidates for the lower house of parliament[8] are largely settled in a special body, the electoral council. This body, which meets under the chairmanship of the party chairman, is composed of representatives of the 19 district organisations (again weighted by their share of the national membership of the party), who meet jointly with all members of the *Partijraad* who are not themselves members of parliament, those members having an advisory status only. The electoral council must decide on the ranking order of candidates on party lists which are presented in each of the 19 electoral districts. This ranking order is practically decisive for actual election, voters being largely unable to affect the election of candidates within the list. (In fact, between 1946 and 1986 only two – Catholic – members had ever been elected to parliament outside the ranking order established by the party nominating them.[9] But in the most recent parliamentary election one maverick liberal member of parliament, Theo Joekes, who had strongly criticised the liberal deputy premier in a parliamentary committee of enquiry, and who had subsequently been duly penalised by being put low on the party list, was indeed elected to parliament against the party-determined order through a massive personal vote.) As the electoral council is composed of relatively few members, each one representing special regional interests, the process of decision-making on party nominations is shot through with regional conflict, with representatives of different regions entering into informal voting coalitions to push particular candidates. Partly to offset the influence of such regional pressures, the party rules allow the party congress to change the order of candidates as it is issued from the electoral council, provided a two-thirds majority of the party congress approves the changes.

Can one distinguish any further trends in organisational developments within the VVD over the last few decades? Generally speaking, in earlier days the political leadership tended to have rather great discretionary powers. Initially, even the rather general push for 'greater democracy' in Dutch society in the 1960s hardly seemed to affect that situation. However, in recent years, following the expansion of the party membership, there are signs of greater vitality and even turmoil in the party. The adoption of a new programme of principles in 1981 was accompanied by comparatively vigorous debate, and during recent election periods there were many attempts to change points in the proposed election platform.[10] Also, the growth of the party brought many young liberals into the party. Not a few showed a distinct ambition to get into parliament. Given the increased competition for places on party lists on the one hand, the enhanced importance of regional pressures in nomination processes on the other, the VVD has tended to experience competition and conflict on a scale not found earlier. Since 1971, the leadership of the party in parliament has been in the hands of relatively young, clearly self-starting politicians, the party thus losing much of an earlier, patriarchical style. Working in a climate of increased publicity, the party has also had more than its share of trouble in recent years. Losing the 1986 elections (when the party lost 9 of its previous 36 seats) led to further altercations – within the parliamentary group and within the party outside parliament.

ORGANISATION AND STRUCTURE: D'66

As for the organisational development of D'66, there could hardly be a greater contrast than that with the VVD. D'66 originated, as we saw, very much from a turning towards political action of groups of young intellectuals who were largely political novices. Campaigning on a platform which emphasised the need for greater democracy in political life, the new party tried to practise for itself what it proclaimed for society as a whole. Thus, the party rejected more elaborate forms of institutionalisation – permitting any member of the party to attend and vote at party congresses. These tended to be joyous, amateurish, and often confusing affairs. In the same vein, placement of the first 25 candidates on party lists – with the exception of the party flag-bearer who is placed at the top of the list through a decision of the plenary congress – depends on a referendum among all party members. However, the degree of political participation tends to vary greatly over time, as did the total number of members formally associating themselves with the party. Table 7.1 makes abundantly clear how much party membership changed over the years while even the highest number of members (somewhat below 18,000 in the *annus mirabilis* of 1981) remained only a smattering compared to the membership of its three very much larger competitors. What the party lacked in institutionalisation and in faithful membership, it tended to make up for by improvisation and a rather acute sense of the importance of publicity.

FINANCE AND GOVERNMENT SUPPORT

Dutch politics is a low-cost affair.[11] Even political campaigns see very little actual spending, when compared to other European countries. The VVD has an annual budget of about 4,000,000 Dutch guilders (less than 1 million pound sterling), D'66 not even a quarter of that sum. More than 60 per cent of VVD income derives from direct membership dues, some 20 per cent from gifts (largely small gifts for a special campaign fund), and the remainder from indirect government subsidies. The government does not finance political parties or elections directly. It makes radio and television time available for special party broadcasts and provides a very small subsidy for parties to meet special broadcasting costs. The budget of parliament provides funds for staff aid to parliamentary parties and individual members of parliament. There are special subsidies for the party affiliated *Teldersstichting* which is the major liberal research organisation, and for political 'education'. Some ancillary organisations of the parties, notably the organisation of liberal youth, can sometimes get additional government funds, as can liberal women under certain programmes to advance women's emancipation. Such subsidies do not detract from the general statement, however, that Dutch politics remains a low-cost affair. There are no special legal limits on campaigning expenditures. Also, there are no special rules preventing special political gifts from private interests. After the Second World War, the newly-formed Liberal Party had been the recipient of special gifts from private firms,[12] but such practices seem to have largely disappeared, not least because parties tend to remain extremely cautious in accepting gifts, let alone large gifts from a single source. If even the Liberal Party – which has a far more stabilised organisational life – is hardly characterised by large-scale resources, this is even more true for D'66 which in its very chequered existence has often had to improvise to keep active and solvent.

LINKS WITH OTHER GROUPS

In the heyday of Dutch *verzuiling*, when society was to a great extent divided along strong ideological lines, there tended to be a rather close network of social organisations within any one subculture. This implied that parties had many informal links with special interest groups in their own subculture, even though such links would fall far short of formal organisational ties. In an era in which such ideological worlds have rapidly disintegrated, the links that did exist have tended to disappear for all Dutch parties. Older liberals and newer Democrats '66 hardly had such formal links. Of course, parties enter into common actions with certain pressure groups, as D'66 did for instance with a wide-based 'Committee Opposing the Stationing of Cruise Missiles', or the VVD and D'66 with the European Movement. There is also little doubt that mutual sympathies and informal contacts exist between certain interest groups and certain parties.[13] Thus, the VVD has clearly been the major protagonist of private enterprise, supporting both the world of large-scale finance and industry, and the world of the small-scale entrepreneur in trade and farming. But so have other parties, including notably the Christian democrats. Practically all Dutch parties tend to wish to be spokesmen of the interests of certain not always well-organised social categories, including notably public employees, the young, the aged, women seeking emancipation, etc. But all this falls far short of what one usually describes as 'interlocking directorates',[14] let alone a world of formal corporatism.

THE ELECTORAL BASE OF VVD AND D'66

Maximal, minimal and average electoral strength of the major liberal parties in the period between the two World Wars are given in Table 7.2, actual election figures for the VVD and D'66 for all post-war

Table 7.2 *Electoral performance of Dutch liberal parties between the two World Wars*

	Liberale Staatspartij		Vrijzinnig-Democratische Bond	
	%	year	%	year
Minimum	3.9	1939	4.2	1922
Maximum	9.3	1922	6.2	1929
Mean	7.3		5.5	

Table 7.3 *Electoral performance of Dutch liberal parties after the Second World War*

	Parliament		Provinces	Parliament		Provinces
Year	%	seats	%	%	seats	%
Partij van de Vrijheid						
1946	6.4	6	6.4			
Volkspartij voor Vrijheid en Democratie						
1948	8.0	8				
1950			8.5			
1952	8.8	9				
1954			8.8			
1956[a]	8.8	13				
1958			11.4			
1959	12.2	19				
1962			10.0			
1963	10.3	16				
1966			10.0			
				Democraten '66		
1967	10.7	17		4.5	7	
1970			12.1			7.7
1971	10.4	16				
1972	14.4	22		4.2	6	
1974			19.0			1.0
1977	17.9	28		5.4	8	
1978			16.9			5.2
1981	17.3	26		11.1	17	
1982			22.2			8.3
1982	23.1	36		4.3	6	
1986	17.4	27		6.1	9	

[a] The total number of seats in the lower house was increased in this year from 100 seats to 150 seats; under the old law the number of seats for the VVD would have been nine.

elections in Table 7.3. For the first twenty-five years after 1945 the VVD never passed 12.2 per cent of the national vote. After 1971 the party began to climb, reaching its maximum strength in 1982 with 23.1 per cent, or close to a quarter of the national vote, to fall back again to 17.4 per cent in 1986 (although this last result represented a considerable psychological loss, this percentage was – as Table 7.3 shows – in a longer time-perspective still a comparatively high figure). In fact, liberals arguably profited more between 1967 and 1982 from the considerable loss of votes of the religious parties than did parties on the left. The figures for elections to the provincial councils show a very similar trend (and as the composition of the Dutch upper house is indirectly determined by those councils, the party political strength of the VVD in the upper house tends not to diverge greatly from its proportionate share in the lower house).

Figures for D'66 are rather more erratic, hugging the 5 per cent mark for most elections except the early 1970s and 1981/2. Both Liberals and D'66 have fewer constant voters than the other major parties in the Dutch political system. Given the rather looser ties liberals have traditionally had to a particular subculture as compared to either Catholics, Calvinists or socialists, this hardly comes as unexpected. D'66 has had a particularly fickle electorate. When the party first entered elections in 1967, it attracted a very large youth vote. But voting studies have found few rather faithful supporters. The chief strength of D'66 – one well realised by party strategists and public relation specialists – has been that it is potentially an attractive electoral alternative for many forces in the political spectrum: disappointed moderate socialists, liberal Liberals, former supporters of Christian democrat parties, who are all seeking a new home without wishing to commit themselves as yet to parties which for many generations had represented an alien subculture – not to speak of new voters. Hence, the party has deliberately chosen a posture felicitously captured in its campaign slogan for its most successful election of 1981: 'Vote for a reasonable alternative!' This has not enabled the party, however, to establish itself as a really crucial actor in the complex party landscape.

As for the location of floating voters more generally: there are considerable cross-currents between the VVD and D'66, as there are between the Socialist Labour Party and D'66. Although VVD and socialists have for long shared the traditional secular vote, there is rather less floating going on between these two parties who are consciously opposing each other on the left–right political spectrum. As for the Christian Democrat Appeal Party (CDA), it experiences some competition from smaller, especially Calvinist, fundamentalist

Table 7.4 *The composition of the electorate of the main Dutch parties and of the total electorate, 1982 and 1986,* %

	PvdA		CDA		VVD		D'66		NL	
	1982	1986	1982	1986	1982	1986	1982	1986	1982	1986
Sex										
Men	44.2	50.3	47.2	45.5	48.8	51.7	50.7	57.6	47.2	48.9
Women	55.8	49.7	52.8	54.5	51.2	48.3	49.3	42.3	52.8	51.1
N	425	435	358	402	332	211	71	85	1,337	1,247
Age										
18–24	15.5	15.6	11.1	15.3	21.0	20.6	22.8	22.0	17.3	17.4
25–34	25.2	24.5	14.4	16.9	22.9	20.1	33.8	29.3	22.2	21.9
35–49	24.6	26.6	27.0	27.7	29.3	29.6	28.0	30.9	26.0	27.3
50–64	21.8	20.4	25.1	23.8	17.9	19.6	11.8	12.8	20.7	20.5
65+	12.9	12.9	22.4	16.3	8.9	10.1	3.6	5.0	13.9	13.0
N	10,625	12,142	10,932	12,345	9,059	6,339	1,519	2,392	36,796	36,424
Religion										
Roman Catholic	21.2	22.5	58.1	50.7	33.0	29.2	22.5	22.6	33.1	31.7
Dutch Reformed	15.8	11.6	18.2	20.0	18.8	12.3	18.3	14.3	17.0	15.2
Gereformeerde Kerken	1.7	1.4	16.8	10.6	3.6	2.4	4.2	3.6	8.5	5.9
Other	5.0	4.3	1.4	2.5	4.8	5.2	8.5	0.0	4.6	4.1
No Church	56.4	60.2	5.6	16.1	39.7	50.9	46.5	59.5	36.8	43.1
N	424	432	358	404	330	212	71	84	1,334	1,246
Self-reported social class										
Upper and upper-middle class	7.7	9.8	11.0	14.9	26.2	40.8	21.7	29.2	15.1	18.5
Middle class	38.9	38.5	55.7	52.8	57.2	48.1	58.0	45.1	49.4	46.0
Upper working class	13.4	15.2	9.0	9.7	7.8	7.3	7.2	8.5	10.0	11.1
Working class	39.9	36.6	24.3	22.6	8.7	3.9	13.0	17.1	25.4	24.4
N	411	421	345	390	320	206	69	82	1,285	1,208

Source: Dutch National Election Studies 1982 and 1986, except for the data on age, which are from NOS-Intomart Precinct Surveys 1982 and 1986.

parties, but is otherwise in competition with socialists, liberals and D'66. In the last decade, with the CDA moving more clearly towards an anti-socialist stance, while posturing as the government party *par excellence*, there has been a particularly massive floating vote between the CDA and the VVD. Traditionally, the Christian democrats in Dutch politics tended to be restricted to the more religiously observant part of the population. But in 1986, the party succeeded for the first time in its history to attract a sizeable number of more secular voters.

Figures on the background of liberal and D'66 voters are given for the 1982 and 1986 elections in Table 7.4. For the sake of comparison, similar figures are presented for Christian democrats, socialists, and the total electorate. The table offers data in line with expectations: for example, the rather higher social-status background of the two liberal parties, their largely secular constituency, a rather strong presence of voters in middle-age brackets, and also a substantial attraction of young voters for both parties (other figures show that the VVD captured indeed almost a third of the youth vote in its great year of electoral gains in 1982, a feat which was not repeated in 1986 when its share of the youth vote fell to about one fifth) etc. Against this, one might note the rather aged constituency which Christian democrats had in 1982, as in earlier years, and their rather more impressive showing regarding a youth vote in 1986, as well as the appearance for the first time of a substantial number of secular voters in their electorate. Notably the socialists, but also the Christian democrats, show a much stronger ability than the two liberal parties to attract the working-class vote, although in becoming more of a popular mass party, the liberal VVD did attempt to make some inroads into the working-class vote. Both socialists and Christian democrats continue to have a more outspoken inter-class character than either VVD or D'66.

GOVERNMENT PARTICIPATION[15]

Cabinet formation in the Netherlands tends to be of a kind that Giovanni Sartori has called 'peripheral turnover'.[16] In all governments since World War II Christian democrats[17] have played a key role, governing sometimes in a centre-left and sometimes in a centre-right coalition. But such preferences tended to change considerably over time. Thus, in the immediate post-war period, one or more Christian democrat parties governed for thirteen years in five successive cabinets with the socialists, until December 1958. In two of these cabinets liberals joined, for a total period of 1,487 days. In

Table 7.5 *Pre-Second World War national government participation*

	No. of times	Total length
Liberale Staats-partij	2	4 yrs 29 days
Vrijzinnig-Democratische Bond	2	4 yrs 29 days
All cabinets	9	20 yrs 39 days

Note: The *Liberale Staatspartij* and the *Vrijzinnig-Democratische Bond* both participated in two cabinets between 1933 and 1937. In some other cabinets liberals sat not as representatives of their party, but in an individual capacity. This was not notably true of the so-called Intermezzo Cabinet-De Geer from 1926 to 1929.

December 1958 the long-standing coalition which had joined socialists and Christian democrats broke up. Since then there have been thirteen cabinets, for a total of just over 10,000 days. In three of these socialists sat, for a total of 2,530 days, or about 25 per cent of the time. Liberals, on the other hand, joined Christian democrats in seven cabinets, for a total of 7,114 days, or over 70 per cent of the time. The remaining three cabinets were interim cabinets, formed with Christian democrats as their core after a coalition between Christian democrats and socialists broke up, to tie over a period until new elections were held, which in each case resulted in a renewed coalition of Christian democrats and liberals. All three cabinets of Christian democrats and socialists since 1958 broke up in acrimony. Only in one case of a Christian democrat–liberal coalition (1965) did a cabinet fall through internal dissension between these two coalition partners. Liberals, then, have become a natural governing party since 1959, albeit always one which numerically remained the junior partner to a larger Christian democrat party, which always had it in its power to make the alternative choice of a coalition with the socialists. Socialists and liberals, on the other hand, have never sat in a government together since 1952.

While socialists and liberals have remained at opposite poles, so to a lesser extent also have D'66 and the liberals. As we saw, in the early 1970s D'66 temporarily joined with socialists and a left splinter from the religious parties in a Progressive Alliance. They took part in what was practically a five-party cabinet under the Socialist Premier J.M. den Uyl between 1973 and 1977, but tended to lose their identity in the process, and decided instead to seek a more independent profile. The strategy paid off in 1981, when D'66 scored a remarkable success and seemed for a time of pivotal importance in the building of a new cabinet coalition. Before the 1981 election, D'66 publicly announced that the party would support only two alternative cabinet coalitions:

Table 7.6 *National government participation after the Second World War*

	No. of times	Total length
Volkspartij voor Vrijheid en Democratie	9	23 yrs 203 days
Democraten '66	3	5 yrs 275 days
All cabinets	18	40 yrs 30 days

Note: Liberals sat in two cabinets with Christian democrats and socialists under a socialist prime minister between 1948 and 1952; all other cabinets consisted of a coalition of Christian democrats and liberals under a Christian democrat prime minister (in one cabinet further reinforced by the participation of a dissident social-democratic party).

D'66 ministers sat in one five-party cabinet under a socialist prime minister (1973–7), in one three-party cabinet of Christian democrats, socialists and D'66 between 1981 and 1982, and in a two-party caretaker cabinet with the Christian democrats in 1982.

one composed of socialists, D'66 and Christian democrats, or one composed of socialists, D'66 and liberals, but not one of D'66, Christian democrats and liberals. If, in the latter case, D'66 would have to make up for the lack of a majority of the two other parties, it would occupy the unenviable position of a small progressive party in a right-of-centre coalition, instead of occupying the much more preferable position as the centre of a coalition with two larger parties on either side. The outcome was a cabinet under a Christian democrat premier, with socialist and D'66 vice-premiers. This cabinet soon got into great conflict, and ended with a resignation of the socialists from the cabinet. In anticipation of new elections the Christian democrats and D'66 then formed a rump cabinet together. This new 'centrist' stance of D'66 – co-operating in a temporary minority coalition with the Christian democrats – was one factor in the disastrous election results in 1982 which reduced its parliamentary strength from 17 to 6 seats.

The period of time and the size of D'66 participation in only three cabinets (two of them very short-lived) were too small to allow clear conclusions on the type of ministries that party tended to covet. At most, one might see a certain preference for departments related to the application of modern technology. As for the VVD: the party participated in nine out of the eighteen cabinets which were formed since 1946. In four cases, the party had the Ministry of the Interior and the Ministry of Defence, three times the Ministry of Economic Affairs, twice the Ministry of Finance, Justice or Transport. The party never had the Ministry of Social Affairs, the Ministry of Social Welfare or the Ministry of Agriculture, and only once the Ministry of Education.

LOCAL GOVERNMENTS AS ARENAS FOR PARTY COALITIONS

As for coalitions on the local level: they are not easily comparable to politics at the national level.[18] The Netherlands being a unitary state, local government is a rather less important political arena than, e.g., the states in the German Federal Republic. Both at the level of the twelve provinces, and the roughly 700 municipalities, elected councils choose members from their own ranks of an executive board which meets under the chairmanship of the centrally appointed royal commissioner or burgomaster respectively. Office at the provincial level carries considerable prestige, but on the whole the provinces are less politically visible than either the national government or municipal governments. At the provincial level, a tendency for proportional power-sharing among the larger parties has tended to prevail.

The situation at the level of municipalities is rather more complicated. Given considerable differences in political preferences in different geographical areas, the political make-up differs greatly from one municipality to another. Thus, in many of the smaller, mainly rural communities religious parties have had a majority, so that no real choice of coalition parties arises. But there are some rural regions in the country where a more secular orientation prevails. In the latter communities, both liberals and socialists are generally comparatively strong; in the executive boards of such municipalities a socialist–liberal combination is rather common. In the largest cities, secular parties are also relatively strong. But here parties on the left, including notably the socialists, often have an independent majority. This has allowed the formation of exclusive left-oriented coalitions, in which D'66 sometimes participates, generally in a very junior role. Such left coalitions (which often also included smaller parties on the left of the socialists) not seldom had a record of considerable conflict. This has led to a return of more proportional arrangements, in which not only left parties, but also other parties obtained seats in the executive board. While dominant left forces were generally more open to coalitional arrangements with Christian democrat forces, liberals have also often been included in what were in fact wide-based cartels of all the larger parties. For the rest: the tendency for the left to form exclusive left coalitions was sometimes answered by equally exclusive coalitions of Christian democrats and liberals. But one should not exaggerate such events. Generally speaking, local government arenas have remained largely autonomous from inter-party conflicts and alignments at the national government level.

In the 1970s, liberals have become increasingly active in local politics. For a long time they were often satisfied with local lists not endorsed by, or even fully representative of, liberal concerns. They have also increasingly used the power of central government to secure a more favourable share in the appointment of burgomasters. D'66 as a rather novel, and less socially-rooted, political movement has remained conspicuously weak at the level of local government, compared with their (even then not particularly powerful) position at the level of the national government.

The liberal VVD, then, is in no way a pivotal actor, or king-maker in Dutch politics. Its position is mainly on the right of the political spectrum. But this position is neither uncontroversial nor unchallenged. Of late, the Christian democrats have abandoned their habitual position as the arbiter of coalition politics. Rather than maintaining their refusal to indicate a coalition preference until after an election, they have instead campaigned on their record as the senior partner in a coalition of Christian democrats and liberals, asking for an electoral mandate for that coalition. As this made the liberals an indispensable partner for the Christian democrats, this new development might seem to strengthen the power of the Liberal Party. However, in moving to the right, where the liberals traditionally located themselves, the Christian democrats have in fact proved to be uneasy bedfellows, as the liberals were to experience to their disadvantage in the 1986 elections. The Christian democrats under a popular prime minister, Ruud Lubbers, indeed greatly increased their strength in a plebiscitary appeal for a new mandate. Although that required the continuation of a coalition between Christian democrats and liberals, such an appeal proved costly indeed for the latter: in the 1986 elections, they lost nine seats, the very number which the Christian democrats won. If the Lubbers cabinet retained its working majority of 81 out of 150 parliamentary seats, the power ratio of the two parties changed greatly, from 45–36 to one of 54–27.

LIBERAL POLICIES AND PARTY PROGRAMMES

If one surveys the programmes (whether declarations of principle, or election programmes) published by the liberal VVD (or its predecessor the *Partij van de Vrijheid* in 1946), two constant elements come consistently to the fore: a strong desire to promote private enterprise, and a clear insistence on individual liberties. If the first makes the party a political actor on the right of the economic political spectrum – fulfilling a role that in other countries one would readily identify with a conservative party – the latter places the party rather more in the world of liberal or even radical traditions on the European continent.

Of course, pronouncements of principle are not everything. Within the liberal party, different individuals and groups have rather different priorities. While some may lay strong emphasis on 'radical' issues – such as easing restrictions on abortion or euthanasia, doing away with censorship laws and enforcing new anti-discrimination legislation which would outlaw discriminatory practices not only on the basis of gender, religion, or ethnic background, but also on homosexuality – other liberal activists lay greater stress on the need to preserve law and order, and to expand police forces and prison facilities.

On the economic front, too, there are considerable differences in the practical elaboration of policies, not only as regards the need for state support to ailing industries or firms in difficulties, but also on the specific degree of social security which society should provide. For all its free enterprise preferences and emphasis on individual self-reliance, the liberals have in fact consistently contributed to the extension of the Welfare State in the 1960s and 1970s. Whereas the emphasis has now changed to the need to curtail public expenditure, and in general to give preference to the claim of the active working population over those who enjoy social security benefits, actual policies (proposed or adopted) are yet far from drastic when looked at in a comparative European perspective. Apart from a streak of traditional radicalism within the liberal tradition, and a somewhat wide spread of opinions within the party, the necessities of coalition government powerfully contribute to keep the party from straying too far from the centre of Dutch politics.

As for D'66, its prevailing temper is definitely more radical than that of the VVD, particularly in its openness to new 'post-materialist' issues. D'66 has deliberately identified with the need to take strong measures to protect the environment: jointly with similarly oriented parties it has cut away the ground for independent ecological movements which, following the example of the German Greens, have tried to form separate ecological parties. D'66 has also given substantial support to the activities of the peace movement: although its specific policies have shown many nuances, they have generally opposed the stationing of Pershing and cruise missiles in Western Europe. But when a narrow majority in parliament eventually followed the Christian democrat and liberal coalition government in accepting the stationing of 48 cruise missiles, D'66 (whose leader H.A.F.M.O. van Mierlo had been Minister of Defence in 1981–2) refused to follow the socialists in the latters' refusal to accept that decision as a *fait accompli*. The liberal VVD, on the other hand, has undoubtedly been the staunchest supporter in Dutch politics of the NATO-Alliance, and of American positions within it.

If one concentrates more specifically on pronouncements in the VVD programme in the last few years, the following issues deserve consideration.[19] In economic matters, the idea of 'more market, less government' stands out. The VVD propagates an active policy of privatisation, e.g. in such areas as social security, social welfare and health. It lays considerable emphasis on the need for technological innovation, the promotion of exports, cutting labour costs, strengthening the capital situation and the profitability of private firms. The party actively campaigns for deregulation, notably for private enterprise. It lays little emphasis on co-determination, except in the context of harmonising EEC legislation. The VVD has some electoral strength in agrarian areas and normally promotes the cause of agricultural interests, but not noticeably more so than other political parties – the 'green lobby' or corporate agricultural interests seeking political support across parties in Dutch politics. The party is a clear advocate of free trade, and has expressed a concern about the dangers of a revival of American protectionism.

In social matters, the VVD is a traditional advocate of individual rights, emphasising the need to respect privacy and taking a favourable attitude towards women's emancipation. It accepts the freedom of education (and therefore does not wish to upset the long-time settlement by which the state finances religious schools on a par with government schools). It stresses the principle of equal opportunity in educational matters, but it also argues that due regard should be paid to differences in intellectual gifts of different pupils. The VVD has, on the whole, resisted any tendency towards enforcing a standardised system of comprehensive secondary education which would do away with special *gymnasia* or other forms of pre-university schooling.

In international affairs, the VVD propagates an active concern with international law, including the observance of human rights. With other Dutch parties, it embraces an active policy of development aid (which is kept largely immune from government spending cuts at about 1.5 per cent of national income), but it advocates a more immediate participation of private enterprise in the granting of specific aid. As mentioned, the VVD is a staunch advocate of NATO. It was the earliest and firmest proponent of the stationing of cruise missiles, and it has taken a positive stand on the Strategic Defense Initiative as promoted by President Reagan. The VVD is an equally active advocate of European co-operation, notably in economic matters (including an active policy of technological research and development). If there is a certain ambiguity in whether on balance the party will take a more 'European', or a more 'Atlanticist' position in foreign policy matters, this is not really different from a similar ambiguity shown by other Dutch political parties.

As for D'66: it shares the VVD view on the need to rely on markets, differing from the socialists notably in the degree of state intervention for which the party pleads. But in practice, D'66 accepts state intervention somewhat more readily than does its larger liberal rival. The party also accepts the need for cutting government expenditures, but at a slower pace than the VVD deems necessary. D'66 is much more explicit than the liberal VVD on the need to increase the level of democratic participation in both private and semi-public organisations. It wishes to base all systems of social security, not on groups (such as the family or the household) but on the individual, being particularly concerned with the separate rights of women (whether married or not). By far the most characteristic points of the D'66 programme, however, relate to the need for political reforms. In 1986 the party deliberately returned to its older emphasis on this point. It continues to advocate the direct election of a prime minister and a district electoral system, it wants the formal introduction of a referendum by which a stated number of citizens can demand a popular vote on any bill passed by parliament, it urges a strengthening of parliament, and it pleads for a far greater decentralisation of political power to local authorities. Apart from the greater reluctance shown on the stationing of cruise missiles, the foreign policy stand of D'66 does not noticeably deviate from that of the VVD. The party shares the ambiguity on a 'European' versus an 'Atlanticist' orientation. It has come out in favour of a special 'European identity' in military security policy.

THE LIBERALS IN THE DUTCH POLITICAL SPECTRUM: PAST, PRESENT AND POSSIBLE FUTURE STRATEGIES

What, then, has the position been of Dutch liberal parties in the past? What dilemmas do they face? What future options do they have?

Although liberalism in the Netherlands represented a political movement with ancient roots in Dutch society, its position came increasingly to be determined by the development of other political parties. If the rise of religious parties pushed the liberals to the more secular part of a secular–religious continuum, the rise of the socialists tended to push them to the right on a socio-economic spectrum. At the same time, liberal organisational strength remained rather inferior to that of rival parties, reminiscent of a period in which liberals had been strong as an unorganised political elite, and did not think it necessary to organise as a mass movement. Liberals, moreover, were often divided, between more conservative and radical elements, supporting until 1940 at least two separate parties.

The traditional position of the liberals began to change substantially once other political parties in the Netherlands began to lose much of their one-time cohesion as a result of the growing disarray in which their subcultures began to fall. This created new opportunities, not only for the liberals (who had anyhow relied more on catch-all political strategies than the parties of 'social integration'[20] in Dutch politics such as Catholics, Calvinists and socialists), but also for the entrepreneurship of the *homines novi* of D'66. Notably the liberal VVD substantially increased its membership and organisational presence. As the Christian democrats had grown increasingly alienated from the socialists with which they had been in coalition for more than a decade after the Second World War, the strategic importance of the VVD for the formation of coalitions increased greatly. The growing strength of liberals at the national level was only partly reflected at lower levels of government, but certainly in the 1970s and 1980s VVD became consciously more active in such political arenas as well.

Compared to the VVD, D'66 had a much more chequered record, both in electoral performance and in its actual role in central or local government. If its newness made it a potentially acceptable alternative to old voters from other parties – and to new voters – its lack of stable social roots was such that it has never obtained a really secure existence, apart from the sudden spurts of certain conspicuous leaders, and a rather special combination of public relations skills and temporary amateur activism. Whereas such improvised tactics might work in (some) national elections, they hardly facilitated the building up of a strong presence in local government. D'66 arose in an attempt to cut across all existing cleavage lines of Dutch politics, posing deliberately as a party which wished to explode an antiquated party system. But it landed soon in a rather limited area of the Dutch party spectrum. It became mainly the radical alternative to the liberals, and the non-socialist alternative to the socialist PvdA, reminding political observers of the position which radical Vrijzinnig-Democraten had earlier occupied at the left wing of the liberals. D'66 gave some voice to new movements (partly of a 'post-materialist' kind), which helped the Dutch political system to absorb the 'new politics' more easily than other countries had managed to do. But here again, D'66 could not lastingly 'appropriate' such issues which in any case were soon also claimed by other Dutch political parties and which by their nature lacked a sufficient degree of specificity to make them the basis for the formation of a really sizeable and lasting political movement.

Both the liberal VVD and D'66 must accommodate to the realities of coalition politics in a rather fragmented multi-party system. We have shown that D'66 had few real chances, running the danger of being embraced too closely by the Socialist Party, in a situation in which even the joining of D'66 in an exclusive left coalition would not give the aggregate left an independent majority. A movement away from the socialists to a more centrist position also did not furnish the party with real gains: for near the centre they found themselves uncomfortably close to Christian democrats, and even liberals, being at most invited to provide these two parties with a majority for a right-of-centre coalition which it found clearly uncongenial.

As compared to the position of D'66, the place of the liberal VVD in coalition politics has been far more assured. We have shown that the party has governed, always in coalition with the Christian democrats, for more than 70 per cent of the time since 1959. The party grew rather steadily in size from 1971 to 1982, being clearly the greatest profiteer from the decline of the vote for the once dominant religious parties. But numerical relations remained such even then that the party could at most hope being the junior partner in a coalition in which the Christian democrats dominated. Moreover: whereas the Christian democrats could always opt for an alternative coalition with the socialists, liberals did not have such a choice. Of late, the liberal VVD has even had to experience that Christian democrats were far from reluctant to steal their clothes: moving over more to the right of politics, assuming a rather clearer anti-socialist stand, and posturing strongly as the natural and reliable governing party.

What options does this leave the VVD? Should the party in turn move more towards the centre, possibly acquiring a key position there rather in the manner of the German FDP, which can decide the formation of either a Christian democrat-cum-liberal coalition or a socialist-cum-liberal coalition? Such a move in a country where liberals and socialists have not sat in one cabinet for over thirty years, would seem to demand a rather considerable change on the part of liberals and socialists alike. There have been non-committal contacts between individual socialists and individual liberals seeking to explore new possibilities of co-operation. In such contacts, common preferences on 'liberal' values have been a catalyst of some value, as has been a growing resentment against the Christian-democrat hold on political power. However, the force of economic factors (which have kept socialists and liberals in the Netherlands apart) and the feeling on the part of liberals that Christian democrats could offer them a share of power which socialists could not rival with any degree of certainty, or pay-off in policies or portfolios, have made such 'moves' so far largely a theoretical affair.

Dutch liberals then tend to occupy a position in Dutch politics which resembles that of a conservative party in other countries, albeit with two qualifications. First, policy positions of parties are not really far apart if one compares inter-party relations in the Netherlands with those in other systems in Western Europe. In a comparative perspective Dutch liberals are therefore rather less conservative than many conservatives in other countries. And secondly, on non-economic issues, the VVD has remained enough of a liberal party to make it something more than a conservative party with another name. As for D'66, it remains a party which retains some of the trappings of a traditional radical party in Dutch politics. At the same time, its particular political platform also makes it a party *sui generis*.

NOTES

1 There is little literature in English on Dutch liberalism. For a general overview of Dutch political parties in the nineteenth and twentieth centuries see, however, W. Verkade, *Democratic Parties in the Low Countries*, Leiden: Stenfert Kroese, 1969; Ernst Kossmann, *The Low Countries 1780–1940*, Oxford: Oxford University Press, 1978; and Hans Daalder, 'Opposition in a segmented society' in: Robert A. Dahl (ed.), *Political Oppositions in Western Democracies*, New Haven: Yale University Press, 1966, pp. 188–236; see also Hans Daalder, 'Dutch liberals in the nineteenth century: a dominant, yet unorganized minority', paper presented to the Erstes Symposium deutscher und niederländischer Historiker, Aachen, 12–16 April 1983 (which in a translated German version has been published as 'Niederländische Liberale im 19. Jahrhundert: eine herrschende, aber unorganisierte Minderheit', in: Hermann W. von der Dunk und Horst Lademacher (eds.), *Auf dem Weg zum modernen Parteienstaat. Zur Entstehung, Organisation und Struktur politischer Parteien in Deutschland und den Niederlanden*, Kassel: Kasseler Forschunger zur Zeitgeschichte, 1986). In Dutch the most important monograph on the liberals and radicals in the nineteenth century is G. Taal, *Liberalen en Radicalen in Nederland 1872–1901*, Den Haag: Nijhoff, 1980.

2 See the seminal treatment in Arend Lijphart, *The Politics of Accommodation: Pluralism and Democracy in the Netherlands*, Berkeley: University of California Press, 1968, 2nd edn 1975.

3 See for interesting analyses Rudy B. Andeweg, *Dutch Voters Adrift: On Electoral Change in the Netherlands*, Leiden: Department of Political Science, 1982; C. van der Eijk and B. Niemoller, *Electoral Change in the Netherlands*, Amsterdam: CT Press, 1983; Galen A. Irwin and Karl Dittrich, 'And the walls came tumbling down . . .' in: R. Dalton et al. (eds.), *Electoral Change in Advanced Industrial Democracies*, Princeton: Princeton University Press, 1984, pp. 267–97.

4 For data see J.J. Godschalk, 'Enige politieke en sociale kenmerken van de oprichters van D'66', *Acta Politica* 5: 1969–70, pp. 62–74.

5 For a theoretical analysis which had a powerful effect on the D'66 electoral programme, see J.F. Glastra van Loon, 'Kiezen of Delen', *Nederlands Juristenblad* 39: 1964, pp. 1135–42 and pp. 1161–7. For an analysis in English see Hans Daalder, 'Changing procedures and changing strategies in Dutch coalition-building (1963–1986)', *Legislative Studies Quarterly* (forthcoming).

6 Maurice Duverger, *Political Parties: Their Organization and Activity in the Modern State*, London: Methuen, 1984. There are, however, problems both in definition and in chronology in this statement. Undoubtedly, the early liberal parties had tended to resemble Duverger's 'caucus parties', and D'66 was at its foundation very much an initiative of a small group of new politicos without any mass base. At the same time, both parties developed in the direction of mass parties to the extent that political recruitment came to be party-controlled, and party finance became largely a matter of dues-paying membership, as is still the case for the two parties today.

7 Events are graphically described in the diary of the D'66 leader, who was also deputy-prime minister between 1981 and 1982, Jan Terlouw, *Naar Zeventien Zetels en Teruq*, Utrecht: Veen, 1983.

8 For a survey of nomination procedures in Dutch parties, see Ruud Koole, 'Candidate selection in the Netherlands', paper presented to the Workshop on Candidate Selection in Comparative Perspective, European Consortium for Political Research, Barcelona, 1985.

9 For a good analysis of preference voting and its effect, see R.C. Hessing, 'Bij Voorkeur: Een Onderzoek naar het Gebruik van Voorkeurstemmen', *Acta Politica* 20: 1985, pp. 157–76.

10 Data on the increase in the number of amendments to various types of party programmes introduced by party members are given in the M.A. thesis of J. de Boer and M. Klück, *Spreken is Zilver: Zwijgen is Goud*, Leiden: Department of Political Science, 1984.

11 For a more detailed analysis on sources of income and expenditures of Dutch political parties, see Ruud Koole, 'The modesty of Dutch party finance' in H.E. Alexander (ed.), *Comparative Political Finance* (forthcoming).

12 For details see Ruud Koole, 'Partijfinanciën en Bedrijfsleven: De Giften vanuit Ondernemerskringen aan de partij van de Vrijheid', *Jaarboek Documentatiecentrum Nederlandese Politieke Partijen 1984*, Groningen, pp. 108–28.

13 Interesting data on the degree of sympathy felt for different interest groups by party activists of Dutch political parties in 1978–9 are available in the Dutch part of the so-called Middle-Level Elites-Project. Whereas 98% of socialist activists and 67% of D'66 activists voiced a definite sympathy for the Trades Union Congress (FNV), figures for the CDA were only 28% and for the VVD 17%. In contrast, only 13% of the socialist activists and 36% of D'66 activists expressed a definite sympathy for the Association of Dutch Industries, as against 61% of the CDA activists and 93% of VVD activists. Data in W.H. van Schuur, *Structure in Political Beliefs: A New Model for Stochastic Unfolding with Application to European Political Activists*, Amsterdam: CT Press, 1984, Appendix 7, p. 288.

14 This is a key element in the analysis of Arend Lijphart, *The Politics of Accommodation*, *passim*.

15 See, in addition to Tables 7.5 and 7.6, for a rather more detailed analysis of the composition of Dutch cabinets A. de Swaan, 'Coalitions in a segmented polity' in: Eric C. Browne and John Dreijmanis (eds.), *Government Coalitions in Western Democracies*, New York: Longman, 1982, pp. 217–37, and Hans Daalder in *Legislative Studies Quarterly*, (forthcoming). More detailed source material can be

found in H. Daalder and C.J.M. Schuyte (eds.), *Compendium voor Politiek en Samenleving*, Alphen aan den Rijn: Samsom, 1986– , ch. 5.

16 E.g., Giovanni Sartori, 'European political parties: the case of polarized pluralism' in: Joseph LaPalombara and Myron Weiner (eds.), *Political Parties and Political Development*, Princeton: Princeton University Press, 1966, pp. 137–76.

17 We speak consistently of Christian democrats in this paper for what were in fact until 1980 three distinct political parties: the Catholic People's Party and two orthodox-protestant parties – the Anti-Revolutionary Party and the Christian Historical Union. Catholics were members of *all* cabinets since 1946. Anti-Revolutionary ministers sat in all cabinets since 1952, Christian Historical ministers were members of most cabinets, except for some interim cabinet and a few later cabinets in which the socialists also participated (e.g., one cabinet between 1965 and 1966, and the left-oriented cabinet under the socialist J.M. den Uyl in which in addition to socialists and one minister of D'66 as well as two left radicals, two ministers served from the Anti-Revolutionary Party, and four ministers from the Catholic Party). In 1976 the three Christian parties decided to federate, and to present a joint list for the 1977 parliamentary elections. The parties formally amalgamated in the Christian-Democratic Appeal (CDA) in 1980.

18 For an analysis of political parties in local government councils, see K.L.L.M. Dittrich, *Partijpolitieke Verhoudingen in Nederlandse Gemeenten 1962–1974*, Leiden: Department of Political Science, 1978.

19 For a short but incisive review in English, see Paul Lucardie, 'New conservatism in the Netherlands?', paper presented to the Workshop on Conservative Parties: Adaptability and Change in Western Democracies, European Consortium Political Research, Göteborg, 1986. For an earlier and fuller review in Dutch by the same author, see 'Waar Blijft Nieuw Rechts in de VVD: Een Voorstudie over de Continuïteit van het Sociaal-Economisch Denken in de VVD', *Jaarboek Documentatiecentrum Nederlandse Politieke Partijen 1981*, Groningen, 1982, pp. 138–57.

20 The reference is to the typology of Sigmund Neumann (ed.), *Modern Political Parties: Approaches to Comparative Politics*, Chicago: University of Chicago Press, 1956.

8

The Belgian liberal parties: economic radicals and social conservatives

Christopher Rudd

HISTORICAL BACKGROUND

During the 1820s, an alliance between Catholics and Liberals had successfully brought about the independence of Belgium from the Netherlands. This Catholic–Liberal alliance – or unionism as it came to be known – continued until 1840 given the need for national unity whilst the Netherlands refused to accept the legitimacy of Belgium's separate existence.

Unionism was characterised by the formation of bipartisan Catholic–Liberal coalition governments regardless of parliamentary strengths. The latent church–state conflict was kept off the political agenda and the main political battles were not between clericals and anti-clericals but between conservatives and progressives over issues such as the extension of the electoral franchise. The difference between the conservatives and the progressives was, as Kossmann points out, one of temperament rather than doctrine or social origin (see Kossmann (1978) 167).

Unionism effectively ended in 1839 with the recognition by the Dutch of Belgian independence, a move which led to greater and more open hostility between Catholics and Liberals. The Liberals, in particular, were the aggressors, feeling that too many concessions had been made to the Catholics in order to gain the support of the Roman church in the struggle for national independence. Although the Liberals were not anti-religious, (indeed, many were practising Catholics), the party demanded a clearer separation between church and state as well as a recognition that the church was subordinate to the state in all temporal matters. For many Liberals, the main bone of contention surrounded the Catholic church's monopoly control of primary education and its attempt to gain a similar position within the sphere of secondary education.

At this time, neither the Liberals nor the Catholics had formed an organised political party. The Catholics had not done so primarily due to opposition from the church itself, opposition which lasted until the 1880s. For the Liberals, however, the end of unionism saw the beginning of moves towards the establishment of a national political organisation. In 1841 the Liberal Alliance of Brussels was formed with the intention of uniting all anti-clerical forces behind a common programme. It was this alliance which was responsible for bringing together the various Liberal groupings in Brussels in June 1846 to take part in the first Liberal congress.

It was hoped that the congress would help heal the growing rift in the Liberal camp between the 'moderates' and 'progressives'. The latter pressed for an immediate and extensive widening of the suffrage, a proposal rejected outright by the former. As the moderates were clearly in the majority at the congress, it was no surprise that a decision to support only a minor extension of the franchise was taken. Other resolutions called for a 'real' independence of civil power and the organisation of all education under control of the state. Most significant from an organisational point of view was the decision to establish a permanent *comité* in each electoral constituency (*arrondissement*) with the responsibility for preparing and disseminating electoral propaganda.

The congress failed, however, in its efforts to reconcile the differences between the moderates and the progressives. After the congress, the moderates or 'doctrinaires' as they became known (after the name given to the followers of the French romantics) formed the Liberal Party (Association Libérale et Constitutionnelle).

The Liberal Party met with immediate electoral success at the 1847 election, winning an absolute majority of seats. Not only did the Liberals then form the first strictly partisan government but they were also to dominate Belgian politics for the next thirty-seven years. Between 1847 and 1884 there were only three non-Liberal governments. For the remainder of this period, the Liberals were in power. Their overall dominance was greatly reinforced by the network of masonic lodges which provided the organisational framework for many local Liberal Party organisations. In addition, the Liberals manipulated the franchise regulations so as to increase the numbers of voters in urban areas where Liberal support was stronger.[1]

From 1884 until the end of the First World War, the Liberals found themselves in opposition. Three factors in particular help to account for this dramatic turnaround in Liberal fortunes.

First, the Catholics had finally decided to establish a formal party structure, thus depriving the Liberals of the organisational advantage they had enjoyed for over forty years. Secondly, the introduction of male universal suffrage in 1893, albeit tempered by plural voting, had served to extend the franchise to those social groups less inclined to support a party which defended the existing social order. The third factor, which is linked to the second, was the formation of the Belgian Socialist Party in 1885. The Socialists were the main beneficiaries of the suffrage extension and they were to become Belgium's second largest party after 1919, forcing the Liberals into third place.

The combined impact of the widening of the franchise and the establishment of the Socialist Party was to reduce the Liberal vote from 45 per cent (60 seats) in 1892 to 28 per cent (20 seats) in 1894 (Table 8.1). It is likely that the Liberal Party was only saved from becoming politically irrelevant through the introduction of proportional representation in 1899.

During the years between the two World Wars the Liberals participated in seventeen of the twenty peacetime governments. But it would be misleading to interpret this statistic as an indication of a Liberal revival for, in electoral terms, the Liberal Party in both the 1920s and 1930s recorded some of its worst results since 1847 (Table 8.1). Moreover, Liberal participation in government was achieved by the virtual inevitability of the formation of coalition governments following the introduction of universal male suffrage without plural voting in 1919. This, combined with an electoral system based on proportional representation, effectively deprived any one party of the ability to win an absolute majority of the available seats. As the Catholic and Socialist parties were unable to reach any lasting compromise over economic policy, the Liberals, almost by default, found themselves placed in the role of being the permanent coalition partners of the Catholics.

In terms of policy, the nineteenth-century Liberal governments of 1850–80 adhered to the philosophy of economic free-trade. Protectionism was considered to be a retrograde step as well as an infringement of individual liberty. Individual prosperity – and by extension, national prosperity – could only be maximised if there were no restrictions or obstacles in the way of economic development. External tariff barriers were reduced, domestic tolls were abolished, interest rates were allowed to find their own level and companies were permitted to form without any need for prior government authorisation.

Table 8.1 *National share of votes and seats (Lower House): 1847–1939*

Year[a]	Liberal % Seats	Liberal–Socialist cartel
1847	52.12 (55)	
1848(D)	69.52 (83)	
1850	54.80 (69)	
1852	57.36 (57)	
1854	57.44 (54)	
1856	45.12 (45)	
1857(D)	54.72 (70)	
1859	54.19 (69)	
1861	57.52 (66)	
1863	45.51 (59)	
1864(D)	49.74 (64)	
1866	58.20 (72)	
1868	44.33 (73)	
1870	55.63 (62)	
1870(D)	44.53 (52)	
1872	31.03 (53)	
1874	52.50 (56)	
1876	46.30 (57)	
1878	52.61 (72)	
1880	50.31 (74)	
1882	52.77 (79)	
1884	38.86 (52)	
1886	51.33 (40)	
1888	37.31 (40)	
1890	54.51 (44)	
1892(D)	45.37 (60)	
1894(D)[b]	27.9 (20)	1.7
1896	21.8 (13)	18.8
1898	21.3 (13)	3.0
1900(D)[c]	24.5 (34)	—
1902	22.6 (34)	—
1904	25.4 (42)	—
1906	21.3 (46)	15.5
1908	18.6 (43)	12.4
1910	22.0 (44)	15.3
1912(D)	11.6 (44)	26.4
1914	24.5 (45)	
1919	17.6 (34)	
1921	18.2 (33)	
1925	14.6 (23)	
1929	16.5 (28)	
1932	14.2 (24)	
1936	12.4 (23)	
1939	17.3 (33)	

[a] Half of parliament was renewed every two years except on dissolution (D) when the whole of parliament was re-elected.
[b] Introduction of male universal suffrage with plural voting.
[c] Introduction of proportional representation.
Sources: Gilissen (1958); Moiné (1970) 128–9; Witte and Craeybeckx (1981) 168–71.

The Liberal doctrinaires were not, however, akin to the classical nineteenth-century liberals of the Manchester School. Whilst liberalism was undoubtedly a middle-class movement furthering the materialistic interests of probably the most bourgeois society in Western Europe at the time, there were at least two distinct aspects to Belgian economic liberalism. First, it was by no means unqualified in its promotion of *laissez-faire* policies. The various Liberal Party governments did not pursue a free-trade policy purely on principle but equally as a means of strengthening the Belgian nation-state. As such, the state was prepared to intervene and play an active role when economic factors required it to do so. Examples of such positive state intervention were the provision of financial guarantees for savings banks, the establishment of *Crédits Communaux*, the setting up of the Belgian National Bank, the establishment of a financial structure for the development of the railways and the state take-over of the administration of the transport and communications network. This type of state intervention by the Liberal governments led to the creation of a massive public debt and frequent tax increases which brought in their wake criticisms from both Liberals and Catholics concerning excessive state interventionism and the consequent bureaucratisation of economic life.

The second aspect of Belgian economic liberalism was its nationalistic element. Economic liberalism was intended to facilitate economic prosperity as this was seen as being indispensable to increasing national power and prestige (Pirenne (1948) 161). As a relatively new nation-state, the Liberals viewed Belgian economic growth as a means to gain international recognition and acceptance. Outside the specific economic field, Liberal nationalism was also exhibited in their favouring a large standing army and the strengthening of Belgium's military fortifications.

Whilst in economic affairs *laissez-faire* principles were tempered in line with perceptions of national interest, these principles were allowed full rein as regards social issues (Chlepner (1983) 73). Liberals were opposed to any form of labour organisations, regulation of working conditions or compulsory education. There was also an anti-democratic element in Liberal thinking in that the doctrinaires steadfastly refused to consider any widening of the franchise. For the doctrinaires, 'liberty' gave the less fortunate the means of improving their social conditions. That such improvement was unforthcoming is substantiated by the appalling working conditions and widespread poverty suffered by the Belgian working class during the latter half of the nineteenth century.

The progressive liberals in the Liberal Party had opposed the doctrinaires ever since the 1846 Liberal congress. The progressives, however, received very little electoral support, particularly after the conservative reaction to the revolutionary upheavals of 1848. At most, the progressives only had six or seven representatives in parliament throughout this period. The progressives were not against the liberal economic system as such, but they rejected the lack of consideration given to social issues such as the regulation of child and female labour, compulsory education and the widening of the franchise.

Following the Liberal Party's ejection into opposition in 1884, moves were begun by the progressives to form an independent political party. Under the leadership of Paul Janson, a Progressive Party was finally set up in 1887. Its programme was greatly influenced by that of the Socialist Party which had been established two years earlier.

This organisational split in the liberal family only lasted until 1900. The short life of the Progressive Party was largely due to the fact that some of its policies were hardly distinguishable from those of the Socialist Party (protection of workers and state ownership of public utility services, for example) as well as other policies which eventually became acceptable to the doctrinaires (extension of the franchise and compulsory education). Those progressives who did not return to the Liberal Party fold usually found themselves most at home on the social-reformist wing of the Socialist Party.

Until the Liberals lost power in 1884, there had been few differences between themselves and the Catholics over the broad thrust of economic and social policy. Both were committed to the existing social order, a restricted franchise, non-intervention by the state in social affairs (for the Catholics, the church would look after the plight of the working classes) and a minimal but important strategic role for the state in economic affairs.

On the question of church–state relations, however, the Catholics and Liberals found themselves in sharp disagreement. The Catholics believed that religious society was superior to civil society, while the Liberals held that the church should be subordinate to the state. Both sides saw education as the crucial issue, as whoever controlled the schools controlled a crucial agent for the socialisation of future generations. The electoral victory by the Catholics in 1884 effectively won for them the 'Schools War', although a further outbreak of hostilities was to occur in the 1950s.

After 1900, the Liberal Party retained its anti-clericalism despite other economic and social issues increasingly coming to dominate the political agenda. With regard to these other issues, the Liberals did show some signs of greater radicalism and the party joined in a number of electoral alliances with the Socialists in support of male universal suffrage and compulsory education. This, however, was more the result of strategic considerations (how to dislodge the Catholics) than of any fundamental change in traditional Liberal policy. By 1916, when the Liberal Party rejoined the government, 'the party had lost so much of its radicalism that it could be considered conservative' (Kossmann (1978) 297).

At the 1919 party congress, the Liberals set out what appeared to be a refutation of any conservative label. The adopted programme called for a minimum wage, progressive taxation, fixed hours of work and the right of all to 'dignity, security and well-being' (Chlepner (1983) 332). That this was only yet another strategic move in response to the introduction of male universal suffrage in 1919 was emphasised when no further mention was made of the earlier demands for social reform at the 1920 congress. Instead, calls for a balanced budget, a legal framework for the settling of labour disputes and the regulation of employer–employee agreements were articulated. Again in 1935, the party programme contained measures which, for the Liberals, amounted to proposals for far-reaching social reforms. But once more, not only was the programme framed in very general and vague terms, it was also essentially an opportunistic response to prevailing public opinion. Following the depression years of the late 1920s and early 1930s, any reference to *laissez-faire* economics would have receieved very little support from the electorate.

By the outbreak of the Second World War, the Liberals had come to lack any widespread appeal or distinctive identity. *Laissez-faire* economics had been discredited, whilst even lip-service to social reformism sounded much more convincing coming from the Socialists and the left-wing of the Catholic Party. Anti-clericalism was no longer a source of electoral attraction, particularly after the secular parties agreed to state subsidies for free (mainly Catholic) schools in 1919. At the Liberal elite level, anti-clericalism was toned down following the First World War but many local party organisations still expressed antagonism towards what they considered excessive church influence in civil affairs. In Brussels, a traditional Liberal stronghold, this anti-clerical feeling remained particularly strong.

On the linguistic issue, which came to assume greater salience in the years between the two World Wars, the liberals took an unambiguous unitarist and pro-Francophone position. This was understandable given that the Liberal Party was a party of the bourgeoisie and the bourgeoisie were overwhelmingly French-speaking, whether they lived in Flanders or Wallonie. Furthermore, as supporters of a strong nation-state, the Liberals opposed any form of federalism.

DEVELOPMENTS AFTER THE SECOND WORLD WAR

After participating in nearly every government between the two World Wars, the post-war period has seen the Liberals excluded from half of all the governments formed (Table 8.2). The major factor accounting for this lower rate of Liberal participation has been the 'acceptability' of alternative centre-left coalitions between the Socialists and Christian-Socials (formerly the Catholic Party). This was a coalition type which had been successfully formed only once between 1919 and 1939, and even then it only lasted for less than a year.

In the years immediately after the Second World War, the Liberals joined a number of *coalitions de gauche* with the Socialists and the Communists. These coalitions presided over a period of rapid economic reconstruction largely financed by American aid. This economic growth allowed numerous improvements to be made to various social-welfare services and facilitated close co-operation between employers and trade unions. Such 'progressive' coalitions, however, became increasingly difficult to maintain partly as a result of the growing intransigence of the Communist Party with the onset of the cold war. There was also an underlying conflict between the Socialists and Liberals over long-term economic policy, particularly with regard to state nationalisation of industries.

The Liberals were in opposition from 1947 until 1954, except for a brief coalition with the Christian-Socials between 1949 and 1950. During this period, two major events in Belgian domestic politics occurred. First, there was the 'Royal Question', the dispute primarily between the Socialists and Christian-Socials, concerning the powers of the monarchy in matters of defence and foreign policy and in particular the conduct of the Belgian king during the German occupation of 1940–4. Although a majority of the liberals sided with the Socialists in calling for the abdication of the king, this did not represent republican sentiments but rather an attempt to replace a monarch whose continued reign threatened to create severe social unrest and political chaos.

Following the 'Royal Question', which was resolved by the king's abdication in 1950, there began what became known as the 'Second Schools War'. The three single-party Christian-Social governments of 1950–4 introduced legislation guaranteeing increased subsidies for Catholic schools. This was done in order to ensure that high school

Table 8.2 *Government participation, 1944–85*

Date of formation	Name of prime minister	Parties represented	Date of resignation
27.9.1944	Pierlot (V)	C – L – S – Co	16.11.1944
16.11.1944	Pierlot (VI)	C – L – S	7.2.1945
12.2.1945	Van Acker (I)	C – L – S – Co	2.8.1945
2.8.1945	Van Acker (II)	S – L – Co – VU	9.1.1946
13.3.1946	Spaak (II)	S	19.3.1946
31.3.1946	Van Acker (III)	S – L – Co	10.7.1946
3.8.1946	Huysmans	S – L – Co	12.3.1947
20.3.1947	Spaak (III)	C – S	27.11.1948
27.11.1948	Spaak (IV)	C – S	27.6.1949
11.8.1949	G. Eyskens (I)	C – L	6.6.1950
8.6.1950	Duvieusart	C	11.8.1950
16.8.1950	Pholien	C	9.1.1952
15.1.1952	Van Houtte	C	12.4.1954
22.4.1954	Van Acker (IV)	S – L	2.6.1958
23.6.1958	G. Eyskens (II)	C	6.11.1958
6.11.1958	G. Eyskens (III)	C – L	2.9.1960
2.9.1960	G. Eyskens (IV)	C – L	27.3.1961
25.4.1961	Lefèvre	C – S	24.5.1965
28.7.1965	Harmel	C – S	11.2.1966
19.3.1966	Vanden Boeynants (I)	C – L	7.2.1968
17.6.1968	G. Eyskens (V)	C – S	8.11.1971
20.1.1972	G. Eyskens (VI)	C – S	22.11.1972
26.1.1973	Leburton	C – S – L	19.1.1974
25.4.1974	Tindemans (I)	C – L	11.6.1974
11.6.1974	Tindemans (II)	C – L – RW	8.12.1976
8.12.1976	Tindemans (III)	C – L – RW	4.3.1977
6.3.1977	Tindemans (IV)	C – L	18.4.1977
3.6.1977	Tindemans (V)	C – S – FDF – VU	11.10.1978
20.10.1978	Vanden Boeynants (II)	C – S – FDF – VU	18.12.1978
3.4.1979	Martens (I)	C – S – FDF	16.1.1980
23.1.1980	Martens (II)	C – S	9.4.1980
18.5.1980	Martens (III)	C – S – L	7.10.1980
22.10.1980	Martens (IV)	C – S	2.4.1981
6.4.1981	M. Eyskens	C – S	9.11.1981
17.12.1981	Martens (V)	C – L	14.10.1985
7.12.1985	Martens (VI)	C – L	

Abbreviations: C = Christian-Social
S = Socialist
L = Liberal
Co = Communist
UDB = Union Démocratique Belge
VU = Volksunie
RW = Rassemblement Wallon
FDF = Front Démocratique des Francophones

fees did not prohibit parents from sending their children to Catholic schools. Although this was considered by the Christian-Socials to be quite justified, given the greater popularity of free schools compared to state schools, it provoked outrage from the opposition Socialists and Liberals.

Frustrated by four years of Christian-Social government and with the Christian-Social schools legislation reawakening anti-clericalist feelings, the Socialist and Liberal Parties found themselves forming in 1954 Belgium's first, and so far only, Socialist–Liberal two-party coalition. It was a coalition founded much more on negative feelings towards the Christian-Social Party than on any mutual attraction between the Liberals and Socialists, whose common desire to reverse Christian-Social schools legislation existed side by side with almost complete disagreement over the direction of fundamental economic policies.

After the anti-clerical coalition lost support at the 1958 election, a number of Liberal leaders began to question the utility of pursuing an electoral strategy based upon anti-clericalism and compromise with the Socialists. They argued that more would be gained from widening the party's appeal to both Catholics and non-Catholics alike – seeking, in particular, to win over the support of the Catholic middle classes traditionally attached to the Christian-Social Party for religious rather than economic reasons.

To this end the Liberal leadership initiated a number of changes during the party congresses of 1961 and 1963 giving the old Liberal Party a new name, structure and programme (see below, next section). Following these changes, the newly named Party of Liberty and Progress – *Partij voor Vrijheid en Vooruitgang/Parti de la Liberté et du Progrès* (PVV/PLP) – entered a number of bipartite coalitions with the Christian-Socials, as well as Grand Coalitions which also included the Socialists (Table 8.2). However, at no point have the Liberals ever seriously considered re-forming a two-party coalition with the Socialists. Even the Grand Coalitions with the Socialists caused unease for the Liberals and were agreed to as the only way of resolving the community crisis.[2]

PARTY ORGANISATION AND STRUCTURE

The Belgian Liberal Party of the nineteenth century corresponded very closely in its structure to the cadre party discussed in some detail by Duverger (see Duverger (1978) 63–71). It was decentralised, loosely knit and had only a small membership. Power resided at the local level and although Liberal members of parliament tended to be loyal to the party when it came to voting, any attempt to enforce a 'party line' was strongly and widely resisted.[3] Loyalty was, in fact, based on a 'common state of spirit' rather than a commitment to a specific party programme. At a time when the franchise was restricted and campaign costs low, there was little incentive to recruit a mass membership. What members there were, however, quite often participated in the pre-selection of candidates for the electoral lists following the introduction of a proportional representation electoral system in 1899. This practice of pre-selection was most common in the large multi-member *arrondissements* of Brussels, Liège, Ghent, Mons and Charleroi.

There was no attempt to carry out any major reform of the party structure during the years between the two World Wars, although some token effort was made in 1919 to create a more modernised party. Power still resided at the local and regional levels, with the 'regional liberal organisations (the Liberaal Vlaams Verbond, the Féderation Bruxelloise and the Entente Libérale Wallonne) being more important than the national party organisation in the formulation of policy' (Hill (1974) 64).

It was not until the 1960s that any organisational or structural reforms were implemented. The main impetus for change came from the national leadership, particularly Omer Vanaudenhove, who had been elected party president in May 1961. Vanaudenhove had immediately set about a 'renovation' of the old Liberal Party, by establishing various commissions whose aims were to draw up new party statutes and policies. These commissions presented their reports in August of that year and after internal party discussions, the PVV/PLP was launched on 7 October 1961.

The various policy reforms which were implemented will be discussed in the section on policy, pp. 201–7. As regards the new party statutes, their most important characteristic was a reinforcement of the president's powers by giving greater authority to the national organs of the party as well as the supremacy of national statutes over the statutes of the local and regional federations.

A major aim of such a centralisation of authority was to ensure that the PVV/PLP overtures to middle-class Catholics did not remain merely empty gestures. Before 1961, the national organs were unable, except in very exceptional cases, to intervene in the drawing up of electoral lists by each local federation. Vanaudenhove wanted the party to offer safe positions on some electoral lists to well-known Catholics with no previous attachment to the old Liberal Party. The problem was how to overcome the resistance of the local party organisations to this move. Vanaudenhove sought the solution in the reform of the party statutes. After 1961, the new statutes gave the national *Bureau Politique/Politiek Bureau* the power to reject any list which did not 'equitably represent all the different tendencies found in the PLP' unless such a list was approved by 40 per cent (or 8,000 members) of the federation's membership (article xvii). Furthermore, the *Comité de Direction* could even appeal against lists which did meet the 40 percent/8,000 members criterion (article xviib). As a result of these changes, the national leadership was able to give eighteen Catholic candidates safe or competitive places on PVV/PLP lists – 16 per cent of all Liberal safe and competitive seats – for the 1965 election (Obler (1972) 173). Although only four of these Catholics were elected (all in Wallonie), the overall success of the PVV/PLP seemed to justify Vanaudenhove's tactics, even if they had created tensions between national and local organisations within the party (Debuyst (1967) 258–9). Resistance at the local level to articles xvii and xvii(b) continued after 1965 and they were eventually modified as a result. The Francophone Liberals now have a Commission of Conciliation and Arbitration which can be requested to arbitrate over conflicts occurring during the drawing up of electoral lists.[4] For the PVV, the *Partijbureau* or *Partijraad* are able to make recommendations regarding the candidate list and the chairman of the *arrondissement fédération* is bound to submit this recommendation either to a poll of members or to the competent electoral committee (article xvii).

As regards internal party democracy, there has been a growing trend amongst the executives of the local Liberal Federations to decide upon the composition of the electoral lists without any polling of party members. In fact, it is often just the chairman and one or two other members who draw up the list of candidates, which is then submitted for approval by the full executive.[5] In 1958, over 50 per cent of elected Liberal members of parliament had been pre-selected by a poll of members. In 1971, this figure had fallen to less than 10 per cent and it has remained around this level ever since.[6]

After 1961, the next major organisational reforms within the PLP/PVV were those resulting from the growing linguistic tensions within the liberal family. In May 1972, the Flemish Liberals held a separate party congress at Blankenberge. Since this congress, the PVV has been established as an autonomous political party, with W. De Clercq elected as its first president. For the Francophone Liberals, however, there was a great deal of conflict between the PLP Wallon and PLP Bruxellois. Even before the setting up of an autonomous Walloon PLP in May 1972, a group of Liberals had already split from the Brussels PLP to form an electoral cartel with the FDF at the 1971

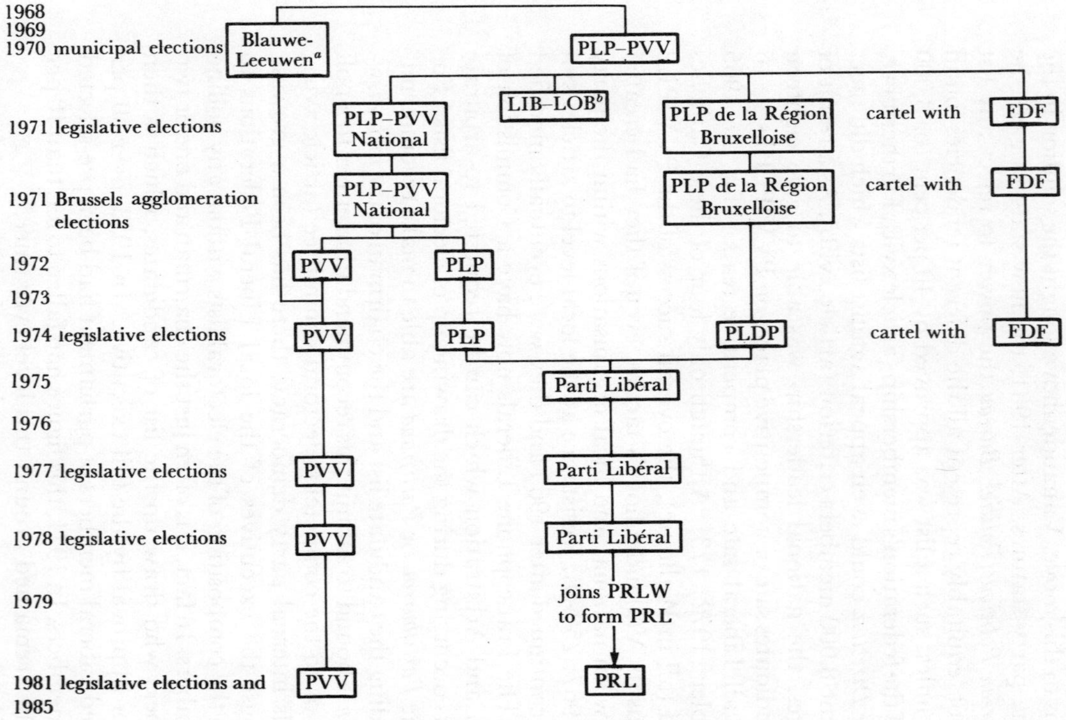

Diagram 8.1 Development of Liberal Parties in Brussels: 1968–85

Notes:

a A group of Flemish liberals who split from the PVV to form the Blauwe Leeuwen on 5 December 1969. The Blauwen Leeuwen wanted linguistic parity in the Brussels federation of the PLP–PVV.

b Parti Libéral Indépendent Beïge – Liberaal Onafhankelijk Belgische Partij, formed 31 March 1971.

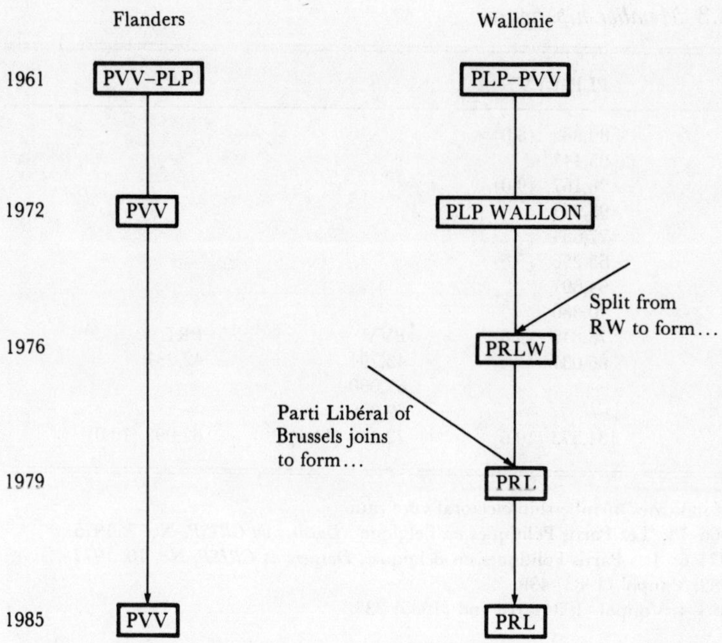

Diagram 8.2 Development of Liberal Parties in Flanders and Wallonie: 1961–85

election. This pro-FDF group, originally called the PLP de la Région Bruxelloise, fought the 1974 election under the name Parti Libéral Démocratique et Pluraliste (PLDP), again in a cartel with the FDF. The PLDP once more changed its name, this time to Parti Libéral (PL), and in 1975 most of the old unitary Brussels PLP was reabsorbed within its ranks (Diagram 8.1).

At the same time as the PL emerged, the Walloon PLP was moving towards a merger with part of the RW to form the Parti des Réformes et de la Liberté en Wallonie (PRLW) in 1976 (Diagram 8.2). Pressure for a reuniting of the PL Bruxellois and PRLW increased after a poor electoral performance by the Francophone Liberals at the 1978 election. This move eventually took place in the summer of 1979, with the creation of the PRL (Parti Réformateur Libéral). The first president of the PRL was the former RW member, Jean Gol – an indication of the extent to which the traditional unitarism of the Francophone Liberals had been modified in less than a decade.

The respective structures of the PVV and PRL are fairly similar, with a system of associations at the common level and federations at the *arrondissement* level as well as a congress, executive/bureau and a

Table 8.3 *Membership figures*

	PLP–PVV		
1966	89,882 (8.0)		
1967	95,147		
1968	98,167 (9.0)		
1969	93,273		
1970	77,654		
1971	65,256 (7.5)		
1972	64,607		
1973	70,380		
1974	76,842 (9.6)	PVV	PRL
1975	86,031	43,794	42,237
1982	—	67,000	—
1983	—	69,329	—
1984	134,573 (10.6)	72,480 (11.1)	62,093 (10.0)

Notes: ( ) indicates membership/electoral vote ratio
Sources: 1966–73: 'Les Partis Politiques en Belgique', *Dossiers du CRISP*, No. 7, 1975.
1974–6: 'Les Partis Politiques en Belgique', *Dossiers du CRISP*, No. 10, 1977.
1982: Vanpol (1983) 439.
1983–4: Vanpol (1984) 518 and (1985) 333.

permanent committee/council at the national level. Both parties have similar membership figures (Table 8.3). The 1984 figures of 72,480 for the PVV and 62,093 for the PRL represent around 10–11 per cent of their respective 1985 vote shares.

An attempt was made in the early years following the linguistic split in the liberal family to maintain some organisational links between the Flemish and Francophone Liberals. A post of joint PVV/PLP president was retained although this was finally abolished in 1976. Nevertheless, the two parties continue to share the same research institute, the Paul Hymans Centre in Brussels. Of more significance is the fact that the PVV and the PRL have, since 1979, formed in the House of Representatives (but not the Senate) a single parliamentary group with regular joint meetings, though both parties still retain an independent operational autonomy.

ELECTORAL PERFORMANCE

Since the introduction of male universal suffrage in 1919, the Liberal Party has always been Belgium's third largest party in electoral terms. Its fortunes after 1945, however, have been mixed (Table 8.4). From 1950 until 1965, the party went through a difficult period, recording some of its worst ever electoral performances. In contrast, after the

Table 8.4 *National share of vote (Lower House): 1946–85*

Year	Christian-Social	Liberal	Socialist	Communist	FDF		RW	Volksunie	Liberal–Socialist Cartel	Ecologist	Other
1946	42.5	8.9	31.6	12.7	—		—	—	1.6	—	2.7
1949	43.6	15.2	29.7	7.5	—		—	—	—	—	4.0
1950	47.7	11.2	34.5	4.7	—		—	—	1.8	—	0.1
1954	41.4	12.2	37.3	3.6	—		—	2.2	2.1	—	1.5
1958	46.5	11.0	35.8	1.9	—		—	2.0	2.1	—	0.7
1961	41.5	12.3	36.7	3.0	—		—	3.5	—	—	3.0
1965	34.4	21.6	28.3	4.6	1.3		1.0	6.7	—	—	2.1
1968	31.7	20.9	28.0	3.3	2.5		3.4	9.8	—	—	—
1971	30.0	16.4	27.3	3.1		11.3		11.1	—	—	—
1974	32.3	15.2	26.7	3.2		10.9		10.2	—	—	—
1977	35.9	14.4	26.8	2.7		7.3		9.7	—	—	3.2
					FDF	/	RW				
1978	36.3	15.5	25.4	3.2	4.3		2.9	7.0	—	—	5.0
1981	26.4	21.5	25.1	2.3		4.2		9.8	—	5.1	5.6
1985	29.3	20.9	28.4	1.2		1.2		7.9	—	6.2	11.1

Source: Witte and Craeybeckx (1981) 266; Ministry of Interior (1981 and 1985).

Table 8.5 *Liberal share of regional vote (Lower House): 1946–85*

Year	Flanders	Wallonie	Brussels Cantons
1946	7.7	9.3	13.4
1949	13.3	14.8	25.0
1950	9.4	11.5	18.4
1954	10.7	11.7	19.4
1958	9.8	10.5	18.2
1961	11.6	11.8	17.0
1965	16.6	25.8	33.4
1968	16.2	26.5	26.3
1971	16.4	17.3	13.5
1974	17.3	15.0	5.9
1977	14.4	18.8	11.8
1978	17.2	16.7	10.1
1981	21.1	21.8	21.5
1985	17.3	24.2	30.9

Source: Witte and Craeybeckx (1981) 269–70; Ministry of Interior (1981 and 1985).

reforms of the early 1960s, the Liberal vote almost doubled between the 1961 and 1965/8 elections.

However, the Liberals were unable to maintain their improved position. In 1971, the Liberal Party vote fell from 21 per cent to 16.4 per cent and afterwards fluctuated between 14 and 15 per cent until 1981. The elections of 1981 and 1985 saw a resurgence once more of the Liberal vote back to the levels of 1965–8. With the fall in the Socialist and Christian-Social vote since 1965–8, the Liberal Party is now much more on equal terms with these parties and it is certainly no longer merely the 'half' party of a 'two-and-a half' party system.

At the regional level, the Liberal Party has tended to perform better in Brussels and Wallonie than in Flanders (Table 8.5). Brussels had been a Liberal stronghold in the early decades of Belgian independence with the capital city being the centre of free-thinkers and the French-speaking commercial and industrial elites. The extension of the suffrage and the growth of working-class suburbs undermined the Liberal dominance in Brussels, even though it remained the party's strongest region until after the First World War. A continued source of Liberal appeal in Brussels and, to a lesser degree, in Wallonie was the Liberal defence of the unitary Belgian state and, as a consequence, the continued privileged position of the Francophone elites. It was, however, the failure of the Liberal Party to be sufficiently radical in the defence of the French-speaking community in Brussels which led to the collapse of the Liberal vote in the capital during the 1970s. It was only in 1985 that the Liberals recouped enough of their losses to become the largest party in Brussels for the first time since 1965.

In Wallonie, as in Brussels, the Liberals suffered heavy electoral losses during the 1970s. The Walloon Liberals (PRL) were unwilling to support the idea of greater Walloon autonomy. They were replaced by the Walloon Federalist Party, Rassemblement Wallon (RW), as Wallonie's third-largest party in 1971 and again in 1974. Liberal support increased, however, once the party came to pursue a more pro-Walloon policy following the defection to the Liberals in 1976 of a number of leading RW members, one of whom, Jean Gol, was to hold the presidency of the PRL from 1979 until 1982. By 1981, the PRL had replaced the Christian-Socials as Wallonie's second-largest party, a position it retained at the 1985 election.

For the Flemish Liberals (PVV), the gains made in 1965 and 1968 were not as significant as those for the Francophone liberals. Yet the PVV did much better than the PRL in retaining these new voters, despite being replaced by the Volksunie as Flanders' third-largest party in 1968, 1971 and 1977. Frognier provided a possible explanation for the PVV's relatively greater success than the PRL's in combating the threat posed by the community parties in his analysis of party preference spaces (Frognier (1976) 189–202). He found that voters perceived the PVV and Volksunie as being far apart, while the Liberal Parties in Brussels and Wallonie were viewed as being quite close to the FDF and RW respectively. A transfer of votes from the Liberals to the community parties was more likely, therefore, in Brussels and Wallonie than in Flanders.

In 1985, however, the PVV, unlike the PRL, suffered an electoral decline, partly due to dissatisfaction amongst PVV supporters with the party's inability to implement any radical fiscal reform or reorganisation of the social security system during three-and-a-half years in government (the measures had been similarly supported by the PRL although somewhat less publicly).

THE SOCIO-ECONOMIC COMPOSITION OF LIBERAL PARTY SUPPORT

Tables 8.6 and 8.7 set out the social composition of the electorates of the Belgian Liberal Parties over the last two decades. Both parties receive the largest share in their support from the 'middle classes' – executives, independents, professionals and white-collar workers. This is a finding consistent with the image of the Liberal Parties as promoters of free trade, private initiative, reduced taxation and less

Table 8.6 *PVV: socio-economic bases of electorate, 1965–84*

	1965–8		1975–7		1979–81		1982–4	
	%	Regional deviation	%	Regional deviation	%	Regional deviation	%	Regional deviation
Farmers	9.3	+0.3	3.0	+1.5	0.7	−0.3	0.9	+0.1
Executives, independents, free professions	38.8	+14.7	22.2	+8.0	24.9	+10.7	25.4	+15.2
White-collar workers	24.3	−1.1	16.2	+1.2	16.3	−0.8	16.4	−2.9
Blue-collar workers	25.7	−10.9	24.5	+0.7	18.3	−1.0	12.0	−9.2
Retired	2.1	−3.0	12.2	−4.9	22.5	−2.1	19.3	−2.1
Housepersons			21.8	−6.5	17.3	−6.4	25.1	−2.1
Practising Catholics	65.6	−8.4	47.2	−9.4	—	—	45.7	−4.4
Non-practising Catholics	34.5	+8.4	52.9	+9.4	—	—	54.4	+4.4
Rural areas	—	—	45.0	−11.2	57.4	−1.7	61.0	+7.4
Medium-sized towns	—	—	36.3	+6.8	24.1	−1.9	22.6	−6.3
Large towns cities	—	—	18.7	+4.4	18.6	+3.7	16.4	−1.0
Female	51.7	+1.7	45.2	+4.4	38.1	+9.0	50.9	−0.7

Source: Calculated from Delruelle et al. (1970) and Eurobarometers Nos. 3, 5, 7, 11, 13, 15, 17, 20 and 21.

Table 8.7 *PRL: socio-economic bases of electorate, 1965–84*

	1965–8		1975–7		1979–81		1982–4	
	%	Regional deviation	%	Regional deviation	%	Regional deviation	%	Regional deviation
Farmers	11.2	+3.8	11.6	+8.8	0.0	−1.7	0.7	−1.3
Executives, independents, free professions	43.9	+20.9	27.5	+13.7	31.8	+18.6	19.3	+10.0
White-collar workers	23.0	+0.94	12.0	−2.6	30.0	+9.7	25.1	+4.5
Blue-collar workers	15.8	−25.7	18.6	−1.1	4.8	−10.0	13.8	−9.7
Retired Housepersons	6.11	+0.1	14.9 15.6	−10.1 −8.4	20.9 12.6	−5.6 −11.3	19.2 21.8	−5.2 +0.5
Practising Catholics	43.9	−0.2	25.0	−6.4	—	—	8.4	−19.7
Non-practising Catholics	56.1	+0.2	75.1	+6.4	—	—	91.7	+19.7
Rural areas	—	—	43.3	+6.3	32.1	−13.8	20.8	−11.5
Medium-sized towns	—	—	17.4	−16.5	37.9	+6.8	27.0	+1.5
Large towns/cities	—	—	39.2	+10.3	29.9	+6.9	52.2	+10.0
Female	51.0	−1.8	47.4	−4.8	42.3	−12.6	5.0	+2.6

Source: see Table 8.6.

government bureaucracy. It was precisely these middle-class groups to whom the community parties appealed most during the late 1960s and 1970s, and it was this that made Liberal voters particularly prone to unpredictability in their partisan preferences (Hill (1974) 82–7). Amongst blue-collar workers on the other hand, both the PVV and PRL electorates have consistently under-represented this social group, a reflection, no doubt, of the lack of appeal of liberal economic policy to lower-income earners.

There has been an appreciable decline in the support of farmers for the Liberal Parties, almost certainly due to the overall shrinkage of this occupational group as a percentage of the total work-force, from 7.5 per cent in 1961 to 3 per cent in 1981. This, however, still leaves the Liberal Parties well represented amongst farming groups, something which does not seem to conform to the widespread view of liberalism as essentially originating and developing in a secular and urban environment. Yet it must be remembered that the clerical–anti-clerical divide in Belgium has never been simply a reflection of an urban–rural cleavage. As in both Italy and France, anti-clericalism flourished in many rural areas, where it still continues to find occasional expression even today. Since the Catholic church and the Catholic Party were so dominant in rural areas, where pockets of anti-clericalism remained, such perceptions became more resilient and ideologically entrenched precisely because of their isolated position. The PRL in particular has retained strongholds of support in the rural areas of the Ardennes, even though the bulk of Francophone Liberal support comes from the more urban and industrial areas of Wallonie.

In the absence of earlier surveys, it is difficult to assess the full impact on the Liberal appeal to practising Catholics resulting from the rejection of anti-clericalism at the 1961 Liberal Party congress. It is certainly clear, however, that the PVV's electorate, unlike that of the PRL, closely reflects the regional distribution of practising Catholics. This discrepancy between the two parties may be due to the fact that the level of religious practice in Wallonie has fallen to such a low point (less than 30 per cent in 1984, compared with 50 per cent for Flanders) that there remains a hard core of religious practicants unwilling to consider supporting the PRL. In a certain respect, such practising Catholics become as entrenched in their support for the Walloon Christian-Social Party as the anti-clerical farmers in their backing of the PRL.

In general terms, although neither of the Liberal Parties could claim to be 'catch-all' parties, their distribution of support amongst the religious and occupational categories is such that to consider the

Table 8.8 *Ministerial posts held by Liberals, 1944–81*[a]

Ministry	Number of governments in which post held	Total length of time (in years)
Justice	13	16.90
Education[b]	13	13.88
Foreign Trade	11	12.37
Finance	10	15.57
Economic	9	10.59
Middle Classes	9	12.84
Public Works	9	14.66
Defence	8	8.31
Interior	7	6.06
Vice-Prime Minister[c]	6	9.56
Institutional Reform	5	5.17
Agriculture	4	5.85
Reconstruction (ceased 1958)	4	7.85
Colonies (ceased 1958)	4	5.85
Communications	2	4.24
Budget[d]	1	1.91
Public Health	1	0.83
Brussels Region[e]	1	3.83

Footnotes:

[a] After the 1985 election the Liberals were given the following posts in the Martens VI government: Vice-Prime Minister, Justice, Institutional Reform, Budget, Science and Planning, Public Works, Transport, Foreign Trade, Defence, Middle Classes, Brussels Region, French Education.

[b] In 1968, the Education portfolio was split into two, Flemish and French.

[c] This post was first created in 1958 and was excluded from the first four Tindemans governments.

[d] This post has often been held in conjunction with another (such as Vice-Prime Minister), and has not always had full cabinet status nor been included in all governments since the Second World War.

[e] This post has only existed since 1973 and is quite often held in conjunction with another cabinet post, usually Defence or Communications.

parties as 'secular and middle class' would be misleading. Certainly their policies of lower taxes and less government bureaucracy have had considerable attraction for the affluent Belgian blue-collar worker, whilst their position on issues such as abortion and education has emphasised Liberal neutrality on religious issues (see below, section on policy, esp. p. 204).

GOVERMENT PARTICIPATION

In examining the types of ministries held by the Liberals, Table 8.8 gives a list of the portfolios most frequently held by the Liberal Party during the period 1944–85. The first point to note is that the Liberals have never held the post of Prime Minister or Foreign Minister, an indication that they have always been considered the junior member in whichever coalition they have participated. The ministries occupied frequently by Liberals correspond by and large to those we would expect liberals to be most interested in, given what has been said above concerning Liberal policy priorities, that is, concern with economic affairs and the interests of the bourgeoisie (Foreign Trade, Finance, Economic, Middle Classes, Education) and the security and stability of the state (Defence, Justice, Interior). Equally revealing is the complete absence of liberals in the 'social' departments such as Social Security, Health, Employment, Labour, Housing and Family. This results from both Liberal antipathy towards these posts as well as the greater concern for social issues expressed by the Socialist and Christian-Social Parties.

Table 8.9 compares the percentage of governmental coalition seats contributed by the Liberal Parties with the Liberal share of cabinet posts. It can be seen that until 1961 the Liberal share of ministerial portfolios was nearly always twice its seat contribution to the coalition. From 1965 until 1985, however, the Liberal shares of seats and cabinet posts was about the same. In fact, between 1966 and 1976, the Liberal Parties received slightly less than their 'fair' share of government posts. This change in situation had been brought about by the weakened bargaining position of the Liberal Parties after 1961 despite, ironically, their improved electoral performance. In the fifteen years after the Second World War, when the religious cleavage was salient and when the likelihood of a stable Christian-Social–Socialist coalition was remote, the Liberals held a pivotal position similar to that occupied during the period between the two World Wars. While the Liberals were no less anti-clerical than the Socialists, Liberal economic policy was more acceptable to the majority inside the Christian-Social Party. This position altered, however, during the 1960s. First, the religious cleavage declined in political saliency, a process to which the Liberals themselves contributed with their party reforms of 1961. Secondly, the Liberals' unitarist stand on the linguistic question and their shift to the right on economic issues, deprived them of a pivotal position on either of these two policy dimensions. With a Christian-Social–Socialist coalition successfully lasting a full four-year term of office between 1961 and 1965, the Liberals were no longer as indispensable for coalition formation as before.

POLICY

Following the end of the Second World War, the Liberal Party was influenced in the drawing up of its policy programmes by the post-war atmosphere of national solidarity and the need for national unity. The Liberals adopted a *Charte Sociale* which called for the constitutional recognition of the right to work, an increase in the number of paid holidays and the 'organisation of the economy' (Chlepner (1983) 355). At the Doctrinal Congress in April 1951 a programme was drawn up which devoted attention to both economic liberalism – private initiative, the market economy, reduced taxation, an end to nationalisations and state subsidies – as well as social objectives, such as the right to work and the maintenance of the social security system.

In the 1954 party programme, certain neo-liberal ideas began to appear for the first time, in particular the regulation of the economy by monetary policy. There was also mention of social justice and the right of the labour movement to organise and to be recognised by employers. Furthermore, the programme stated that there should be no discrimination against any social group and that the state should ensure equality of opportunity for all.

No doubt the willingness of the Liberal Party to talk about social reforms and to assign a positive role for the state to play in socio-economic life facilitated the formation of the Socialist-Liberal coalition in 1954. However, the Liberal programme remained vague in its commitment to the preservation of the Welfare State, while there was always an unmistakable emphasis placed upon the values of individualism and private initiative.

After the signing of the Schools Pact in 1958, the Liberals gradually began to shift away from their brief flirtation with the policies of social-welfare liberalism. Increasingly, the Liberal Party came to present itself as the sole defender of economic freedom and the interests of the middle classes (both Catholics and non-Catholics). It criticised the Christian-Social Party for being a 'prisoner of its Flemish wing, a party of taxes and giving in to trade-union pressures' (*Courrier Hebdomadaire* 1964, p. 5; author's translation). The Liberals blamed Christian-Social weakness for the failure of the Christian-Social–Liberal coalition of 1960–1 to introduce wide-ranging economic austerity measures.

When the PVV/PLP was formed in 1961, even though Vanaudenhove had initially talked of setting up a new party of the centre, the PVV/PLP's programme was clearly oriented towards the middle classes with the hope of 'regrouping the right' and fostering *bipartisme*

Table 8.9 *Liberal Party government participation: seats and cabinet posts, 1946–85*

Government	Coalition partners	% Liberal seats of total coalition seats	% Liberal Cabinet Posts[a]	Cabinet posts
Van Acker III (1946)	Socialist, Communist	15.6 (17)	31.5 (6)	Interior, Justice, Agriculture, Economic, Colonies, Foreign Trade.
Huysmans (1946–7)	Socialist, Communist	15.6 (17)	31.5 (6)	Interior, Justice, Agriculture, Economic, Colonies, Foreign Trade.
Eyskens I (1949–50)	Christian-Social	21.6 (29)	47.0 (8)	Education, Justice, Finance, Public Works, Defence, Public Health, Reconstruction, W.P.[b]
Van Acker IV (1954–8)	Socialist	22.5 (25)	43.8 (7)	Justice, Finance, Agriculture, Economic, Colonies, Middle Classes, Public Works and Reconstruction.
Eyskens III (1958–60)	Christian-Social	16.8 (21)	36.8 (7)	Vice-PM, Foreign Trade, Interior, Education, Justice, Economic, Public Works and Reconstruction.
Eyskens IV (1960–1)	Christian-Social	16.8 (21)	35.0 (7)	Vice-PM and Interior, Foreign Trade, Education, Justice, Economic, Institutional Reform, Public Works and Reconstruction.
Vanden Boeynants I (1966–8)	Christian-Social	38.4 (48)	36.8 (7)	Vice-PM and Budget, Economic, Finance, Education, Interior, Defence, Foreign Trade.
Leburton (1973–74)	Christian-Social, Socialist	21.0 (34)	18.2 (4)	Vice-PM and Finance, Justice, Middle Classes, Education (Francophone)
Tindemans I (1974)	Christian-Social	31.4 (33)	30.0 (6)	Justice, Finance, Foreign Trade, Middle Classes, Public Works, Education (Flemish)
Tindemans II (1974–6)	Christian-Social, RW	28.0 (33)	26.0 (6)	as above
Tindemans III (1976–7)	Christian-Social, RW	28.0 (33)	32.0 (8)	as above, plus Civil Service and Institutional Reform (Francophone).
Tindemans IV (1977)	Christian-Social	31.4 (33)	32.0 (8)	as above

Martens III (1980)	Christian-Social, Socialist	20.3 (36)	22.2 (4)	Vice-PM and Justice and Institutional Reform (Flemish), Finance, Defence, Communications
Martens V (1981–5)	Christian-Social	46.0 (52)	46.7 (7)	Vice-PM and Justice and Institutional Reform (Francophone), Vice-PM and Finance and Foreign Trade, Public Works, Communications, Defence, Education (Francophone), Brussels Region and Middle Classes
Martens VI (1985–)	Christian-Social	40.0 (46)	46.7 (7)	Vice-PM and Justice and Institutional Reform (Francophone), Vice-PM and Budget and Science and Plan, Public Works, Transport and Foreign Trade, Middle Classes, Defence and Brussels Region, Education (Francophone)

Notes:
[a] The number of cabinet posts is based on the total number of ministers and not the total number of ministerial portfolios.
[b] W.P. = without portfolio.

(Trencavel (1970) 391). The emphasis was clearly on economic growth, the need to reduce taxation and achieve a balanced budget. In seeking to protect the individual from pressure groups, the Liberals gave little recognition to the role played by such groups, particularly trade unions. Before 1961 there had been fairly close links between the Liberal Party and the Centrale Générale des Syndicats Libéraux de Belgique/Algemene Centrale der Liberale Vakbonden van Belgie (CGSLB/ACLVB). With the increasingly anti-trade union stance of the Liberals, however, the CGSLB/ACLVB has come to distance itself from the PVV/PRL.

Since shedding its anti-clerical image in 1961, the PVV/PRL has attempted to remain neutral on questions of religion and private morality. With the resurfacing of the schools issue which brought a halt to the work of the Commission du Pacte Scolaire/Schoolpactcommissie in 1985 for the first time since its establishment in 1958, the Liberals were careful to allow the Socialists to take the responsibility for criticising the alleged unfair advantages given to Catholic schools in the proposed government legislation over education subsidies.

With regard to abortion, there has been a difference of opinion between the PVV and PRL, something which is no doubt partly a reflection of the differences in the respective electorates of the two parties (Tables 8.6 and 8.7). In a parliamentary vote in 1982 on the temporary suspension for two years of those articles of the criminal code relating to abortion, twenty-one Liberals voted against (PVV 17, PRL 4) whilst twenty-two voted in favour (PVV 7, PRL 15) (*Courrier Hebdomadaire* (1982)). These figures indicate a difference not only between the PRL and the PVV but also show that both parties face the problem of reconciling their support for individual freedom in the economic field with conservative positions on moral issues. There is, also, no doubt that the fact of the need to attract Catholic voters encourages a more pragmatic approach to the question of abortion than would otherwise be the case, particularly as the Christian-Social Parties are the only realistic coalition partners for the PVV/PRL (at the national level, at least).

The one area in which there has been a significant shift in the Liberal Parties' position during the last twenty-five years has been over linguistic conflicts. In the 1961 manifesto, the Liberal Party expressly committed itself to maintaining Belgium as a unitary state with the party itself remaining organisationally united at the national level. This was not just a reflex defence of the status quo but a reflection of genuine opposition to any movement which would weaken the nation-state, hinder Belgian economic development and infringe individual free choice over the use of language. The most the Liberals would concede was a limited decentralisation in the sphere of cultural affairs.

Such a unitarist strategy chosen by the national leadership did not, however, meet with the universal approval at the grass-roots level. In May 1962, a break-away group of Liberals in Liège established the Mouvement Libéral Wallon, whilst in Brussels a separate group of Flemish Liberals was formed as one result of the official Liberal Brussels Federation's refusal to guarantee places on the electoral lists for Flemish Liberals. During the 1970s, the PVV and PRL came to adopt clearer policies in defence of specific regional and community interests. This has often led to conflicts between the two, particularly with regard to the status of Brussels.

Outside the linguistic field, there are no really fundamental disagreements between the PRL and the PVV over policy. There are, however, some differences as regards both style and short-term political tactics with such differences becoming more pronounced during the first half of the 1980s. The PVV has projected a much stronger ideological profile since its 1979 Kortrijk conference than its sister Francophone party. Whilst the PVV has publicly committed itself to radical reforms of the tax and social security system, the PRL, although equally committed to these aims, has chosen to present a more pragmatic image to the electorate.

Also, while both parties have tried to present themselves as parties of the centre, the PRL has sought to do so by emphasising its differences from its usual coalition partner and the other contender for the political centre in Wallonie, the Walloon Christian-Socials. The PVV has not done the same *vis-à-vis* the Flemish Christian-Social Party. In fact, during the 1985 election campaign the PVV leader, Guy Verhofstadt, announced that a vote for the PVV was also a vote for the CVP given that both parties had publicly announced their willingness to participate together once again in a Christian-Social–Liberal coalition government. This was a major electoral blunder on the part of the PVV, almost certainly contributing significantly to its loss of votes in 1985.[7]

Allowing for the differences in linguistic policy as well as electoral tactics, Table 8.10 summarises the results of a content analysis of Liberal Party manifestos divided into two periods, the first before and the second after the reform of 1961.[8] Issues that are common to both periods are as follows: free enterprise, economic orthodoxy, middle classes, government efficiency, and agriculture and farmers. The old Liberal Party of 1946–61 devoted more attention to social justice and labour groups and they were also opposed to the division of society

Table 8.10 *The top eleven issues most frequently mentioned in Liberal Party manifestos*

	1946–61	1965–81
1.	Free enterprise[a]	Middle classes[a]
2.	Economic orthodoxy[a]	Free enterprise[a]
3.	Middle classes[a]	Decentralisation (positive)
4.	Agriculture and farmers[a]	Economic orthodoxy[a]
5.	Technology and infrastructure[a]	Unemployment
6.	Government efficiency[a]	National effort and social harmony[a]
7.	Underprivileged minorities[a]	Democracy
8.	Communalism (negative)[a]	Freedom and human rights[a]
9.	Social justice	Art, sport, leisure, media
10.	Congo	Agriculture and farmers[a]
11.	Labour groups (positive)	Government efficiency[a]

[a] Denotes these issues mentioned more by the Liberal Parties than any other party
Source: see note 9.

into religious, class or linguistic sub-groups (*Communalism negative*). This reflects the Liberal Party's unitarist stand, its opposition to a separate Catholic educational system, its recognition of trade-union rights and a clearly positive evaluation of Belgium's welfare system. After 1961, there is a shift of emphasis away from social welfarism towards the defence of individual freedoms (for example, freedom from bureaucratic control, freedom of choice in education) and a more explicitly expressed support of domestic institutions in general.

Overall, the Belgian Liberals have, in terms of policy at least, moved towards a position of radical liberalism since the 1960s.[9] This neo-liberalism as it has been called, with its attacks on the bureaucratisation of society and high taxation, has popular backing in Belgium as demonstrated by the upsurge in Liberal electoral support in the 1980s. Such principles can be clearly contrasted with the social-welfare liberalism of the 1940s and 1950s. Many former 'moderate' Liberals have become converted to this radical liberalism.[10]

This radical liberalism has, however, coexisted rather uneasily with the very conservative position taken by the PVV/PRL with regard to individual behaviour and civil liberties. The Liberals have consistently emphasised the need for a strong nation-state and the guaranteeing of a high priority for the maintenance of law and order. Of all the major political parties in Belgium, the Liberals are the ones most committed to continued NATO membership, the siting of cruise missiles in the country and the lengthening of compulsory military service. As Justice Minister (1981–), Jean Gol has been the motivating force behind the legislation restricting immigration (*Loi Gol* of June 1984), the strengthening of the security forces (one of the few areas where greater public spending is supported by the Liberals), wider police powers in respect of the prevention of acts of terrorism and greater control over public demonstrations.

It is interesting to note that the radical liberalism of the PVV/PRL has not gone unnoticed by the other liberal parties of Western Europe. During the Liberal International conference in 1985, the Belgian liberals found themselves in a minority over issues such as voting rights for immigrants working in the EEC, more popular control of police forces and opposition to the American Strategic Defense Initiative (SDI). This brought an accusation by Gol that the Liberal International was too much to the left. He threatened to withdraw the PRL and to ask for observer status in the International Democratic Union (a group which includes the British Conservative Party).

STRATEGY OF THE BELGIAN LIBERAL PARTIES

In examining the coalition of strategy of the Liberal Parties, a distinction needs to be made between the national, regional and provincial levels of government.

At the national level, the Liberals have rarely considered the Socialist Parties as viable long-term coalition partners. With hindsight, the 1954–8 Liberal–Socialist alliance was an exception, unlikely to be repeated in the foreseeable future. Once economic issues became a major political priority, with the main policy options being reflation versus deflation, little common ground remained between the Socialists and Liberals. Even in the three-party Grand Coalitions, the Socialists and Liberals found it difficult to cohabitate, a fact exemplified by the latter leaving the Martens III coalition in 1980 over Socialist opposition to further austerity measures.[11] The Socialists in turn refused to consider any future coalitions which included the Liberals, preferring if necessary to go into opposition as in 1981.

The departure from the Martens III government demonstrated that the Liberal Parties are not purely power seeking. Recognising the growing electoral popularity in the late 1970s of neo-liberal policies, the Liberal leadership emphasised more and more their detailed policy solutions for Belgium's economic problems. It was precisely this emphasis on policies which was to lose the PVV votes at the 1985 election (Rudd (1986) 284). Similarly, the negotiations between the Christian-Socials and Liberals for the forming of the

Martens VI coalition were unexpectedly lengthy due to the Liberal leaders, especially the Flemish, demanding the discussion of policy details rather than just general agreements on broad policy objectives.

In 1980, another level was added to the Belgian system of government – the regional and community councils. Until 1985, the composition of the executives of these councils was based on a strict proportional representation of the parties with the presidency of the executive going to the largest political group. Following the 1985 national election, the proportionality principle for the executive was abandoned, thus opening the way for the 'normal play' of coalition bargaining. Given the movement towards a Christian-Social–Liberal coalition at the national level, pressure was exerted on the various party leaderships to achieve the same coalition formation in the regions and communities. In Flanders, the PVV readily accepted a coalition with the Christian-Socials. An alternative majority coalition between the PVV, Socialists and Flemish Nationalists was unacceptable to the PVV because of the Socialists' radical economic policy and their demand that the US cruise missiles be unconditionally withdrawn from Belgian territory. In Wallonie, however, the PRL was more receptive to a coalition involving the Francophone Socialists. The Francophone Socialists were more moderate in their economic proposals than their Flemish counterparts and were opposed to any unilateral withdrawal of the cruise missiles. The Francophone Christian-Socials, however, wanted to exclude the Socialists from both the Francophone community and Walloon regional executives. This factor, together with the pressure from the national party leaders to avoid asymmetrical coalitions at the national and community or regional levels, eventually brought about a Christian-Social–PRL coalition for both executives.

When looking at the third tier of government in Belgium, the nine provinces, two points have to be kept in mind. First, the provinces have very few powers and, consequently, limited political influence. Secondly, there is an incompatibility between the holding of provincial and national offices (Loeb-Mayer (1986) 21). Both these points reduce the interest of the central party leadership in the political affairs of the provinces, enabling local factors to play a greater influence in coalition formation. In the Walloon province of Luxemburg, Socialist–Liberal coalitions have been formed since 1968, following the tradition of the anti-clerical Socialist–Liberal electoral cartels for the national elections of 1946, 1950 and 1954. Socialist–Liberal coalitions were also formed in the Walloon provinces of Liège and Namur in 1985 despite the simultaneous formation of Christian-Social–Liberal coalitions at the national, regional and community levels.

In the Flemish provinces there is less of a tradition of anti-clerical coalitions between Liberals and Socialists than in Wallonie. Instead, the usual alliance is between the Christian-Socials and Socialists. So, while the PRL benefited from the relative autonomy of the provincial electoral arena by coalescing with the Socialists in three of the four Walloon provinces in 1985, the PVV found itself excluded from power in all but one of the Flemish provinces.

CONCLUSION

During the one hundred and forty years of its existence, the Belgian Liberal Party(-ies) has (have), not surprisingly, undergone a number of important changes. Most dramatic of these was undoubtedly the dropping of the liberal anti-clerical heritage in 1961 and the acceptance during the 1970s of the end of the traditional Belgian unitary state.

Despite such changes, however, many continuities and similarities run throughout the history of organised liberalism in Belgium. Although the structure and organisation of the parties were significantly modified in 1961, the greater centralisation of decision-making still left a cadre party intact, essentially a party of local notables and political personalities such as De Clercq, Daems, Vanderpoorten, Grootjans, De Croo, Gol, Michel and Damseaux. The party remains small in terms of members, a factor that helps to prevent internal factionalism by fostering *tendances* around individuals rather than different policy priorities.

Liberal policy, in the nineteenth century, combined social *laissez-faire* with a similar principle held in the field of economics except for the recognition that the need for a strong nation-state might sometimes require active government participation. These liberal principles were retained unchanged throughout the period between the two World Wars. After 1945 the Liberal Party came to accept the establishment and the underlying principles of a Welfare State system. It became openly committed in its party manifesto to genuine social change although it always asserted the necessity of preserving the central tenets of a free market economy. It is certainly revealing to note that there is little or no mention in any post-Second World War Liberal manifesto of issues such as nationalisation, economic planning, regulation of capitalism or Keynesian demand management.

After 1961, as if in reaction to an 'excessive' growth in the Welfare State, Liberal policy became increasingly radical with regard to economic policy. On social issues, however, the contemporary Belgian Liberals have clearly become more conservative than their predecessors. Judging from the recent electoral successes of the PVV/PRL, it would appear that this particular combination of radical economic liberalism and social conservatism has found considerable popular support in Belgium, although its long-term attraction cannot be predicted on the basis of a couple of good election results. After all, similar predictions were made and unfulfilled following the 1965 and 1968 elections.

NOTES

* I am grateful to David Broughton, Emil Kirchner, Nicole Loeb-Mayer, Hugh Berrington and John Fitzmaurice for their comments on earlier drafts of this chapter. My special thanks go to Jan Engels, Director of the Liberal Research Centre in Brussels, for all his help and assistance and to the Department of Government, University of Essex, for providing financial support for this research.

1 Between 1848 and 1893, the right to vote was only given to those paying a minimum of 20 florins in direct tax. Such a system was open to manipulation by governments simply by means of fiscal legislation which could increase or decrease the amount of tax paid. Such manipulation was practised by the Liberals to the detriment of the Catholics in 1878, 1879 and 1881 (Jan De Meyer (1969) 50).

2 During the 1970s, the community conflict revolved around the question of the composition and competences of the newly created community and regional councils. The constitution stipulated that legislation concerning these bodies 'must be passed with a majority vote within each linguistic group' as well as a two-thirds majority of the total votes cast. A coalition of the three largest parties was the only way to guarantee such majorities, once it became obvious that coalitions including the community parties were unworkable.

3 Voting discipline in parliament after 1945 has remained very high for the Liberal Parties (see L. Holvoet (1980)).

4 The request can be made by the party president, the bureau of the party, a provincial or *arrondissement* federation, the federation of Young Liberals or the Brussels region (article 8.2).

5 J. Engels, Director of the Centre Paul Hymans/Paul Hymans Centrum, communication with the author.

6 A similar decline in the use of internal party polls is also found in the Christian-Social and Socialist Parties (De Winter (1980)).

7 Analyses of voter changes between 1981 and 1985 show that there was a net gain of voters by the CVP from the PVV of around 63,000–72,000 (Swyngedouw (1985) 6).

8 The author wishes to thank Dr Derek Hearl of Essex University who gave permission to use the results of his analysis of post-Second World War Belgian party election manifestos.

9 This term should not be confused with the radical liberals of the late nineteenth and early twentieth century who were to the left of the progressive liberals. These radical liberals found themselves equally at home in the Socialist Party. The contemporary radical liberal, however, is clearly on the right wing of the party. A leading radical liberal has been Guy Verhofstadt, former PVV youth leader and

chairman of the party from 1982 to 1985. He became Vice-Prime Minister and Minister for Budget in the Martens VI government. Verhofstadt was influential in drawing up the 1979 PVV Kortrijk manifesto in which the term 'radical liberalism' was used in reference to the various proposals to reassert the freedom of the market, encourage private initiative and 'roll back the state'.

10 One well-known 'convert' to radical liberalism has been the recently elected president of the PVV, Annemie Neyts (see *Le Soir*, 24/25 December 1985 and *De Standaard*, 21/22 December 1985).

11 See M. Platel (1981) and H. Lemaître (1982) ch. 12.

REFERENCES

Chlepner, B.S. (1983) *Cent ans d'histoire sociale en Belgique* (Brussels: Editions de l'Université de Bruxelles).

Courrier Hebdomadaire (1961) 'La réforme du parti libéral: naissance du parti de la liberté de du progrès – PLP' no. 125 (Brussels: Centre du Recherche et d'Information Socio-Politiques – CRISP).

Courrier Hebdomadaire (1962) 'Le PLP: situation interne et perspectives politiques' no. 160 (Brussels: CRISP).

Courrier Hebdomadaire (1964) 'Facteurs de changements dans le monde catholique, socialiste et libéral, à la veille des élections communales d'octobre 1964' part 4, no. 257 (Brussels: CRISP).

Courrier Hebdomadaire (1965) 'Le PLP et les élections du 23 mai 1965' no. 289 (Brussels: CRISP).

Courrier Hebdomadaire (1966) 'Le Congrès du PLP des 22 et 23 janvier 1966' no. 313 (Brussels: CRISP).

Courrier Hebdomadaire (1969) 'Bilan d'une présidence au PLP: Omer Vanaudenhove (1961–1969)' nos. 434–5 (Brussels: CRISP).

Courrier Hebdomadaire (1971) 'Structure et évolution du "Monde Libéral" en Belgique' nos. 523–4 (Brussels: CRISP).

Courrier Hebdomadaire (1982), 'Les partis devant le problème de l'avortement' no. 962 (Brussels: CRISP).

Debuyst, F. (1967) *La Formation Parlementaire en Belgique* (Brussels: CRISP).

Delruelle, N. and R. Evalenko and W. Fraeys (1970) *Le comportement politique des électeurs belges* (Brussels: Institut de Sociologie de l'Université Libre de Bruxelles).

Duverger, M. (1978) *Political Parties: Their Organisation and Activity in the Modern State* (London: Methuen).

Dossiers du CRISP (1975) *Les Partis Politiques en Belgique*, no. 7 (Brussels: CRISP).

Dossiers du CRISP (1977) *Les Partis Politiques en Belgique*, no. 10 (Brussels: CRISP).

Fitzmaurice, J. (1983) *The Politics of Belgium* (London: Hurst).

Frognier, A.-P. (1976) 'Party preference spaces and voting change in Belgium' in *Party Identification and Beyond*, ed. by I. Budge and I. Crewe and D. Darlie (London: Wiley).

Gilissen J. (1958) *Le régime représentatif en Belgique depuis 1790* (Brussels: La Renaissance du Livre).

Gol, J. (1985) *L'Optimisme de la volonté* (Brussels: Legrain).

Hartmann, J. (1978) 'Belgien' in *Die Politischen Parteien in Westeuropa*, ed. by J. Raschke (Hamburg: Rowohlt) 46–67.

Hascal, V. (1977) *Parti Libéral et P.L.P. Brève histoire de la famille libérale au XXe siècle* (Brussels: Centre Paul Hymans).

Hascal, V. and M. Detaille (1981) 'Vingt ans de libéralisme en Wallonie et à Bruxelles', *Res Publica* 23: 2–3, 345–58.

Hill, K. (1974) 'Belgium: political change in a segmented society' in *Electoral Behaviour*, ed. by R. Rose (New York: Free Press) 29–107.

Höjer, C.-H. (1969) *Le régime parlementaire belge de 1918 à 1940* (Brussels: CRISP).

Holvoet, L. (1980) 'De stemmingen over het investituurdebat in kamer en senaat', *Res Publica*, 22: 1–2, 35–76.

Hymans, P. (1930) *L'Oeuvre Libérale d'un Siècle (1830–1930)* (Brussels: Conseil National du Parti Libéral).

Kossmann, E.H. (1978) *The Low Countries* (Oxford: Clarendon Press).

Lemaître, H. (1982) *Les gouvernements belges de 1968 à 1980. Processus de crise* (Stavelot: Editions J. Chauveheid).

Loeb-Mayer, N. (1986) 'Sub-national coalitions in Belgium. Linkages with the national coalitions and the party system', paper presented at the ECPR Workshop on *Political Parties and Coalition Behaviour in Western Europe: the perspective of local politics*, Göteborg.

Luykx, Th. (1978a) *Politieke geschiedenis van belgië 1789–1944* (Amsterdam–Brussels: Elsevier).

Luykx, Th. (1978b) *Politieke geschiedenis van belgië 1944–1977* (Amsterdam–Brussels: Elsevier).

Mabille, X. (1979) 'Le système des partis dans la Belgique post-unitaire (1971–1979)', *Courrier Hebdomadaire*, no. 864, (Brussels: CRISP).

De Meyer, J. (1969) 'Elections et partis en Belgique', *Verfassung und Verfassungswirklichkeit* 4, 49–81.

Ministère de l'intérieur (1981) 'Résultats officiels du 8 novembre 1981' (Brussels).

Ministère de l'intérieur (1985) 'Résultats oficiels du 13 octobre 1985' (Brussels).

Mirroir, A. (1982) 'Le syndicalisme libéral (1894–1961). Contribution à l'étude des familles politiques', *Belgisch Tijdschrift voor Geschiedenis*, 13: 1, 59–82.

Moiné, W. (1970) *Résultats des élections belges entre 1847 et 1914* (Brussels: Bibliothèque de l'Institut Belge de Science Politique).

Obler, J. (1972) 'The role of national party leaders in the selection of parliamentary candidates'. *Comparative Politics* 5, 159–84.

Pirenne, H. (1948) *Histoire de Belgique*, Vol. 7, (Brussels: Lamertin).

Platel, M. (1981) 'Martens I, II, III, IV', *Res Publica*, 23: 2–3, 239–76.

Rudd, C. (1986) 'The aftermath of Heysel: the 1985 Belgian election', *West European Politics*, 9: 2, 282–8.

Swyngedouw, M. (1985) 'De veranderingen van het kiesgedrag in Vlaanderen bij de parlementsverkiezingen van 1981 en 1985. Een statistische analyse', Bulletin no. 10 van de vakgroep 'Methoden van Sociologisch Onderzoek', Sociology Department, Louvain University, Belgium.

Trencavel (1970) 'Le PLP désemparé', *Revue Nouvelle*, 389–97.

Vanpol, I. (1983) 'Morfologie van de Vlaamse politieke partijen in 1982', *Res Publica*, 25: 2–3, 417–73.

Vanpol, I. (1984) 'Morphologie des partis politiques francophones en 1983', *Res Publica*, 26: 4, 502–40.

Vanpol, I. (1985) 'Morfologie van de Vlaamse politieke partijen in 1983 en 1984', *Res Publica* 27: 2–3, 311–67.

De Winter, L. (1980) 'Twintig jaar polls, of de teloorgang van een vorm van interne partijdemocratie', *Res Publica*, 22: 4, 563–85.

Witte, E. and J. Craeybeckx (1981) *Politieke geschiedenis van Belgie sinds 1830* (Antwerp: Standaard Wetenschappelijke Uitgeverij).

9

The Freiheitliche Partei Österreichs: protest party or governing party?

K.R. Luther

INTRODUCTION

The subject of this essay is the Freiheitliche Partei Österreichs (FPÖ), traditionally translated into English as the Freedom Party of Austria. It is a party with numerous internal contradictions, especially of an ideological nature. For years after its launch in 1956, it was almost universally reviled in Austria as a party of old Nazis. In 1979 it joined the Liberal International and now wishes to be known in English as the Liberal party of Austria. In 1983, the FPÖ commenced its first ever period of federal governmental office, and in a coalition with the Socialists at that.

This essay seeks to explain the FPÖ's transition from a party of protest to a party of government. First, it will show that the FPÖ's contradictions are a hallmark of the political tradition from which it derives. Secondly, it will examine the current tensions and conflicts in the FPÖ's organisation. Thirdly, I shall look at the party's often precarious electoral situation, concentrating in particular upon the profile of its protest voters, who have traditionally constituted a substantial proportion of the FPÖ's electoral support. Then, I shall outline the programmatic development of the party, with special reference to the most recent developments in the relationship between the FPÖ's national and liberal traditions. The penultimate section of this paper will concentrate upon the party's experience in government. Here the party appears to have had some success in one of its major objectives, namely to start reducing the influence of Austria's very powerful and ubiquitous system of *Proporz* (the party-political allocation of public offices). Finally, the threads of this exposition will be drawn together and some consideration given to the strategy and likely prospects of this very interesting, but academically neglected, political phenomenon.

THE HISTORY OF THE 'THIRD LAGER'

The monarchy

According to its self-perception and the judgement of most political observers, the FPÖ is merely the latest party-political manifestation of the third of Austria's *Lager* or camps: the National-Liberal one.[1] The *Lager* theory (Wandruszka (1957)) – though not without its critics (Fritzl and Uitz (1975)) – still constitutes the most widely utilised paradigm for the analysis of Austria's party system. Wandruszka argues that Austrian politics has been characterised by the coexistence of three encapsulated subcultures, each with its own political party, which emerged in the 1880s in response to the perceived failings of Austria's short-lived experiment with *laissez-faire*. These *Lager* were organised in defence of economically marginalised groups. The Socialists' clientele was primarily the urban proletariat, the Christian-Socials' was the *petite bourgeoisie* and peasantry, while the *völkisch* National-Liberals recruited especially well among intellectuals and *Beamte* (civil servants). Academic groups had always been in the vanguard of German nationalism. *Beamte*, imbued with a Josephinian ethic of enlightened state service and respect for constitutional authority, had traditionally been a pillar of liberalism. The discrediting of economic liberalism was one reason for the marriage of these two groups. Another was the fear of the *Beamte* that the German speakers' cultural, political – but above all their administrative – ascendancy within the monarchy, was now severely threatened by the other nationalities. German nationalism was seen as the answer.

But the *Third Lager's* nationalism soon changed from the rational, liberal variety of 1848 to an irrational racism tinged with Darwinism. This was clearly inconsistent with social liberalism. Having repudiated economic liberalism, the *Lager's* remaining liberal principles were anti-clericalism and constitutionalism. The former was shared by the nationals, but was interpreted much more aggressively as opposition to the Catholic Habsburg state, which was seen as dependent upon Rome and antithetical to German unity. Some vociferous factions openly advocated German unity under Prussian leadership. Such sentiments grew at the expense of constitutionalism and liberalism, highlighting the tension between national and state loyalties. This ambivalence has been a characteristic of the *Lager*, with attitudes ranging from national anti-system protest to liberalism and governmental participation.

Consequently, while the Socialists and Christian-Socials developed into highly-organised mass parties with vertically integrated and encapsulated subcultures, the National-Liberals did not. They were fragmented at the elite level into a multitude of parties and factions based upon notables, while at the grass-roots level they were organised around a plethora of sporting and similar cultural associations. This organisational deficit was never made up and helps explain the relative weakness of the *Third Lager* ever since.

The First Republic

In 1920 the Greater German People's Party (GdVP) emerged as a union of seventeen *Third Lager* parties, and in 1922 rural National-Liberals set up the Landbund (Agrarian League). Meanwhile, the radical National Socialists spurned all merger suggestions. The genesis of the GdVP testifies to the independence from the grass-roots of the parliamentary notables, as does the fluidity of First Republic electoral alliances, which make analysing the First Republic vote hazardous. Nonetheless, the unmistakable message of Table 9.1 is a gradual decline in the *Third Lager* vote. No consistent geographical pattern is visible, other than that Carinthia always had the highest concentration of the vote, usually closely followed by Burgenland. This was partly a reflection of the enduring problem of frontier demarcation and, in the case of Carinthia, of the status of the non-German ethnic minority. GdVP voters were largely urban and Landbund voters overwhelmingly rural (Simon (1957) 182 and 193). *Third Lager* support was greatest in Protestant communities (historically opposed to the Catholic, state-building Habsburg elite) and among the middle-class intelligentsia (Simon (1957) 223ff. and 138ff.).

Though the National-Liberals never succeeded in gaining more than 15.1 per cent of the National Council seats, the GdVP and Landbund were virtually indispensable for coalition formation. One or other party was in almost every government from 1919 to 1933. Of the ministerial portfolios held in these years, those of Justice, Trade, and the Interior were most frequent. To these was added the post of vice-chancellor.

Why this persistent success in achieving federal governmental office should have had an adverse effect upon the *National Lager* can perhaps best be explained by a consideration of its programmatic goals (Berchtold (1967)), the two main themes of which were *völkisch*

Table 9.1 *National electoral performance between the two World Wars*

	1919[a]	1920 German Nationals	1923 GdVP and Landbund	1927 GdVP	Landbund[c]	1930 National Economic Block and Landbund
Vote %	18.4	16.7	12.8	—	6.3	11.6
Seats %	15.1	15.3	9.1	—	12.7	11.5
Number of seats	(26)	(28)	(10)(5)	(12)	(9)	(10)(9)
Vienna	14.4	10.5	5.2	—	0.3	10
Lower Austria	20.8	16.4	10.4	—	3.0	8
Styria	25.6	23.4	19.0	—	16.0	17
Upper Austria	25.8	17.3	15.2	—	9.0	7
Carinthia	32.7	31.5	38.1	—	27.0	22
Tyrol	17.2	15.0	10.0	—	1.0	1
Salzburg	27.3	23.9	15.1	—	6.0	13
Burgenland[b]	—	30.1	21.9	—	17.0	16
Vorarlberg	16.2	21.6	17.3	—	5.0	21

Source: Total Austrian result cf. ÖJP, 1980, Vienna 1981, 606f. Land details cf. data supplied in 1981 by Austrian Central Statistical Office.
[a] Includes all German-national parties except German–Austrian People's Party and (in Vienna and Lower Austria) four small 'democratic' parties.
[b] Burgenland joined the Republic late. Its first national council election was on 18.6.1922.
[c] In 1927 the GdVP campaigned on a 'unity list' with the Christian-Socials. Therefore no data on the GdVP vote are available.

community and *Anschluss*. The former provided a rationalisation for economic intervention and anti-Semitism, while the long-term nature of the latter goal meant that, in the short term, the party undertook to execute both domestic and foreign policy decisions in a manner that would facilitate the synchronisation of Austria and Germany.

The GdVP and Landbund's 'pragmatism' once in office clearly enhanced their image as responsible parties of government, but there was a price to pay. First, a coalition with the Christian-Socials offended the *Third Lager's* strong anti-clerical tradition. Second, the bourgeois coalition implemented a number of economic austerity policies, including cutting 100,000 civil servants. These people were core supporters of the GdVP and thus, while agreement to the cuts might be viewed as placing the interest of the state over self-interest, it was politically disastrous, resulting in a loss of half the party's parliamentary seats. The final and most general point is that the very fact of participation in the Austrian state led to the GdVP and

Landbund being perceived by the more radical elements in the *Lager* as collaborators in, and thus maintainers of, an externally imposed system fundamentally incompatible with the goals of German *Volksgemeinschaft* and *Anschluss*. The long-standing conflict between the constitutionalist/statist tradition and that of anti-system protest grew apace. In January 1932 the parliamentary GdVP was forced to withdraw from the coalition. The more homogeneous Landbund, in tune with the increasingly influential corporatist ideas, continued in government until September 1933.

Meanwhile, at the grass-roots level of the *Third Lager*, a number of fateful developments occurred in the early 1930s. As the already tenuous links of the numerous associations to the parliamentary parties became even more strained and disaffection from the state grew, the National Socialists' influence increased. The relentless surge of the Nazis eventually engulfed the parliamentary elite also. In May 1933, the National Socialists signed an agreement with the GdVP, which effectively signalled the end of the latter's independence.

The Second Republic

Broadly speaking, there have been two interpretations of the process by which the *Third Lager* became national socialist. The more charitable version (e.g. Wandruszka (1957)), is that the *Lager* was captured or 'conquered' by the National Socialists, who are thus depicted as external and antithetical to the *Lager*. The less charitable version (e.g. Perchinig (1983)), however, sees the National Socialists as the embodiment of a long-standing tradition within the *Third Lager* and their success in assimilating the other component parts of the *Lager* as indicative of the whole *Lager's* sympathy for pan-Germanic, anti-Semitic, anti-democratic, and similar values. The FPÖ, the current party of the *Third Lager*, argues that German nationalism was common to all parties and anti-Semitism was at least as strongly articulated by the conservative *Lager*. Moreover, the FPÖ points to what it perceives to have been a strong and enduring commitment of the *Third Lager*, namely to constitutionalism and political liberties (Kroupa (1984)).

Given the ambiguous history of the *Third Lager*, there is clearly evidence to support both views. Nonetheless, the most popular interpretation has been that which equates the *Third Lager* with national socialism. It is indispensable to a rounded appreciation of the FPÖ and of its immediate predecessor to bear this fact in mind. As will be shown below, this perception of the party strongly militated against its chances of governmental participation. It coloured the attitudes of other political actors and political observers, as well as the actions of the party itself. Thus it is only since the party actively stressed its liberal, as opposed to its national, ideals that it finally entered government.

Allied suspicion of the *Third Lager* delayed until 1949 the establishment of the League of Independents (VdU) as the political expression of that camp.[2] The initiators of the League (Kraus and Reimann), were liberal journalists from Salzburg. While the Sozialistische Partei Österreichs (SPÖ) supported the foundation of the VdU as a means of splitting the bourgeois vote, the Österreichische Volkspartei (ÖVP) was strongly opposed and added its voice to that of the large group of persons who saw in the League nothing but a revival of national socialism. Though high among the aims of the VdU was provision of a political voice to the 500,000 or so Austrians disenfranchised by the de-Nazification process, the League was more than a party for ex-Nazis. It was also supported by repatriates, liberals, and elements of the *petite bourgeoisie*, alienated from the post-war system. One of the prime concerns of the League was to counter what it regarded as the ÖVP and SPÖ's unhealthy monopolisation of Austrian public life. This antipathy to the party cartel accounts for the name of 'League of Independents'. The VdU recruited well amongst anti-clerical and anti-socialist voters who wanted a 'third way' between SPÖ and ÖVP.

What this entailed was articulated in the VdU's 1949 programme (cf. Berchtold (1967) 484ff.). Its opening section contains commitments to political liberalism, for example to constitutionalism, legal equality and protection of the individual, as well as proposals for the introduction of direct democracy. Some of these commitments (notably the abolition of all privileges and the rejection of retrospective legislation) were clearly directed against the de-Nazification laws. Critics also interpreted the advocacy of a 'United States of Europe' and the League's commitment to German *Volkstum* as thinly-veiled assertions of pan-Germanism. The programme's section on domestic policy was characterised by an emphasis upon integrity and a rejection of *Proporz*. There were calls for a reduction in the bureaucracy and a condemnation of corruption. The programme advocated a mixed economy based upon sound money and minimal nationalisation. Fiscal policy was not to undermine the principles of thrift and enterprise. The VdU supported public works in order to guarantee full employment, and spoke of health education, fair rents, and insurance-based welfare provision. The League rejected class struggle and argued for the establishment of a system where effort was matched by rewards. Summing up the programme were the three principles of justice, integrity, and excellence (*Leistung*).

Table 9.2 *Performance of VdU at National Council, Landtag, and Chamber of Labour elections (percentages)*

	National council		Landtag				Chamber of Labour	
	1949	1953	1949	1953	1954	1955	1949	1954
Vienna	6.9	10.6	6.8		5.9		5.6	1.1
Lower Austria	4.4	5.3	4.4		2.6		0.0	0.4
Styria	14.6	13.6	14.6	13.6			14.6	2.7
Upper Austria	20.8	12.2	20.8			9.6	28.8	5.3
Carinthia	20.6	16.6	20.5	16.9			19.9	3.7
Tyrol	17.4	13.1	17.4	9.9			17.2	3.5
Salzburg	18.5	19.0	18.5		13.2		27.3	6.5
Burgenland	3.9	3.7	3.9	3.6			0.0	0.9
Vorarlberg	21.9	18.8	22.1		13.7		21.0	7.6
Austria: %	11.7	10.9					11.7	2.5
Austria: Seats	16	14					117	19

Sources: National council and Landtag: Verbindungsstelle (1981) 26f.; chamber of labour: Ulram (1985) 125ff.

The VdU's initial political success was impressive (see Table 9.2). It gained 11.7 per cent of the 1949 national council vote and 16 seats. In Vorarlberg, Carinthia and Upper Austria it actually got over 20 per cent. The worst performances were in the Soviet Zone, where the *Third Lager* was allegedly actively undermined. At the chamber of labour elections the VdU also achieved 11.7 per cent of the vote. The VdU's candidate in the 1951 presidential election obtained a creditable 15.4 per cent of the total vote and forced a second ballot between the SPÖ and ÖVP candidates.

However, 1951 was to prove the zenith of the VdU. Contrary to the party's policy of not issuing voting recommendations for the second round of the presidential election, Kraus declared his support for the ÖVP. This was perhaps to be expected from an anti-socialist and practising Catholic, but was too much for the vehemently anti-clerical national wing. The most outspoken was the Viennese radical Stüber, who had regarded Kraus and Reimann as ultimately dispensable political fig-leaves who would allow the nationals access to the parliament (Perchinig (1983) 71). The opposition of Stüber et al. eventually forced Kraus's resignation. The new leader was Stendebach, a retired colonel born in Saxony. Electoral defeats exacerbated the VdU's internal conflict. Though in 1953 the VdU's total share of the vote fell by only 0.8 per cent, this resulted in the loss of two MPs. Moreover, had Stüber's radical right-wing Viennese party not managed to increase its vote in the populous capital by 60 per cent, the overall figure would have been much worse, a fact Stüber considered an endorsement of his uncompromising approach. The disastrous 1954 elections to the chamber of labour and a series of very poor Landtag results made the internal battles worse.

The VdU was on its way out. At the parliamentary level it made no headway in face of the Grand Coalition, which had 90 per cent or more of the seats. Approaches to the ÖVP in 1953, with a view to achieving VdU governmental participation, were scuppered by the Socialist federal president and strongly opposed by the party's own national wing. The VdU was stuck in the role of a party of protest. Yet, at the same time, the reservoir of support for such protest was dwindling, because of economic revival and deliberate attempts by the two major parties to attract the repatriates, ex-Nazis, and other groups which had given the VdU its initial support. The 1955 State Treaty enhanced the prestige of the Grand Coalition parties and further undermined the VdU. The party's *raison d'être* vanished and the incompatibility of its factions became ever more evident.

The eventual outcome was the demise of the short-lived VdU and the establishment in April 1956 of the new Freiheitliche Partei Österreichs under Anton Reinthaller, an ex-SS officer and National Socialist minister. Kraus and Reimann refused to join. Their intention had been to use the VdU as a vehicle for integrating ex-Nazis and other disaffected groups into the liberal camp and thus into Austrian political life. The VdU's organisational weakness, its lack of ideological or sociological homogeneity and the unfavourable nature of the party system all contributed to its demise. Once again, the *Third Lager's* mix of political liberalism and anti-system protest had proved irreconcilable. Neither Kraus nor Reimann were prepared to participate in a successor party led by Reinthaller and geared towards a policy of nationalism designed to gain the support of those 24 per cent or so of the population who had been NSDAP members at the end of the war (Kraus (1979) 27f.).

THE FPÖ: ORGANISATION AND STRUCTURE

The chairman

The character of the leader has always been an important factor for the FPÖ. The party has had four chairmen, the first the above-mentioned right-winger Reinthaller, who died in 1958. His successor was Friedrich Peter, an ex-Nazi, but a man whose political values appear to have been considerably modified during his twenty years as chairman. He succeeded in creating links to the SPÖ as well as to the ÖVP and is generally held to have facilitated the FPÖ's transition to a more liberal course.[3] Peter's replacement in 1978 was Alexander Götz, the anti-Kreisky figure within the party. His aim was to introduce at the federal level the kind of coalition with the ÖVP which in his native Graz had given him the post of mayor. Under Götz the FPÖ increased its vote and gained an additional seat at the 1979 elections. Yet his credibility as chairman was undermined by the fact that the SPÖ actually increased its majority and the ÖVP vote declined. This encouraged those in the FPÖ who opposed a coalition with the ÖVP and who were alienated by Götz's aggressive style. The upshot was Götz's resignation in December 1979.

In March 1980, the leadership was won by Norbert Steger, a Viennese lawyer born in 1944, who symbolises the new generation of upwardly mobile technocrats, young enough not to have a Nazi background. Together with Frischenschlager, Steger was a leading figure in the group of liberal 'Young Turks' of the *Atterseekreis* (Attersee Circle).[4] Steger's rise to high office started in Vienna, where he gained the post of chairman of the *Land* party in 1977. In 1979 he was elected to the national council. From 1980 to 1983 he chaired the national council's justice committee and, in a move which helped enhance the image the party wished to convey of itself as a party of men of integrity (*Saubermänner*), he became the chairman of the committee of investigation into the corruption scandal surrounding Vienna's general hospital. After the 1983 elections Steger led the party into its first ever period of federal governmental office.

The formal structure

The formal structure of the party is set out in its statutes.[5] Nominally, sovereignty resides with a biennial conference made up of the members of the FPÖ federal directorate and delegates from each of the nine *Land* groups in proportion to their respective membership figures. The conference approves the party programme and elects the chairman, presidium, and a proportion of the executive and directorate of the party. The directorate numbers some 90 persons. Membership of the directorate is automatic for those in the executive and for all National Council MPs and all FPÖ members of *Land* and federal governments. The remaining members are elected for a two-year period by the conference, usually on a slate previously agreed between *Land* groups (Reiter (1982) 17).

The directorate is too large for effective decision-making and this is therefore left to the higher organs. The first of these is the executive, which presently has twenty members. The chairmen of all nine *Land* groups have a guaranteed seat, as does the leader of the parliamentary party. The remaining members (the chairman, his deputies and four additional members) are elected by the conference biennially. Since 1976, the party has had a presidium, currently comprising the chairman, his six deputies, and the leader of the parliamentary party. FPÖ statutes give the chairman wide-ranging powers. He chairs the party conference, the directorate, executive and presidium. He prepares the directorate's meetings, implements its policies and is responsible for 'the supervising of the whole of the party's activities' (Statutes, 15 [2]). He appoints both the party manager – with the agreement of the executive – and the secretariat's staff. He also has the sole right of nominating the general-secretary.

The office of general-secretary[6] dates from 1978 when Krünes was appointed to protect Götz's interests in the Vienna headquarters while the latter was busy fulfilling his duties as mayor of Graz. Both men retired at the end of 1979 and there was no replacement general-secretary until 1982, when the directorate endorsed Steger's nomination of Grabher-Meyer, who subsequently convinced the executive to limit the general-secretary's term of office to two years. A time-served printer in his early forties who now owns a textile business, Grabher-Mayer conforms to the new image the FPÖ wants to project as a party of the upwardly mobile, young, articulate liberal. One of his major aims on assuming office was to modernise the federal party's organisation.

The general-secretary is nominally a powerful party figure. He can speak on behalf of the chairman on all political matters, has powers of appointment and direction *vis-à-vis* FPÖ staff and is chief executive of the party newspaper. He is also the parliamentary party's deputy-leader and whip. However, Grabher-Meyer's main problem – and one which, he admits, initially almost defeated him – has been to maintain unity between the jealously independent *Land* groups and the centre. The very decentralised nature of the FPÖ has been a perennial problem for the federal leadership and is exacerbated by the weakness of the party machine, much of which is controlled by the Länder.[7] The general-secretary has no formal rights over the *Land* groups, though they for their part are strongly represented in the organs of the federal party.

The most strident opposition to the whole Vienna-based leadership has come from Jörg Haider, the Carinthian party boss and Steger's *bête noire*. Strong criticisms have also been voiced from Tyrol and elsewhere against what these persons see as over-centralisation and the unilateral imposition by Steger and his Attersee yuppies of a too liberal line, at odds with the more national views prevalent in many

Länder. Such opposition became especially vociferous in the months following the FPÖ's assumption of federal government office. There were even resignations from the party.[8]

The membership: regional and other factors

If one examines the regional distribution of FPÖ membership, it becomes clear why the leadership cannot ignore Haider et al. (see Table 9.3). First, it is precisely in *Länder* such as Carinthia that the party has most members. 45 per cent of the total membership is from two, and 75 per cent from four of the nine *Land* groups. A second reason why Steger cannot ignore Haider is that, while the gradual increase of the FPÖ's total membership suffered its first reversal after Steger's entry into government in 1983, Haider's Carinthian party has been able to increase both its membership and Landtag vote. Haider uses these successes as a vindication of his more national approach. A third cause of conflict lies in the differences between the *Länder* and between them and the centre in terms of their relationships to the two major parties. In Carinthia, for example, the FPÖ's traditional opponent has been the SPÖ, which made acceptance of the federal SPÖ–FPÖ coalition difficult. Similarly, there was dissent in Tyrol, where co-operation with the ÖVP had been preferred (*Profil*, 19.12.83).

Table 9.3 also shows the FPÖ's membership density as measured at the last four national council elections.[9] In contrast to the two main parties, the FPÖ is very much a *Wählerpartei* (voters' party) rather than a *Mitgliederpartei* (members' party or mass party). The former type typically relies upon notables, a characteristic applicable to the FPÖ and a consequence of which – namely, persistent personality disputes – is endemic in the party.

No detailed sociological profile of FPÖ members exists. The information that is available points to a high percentage of graduates and an under-representation of women. It is widely believed that civil servants, the free professions and the self-employed are over-represented. This would tie in with the data on the voter profile of the party and is partly reflected at the very highest echelons of the FPÖ. Thus the occupational background of the present executive is 61 per cent free professions, 22 per cent self-employed, 11 per cent farmers and 6 per cent white-collar workers, while the presidium consists of 83 per cent from the free professions and 16 per cent self-employed.[10]

Finance

Traditionally, all Austrian parties have been secretive about their finances, but since the 1975 statute on state financing of political parties, they are obliged to publish at least their annual accounts.

Table 9.3 *Size, density and distribution of FPÖ membership*

			Regional distribution, %								
Year	Total	Density, %	UA	C	St	Sa	Vo	T	LA	Vi	B
1959	22,000										
1970	28,000	11.1									
1971		11.3									
1975	33,000	13.2									
1976	34,000										
1977	35,000										
1978	36,761										
1979	37,288	13.0									
1980	37,380										
1981	37,568		25	19	18	14	6	6	5	5	2
1982	37,606		25	19	18	14	6	6	5	5	2
1983	37,233	15.4	25	19	18	14	6	6	6	5	2
1984	36,377		25	19	18	13	6	6	6	5	2
1985	37,057		25	20	18	13	6	5	6	5	2

Sources: Gerlich and Müller (1983) 160 and FPÖ internal records, supplied December 1985.

Though these remain very sketchy, they offer a few clues as to finance. First, they show that the declared income of the FPÖ is relatively modest when compared to that of the two main parties. Thus the public accounts for 1979 show party incomes to have been (in million Austrian shillings): SPÖ 175; ÖVP 105; FPÖ 26 (Kadan (1981) 13ff.). Yet this presents a very incomplete picture. It has been estimated by Pelinka that the true figures are nearer 396, 457 and 75 million respectively (cited in Kadan (1981) 17). This enormous discrepancy is in part due to the fact that only the federal party is obliged to publish its income, while the regional organisations are not. The disparity is, however, also mirrored in the wide-spread public cynicism of Austrians regarding party finances. Allegations of clandestine dealings of a dubious legal or moral nature abound and there has in recent years been a steady stream of scandals and corruption trials. With the exception of the damaging 'Olah affair' in the early 1960s[11] and an accusation in 1970 which came to nothing, the FPÖ has emerged relatively unscathed. This is just as well in view of its wish to be seen as the anti-corruption party.

Bearing in mind the above caveats regarding the incompleteness of the published accounts, there is a second type of analysis possible, namely of the relative importance of the different sources of party income. Table 9.4 provides such a breakdown of FPÖ income during

Table 9.4 *Sources of finance of federal FPÖ, 1975–84, %*

Year	State	Membership dues	Party tax and assets	Donations	Savings	Loans	Other
1975	10	—[a]	5	83			2
1976	56	11	7	26			1
1977	45	10	8	30	1		5
1978	46	9	7	32	3		5
1979	26	7	6	47	13		1
1980	42	8	30	8	12		2
1981	47	10	8	35			1
1982	39	5	7	47			1
1983	32	4	7	8	41	8	1
1984	51	6	10	31			1

[a] Not listed as separate item in 1975.
Source: Party accounts, as supplied in January 1986 by FPÖ Federal Secretariat.

a ten-year period. Membership dues are shown to be relatively insignificant as a contribution to the federal party's income. These monies tend to remain with the *Land* groups. In comparison, in 1979 this rubric accounted for 34 per cent and 18 per cent of the respective incomes of the SPÖ and ÖVP (Kadan (1981) 13f.). A further source of funding is the party tax. This is a levy each Austrian party raises on the salaries of those persons who owe their political, administrative or business posts to the party. The levy is reported to range between 12 and 40 per cent of the relevant salary (Gerlich and Muller (1983) 253). Party taxes do not account for a very large proportion of FPÖ income, though this may increase, now that the party is in a better position to dispense patronage.

The FPÖ's two most important sources of funding are the state and donations. At election time, donations replace state subsidies as the prime contributor to the party's coffers. Though the FPÖ does not identify its sponsors, it is an open secret that a large proportion of its donations comes from the Austrian assocation of industrialists. There is speculation that this has had an impact upon the party's economic policy, making it more market-orientated.

The group environment

This brings us to a consideration of the FPÖ's relationship to the various extra-parliamentary groups in Austria. The party has a number of auxiliary associations, based upon groups such as entrepreneurs, teachers, pensioners, and the youth (Reiter (1982) 22ff.). Additionally, there are working groups targeted on employees, railway workers, military personnel, and farmers. The FPÖ's links to the student, cultural, and sporting associations so typical of the *Third Lager* in earlier times are now much more tenuous. The once influential 'Ring Freiheitlicher Studenten', from which people such s as Steger, Frischenschlager and Reiter were recruited, has become an organisation of peripheral impact. Like some of the other academic and student groups, it has adopted extreme right-wing ideas.

Outside its more immediate political milieu, the party is almost completely devoid of the kind of representation which the ÖVP and SPÖ enjoy in the key economic institutions of the corporate system. The three crucial bodies are the chambers of labour, commerce, and agriculture. In the first, the FPÖ only won 2.5 per cent of the vote and 13 of the 840 seats in the 1984 elections. Even in Carinthia it only managed 6.5 per cent. Despite its keenness to challenge the ÖVP hegemony in the other two chambers, the FPÖ's performance has been disappointing, with a large defeat in the 1985 elections to the chamber of commerce. Given the political significance of the system of social partnership, it is essential for the FPÖ to be better represented here if it wants to increase its political saliency.

Publicity

The party has at its disposal a range of channels for the dissemination of its political ideas. The various associations mentioned above clearly function as such channels. The over-representation of the party among academics also helps, albeit in an unquantifiable manner. Newspapers are perhaps the most traditional medium for spreading the word. Every *Land* group publishes its own newspaper, while the federal party publishes the weekly *Neue Freie Zeitung*. More substantive discussions appear in the party's quarterly journal *Freie Argumente*, which constitutes an invaluable source of information on internal ruminations about the FPÖ's programmatic and strategic options. Indicative of the FPÖ's desire to present itself as liberal is the fact that in recent years the *Freie Argumente* have regularly published profiles of historical persons who exemplify those aspects of the tradition of the *Third Lager* which the party currently wishes to promote, and whom the FPÖ claims as its own. Similar endeavours have appeared in material published by the Freiheitliches Bildungswerk, the state-financed political academy of the party.

THE ELECTORAL ARENA

Having considered the organisation and structure of the FPÖ, it is time to examine the major object of all that effort: the electoral arena.

The basic facts of the FPÖ's performance at National Council elections are set out in Table 9.5, which clearly shows the impact of the 1970 electoral reforms. After 1970, the party's mean share of the vote decreased, whilst its absolute and relative parliamentary strength increased. The iniquity of the old system is shown in the figures on the number of votes each party required to gain a seat. For the FPÖ, this sank by 43 per cent after 1970, to a figure virtually identical with that of the major parties. In fact, in 1983 it was the FPÖ whose seats were 'cheapest', costing about one fifth less than those of the SPÖ and ÖVP. 1983 provided a further irony, for despite registering its lowest ever vote (4.98 per cent), the FPÖ not only gained its highest ever number of seats, but also entered the federal government for the first time.

The FPÖ's electoral vulnerability has much to do with its low proportion of stalwart voters, estimated by some to constitute a mere 50 per cent of the party's vote (Haerpfer (1985) 249f.). Others have concluded that only 32 per cent are stalwart voters, 37 per cent partially and 30 per cent not at all committed to the FPÖ (Plasser and Ulram (1985) 20). The reasons for this are, first, the party's lack of an extensive network of auxiliary associations analogous to those of the ÖVP and SPÖ, which facilitate political socialisation and mobilisation. Secondly, the FPÖ, like many previous parties of the *Third Lager*, relies heavily upon protest voters. This is one reason why the Green parties pose such a threat, another being the sociological similarity of their vote. It appears that about a fifth of the FPÖ's 1979 voters who switched parties in 1983 moved to the Greens (Birk et al. (1983) 317). Moreover, when the FPÖ entered government in 1983, it became less attractive for protest voters, which helps explain the considerable losses it experienced in all but one of the Landtag elections subsequently (see Table 9.7) and augurs badly for the future.

Despite the decline at the 1983 elections of the FPÖ vote in some *Länder* – notably Vorarlberg and Tyrol – the *Länder's* relative FPÖ voting strength has remained fairly stable (see Table 9.6). This continuity has much to do with Austria's demographic immobility and the resultant 'stable interpersonal networks' (Haerpfer and Gehmacher (1984) 44). At *Land* and communal level, the interpersonal dimension is even more important. Within almost any given *Land*, the FPÖ is more successful at Landtag rather than National Council elections (see Tables 9.6 and 9.7). In some communal strongholds it even achieves absolute majorities, while in its Carinthian, Salzburg and Vorarlberg heartland, it has almost always achieved representation in the *Land* governments (see Table 9.7).

Before proceeding to consider the sociological profile of the FPÖ

Table 9.5 *FPÖ National Council vote and seats, 1956–83*

Year	Votes Absolute	Votes %	Seats Absolute[a]	Seats %	Votes per seat FPÖ	Votes per seat SPÖ	Votes per seat ÖVP
A							
1956	283,749	6.5	6	3.6	47,292	25,315	24,390
1959	336,110	7.7	8	4.8	42,014	25,050	24,406
1962	313,895	7.0	8	4.8	39,237	25,798	24,994
1966	242,570	5.4	6	3.6	40,428	26.067	25,778
1970	253,425	5.5	6	3.6	42,238	27,432	26,295
B							
1971	248,473	5.5	10	5.5	24,847	24,518	24,559
1975	249,444	5.4	10	5.5	24,944	25,013	24,766
1979	286,743	6.1	11	6.0	26,068	25,402	25,737
1983	241,789	5.0	12	6.6	20,149	25,695	25,899
Mean A	285,950	6.4	6.8	4.1	42,242	25,932	25,173
Mean B	256,613	5.5	10.8	5.9	24,002	25,157	25,240

[a] Total number of seats 1956–70 was 165; 1971–83 it was 183.
Sources: Haerpfer (1983) 143ff., and Plasser and Ulram (1983) 129f.

Table 9.6 *Regional distribution of FPÖ National Council vote, 1956–86*

	1956	1959	1962	1966	1970	1971	1975	1979	1983	1986
Vienna	5.6	7.4	6.5	4.0	4.1	4.3	4.1	4.7	4.4	5.8
Lower Austria	3.0	4.3	3.4	2.3	2.7	3.1	2.9	3.6	3.0	6.1
Styria	6.9	6.8	6.8	4.9	5.0	4.9	4.6	6.1	4.0	9.9
Upper Austria	7.1	8.7	8.0	6.5	6.7	6.5	6.7	7.2	6.0	11.0
Carinthia	15.1	13.5	12.5	11.5	9.7	9.7	10.0	10.0	10.7	20.9
Tyrol	6.0	7.9	6.5	4.9	5.5	5.2	5.3	5.7	4.4	11.3
Salzburg	14.4	15.2	13.7	12.5	13.0	11.5	12.1	11.4	8.0	15.9
Burgenland	3.0	5.0	4.0	2.4	2.7	2.9	2.5	2.7	2.2	5.4
Vorarlberg	10.3	12.1	14.9	12.9	13.6	11.1	10.2	10.7	7.2	11.9
Austria	6.5	7.7	7.1	5.4	5.5	5.5	5.4	6.1	5.0	9.7

Sources: Verbindungsstelle (1981) 26f., and Plasser and Ulram, (1983) 130.

Table 9.7 *FPÖ vote at recent Landtag elections*

	1977	1978	1979	1980	1981	1982	1983	1984	1985
Vienna		6.5					5.4		
Lower Austria			3.2				1.7		
Styria		6.4			5.1				5.0
Upper Austria			6.4						
Carinthia			11.7[a]					16.0[a]	
Tyrol			6.6					6.0	
Salzburg			13.2[a]					8.7	
Burgenland	2.2					3.0			
Vorarlberg			12.5[a]					10.5[a]	

[a] As a result of these elections, the FPÖ held one seat in the respective *Land* government.
Sources: ÖJP 1984 and *ÖJP 1985*, 626ff. and Kukacka (1985) 17.

vote, it is worth noting that the size of the FPÖ cohort is in many surveys so small that conclusions regarding the party have to be treated with caution. In order to mitigate this problem, we shall rely upon the findings of a relatively large (10,000-case) 1982 survey.[12] For comparative purposes, Table 9.7 also includes some data from a smaller (2,000-case) 1977 poll (Haerpfer and Gehmacher (1984)). The latter is broadly in agreement with the 1982 results.

The data show the sociology of the FPÖ vote to be very similar to that of previous *Third Lager* parties. The FPÖ is predominantly a middle-class party of the small and medium-sized towns, under-represented amongst the working class, in rural communities and in socialist Vienna. True to the anti-clerical tradition of the *Third Lager*, FPÖ voters exhibit the lowest degree of religiosity of all three main parties (Haerpfer and Gehmacher (1984) 34f.). This is positively correlated with the educational profile of the FPÖ, which is the party of the well educated. The 1982 results show that only in the FPÖ is the percentage of males above the national mean. Indeed, the 1977 survey found that a full two-thirds of the party's vote came from males. This over-representation is at least in part explicable by the positive correlation between women and religiosity (Haerpfer and Gehmacher (1984) 43).

The data give a number of clues as to the character of the protest vote within the FPÖ. The regional dimension demonstrates an under-representation in Austria's political, economic, cultural and administrative centre, but an over-representation in the periphery (see Tables 9.6 and 9.7). Detailed examination of the 1977 data on

Table 9.8 *Social composition of FPÖ vote %*

	1977		1982	
	Survey Mean	FPÖ	Survey Mean	FPÖ
Class:				
Working	38	19	42	35
Middle	47	70	36	38
Upper-middle			13	18
Farmers	14	12	9	10
Income: (AS p.m.)				
<10,000			29	31
<14,000			26	20
<18,000			20	20
>18,000			26	30
Education:				
Basic	48	33	40	34
Intermediate	40	42	46	46
Higher	13	25	14	20
Urban Rural:				
<5,000			44	39
<50,000			21	25
<250,000			13	16
Vienna			22	20
Region:				
East			45	31
South			23	27
Central			22	25
West			11	17
Age:				
<25			18	17
25–39			29	26
40–59			37	38
>60			17	19
Sex:				
Male			46	49
Religiosity:				
Non church-goers	44	63	—	—
Occasional church-goers	30	26	—	—
Regular church-goers	27	11	—	

Sources: IFES (1982) and Haerpfer and Gehmacher (1984).

Table 9.9 *Responses to the question 'Is Austria a nation?'*

	1965		1977		1980	
	FPÖ	average	FPÖ	average	FPÖ	average
Yes	22	48	51	62	68	67
Gradually becoming one	20	23	15	16	15	19
No	53	15	23	11	17	11
Don't know	5	24	11	12	—	3

Sources: Sozialwissenschaftliche Studiengesellschaft, Report nos.: 34, 5f. and 135, 2f. Also IFES/Fessel Survey by Lazarsfeld-Gesellschaft 1980, 15f. Material kindly supplied by Dr Haerpfer.

working-class FPÖ support shows it to be far greater amongst skilled workers (Haerpfer and Gehmacher (1984) 29), who presumably have greater aspirations to upward social mobility. The FPÖ also has proportionately more workers among the lower rather than the higher echelons of the public service and has a greater proportion of self-employed than any other party (Haerpfer and Gehmacher (1984) and *Zukunft*, 1979/6, 12). Finally, Table 9.8 shows FPÖ voters to be over-represented in both the highest and lowest of the four income groups. One might hypothesise that, taken together, these factors suggest that the FPÖ vote contains a sizeable group of persons who might feel estranged from, or marginalised by, Austrian society.

The attitudinal profile of the FPÖ protest vote has long been a vexed question. *Third Lager* parties have in the past contained persons of pan-Germanic, anti-system, authoritarian, and even racist persuasion and both the VdU and early FPÖ recruited well amongst ex-Nazis. However, while there is broad agreement on these facts, there is considerable debate over whether or not the aforementioned attitudes constitute a significant element in today's FPÖ. Not surprisingly, the party is at pains to stress that they do not. Steger has made it clear that there is no room in his party for anyone whose attitudes even remotely resemble those of Nazism (interview in London, 26.2.86) and other leading FPÖ figures argue that the party's national principle is now not pan-Germanic, but a form of Austrian patriotism (interview with G. Stix). Notwithstanding such statements, the FPÖ still has a popular image as a party whose supporters have both little commitment to the Austrian political system and a susceptibility to authoritarianism.

One way to assess FPÖ supporters' commitment to the Austrian system is by examining opinion-poll data on questions such as whether or not Austria is a nation (see Table 9.9). Results show FPÖ attitudes to have undergone a radical change on this issue between 1965, when only 22 per cent replied yes, and 1980, when 68 per cent did so. This appears to suggest that most supporters of the FPÖ's national ideology now see it as compatible with Austrian nationhood and cannot therefore be considered anti-system in this respect. Nonetheless, the percentage of FPÖ supporters denying the existence of an Austrian nationhood remains significantly higher than the national average.

The opposition of the FPÖ and its predecessor to some of the key features of Austria's political system has also been interpreted as indicative of anti-system or even anti-democratic predispositions. However, while survey results show an above average desire to see a strong man rule (Nick and Pelinka (1984) 77), one must beware of confusing opposition to *Proporz* with opposition to liberal democracy. From the FPÖ's perspective, its criticisms have been against a system of party cartel based upon patronage, which is itself undemocratic and open to abuse. It is also not surprising that a party excluded from government for about thirty years should be cynical about the political system. Moreover, the disenchantment with Austrian politics and politicians has in recent years increased throughout the population. (Plasser and Ulram (1985); Haerpfer and Gehmacher (1984)).

That is not to say that the FPÖ is devoid of authoritarian attitudes. Surveys regularly find that it has the largest party concentration of authoritarian, anti-semitic and similar attitudes (Pelinka (1979) *Profil*, 1.4.85, 26f.). Other sources find evidence of praise for Nazis and even biological racism (Neugebauer (1979)). Nor are these confined to voters rather than members. Some of the most radical ideas stem from Carinthia's Scrinzi, an FPÖ national council member for over ten years and an 'independent' candidate at the 1986 presidential election.[13] However, one must also note that even if such ideas are significant numerically or in terms of their extremeness, this does not mean that they are significant in determining party policy. For the leadership – at least nationally – is now composed almost exclusively of persons from the FPÖ's liberal wing.

Nonetheless, such radical attitudes are significant in at least three respects. First, they persistently militated against the coalition potential of the VdU and the FPÖ (see the section on government participation, pp. 238–42, below). Secondly, they contribute greatly to the intra-party conflict mentioned in the section on organisation and structure pp. 220–6, above. Thirdly, they undermine the credibility of the attempts under Norbert Steger to portray the FPÖ as a liberal party. Polls have shown the Austrian electorate evenly split between those who see the FPÖ as liberal and those that see it as national (*Wochenpresse*, 21.2.84, 13). The national ideology is widely perceived as illiberal, which means that in order to achieve his declared aim of increasing the FPÖ vote in the middle class (interview), Steger will have to divest the party of at least the more extreme national elements. A change in the FPÖ's programmatic image could also help in this recruitment strategy. Developments in FPÖ ideology are the subject of the next section of this essay.

THE PROGRAMMATIC DIMENSION[14]

Common to the FPÖ's rather superficial first four programmes (1955, 1957, 1964 and 1968) were anti-communism, antipathy to *Proporz*, an organic vision of one German *Volk*, as well as commitments to freedom and excellence (*Leistung*). 'Liberalism' was only used to describe economic *laissez-faire*, which the party repudiated. The FPO's popular image was of a national-conservative, illiberal and, according to some, an extreme right-wing party (Neugebauer (1979)). This was reinforced by charged statements such as the one in the 1968 programme which said that a state priority should be the application of modern genetics to ensure that the *Volk* remained of healthy stock (Reiter (1982), 86).

Aware of the strategic handicap of this anti-system image, the leadership began to change party ideology. Thus 1964 and 1968 already saw declarations of willingness to participate in government and a self-assessment as a party of the centre. The 1970 and 1971 electoral manifestos incorporated liberal ideas and in 1970, young liberals under Frischenschlager and Steger set up the Attersee Circle to generate new ideas with which the FPÖ's liberal and intellectual profile could be enhanced. These developments resulted in the 1973 social manifesto, significant as the first policy statement not formulated by a closed party elite. It was also deemed by at least one external observer to be the first time the FPÖ had given a clear priority to liberal ideas (Kadan and Pelinka (1979) 39).

The manifesto offers a distinctive view of man and society. There is great emphasis upon individual freedom, but mechanistic notions of society are explicitly rejected in favour of an assertion of communal loyalties to family and *Volk*. Freedom, it is said, can only exist in an ordered society. According to the manifesto, man is naturally unequal, in terms, for example, of skills and physical attributes, but above all in his psychological predisposition to the pursuit of freedom and self-fulfilment. A concomitant and central concept of the manifesto is that of the 'active element'. This denotes a relatively small group, held to exist in all societies, which is characterised by a 'vigorous and courageous approach to life, self-confidence, an urge to creativity or knowledge and the courage to undertake change, as well as a striving for higher things' (Reiter (1982) 96). This active element is considered to be the 'engine of society' (Reiter (1982) 97).

The manifesto's prescriptions derive from these fundamental beliefs. Hence the predominant demand is for greater personal freedom, especially for the active element, the liberation of whose personal enterprise and initiative will be of general benefit. Similarly, the manifesto argues for a more meritocratic society, with increased differentials and less progressivity in taxation, in order to reward effort and encourage enterprise. Since people are held necessarily and legitimately to make differing use of freedom, egalitarian policies are rejected. They are seen as depriving individuals of the opportunity for social, economic and cultural advancement (*Aufstieg*). The manifesto recognises a tension between freedom and security, but clearly values the former more highly. Accordingly, it argues that state social welfare provision should be merely a supplement to private insurance and familial obligations. It should grant minimal benefits to persons in temporary need, but avoid creating dependence upon state support. The function of social policy ought to be the promotion of self-reliance.

In sum, the manifesto is an anti-egalitarian mix of individualism and organicism, with an emphasis upon personal freedom and unmistakably elitist features. It does not use the term 'liberal', but does still employ phrases to which Austrians have been sensitised and which many consider symptomatic of the persistence in the FPÖ of national and illiberal elements, e.g. the commitment to the German *völkisch* and cultural community, and albeit in a milder form than 1968, continued reference to maintaining a healthy genetic stock. Though the manifesto soon became the *de facto* basic programme of the party, it was formally merely an extension of the conservative 1968 programme, which remained in force.

Throughout the 1970s, the FPÖ engaged in a sustained major debate on liberalism. It also gradually developed detailed policies on a wide range of issues. Externally the party proclaimed itself the liberal party of Austria, a claim supported by its accession to the Liberal International in 1979. The FPÖ undertook an exercise in political genealogy, designed to demonstrate the liberal pedigree of the *Third Lager*, the party's descent from which was then increasingly stressed. After a brief hiatus under Götz, the FPÖ has placed ever greater emphasis upon liberalism.

In 1982, the party conference approved Frischenschlager's proposal to consolidate the ideological developments of the 1970s by integrating them into a new programme. Adopted in June 1985, the new programme constitutes an important milestone in the FPÖ's programmatic history. It has two parts. The first contains a declaration of the party's basic principles, elucidated under the following ten rubrics: freedom, human dignity, *Volk* and homeland, Europe, culture, just society, excellence, property and market economy, state and law, and environment. The second part has twelve chapters, in which these principles are converted into a variety of specific policy goals. The 1985 programme differs in important respects from earlier programmes. It is the product of much more internal discussion. It is far more detailed and makes frequent express commitments to liberalism. FPÖ ideology is now undeniably no longer one of anti-system protest. Indeed, a senior party figure argues that 1985 marks such a dilution of FPÖ ideology that the party has lost its distinctiveness. He largely attributes this to the fact that the programme was drafted whilst the party was in office (Reiter interview).

However, inspection of the programme reveals many customary components of FPÖ ideology. The active element is still an important feature and the programme's social policy relies heavily upon the manifesto. The greatest single influence is again that of Hayek, whose impact is nowhere more apparent than in the pivotal concept of freedom. 'Freedom is our highest value', the opening sentence reads. This principle permeates the whole document and the aforementioned sentence adorns the cover of the programme. More significant, however, is that the framers of the programme see in freedom a concept to unite the FPÖ's two conflicting ideological traditions: the national and the liberal (Stix interview). These are presented as mere variations upon the central theme of freedom; one can espouse both freedom of the individual and freedom of the national collectivity. Seen thus, the two traditions are, they maintain, not mutually exclusive, but co-ordinate.

Both traditions appear in the programme. The first part was deliberately structured to highlight a natural organic progression from the individual, via family and *Volk*, to the FPÖ's ultimate aim of a European union of nations (Stix interview). There is also the traditional declaration of Austrian membership of the German *völkisch* and cultural community, but it is qualified by the novel recognition of the existence and value of Austria's ethnic minorities. Steger sees this as a liberal advance upon previous FPÖ programmes and is very proud of it (interview). The first part contains other liberal principles, such as tolerance and humanity, the uniqueness and equality of man (and woman), and a commitment to equal opportunity rather than sameness. There are calls for more freedom and less state, but with the proviso that the state may not renounce its social obligations.

In economic policy, the programme does not follow Hayek, whose system Stix terms 'jungle liberalism' (interview). Instead, the programme draws freely upon the Liberal International's 'Liberal Appeal 1981' of Rome. On the one hand it demands more efficiency and less bureaucracy in the state sector, as well as judicious reprivatisation. Predictably, the market is preferred to a centrally planned economy, and the importance to the economy of small and medium-sized firms is asserted. On the other hand, unrestricted economic freedom is considered to be exploitative of society's weakest members and potentially antithetical to the general interest. Intervention is justified for social or ecological reasons, one specific suggestion being international controls on multinationals.

The programme also contains traditional FPÖ demands such as increased control of the executive and greater rights of popular participation. Antipathy to *Proporz* is reflected in calls for greater (party-political) independence of the judiciary, for restrictions in the scope of social partnership and for democratisation of the corporate structure. The anti-corruption topic is also present. Recurrent themes of the programme include individualism, self-help, voluntarism, excellence, more selectivity of state benefits and checks against abuses of the system. Organicism is also expressed, notably in the emphasis upon various communal responsibilities and in declarations of rights, such as the right to work. Last but not least, the whole programme is pervaded by ecological considerations, an FPÖ issue since 1968.

Having briefly outlined the FPÖ's programmatic development, the next task is to evaluate that ideology. To date, most evaluations (except Frischenschlager (1978)) have been exercises in nomenclature, seeking to adjudicate upon the FPÖ's recent claims to be liberal. While there appears to be agreement that the party's official pronouncements are more liberal than they were, considerable differences remain over whether the FPÖ can therefore legitimately be classified as liberal. Frischenschlager maintains that it can, albeit with the qualification that it is a 'right-liberal' ((1975) 48) or 'conservative-liberal' (1978) party. Similarly, Reiter concludes that the manifesto betokens 'an independent liberalism with a strong regional flavour' ((1982) 78). Others refute such claims. They consider the party's national and liberal traditions to be incompatible and, inasmuch as the former still informs the ideas and actions of FPÖ members, these observers cannot credit the party with being genuinely liberal (Neugebauer (1979), Kubinzky (1981), Perchinig (1983)). Moreover, some allege that it is inappropriate to assess the FPÖ by reference to its official programmes, since it is not they, but the nature of the party notables which determine the character of the party. The present ideological line is seen by these critics as no more than an expression of the priorities of the current leadership and easily reversible once that leadership is replaced (e.g. Kubinzky (1981)).

When considering these differing opinions, two points must be borne in mind. First, they all precede the 1985 programme, of which there has as yet been no academic assessment, and they are thus out of date. As demonstrated earlier, the programme is explicitly liberal and although the national tradition survives, it takes a decidedly second place to liberalism. One might, therefore, conclude that FPÖ ideology is now considerably more liberal than it was when the above evaluations were made. The second point is that no definitive judgement of the FPÖ's liberality is possible anyhow, for we lack an undisputed yardstick of liberalism. This means that debates on the subject run the risk of descending into politically irrelevant semantics.

Potentially much more instructive would be to assess FPÖ ideology by reference to its political functions. Internal functions include providing a framework for the selection and articulation of a party's political demands. As the FPÖ moved out of the political wilderness, this function became ever more relevant. Political ideologies can also function as agents of party integration. However, this has traditionally not applied to *Third Lager* parties. Instead, ideological discussions have usually had a centrifugal effect, as was evident during the preparation of the 1985 programme. It remains to be seen whether Stix's conviction about the programme's philosophical integration of the national and liberal traditions will be translated into more worldly unity.

Externally, ideologies can have an impact upon the recruitment of voters and members. Prima facie, the enhancement of the FPÖ's liberal image and its emphasis upon greater personal freedom and greater rewards for enterprise, as well as the notion of the active element, all appear well suited to attract the young, upwardly-mobile new middle classes upon whom Steger has set his sights. Whether or not the ideology does facilitate this recruitment will become clear in due course. Finally, when evaluating the FPÖ's ideological development one must remember why the liberal course was adopted, namely to achieve government participation. The party's success in this respect introduces a new consideration. While early FPÖ programmes were insignificant in policy terms because the party was unlikely ever to be in a position to implement them, the 1985 programme is different. It is the first programme which can be assessed in terms of its impact upon government. It is to the question of the FPÖ's governmental participation that we now turn.

GOVERNMENT PARTICIPATION[15]

Until 1983, the *Third Lager* was excluded from every Second Republic federal government. Though participation often appeared tantalisingly close, all negotiations failed. Frequently, this was because the FPÖ's 'brown' past was felt to make it unsuitable. At other times, the FPÖ's negotiating partner was using those discussions merely to exert pressure upon the actual focus of its coalition preference: the other major party. Austria's party system itself militated against the FPÖ's governmental aspirations. From 1949 to 1966 the grand coalition controlled over 90 per cent of national council seats, leaving the FPÖ, for the first ten years of its existence, as the sole opposition party. This understandably led to the FPÖ's self-perception as *the* parliamentary party, upon which any hope of controlling the two-party monopoly rested. The party considers its successes during this period to include measures enhancing parliamentary control of the executive, the introduction of the ombudsman, as well as campaigns for increased democracy and against corruption (Piringer (1982) 113ff.). The FPÖ's political role was essentially reactive. In 1957 it supported a joint presidential candidate with the ÖVP, but in 1963 allied with the SPÖ to defeat the ÖVP proposal that Otto von Habsburg be readmitted to Austria.

The first majority government (1966–70) signalled a radical change in Austria's party system and boded well for the FPÖ's desire for a pivotal role like that of the German Free Democrats. Aware of the changed circumstances, Kreisky was wooing the FPÖ with a view to an anti-bourgeois coalition. This found favour with some in the FPÖ and encouraged the party's tentative first moves towards programmatic reform. It also unleashed protest by the anti-socialists. The result was a pre-electoral assurance by the party that there would be no red chancellor. Thus compromised, the FPÖ was unable to coalesce with the SPÖ, which unexpectedly emerged from the 1970 election to form a minority government. Nonetheless, the FPÖ did give the SPÖ tacit parliamentary support. The advantages for the FPÖ were that it was able to project a new image as a potential governing party and that it managed to get a number of policy demands fulfilled. The most significant was the introduction of a new electoral system that no longer militated against the party.

However, FPÖ expectations that its parliamentary support for the SPÖ would lead to full-scale coalition were thwarted by the SPÖ's achievement of absolute majorities in 1971, 1975 and 1979. FPÖ attention shifted to the ÖVP; yet there were also problems here. Even when the respective leaders agreed that an anti-socialist coalition would be mutually beneficial, there was little chance of the parties' grass-roots accepting this. Opposition was particularly strong in ÖVP factions such as the '*Cartel Verband*' which have traditionally been hostile to the *Third Lager's* anti-clericalism and nationalism. Götz had hoped his strident anti-socialism would help cement an ÖVP/FPÖ alliance, but the accompanying reassertion of the national ideology of the party's right wing in fact alienated many ÖVP supporters.

Under Steger's liberal leadership, FPÖ strategy changed again. At the 1983 election there was a clear leadership preference for an SPÖ–FPÖ coalition, though in view of the 1970 experience, the FPÖ publicly declared itself willing to negotiate with either major party. In reality, the only viable coalition was the one that emerged, for Kreisky would not countenance a grand coalition, and the ÖVP grass-roots would not have accepted an alliance with the FPÖ, even though their chairman was prepared to consider it.

The FPÖ–SPÖ coalition negotiations were relatively brief and centred on two main areas.[16] First, the FPÖ was determined to negotiate reductions in the SPÖ's proposed tax increases, in particular in respect of private savings, supertax, and small and medium-sized industry. This concern follows logically from the party's programmatic commitments, as outlined in the preceding pages. In the event, some concessions were achieved, but not enough to assuage elements in the FPÖ's right wing, a prominent member of which described the package as 'purest communism' (*Wochenpresse*, 15.11.83). The final coalition agreement was deliberately vague and excluded potentially divisive issues such as nuclear power.

The second topic of the coalition negotiations concerned the distribution of portfolios. The FPÖ got the Ministries of Trade and Industry, Defence and Justice, as well as three state secretaries and the vice-chancellorship. The significance of these Ministries to the party is at least twofold. First, they have a symbolic importance. Defence provides a patriotic focus for the FPÖ's national element, thereby helping to affirm the party's commitment to the Austrian state. The Justice Ministry underscores the FPÖ's self-image as a party of *Saubermänner*. Finally, the Ministry of Trade offers the party a platform from which to present itself as the party of economic expertise.

The second and more obvious significance of the ministries to the party is that they are responsible for policy areas in which the party perceives itself as having a distinctive contribution to make. In Defence, the FPÖ sees itself as replacing traditional SPÖ ambivalence to the military with a much more positive approach. The FPÖ rejects mere 'symbolic defence', arguing that what is needed is a clear commitment to effective defence, fully accepting the costs involved (Reiter interview). Frischenschlager's priorities were to improve military equipment, provision and morale. He also set great store by political education, especially of the youth, regarding the need for active national defence. He started his tenure of office very well, with an oath-taking ceremony symbolically located in an ex-concentration camp and went on to achieve an increase in the defence budget. However, he was politically fatally damaged by the 'Reder affair' when, to public dismay, he welcomed back to Austria a Nazi war criminal. Frischenschlager also ran into controversy over his purchase for the Austrian air force of Swedish fighter aircraft, the suitability and local acceptance of which soon became a matter of some debate. Frischenschlager was eventually replaced in April 1986 by ex-general-secretary Krünes and himself assumed the post of leader of the parliamentary party. Early indications suggest Krünes to be considerably less committed to the purchase of the Swedish fighters.

FPÖ justice policy seeks to reverse a perceived tendency to favour the perpetrator over the victim of crime, as well as to fight (political) corruption, of which Austria has had numerous cases in recent years. One of Steger's priorities as Minister of Trade, Commerce and Industry is promoting small and medium-sized firms, the health of which the party considers a precondition for Austria's economic growth. This has meant deregulatory policies such as revision of the rent protection laws and more flexible shop trading hours. It also involves reducing the tax burden of these industries and a general preference for indirect over direct taxation, as the former is held to reward enterprise more. While Steger in principle approves of reprivatisation, his approach is pragmatic, with less emphasis upon ownership than upon management of the state sector. In particular, he argues that state industries must be run on economic (i.e. market) principles and that party membership should cease to be a criterion in staffing decisions. Steger sees the latter practice as symptomatic of the excessive politicisation of Austria's economic and public life. The gradual dismantling of this system is, he says, the overriding goal of the FPÖ in the present coalition (interview). Moreover, the party believes it has achieved considerable initial successes in dismembering

Proporz. The most noteworthy example concerns the VOEST, Austria's most prestigious state sector company, which collapsed at the end of 1985 with enormous debts, largely incurred via dubious commodity speculation deals. The FPÖ was quick to attribute the crash to *Proporz*, for company supervision was not in the hands of professional managers, but had long been statutorily divided between the two main parties in proportion to their electoral strength. The FPÖ claims a large amount of credit for abolishing the relevant legislation and introducing new regulations designed to remove party control and ensure that VOEST is henceforth run on market lines (*Neue Freie Zeitung*, 20.2.86 and Steger interview).

On the other hand, the party has experienced a number of problems in government. First, it took considerably longer than it had expected to learn the ropes of government. Secondly, there have been problems with the SPÖ, whose trade-union and intellectual wings were never supporters of an alliance with the FPÖ. The problems were particularly acute as a result of the Reder affair, when the very survival of the coalition appeared in doubt, with SPÖ ministers threatening resignation. Thirdly, the party has to strike a difficult balance between, on the one hand, the political and administrative benefits of giving jobs to FPÖ supporters and, on the other hand, its oppositions in principle to political patronage. Thus the rapid transition of Peter from leader of the parliamentary party to member of a supervisory board in the public sector did nothing to convince sceptics of the sincerity of the FPÖ's claim to be opposed to patronage (*Profil*, 23.6.86, 27).

Government participation has also had internal effects upon the FPÖ. The party's electoral strength has been undermined by the loss of the protest vote. The hope is that these voters will be replaced by middle-class voters won over by the FPÖ's policies and by its new role as a governing party. This explains the frequent reference in party literature to Steger as the 'champion of the middle classes'. There has also been considerable internal protest from the party's right wing about the compromises which the FPÖ has entered into. The party has been accused by its own members of being but a pawn of the SPÖ (*Wochenpresse*, 21.5.83). In reply, the leadership argues that it is better for the party to have some influence upon government policy rather than none at all, as would be the case if it were in opposition (Grabher-Meyer interview). Moreover, Steger states that the cabinet's principle of unanimity in reality gives the FPÖ a potential veto over SPÖ proposals and therefore means that the party's influence in the coalition is, in fact, much greater than critics suggest (interview). Finally, the leadership points out that the FPÖ's goals are long-term ones. They involve a radical reform of a deeply-entrenched system. Steger says that this will require more than one term of office and believes that the party will have at least two more terms in which to exercise its role as a 'catalyst of reform' (interview).

STRATEGY AND PROSPECTS

The picture of the FPÖ which emerges from the preceding sections is that of a party which has many similarities with previous *Third Lager* parties. Included among these resemblances are a decentralised, notable-led organisation, with similar strongholds and comparable centre-regional friction. The sociology of the *Third Lager's* membership and vote appears also to have remained fairly constant over time. There is still an over-representation of the well-educated, urban, male, middle class with a low degree of religiosity. A strong protest vote, reflected in an above-average predisposition to authoritarian and racist attitudes, is another traditional feature of the *Third Lager*. However, anti-system attitudes based upon pan-Germanism now appear to be the preserve of a minority, while authoritarian inclinations have declined significantly in recent years.

The second section explained the reasons for the *Third Lager's* distinctive and often uneasy mix of nationalism and liberalism. The FPÖ's recent programmatic development has to be seen as part of a strategy aimed at improving the party's prospects by projecting a more favourable ideological image than in the past. The newest programme has decidedly reversed the *Lager's* traditional subordination of liberalism to nationalism, but the FPÖ continues to articulate both individualism and organic ideas. Elitist notions such as the 'active element' remain, alongside the recognition of Austria's membership of the German *völkisch* and cultural community. Similarities between 1985 and the VdU's 1949 commitment to the principles of justice, integrity and excellence are also evident. The 1985 programme is certain to reanimate the debate about the FPÖ's liberal credentials. Clearly, a programme cannot of itself make a party liberal, but the arguments supporting the FPÖ's claim to be liberal have, despite incidents such as the Reder affair, never been stronger.

However this debate ends, one thing is certain. The most dramatic change for the party has been its transition from party of protest to party of government. Yet even here there is some historical continuity, inasmuch as the FPÖ holds portfolios very similar to those typical of the *Third Lager* in the First Republic and also has analogous internal conflict over the inevitable compromises of office. The party's newly found governmental role has cost it considerable support amongst protest voters, whilst its heightened liberal profile has alienated many on the national right wing. For a party whose share of the 1983 vote was barely 5 per cent, such developments augur badly for the next general election, which is due no later than May 1987. Though in late 1985 one likely scenario for that election had appeared to be a continuation of the SPÖ–FPÖ coalition (Luther (1986) 41), immediately after the 1986 presidential contest the outlook seemed bleaker.

The FPÖ did not field an official candidate of its own and was formally neutral as between the contenders for the presidency, but the outcome of the election was still of concern for the party. Waldheim's 53.9 per cent in the second round underscored the progress the ÖVP had been making at *Land* and communal elections. Moreover, the very poor showing of the SPÖ candidate (46.1 per cent) was equally ominous, since his defeat was widely seen as an anti-government vote. Indeed, Chancellor Sinowatz felt obliged to resign as a result of this first ever defeat of a Socialist presidential candidate. The 1986 election was uncomfortable for the FPÖ in other respects. First, the controversy surrounding Kurt Waldheim's war record raised the public temperature in Austria on issues such as anti-Semitism and the Nazi past. Such debates have in the past left the FPÖ very vulnerable to attack. Secondly, while the leadership in practice clearly favoured the presidential candidate of its Socialist coalition partner, preliminary research suggests that FPÖ supporters voted two to one in favour of Waldheim (Plasser and Ulram (1986) 8). Finally, the candidature of Otto Scrinzi was unwelcome to the party leadership, contrary to whose wishes he was deemed still to be an FPÖ member, albeit with a non-active membership (*ruhende Mitgliedschaft*). Though he stood as an independent candidate, it was a considerable embarrassment to the leadership that Scrinzi received support for his very right-wing campaign from a number of FPÖ officials and supporters, including ex-chairman Götz.

The FPÖ now finds itself in the classic dilemma of a junior coalition partner tied to a political party whose electoral fortunes are waning. There appear basically to be two strategic options. First, the party could retain its commitment to the SPÖ and hope that the new Vranitzky government will rescue the coalition's image before the next election. The FPÖ leadership is currently banking on this strategy, arguing that the present coalition is united by a common commitment to equality of opportunity and that there is no basis for a coalition with the ÖVP, with whom relations have in recent years been very acrimonious (Steger and Grabher-Mayer interviews). The alternative strategy would be to seek ways in which openings could be made to the ÖVP. Despite protestations to the contrary, possible bases for an ÖVP–FPÖ coalition do seem to exist, for example in economic policy, where the parties share a much more market-orientated approach than the SPÖ. Yet to be seen even considering such a switch of coalition partner involves no small risks. It would be perceived as a tacit admission of failure by the government of which the FPÖ has been a part since 1983 and would itself be likely to damage both SPÖ and FPÖ electoral prospects.

Notwithstanding these risks, there is a strong and vociferous group within the FPÖ which argues that the party is tying itself too closely and uncritically to the SPÖ and that it ought instead to leave its options for the period after the next election more open. Friction between those of this persuasion and the party leadership has of late become intense. Thus in February 1985 Haider threatened to lead his *Land* group into a breakwaway party, and in 1986 he has been a key figure in a number of moves against the leadership. These have included a well-publicised campaign to replace both the chairman and general-secretary. Yet in a statement on 2 June 1986, all the chairmen of the *Land* groups (including Haider) agreed that the damaging internal disputes were to end and that they would all propose Steger's re-election as chairman of the federal party at the party conference in September. However, it is not at all clear whether it will prove possible to maintain this fragile unity between the mainly Vienna-based liberal leadership and the national wing.

Two of the possible outcomes of this strife are a formal split in the party or the re-emergence of a nationally orientated leadership. Both would be likely to result in the FPÖ losing its governmental status and thus its opportunity to act as 'a catalyst for the reform of the Second Republic's incrusted political structures' (Steger interview). A substantial lurch to the right would be electorally suicidal, as Scrinzi's mere 1.2 per cent of the ballot in the first round of the presidential election demonstrated. Furthermore, such a change in political direction would also have potentially very damaging effects upon the party's prospects of fulfilling its long-term strategy of becoming a hinge-group in the Austrian party system. For it would be essential to such a pivotal role that the FPÖ was popularly accepted as a party of the centre. Yet if the federal party did adopt a national leadership, the FPÖs chances of being an acceptable coalition partner for either the SPÖ or the ÖVP would be remote. The fate of the FPÖ might then well be to revert to the role of a protest party of peripheral political salience.

POSTSCRIPT

The FPÖ's June 1986 agreement proved ephemeral. Amidst scenes of high drama, Haider defeated Steger for the chairmanship of the party by 263 to 179 votes. Many reports on the conference (e.g. *Profil*, 22.9.86, 18ff. and 29.9.86, 18ff.; *Presse*, 15.9.86, 5 and *Falter* Nr. 19/86, 5f.) speaks of events such as '*Sieg Heil*' calls and a delegate informing Mrs Steger that her husband 'ought to be gassed'. One prominent FPÖ figure dismisses such reports as 'pure nonsense'. Another argues that, in the absence of evidence, the party has been able to discipline only one person, a functionary expelled for bringing the party into disrepute by displaying a Hitler medallion at the conference (interviews on 25.11.86 with Stix and new general-secretary Gugerbauer).

A more profound consequence of Haider's election was the SPÖ's unilateral annulment of its coalition with FPÖ and the announcement of a snap election for 23 November 1986.[17] A characteristic of the campaign was the great emphasis on personalities, which favoured the young, rhetorically skilled and charismatic Haider. The FPÖ's whole campaign revolved around Haider, whom it presented as 'a politician of the new type' and was directed against the widely expected re-establishment of an SPÖ–ÖVP Grand Coalition. Though he had been forced to let Steger lead the FPÖ in the caretaker federal government, Haider was successful in presenting the FPÖ as *the* party of opposition. This was possible because the ÖVP seemed to be tempering its criticism of Vranitzky's SPÖ considerably during the election, since it expected to coalesce with it after the election, while Haider, whose party had fallen to circa 3 per cent in the August opinion polls, had nothing to lose and mounted a no-holds-barred attack on both parties and in particular on Vranitzky.

The FPÖ conducted an emotive, populist campaign whose message of protest was targeted on about six issues of widespread public concern. These were the alleged exploitation of farmers by an omnipotent, uncaring co-operative agricultural bank; the baleful effects of *Proporz*, as epitomised by the VOEST scandal; the multiplication of social security agencies whose bureaucratic waste militates against claimants; 'social security scroungers'; politicians' 'privileges'; and the need for more national pride. As was perhaps to be expected, there were a number of attacks on the 'brown' FPÖ under Haider for at best not distancing itself from the far right, including neo-Nazis, or at worst actively courting such support.[18]

The outcome of the election exceeded the party's wildest dreams. The FPÖ vote rose a full 95 per cent from 4.98 per cent of the total vote in 1983 to 9.73 per cent and its tally of seats rose from 12 to 18. In Carinthia, the FPÖ achieved 20.9 per cent and in Salzburg 15.9 per cent. These are levels unprecedented for the *Third Lager* since the heady early days of the VdU (see Table 9.3). The success is due to winning over a number of groups: first, the *Third Lager's* national 'core' alienated from the FPÖ by Steger's liberals; secondly, a large number of young, non-ideological voters attracted by Haider's personality and his audacity *vis-à-vis* the famous and the good in Austrian political life; thirdly, Haider was successful in winning both from the ÖVP and the SPÖ voters disenchanted with the two big parties; finally, he appears to have attracted almost all the non-Green protest potential. Early evidence indicates that FPÖ voters were predominantly male. They were also young – a third being under thirty – and 12 per cent of all first-time voters voted FPÖ. That most radical right-wing voters also voted FPÖ is evident from a survey showing that 89 per cent of those voting Scrinzi in May 1986 voted FPÖ in November (*Profil*, 1.12.86, 28ff.).

The coalition negotiations are still under way. Vranitzky has ruled out a coalition with Haider and despite the FPÖ's willingness to coalesce with the ÖVP (*Wochenpresse*, 12.12.86, 16ff.) the latter is unlikely to accede to this suggestion, notwithstanding the similarities in the parties' economic policies. Since neither the SPÖ (80 seats) nor the ÖVP (77 seats) have a majority, and a grand coalition leaving the FPÖ in opposition with the 8 Green MPs seems most likely. The new FPÖ general-secretary argues that an oppositional role for the party is strategically best, for the near certainty that Austria's economic problems will increase is bound to exacerbate political discontent and thus enhance the FPÖ's vote at the next election (interview 25.11.86).

This postscript will conclude with a consideration of two issues. The first concerns the factors causing the change of leadership, the second pertains to how one might assess the 'new' FPÖ. The leadership change was partly caused by external factors such as the inevitable compromises of government and a media largely hostile to Steger. Secondly, there were a series of political blunders by the leadership, the most damaging of which was probably the Reder affair. Thirdly, the liberals were a relatively small group in the party, the liberalisation of which they overestimated. Many provincial functionaries had at best been reluctant followers of the new liberal and governmental roles. Fourthly, the smallness of the liberal group left it overstretched by the twin pressures of government and party work. The consequence was that the latter lost out. The communication to provincial functionaries of government successes was ineffective, whilst the leadership for its part became increasingly oblivious to the strength of grass-roots disaffection. Into this vacuum stepped Haider and his supporters, who were able to convince the local party functionaries that only Haider could reverse the continuing decline in the party's electoral prospects. Without holding any of the key posts at the federal level, they took over the party's leadership via the real power base: the *Land* groups. Steger and his group failed to perceive the seriousness of the threat until it was too late.

The implications of the FPÖ's leadership change appear to be far-reaching. This was to be expected, given the influence which the character of FPÖ leaders has traditionally exercised on the party (see the section on organisation and structure, pp. 220–6). First, Haider's success has already affected the ideological profile of the membership. A number of the previously leading liberals have left the FPÖ including many from the Attersee Circle. The party manager and general-secretary both left, with the latter arguing that 'liberalism has no future in the FPÖ . . . [under] an ideologically suspect new *Führer*'.[19] Others have had equally scathing things to say about the new FPÖ. The right-wing shift in the membership's ideological profile is likely to be enhanced by new recruits coming mainly from the right. Indeed, the party itself perceives a threat of extreme right-wingers infiltrating the FPÖ and has decided to adopt measures to counter this problem (Stix interview).

Secondly, the leadership style of Haider is likely to differ from that of his predecessor. Early indications are that he will conduct the party on the basis of an ongoing dialogue with 'his' grass-roots, whose wishes he will intimate and implement. In short, his leadership style is likely to be populist. Thirdly, the content and delivery of his political message might well be different from Steger's. Even if the party's formal programme remains unaltered, the evidence of the recent electoral campaign and of Haider's speech on assuming the chairmanship suggest an approach which has many of the classical features of Poujadism. However, it must be noted that Haider's political career testifies to his remarkable ideological agility. This chameleon-like quality saw him start his political life as an Upper Austrian national, become a liberal in Vienna and then a national again in Carinthia. It could well see him resume a more liberal tone. He has apparently already argued in the FPÖ's executive committee for a 'social-liberal policy' (Stix interview). Finally, however, it does appear that under its new leadership the FPÖ has opted – at least for the next few years – to revert to its traditional role of a party of protest rather than a party of government.

NOTES

For an earlier version of this paper see K.R. Luther (1986) 'The transformation of the Freedom Party of Austria from old Nazi to liberal party', Staff Papers of School of Public Policy and Administration, Lancashire Polytechnic.

1 Different labels have been applied to the *Third Lager*. Wandruszka's seminal essay almost exclusively refers to it as the '*National Lager*', but in his application of Wandruszka's theory, Berchtold labels the same camp 'German-National/Liberal'. More recently, the term 'National-Liberal' has been used. This essay also employs this designation, since it appears more accurately to reflect topical debates within the camp. The following is a selection of the literature consulted prior to the drafting of the section on the *Third Lager* during the monarchy and First Republic: Berchtold (1967), Fuchs (1949), Kroupa (1984), Sauer (1974) and (1976), Simon (1957), Wandruszka (1957) and (1974) and Wolfram (1974) and (1977). The author is also grateful to Dr Manfred Sauer for his useful explanation of *Third Lager* history.

2 On the VdU, see the following: Berchtold (1967), Kraus (1979), Muller-Klingspor (1972), Perchinig (1983), Reimann (1980), Riedelsperger (1978), Stäuber (1974), Wandruszka (1957). Also very useful regarding the VdU and early FPÖ were an interview with Dr Piringer on 13.12.85, as well as Piringer (1974) and (1982).

3 Kraus recalls a conversation in the late 1960s in which Peter told him that he, too, wanted to bring the ex-Nazis into the liberal *Lager*, but while that had proved impossible for Kraus, it was precisely because Peter was, by contrast, not a liberal but an ex-SS man that he would succeed (Kraus (1979) 28). On the other hand, Peter's SS background frequently caused political controversy, not least as regards the ill-fated proposal that he be elected deputy president of the National Council.

4 On the Attersee Circle see Reiter (1983) and the section on the programmatic dimension, pp. 233–8. Frischenschlager was Defence Minister from 1983 to 1986 (see the section on government participation, pp. 238–42) and Reiter his *chef du cabinet*. Both were academics. For an interesting profile of Steger, see *Das Magazin*, 1983/1, 45ff.

5 Printed in *Freie Argumente*, 1975/2 and /8 and in Reiter (1982) 289ff.

6 Most of the following information derives from an interesting interview with the current general-secretary, Grabher-Meyer, on 12.12.85.

7 Reiter (1982) 20f. estimated the FPÖ staff at all levels to amount to no more than an equivalent of 130–40 full-time posts.

8 See the Austrian press in autumn and winter 1983, especially *Wochenpresse*, and *Profil*.

9 This disguises large regional disparities. In 1983, *Länder* membership density was as follows: Salzburg 23.6%, Styria 21.9%, Upper Austria 19.7%, Carinthia 19.1%, Vorarlberg 17.9%, Burgenland 16.6%, Tyrol 13.3%, Lower Austria 7.2%, Vienna 4.1%. According to information kindly supplied by Dr Müller of Vienna University, the figures for the SPÖ and ÖVP are 30.3% and 34.1% respectively.

10 My own calculations based upon biographical information supplied by the FPÖ in December 1985.

11 While president of the Austrian Trade Union Federation, Olah secretly diverted large sums of money to the FPÖ. When uncovered, these dealings caused considerable controversy not only for Olah's party (the SPÖ), but for the FPÖ also (see Piringer (1982) and Reimann (1980)).

12 Extensive tabulation of the results of this survey were generously supplied by Dr Christian Haerpfer of the Viennese Institute for Conflict Research, whose valuable assistance the author gratefully acknowledges. Discussions in December 1985 with Dr Fritz Plasser of the ÖVP were also very helpful.

13 Though formally not an FPÖ candidate, Scrinzi received support from many local FPÖ officials and members, including ex-Chairman Götz. Declaring himself the only truly 'German' candidate, Scrinzi won 1.2% of the total vote. Yet in Carinthia he achieved 2.8% and in Salzburg 1.7% (*Neue Freie Zeitung*, 8.5.86, 3).

14 I am grateful to the president of the national council, Dr Stix, for his interesting elucidation of the FPÖ's 1985 programme (interview, 12.12.85). Stix was joint chairman with Frischenschlager of the committee responsible for drafting the programme. *Third Lager* programmes up to 1964 can be found in Berchtold (1967). A much wider range of programmatic documentation up to 1980 is contained in Reiter (1982). For the 1985 programme, see bibliography.

15 In this section I was assisted by interviews with FPÖ members, including Vice-Chancellor Steger (26.2.86), General-Secretary Grabher-Meyer (12.12.85), Dr Reiter (11.12.85), and FPÖ press spokesman Kabas (13.12.85). SPÖ MP Professor Nowotny also provided useful insights in an interview on 11.12.85.

16 See note 6 above.

17 For a more detailed evaluation of the election than I can give here, see my 'Austria's Future and Waldheim's Past: the Significance of the 1986 Elections' in *West European Politics*, Vol. 10 (1987).

18 See, for example, *Presse* 6.11.86, 4, *Falter* 19/86, 5f., *Salzburger Fenster* 16/86, 3f., *Klartext* Nr. 141, 10/86, *National freiheitliches Gewissen*, Nr. 6/1986; *Wochenpressse* 23.9.86, 24f. and open letters to the FPÖ by Grabher-Meyer and Kier on 21.11.86 and 12.11.86 respectively. These claims were naturally rejected by the party leaders (Stix and Gugerbauer interviews of 25.11.86). Nonetheless, some Liberal International members were sufficiently concerned to call, albeit in vain, for the FPÖ's exclusion from that organisation.

19 Quoted from Grabher-Meyer's letter. See also Kier's letter (cf. n. 18) and Allesch in *Falter* 19/86, 5f., who argues that the new FPÖ is attracting the authoritarian type who waits for the *Führer* to tell him what to do and is not amenable to rational persuasion. See also the news items of the 'Liberal Initiative' founded by Kier.

REFERENCES

Abbreviations

B: Burgenland
C: Carinthia
FA: *Freie Argumente*
LA: Lower Austria
ÖJP: *Österreichisches Jahrbuch für Politik*
ÖM: *Österreichische Monatshefte*
ÖZP: *Österreichische Zeitschrift für Politikwissenschaft*
Sa: Salzburg
St: Styria
T: Tyrol
UA: Upper Austria
Vi: Vienna
Vo: Vorarlberg

Berchtold, Klaus (ed.) (1967) *Österreichische Parteiprogramme 1868–1966*, Vienna.

Birk, Franz, Gehmacher, Ernst and Traar, Kurt (1983) 'Eine veränderte politische Landschaft. Ergebnisse der Umfrageforschung zu den Nationalratswahlen 1983', in *Journal für Sozialforschung*, 1983/3, 311–24.

Frischenschlager, Friedhelm (1974)'Die Freiheitliche Partei Österreichs' in *Liberal*, 1974/7, 535–46.

Frischenschlager, Friedhelm (1975) 'Österreichische Demokratie und FPÖ' in *FA*, 1975/7, 32–48.

Frischenschlager, Friedhelm (1976) 'Was will der Liberalismus?' in *FA*, 1976/10, 10–27.

Frischenschlager, Friedhelm (1978) 'Funktions- und Inhaltswandlungen von Parteiprogrammen am Beispiel der FPÖ-Programme' in *ÖZP*, 1978/2, 209ff.

Frischenschlager, Friedhelm (1981) 'Wie liberal ist die FPÖ?' in *ÖJP 1980*, 135–81.

Frischenschlager, Friedhelm and Reiter, Erich (1984) *Liberalismus in Europa*, Vienna.

Fritzl, Hermann and Uitz, Martin (1975) 'Kritische Anmerkungen zur sogenannten Lagertheorie' in *ÖZP*, 1975/3; 325–32.

Fuchs, Albert (1949) *Geistige Strömungen in Österreich 1867–1918*, Vienna.

Gerlich, Peter and Müller, Wolfgang (eds.) (1983) *Zwischen Koalition und Konkurrenz. Österreichs Parteien seit 1945*, Vienna.

Haerpfer, Christian (1983) 'Nationalratswahlen und Wahlverhalten seit 1945' in Gerlich and Müller (1983).

Haerpfer, Christian (1985) 'Abschied vom Loyalitätsritual? Langfristige Veränderungen im Wählerverhalten' in Plasser and Ulram and Welen (1985).

Haerpfer, Christian and Gehmacher, Ernst (1984) 'Social structure and voting in the Austrian party system' in *Electoral Studies*, 1984/3, 25–46.

Institut für empirische Sozialforschung (IFES) (1982) 10,000-case polled survey, directed by Ernst Gehmacher, Vienna.

Kadan, Albert (1979) 'Die Freiheitliche Partei Österreichs (FPÖ)' in *Republik*, 1979/1, 16–24.

Kadan, Albert (1981) 'Parteifinanzierung in Österreich und der Bundesrepublik Deutschland' in *Sozialwissenschaftliche Schriftenreihe des Institutes für Grundlagenforschung*, 1981/1, 7–27.

Kadan, Albert and Pelinka, Anton (1979) *Die Grundsatzprogramme der österreichischen Parteien, Dokumentation und Analyse*, St Pölten.

Kraus, Herbert (1979) 'Österreich zwischen 1945 und 1955' in *Schriftenreihe des freiheitlichen Bildungswerkes*, Nr. 2.

Kroupa, Wilhelm (1984) 'Der freiheitliche Beitrag zur Geschichte Österreichs' in *Informationen, Zeitung des Freiheitlichen Bildungswerkes*, 1984/4.

Kubinzky, Karl (1981) 'Wie liberal ist die FPÖ?' in *ÖJP 1980*, 183–7.

Kukacka, Helmut (1985) 'Ein Sieg der Persönlichkeit und der politischen Leistungsfähigkeit' in *ÖM*, 1985/5, 19–24.

Luther, K.R. (1986) 'The transformation of the Freedom Party of Austria from old Nazi to liberal party', Staff Paper of School of Public Policy and Administration, Lancashire Polytechnic.

Müller-Klingspor, Werner (1972) *Die Neuformierung des Freiheitlich Nationalen Lagers in Österreich 1945–1949*, Phd Vienna.

Neugebauer, Wolfgang (1979) 'Die FPÖ – zwischen rechtsextrem und liberal' in Dokumentationsarchiv des österreichischen Widerstandes, *Rechtsextremismus in Österreich nach 1945*, Vienna.

Nick, Rainer and Pelinka, Anton (1983) *Bürgerkrieg–Sozialpartnerschaft. Das politische System Österreichs 1. und 2. Republik: ein Vergleich*, Vienna.

Nick, Rainer and Pelinka, Anton (1984) *Parlamentarismus in Österreich*, Vienna.

Pelinka, Anton (1979) 'Die Grossparteien und der Rechtsextremismus' in Dokumentationsarchiv des österreichischen Widerstandes, *Rechtsextremismus in Österreich nach 1945*, Vienna.

Perchinig, Bernhard (1983) 'National oder liberal: Die Freiheitliche Partie Österreichs' in Gerlich and Müller (1983).

Piringer, Kurt (1974) '25 Jahre Dritte Kraft' in *FA*, 1974/2, 39–55.

Piringer, Kurt (1982) *Die Geschichte der Freiheitlichen. Beitrag der Dritten Kraft zur österreichischen Politik*, Vienna.

Plasser, Fritz and Ulram, Peter (1983) 'Die Nationalratswahl 1983: Dokumentation, Analyse und politische Konsequenzen' in *ÖM*, 1983/4, 127–35.

Plasser, Fritz and Ulram, Peter (1983a) 'Wahlkampf und Wahlentscheidung 1983: Die Analyse einer "kritischen" Wahl' in *ÖZP*, 1983/3, 277–92.

Plasser, Fritz and Ulram, Peter (1985) 'Entsteht ein neues Parteiensystem?' in *ÖM*, 1985/2, 19–22.

Plasser, Fritz and Ulram, Peter (1985a) 'From stability to diffusion: dealignment in the Austrian party system', Paper given at the American Political Science Association, New Orleans, 29.8.–1.9.1985.

Plasser, Fritz and Ulram, Peter (1986) 'Ein Beben mit Folgen, Die Präsidentschaftswahl 1986' in *ÖM*, 1986/4, 6–10.

Plasser, Fritz, Ulram, Peter and Welan, Manfred (1985) *Demokratierituale*, Vienna.

'Parteiprogramm der FPÖ 1985 beschlossen am Programmparteitag 1. and 2. Juni 1985 in Salzburg' (1985) in *Informationen, Zeitung des Freiheitlichen Bildungswerkes*, 1985/4.

Reimann, Viktor (1980) *Die Dritte Kraft in Österreich*, Vienna.

Reiter, Erich (1982) *Programm und Programmentwicklung der FPÖ*, Vienna.

Reiter, Erich (1983) 'Der Atterseekreis innerhalb der Freiheitlichen Partei' in *ÖJP 1982*, 103–24.

Reidelsperger, Max (1978) *The lingering shadow of Nazism: the Austrian Independent Party Movement since 1945*, New York.

Sauer, Manfred (1974) 'Die "Grossdeutsche Volkspartei" und der "Landbund für Österreich" in der Ersten Republik' in *FA*, 1974/2, 12–19.

Sauer, Manfred (1976) 'Josephinismus, Liberalismus und imperiale Idee' in *FA*, 1976/10, 47–70, /11, 25–43, and /12, 55–66.

Simon, Walter (1957) *The Political Parties of Austria*, PhD Columbia.

Stäuber, Roland (1974) *Der Verband der Unabhängigen und die Freiheitliche Partei Österreichs*, PhD, Zurich.

Sully, Melanie (1981) *Political parties and elections in Austria*, London.

Ulram, Peter (1985) 'Ein politischer Erdrutsch: Die Wahlen zur Kammer für Arbeiter und Angestellte 1979 und 1984' in *ÖJP 1984*, 113–32.

Verbindungsstelle der Bundesländer (1981) *Die Wahlen in den Bundesländern seit 1945. Nationalrat und Landtage*, Vienna.

Wandruszka, Adam (1957) 'Österreichs politische Struktur. Die Entwicklung der Parteien und politischen Bewegungen' in Benedikt, Heinrich (ed.), *Geschichte der Republik Österreich*, Vienna.

Wandruszka, Adam (1974) 'Liberalismus in Alt-Österreich' in *FA*, 1974/2: 3–11.

Wolfram, Fritz (1974) 'Die deutschnationale Bewegung in der Monarchie' in *FA*, 1974/2: 12–19.

Wolfram, Fritz (1977) 'Die Programmatik der national-freiheitlichen Parteien in der Ersten Republik (1918–1938)' in *FA*, 1977/3: 1–16.

10

The Swedish Liberal Party: The politics of unholy alliances

Ulf Lindström and Ingemar Wörlund

INTRODUCTION

Sweden is commonly looked upon as the middle-way *Schlaraffenland*,[1] yet its citizens have not found the middle parties to their liking. Rather, the Liberal Party, (Folkpartiet) has often been made an object of ridicule by its opponents and in the media; television cannot resist the temptation to portray the party as an unholy alliance of atheist social science professors from Stockholm and pietist smallholders from the hinterland.

The Liberal Party's overall performance has not generally been applauded by the Swedish electorate. The party's reluctant stance on whether to join bourgeois coalition cabinets engendered much antipathy towards them among the public at large. The Liberal Party was seen as the champion of the 'alternating-majority formula' of governing, i.e. minority cabinets depending on either bourgeois or socialist support to pass legislation in parliament. Political tightrope walking is alien to the rationalist political culture of Sweden.[2]

Time and again political commentators have prophesied the demise of the Liberal Party. Predictions of this kind have repeatedly turned out to be premature, most obviously in 1985 when the Liberal vote soared to 14.2 per cent from a previous all-time low of 5.9 per cent in 1982.

This chapter is meant to be an introduction to the nature and trends of Swedish liberal politics. The various topics raised in the course of the empirical analyses will be synthesised in a concluding discussion on whether Sweden is an illiberal society or, on the contrary, too liberal to be in need of a liberal party, or if the Liberal

Party (until very recently) has misconceived its mission in Swedish politics.

THE EARLY CONDITIONS FOR SWEDISH LIBERALISM

Sweden is one of the most homogeneous countries of the world. She has never been occupied by foreign troops, and her own imperialist era of the seventeenth century[3] came to a close without leaving diasporas of Swedes beyond the Baltic Sea longing for reunion with the fatherland. The Swedish state- and nation-building processes never encountered anything reminiscent of a *Stunde Null*. Having lost the countries east of the Gulf of Bothnia to Russia in 1809 (after 1917 known as the Independent Republic of Finland) the Swedish elites embarked on a large-scale revision of the country's history with the aim of proving that Finland had never been a 'natural' part of Sweden. Faced with Norwegian demands for complete independence from the union with the Swedish royal court,[4] the resistance of the Swedish bourgeoisie finally broke down in 1905; the moneyed section of that group had come to the conclusion that its interests as industrialists were being damaged by Swedish megalomania. When European capitals were set ablaze in 1848, Stockholm got away with stone-throwing in the Old Town; and when the labour movements in Germany, Poland, Hungary, Russia and Finland threw themselves into revolution in the wake of the First World War, Swedish social democracy – in contrast – assumed cabinet portfolios in the government.

According to the Rokkan schema on the conditions of political mass mobilisation, the following were particularly significant in Sweden.[5]

The threshold of legitimisation: Individuals and groups giving voice to deviant political ideas have never been subject to arbitrary, let alone institutionalised, repression. Sweden developed a tradition of *Gemeinschaft* regulation of expression. In the tight and homogeneous social context of the rural areas and small towns, everyone was expected to know his/her place and to obey what was considered *comme-il-faut* in public life.

The threshold of incorporation: Sweden stands out for her very gradualist extension of the suffrage combined with a host of qualifying criteria for gaining the right to vote. In 1866 about twenty per cent of adult males were enfranchised; manhood suffrage came into effect for the first time in 1911; finally, in 1919, women were given the vote and all tax qualifications were abolished.

The threshold of representation: The constitution of 1807 revitalised the Riksdag within the structure of the four-estate diet. It was thanks to two of the estates, those of the burghers and peasants, that the diet managed to survive until 1866, when it was abolished. There was no strict rule as to who would be eligible to qualify as a peasant or a burgher, and that guaranteed a minimum of flexibility in the diet adapting to society's development as a whole. The bicameral Riksdag assembled on the basis of very cumbersome procedures until 1911 when proportional representation was introduced. Prior to this reform, the Liberals and Social Democrats occasionally appeared on joint tickets in parliamentary elections. Finally, in 1970, the unicameral Parliament convened for the first time, elected by strict proportionality except for the effect of the *Sperrklausel:* parties polling less than four per cent of the vote nationwide do not win parliamentary seats (and do not qualify therefore for government subsidies).

The threshold of executive power: Parliamentarism made its major breakthrough in 1917 with the inauguration of the Liberal–Social Democratic Edèn cabinet. Before that, the king retained his constitutional right to make and unmake cabinets. In 1914, for instance, Gustavus V indirectly forced Liberal Party Leader Staaff's cabinet out of office following the so-called courtyard crisis. Cabinet formations have been somewhat complex in Sweden due to ambiguous constitutional procedures and inconsistencies in expert interpretation of the articles guiding dissolutions of Parliament for fresh elections. This problem was felt most acutely during the bicameral era, which provided for the coming and going of weak minority cabinets. It was during the 1920s that the Liberal Party was subject to much criticism by practising the opportunist 'alternating-majority formula' of staying in executive office. The party repeated this option in 1978 only to face the same reaction from the general public.

While the national revolutions of the nineteenth century bypassed Sweden, thus eliminating the likelihood of parties being created from religious, cultural, and ethnic cleavages, the industrial revolution rearranged the conditions for organised liberalism. From their already vulnerable position as parties mobilising a nondescript cross-section of enfranchised Swedes, the liberal force now ran the risk of being deprived of political space in a mass society increasingly ridden by class antagonisms.[6] The mind-boggling genealogy of political liberalism in Sweden is illustrated in Diagram 10.1. Two explanatory comments are particularly appropriate here.

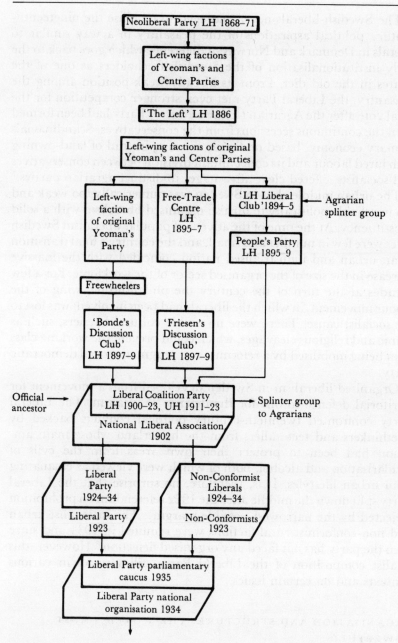

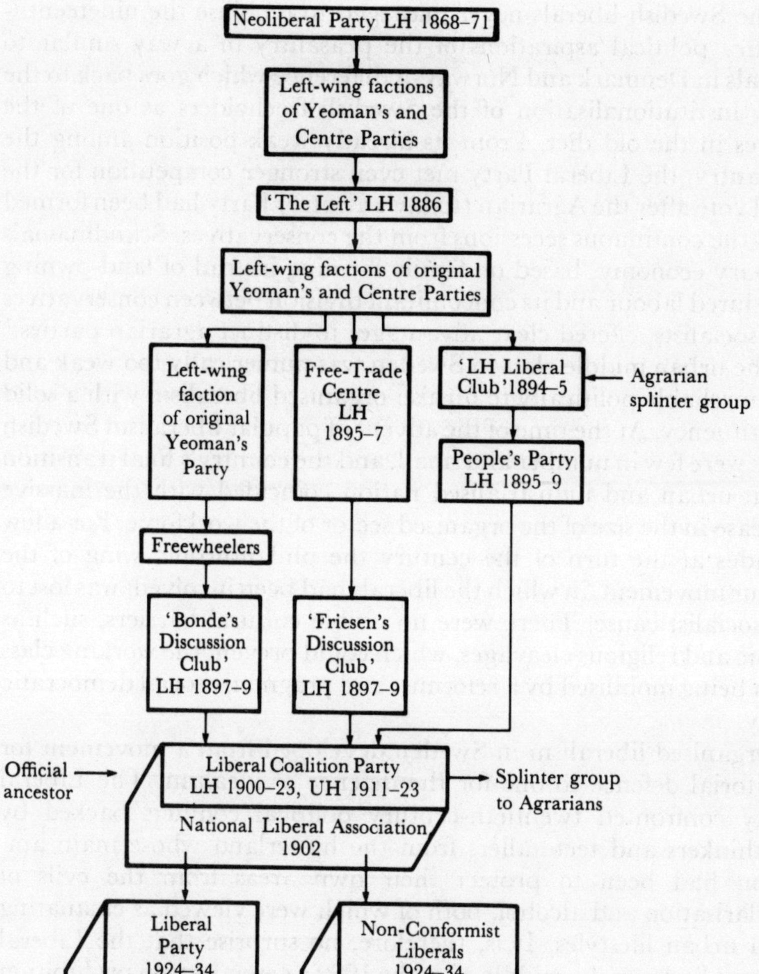

Diagram 10.1 Genealogy of organised liberalism in Sweden, 1868–

Notes:
Inverted commas indicate network rather than party formation
LH = Lower House
UP = Upper House
Names in lower half of boxes = Party member organisation

Source: based on H. A. Larson (ed.), *Centern – en vital 70-åring*, Stockholm: Centerns Riksorganisation, 1980.

The Swedish liberals never managed to mobilise the nineteenth-century political aspirations of the peasantry in a way similar to liberals in Denmark and Norway, a difference which goes back to the early institutionalisation of the Swedish freeholders as one of the estates in the old diet. From its already weak position among the peasantry, the Liberal Party met even stronger competition for the rural vote after the Agrarian (today's Centre) Party had been formed from the continuous secessions from the conservatives. Scandinavia's primary economy, based on family farming instead of land-owning with hired labour and its concomitant division between conservatives and socialists, offered clear advantages to distinct agrarian parties.[7]

The urban middle class in Sweden was numerically too weak and too unreliable politically to furnish organised liberalism with a solid constituency. At the time of the advent of popular liberalism Swedish cities were few in number and small, and the country's final transition to an urban and industrialised nation coincided with the massive increase in the size of the organised sector of the workforce. For a few decades at the turn of the century the philanthropic wing of the labour movement, in which the liberals had been involved, was lost to the socialist cause. There were no visible cultural barriers, such as ethnic and religious cleavages, which could prevent the working class from being mobilised by a reformist and pragmatic social democratic party.

Organised liberalism in Sweden developed from a movement for territorial defence to one for the defence of idealism. The Liberal Party confronted twentieth-century political conflicts backed by freethinkers and teetotallers from the hinterland whose main ambition had been to protect their own areas from the evils of secularisation and alcohol, both of which were viewed as emanating from urban lifestyles. It is, therefore, no surprise that the Liberal Party split down the middle after the 1922 referendum on prohibition (rejected by the narrowest possible margin). The rationalist urban and non-conformist rural factions were reunited in 1934 and since then the party has not faced any organised defection.[8] However, this dualist composition of the Liberal Party still surfaces in various contexts and on certain issues.

ORGANISATION AND STRUCTURE: THE WORLD'S MOST POWERFUL?

Election nights in the West have one common feature. Having watched the disappointing figures flash over the television screen the fatigued party leader has one standard explanation to offer the reporters: we lost because we didn't get enough exposure and enough money. Of course, party leaders are not expected to admit that their platforms are out of touch with the sentiments of the electorate. Hints to the effect that the party would have done even worse had it secured more exposure are brushed aside as academic wisecracks. Nevertheless, party headquarters operate on the basis that all it takes to win is convertible assets.

The relationship between electoral returns and party organisation (convertible assets) is next to impossible to confirm other than by theoretical statements concerning the causal links involved:

Socio-economic structure ⟶ corporate party hierarchies ⟿ party organisation ⟶ vote

The Liberal membership statistics for the period after the Second World War do not lend support to the idea behind the right-hand side of the above chart. At times it seems as if a growing number of members subsequently pays off at the polls; at times it looks like an electoral success helps the recruitment of new members. For instance, between 1945 and 1951 the Liberal rank-and-file rose from 34,000 to 97,000 members, a trend which culminated with the all-time high of 24.4 per cent of the vote in the 1952 election. However, for the last twenty-five years of Liberal ups and downs at the polls, its membership has been shrinking. In 1985, the Liberal Party had 42,400 members (it obtained 792,268 ballots among the 6,249,445 entitled to vote, of which 5,615,242 actually turned out to vote).[9]

Rank-and-file members are no longer of vital concern to any party in Sweden. The Liberal member has been the most expendable of all; ever since the 1920s the liberal press has accounted for about half the total circulation of newspapers. While not as partisan as that of the labour movement, the liberal press nevertheless gives more space to liberal politics than would be warranted from a neutral news editor's point of view.

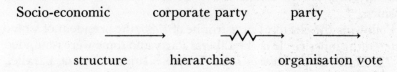

Since the parties voted themselves public subsidies in the sixties, it is the taxpayers who finance Swedish parties. In 1983, the combined national, regional, and local expenditure on all parties amounted to SEK 280 million (appr. 28 million pounds sterling or 5.00 pounds sterling per voter). Each party is reimbursed according to its proportion of the vote or its number of seats in elected assemblies. For the Liberal Party's financial status in 1983 this meant that the party collected SEK 23.4 million in combined public subsidies. The bookkeeping of the party's national organisation in 1986 shows that SEK 11.8 million were obtained from taxpayers and 2.2 million were raised by the party itself.

As the bills calling for public subsidies to parties (and the press) were passed by the Communists, the Social Democrats and the Centre Party in parliament, fearful voices were heard prophesying fatal consequences for the spiritual and financial commitment of party members. Indeed, more than half of the Liberal Party's local organisations no longer have any substantial sources of revenue other than that provided by public subsidies. From the early seventies, the Liberal Party has no longer accepted cash contributions from big business.[10]

Following the electoral catastrophe of 1983, the president of Volvo entered the inner circle of the Liberal Party and some were reminded of *The Eighteenth Brumaire of Louis Bonaparte*. It is a tempting parallel, but nonetheless a misleading one. Neither big business nor teachers have had the party under either overt or covert control. The only liberal faction of any stability is that of the non-conformists, the old *frisinnade*, whose leverage is inversely correlated with the popular strength of the party. The non-conformists are not in the habit of fighting widely-publicised show-downs with the rationalist liberals. Instead they toil in silence, ready to raise their voices at caucus meetings against close alliances with the Conservatives (see below), eager to strengthen the ties between the grass-root organisations, the parliamentary caucus, and the party leadership.

As can be seen from Diagram 10.2, the Liberal Party is organised on the basis of its mass-membership, emphasising territorial representation but also accommodating three subgroups, namely, women, youth, and the liberal press. One group is officially excluded from the diagram: the parliamentary caucus, which has always been the most powerful element. Ever since the Second World War, internal party democracy has been an important issue among the Liberals. The party's youth branch and the non-conformists have demanded that the parliamentary caucus should be made answerable to the national convention. Those who plead for the retaining of the autonomy of the parliamentary caucus prefer to regard the national convention as an opportunity for the manifestation of party cohesion. Bertil Ohlin, a well-known Professor of Economics and party leader during the heyday of Swedish liberalism between 1945 and 1958, strongly resisted calls for extended democracy within the party. He was against roll-calls as a method of decision-making at both the meetings of the party board and at national conventions. Indeed, on average, two motions were listed on the agenda![11] Measures have since been taken to invigorate internal party democracy.

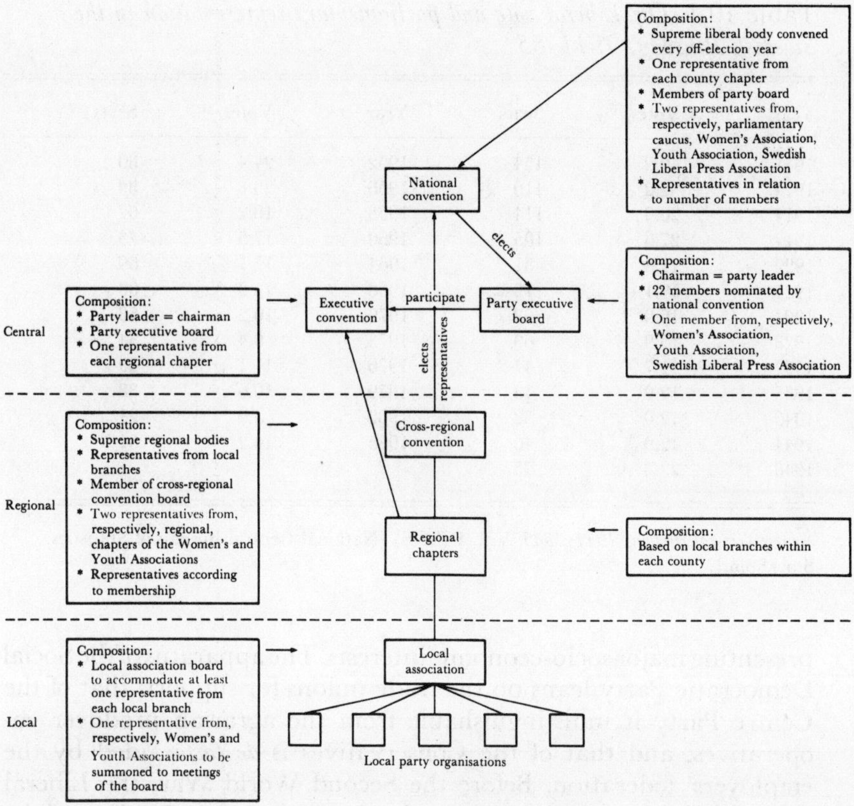

Diagram 10.2 Organisational structure in the Liberal Party

All Liberal Party leaders having held office between 1967 and 1983 have experienced the same pattern in terms of popularity: during the early period after having assumed office their popularity figures rose markedly only to fall equally markedly soon afterwards.[12]

Bengt Westerberg, who assumed this task after the 1982 election, is so far no exception to the rule. In fact, media reports have it that he went on a honeymoon trip with the Swedish people after election day in 1985. In the first post-election poll, the Liberals received 23.5 per cent of the vote.

The reason why the Liberal Party – its leaders, members, and voters alike – is so vulnerable to external forces is hinted at in Diagram 10.2 above. In terms of access to financial sources and the printed media, the Liberal Party is not (relatively speaking) worse off than any of the other Swedish parties. What the Liberal organisation lacks is the backing of powerful and reliable corporate hierarchies re-

Table 10.1 *The Liberal vote and parliamentary representation in the Swedish Riksdag, 1911–85*

Year	Votes, %	Seats	Year	Votes, %	Seats
1911	40.2	154	1952	24.4	80
1914	32.2	119	1956	23.8	88
1914	26.9	114	1958	18.2	67
1917	27.6	105	1960	17.5	73
1920	21.8	81	1964	17.1	69
1921	19.1	79	1968	14.3	60
1924	16.9	68	1970	16.2	58
1928	15.9	63	1973	9.4	34
1932	11.7	47	1976	11.1	39
1936	12.9	43	1979	10.6	38
1940	12.0	38	1982	5.9	21
1944	12.9	40	1985	14.2	51
1948	22.8	75			

Source: General elections 1911–1985, Vol. 1 (SOS) (National Central Bureau of Statistics, Stockholm).

presenting major socio-economic interests. The apparatus of the Social Democratic Party leans on the trade unions for support; that of the Centre Party is indistinguishable from the agrarian producer co-operatives; and that of the Conservatives is *de facto* aided by the employers' federation. Before the Second World War, the Liberal Party probably drew on scattered support from local lodges of the teetotalist movement and freethinking congregations. Today, these voluntary associations are of marginal importance in the party's endeavours in mobilising its vote.

ELECTORAL BASE: MOBILISING EVERYBODY AND NOBODY

Just because the Liberal Party pledges itself to ideas instead of interests does not mean its constituency exists in a social vacuum. However, the structural properties that work in favour of the Liberal vote (see Table 10.1) cannot be identified through the use of bivariate discriminants. This is forcefully brought out by the various data compiled in Tables 10.2–5: few single coefficients and percentage distributions are of much help in trying to pin down the typical Liberal constituency or individual voters.

Between the two World Wars Liberals could obviously be found in urban as well as rural areas, and in the latter, the proportion of smallholders rather than freeholders and landowners was the only variable with a minimum of correlation with the Liberal vote.[13] Some, but far from conclusive, evidence for the notion of the Liberal party mobilising the two counter-cultural communities can also be presented. It was primarily the non-conformist context that was an asset to the party's electoral strength. Moreover, there is little or no evidence to suggest that the Liberals capitalised on a purported generation and gender gap. The Liberal attraction to the working class is very modest indeed. In 1982, only one out of a hundred workers voted Liberal! Otherwise expressed (but not shown in Table 10.2), 63 per cent of the Liberal constituency consists of people holding middle-class occupations.[14]

This does not mean that all conceptions of a Liberal 'core' are academic phantoms or inventions by the media. Why is it that we readily believe a district attorney in a small picturesque town, a schoolteacher or a smallholder in an egalitarian countryside to be Liberals? It is the spatial distribution in particular that sets our minds working this way. Here geography alone must not be confused with the most significant four points. Rather, the term subsumes the historical, social, and cultural factors which once went towards cementing the Liberal core.

Although Sweden was undergoing a complete transition at the turn of the century, civil society changed and evolved without wrecking its basic continuity. Family bonds guaranteed inter-generational stability in political alignments; the children also inherited partisan affiliations from their parents. As long as social mobility, (working-class children turning into white-collar workers) remained low, so did the level of cross-pressure on the electorate.

Sweden's entry into the welfare era may be dated to the early 1960s. Ever since, civil society has been exposed to processes slowly eroding its basic structure, namely work and residence. People have moved – six out of ten Swedes no longer live where they were born and raised[15] – to take up work not easily classified according to traditional socio-economic criteria, and the residential areas in which this so-called 'dessert generation' settled never acquired a tight and united politico-cultural network. In the meantime, the local contexts prevalent at the time of the breakthrough of mass politics – isolated industrial towns of the provinces where people were born into the labour movement, municipalities dominated by the free-thinking culture where people were born into the Liberal community – have withered away. The total number of voters still living in the latter enclaves, where party disloyalty is tantamount to a serious public indiscretion, is now simply too small to ensure a Liberal core of more than, say, five per cent of the total electorate.

Table 10.2 *The Liberal constituency 1921–85: highlights*

	Economy			Culture		Geography				Sociology								Politics							
	Industry (1940)	Agriculture (1940)	Smallholders (1932)	Non-conformists (1920–40)	Teetotallers (1920–40)	Rural areas	Municipalities	Cities	Stockholm, Göteborg, Malmö	Blue-collar workers	Other workers	Lower white-collar workers	Middle white-collar workers	Upper white-collar workers	Small businessmen	Farmers	Students	Communists	Social Democrats	Liberals	Christian Democrats	Centre Party	Conservatives	Turnout	Sources
1921	−0.14	0.11	0.17	0.00	0.00	Coefficients; Liberal vote – % of population in two sectors (census years), % of all farmsteads (census year), % of population members (years). N of minor civil-divisions approx. 2,500.																			1
1936	−0.07	0.01	0.15	0.27	0.10																				
1978				26	15	% voting Liberal according to sample survey 1978.																			2
1982						12	26	50	12	Spatial composition of the Liberal vote 1982, %															3
1976										5	7	16	20	19	21	5	12	Where did the Liberal 1979 vote go in 1982?, %							
1979	Class distribution of the vote, %									5	8	16	14	20	14	5	7								
1982										1	4	8	8	11	7	3	9	1	10	44	3	10	27		4
1982	Party distribution of the vote and turnout 1982 and 1985, %																	5.6	45.6	5.9	—	17.4	23.6	91.4	5
1985																		5.4	44.7	14.2	—	12.4	21.3	89.9	

Sources:

1. Ecological data bank with the Dept. of Political Science, University of Umeå, supplemented by data from the Dept. of History, University of Uppsala (non-conformist and teetolalist membership).
2. *Frikyrko-Sverige – en livsstilsstudie*, (Stockholm: Moderna Läsare, 1979); *Nykterhets-Sverige – en livsstilsstudie* (Stockholm: Sober, 1979).
3. Sören Holmberg, *Väljare i förandring* (Stockholm: Liber, 1985) p. 113.
4. Sören Holmberg, *Väljare i förandring* (Stockholm: Liber, 1985) p. 95, p. 29.
5. Election statistics. In 1985 the Christian Democrats appeared on a joint list with the Centre Party.

Table 10.3 *Party preference among first-time voters, 1956–82%*

Year	Communists	Social Democrats	Centre Party	Liberals	Conservatives	Others	Total	N
1956	0	54	9	26	11	0	100	35
1960	0	65	10	6	19	0	100	43
1964	0	52	13	23	7	5	100	87
1968	2	57	14	18	6	3	100	100
1970	11	46	28	10	5	0	100	226
1973	12	36	36	3	10	3	100	126
1976	9	41	26	12	10	2	100	211
1979	11	33	20	13	20	3	100	133
1982	7	45	13	6	23	6	100	139

Source: Sören Holmberg, *Väljare i förändring*, (Stockholm: Liber, 1985).

Table 10.4 *Proportion of women in the Liberal constituency, 1970–82, %*

	1970	1973	1976	1979	1982
Women	53	51	47	50	57

Source: General elections 1970–1982, Vol. 3 (SOS) (National Central Bureau of Statistics, Stockholm).

Table 10.5 *Liberal Party preference by sex, 1970–82, %*

	1970	1973	1976	1979	1982
Women	14	9	12	11	7
Men	14	8	12	11	5

Source: General elections 1970–1982, Vol. 3, (SOS) (National Central Bureau of Statistics, Stockholm).

This dealignment of voting behaviour may be seen as an opportunity for an issue-oriented party such as the Liberal Party; its successful gains in the 1985 election seems to confirm such a possibility. However, before we predict another glorious era for the Liberals, two things must be kept in mind. First, voters who have been taken from the close *Gemeinschaft* of their immediate surroundings have not been atomised and become targets for just about any political entrepreneur. Developments like that were stifled by the massive growth of interest organisations with more or less formal ties to the political parties, especially trade unions organising middle-class people – the Liberal target group *par excellence*. They have grown strong and increasingly social democratic (at least among the union officials). Second, opportunity means risks, risks of misinterpreting the perception of the electorate, risks of being outgunned by the opposing parties, and risks of making strange bedfellows or being left out in the cold in parliament.

GOVERNMENT PARTICIPATION: THE POLITICS OF RELUCTANCE[16]

Cabinet formation in multi-party systems need not necessarily be an incomprehensible process replete with conflicting means and goals. Formalised models on coalition building reduce the problem to a matter of arithmetic: if parliament houses five parties of about equal representation in terms of seats, a three-party majority cabinet is expected to take office. Should this prediction fail, the mathematician swiftly adds one or two qualifying variables to support the initial hypothesis. The student of Swedish cabinet formation is well advised to prepare himself for more than simple calculations. Two factors limit the usefulness of formalised models: the dominance of the Social Democratic Party, and the variegated character of Swedish party politics.

The Liberal Party always runs the risk of alienating its left-leaning constituents and party members whenever it reaches for agreements with the Conservatives. The reverse is true if the Liberal Party approaches the Social Democrats. Diagram 10.3 sets out the Liberal options in parliament and lists the portfolios held by the Liberal Party when it has shared cabinet responsibility.

Modern Swedish parliamentarism knows of three instances when the Liberal Party has controlled the executive in its own right, in 1926–8, 1930–2, and 1978–9. Complex circumstances rather than the party's own wishes helped thrust the Liberals into cabinet positions. However, there is a liberal wing which explicitly advocates such a role for the party. The arguments heard in favour of the 'alternating-majority formula' – voiced mainly by those with ties to the old non-conformist faction – refer to the party's responsibility as a moderating force between a too radical Social Democratic Party and a too reactionary Conservative Party. By leaning on tacit or open support from the Social Democrats, the Liberal cabinet can push bills improving social security and jobs through parliament and by turning to the Conservatives, the Liberal cabinet serves as a bulwark

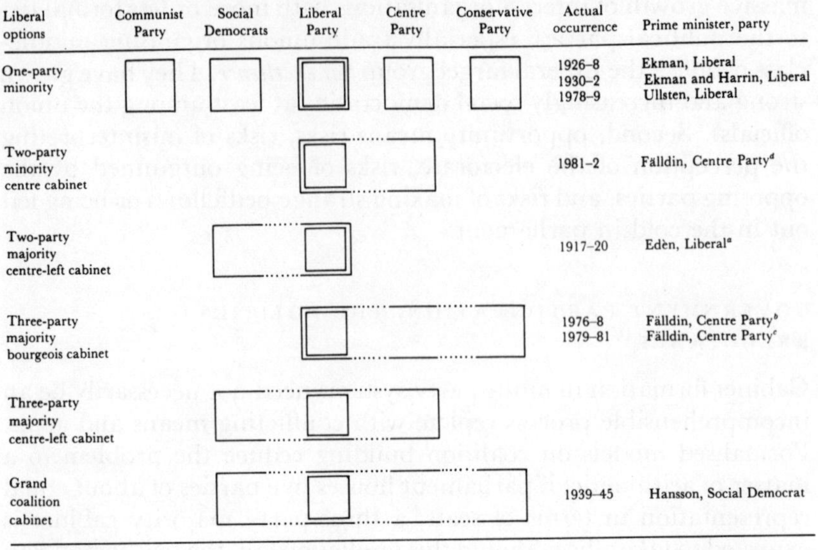

Liberal options	Communist Party	Social Democrats	Liberal Party	Centre Party	Conservative Party	Actual occurrence	Prime minister, party
One-party minority						1926–8 1930–2 1978–9	Ekman, Liberal Ekman and Harrin, Liberal Ullsten, Liberal
Two-party minority centre cabinet						1981–2	Fälldin, Centre Party[d]
Two-party majority centre-left cabinet						1917–20	Edèn, Liberal[a]
Three-party majority bourgeois cabinet						1976–8 1979–81	Fälldin, Centre Party[b] Fälldin, Centre Party[c]
Three-party majority centre-left cabinet							
Grand coalition cabinet						1939–45	Hansson, Social Democrat

Note: [a] Total 11 [b] Total 21 [c] Total 20 [d] Total 18

Liberal members of cabinet:

M of Foreign Affairs	M of Finance	M of Foreign Affairs	M of Foreign Affairs
M of Justice	M of Education	M of Finance	M of Finance
M of Civil Service Affairs	M of Labour	M of Education	M of Education
M of Agriculture	M w P	M of Labour	M of Commerce
M w P*		M of Housing	M of Labour
M of Defence			M of Housing
			M w P
			M w P
			M of Transport

* M w P = Minister without Portfolio

Diagram 10.3 Cabinet formations in Sweden, with special reference to Liberal Party options

against encroachments upon free enterprise and against leaving too much power in the hands of organised interests. In addition, the Liberal Party will be the focus of media coverage and this may help the party in recruiting a growing number of uncommitted voters. Rejections of this one-party minority option can easily be found. Swedes have grown accustomed to predictability in the government process; they appreciate neither the alternation of socialist and bourgeois weeks, nor the combination of a socialist foreign policy and a bourgeois economic policy. Second, the opposing parties will certainly not miss the opportunity to promise more of what is generally thought of as most attractive in the Liberal record, thus leaving the cabinet with the blame for what is considered a failure, such as increasing inflation rates and rising unemployment figures.

The most recent Liberal minority cabinet took office in 1978 and it lasted for less than a year.[17] It succeeded the first bourgeois majority cabinet to break the 44 years of uninterrupted Social Democratic rule. However, in October 1978, the Centre Party broke with the Liberals and Conservatives on the issue of nuclear energy policy. Why did the Liberals subsequently opt for a one-party cabinet on their own, rather than carrying on with the Conservatives for the remaining year of the parliamentary term? At the first meeting of the Liberal Riksdag caucus following the cabinet crisis, only three out of the 39 MPs were in favour of a Liberal–Conservative deal. Some said that the Conservatives were unacceptable on historical grounds; the two parties had once been arch-rivals on the issues of universal suffrage and parliamentarism, and the non-conformist subculture within the Liberal Party especially could not easily forget that. Liberal MPs, less concerned with historical conflicts but equally in favour of rejecting the Conservatives, saw that the one-party solution would put an end to time-consuming negotiations within the cabinet on government proposals, energy better spent in steering bills through parliament. In addition, an alliance with the Conservatives would give both the Centre and Social Democratic Parties ample opportunity for attacking the Liberals for going right, allegedly alienating left-leaning Liberal voters.

Despite such reasons, the Liberals have taken part in a two-party minority cabinet. This was in 1981–2, following a second exodus from a bourgeois majority coalition. This time, it was the Conservatives who felt their position was becoming untenable since the two centre parties were not prepared to adopt the proposed Conservative tax cuts. All that remains in favour of the Liberals embroiling themselves in this type of minority cabinet comes down to affective ties. A few Liberals still entertain the dream that one day the centre parties will become the dominant force in Swedish politics, reducing the Social Democratic and Conservative Parties to positions comparable to that of today's combined strength of the political centre.

Why is it that a Liberal–Social Democratic coalition has not been repeated after the experience of 1917–20? First and foremost, this solution (common in Denmark) has not been attractive enough to the powerful Social Democratic Party. But what about Liberal views? No doubt, such a coalition is embraced by a few liberal so-called 'social engineers', but this faction is hard pressed to convince the party leadership that a deal with the Social Democrats would not reduce the Liberal Party to nothing but an appendix in Swedish politics. One thing is certain: an actual attempt at a Liberal–Social Democratic coalition would be met with vociferous accusations of betrayal from the Conservatives.

If the overwhelming majority of Liberal MPs find the Conservatives such a repugnant party, how come that they have entered a bourgeois coalition on two occasions and are prepared to re-enter such a coalition today? It is only recently, (in the early seventies) that the Liberal Party explicitly and in advance of the elections, began to reconcile itself with the concept of a bourgeois coalition. (However, all three parties presented separate manifestos for the elections.) One reason for this change of opinion is that few liberals seriously believe in a permanent revitalisation of the party comparable to its period of strength during the forties and fifties. Thus, if accompanied by the Centre Party (a definite requirement), the Liberal Party sees the middle parties as a sufficiently potent counterbalance to Conservative influence in a bourgeois coalition. Since this cabinet format is the only realistic chance for the Conservatives to gain office, not only may the Liberals feel content that the Conservatives will bend over backwards to accommodate the middle parties, but also ensure that the right wing of the Conservative Party tows the line. The Liberals may also argue that the Social Democrats will stop at nothing to stigmatise a bourgeois coalition as one being run by the Conservatives, and if this attack is successful, the two middle parties will lose their left-wing constituents to the Social Democrats at the next election, thus eroding the potential parliamentary plurality of the non-socialist bloc.

Diagram 10.3 contains one highly hypothetical option for the Liberals: a majority cabinet including the Social Democratic, Liberal, and Centre Parties. This centre-left formation rests upon a concept of an 'anti-extremist coalition', in so far as it would be flanked by a weak Communist and a strong Conservative Party. It takes at least two major changes in Swedish – and possibly one in international – politics before this option can realistically be discussed outside the academic community. First, the Social Democratic Party would have to be weakened at the polls to a 'Danish' level, one at which forty rather than fifty per cent of the vote is attainable in the near future (not to be expected in the face of what the assassination of Olof Palme did to the popular appeal of Swedish Social Democracy). Second, the Social Democratic Party must get a clear response from the public at large about the Conservatives not being altogether reliable with respect to the country's foreign policy of neutrality and non-alignment. However, it would also require another movement away from *détente* in Europe before the Social Democrats would be able to convince the Swedish people about the risks inherent in the allegedly pro-NATO stance of the Conservatives. Should these requirements be met however, it is not unlikely that some kind of centre-left crisis agreement could be reached, an agreement based on, first, a purported community of interest in defending the Welfare

State against unrestrained *laissez-faire* politics, and, second, a nationalist façade of Swedish neutrality in the face of international tension.

The last entry in Diagram 10.3, the Grand Coalition cabinet (excluding the Communists), was a war-time phenomenon to ensure a maximum of national unity. While this option used to attract the Conservatives during the years immediately after the Second World War, it has never registered much sympathy among the Liberals. There are two important exceptions to this. Herbert Tingsten, one-time Social Democrat, and later editor-in-chief of the largest Liberal morning paper, *Dagens Nyheter*, came out strongly for the idea of permanent coalitions, a system akin to the Swiss model. Tingsten, the Swedish proponent of the 'end-of-ideology' thesis of the mid-fifties, saw no reason for the parties to hold fast to obsolete antagonisms. A permanent coalition would exert a healthy impact on the quality of the political debate, eliminating outdated rhetoric and irresponsible overbidding among the parties in favour of informed arguments subject to intellectual scrutiny.[18] Six months before the 1985 Riksdag election which gave the Social Democratic cabinet three more years of parliamentary control, *Dagens Nyheter* reopened the debate about permanent coalitions. For most Liberals, however, this concept violates the leading rationale of parliamentarism represented by the once influential British tradition.

Parliamentary caucuses do not consist of integrated bodies. Nothing is said in the Swedish constitution about MPs having to obey the party whips. Once elected, the individual MP is at (theoretical) liberty to follow nothing but his or her conscience. Although the Riksdag is known for its faithful roll-calls according to party, occasionally parliament is disturbed/reinvigorated by mavericks. Whilst most non-partisan roll-calls are harmless, whenever the main economic bills are placed before the Riksdag, the party whips are not indulgent with regard to individual preferences. It does not come as a surprise that the socialist parties show the highest level of party cohesion in parliament. Nevertheless, it is a fact that the Liberal Party, usually along with the Centre or all bourgeois MPs, has always been known to register more frequent defections from its ranks than the other parties.[19] It is true that this observation makes sense in view of the Liberal position as a party squeezed in between the left and the right. Liberal free-wheeling may also be explained on the grounds of the division between the non-conformist and urban liberals. Indeed, issues involving matters such as religion and alcohol are generally judged by individual MPs irrespective of party affiliation. One would, nonetheless, expect the Liberal Party to be very concerned about party unity. The Liberal caucus is not very large, but the Liberals can sometimes win the attention of Social Democratic cabinets which more often than not are in need of votes from other parties to have legislation passed by the Riksdag. Since there is a traditional reluctance amongst many Social Democratic MPs to depend on the Communists for passing bills in parliament, the Liberal Party can exert influence on Social Democratic cabinets through the method known as 'anticipated reactions'. Empirical data do not suggest that this type of roll-call co-operation is common practice. On the contrary, of all the bourgeois parties, the Liberal Party is the least frequent ally of the Social Democrats. However, it is more than educated guesswork to suspect that this pattern reflects Social Democratic, Centre, and Conservative ties to corporate interests, whose mode of operation tends to be reflected in the parliamentary arena as well.

We may thus conclude that the Swedish Liberals, as a party as well as individual MPs, have been leading an uncomfortable life in parliament. In whatever direction the Liberal Party turns for allies – and it cannot avoid taking sides – there will always be MPs, party officials, members, and voters whose instincts and feelings are ignored.

LIBERAL POLICY: FIGHTING FOR THE ILLUSORY AVERAGE

The Liberal Party is at pains to defend its own issues whenever they fit along the left–right dimension of conflict. Historically, many Liberal demands were borrowed and eventually refined into causes championed by the Conservatives and Social Democrats (of course the reverse is also true). Political moderation is indeed the imprint of the typical Swedish voter. While, in this sense, the Liberal Party is in tune with the sentiments of the vast majority of the electorate, the media (and television in particular) contribute towards making public debate polarised. In the sixties, it was the left who asked the questions with the right on the defensive; today it is the other way around and few care about the opinion of the political centre. We should not be surprised by this. The media and political centrism traditionally do not mix; the media's task is to make the complex simple, the fate of liberalism is to make the simple complex. Diagram 10.4 bears witness to this. Irrespective of the *Zeitgeist* the Liberal elite, as opposed to those of the Social Democratic and Conservative Parties, has been reluctant to take a firm position on the issue of more or less state intervention in society.

At regular intervals we have been told that the left–right cleavage is

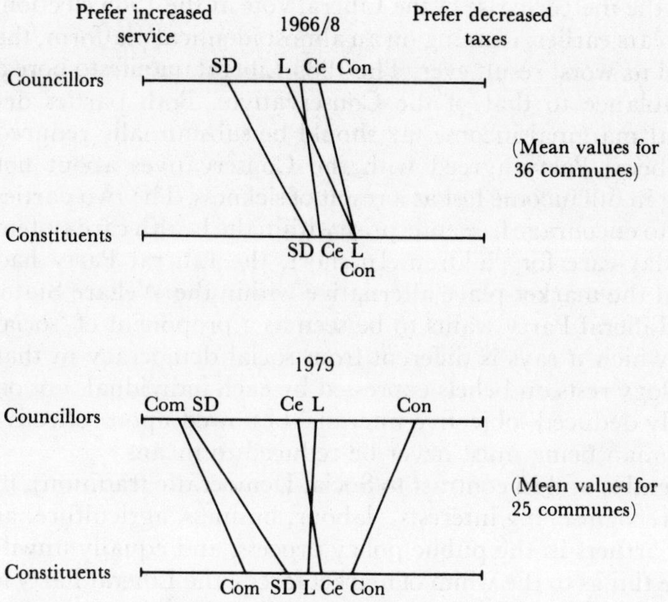

Diagram 10.4 Profiles of opinion on taxes and services among elected members of local councils and constituents, 1966–8 and 1979

Notes:
Com = Communists
SD = Social Democrats
L = Liberals
Ce = Centre Party
Con = Conservatives

Source: L. Strömberg and J. Westerståhl, *The New Swedish Communes* (Stockholm: Liber, 1984) 47.

obsolete expressed through the end-of-ideology thesis of the fifties and the green wave of the early seventies. While the former trend coincided with the heyday of Swedish liberalism, the latter became a burden for the Liberals in so far as the Centre Party monopolised the ecologists and the rurally romantic. The Liberal Party certainly did not follow in the footsteps of its Norwegian sister party. In the 1980 referendum on nuclear energy development, the Liberal Party joined the Social Democrats in advocating a substantial nuclear power plant programme.

It is true that the Liberal Party has registered some success in introducing issues at variance with the left–right conception of Swedish politics. Quite a number of the electorate identify equality between the sexes and aid to developing countries as Liberal causes.[20] However, one must not jump to the conclusion that these issues alone account for the meteoric rise of the Liberal vote at the 1985 election; only three years earlier, running on an almost identical platform, the party scored its worst result ever. The 1985 Liberal manifesto bore a basic resemblance to that of the Conservatives. Both parties demanded that marginal income tax should be substantially reduced and the Liberal Party agreed with the Conservatives about not reimbursing in full income lost as a result of sickness. The two parties also agreed to encourage free enterprise within the health care system as well as day-care for children. In short, the Liberal Party had rediscovered the market-place alternative within the Welfare State.

Yet, the Liberal Party wants to be seen as a proponent of 'social liberalism' which it says is different from social democracy in that liberal ideology rests on beliefs expressed by each individual, not on teleologically deduced 'objective interests' bestowed upon collectivities; the human being must never be reduced to means.

Consequently (and in contrast to Social Democratic tradition), in refusing to recognise 'big interests' (labour, business, agriculture) as legitimate partners in the public policy process, and equally unwilling to leave things to the whim of market forces, the Liberal Party is trapped in an awkward situation. For the Liberals, only one tool of governing remains, viz., government in the old constitutionalist term of the word (or the *Rechtsstaat*), an institution which cannot but grow into big government if it is to face up to the challenges of a modern welfare society. This Liberal dilemma is very concrete in the case of tackling industrial relations. Government committees are to be given a greater say in wage contracts through arbitration so that each party concerned, including the Ministry of Finance, gets a fair deal.

One can only assume that Sweden, according to the Liberals, is to be governed by bookish laws drafted by the meritocracy and not by bargaining among giant interests. This explains why, amongst the informed observers of Swedish politics, the Liberal Party is associated with restrictions on more than just the consumption of alcohol. Liberalism is not, however, to be confused with libertarianism. Nonconformism, as one expression of the extensive social responsibilities assumed by the Swedish Liberals, acts as a belief in the rational solving of societal malfunctions, with a moral *raison d'être*. The two – sectarianism and hierarchy[21] – mix perfectly well in a country which has never experienced a liberal revolution.

LIBERAL STRATEGY: NO LONGER THE BOURGEOIS MODERATOR?

'Being Liberal is to be split', Liberal Party Leader Gunnar Helen once blurted out and he earned himself a reputation as being naïve as a result. Liberal ideas fare badly in Swedish political debate, which tends to drown voices if there are more than two at a time, one of which is always that of social democracy. The Liberal Party once – during the late forties and early fifties – occupied the position which has recently been held by the Conservatives. Large portions of the middle-class vote were then moving leftwards whereas, up until the 1982 election, the bulk of the floating non-Socialist vote acted to increase the Conservative constituency. In 1985, however, the tide turned in favour of the Liberals again.

The Liberal Party faces the classic Downsian dilemma: multi-party systems encourage all interests to try their fortunes at the polls, while, at the same time, the one-dimensional left–right cleavage tells them that all but two parties are expendable. What has the Liberal leadership done to overcome this paradox? Has it left the problem in the hands of party strategists thoroughly familiar with Downs's vote-maximisation thesis, or with those who know Sjöblom's concepts by heart and who, therefore, argue for the party to pursue the contradictory aims of maximisation of parliamentary influence and party cohesion?[22]

Swedish politics is marked by pragmatism. The question of who is to control the executive constantly ranks high among the concerns of the voters, even above specific issues such as government interference in the economy. In 1985, for instance, the Social Democrats won the election partly on their image as the only reliable possibility when it comes to executive stability. The Liberal Party, too, is preoccupied with how to get the most out of its position in parliament. This, of course, makes life less pleasant for the party's ideologues whose conception of true liberalism does not easily permit the accommodation of Centre Party demands for increased subsidies to agriculture. The party's election strategists also have to accept less than satisfactory solutions in order to let the party leadership have their say in cabinet.

Party strategists, however gifted, cannot perform miracles. The best they can do in a party landscape where firm class alignments have reduced the proportion of volatile voters to about twenty per cent of the electorate is to try and mould the *Zeitgeist* into attractive policies. Of course, for the Liberal Party, which fights for the large proportion of uncommitted bourgeois voters, this can mean the difference between success and failure.

The campaign output of the sixties confirmed that Liberal propaganda was addressed not to classes but to groups: the retired, the young, families with children, etc.[23] For a party whose cross-class appeal is well known, this may indeed seem a wise strategy. The problem is that age, sex and similar characteristics carry little weight in terms of party preference (cf. Tables 10.3–5), once class-related discriminants are brought to bear on voting behaviour.

When a party finds it difficult to convince the voters about its own qualities, it can always try to make its opponents look worse. In this respect, the Liberal Party has waged unbalanced campaigns, primarily attacking the incumbent Social Democratic Party whilst leaving the Centre and Conservative Parties untouched.[24] Although there is an exchange of voters between the Social Democratic and Liberal Parties, the bulk of 'floating voters' consists of non-Socialists, all theoretically within the reach of the Liberal Party. The reason why the Liberal leadership puts restrictions on the party's vote-winning formulae is that there is much to come *after* election day. In order to maximise parliamentary influence, the Liberals, together with the Centre and Conservative Parties, have to push the Socialist representation in the Riksdag below half the total number of seats. Second, the forming of a bourgeois majority cabinet is, as was shown above, a process painstaking enough not to need fresh wounds inflicted on it by bourgeois infighting during the election campaign.

Partly self-inflicted and partly engendered by the media, it has been the responsibility of the Liberal Party to mediate between conflicting bourgeois standpoints. For example, the Liberals are expected to find a workable compromise between Conservative calls for cuts and Centre Party calls for increases in subsidies to farming. This takes the momentum out of the Liberal campaign, energy needed to promote specifically Liberal proposals.

In the 1985 campaigns the Liberals dropped their role as mediators. The election result was the outcome of a triangular drama featuring a head-on confrontation between the Social Democrats and Conservatives, with the Liberal Party picking up momentum at the expense of the Conservatives, whose credibility as a serious alternative to the Social Democratic cabinet wore thin in the course of the election campaign. Those voters who felt a need to disassociate themselves from a Conservative Party on the decline had no difficulty in finding their way to the Liberals.

CONCLUSION – SWEDEN ILLIBERAL?

Organised liberalism in Sweden is weak. Is Sweden as a body politic hostile to a liberal party, or has the Liberal Party been inept in its choice of policy and leadership?

Sweden's transition from an underdeveloped to a modern society has not left the Liberal Party with a rich and glorious legacy. Rather, it was the era of lost opportunities for organised liberalism.

With a cultural homogeneity like few other European nations, Sweden's late socio-economic restructuring from self-supporting agriculture to an industrial division of labour soon found political expression along the left–right dimension of partisan conflict. In the wake of the introduction of universal suffrage, almost nine out of ten ballots were cast for parties with a distinct class appeal; not one single vote was recorded for parties representing specifically regional, religious, linguistic or ethnic interests.

Sweden did not go through an extended period of political repression of the developing classes and their interests before complete democracy was assured. The liberal sister parties in Norway and Denmark can point to successes in 1884 and 1901 respectively when parliamentarism was gained in one single step in opposition to a distinct right, the latter group subsequently stigmatised in both Norwegian and Danish history. Both 1884 and 1901 remained years of highly symbolic meaning long after they turned into myths cultivated by the early liberal generations of Norway and Denmark. The Swedish Liberal Party is not similarly associated with any symbolic year or action at all.

It is a commonly held opinion among Swedish as well as foreign scholars and intellectuals that Sweden is a tightly-knit society, intolerant of individual idiosyncracies, but open to societal experiments as long as they are group-oriented and well organised, preferably sanctioned and planned by some public agency. Sweden is liberal in the sense that few, if any, ideas are ruled out on the basis of cultural and religious bigotry. However, when it comes to the implementation of new ideas, typically codified by an investigative committee representing all organised interests of importance, very few potential solutions dare ignore the official bureaucracy and its standards of what is feasible. This may, of course, be construed as evidence of how anticipated reactions limit the scope of Swedish political debate. What at first glance may look like a society with a well-conducted political debate and centrally monitored implementation does, in fact, possess both heretical values and a good portion of bureaucratic disobedience at local level. Whether this is a sign of civil health, neo-individualism or cynicism is a moot point.

Swedish society has been subjected to a wide and deep political penetration during the last thirty years. In addition to the expanding public sector (now about 65 per cent of GNP), the strength of organised interests sees to it that few citizens today are able to escape politics. Indeed, Swedes are not in the habit of resorting to any other means; practically all extra-parliamentary citizen initiatives never consider any option other than (re-)turning to government for help.

The Swedish so-called 'middle-way' is therefore political, not societal. The legitimacy of governmental regulations is not seriously questioned in Sweden. Swedish politics is so preoccupied by confrontations about tangible matters (taxes, wages, and dividends) that few ever bother to ask about the kind of politicians and officials who continue to run Swedish society. The typical news story on television identifies an issue accompanied by an interview with a government official who is asked what government will do to solve the problem.[25]

For the Liberal Party, this simply means politics according to social democracy; whenever similarities between Liberal and Social Democratic policies are observed, the comparison invariably challenges the *raison d'être* of the Liberal Party. Whenever the Liberals propose a clear-cut, non-socialist alternative, they are accused of acting as a proxy for the Conservatives.

Douglas Verney believes that Sweden experienced a liberal era between 1900 and 1920.[26] His way of testing his thesis, by reference to social welfare policies enacted by the Liberal cabinets of that time, is also significant for present day conceptions of the party's role in Swedish politics: a social engineer balancing at the apex of society above giant organised interests accustomed to giving rather than taking orders from government. Nobody knows this better than the Social Democrats, whose success in governing the Welfare State has also been contingent upon an 'entrepreneurisation' of political power. In return for responsible behaviour on the part of organised interests, voluntary associations have been entrusted with the implementation of the finer details of public policy.

In the meantime Sweden has come to forget what the term society, *samhälle*, once denoted, i.e. the civil sector. This blurring of the words 'state' and 'society' is commonly noted by foreigners. However, they are mistaken to conclude that Swedes do not lead a life outside the reach of the state. In some respects civil society continues to flourish – getting by in the unofficial economy, for example. Such a society of petty transactions among friends and neighbours has no political conception other than that it serves as a miniature forerunner for the conservative blueprint of the Sweden of tomorrow. If the Liberals bothered to consult their continental precursors they would perhaps muster enough courage to reconsider the value of a project to furnish civil society with something more than just 'neo-rightist greediness'.

Sweden as a body politic is hostile to a liberal party, especially one which has been notorious in trespassing onto Social Democratic territory and afraid to advocate the kind of liberal values and ideas with which it rose in the nineteenth century.

NOTES

1 Cf. Childs, *Sweden: the Middle Way*.
2 Cf. Hanson, 'Returning from Sweden'.
3 Michael Roberts, *The Swedish Imperial Experience 1560–1718*.
4 The Swedish–Norwegian union of 1814 through 1905 was never more than a personal union in the sense that the king of Sweden was also formal head of state in Norway which meant that laws enacted by the Norwegian Storting needed the king's signature before becoming effective.
5 The following section draws on data from Lafferty, *Economic Development and the Response of Labor in Scandinavia*.
6 Cf. Vallinder, 'Folkpartiets ideologiska och organisatoriska bakgrund 1866–1934', and Ronnblom, *Frisinnade landsforeningen 1902–1927*.
7 Urwin, *From Ploughshare to Ballotbox*.
8 Johansson, *Liberal splittring, skilsmassa – och aterforening 1917–1934*.
9 Internal party archives.
10 On party finance, see Gidlund, *Partistod*.
11 Johansson, 'Frisinnade och liberaler 1934–1984'.
12 Esaiasson, *Partiledarna infor valjarna*.
13 See also von Bonsdorff, *Studier rorande den moderna liberalismen i de nordiska landerna*.
14 Holmberg, *Väljare i förändring*.
15 Petersson, *Väljarna och valet 1976*.
16 This section does not discuss the executive aspects at regional and local levels since the county councils and local governments operate on the basis of the proportional distribution of seats on executive bodies.
17 Petersson, *Regeringsbildningen 1978*.
18 Ruin, *Mellan samlingsregering och tvapartisystem*.
19 Bjurulf and Nils Stjernquist, 'Partisammanhallning och partisamarbete'.
20 Holmberg, *Väljare i förandring*.
21 Cf. Wildavsky, 'The logic of public sector growth'.
22 Downs, *An Economic Theory of Democracy* and Sjöblom, *Party Strategies in Multiparty Systems*.
23 Isberg et al., *Partierna infor väljarna* (Stockholm: Allmanna Forlaget, 1974).
24 Isberg et al., *Partierna infor väljarna*.
25 Westerståhl and Johansson, *Bilden av Sverige*.
26 Verney, 'The foundations of modern Sweden: the swift rise and fall of Swedish liberalism'.

REFERENCES

Bjurulf, B. and Stjernquist, N., 'Partisammanhallning och partisamarbete', *Statsvetenskaplig Tidskrift*, Vol. 71, 1968.
Bonsdorff, G. von, *Studier rorande den moderna liberalismen i de nordiska landerna* (Lund: Gleerup, 1954).
Childs, M., *Sweden: the Middle Way* (New Haven: Yale University Press, 1936).
Downs, A., *An Economic Theory of Democracy* (New York: Harper & Row, 1957).
Esaiasson, P., *Partiledarna infor valjarna* (Göteborgs Universitet: Forskningsrapport 1985: 4, Statsvetenskapliga institutionen).
Gidlund, G., *Partistod* (Lund: CWK Gleerup, 1983).
Hanson, B., 'Returning from Sweden', *Politologen*, No. 1, 1986.
Holmberg, S., *Väljare i förändring* (Stockholm: Liber, 1985).

Isberg, M. et al., *Partierna infor valjarna* (Stockholm: Allmanna Forlaget, 1974).
Johansson, G., *Liberal splittring, skilsmassa – och aterforening 1917–1934* (Göteborg: Bokförlaget Folk & Samhälle, 1980).
Johansson, G., 'Frisinnade och liberaler 1934–1984' in *Liberal ideologi och politik* (Stockholm: A.B. Folk & Samhälle, 1984).
Lafferty, W.M., *Economic Development and the Response of Labour in Scandinavia* (Oslo: Universitetsforlaget, 1971).
Petersson, O., *Valjarna och valet 1976* (Stockholm: Liber, 1979).
Petersson, O., *Regeringsbildningen 1978* (Stockholm: Raben & Sjogren, 1979).
Roberts, M., *The Swedish Imperial Experience 1560–1718* (Cambridge: Cambridge University Press, 1979).
Ronnblom, H.-K., *Frisinnade landsforeningen 1902–1927* (Stockholm: Saxon & Lindström, 1929).
Ruin, O., *Mellan samlingsregering och tvapartisystem* (Stockholm: Bonniers, 1968).
Sjöblom, G., *Party Strategies in Multiparty Systems* (Lund: Studentlitteratur, 1968).
Urwin, D.W., *From Ploughshare to Ballotbox* (Oslo: Universitetsforlaget, 1980).
Vallinder, T., 'Folkpartiets ideologiska och organisatoriska bakgrund 1866–1934' in *Liberal ideologi och politik* (Stockholm: AB Folk & Samhalle, 1984).
Verney, D., 'The foundations of modern Sweden: the swift rise and fall of Swedish liberalism', *Political Studies*, Vol. 20, 1972.
Westerståhl, J. and Johansson, F., *Bilden av Sverige* (Stockholm: SNS, 1985).
Wildavsky, A., 'The logic of public sector growth' in J.-E. Lane (ed.), *State and Market* (London: Sage, 1985).

11

Liberalism in Denmark: agrarian, radical and still influential

Alastair H. Thomas

INTRODUCTION

The first task in any study of liberalism in Denmark is to decide which parties can justifiably be classified as 'liberal', given the country's fragmented party system, particularly since 1973. There are two main candidates for this label and both will be dealt with in this chapter.

The name of the first, Venstre, (founded in the 1870s) translates literally as 'The Left', which relates to the party's nineteenth-century origins as the proponent of electoral reform and the parliamentary principle of governmental responsibility to the popularly elected majority. Under the name 'The United Left', Venstre issued Denmark's first political party manifesto in 1872, emphasising reformist aims and opposition to the anti-parliamentary government of 'The Right' which continued to hold power under the monarch until 1901.

The name Venstre is sometimes translated into English as the Liberal Democratic Party, and sometimes as Agrarian Liberals, in recognition of the main source of their electoral support, both originally and currently. In 1970 the party confirmed its own claim to its liberal inheritance by formally adopting a suffix to its name, becoming Venstre – Danmarks liberale Parti.

The second candidates for the 'liberal' label are the Radical Liberals, Det radikale Venstre (often referred to as the Radicals). They broke away from Venstre in 1905, partly reflecting dissatisfaction among smallholders that Venstre's tax reforms bore more heavily on them than on large farms, and partly because of their objection to proposed increases in defence expenditure. Nevertheless, the Radicals shared Venstre's orientation towards individual political participation and limited government.

From 1929 to 1964 the Radicals were closely aligned with the Social Democrats and are therefore sometimes referred to as 'social liberals'. They certainly belonged during that period to the radical-liberal category (as defined by Smith 1972). Ever since then they have been clearly in the centre of the Danish party spectrum, whereas Venstre has equally clearly located itself as a conservative-liberal party with the Conservatives in a bourgeois group to the right of centre. These placings were disrupted in 1973 but were increasingly resumed over the years 1975–9 (Nannestad (1984) 173–8).

Both the liberal parties were integral to the growth of the Danish party system. During the period 1870–1905 the main contest was between the left (Venstre) and the right. The Social Democrats, founded in 1871, were steadily building up their organisational strength. The Radical Liberals, splitting away from Venstre in 1905, made the fourth of 'the four old parties' which formed all cabinets until 1982. The only brief exceptions were the broad-based national coalition of 1945 and the inclusion of the Justice Party in the 1957–60 cabinets.

In the 'earthquake election' of 1973 the number of parties doubled with the Justice Party again being represented after an interval of thirteen years. There were three completely new parties – the Christian People's Party, the Centre Democrats and the Progress Party – none of which could lay claim to the 'liberal' label; nor does there seem much in the programme content of either the Centre Democrats or the Christian People's Party to justify the term liberal rather than centre. Other parties clearly in the socialist block are the Social Democrats, the Communists, the Socialist People's Party, and the Left Socialists.

On the basis of their party manifestos for the entire period since the Second World War, there is little difference between the two Danish liberal parties on a 'conservative–radical' scale. On a 'left–right' dimension, Venstre is located well to the right along with the Dutch VVD and the Danish Centre Democrats, although not so far to the right as the Danish Conservatives. RV is located centrally, in a group which includes such other liberal parties as the German FDP and the British Liberals.

Both Venstre and the Radicals were members of the Liberal International from the outset and Venstre has been represented in the European Parliament since Denmark joined the EC. The Radicals did not, however, win any seats at either the 1979 or the 1983 European elections.

THE HISTORICAL DEVELOPMENT OF THE DANISH LIBERAL PARTIES

The impetus for the constitutional and electoral developments which built the modern Danish nation came from the liberal movement, initially from National Liberals and after 1870 from the United Left (Venstre), increasingly organised as the parliamentary and popular opposition to 'the right'. Manhood suffrage with secret ballots was gained as a result in 1901, followed by universal suffrage in 1915. Proportional representation replaced plurality voting in single-member constituencies from the 1918 elections.

In Denmark, liberalism has never stood for anti-clericalism, though in championing a nationalism of popular culture and self-renewal, it opposed the narrow pietism and self-interest of the nineteenth-century religious and political establishment. The National Left were also distinguished by pan-Scandinavianism, and a keenness on national defence which placed them close to the National Liberals.

In 1870, the programme of the 'United Left' was clearly in the interests of the peasant farmers who supported the new party and opposed the large landowners. There was, however, little cohesion or discipline among the parliamentary group until the early years of the twentieth century. It consisted largely of the personal followings of such leaders as Frede Bojsen, Christen Berg and Viggo Hørup. The parliamentary origins of both Venstre and the right contrast with the growth of the Social Democratic Party which was first set up in 1871 and was based in the trade-union movement. When the Radicals broke away from Venstre in 1905 they sought to develop a party structure which would subject the activities of their parliamentary representatives more to the influence of their voters.

The four-party system established in 1905 allowed the expression of the principal cleavages in Denmark. Capital, land and labour were represented by the Conservatives, Venstre and the Social Democrats respectively. The Radicals were never so closely identified with a single economic interest, but they were supported by smallholders, teachers and other professionals, and those whose values included the rural culture, pacifism, internationalism, and social reforms which favoured voluntary co-operation rather than centrally-directed collectivism. Proportional representation stabilised this four-party configuration, rescued the Conservatives from under-representation, ended Liberal over-representation, and prevented the Social Democrats attaining an outright majority.

Having suffered severely from factionalism and fission around the turn of the century, once they had parted company from each other in 1905, the two Danish liberal parties remained remarkably free from these problems. The one relatively minor exception to this generalisation occurred in the 1960s, when Venstre was in some internal disorder. The party's national vote was falling and there were some who preferred to see their party oriented towards the centre rather than the Conservatives. A faction called Liberal Centre formed in 1965, but its existence as a separate party was brief and the split was healed in 1968.

One measure of party cohesion is the extent to which individual members of the Danish parliament (Folketing) (MFs) break the unity of the parliamentary group by voting differently from the majority of their party colleagues on legislative issues. Studies by Pedersen (1967) and Svensson (1982) of consensus and conflict in the Danish Folketing have shown (see Table 11.1) that, while breaks in party discipline were quite clearly the exception and the majority of divisions were unanimous, there were significant variations in the degree of internal dissent between the parties.

In the earlier of the two periods, unity was highest among the Social Democrats and lowest for Venstre. In both Venstre and the Conservative Party, but not in the other two parties, breaches of unity were not only in the form of dissension by one or two individuals but also included a significant number of cases where a more comprehensive break in party lines occurred (Pedersen (1967) 147). In 1953–65 Venstre was the least united of the five parties, with the highest levels of dissension in 1954–5 and 1960–1, and the lowest in 1963–5.

We next compare and contrast the organisation and structure of Venstre and the Radicals in terms of their internal decision-making procedures and the role of their respective members.

THE ORGANISATION AND STRUCTURE OF THE DANISH LIBERAL PARTIES

The two Danish liberal parties differ significantly in their organisation and structure. Venstre is a decentralised mass party, with a large membership and a correspondingly highly-developed system of local branches. It is well represented in the local (*kommune*) and county (*amt*) councils, where it is second only to the Social Democrats.

By contrast with Venstre and with their original intentions, the Radicals are a small, more cadre-like party with a low ratio of

Table 11.1 *Percentage of parliamentary divisions in which parties acted with unity*

Party	1953–65	1971–9
Socialist People's Party from 1960	98.4	98.0
Social Democrats	98.8	96.3
Radical Liberals	97.4	93.9
Venstre	94.9	96.7
Conservatives	96.3	97.7
Left Socialists		98.6
Centre Democrats		97.6
Christian People's Party		97.6
Justice Party		97.9
Progress party		95.4

Sources: Pedersen (1967), Svensson (1982).

members to voters and few local councillors. They rely heavily on the parliamentary group and on the ability of their leaders to make an effective impact through the news-media. From their origins in 1905, internal democracy within the Radical Party has been asserted by the party branches. A continuing sign of this is that the party chairman is not normally a member of parliament (Tågholt (1971) 130).

No party in Denmark can afford to become too centralised, since the electoral system requires nomination in districts which are smaller than the multi-member constituencies and which give advantages to locally organised parties. Of the two parties, Venstre is more decentralised than the Radicals.

Venstre's collective body is the national organisation (Venstres Landsorganisation), comprising the 991 associations at district (*kommune*) level. This branch network retains the party's large membership and gives it the highest organisation ratio of all the Danish parties. Several district associations make up associations at constituency (*kreds*) and county level. County organisations nominate parliamentary candidates. The constituency level promotes the party's ideas and activities, supports nominated candidates, maintains contact with county councillors and ensures that the district associations are working effectively.

The national assembly (*landsmødet*) is the decisive authority on party policy, held annually, with extraordinary meetings if necessary. Most representatives come from constituencies, which can send their chairman and one delegate for each 300 members or part thereof. (The corresponding figure for the Radicals is one delegate per 30 members.) Others with voting rights on the national assembly are members of the party executive (*hovedbestyrelse*), the parliamentary group, ministers and parliamentary candidates, editors, the national executive of the youth wing, and members of or nominated candidates for the European Parliament. Constituency chairmen also have their own annual meeting. Venstre's national chairman is usually the party leader and the position is often combined with chairmanship of the parliamentary group.

The Radicals' organisation is based on associations at constituency rather than local level, with several combining to form the county level organisation which may comprise constituency delegates or a county assembly. Local associations may also operate below constituency level, so that RV can operate very flexibly in response to variations in the number of local members. Association officers are elected by the members. Constituency associations nominate parliamentary candidates and elect officers and delegates to the national assembly and to county delegate meetings.

The Radicals' annual national assembly is the party's highest authority. It alternates between a central and a peripheral location – in 1985 it was held at Aabenraa in south-east Jutland, near the German border. All party members have the right to attend and speak, but only constituency delegates may vote. There is a large executive comprising chairmen plus two elected members from the 14 county organisations plus another 40 elected members distributed in proportion to the party's votes at the last parliamentary election. In addition to the county delegations, national assembly delegates elect to the executive a further fifteen members, plus five Folketing representatives or ministers. The Young Radicals have three members and the radical editors' association two. This makes a body of just over one hundred members which meets quarterly and functions as a party council between annual assemblies. The elected national chairman chairs the assembly, the executive and the thirteen-member business committee. The latter is responsible for the national organisation's direction and finance between executive meetings and carries out executive decisions.

The high membership level in Venstre over the mid-twentieth century reflects the party's character as an agrarian class party. Membership is a useful indicator of willingness to support the party financially and by voluntary activity. It is therefore of serious concern to all the Danish political parties that total party membership has fallen from 24 per cent of the electorate in 1953 to 8 per cent in 1984, while the six parties of 1953 have become nine (H.J. Nielsen (1984) 5).

Both Venstre and the Social Democrats have relied on well-defined social groups (farmers in Venstre's case and the proletariat in the Social Democrats'). Compared with the figures in Table 11.2, party membership as a percentage of voters (the organisational percentage or membership ratio) for the Social Democrats fluctuated within the 25–30 per cent range during 1920–45, rose to almost 40 per cent immediately after 1945, and declined steadily to about 15 per cent over the ensuing thirty years (Thomas (1977) 238).

Both Venstre and the Social Democrats have suffered a steady decline in their membership numbers and membership ratio. Venstre's membership in 1983/4 was less than half the peak they reached in 1950. For the Social Democrats, their 1983/4 membership (107,000) is 37 per cent of the number it was in 1953 (283,000). While Social Democrat strength was, of course, urban-based, Venstre has had persistent problems establishing itself in the capital as strongly as in the provinces. Before 1948 Venstre formed a legally separate party in Copenhagen so as to qualify for supplementary mandates. The electoral law was changed that year to make such a tactic unnecessary, but Venstre is still weak there.

Membership data for the Radicals are less comprehensive than for Venstre, but they do show an even more severe recent decline. The 18 per cent membership ratio for 1977 reflects severe electoral losses rather than improved membership numbers. Indeed, their membership figure for 1983/4 is only 28 per cent of what it was in 1953. This is much the worst membership decline of any of the four 'old parties'.

Membership fluctuations from one year to the next within such highly-decentralised voluntary organisations as political parties may reflect local variations in the efficiency or accounting practices of party officials. Long-term trends, however, are an important indicator of the number of individuals prepared to show their commitment to a party by paying a regular subscription. Clearly, such commitment has declined sharply for both the mass membership parties, though more for the Social Democrats than for Venstre. For the Radicals, individual membership has not been so significant, but its decline has been even more marked.

There can be no simple explanation for the decline of party membership, common not only to Venstre and the Social Democrats, but to all the large Danish parties over the past two decades (H.J. Nielsen (1984)). One factor, whether as a cause or a symptom, is the decline of a provincial party press with a clear commitment to each of the four 'old parties'. In the 1930s, for example, the Radicals alone could count on the support of 30 papers throughout the country, some of them with a national circulation, but by 1980 only two remained

Table 11.2 *Membership numbers and voters at the immediately preceding election, and membership as a percentage of voters, for Venstre and the Radicals for various years*

	Venstre			Det radikale Venstre		
Year	Members	Voters	%	Members	Voters	%
1930	166818	402121	42		151746	
1932	164975	381862	43		145221	
1935	136296	292246	36		151507	
1939	129545	309355	42		161834	
1942	139227		45			
1943	146118	376850	39		175179	
1945	154541	479158	32		167073	
1947	193094	574895	40		144206	
1950	201429	438188	46		167969	
1953	186854	456896	41	36000	169295	21
1957	189104	578932	33		179822	
1960	192629	512041	38		140979	
1964	181272	547770	35		139702	
1966	168580	539027	31	30000	203858	15
1970	136207	530167	26	25638	427304	6
1971		450904			413620	
1973	112543	374283	30	25000	343117	7
1977	105500	371728	28	20000	113330	18
1979	98500	396484	25			
1980	100000	396484	25	13400	172365	8
1983/4	89500	405737	22	10000	184642	5

Sources:
Venstre:
1930–58: *Venstres organisations-meddelelser* 1959
1959–74: *Venstre medlemsopgørelse* for relevant years
1979: Tom Matz, personal communication, 16.2.1982
Det radikale Venstre:
1970: Helge Larsen (ed.), *Det radikale Venstre i medvind og modvind*, 1955–1980 (1980) 149.
1974: *Weekendavisen Berlingske Aften*, 26 July 1974, p. 4.
1953, 1966, 1977, 1980, 1983/4: Hans Jørgen Nielsen, 'De store partier har på får år mistet 60% af medlemmer', *Politisk Ugebrev*, 22, 4 June 1984, pp. 4–5.
Venstre i 100 aar, 1939–70, p. 132.

(Helge Larsen (1980) 137). Venstre, by contrast, has had only local papers during the post-Second World War period, 43 in 1945 declining to 22 in 1979 (Helge Larsen (1980) 139). The Conservatives and the Social Democrats also have a party press.

Another reason for the decreases in party membership lay in changes affecting the Danish economy. In the late 1950s agriculture became more capital intensive and full-time rural employment declined, while industrial and technical employment increased. These changes inevitably affected the hitherto strong rural roots of the two liberal parties. For some time voters retained earlier membership and voting patterns, but they were becoming more volatile. The full effects of these changes were seen in high levels of voter mobility, fierce competition for electoral support from new or revived parties, and the high level of mistrust of the four 'old parties' in the elections of the 1970s, especially in 1973.

In terms of its financial position, Venstre has benefited greatly from its large and relatively stable membership. In 1982 members paid annual subscriptions of between 50kr. and 125kr. (about £4–£10) to their local branch, the figure being set individually by each branch, which then passed on 38kr. (about £3) to the national organisation. In addition, the party received many small and some large donations. The Radicals have had to plan a sharp rise in their membership contributions, from 90kr. in 1985 to 120kr. in 1986, 150kr. in 1987 and 165kr. in 1988, and in the past they have also had to make special financial appeals to their members. There is no state subsidy to political parties in Denmark, but a contribution is made to the office and research costs of the parliamentary groups geared to their size. This amounts to about half the Radicals' total income at national level.

As we shall see in the next section on electoral support, however, financial constraints on the two liberal parties have not prevented them from achieving contrasting profiles with regard to the most commonly employed social background variables structuring partisan choice.

ELECTORAL SUPPORT

At the beginning of the twentieth century the three components of the party system, the Right, Venstre and the Social Democrats, corresponded closely with, respectively, the business world, with its employer and trade organisations; agriculture, with organisations of farmers, smallholders and the co-operative movement; and labour, organised by the trade unions. At this stage the Danish party system illustrated Rokkan's functional-economic model of the electoral fronts in Norway (Rokkan (1966) 93). These three parties still organise important class-based components of the Danish party system of the 1980s, but both fissions and additions have increased the diversity of choice for the voter.

Until 1966, the socialist bloc had never had an overall majority and the Social Democrats generally relied on Radical support, while

Table 11.3 *National electoral performance of Danish liberal parties, 1945–84*

Election year	Venstre		Radikale Venstre	
	vote, %	seats	vote, %	seats
1945	23.4	38	8.1	11
1947	27.6	49	6.9	10
1950	21.3	32	8.2	12
1953, April	22.1	33	8.6	13
1953, Sept.	23.1	42	7.8	14
1957	25.1	45	7.8	14
1960	21.2	38	5.8	11
1964	20.8	38	5.3	10
1966	19.3	35	7.3	13
1968	18.6	34	15.0	27
1971	15.6	30	14.4	27
1973	12.3	22	11.2	20
1975	23.3	42	7.1	13
1977	12.0	21	3.6	6
1979	12.5	22	5.4	10
1981	11.3	20	5.1	9
1984	12.1	22	5.5	10

Sources: Tågholt (1971) 28, Hvidt (1984) 298–300.

Venstre and the Conservatives provided the non-socialist alternative. Until 1973, the Danish party system comprised socialist and 'bourgeois-liberal' blocs. From 1966 to 1973 the Radicals joined the non-socialist bloc. Thereafter, they have pursued a centrist strategy, although their parliamentary strength was only sometimes sufficient to allow them to have effective influence on decisions.

Unlike the other three 'old parties', each with their clear-cut social base, Radical support came from a cross-section of the electorate, attracted by the party's radical reformism, its programme of social change in favour of the smallholder and the other disadvantaged members of society, and its pacifist internationalism.

As recently as the mid-1960s, Venstre could justifiably be labelled 'the Agrarian Liberals' and treated as comparable with the farmers' parties of Norway, Sweden and Finland. At that stage, 78 per cent of Danish farmers supported the party, clearly confirming its function as an agrarian class party, while fewer than one Venstre voter in twenty was a blue-collar worker and only one in nine a white-collar worker. At the 1968 election their 18.6 per cent average national vote ranged from 26.5 per cent in rural Jutland, to only 3.4 per cent in

Copenhagen (Elder et al. (1982) 73). The party's losses between 1957 and 1960 averaged 2.9 per cent but ranged from 4.4 per cent in the least urbanised areas to 2.5 per cent in the most urbanised ones. This trend continued at a slower rate between 1960 and 1964.

Radical losses were much smaller and were slightly heavier than Venstre's in the most urbanised areas (Borre and Stehouwer (1970) 60, 63). Venstre's problem was the decline in its core electorate in agricultural occupations and rural residence, as the service sector of the economy grew and agriculture declined in the number of people it employed. Venstre's decline continued increasingly rapidly to 1973 (see Table 11.3), with the greatest losses being to the Radicals in 1971 and to the Progress Party in 1973 (Borre et al. (1974) 5, 8).

The Radicals began to revive in 1966 and made spectacular gains in 1968, campaigning for a centrist course which would avoid 'extremism' of the left or the right. Their strongest gains on each occasion were in rapidly growing middle-class areas of the largest towns (Borre and Stehouwer (1970) 137–8). Over the following two years they collected support from former voters of the Justice Party, the Liberal Centre, and from many middle-class former Social Democrat and Socialist People's Party voters, disappointed by the break-up, after a year, of relationships within the 'labour majority' (H. Larsen (1980) 59).

Venstre tried to change its image and appeal in 1970 by adopting the label of 'Denmark's Liberal Party', but the electoral decline continued at the 1971 election. In the short term, the Radicals retained their high level of representation at the 1971 election, called towards the end of the Folketing's four-year term to capitalise on progress made in the EC entry negotiations.

In the medium term the issue of permissiveness versus morality, and especially the abortion question, gave impetus to the formation of the Christian People's Party in 1970. Allegations of excessive taxation and bureaucracy gathered support for the new Progress Party in 1972, and house owners' taxation problems contributed to the 1973 Social Democratic Party split which formed the Centre Democrats. These new issues and the personalities which they threw into prominence to champion them caused the new cleavages underlying the drastic fractionalisation and reshaping of the party system at the 'earthquake' election of 1973.

In terms of net change as well as gross turnover between parties, the 1973 election constitutes the high point in electoral instability. Panel data suggest that of those who voted in both 1971 and 1973, 40 per cent voted for different parties (Borre (1977) 9). Worre's earlier study showed that the Social Democrats were reduced to reliance very

Table 11.4 *Party voting by previous voting preference, 1973, %*

Party	A	B	C	D	N
Socialist People's Party	29	52	4	15	27
Social Democrats	86	9	1	4	139
Radicals	54	39	2	5	54
Venstre	68	22	2	8	78
Centre Democrats		71	26	3	35
Conservatives	64	32	—	4	25
Progress Party		59	29	12	59
Small parties	14	51	30	5	37
Total	49	32	9	10	469

Columns:
A Core voters
B Changed preference once at 1968, 1971 or 1973 elections
C Changed preference twice at 1968, 1971, and 1973 elections
D Previously non-voter
N Number of respondents
Source: Worre (1974) facing p. 34.

largely (86 per cent) on core voters, while this proportion for Venstre was 68 per cent and for the Radicals 54 per cent. Both liberal parties were much more successful than the Social Democrats in attracting first-time changers (Table 11.4).

The social basis of support for the two liberal parties in 1975 is shown in Table 11.5. Venstre's reliance on farmers is clear, as is the Radicals' on lower-salaried workers. Both parties relied on the 40–64 age group and on those in the highest income band. Both relied heavily on rural voters, but the Radicals also had a good following in urban Copenhagen, something which Venstre has never achieved. Venstre had a fairly even balance of men and women supporters, while men predominated among the Radicals. The two parties were similar in their attraction of the better educated segment of the electorate.

In 1979 Venstre still accounted for 61 per cent of the farming vote (Borre (1983) 64). But whereas half its total vote came from this source, in 1979 this proportion was down to one quarter, with a corresponding increase among those who gave their occupation as 'helping their spouse'. The party was weakly represented among urban occupations, but there was an important growth in the significance of 'lower-salaried employees' (from 18 per cent to 27 per cent) as a component of the party's vote (Borre (1983) 69). Venstre voters were more likely than the rest of the electorate to live in their

Table 11.5 *The social basis of support for Danish liberal parties, 1975,* %

	Venstre	Radicals	Whole population
Occupation:			
Farmers	38	15	16
Independents	15	3	11
Higher-salaried employees	14	21	14
Lower-salaried employees	15	33	23
Skilled workers	7	12	16
Unskilled workers	10	15	20
Age:			
20–9 years	15	17	18
30–9 years	22	19	19
40–64 years	48	49	45
65 and over	15	15	19
Income:			
0–60,000kr.p.a.	38	45	43
60,000–100,000kr.p.a.	27	15	31
Over 100,000kr. p.a.	35	40	26
Urban/rural:			
Copenhagen	20	35	31
Provincial towns	33	21	38
Country areas	47	44	31
Region:			
Copenhagen	20	23	30
Islands	24	34	23
Jutland, south and east	18	26	23
Jutland, north and west	38	18	24
Sex:			
Men	55	61	51
Women	45	34	49
Education:			
Non-academic (*folkeskole*)	64	62	70
Certificate (*realskole*)	24	25	21
University entry (*studentereksam*)	12	13	9
	N = 238	53	879

Source: Worre (1976) 84.

own houses, to be aged over 40, and to identify with the middle class. Venstre has always been weak in and around Copenhagen, and in 1973 it also suffered a relative weakness in the southern islands of Lolland–Falster (Berglund and Lindström (1978) 131). Strong areas in 1983 were Sorφ (west of Copenhagen), Bornholm, and most of Jutland outside the larger towns (*Statistisk Årbog* (1983) 376–81).

Regionally, the Radicals were strong at the 1981 election in the west of Jutland (especially around Skive) and in the islands (strongest of all in Holbaek and Nykobing Sjaelland), and weak in Copenhagen and its suburbs and in north, east and south Jutland (*Statistik Årbog* (1983) 376–81). This pattern held true over the 1932, 1964 and 1973 elections (Berglund and Lindström (1978) 126).

To what extent have these changes in electoral support influenced the ability of the liberal parties to participate in national government? We now want to consider the roles of each party in office.

GOVERNMENT PARTICIPATION

Venstre has been in govenment during substantial proportions of each of the successive periods into which the twentieth century is subdivided in Table 11.6, least during 1945–73, but almost half the time between 1973 and 1986. The Radicals were in government for a large proportion of the 1920s and 1930s, although not so long as their then allies, the Social Democrats. The same is true for the century as a whole. Since leaving office in 1971 the Radicals have not taken part in cabinet deliberations, but they have given parliamentary support to governments throughout the period since 1973, with the single exception of the 1978–9 Social Democrat – Venstre government. Radical support has been given since 1982 to many of the Schlüter four-party coalition's policies, but it has been withheld on certain aspects of defence and foreign policy, including financial contributions to NATO's costs for cruise and pershing missiles, and the European Community's 1986 moves to limit the veto power in the Council of Ministers.

We can see from Table 11.7 that Venstre has taken part in the formation of cabinets less frequently than the Social Democrats, with the Radicals in third place and the Conservatives fourth. Of post-1945 prime ministers, the Social Democrats have provided six, Venstre three, and the Radicals and Conservatives one each.

Most Danish governments since 1945 have been minority governments, with the cabinet being formed by a single party which then relies on parliamentary support from its own and other parties. Since 1945 (excluding the unity cabinet of May–October 1945 formed in the special circumstances of the liberation), there have been eight coalition cabinets formed in the period to June 1986. In each of these coalitions, one of the two liberal parties was represented – only in the Radical-led Baunsgaard coalition (1968–71) were both liberal parties in cabinet simultaneously.

The Radicals have always seen their central role as opposing the

Table 11.6 *Percentage duration of government participation by Danish political parties*

Party:	S	R	V	K	DS	Rf	DKP	CD	KrF
1901–20	0	40	60	0					
1920–43	73	62	46	19					
1945–73	69	40	32	25	2	12	2		
1973–86 (10 June)	61	0	48	30				30	30
1901–86	53	40	35	19	1	4	1	5	5

Table 11.7 *Number of cabinets formed or participated in by Danish political parties*

(In this table a 'cabinet' is taken to be a government led by a single prime minister and relying on the same sources of parliamentary support.)

Party:	S	R	V	K	DS	Rf	DKP	CD	KrF
1901–20	0	2	5	0					
1920–43	5	4	2	0					
1945–73	12	6	5	4	1	2	1		
1973–86 (10 June)	4	0	3	1				1	1
Total	21	8	15	5	1	2	1	1	1

Party abbreviations:
CD Centrums Demokraterne: The Centre Democrats
DKP Danmarks Kommunistiske Parti: The Communist Party of Denmark
DS Dansk Samling: The Danish Union
K Det Konservative Folkeparti: The Conservative People's Party
KrF Kristeligt Folkeparti: The Christian People's Party
R Det Radikale Venstre: The Radical Liberals
Rf Retsforbundet: The Justice League
S Socialdemokratiet: The Social Democrats
V Venstre – Danmark's Liberale Parti: The Danish Liberal Party

Sources: Hvidt (1984) 320–6, Elklit and Tonsgaard (1984) 58–9, Tågholt (1971) 17ff.

formation of blocs, whether of the left or the right. They therefore broke with the Social Democrats in 1966 when, for the first time, the SD and the Socialist People's Party together had a majority, a circumstance which has only recurred once (1971–3). Since then, the Radicals have used their support to encourage successive governments not to make themselves dependent on either extreme of the political spectrum: the Progress Party on the right and the Socialist People's Party, Left Socialists or Communists on the left.

In single-party governments the allocation of portfolios is not at issue, but the party forming the government has to find competent individuals to cover the full range of government responsibilities. This task is eased by the Danish convention which allows the appointment of ministers who are not MFs. Such ministers may not vote but are fully entitled to speak in the Folketing.

Table 11.8 shows the allocation of portfolios to Radical and Venstre ministers in each of the post-1945 coalitions. Agriculture was the one ministry which has been held by a liberal in every coalition, reflecting the close relationship of both parties (especially Venstre) with the organised interests in this sector of the economy. The other strong interest which both parties share is in Education, and this is also reflected in the allocations.

Conversely, neither party has taken responsibility for Greenland or for Housing (which mainly involves the financial and public health aspects, since housing in Denmark is built and administered either privately or by housing societies, with only a 5 per cent public sector involvement). On several occasions the parties have held a portfolio only once: Venstre held the Defence portfolio between 1950 and 1953 and Social Affairs only in the 1968–71 government. The Radicals had the Labour and Cultural Affairs portfolios only once (1968–71). SD's close personal links with the labour movement meant they would always expect to hold the Labour portfolio, and they have also retained control on the patronage exercised by the Cultural Affairs Ministry. Otherwise, continuities reflect either the seniority or the interests and experience of individual politicians.

It is sometimes argued in coalition theory that large parties tend to be under-represented in coalition cabinets as the price they have to pay for the co-operation of their smaller coalition partners. This can be tested (Tables 11.9a–d) by comparing the percentage of ministers of each party to the relative strengths of their respective parliamentary groups. In the Hansen/Kampmann/Krag series of coalitions the hypothesis turns out to be well supported. The large SD parliamentary group was quite heavily under-represented in cabinet, to the Radicals' advantage. The same was true to a lesser extent in the SD and Venstre coalition. The main explanation relates to the need to maintain the coalition once formed, to hold the team together despite party differences.

One obvious way of achieving this is for policy agreement between the parties to be reached on the major issues of the day. We now want to consider the main policies of Venstre and the Radicals.

Table 11.8 *Ministries held by Venstre and the Radicals in coalition governments, October 1945–86*

Portfolio	Government								
	1	2	3	4	5	6	7	8	9
PM	V	—	—	—	—	R	—	—	—
Foreign	—	—	—	—	—	V	V	V	V
Assistant Foreign							—		
Finance	V	—	R	R	—	—	—	V	V
Defence	V	—	—	—	—	—	—	—	—
Church	V	—	—	—	—	V	—	V	V
Education	—	R	R	R	R	R	—	V	V
Justice	V	—	—	—	—	—	V	—	—
Interior	—	—	—	—	—	—	V	V	V
Environment							—		
Environment and Nordic Affairs								—	—
Labour and Social	—								
Labour and Housing		—							
Labour			—	—	—	R	—	—	—
Social		—	—	—	—	V	—	—	—
Housing			—	—	—	—	—	—	—
Public Works	—	—	—	—	—	V	V	—	—
Agriculture	V	R	R	R	R	V	V	V	V
Energy								V	V
Fisheries	V	—	—	R	R		—	—	—
Fisheries and Greenland						R			
Greenland				—	—		—	—	—
Trade	—	R	—	—/R	R	—	V		
Industry								—	—
Economic reorganisation							—		
Economy and Nordic Affairs		R	R	R	R	V	V		
Economy and Tax							V		
Tax and Excise								—	—
Economy									V
Culture				—	—	R	—	—	—

Notes: Key: R or V indicates that a portfolio was held by the Radicals or by Venstre respectively. (—) indicates that the portfolio was held by another party. —/R indicates that the portfolio was held initially by another party and then by a Radical. The column is blank where a portfolio was not filled.

Governments:

1	Eriksen's V and K minority coalition	1950–3
2	Hansen's SD and R and Rf majority coalition	1957–60
3	Kampmann's SD and R and Rf majority coalition	1960
4	Kampmann's SD and R majority coalition	1960–2
5	Krag's SD and R majority coalition	1962–4
6	Baunsgaard's R and V and K majority coalition	1968–71
7	Jøgensen's SD and V minority coalition	1978–9
8	Schlüter's K and V and KrF and CD minority coalition	1982–6
9	Schlüter's K and V and KrF and CD coalition, reshuffled	1986–

Sources: Tågholt (1971) 22–7, Hvidt (1984) 306–26, *Nordisk Kontakt* 16/85, 1185.

Tables 11.9a-d *Party participation in coalition cabinets, Denmark, 1946–86*

Table 11.9a *Number of ministers by party*

Government:	1	2	3	4	5	6	7	8	9
S		9	9	12/13	11		14		
R		4	4	6/5	5	5			
Rf		3	3						
V	8					6	7	8	9
K	8					6		8	8
Non-party					1				
CD								4	3
KrF								1	1
Total	16	16	16	18	17	17	21	21	21

Table 11.9b *Percentage of ministers allocated per party*

Government:	1	2	3	4	5	6	7	8	9
S		56	56	67/72	65		67		
R		25	25	33/27	29	30			
Rf		19	19						
V	50					35	33	38	43
K	50					35		38	38
Non-party					6				
CD								19	14
KrF								5	5

Table 11.9c *Relative strengths (per cent) of parliamentary groups of parties represented in coalition cabinets*

Government:	1	2	3	4	5	6	7	8	9
S		75	75	87	87		76		
R		15	15	13	13	27			
Rf		10	10						
V	54					35	24	31	29
K	46					38		40	55
CD								23	10
KrF								6	6
N[a]	59	93	93	87	87	98	86	65	77

([a] total parliamentary seats held by all cabinet parties)

Table 11.9d *Over- (+) or under-representation (–) in cabinet compared with parliamentary party strength (difference of percentages)*

Government:	1	2	3	4	5	6	7	8	9
S		– 19	– 19	– 20/ – 15	– 22		– 9		
R		+ 10	+ 10	+ 20/ + 15	+ 16	+ 3			
Rf		+ 9	+ 9						
V	– 4					0	+ 9	+ 7	+ 14
K	+ 4					– 3		– 2	– 17
Non-party					+ 6				
CD								– 4	+ 4
KrF								– 1	– 1

Source: Hvidt (1984) 296–326.
Notes: Governments 1–9 as for Table 11.8.

PARTY POLICIES AND PROGRAMMES

The Radicals' most recent 'programme of principles' dates from 1976. This has been supplemented by several 'working programmes' on specific sectors of policy, such as the one on 'Aims and means in economic policy' passed by the party's national assembly in 1985. In addition, the party publishes numerous sheets headed 'Radical Policy' which either relate past assembly resolutions to current concerns or publicise the positions taken by the party's MFs speaking in the Folketing or negotiating the terms of their support for policy proposals with the government or other parties.

Venstre has operated similarly, with a programme of principles, 'Forward to the year 2000' agreed in 1970 and a later programme in 1979 based on resolutions at the 1978 national assembly, on the theme: 'A society based on freedom'. In addition, the party operates a publishing house, Forlaget Liberal, from its headquarters just north of Copenhagen which has put out a series of small books together with numerous shorter items giving publicity to current policy thinking.

This pattern is followed by most parties in Denmark, with a 'programme of principles' published in each generation or decade, and more frequent working programmes applying the principles to the current situation. With a series of elections at little more than biennial intervals during 1971–84, it could hardly be otherwise.

Venstre's economic policy is based on market forces as the best route to economic progress, while the Radicals are more sympathetic to state intervention. Venstre wishes to halt the growth of the public sector, including public sector employment, whilst at the same time modernising and improving the service which it offers. This would be achieved by responsiveness to market forces, decentralising powers and responsibilities, and greater use of new technology.

The Radicals agree on decentralisation but with a community rather than an individual emphasis, with a continuing role for the state in determining a uniform framework within which local authorities and groups of individuals can allocate resources. The Radicals would encourage experiments to allow local communities to take over the administration of common tasks such as care of children or the elderly, tasks given financial support by local governments.

Both parties oppose growth in the public sector for its tendency to increase bureaucracy, problems of accountability to the public, and obstacles to enterprise. For the Radicals, private ownership of the means of production should be retained, but state and local government may be the most appropriate means of meeting common objectives such as communications or energy supply.

Both Venstre and the Radicals have had a long-standing commitment to free trade in the interests of the export markets sought by most of Danish agriculture. The EC's Common Agriculture Policy has the advantages of securing a large market and minimum prices above world levels. This allows both parties to advocate the abolition of national subsidies and monetary compensations, with their distortions of competition. They also both agree on the adverse effects of customs duties and trade restrictions on developing countries.

Both liberal parties place great importance on the legal protection of individual rights, but the theme is largely taken for granted and it does not figure very prominently in their programmes. Individual rights have been more of a problem to liberal parties in the employment and economic rather than in the legal spheres. In principle, the Radicals seek the removal from legislation and collective agreements of conditions that require membership of specific unions or organisations as a prerequisite for employment or for the practice of a trade or profession. Both liberal parties supported 1982 legislation restricting the closed shop following a decision of the European Court of Human Rights.

Denmark has an established Evangelical-Lutheran church, with a 94 per cent level of church membership (*Statistisk Årbog* (1984) 376) but a low level of attendance. The Reformation was accepted without controversy. Subsequent argument since the nineteenth century has been about the relationship of free-thinking congregations to the established church, and about the role of religion and the church in the national culture and its transmission – believers versus the indifferent. Advocates of national church revival are more likely to be found within Venstre, while spokesmen for freedom of thought are more often found among the Radicals. In terms of policy, Venstre wishes to preserve the church's tradition of freedom, while leaving its administration to the state, which should not interfere with the inner life of the church. The Radicals consider a broad church with a tolerant outlook to be the necessary condition for a free life (Garodkin (1985) 218).

In international policy, the two liberal parties differ considerably, and they have done so ever since the Radicals broke from Venstre over defence in 1905. While giving the support which makes up a majority for the Conservative and Venstre four-party minority coalition on economic policy, the Radicals have acted with the Social Democrats and the two socialist parties to form an opposition majority to the government coalition on several international issues. For example, they have imposed significant reservations in relation to NATO missile deployments and East–West missile negotiations, while not bringing the country's continued NATO membership into question (Thomas (1986) 209–20).

Generally speaking, in setting policy priorities, the parliamentary leadership of Venstre appears to be under less constraint from the rest of the party than the Radicals' leaders, whose national assembly can often be highly critical of parliamentary policy developments if they conflict with the views of party activists.

Policy content is often important in terms of relationships between parties as well as perceptions of ideological distance between them. The precise impact of policy agreement or disagreement is crucially dependent upon the strategy which each party is trying to pursue, in particular the interests they are defending and the influence they are attempting to exert.

LIBERAL PARTY STRATEGY

For much of this century SD and Venstre regarded it as normal that their interests were opposed to each other. One stood for socialism and the urban workers by hand and brain and the other was anti-centralist and drew its support very heavily from self-employed farm owners, the agricultural sector of the economy and the rural community. The natural allies of each were on the left and the right respectively. Yet SD's most effective periods of government have been in alliance with the Radicals, who exerted a steady and perceptible liberalising influence on the larger party. Venstre tried to take over this role, but the party's losses in 1977 were in part a reversion towards their previous 'natural' level of support after the spectacular and transitory gains of 1975. This electoral reversal was also seen as a judgement by the voters on the party's unbending line. After the SD–Venstre coalition was formed, initial poll results indicated some popular approval of the ability of the two parties to work together.

The brief 1978–9 coalition of the Social Democrats with Venstre, the latter with their strong agrarian base, invites comparison with the 'red–green alliances' which ruled in Finland throughout the post-1945 period (except for the decade 1957–66) (Nyholm (1982) 84–5) or in Sweden in 1936–9 and 1951–7. In both the Finnish and Swedish cases, the link was between the Social Democrats and the Agrarian (later Centre) Party, representing a link between the urban and rural lower classes, proletarian and peasant, a link which relied for much of its success on two factors – the unusually strong position of the independent peasantry in the politically mobilising societies of the time, and on the relative lateness of industrialisation in those societies (Castles (1978) 134 and *passim*).

In the much richer agricultural conditions of Denmark, there was not the scope for an independent peasantry. Instead, the estate owners generally supported the Conservatives, at least in the nineteenth century. The farmers, increasingly significant economically during the first half of the twentieth century, voted mainly for Venstre, while the smallholders voted for the Radicals. As agricultural interests were most closely identified with the Liberals, it is arguable that the term 'red–green alliance' could be applied both to the Social Democratic–Radical governments of 1929–40 or 1957–64, and also to the Social Democratic–Venstre government of 1978–9.

The character of Venstre's support has changed with the changing structure of the Danish economy. In 1950, 15.8 per cent of the economically active population were self-employed farmers. In 1970 this figure was exactly half of the previous figure, while salaried employees had increased from 22.6 per cent to 36.4 per cent of the work-force. 61 per cent of self-employed farmers preferred Venstre in 1974, but Venstre's problem has been to attract salaried and urban employees to compensate for the declining rural base. Even if Venstre might once have been described as 'green' in terms of its agrarian base, it has become decreasingly so in the 1960s and 1970s. While still laying claim to the 'green' label for themselves, that claim is challenged by both the Radicals and the Socialist People's Party: both parties have included appeals to the environmentalist vote in their recent programmes. A different and more radical claim to the 'green' label is made by 'the Greens', a movement which was very slow to start in Denmark by comparison with its impact in West German politics, but which gained its first ten seats at the local (*kommune*) elections in November 1985.

CONCLUSION

The emergence of the Conservative-led coalition of 1982 which included Venstre and was supported selectively by the Radicals can be traced back at least as far as 1950–3, and more immediately to 1976–8. Between the latter dates the Conservatives, Venstre, Centre Democrats and Christian People's Party began to act together as a constructive alternative to the succession of minority Social Democratic governments and to the mood of 'opposition for opposition's sake' provoked by the Progress Party.

Since 1945, the two Danish liberal parties together have achieved as much as one third of the total vote (1947 and 1968), with another peak as recently as 1975, but their support since then has been nearer half that level. The decline of support for Venstre in the 1960s seems nearly to have halted since 1977. There are some signs of increasing support among the lower stratum of salaried workers. Radical support seems also to have stabilised after the turbulence of the 1970s.

In the Danish multi-party system, this base has been sufficient for one or other of the liberal parties, and occasionally both, to exert a persistent influence on government policy. While the Radicals have emphasised a liberal concern for the weaker members of society and have kept alive a long tradition of internationalist pacifism, Venstre has defended agriculture and pressed for greater economic and technical efficiency in the services of the Welfare State. Together, they richly illustrate the diversity of liberal thought which has so greatly influenced the twentieth-century development of Danish society.

The government formed in 1982 has been led by the first Conservative prime minister the country has had since the transition to parliamentary democracy in 1901. It has depended on Venstre participation and Radical parliamentary support. It was confirmed in office, with some increase in support, at the 1984 parliamentary election and was encouraged to continue by favourable results in the November 1985 local elections and the February 1986 consultative referendum on institutional development of the European Community.

As we saw in the discussion of government participation earlier in this chapter, Venstre have the secondary position within the four-party coalition, and they have found it far easier to work effectively in this context than in coalition with the Social Democrats.

The Radicals consistently and conditionally supported much government policy throughout the 1973–87 period. But they withheld that support for the Schlüter government on many foreign policy issues, as well as on some environmental policies. Instead they formed part of a parliamentary majority which was opposed to US motivated NATO decisions to station cruise and pershing II missiles anywhere in Western Europe, to recommence manufacture of chemical weapons, and to increase the pace of the East–West arms race. The Radicals also voted with the Socialist bloc in support of efforts to maintain and strengthen the Nordic region as a nuclear-weapons-free zone and to develop a non-offensive security policy.

A problem for any government of whatever ideological complexion is to retain momentum. Danish liberalism often sees itself as setting limits to the powerful – including bureaucrats and monopolists – so that individuals can try out ideas and initiatives for themselves. The special legacy of Danish liberalism includes a Christian heritage centred on the value and inviolability of the individual created in God's image, with the concomitant obligation to develop human talents and inventiveness and to make the world a better place for our successors. While in the 1960s the Social Democrats were the main source of progress, now it is the Liberals who aim to create a freer, richer and more reasonable society (Haarder et al. (1985) 55–61).

In 1986, the price of power for Venstre was increasing criticism from core voters, those hit by the removal of exemptions for agriculture from taxes on land transactions and the imposition under Radical pressure of tax on fertilisers in the interest of preventing water pollution. Aspects of tax reform have also offended investors in shipping and industry who in other respects have benefited greatly from the coalition's economic policy. Its hold on power depends crucially on how well it manages to retain public confidence in its economic policy, but even so it seems likely that the two liberal parties will continue to exert their influence on cabinets and in parliament long into the future.

REFERENCES

Berglund, Sten and Ulf Lindström (1978) *The Scandinavian Party System(s): A Comparative Study* (Lund: Studentlitteratur).

Borre, Ole (1977) 'Recent trends in Danish voting behavior' in *Scandinavia at the Polls: Recent Political Trends in Denmark, Norway and Sweden*, edited by Karl H. Cerny (Washington DC: American Enterprise Institute) 3–38.

Borre, Ole and Jan Stehouwer (1970) *Fire Folketingsvalg 1960–68* (Århus: Akademisk Boghandel).

Borre, Ole et al. (1974) *Vælgerskredet 1971–73: Arbejdspapirer fra en interviewundersøgelse* (Arhus University, Institute of Political Science).

Borre, Ole et al. (1983) *Efter Vælgerskredet: analyser af folketingsvalget 1979* (Århus: Forlaget Politica).

Brixtofte, Peter (1980) *Den truende velstand: en debatbog om, hvordan vi får styr på den offentlige sektor* (Holte: Forlaget Liberal).

Castles, Francis G. (1978) *The Social Democratic Image of Society: A Study of the Achievements and Origins of Scandinavian Social Democracy in Comparative Perspective* (London: Routledge & Kegan Paul).

Elder, Neil, Alastair H. Thomas and David Arter (1982) *The Consensual Democracies? The Government and Politics of the Scandinavian States* (Oxford: Martin Robertson).

Elklit, J. and O. Tonsgaard (eds.) (1984) *Valg og Vælgeradfærd: studier i dansk politik* (Arhus: Forlaget Politica).

Garodkin, Ib (1985) *Håndbog i dansk politik*, 7th and earlier editions (Preasto: Mjølner).

Haarder, Bertel, Tom Høyem and Per Stig Møller (1985) *Mulighedernes Samfund* (Copenhagen: Gyldendal).

Hvidt, K. (ed.) (1984) *Folketingets Håndbog efter valget 10. Januar 1984* (Copenhagen: Schultz).

Larsen, Helge (ed.) (1980) *Det radikale Venstre i medvind og modvind 1955–1980* (Copenhagen: Tidens Tankers Forlag).

Nannestad, Peter (1984) *Dimensioner i vælgernes opfattelse af partisystemet* in Elklit and Tonsgaard (1984) 167–94.

Nielsen, Hans Jørgen (1984) 'De store partier har på får år mistet 60% af medlemmer', *Politisk Ugebrev* 22, 4 June, pp. 4–5.

Nyholm, Pekka (1982) 'Finland: a probabilistic view of coalition formation' in *Coalition Governments in Western Democracies*, edited by Eric C. Browne and John Dreijmanis (New York and London: Longman) 71–108.

Paterson, William E. and Alastair H. Thomas (eds.) (1986) *The Future of Social Democracy. Problems and Prospects of Social Democratic Parties in Western Europe* (Oxford: Clarendon Press).

Pedersen, Mogens N. (1967) 'Consensus and conflict in the Danish Folketing 1945–65', *Scandinavian Political Studies* 2: 143–66.

Rokkan, Stein (1966) 'Norway: numerical democracy and corporate pluralism' in *Political Oppositions in Western Democracies*, edited by R.A. Dahl (New Haven and London: Yale University Press): 70–115.

Smith, Gordon (1972 and subsequent editions) *Politics in Western Europe* (London: Heinemann Educational Books).

Statistisk Årbog 1983 (1983) (Copenhagen: Danmarks Statistik, vol. 87) and other editions.

Svensson, Palle (1982) 'Party cohesion in the Danish parliament during the 1970s', *Scandinavian Political Studies* 5 (n.s.) (1) 17–42.

Tågholt, Knud (1971) *Hvem var minister: Dansk politik gennem 100 år* (Århus: Forlaget Aros).

Thomas, A.H. (1977) 'Social democracy in Denmark' in *Social Democratic Parties in Western Europe*, edited by William E. Paterson and Alastair H. Thomas (1986) 234–71.

Thomas, Alastair H. (1986) 'Social democracy in Scandinavia: can dominance be regained?' in Paterson and Thomas (eds.) (1986) 172–222.

Worre, Torben (1974) 'Partistabilitet og vælgervandringer ved valgene i 1971 og 1973' in Borre, Ole et al. (1974).

Worre, Torben (1976) 'Social baggrund og partivalg', in Borre, Ole et al., *Vælgere i 70'erne* (Copenhagen: Akademisk Forlag) 50–87.

12

The Norwegian Liberal Party: from political pioneer to political footnote

Jørn Y. Leiphart and Lars Svåsand

HISTORICAL DEVELOPMENT

The Liberal Party occupies a central position in Norwegian political history and its origin is intimately linked to crucial events in the development of the Norwegian state from the late nineteenth century onwards. As Diagram 12.1 shows, the Liberal Party was not only one of the first two parties to be formed in the Norwegian political system, but it is also directly linked to the development of several other parties.

However, as we shall see, the history of the Liberal Party is also one of more or less continuous decline: its greatest electoral success was in 1885 when it won 76 of the 123 seats in the Storting (parliament). One hundred years later it was without any parliamentary representation at all. The large number of splits in the party suggests an extreme heterogeneity in its origin, a heterogeneity that could not be continued once the reason for the party's establishment had become unimportant.

Origin

The formation of the Norwegian Liberal Association on 29 August 1884 was one step in the development of the most serious political crisis in Norway after the country had entered a union with Sweden in 1814. At issue was the question of whether the king had the right to veto a constitutional amendment which the parliament had voted in favour of three times.[1] This issue was later referred to as the struggle over parliamentarianism. The first two Norwegian parties, the Liberals and their opponents – the Conservatives – emerged over this issue, with the

Liberals as the reformers. The issue that had brought the Liberals into being however, had simply unified a number of groups and movements which saw the removal of the Conservative cabinet as the solution to their own particular problem, but they agreed upon little else. Mjeldheim (1984) suggests that it is not very likely that the alliance behind the Liberals ever thought of establishing a permanent party. Thus, from the start, the Liberals could be characterised as a coalition of interests. The fundamental problem of the party stemmed from this situation. Naerbøvik (1984) distinguishes between four groups in this coalition: a populistic group, the Christian-laymen's movement, the urban liberal wing – in part associated with the emerging labour movement – and a rural national democratic tradition.

The groups represent several of the most important dimensions in the Norwegian political system – culture, economy and territory. First, there is the urban–rural dimension separating the interests of the towns from those of the countryside. Apart from the obvious differences in the economic interests of the two groups, there were also important political and cultural differences. Politically, the urban intellectuals were interested in extending the voting rights to urban groups previously unenfranchised. This was of less interest to the peasants, most of whom already had the vote. Culturally, the social behaviour of the urban intellectuals contrasted sharply with that of the peasants, particularly in terms of religious observance and attitudes towards the consumption of alcohol. Secondly, the peasants did not constitute a homogeneous group either. In the South and the West, farms were on average much smaller than in the East. On the other hand, the internal variation in farm sizes was much less in the West, which meant that class differences were less significant than in the East. Thirdly, the fundamentalist religious laymen's movement and its teetotalist wing was much stronger in the South and in the West than in the East, particularly in the rural areas.

Finally, as the industrialisation process developed, the Liberals became divided in their attitudes towards the emerging industrial proletariat.

Developments after formation

Within a year of their victory in the struggle over parliamentarianism, the Liberal Party split along the religious cleavage. The fundamentalists in the party were excluded from the Liberal parliamentary association and they formed their own party, the Moderate Liberals, which later fused with the Conservatives (Diagram 12.1).

Although still a very heterogeneous movement, the Liberals avoided further splits until after the dissolution of the union with Sweden in

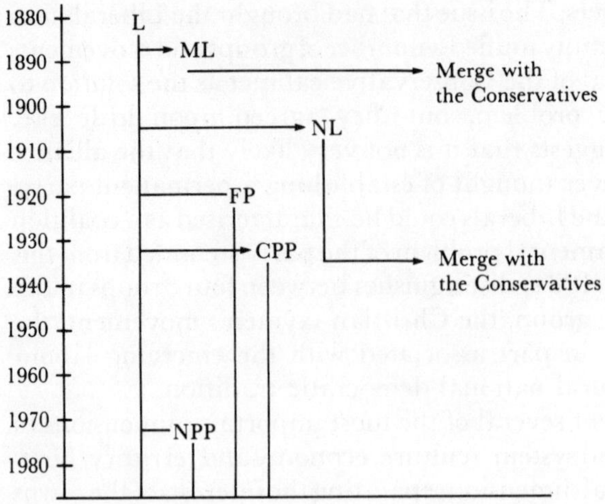

L = Liberals
ML = Moderate Liberals
NL = National Liberals
FP = Farmers' Party, from 1957: Centre Party
CPP = Christian People's Party
NPP = New People's Party, from 1981: Liberal People's Party

Diagram 12.1 The historical development of the Liberal Party

1905. The question over the status of Norway within the union, particularly the management of foreign affairs, had much the same effect as the issue of parliamentarianism had had on the party twenty years earlier; it kept internal conflicts latent by concentrating every effort on fighting the Conservatives whom the Liberals considered as allies of the Swedes. The Liberals soon emerged as the most nationalistic force in Norway and they successfully managed to pull Norway peacefully out of the union. However, an almost immediate effect of this was a split in the party along the 'economic dimension'. The splinter party, the National Liberals, did not share the Liberals' view of state intervention in the economy, symbolised primarily by the state regulation of investment in mines and hydro-electric power plants. Ten years later, in 1918, and especially in 1921, the farmers' association put up its own candidates in the Storting election. With the formation of the Farmers' Party (later the Centre Party) the Liberals lost one of their main pillars. Finally, the religious issue re-emerged in the 1930s leading to the formation of the Christian People's Party in 1933.

In the early 1970s, the whole Norwegian party system was shaken to its foundations over the issue of EC membership. Most Norwegian parties were internally divided and the Liberals were no exception. The chairman of the party was one of the most active favouring Norwegian EC membership, while others in important party positions were equally active in campaigning against. However, the Liberals were more severely split than other parties as the division on the EC question came on top of several other internal divisions within the party. In the referendum, Norwegian EC membership was rejected and the Labour government resigned. A majority in the Liberal Party's national council favoured Liberal participation in the government to be formed among the parties and representatives that had been against EC membership. However, in the Liberal parliamentary group a majority had favoured EC membership. Thus, the party *organisation* collided with a majority of the party *representatives* (MPs). In addition, the idea that the party organisation should be able to give orders to the parliamentary group was alien to the traditions of the party. The Liberal Party did not survive the EC issue intact – it split yet again. The New People's Party (later the Liberal People's Party), consisting mainly of the pro-EC faction of the party, was unable to compete with the main party. After returning one representative to the Storting in 1973, it declined rapidly and it currently polls less than 0.5 per cent of the votes. The main party itself also declined and a provisional final chapter in its history was written when it lost its two final parliamentary seats in the 1985 election.

Thus, the history of the Liberal Party is connected with the problem of containing numerous cleavages within a single party. However, it is also associated with the problem of managing a party without a clear ideological identity. There has never been a strong bond to keep the party together. Originally, the Liberal Party organisation was strong, but it deteriorated in the period between the two World Wars. The schisms suggest that the party has acted as an arena of competing interest groups; religious and teetotalist associations, farmers and labour interests. In view of such complexity, it is not surprising that the party has split several times. However, its decline can be explained not only in terms of internal divisions, but we must also take the party's position in the Norwegian party system into consideration. We will return to these issues in the sections on internal party structure and ideological profile(s).

INTERNAL PARTY STRUCTURE

Norwegian political parties are very similar in terms of their formal organisational structures. With some exceptions it is the same type of units we find in all parties. Beneath this similarity there are important

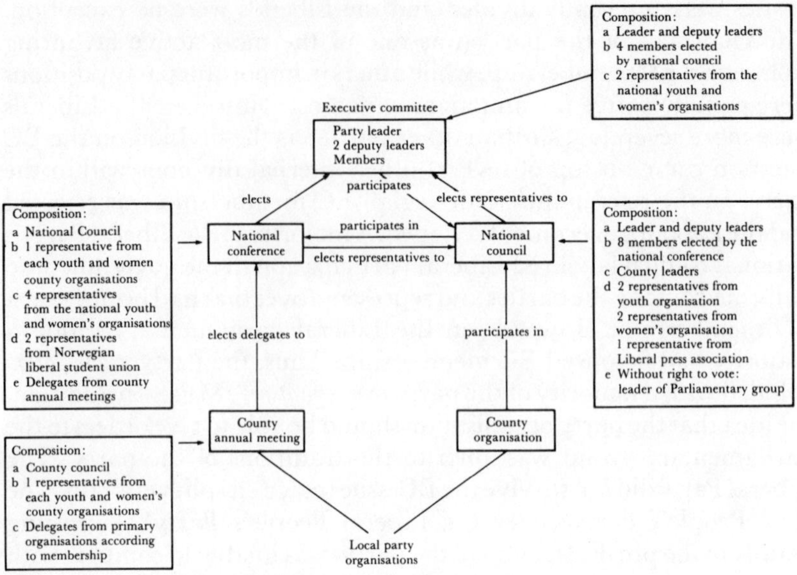

Diagram 12.2 Organisational structure in the Liberal Party

differences in the relationship between units and in the composition of participants in each organisational unit. The party structure consists of units in the party hierarchy and the relationship between the party organisation proper and auxiliary organisations.

The party hierarchy

The basic party structure is displayed in Diagram 12.2. There are three levels in the party hierarchy, corresponding to the Norwegian administrative units that are important for election purposes.

The local government unit, the commune, is the area covered by the party unit at the lowest level. (Occasionally for some cities and some of the larger rural communes there may be area units within the local branch.) The local party organisation has three important functions: a) to nominate candidates for elections to the local councils, b) to carry out election campaigns and c) to recruit party members. At the next level, the province level (*fylke*), the most important task of the party organisation is the nomination of candidates for parliamentary elections, which take place in multi-member constituencies with the *fylke* as the unit of representation. Since 1975, the province association also nominates candidates for the province councils. The province association is also responsible for the co-ordination of election campaigns, which is carried out by the members of the local branches.

The province association also forms the link between the local and national party organisation. The local branches elect representatives to the board of the province association, which in turn is represented at the national level via two channels. First, the province associations elect delegates to the annual national conference, according to their number of members as well as the strength of the party at the last general election. Second, between annual conventions the national council is the highest party organ. In all parties, the province associations are represented in the council, usually by their chairpersons. The province association, therefore, is extremely significant in terms of communication between the national and local levels. Its importance has been pointed out by the deputy chairman explaining the party's loss of seats at the 1985 election – the decision at the national level to support a Labour government had not been communicated and explained properly at the local level. Thus, the change in political alliance had not been understood and supported by the rank and file.

At the national level, there are three organisational units of importance: the annual conference, the national council and the executive committee.

The annual party conference elects the party leadership, a leader and two deputy leaders, for a period of two years. The conference also votes on proposals to be included in the party programme. The composition of the conference is based on three groups: members of the national council, delegates elected by the province associations, and representatives from affiliated organisations, such as the youth, student and women's associations. In the period between the conferences the most representative body is the national council, consisting of the representatives from the province associations and the affiliated associations. However, the day-to-day business is managed by the executive committee consisting of the leadership, four members elected by the national council and a representative from the youth and women's organisations.

Membership development

About 16 per cent of the Norwegian electorate report membership in a political party. In the Liberal Party, 13 per cent of the voters are party members. Prior to the split in the party in 1973 it had a total of ca. 13,000 members (see Table 12.1).

Compared to the Agrarian and the Christian People's Parties, which were about the same electoral size as the Liberals in 1969, i.e. around 10 per cent of the votes, the Liberals were considerably weaker as an organisation. The Agrarians claimed almost 60,000 and the Christian People's Party 44,000 members in 1973. The split in the party cut the

Table 12.1a *Liberal Party members, 1972–81*

Year:	1972	1975	1977	1979	1980	1981	1982	1983	1984
Members:	13,220	6,547	8,793	9,570	12,007	12,664	12,485	12,004	11,647

Source: Lars Svåsand (1985) 52.

Table 12.1b *Party members as percentage of voters in national elections*

Election year:	1957	1977	1981	1985
Percentage:	16	12	13	14

Source: Lars Svåsand (1985) 53.

membership figure in half. By 1980 the figure had climbed back to 12,000, but it has since declined once more to *c.* 11,000.

The party organisation and its affiliates

As we have seen from Diagram 12.2, the Liberal Party comprises of several organisational elements commonly found in Norwegian political parties: youth, women's and student associations, and the association of Liberal newspapers. In addition to these formal organisations, the party's representatives in parliament form an important group. It is common in all Norwegian parties to allow some representation of auxiliary organisations in the decision-making bodies of the party organisation. In the Liberal Party the youth and women's associations are more strongly represented than in other parties. During the 1960s the Liberal Party suffered a series of internal disputes in which the relationship between the youth organisation (and also the women's organisation to some extent) and the party organisation became strained. A series of domestic and international events eventually divided the party. The participation of the Liberal Party in the government coalition of 1965 was reluctantly accepted by the various groups in the party, but the youth movement was generally the strongest opponent of that particular coalition. During the 1969 nomination process the leader of the youth movement even opposed the party leader's bid for renomination. The radicalisation of the universities in the late 1960s and the anti-Vietnam war campaign further widened the gap between the youth movement and the party leadership. A similar schism, although not as prominent, could also be detected concerning Norwegian membership in NATO. The disagreement over the EC membership came on top of these political – and

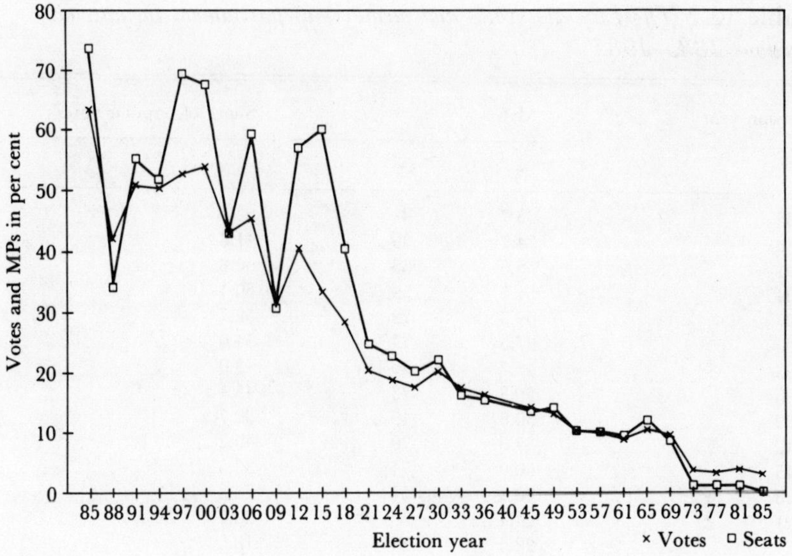

Diagram 12.3 The Liberals: Votes and Members of Parliament in national elections, 1885–1985

Source: Knut Heidar, *Norske Politiske Fakta 1884–1982*, Universitetsforlaget, Oslo

personal – controversies that had built up within the party. Political differences did not, of course, run solely between the party and the youth organisation. In addition, there were divisions within the party itself. However, it was because of the alliances between the external organisations and groups within the party that cleavages became so fierce that the party split in two as a result.

ELECTORAL SUPPORT

The electoral fortunes of the Liberal Party have, with few exceptions, been downhill (Diagram 12.3). This decline is connected with the splits that have occurred throughout its history in which major voting groups have defected.

Although the decline has been more or less continuous there is nevertheless a significant difference between the periods before and after the two World Wars. During the pre-war elections, the Liberals polled on average 35.7 per cent of the votes and obtained 31.3 per cent of the seats. In the post-war period the corresponding figures are 7.3 per cent and 10.9 per cent. Bjørklund (1984) distinguishes between four electoral periods for the Liberal Party: 1) the majority party (1882–1902), 2) *the* centre party (1903–17), 3) *one* of the centre parties

Table 12.2 *The Liberals: votes and members of parliament in national elections 1885–1985*

Election year	MPs		Share of popular votes
	%	N	%
1885	33.7	84	63.4
1888	34.2	39	41.8
1891	55.6	65	50.8
1894	51.7	59	50.4
1897	69.3	79	52.7
1900	67.5	77	54.0
1903	42.7	50	43.0
1906	59.3	73	45.4
1909	30.6	46	30.7
1912	57.0	70	40.2
1915	60.0	74	33.3
1918	40.4	51	28.3
1921	24.4	37	20.1
1924	22.6	34	18.6
1927	20.0	30	17.3
1930	22.0	33	20.2
1933	16.0	24	17.1
1936	15.3	23	16.0
1945	13.3	20	13.8
1949	14.0	21	13.1
1953	10.0	15	10.0
1957	10.0	15	9.7
1961	9.3	14	8.8
1965	12.0	18	10.4
1969	8.6	13	9.4
1973	1.9	2	3.5
1977	1.2	2	3.2
1981	1.2	2	3.9
1985	0.0	0	3.0

(1918–1972), and 4) the green mini-party (1973–83). We will look more closely at two aspects of the electoral base of the party in the post-war period. First, we will examine the geographical distribution of Liberal voters. This is significant, given the party's origin as the party of the periphery (Rokkan (1967)). Second, because of the importance of territory, the Liberal Party has been less indentified with a particular social group or class than is the case with most other Norwegian parties.

Geographical distribution of Liberal votes

The centre–periphery dimension was essential to the formation of the Liberal Party in 1884 and it has remained so ever since, in spite of all the splits that have occurred. Maps 12.1–4 display the strength of the party (*communevise*) at four general elections – 1945, 1957, 1969 and 1981.

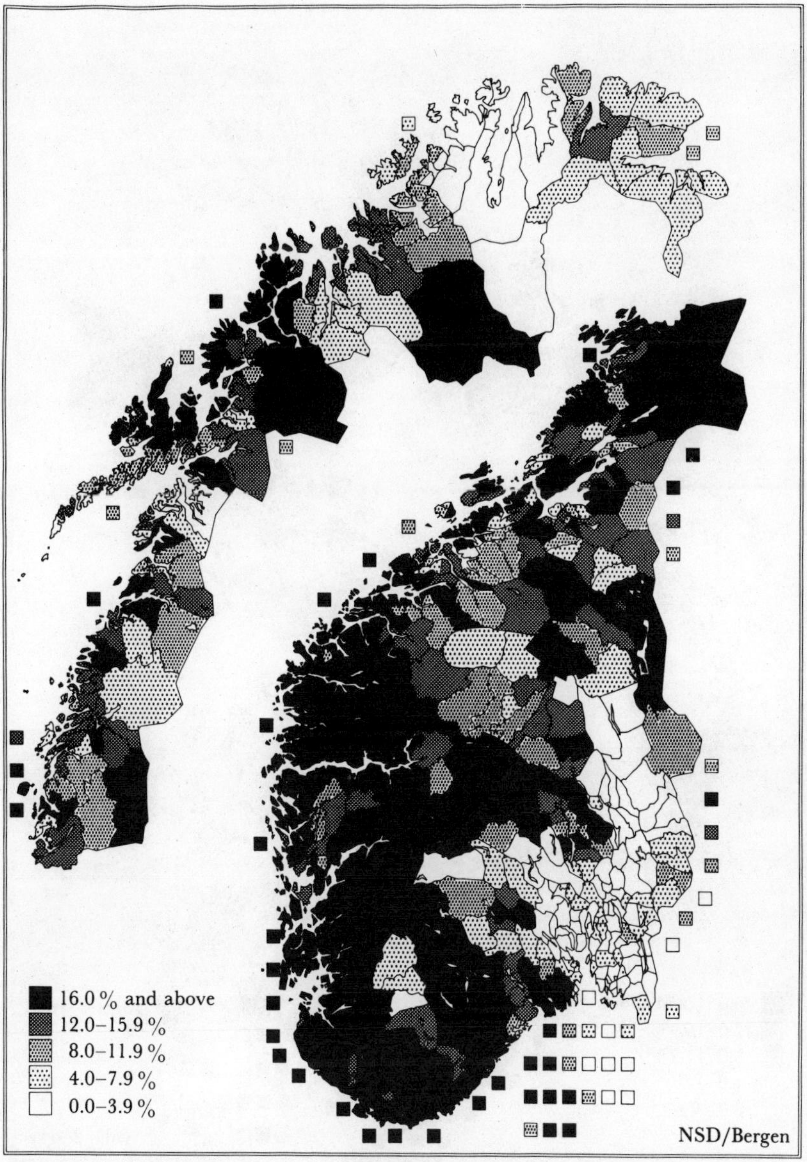

Map 12.1 National election 1945: Geographical distribution of Liberal Party strength (*communes*)

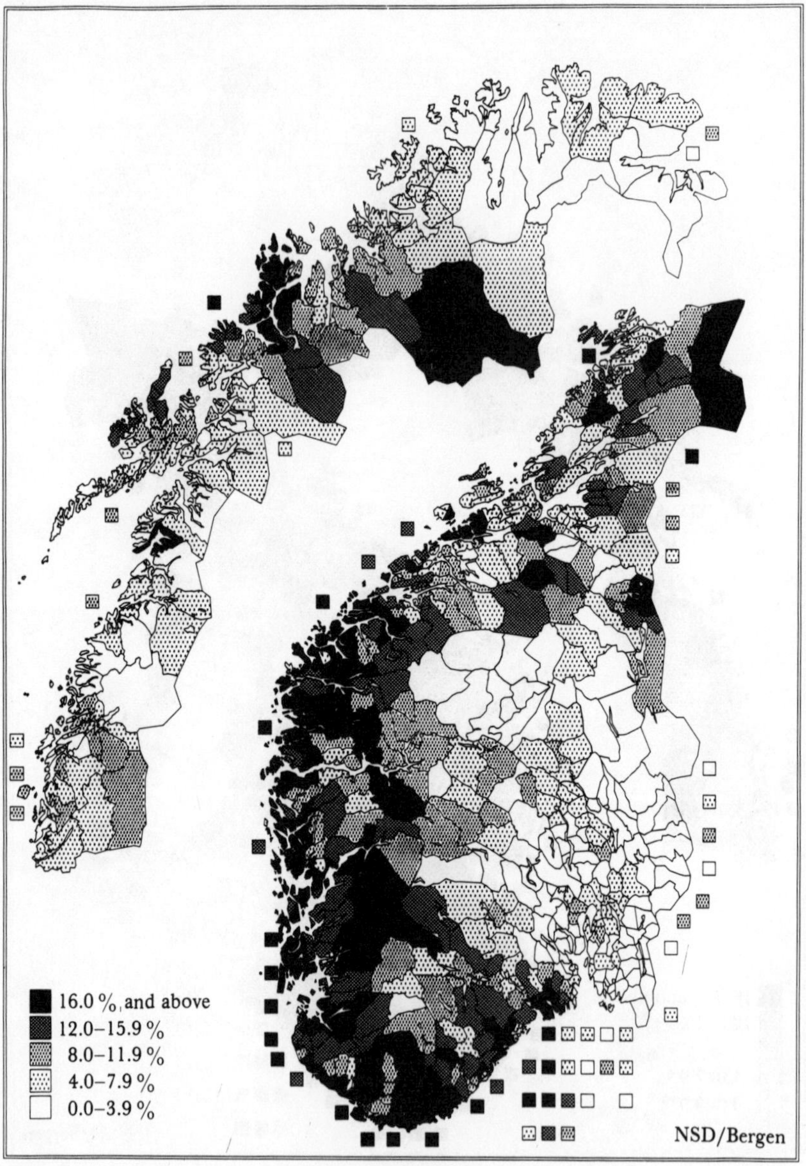

Map 12.2 National election 1957: Geographical distribution of Liberal Party strength (*communes*)

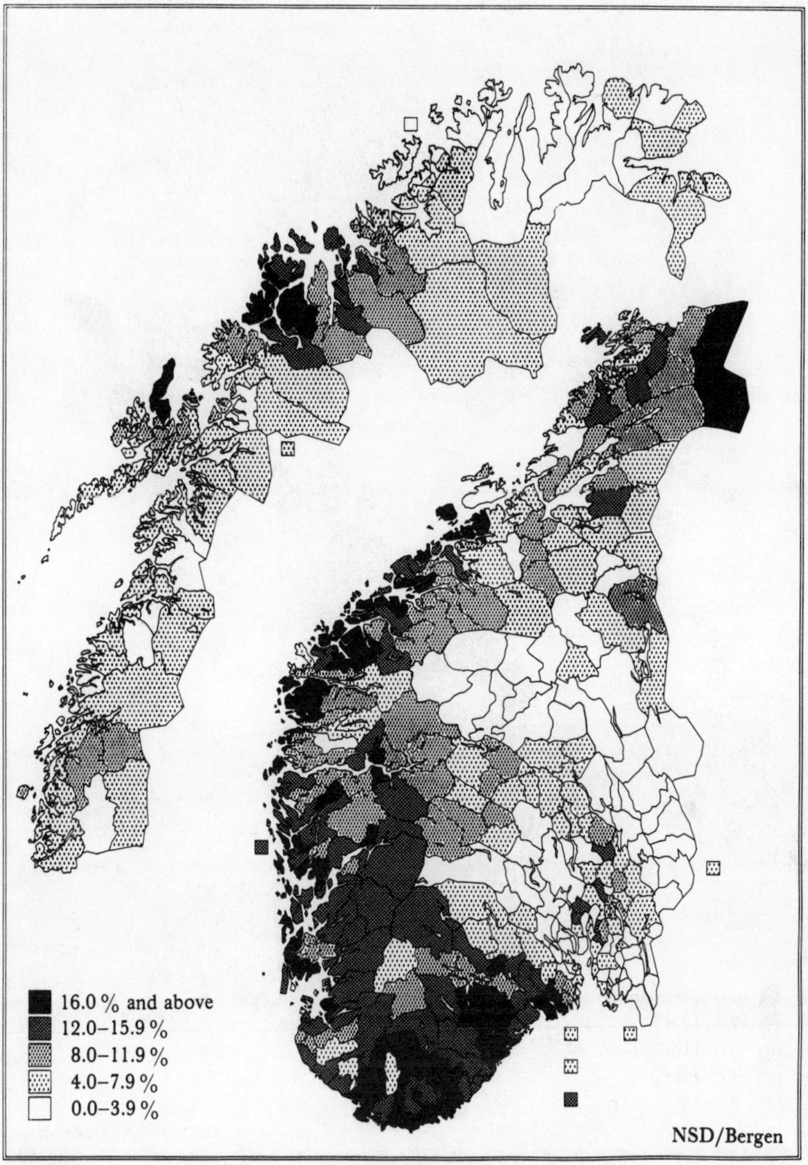

Map 12.3 National election 1969: Geographical distribution of Liberal Party strength (*communes*)

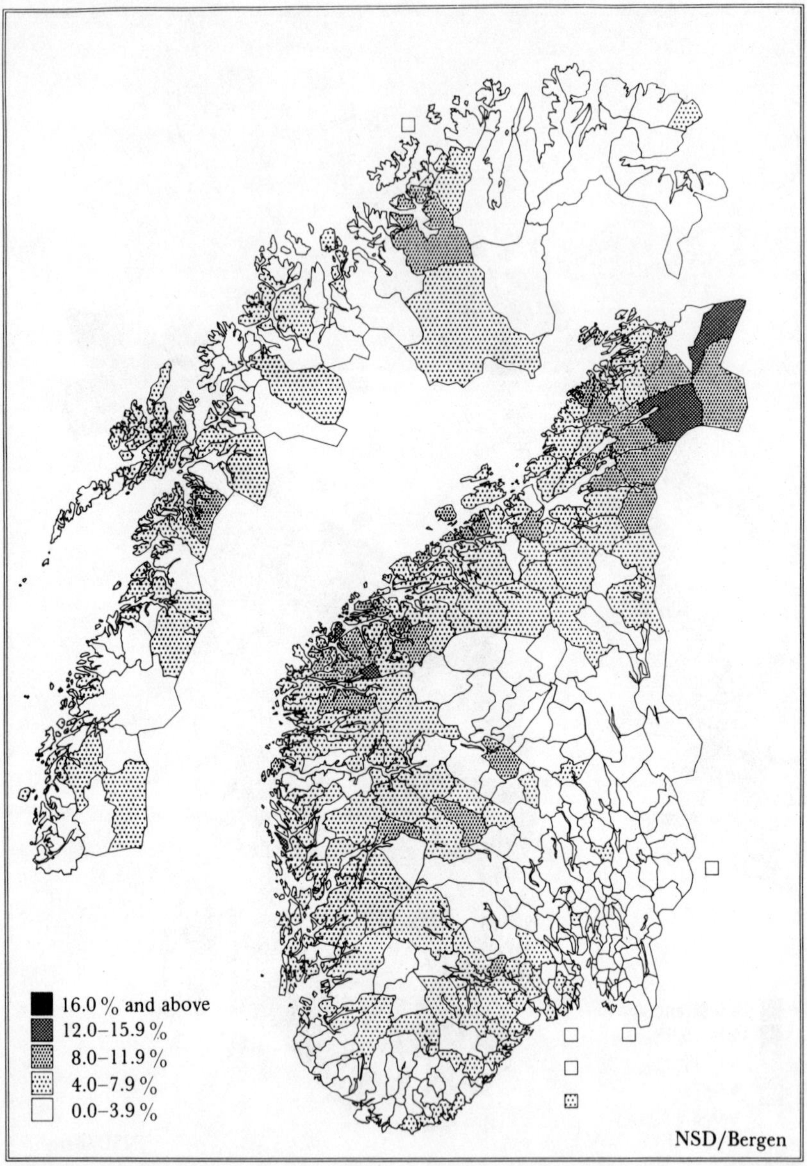

Map 12.4 National election 1981: Geographical distribution of Liberal Party strength (*communes*)

In 1945 the party could still be said to be a truly national party, although it was even then significantly weaker in the south-eastern part of the country, the area close to the capital. The western and the southern parts of the country were solid Liberal areas, as they were in the early days of the party. In the central part of the country and in the North there were scattered areas of Liberal strength. Overall, the party polled almost 14 per cent of the votes in this first post-war election. In the 1957 and 1965 elections the party was down to about 10 per cent nationally. The effect of this decline on the geographical distribution is quite marked: although the party was declining all over the country, the only really strong areas were in the West and South. In 1981 the picture changed again: now its strength is in the north-western part of the country. In the South which used to be the real stronghold, the change from 1965 is dramatic. The reason for this is to be found in the party split in 1973: the new party mobilised those Liberal voters who had been on the centre-right of the party. As a result, the decline of the party has renewed the centre–periphery dimension, but the split in 1973 clearly breaks with the pattern of the past.

Characteristics of Liberal voters

In terms of electoral mobilisation, the nature of the Liberal Party as a coalition had certain advantages. The party was able to rally voters around broad national interests that were not associated with a particular class of a particular group of voters – its lack of identification with group interests was its strength. However, the splits in the party led to the formation of other parties articulating the interests of more clearly defined groups: the Christians in 1888 and 1933, the farmers in 1918, and the industrial workers being mobilised by their own party. This process has left the Liberal Party with no defined group of voters to mobilise. In particular, as Norwegian society became more and more thoroughly organised by interest groups, many of whom supported a particular party, the Liberals were left without any mass organisation to rely upon. This lack of a major social-group basis is evident in survey results. Table 12.3 shows the party's support among various occupational groups in the post-war period.

In 1949 one could still see the remains of the Liberals as a party for the peasants, as it had been originally. A fifth of farmers supported the party at that time, a figure dwindling to its present level of 4 per cent twenty years later. The other major support group was self-employed persons such as lawyers, doctors and artisans. The support among this group reflects the party's character as a non-socialist party, often defending minor business interests. White-collar workers, in particular those employed in the public sector, have been the third major voting

Table 12.3 *Percentage of occupational groups voting for the Liberal Party, 1949–81*

	1949	1957	1965	1969	1973	1977	1981
Workers	6	5	8	7	4	3	3
Farmers and fishermen	21	11	9	4	3	4	3
White-collar workers (public sector)	–[a]	15	16	16	4	4	10
White-collar workers (private sector)	–[a]	13	13	14	3	4	2
Self-employed (excl. primary sector)	25	15	18	7	4	5	1

[a] No distinction in the 1949 survey between public and private sectors.
Source: Valen (1981) 105–13, Valen and Aardal (1983) 190.

group. Civil servants have now emerged as the group with the strongest support for the Liberals.[2] Within this last group, it is possible to identify a subgroup that seems to have been particularly attracted to the Liberals – the teachers. In a survey from 1953, Rokkan ((1970) 302) found that 36 per cent of teachers voted Liberal, by far the strongest party in that profession. Among male primary school teachers support reached 45 per cent. Least support has been given to the Liberals from blue-collar workers due to the very effective mobilisation of the Labour Party. However, this does not mean that such workers are of little electoral importance for the Liberal Party. If we turn Table 12.3 around and look at how important various occupational groups are amongst those voting Liberal, the picture becomes very different (Table 12.4).

Now it appears that the workers have accounted for almost a third of the total Liberal votes in most of the post-war period, and in 1973 for almost half of the votes. The importance of publicly employed white-collar workers is further enhanced, now being one half of the total Liberal electorate. The reason for the attractiveness of the Liberals for some workers is probably associated with the Liberals as a credible party for the so-called 'counter-cultural' movements in Norway, such as religion, teetotalism and support for the rural language (*nynorsk*). In 1969, support for the Liberals was 7 per cent among those using the urban form of the Norwegian language, but 14 per cent among those using the rural variant. Similarly, among those attending religious services once a month, almost 17 per cent voted Liberal, while among those not attending church only 8 per cent voted Liberal. Thus, for workers to whom the language or religious values have been important,

Table 12.4 *Liberal Party vote by occupational groups, 1957–81*

	1957	1965	1969	1973	1977	1981
Workers	31	32	34	45	39	31
Farmers and Fishermen	23	15	6	13	8	6
White-collar workers (public sector)	16	19	37	19	18	50
White-collar workers (private sector)	17	19	17	13	18	11
Self-employed (excl. primary sector)	13	15	6	10	17	2
	100	100	100	100	100	100
	(98)	(161)	(121)	(38)	(51)	(52)

Source: Valen and Aardal (1983) 190.

Table 12.5 *Age distribution among Liberal voters, 1957, 1965, 1981*

Age group	1957	1965	1981[a]
Less than 26 years	4	13	15[b]
26–39	31	22	56
40–59	40	42	19
60 +	25	23	10

[a] Voting age from 18
[b] Less than 23 years
Sources: For 1957 and 1969: Norwegian Social Science Data Services; for 1981: Valen and Aardal (1983) 58.

the Liberal Party may have been a serious alternative to the Labour Party. The increased support for the Liberals among workers in 1973 is probably an effect of the EC debate. With the Liberal Party more on the anti-EC than on the pro-EC side of the debate, the Liberal Party was an alternative for those workers who were against Norwegian EC membership.

One of the most interesting changes to have occurred in the Liberal part of the electorate is the changing age composition of the party's support base.

In 1957 the Liberal Party was dominated by an adult and elderly electorate, $\frac{3}{4}$ of the voters were more than 40 years old, $\frac{1}{4}$ more than 60 years. In 1981 less than $\frac{1}{3}$ of the voters were more than 40.

A younger electorate does not, however, imply a larger electorate over time. Apart from the lack of a clearly identified target group in the social structure, the biggest problem for the Liberal Party is its inability to mobilise a stable electorate. Valen and Aardal ((1983) 59) found that of the 1981 Liberal voters only 17 per cent had voted Liberal in the preceding general election in 1977. 40 per cent came from other parties and 25 per cent were voting for the first time. This suggests that the Liberal Party's electorate is using the party as an intermediary stop on their way between other parties.

THE LIBERAL PARTY IN GOVERNMENT

In the pre-1940 era the Liberals were one of the 'natural governing parties' in Norway. The last Liberal-led government resigned in 1935. During the first 56 years with parliamentarism the Liberals participated in 13 governments for a total period of 34 years and 3 months. With the Labour Party's rise to dominance in the Norwegian party system in the post-war period, it was 1963 before the non-socialists were able to form a government. That government fell after only two weeks, but its political importance was significant: it proved that the non-socialist parties were able to co-operate sufficiently to form a government. These parties, the Conservatives, Liberals, Agrarians, and the Christian People's Party, obtained a majority at the 1965 and 1969 elections. However, the government collapsed in 1971 over the EC issue. As has been explained earlier, the Liberal Party also took part in the government formed after the referendum over the EC membership. In the four post-war governments the Liberal Party has assumed the following portfolios:

1963	Church and Education, Labour and Local Government, Wages and Prices.
1965–71	Finance, Agriculture, Labour and Local Government.
1972–3	Finance, Trade, Defence, Consumer Affairs and Administration.

While the last of these governments only had three parties, the Agrarians, Christians and Liberals, the Liberals had four ministers against three in the governments in which the Conservatives also participated. In any Norwegian government there are three important positions any party would like to control, and other positions in which some parties have a particular interest.

The three most important positions are the prime minister, the foreign minister and the finance minister. In the non-socialist majority governments 1965–71 the Conservatives agreed not to insist on the prime minister position, even if they were by far the largest party. To make the government acceptable to the centrist parties, it was agreed that the prime minister would have to come from one of these parties. Both the Agrarians and the Liberals had a candidate. In the end the Christians opted for the Agrarian candidate, Per Borten. As a compensation, the Conservatives got the Foreign Office, traditionally the second most important position in the government. Finally, the Christian People's Party got two of the ministries of greatest concern to them – Church and Educational Affairs and Social Affairs. Thus, it was natural that the Liberals got the third most important position, Finance. The Liberals controlled the Labour and Local Government Department in all but one of the four governments in which the party has participated. This department can be seen as central to the Liberals' interest since the party has traditionally stressed decentralisation as an important issue in national politics.

IDEOLOGICAL PROFILE(S)

Is there a liberal ideology? The question is frequently asked, but seldom answered. It is not possible to speak of a liberal ideology that would be valid as a characterisation of the Liberal Party throughout its entire history. The very society in which the party functions has changed so fundamentally that an attempt to do so would be pointless. Moreover, a party that has changed so dramatically as the Liberals, with all their splits and their decline from a major party to a political footnote, cannot be characterised easily. As a coalition more than as a homogeneous party, the Liberals have contained conflicting views in their political programme. On the one hand, they have stressed the rights of individuals, but on the other hand the party has also emphasised the rights of the state to intervene in society to prevent the more unwanted consequences of free-market liberalism (Nordby (1984) 135).

The liberals have been torn by their relationship with the Labour Party on the left and the Conservatives on the right. The Conservatives, the traditional opponents of the Liberals, wanted to unite the non-socialist parties against the growing strength of the Labour Party. However, the Liberals, or at least a majority of them, always rejected such a possibility. The Labour Party was equally unacceptable as a coalition partner. Following the split in the party in 1908, the Liberal parliamentary group decided that: 'This parliamentary group cannot enter into political or parliamentary cooperation with the Conservatives or with the Socialist Party.' (Nordby (1984) 125). It was not until 1963 that the Liberals' fear of the Conservatives was overcome.

The Liberals' relationship with the other non-socialist parties

Table 12.6 *People mentioning various issues as important in 1981 election*

	Percentage of Liberals voters	Percentage of all voters
Environment, energy, decentralisation	50	13
Defence and foreign policy	34	20
Abortion, Christian values	11	28
Taxation	9	24
Health/Welfare	23	23

Source: Valen and Aardal (1983) 43 and 45.

changed fundamentally in the decade following the EC issue of the early 1970s. First, the Liberals split, and they were halved in strength as a result, making them less vital as a coalition partner for other parties. Second, the Conservatives clearly emerged as the largest non-socialist party with *c*. 30 per cent of the votes in the early 1980s. The decline of the political centre in Norway meant that any non-socialist majority government would have to include the Conservatives. With anti-Conservative attitudes dominant in the Liberal Party along with its own reduced strength, the party was excluded from governmental participation when the non-socialists were again able to form a government in 1981. The Liberal Party decided to support, and eventually to take part in, a Labour government prior to the election of 1985, should the Labour Party emerge as the biggest party after the election. In the view of the Liberals, the previous government dominated by the Conservatives had become too right-wing, spending too little on health, social affairs and local government. On these issues, the Liberals felt closer to the Labour Party – without becoming more 'socialistic'. The policy change was a disaster as the party lost its two remaining seats in parliament. The position of the Liberal Party in the centre of the political spectrum in Norway, partly leaning towards Labour, partly in a more right-wing direction, has often led to shifting party positions on issues, as well as substantive internal differences of opinion within the party. It has therefore sometimes been difficult to pinpoint what exactly distinguishes the Liberals from their political neighbours. However, from the mid 1970s onwards, the Liberals have attempted to profile themselves as the most environmentally conscious party in Norway. Table 12.6 shows very clearly how Liberal voters perceived various issues at the 1981 election.

Following the disastrous election of 1985 the Liberal Party set up a committee to examine what went wrong, and to make proposals for the reconstruction of the party. The committee points, among other factors, to the extremely narrow focus of Liberal Party policy: the party became almost exclusively an ecological interest group. Other issues, such as regional and housing policy, were pushed into the background, although prominent in the party programme. The committee hints that a partial explanation for this is found in the preferences of a 'well tuned youth organisation that has turned the party profile away from traditional liberal issues'. The party became 'a green party for people in white coats'. Politically, the emphasis on ecological issues led to a conservative position on economic issues: ecological protection was turned into the protection of virtually everything, against any real change. The Liberals became a 'no'-party (Venstre (1986)).

CONCLUSION

The most important question facing the Liberal Party today is its very survival in Norwegian politics. It is indeed somewhat of a paradox that the party which forced the *ancien régime* to resign one hundred years ago is now on its own death-bed, while the Conservative Party is the largest non-socialist party and has been in government from 1981, first as a minority single-party government until mid-1983, later together with the Christian People's Party and the Agrarians, until the government was defeated in a parliamentary vote in the spring of 1986. There seems to have been both long-term and short-term factors explaining the decline of the Liberal Party in Norway. First, as a broad coalition around certain specific issues, rather than relying on a coherent ideology, it has suffered numerous splits and defections. Second, its position in the centre of the political spectrum has made it vulnerable to the manoeuvres of its partisan competitors. The moderate Labour Party, on the left, has often tried to appear as a centrist party. Even more problematic have been the changes in the Conservative Party, which has clearly moved to the left. Thus, the space in the middle of the party spectrum has become considerably narrower. So far, the Agrarians and the Christian People's Party have been able to maintain their positions in their capacity as 'interest parties'. Finally, the latest shift in political alliances, towards the Labour Party, was not acceptable to the rank and file in the Liberal Party. The split in 1973 and the acceptance of the Labour Party as a more credible governmental alternative than the Conservative-led coalition has left the Liberals as a very different party from the one they used to be.

The committee examining the 1985 defeat has recommended far-reaching changes both in the party apparatus and in policy output. It stressed that communication between the central party apparatus and the local units must be improved. More emphasis must be put on involving the party branches in policy-making. In the national council and the executive committee, lines of responsibility have been unclear in the past. The relationship between the party organisation and the party's parliamentary representatives must also be improved.

In terms of policy, the committee proposes six areas where the party should focus its attention: the change from an industrial to a service society; education and business; health and social policies; it must find a new balance between the private and the public sectors; environmental protection and international justice; and cultural diversity.

Recently, the newly-elected party leader and the leader of the Liberal People's Party, which split off from the Liberals in 1973, have started discussing a possible re-uniting of the two parties.

It may be premature to declare the Liberals dead. Other parties have managed to come back to the Storting, and the recent success of the Swedish Liberal Party will certainly encourage the Norwegian Liberal Party to strive for similar goals. However, it will need the regular backing of a substantial number of voters if it is to regain the position it has occupied in the past – backing which appears both unstable and unpredictable. In spite of the differences, the recent success of the Swedish Liberal Party demonstrates how unpredictable voters and parties are.

NOTES

We would like to thank Leiv Mjeldheim and Emil Kirchner for valuable comments on an earlier draft of this chapter.

1 The constitution gave the king a temporary veto. However, if parliament voted in favour of a law three times, the act would become law even without the king's signature. The king and his cabinet insisted that this only applied to ordinary laws, and that in constitutional matters the king's veto was absolute.

2 Among the delegates to the national conference in 1985 civil servants accounted for 58% (Heidar (1985)).

REFERENCES

Bjørklund, Tor (1984) 'Den krympende velgerflokk' in Naerbøvik and Grepstad (1984) 175–95.

Heidar, Knut (1985) 'Notat om landsmøtedelegatene 1985: Venstre', Oslo, Institute of Political Science, unpubl. manuscript.

Mjeldheim, Leiv (1984) *Folkerørsla som vart parti. Venstre 1884–1905* (Olso: Universitetsforlaget).

Naerbøvik, Jostein (1984) 'PA leit etter vinstrelina (1884–1935)' in Naerbøvik and Grepstad (1984) 27–44.

Naerbøvik, Jostein and Ottar Grepstad (eds.) (1984) *Venstres Hundre År* (Oslo: Gyldendal).

Nordby, Trond (1984) 'Kampen om Venstre (1906–1908)' in Naerbøvik and Grepstad (1984) 125–42.

Rokkan, Stein (1967) 'Geography, religion and social class: cross-cutting cleavages in Norwegian politics' in S.M. Lipset and S. Rokkan (eds.), *Party Systems and Voter Alignments* (N.Y.: Free Press).

Rokkan, Stein (1970) *Citizens, Elections, Parties* (Oslo: Universitetsforlaget).

Svåsand, Lars (1985) *Politiske Partier* (Oslo: Tiden).

Valen, Henry (1981) *Valg og Politikk* (Oslo: NKS-Forlaget).

Valen, Henry and Bernt Olav Aardal (1983) *Et Valg i Perspektiv. En Studie av Stortingsvalget i 1981* (Oslo: Statistisk Sentralbyrå, Samfunnsøkonomiske Studier 54).

Venstre (1986) *Tilbake til Venstre. Instilling fra Venstres Gjenreisningkommisjon om vegen framover* (Oslo: Venstre).

13

Liberal parties in Finland: from perennial coalition actors to an extra-parliamentary role

David Arter

INTRODUCTION

At the general election in March 1983, the Finnish Liberal People's Party, Liberaalinen Kansanpuolue (LKP), lost its toehold in the 200-seat national assembly (Eduskunta). This meant for the first time since the creation of a modern legislative system in Finland in 1907, there were no liberal representatives in parliament – precisely the same fate which had befallen the Norwegian Liberals (Venstre) two years earlier. To many observers of the Finnish political scene, this disastrous result for LKP came as little surprise, and the newspaper obituaries to mark the peaceful demise of the party were doubtless composed shortly after the Liberals' decision to become a member organisation of the Centre (formerly Agrarian) Party early in 1982. It was in this twilight world as 'a party within a party' that LKP lost all four of its parliamentarians and plummeted to an all-time nadir of 0.8 per cent of the active electorate in 1983. It seemed the end of the line for Finnish liberalism and its absorption into a federated political centre similar to the UDF in France.

The road back for the party will be long and hard. At the local government elections in October 1984, to be sure, LKP contrived to increase its vote slightly (1.3 per cent of the valid poll) and then emboldened by the resurgence of liberalism in neighbouring Sweden and the 14.3 per cent gained by Folkpartiet at the autumn 1985 general election, LKP seized the opportunity of breaking the knot with the Centre Party. Its target then was to win two MPs and two per cent of the vote at the 1987 general election, whilst recapturing seats on the large councils in the southern population centres, especially Helsinki, Turku and Espoo at the 1988 local government elections. The first part of this target was not, however, achieved. At the 1987 general election, the Liberals polled a meagre 1.0 per cent of the vote and remained without representatives in the Eduskunta. In contrast to this extremely modest performance, the Finnish liberals had in the past savoured the most succulent morsels of *Machtpolitik* – they have boasted two presidents and seven prime ministerships since independence in 1917 and consequent upon a strategic placement at the centre of the political spectrum, liberal parties have participated in approximately two-thirds of all governments in the same period.

When viewed in partisan terms, a long liberal tradition in Finland has been marked by division and discontinuity. Division, in the way that liberalism has failed to embrace and unite the two national cultures – the majority Finnish-speaking and the minority Swedish-speaking culture – and, accordingly, has appeared numerically weak in comparison to liberal parties elsewhere in the Nordic region. Discontinuity, in the sense that there have been several liberal-minded parties identified with different stages in the state-building process. First, there was the Young Finn Party's defence of constitutionalism against tsarism in the final decades of the pre-independence period when Finland was a grand duchy of the Russian empire. Then there was the Progressive Party's advocacy of republicanism against constitutional monarchy in the struggle over a new form of government in 1918. Finally, there was the Finnish People's Party and subsequently the Liberal People's Party's espousal of social liberalism and welfare reformism in the changed climate after the Second World War. In short, whilst liberals have been engaged at the crucial points in the evolution of the modern nation-state, a historic liberal lineage in Finland has spawned several parties and created an overall picture of fragmentation.

Liberalism has deep roots in both national language groups. There have long been liberals among the Swedish-speaking population and the first liberal party in Finland – which emerged in 1880 – was, in fact, based in the ethnic minority. The Swedish People's Party, Svenska Folkpartiet, its mouthpiece since 1907, moreover, might well be regarded as a liberal party and joined the Liberal International in 1983. It is not, however, *exclusively* a liberal party. Rather, it constitutes a distinctive genus which attempts to represent the socio-economic interests of a diverse Swedish-speaking population – the working class in the industrial south, the farmers in north-west Finland, the fishermen in the coastal districts and on the Åland islands and not least the professional and business elements in the towns and the capital city in particular. Significantly, too, the Swedish People's Party contains a right-wing faction, Nordiska Grund, which enjoys observer status at the European Democratic Union.

Among the Finnish-speaking citizenry, there have been four parties generally regarded as bearing the liberal tradition, although only the most recent has been liberal with a capital 'L'. This is not in itself significant since in Scandinavia the 'Liberal Party' designation has appeared as a suffix to traditional names only in the last decade or so (Venstre, Danmark's liberale parti in 1970, for example). The four parties which will form the focus of this essay are – the Young Finn Party (1894–1918), the National Progressive Party (1918–51), the Finnish People's Party (1951–65) and the Liberal People's Party (1965–). They have provided a main artery of the Finnish party system and as one of them has ceased to exist, there has been a transference of leaders and voters to its successor. In the context of the traditionally polarised politics of the small Finnish democracy, the overriding common denominator between these liberal parties has been their centre placement. In the words of LKP's 1971 programme: 'The Liberal People's Party is an independent reformist party situated at the centre of the political spectrum.'

THE DEVELOPMENT OF LIBERAL PARTIES

Facilitated by Tsar Alexander II's decision to convene a diet of estates in the grand duchy in 1863 and influenced by Herder, Pestalozzi and cultural nationalism in Europe as a whole, an embryonic Finnish party system emerged in the 1860s centred on the language question. A Finnish Party (Suomalainen puolue), led by J.V. Snellman, championed the subject Finnish culture of the masses against the dominant Swedish culture of the educated classes.[1] The latter was a legacy of the nation's long association with the Swedish crown which was severed after Russia conquered Finland during the Napoleonic Wars. Swedish was spoken by an urban elite of old aristocratic and commercial families, and it was also the language of the central administration, universities and press, in addition to the senior clergy. Put somewhat simply, the Swedish language distinguished bumpkin from bigwig. Indeed, there were those Swedish-Finnish literati – J.J. Nordström and Emil van Qvanten, for instance, who – in the name of pan-Scandinavianism – urged the Finns to break with Russia and rejoin Sweden.[2]

The first liberal party in Finland was founded in 1880 by a splinter group from this Swedish party. It was led by Leo Mechelin, a man who was to become supremely important in disseminating the concept of a Finnish state across Europe.[3] Liberal ideas had earlier taken root among Swedish-speaking groups closely associated with the newspaper *Helsingfors Dagbladet* founded in 1862 in the capital city. Although this liberal group had no party organisation, its programme issued in November 1880 – relatively early by comparison with the radical programme in the UK, for example – was underwritten by thirty-nine highly prestigious individuals and sought to subordinate the language issue to important social and economic questions.[4] It appealed to liberal elements in the Finnish movement to join forces, but when this co-operation failed to materialise, its fate was sealed. The Swedish-Finnish liberal party survived only five years before reverting to the mother party. None the less, it had boasted the first coherent party programme in Finland.

Ironically, roughly coincident with the demise of this first liberal party, a liberal wing within the Finnish Party emerged based on a younger generation of political leaders, especially among the students, for whom the older leaders of the party like Yrjö-Koskinen were too conservative. Unlike the founders of the short-lived Swedish-Finnish liberal party who had wanted to transcend the language question, the rising group of Finnish Party figures appeared less liberal in initially demanding a stronger stand on the language question than that pursued by the older Finnish Party leadership. They did, however, advocate a liberal and democratic line in cultural and religious matters, wished to respond to liberal currents on the continent and had at their disposal several newspapers with which to articulate their case. In the peasant estate too, a group of these 'Young Finns' gathered around the person of Jonas Castrén. When the Russification programme of Alexander III and subsequently Nicholas II in the 1890s threatened the systematic reduction of Finland's basic institutions, the Young Finns broke with the conciliatory line of the Old Finns and in 1894 issued an independent party programme.

In the form of the Young Finn Party, liberal currents became closely associated in the late pre-independence period with two central political issues. First, there was *constitutionalism* and principled opposition to tsarist designs to reduce the basic rights of the grand duchy. Secondly, there was rural *revivalism* and low church opposition to a higher Lutheran clergy which seemed to have neglected its pastoral duties in favour of maintaining its privileged social status. Liberalism, in other words, achieved an identity by reference to the *national question* and the *church question* – issues of 'high politics' rather than economic creed. During the vital period of state-building between 1917 and 1919, however, the Young Finns split and liberals were divided over the form of government which the newly-independent state should adopt.

The collapse of tsarism in Russia in February 1917 created a highly fluid situation in the grand duchy. The Russian provisional government refused to ratify a sovereign powers bill (*valtalaki*) which would have bestowed on the Finnish parliament competence in all legislative matters excepting foreign affairs and defence and in the face of considerable Finnish resistance, especially from the Social Democrats, the Russian prime minister, Kerensky, dissolved the Eduskunta and called fresh elections for October 1917. The Old Finn and Young Finn Parties formed electoral alliances everywhere except in the single-member constituency of Lapland and achieved a combined total of 30.2 per cent of the poll compared with 44.8 per cent for the Social Democrats, 12.4 per cent for the Agrarians and 10.9 per cent for the Swedish People's Party. Lenin's seizure of power in St Petersburg in November 1917 complicated matters further. The Finnish Social Democrats, under growing pressure from the labour movement, resigned from the domestic government (Senate) and this paved the way for the bourgeois coalition's unilateral declaration of Finnish independence which obtained parliamentary approval on 6 December 1917. The Social Democratic delegates had already absented themselves and against a backdrop of domestic famine and revolution in Russia, Finland became embroiled in a bloody civil war by January 1918. This was eventually won by the whites, with the help of a contingent of highly-trained German infantry, but it created a deep rift in the fabric of political society during the years between the two World Wars. Thus the Finnish Communist Party, which had been founded in Moscow by red exiles, was banned in 1930 and the Social Democrats remained outside government for the bulk of the period before 1939. Liberalism, in turn, was cast in a system-defence role, combining with the non-socialist groups to protect the fledgling bourgeois state against threats from the radical left – and in the 1930s a significant radical right, too.

It was ironic that with the reds imprisoned or exiled, the solidarity of the White bloc of Old Finns, Young Finns, Swedes and Agrarians should disintegrate during the summer and autumn 1918 over the form of the new constitution. Indeed, although the fact was challenged by the right, the republican principle had been incorporated into the declaration of independence in December 1917 and was widely supported by the majority of the Finnish people. In recognising Finnish independence in January 1918, France, Germany and Russia had all referred to the independent republic! From the outset the Old Finns and Swedes adopted an opportunistic stance, arguing in public that the creation of a constitutional monarchy and the installation of a German king on the Finnish throne would permit the acquisition of 'Greater Finland' (the incorporation of the Finnish-speaking parts of Russian Karelia) and noting in private that it would also forestall a future Socialist president. It needs to be emphasised that in 1916 the Social Democrats had gained an absolute majority of parliamentary delegates and despite the split on the left they returned to the Eduskunta with two-fifths of the seats in 1919. The Agrarians, in contrast, consistently advocated republicanism and identified monarchism with an urban elite – the same sybaritic stratum that had long dominated politics. The principal casualties of the form of government struggle were the Young Finns. The party was badly divided and it was this republican–monarchist split in its ranks that led by November 1918 to the formation of the National Progressive Party (kansallinen edistyspuolue).

When the Old Finn Ingman brought a proposal for a constitutional monarchy before the Eduskunta's constitutional committee on 21 May 1918 the balance of republicans and monarchists was fairly even. However, the conversion of many Young Finns gave the monarchists a majority in the House by June 1918 and, according to a Young Finn leader K.J. Ståhlberg, only three or four of the party's parliamentary group remained republicans by early August 1918. The following month a leading Young Finn republican, Nikula, a medical doctor from Helsinki, broached the question of whether the Agrarian Party would be prepared to amend its name and modify its programme if the Young Finn republicans joined it. At a meeting of the Republican Club later in the month, a number of other Young Finns sounded out the possibility of joining the Agrarian Party. The Agrarian leader, Alkio, declined these overtures, asserting that it would be best if the Young Finn 'gentlemen republicans' founded a new and radical urban party of their own.[5] This they did in the shape of the National Progressive Party which was formed in November 1918 – the same month that the defeat of Germany and the abdication of the Kaiser scuppered plans to appoint a German King of Finland. The same month, too, the Old Finn and Young Finn monarchists created a new right-wing party, the National Coalition.

In the fractured climate of Finnish politics in the aftermath of civil war and the form of government crisis, the National Progressive Party (NPP) combined with the Agrarians in a series of coalitions which contrived to develop a greater measure of consensus behind the new republic. In particular, these governments of the political centre between 1919 and 1922 viewed an extensive land reform programme as a means of providing a large rural proletariat with a stake in the country (and capitalist state). The NPP especially also sought to conciliate the Social Democrats by canvassing an amnesty for political prisoners. These centre-based coalitions were backed by the first president, K.J. Ståhlberg, a lawyer and former Young Finn, who set exemplary standards in applying the constitution, thereby ensuring the operation of the parliamentary principle in the complex, polarised conditions of party politics in the early 1920s. In this decade Finland was thus established as a parliamentary democracy, albeit with a high level of government instability, rather than a semi-presidential system.

The National Progressive Party held its political ground in the highly-charged atmosphere of the 1930s aided by astute leadership and tactical electoral alliances. In 1930 the NPP joined the National Coalition's 'Patriotic Front' against communism, but cut away when the National Coalition started to ally itself with the Patriotic People's Movement, IKL (the radical rightist successor to the neo-fascist Lapua movement which attempted an unsuccessful coup in 1932). The NPP provided the prime minister for the first red–green, Social Democratic–Agrarian coalition under Cajander between 1937– and 1939 and in 1939 it polled 4.8 per cent of the vote despite having slates of its own in only two constituencies. When the NPP poll fell to a mere 3.9 per cent in 1948, however, it was plainly time to take stock of the position, particularly as two years later, in November 1950, a small group known as the Independent Middle Class Party emerged to compete among the growing body of electors in the tertiary sector. Accordingly, on 3 February 1951 a new liberal-minded party, the Finnish People's Party (Suomen kansanpuolue) was formed and in its inaugural declaration pledged itself to champion the middle class and to espouse free enterprise, Christian values, individual freedom and strong democracy. In opposition to this venture, a number of former NPP figures founded a Liberal League (Vapaamielisten Liitto) in 1951 with a view to defending what they saw as 'true liberalism'. Not originally conceived as a political party, the Liberal League none the less entered parliament with a single seat in 1962. Such fragmentation of the liberal electorate was obviously undesirable and came to an end in 1965 when co-operation between the FPP and Liberal League led to reunion in the ranks and the inception of the Liberal People's Party.

GOVERNMENT PARTICIPATION

There have been sixty-three governments in Finland in the seventy years of independence, and liberal parties have been involved in forty-

Table 13.1 *Liberal participation in Finnish governments, 1910–80*

Year	Percentage of governments with liberal participation
1910–20	39.5
1920–30	57.1
1930–40	100.0
1940–50	77.7
1950–60	60.0
1960–70	57.0
1970–80	80.0

four or 71 per cent of them. Out of the forty-four governments in which liberals have participated, twenty-seven have been majority coalitions, twelve minority coalitions and five 'caretaker' cabinets of officials. The liberal parties in Finland have been more regular members of government than their counterparts in Norway and Sweden. In Sweden, liberals have been part of eight or nearly 35 per cent of the cabinets between 1922 and 1988 whereas in Norway liberals have been included in approximately half of all governments since 1915. Unlike Norway and Sweden, though, there has never been a single-party liberal cabinet in Finland – only the Agrarians and Social Democrats have governed on their own.

Table 13.1 outlines the differential level of liberal participation in government between 1910 and 1980. It warrants emphasis that for much of the independence period the participation of liberal parties in government has been relatively unaffected by a decline in their electoral fortunes. Thus the National Progressive Party featured in every coalition in the 1930s although its vote had shrunk to a mere 4.8 per cent in 1939. To be sure, its successor, the Finnish People's Party, participated in less than half of the governments between 1951 and 1965 (it held 5 per cent of all cabinet portfolios in this period), but the Liberal People's Party with only 4.3 per cent of the poll in 1975 still contrived to be a member of 80 per cent of all governments in the 1970s. In short, liberal parties in Finland have displayed a high eligibility for government. As Table 13.2 demonstrates, only the Agrarian-Centre, which has taken part in over 87 per cent of all cabinets since independence, has a record of more extensive government involvement than the liberals. The National Coalition, with over 20 per cent of the vote in recent elections, has participated in only 8 per cent of the political coalitions (that is excluding 'caretakers' of officials) since 1944.[6]

Two factors in particular have been conducive to the relatively high liberal involvement in Finnish governments. First, the strategic placement of liberal groups at the centre of a traditionally polarised party spectrum has permitted them to maintain coalition options to both right and left. Since independence, liberal parties have thus co-operated in government with *all* the established parliamentary groups from the Communists to, on one occasion (in 1941), the neo-fascist Patriotic People's Movement. A majority of Finnish coalitions, however, have been centre-based bringing together the liberals, Agrarian-Centre and Swedish People's Party. Despite the historic fragmentation of the political centre in Finland, the close alignment of these centre groups has created a numerically significant factor in the coalition-building process. During the early years of independence, when the party system witnessed a marked centrifugalism, the Agrarian–National Progressive Party governments of the centre defended the embryonic pluralist democracy against the challenges from the Communists (masquerading as the Socialist Workers' Party) on the radical left and the Swedish People's Party (briefly associated with demands for a self-governing Swedish-speaking province in north-west Finland) on the radical right. The Young Finns and NPP were the largest coalition party in the seven short-lived cabinets which covered this vital period of state-building between 1917 and 1922, although both these parties were over-represented in government relative to their strength in parliament. By the 1930s the staple configuration of groups at the political centre had been established. The Agrarians became the dominant governing party; with little attention paid to reflecting the parliamentary balance of power, the liberals remained over-represented in cabinet; and the Swedish People's Party, after its brief flirtation with radical rightism, assumed a position as the third string of the centre bloc.

A second factor accounting for the regular liberal presence in Finnish government has been that unlike the centre bloc, the parliamentary groups to both right and left have intermittently forfeited their elegibility for government and thereby restricted the partisan base of coalition-building. Put another way, with the main parties outside the centre confined to opposition for long periods, the centre has been the principal recruitment ground for governments. Table 13.2 illustrates the point. There was no radical leftist involvement in government before 1944 – pressure from the Lapua movement led to a ban on the Communists in 1930 – and though the Communist Party was re-legalised as part of the armistice with the Soviet Union, the party did not become a regular coalition partner until 1966. Consequently, it has participated in only 14 per cent of Finnish cabinets since 1917. Despite their position as consistently the

Table 13.2 *Participation of main political parties in Finnish governments, 1917–87*

Party	Times in government	Total number of governments	%
National Coalition	27	63	43
Swedish People's	42	63	67
Liberals	44	63	70
Agrarian-Centre	54	63	86
Social Democrats	33	63	52
Communists (SKDL)	9	63	14

strongest electoral party, the Social Democrats did not 'collaborate' in government until 1937. The party split in the late 1950s when it also lost favour 'in high places' (the presidential palace and the Kremlin) on account of the reputedly pro-Western stance of an older generation of leaders and so, like the Communists, did not become a regular governing party until 1966. The incorporation of Communists and Social Democrats into the so-called Popular Front (two left-wing parties and centre bloc) cabinets of the late 1960s, propelled the right-wing National Coalition into the political wilderness where it languished for twenty years. All in all, the calculus of government-building in Finland has involved a type of sum of exclusions – excluding the main groups on the left and/or right has meant that centre coalitions have been something of a residual category.

On a number of occasions, particularly since the last war, liberal parties have contributed the prime minister of 'caretaker' or stop-gap governments appointed by the president to tide the nation over a political crisis. There was a parallel logic in the formation of the Ullsten Folkpartiet minority cabinet in Sweden in 1978–9 or the minority Venstre government under Poul Hartling in Denmark between 1973 and 1975 – both of which were last resorts designed to avoid premature recourse to the polls. In Finland 'caretaker' cabinets have been either 'half political' in the sense of containing some partisan ministers – the cabinet led by Tuomioja of the Finnish People's Party between 1953 and 1954 is a case in point – or have comprised solely officials in the style of two governments led by the liberal mayor of Helsinki in 1970 and 1970–2 respectively. Although the legislative increment of these liberal caretakers has been negligible and they have resigned immediately after an Eduskunta-based cabinet list has been finalised, their recurrence as an institution has been a peculiarity of the Finnish system and the prime minister has been the personal nominee of the head of state.

It must be allowed that for the bulk of the independence period, the office of prime minister (irrespective of the type of government) has been overshadowed by that of the head of state. But among the ten liberal premiers there have been several colourful personalities – A.K. Cajander, for instance, who held the post three times between the two World Wars. Cajander's third government, 1937–9, is notable because it was the first time the producer-based Agrarians and consumer-oriented Social Democrats had joined forces and betokened the staple red (SDP) – green (Agrarian) coalition of the era after the Second World War. Cajander, who owed his position in large measure to the fact that he was an 'outsider', i.e. from neither of the two main coalition groups, was cast in the role of conciliator and mediator, harnessing and reconciling the opposing interests of Social Democrats and Agrarians. To achieve this end Cajander instituted the 'evening class', so called because of the prime minister's didactic manner and headmaster-style moustache, which was conceived as an informal (sauna) gathering of ministers on Wednesday evenings to prepare matters for the Thursday cabinet. The 'evening class', albeit in a much bureaucratised form, has become a durable feature of the Finnish cabinet system.

In addition to the premiership, the liberal parties in Finland have held all the senior cabinet offices including the Foreign Ministry, Finance Ministry, Ministry of Justice and Ministry of the Interior. Until the 1950s at least it cannot be said they were merely trustees of junior portfolios and accordingly bit-part actors on the cabinet stage. The National Progressive Party, in its time, held every cabinet post and, as Table 13.3 indicates, it regularly claimed the senior positions at the Foreign Office and Ministry of Finance as well as holding responsibilities in economic policy management (Agriculture, Trade and Industry) and the welfare sector (Education and Social Affairs). Unlike their close allies, the Agrarians, the pathway to government office for NPP ministers was not through a long term in the Eduskunta: no less than one-third of NPP ministers lacked parliamentary experience at the time of their appointment to the cabinet.[7] By the 1950s, the liberals' failure to gain the really high-ranking cabinet posts reflected the diminishing size of their parliamentary groups. The Finnish People's Party managed only 5 per cent of the cabinet portfolios between 1951 and 1965, and in terms of their distribution there was something of a concentration on the Ministry of Social Affairs (see Table 13.3). The Liberal People's Party, however, claimed six different portfolios – Justice, the Interior, Education, Transport, Social Affairs, and Trade and Industry – during the 1970s (a number of them twice or more often) and although since the Second World War the liberals have tended to hold the less prestigious cabinet posts, they have

Table 13.3 *The distribution of ministerial portfolios among liberal parties, 1917–79*

Cabinet post	YFs	NPP	FPP	LKP
Prime Minister	1	9	—	—
Foreign Minister	1	8	1	—
Minister of Justice	2	9	—	3
Minister of Interior	2	5	2	—
Defence Minister	—	2	1	1
Finance Minister	—	9	1	—
Minister of Education	3	8	2	2
Minister of Agriculture	—	3	—	—
Minister of Communications and General Works	2	6	—	1
Minister of Trade and Industry	2	7	1	2
Minister of Social Affairs	—	5	5	2
National Welfare Minister	—	3	—	—
Minister without Portfolio	1	1	—	—

YF = Young Finns, NPP = National Progressive Party, FPP = Finnish People's Party, LKP = Liberal People's Party.
Source: Klaus Törnudd, 'Ministeristöjen rakenne' in *Valtioneuvoston historia* 1917–1966 III, p. 407. *Liberaalinen kansanpuolue* 1978, p. 10.

maintained an influence in policy-making through membership of cabinet committees and a variety of informal working groups. Incidentally, in both the National Progressive Party and the Finnish People's Party the decision to enter a coalition rested entirely with the parliamentary group. In the Liberal People's Party the influence of the party organisation was increased and the matter decided conjointly by the parliamentary group and the party's executive committee. It was by such a joint decision that the liberals determined not to enter the broad centre–left coalition under Mauno Koivisto in 1979. They have not been in government since.

THE ELECTORAL BASE OF LIBERAL PARTIES IN FINLAND

The electoral catchment of Finnish liberalism has contracted appreciably since independence. During the 1920s the National Progressive Party surrendered its mass base among the small farm proprietors in eastern and northern Finland to the class-oriented Agrarian Party and thereafter came to vie with the conservative National Coalition for the support of essentially middle-class voters in the urban centres in the South. By the 1950s the Finnish People's Party's electorate contained a sizeable floating vote[8] and a measure of this voter instability was inherited by its successor, the Liberal People's Party. In addition to losses to the political right, LKP saw a significant body of young members defect to a new parliamentary group, the Greens, following its merger with the Centre Party in 1982. Historically, liberalism failed to unite the two national cultures in Finland; in the early independence years it failed to bridge the urban–rural cleavage; and in the ensuing decades it failed to make significant inroads on to the bourgeois electorate in the cities. In recent times the liberals' small electoral clientele has comprised predominantly educated persons, many of them employed in education.

Much as in the case of Venstre in Norway – the other 'colony' in late nineteenth-century Scandinavia – support for nascent Finnish liberalism comprised highly disparate elements. There was an essentially urban and urbane leadership of politicians, officials, academics, journalists and owners, and a mass base of independent peasants and low church revivalists in the rural areas of the North and East. The common denominator in this heterogeneous constituency was commitment to a political cause – constitutionalism and the struggle against Russification – rather than a common set of economic interests. From the outset, liberalism was not a class-centred movement; rather it stressed the classical political freedoms and individual rights which reactionary tsarism was threatening.

The regional character of support for pre-independence liberalism deserves emphasis. The Young Finns prospered in the more radical political climate of the North and East and the Old Finns in the conservative South and West. In the 1904–5 session of the peasant estate (part of a quadricameral diet abolished in the wake of Nicholas II's October manifesto in 1905), the majority of Young Finn over Old Finn delegates in the northern and eastern provinces of Oulu, Kuopio, Mikkeli and Viipuri was 23: 11, and the following year this increased to 26:5. The explanation of this lies in the differential progress of liberalism half a century earlier. In the cosmopolitan atmosphere of Viipuri, a town only thirty miles from St Petersburg, the student body adopted liberalism soon after 1848 and it took a more general hold in eastern Finland as a result of the articles in *Viborg*, a newspaper founded in 1855.[9] In western Finland, in contrast, liberalism did not make such good headway and the supremacy of the Old Finns was not seriously challenged. The basic clerical conservatism of the South and West (the Old Finns were closely linked to the higher Lutheran clergy) was well captured by one Suutarla addressing the peasant estate in 1888: 'We peasants represent healthy common sense, not theories or foreign ideas'[10] – like liberalism!

The liberalism of the Young Finns attracted 13.7 per cent of the poll at the 1907 elections when Finland became the first European country to enfranchise women. Throughout the decade 1907–17, moreover, the Young Finns were the third-largest party behind the Socialists (who had refused to participate in elections to the diet of estates) and the Old Finns. This was a period of sham democracy in the grand duchy, however, for by repeated dissolutions of the Eduskunta the tsar attempted to snuff out the parliamentary system which had been a by-product of his October manifesto. By 1912 native Russians were appointed to the Finnish government. Still in 1911 the Young Finns polled 14.9 per cent of the vote – the highest for a liberal group this century – and though this was the fifth general election in little more than four years, the party gained in its stronghold areas, particularly in eastern Finland (Karelia). In this frontier region, the threat of Russia annexing a number of border communes was felt acutely and, contrary to the national trend, turn-out in the constituency of eastern Viipuri increased in consequence.

Since it was founded by republicans in the aftermath of the form of government struggle, it may reasonably be surmised that the National Progressive Party appealed principally to republican sympathisers – a voter market in which there was competition from the Agrarians and by 1919 the regrouped Social Democrats, too. None the less, the NPP polled 12.8 per cent of the vote in 1919 and its strength lay in the capital and parts of eastern Finland. However, during the 1920s, with the constitutional question resolved and hence the major issue of 'high politics' off the agenda, the NPP lacked the class or ethnic base of its main adversaries and struggled to project a distinctive identity to voters. Its support had been almost halved to 5.9 per cent by 1929.

Finnish liberalism never established a significant allegiance among the industrial workforce. When mass democracy was achieved in 1907, the working class comprised a small factory labour force together with a sizeable, landless rural population, and both categories tended to favour social democracy. Liberalism, to be sure, did have a solid platform among the independent small farmers, especially in the North and East, where Young Finn constitutionalism had taken root. Yet with the achievement of independence and the enactment of a republican constitution, liberalism was largely displaced in these farming communities by agrarianism which represented a more instrumental, class-based approach to politics. In 1927, for example, the Agrarian Party won eight seats, seven of them from the NPP which no longer had the support of the farming population in any constituency as it had in east Häme and south Savo in 1924. Liberalism, in short, became a predominantly urban phenomenon; the Finnish-speaking political centre divided along a rural (Agrarian) – urban

(Liberal) axis; and the National Progressive Party found itself increasingly competing with the conservatism of the National Coalition in the larger towns of the South.

In retrospect it is evident that tactical mistakes were made. Despite the social liberalism of its programme, the strongly middle-class bias of the Finnish People's Party made it difficult to distinguish from its main competitors, the National Coalition, and downward shifts in the People's Party's support went hand in hand with upturns in the National Coalition's fortunes. Yet the Finnish People's Party's electoral ground remained fairly firm at just under 6 per cent of the national poll between 1951 and 1965 and in 1954 its 7.9 per cent constituted the best result for liberalism since 1924. The Liberal People's Party vote, too, held up until the mid-1970s (6.2 per cent in 1972) despite a new entrant into the urban vote market – the Centre Party, which jettisoned the label Agrarian Party in 1965 – and the strategic position of the right-wing National Coalition as the main opposition to the centre-left in power. But as Table 13.4 illustrates, the Liberal People's Party went into accentuated decline from 1975. It mustered a mere 4.4 per cent of the vote that year, its lowest poll since the Second World War; only 3.7 per cent in 1979 when it fought a disastrous campaign brazenly championing the middle class; a paltry 1.8 per cent in the presidential college elections in 1982; a fraction under 1 per cent in 1983 when for the first time in nearly nine decades, the liberals lost their status as a parliamentary group; and a mere 1 per cent at the 1987 general election when, again, they went empty-handed.

On the threshold of this decline in the mid-1970s, the ecology of LKP's vote mirrored the shift from the North and East to the South and West that had taken place in the liberal electorate since independence. If the five regions used in Pesonen and Sänkiaho's extensive voter survey *Kansalaiset ja kansanvalta* (*Citizens and Democracy*) are deployed,[11] it can be seen from Table 13.5 that over one-third of the liberals' national vote of 4.4 per cent in 1975 derived from only one of these regions, the South, whereas in the East and North the liberals recruited only about one-seventh of their overall poll. In terms of the social composition of the party's vote, Pesonen and Sänkiaho's study, conducted in the mid-1970s, reveals that one quarter of LKP respondants had completed their student examination and that liberal households enjoyed a slightly higher than average income. A typical liberal voter was likely to be a teacher or office worker and generally younger than the majority of electors for other parties. The Liberal People's Party was also supported by an element of skilled workers and

Table 13.4 *The vote for liberal parties in Finland, 1907–87*

Year	Party	Percentage of active electorate	MPs
1907	Young Finns	13.7	26
1908	Young Finns	14.2	27
1909	Young Finns	14.5	29
1910	Young Finns	14.4	28
1911	Young Finns	14.9	28
1913	Young Finns	14.1	29
1916	Young Finns	12.4	23
1917	Young Finns	—[a]	24
1919	National Progressive Party	12.8	26
1922	National Progressive Party	9.2	15
1924	National Progressive Party	9.1	17
1927	National Progressive Party	6.8	10
1929	National Progressive Party	5.6	7
1930	National Progressive Party	5.8	11
1933	National Progressive Party	7.4	11
1936	National Progressive Party	6.3	7
1939	National Progressive Party	4.8	6
1945	National Progressive Party	5.2	9
1948	National Progressive Party	3.9	5
1951	Finnish People's Party	5.7	10
1954	Finnish People's Party	7.9	13
1958	Finnish People's Party	5.9	8
1962	Finnish People's Party	6.3[b]	13
1966	Liberal People's Party	6.5	9
1970	Liberal People's Party	5.9	8
1972	Liberal People's Party	6.2	7
1975	Liberal People's Party	4.3	9
1979	Liberal People's Party	3.7	4
1983	Liberal People's Party	0.8[c]	—
1987	Liberal People's Party	1.0[d]	—

[a] In 1917 the Young Finns formed part of a national electoral alliance with the Old Finns (except in Lapland) which realised 30.2% of the vote.

[b] In 1962 the Liberal League polled 0.5% of the vote and gained one parliamentary seat.

[c] In 1983 the Liberal People's Party contested elections in its own name, but as a member organisation of the Centre Party.

[d] In 1987 the Liberal People's Party fought as an independent party but formed electoral alliances with the Centre Party and Christian League in many constituencies.

small entrepreneurs. All in all, it may be speculated that in the 1980s the remaining liberal electorate draws mainly on the old middle classes rather than the new salariat and that, crucially since the Second World War, the party has failed to establish itself among electors in the much-expanded tertiary sector.

Table 13.5 *Regional distribution of the liberal vote at the 1975 general election*

Region	Percentage of liberal vote
The South City of Helsinki and Uusimaa constituency	35.5
The South-West Two constituencies of Turku–Pori	16.5
The South-East Three constituencies of Häme and Kymi	18.7
Central zone Constituencies of Mikkeli, Kuopio central Finland and Vaasa	15.3
The East and North Constituencies of north Karelia, Oulu and Lapland	14.0
Total Vote	190,000
Percentage of national poll	4.4

PARTY ORGANISATION AND STRUCTURE

The Liberal People's Party is a conventional mass-based party organised along regional lines. There are fourteen constituency organisations – one in each of the large units (comparable to English counties or German *Länder*) that collectively make up the national territory – and in all of these there is a network of local and district branches. The conditions for membership of these branches are straightforward: namely, that a person is not a member of another party and accepts the basic aims and principles of the Liberal People's Party. The local branches constitute the focal point of party activity at the grass-roots, undertaking a range of matters in the community including selecting and sponsoring candidates at local elections. Contiguous with the decline in the liberal vote at general elections, its performance at local polls, and hence its representation on municipal and communal councils has deteriorated in recent years. At the local elections in 1980 LKP, with 3.2 per cent of the vote nationally, was represented on 203 (out of 484) councils; in 1984 when LKP polled 1.3 per cent this had fallen to 99. There has also been a drop in the number of local party branches – approximately 350 in 1978 against 257 in 1985 – along with the level of membership: 11,000 in 1978 compared with about 8,600 in 1985. Interestingly, the member–voter ratio among the non-socialist parties has traditionally been lower than among the two left-wing parties, and LKP has been no exception to this.

At the national level, LKP's supreme decision-taking organ is the party conference which meets bi-annually, although provision exists for calling extraordinary conferences. Delegates are nominated by their local branch and mandated to vote on its behalf at party conference. LKP's conferences elect the party chairman and two vice-chairmen, consider a report on the work of the party since the previous conference, scrutinise an account of the parliamentary group's activities and elect members of the central council (*puoluevaltuusto*) and executive committee(*puoluehallitus*). The central council has approximately 50 members and meets twice a year (spring and autumn), unless extra sessions are called by the chairman. It exercises decision-making powers in the party between party conferences. At its autumn meeting the central council approves the party's strategy for the forthcoming year, fixes the amount of members' subscriptions and ratifies the party's budget for the next calendar year. At its spring meeting the central council handles the party report on the preceding year together with the parliamentary group report, the party's statement of account and the auditor's report.

LKP's executive committee directs routine proceedings of the party in line with the decisions of party conference and central committee. It prepares matters to come before the two aforementioned bodies and ensures that meetings of the central council and party conference are called and an agenda drafted. It is responsible for keeping a list of party members, for appointing staff to serve in the party and for setting the general guidelines for the party, including planning and preparations for elections. The executive committee generally convenes monthly and is empowered to delegate specific preparatory tasks to a steering group or political committee, *poliittinen toimikunta* (almost an 'inner cabinet') usually comprising the party chairman, party secretary and three executive committee members, which meets on average once a week. The basic organisational structure of the Liberal People's Party is set out in Diagram 13.1.

In addition to the regular party machinery organised on a territorial basis, LKP has created several 'corporate' committees and working groups targeting sectional interests – committees focusing on the needs of small and medium-sized entrepreneurs, civil servants, public-sector workers, consumers and trade unionists, for example. The women's section of the party, whilst also serving a specific clientele, is structured on regional lines. However, with the exception of the branch registered in the city of Turku in 1985, women's sections have not been regarded as independent entities like the local branch organisations (the matter is currently under debate in the party).[12] In addition, there is a liberal youth organisation, a section for senior citizens founded in 1974, *Suomen Ruskaliitto*, and a so-called free study centre, *Vapaa Opintokeskus*, a cultural body formed in 1970 and designed, amongst other things, to encourage those persons with a basic education to undertake further study[13] – that is, engage in continuing education in the field of politics and society. This it does by providing courses, lectures and basic literature.

To articulate its views, LKP has an official organ, *Polttopiste* (*Focus*),

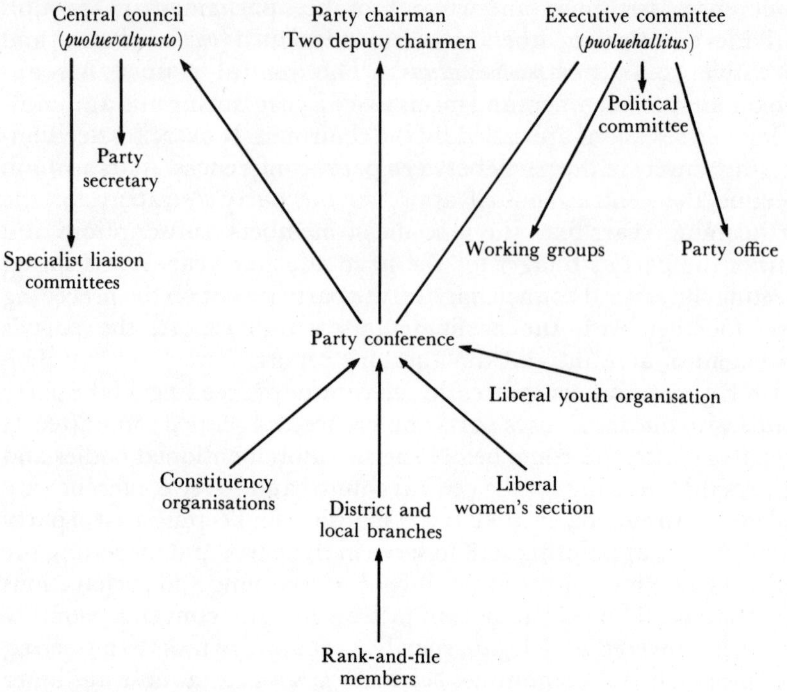

Diagram 13.1 The Liberal People's Party organisation

presently edited by the party secretary, Jari P. Havia, which comes out about twenty times a year. It has only a very small circulation of roughly 12,000, but along with the rest of the party press receives support from the state. One of the largest national daily newspapers, *Helsingin Sanomat*, has traditionally presented the liberal viewpoint although it is formally independent of the political parties. Media coverage of the party, however, has been limited in recent years and this was particularly the case between 1982 and 1985 when its decision to join the Centre Party meant that LKP lost its right to appear on the pre-election debates on television.

Lacking parliamentary representation since 1983, decision-making powers in the Liberal People's Party have tended to devolve upon the leader (party chairman) and, to a lesser extent, the executive committee, whilst the implementation function has been concentrated on the party secretary assisted by a small central party staff. In contrast to the UK, rank-and-file members do not participate directly in the election of the Liberal leader and the sovereign powers of the party conference have been vitiated in practice by the appointment of a higher echelon of policy committees. In short, in violation of the letter of LKP's constitution, the flow of authority in the party runs from the top down, rather than from the grass-roots up. The elitist character of LKP's decision-making is, of course, in line with that found in the majority of West European parties in the late 1980s. It may indeed be that the whole regional basis of the party's apparatus is viscous and outmoded – in the sense of proving insufficiently adaptive to structural and demographic change – and that a more specifically vocational approach is called for, targeting a market at the workplace from among 'non-affiliated' social groups (particularly in the much-expanded public sector). The ossification of its traditional organisation is by no means peculiar to LKP (and is integrally related to the slump in its electoral fortunes), but minus the state support it derived from having members of parliament, and lacking significant funding from industry and commerce, LKP has been in a parlous financial state in the last years. It was this factor which weighed heavily in the decision to join the Centre Party in 1982.

PROGRAMMES AND POLICIES OF THE FINNISH LIBERAL PARTIES

In 1918 the National Progressive Party became the first of the Nordic parties to adopt a programme of social liberalism. This married a classical liberal concern to protect individual rights and freedoms with an active role for the state in social and economic management. The more detailed programme of the NPP's successor, the Finnish People's Party, in 1951 retained the social liberal perspective, although in somewhat diluted form. Its economic thinking in particular was much further to the right than the NPP. The state was vested with only minimal regulatory functions and considerable emphasis was placed on free competition and market forces. The FPP also targeted the middle class which it claimed was a socially disprivileged group. Indeed, the sectional character of this approach was followed by the Liberal People's Party, especially in the late 1970s. By the following decade LKP had witnessed a marked erosion of its traditional constituency and faced the challenge of rapid socio-economic change: Finland had become a service-dominated post-industrial state and the Liberals had to respond to the new order. Accordingly, in its radical action plan for 1984–6, LKP aspired to achieve a qualitative reform of society – to defend the national culture against the international mass culture, the individual against the bureaucratic state, future generations against the destruction and pollution of the national environment, and individual initiative against monopolies and cartels. The

Liberal aim is to mobilise the individual to act for himself whilst endeavouring to create more routes along which to achieve heightened participation in decision-making at all levels. The party's ultimate goal, as defined in the preamble to the 1984 programme is 'a classless, balanced social form in which there are ample opportunities for voluntary self-improvement'.[14] The Liberals at present have perhaps the most modern party programme in Finland.

The programme which the National Progressive Party adopted on 8 December 1918 bore the clear imprint of the lawyer and constitutional theorist, K.J. Ståhlberg.[15] Earlier, Ståhlberg had displayed outstanding vision at a time when the armed conflict between reds and whites was generating deep-seated animosity and prejudice. Already on 16 April 1918, with the civil war still in progress, he had submitted a controversial letter to the leading daily, *Helsingin Sanomat*, looking ahead and stressing the need to preserve the great achievement of the 1906 reforms – a unicameral assembly elected on the basis of a free, equal and universal suffrage. Ståhlberg also insisted on the importance of proceeding with those major reforms – on religious freedom, taxation, legal rights etc. – interrupted by the civil strife and urged that any reprisals against the leaders of the reds should not delay the enactment of essential working-class reforms.

The programme of the NPP alluded neither to liberalism nor liberal principles, but in the contemporary context of acute social and political tension it may be regarded as liberal and reformist in spirit, bringing together republicanism, parliamentarism and individualism with an active role for the state in the management of society and the economy. In the realm of 'high politics', the NPP's commitments were unequivocal. The form of government question (the new constitution) was to be resolved by parliament after fresh elections or submitted to the people at a referendum. The Eduskunta was to be granted the decisive legislative power and governments were to be responsible to parliament. Finland was to pursue a policy of strict neutrality. In order to safeguard Finnish freedom, there was to be an adequate defence force; close relations were to be established with Finland's ethnic neighbours (in the Soviet Union and the Baltic states); and the incorporation of eastern Karelia into Finland was to be supported. The traditional liberal concern for individual freedoms and minority rights is evident in the detailed sections on freedom of religious conscience (the separation of church and state), equality for women in the workplace and at home, and the importance of guarantees for Swedish as the language of the national minority (Finnish was to be the dominant language).

It is important to note, however, that the NPP's conception of government was relatively expansive. The state was to intervene actively to promote the economy, provide for the welfare of its citizens and safeguard the mental and physical health of the nation. The state was given a significant part to play in a land-reform programme, and in order to create land for the landless labourers and crofters it was to be granted compulsory purchase powers and the authority to prevent land being concentrated in the hands of timber companies. Public monies were to be utilised in stimulating the nation's main economic activity, agriculture and fishing, and the development of its natural resources, especially the forest industry. The state was to assume responsibility for unemployment. Job creation work and unemployment benefit schemes were to be fostered in conjunction with the trade unions; there was to be legislation guaranteeing contracts, conditions of work and a minimum wage; and the state was to participate in the provision of compulsory sickness insurance pensions and house-building schemes. Finally, funding for this social reform programme was to be generated by means of a complete overhaul of the existing taxation system and the institution of a progressive income and wealth tax. The spirit of the NPP's programme, in short, was clearly that of social liberalism.

So, too, was that of the Finnish People's Party – at least according to the exposition of principles set out in the programme approved at an extraordinary party conference in April 1951. 'The ideological base of the Finnish People's Party's activities', the preamble noted, 'is a positive and constructive Finnish liberal view of the world, predicated on a Christian conception of life, a national and social view of the state and an unswerving defence of individual freedom and democracy.' After a section on the supreme importance of liberty and the rule of law as a basis of political life, the FPP programme brings out the 'social' element in its thinking by advocating a consolidation of the welfare system. Individuals were to be protected in their hour of need by the provision of adequate health and unemployment benefit, better care facilities for the elderly and a range of dispensations for invalids and war veterans. In its social policy commitments, the FPP was close to the provision of the Agrarians and Social Democrats.

However, in important respects, the Finnish People's Party approximated the views of the right-wing National Coalition, notably in its economic outlook. The FPP thus advocated a minimal role for the state both in the production process and the overall handling of the national economy. Section two of the 1951 programme asserted that 'the FPP stresses the importance of individual ownership and the spirit of free enterprise as the foundation of the economic system. Normal development should occur through free competition and the market.' True, there followed a statement that sound economic development requires broad-gauge planning taking cognisance of market forces, the employment situation, socio-cultural conditions and regional factors. But the paramount objective of planning was ultimately to remove the obstacles to healthy individual initiative. This was perceived to be the corner-stone of national growth and indirectly would facilitate a more equitable distribution of wealth. There is no mention of specific kinds of planning – merely the assertion that the machinery should be democratic in the sense of incorporating all the relevant socio-economic interests. Nor is there any inference that the state would play an active role in the realisation of a just distribution of wealth, although it seems likely that some form of incomes policy was envisaged.

The Finnish People's Party's true colours were revealed later in the programme when it becomes apparent that a fairer distribution of income did not necessarily involve only the poorest members of society. 'The FPP is ready to back demands for the reasonable betterment of the living standards of all disprivileged groups and, accordingly, regards it as imperative to place on record that compared with other income groups, a large section of the nation's middle class has fallen behind.' The FPP committed itself to remedy this situation and in practice presented itself as essentially a sectional party targeting the growing body of middle-class voters.

The Liberal People's Party, too, canvassed the middle-class vote, particularly in the 1979 election campaign, but its disappearance from parliament in 1983 forced LKP to broaden and modernise its appeal. At its 1984 party conference a revised programme containing a number of innovative elements was adopted. Liberalism was called upon to demonstrate its relevance to a late twentieth-century society. True, there was still the old concern to woo the middle classes. Success had been achieved in reducing wage differentials, it was noted, through the biannual incomes policy packages which had become a regular feature of Finnish decision-making. But the incomes of those with an advanced education in positions of responsibility (the 'old middle class') had deteriorated relative to those in less responsible and demanding positions and the Liberals committed themselves to rectify this situation. The basic orientation of the party also remained unchanged. LKP described itself as a liberal reformist party located at the political centre. Its ideological base was depicted as 'constructive political and social liberalism aiming at the spiritual freedom of the individual, a sense of collective responsibility among citizens and social equality'. The deleterious consequences of unrestricted competition and the duties of the state in social and economic management were stressed and, in line with the party's social liberalism, it was held that freedom should not be allowed to lead to concentrations of power and unnecessary restrictions on the liberty of others.

Importantly, however, the 1984 programme displayed a concern both to adapt to, and capitalise on, the post-materialist climate of the 1980s. This had spawned the only parliamentary Green Party in Scandinavia and an increased sensitivity to environmental issues. In its introductory section, the programme asserts that man is to be viewed as an integral part of the ecological system, and among its short-term policy aims LKP urged the case for the storage and recycling of a range of products – paper, glass, metal, rag, pulp etc. – so as to reduce the problems and costs of waste disposal, measures to prevent the further pollution (through acid rain) of Finland's vast natural forests, and an increase in domestic energy supplies, albeit without the construction of more atomic power-stations. The goal of economic activity is defined as improving the quality of life through the provision of a better standard of goods and services, a conducive work environment and a concern to conserve natural resources.

LKP's short-term policy measures were outlined in its action plan for 1984–6. Communes are urged to take the initiative in dealing with the local employment situation by encouraging and safeguarding enterprises (particularly small firms) and creating work opportunities for young persons. It is proposed that steps should be taken to reduce payroll costs by abolishing the insurance (sickness and pension) contributions paid by employers and that purchase tax should be raised to compensate for lost revenues. A simplification of income and wealth taxation is advocated along with a shift towards indirect taxes and the introduction of VAT to stimulate exports. In the field of electoral politics, LKP favours the introduction of direct presidential elections (replacing the present American-style electoral college system),[16] a Swedish-style pool of national seats over and above those allocated on a constituency basis at general elections (the d'Hondt list system has tended to favour the large parties), and the use of consultative referenda. In educational policy the party demands comparable regional facilities for pre-school children to enable all pupils to be sufficiently mature and resilient to embark upon full-time elementary education at the legal starting age of seven. The Liberals want the introduction of an institution offering higher education on a part-time basis along the lines of the Open University and support sabbatical periods of work-leave to facilitate retraining. They are also concerned to ensure that gifted children are not held back in the comprehensive system of secondary education.

In social policy LKP has supported increased spending on house construction and improving care for the disabled, elderly and long-term sick. It has urged that social and health services in the public sector be supplemented by provision organised on a voluntary basis, that a more flexible retirement age be introduced, and that the child-care allowance be organised so that families get the type of arrangement (father/mother at home, employing a nanny etc.) which they believe best suits their needs. Finally, LKP has opposed the artificial obstacles barring the way to local radio stations and cable television and in line with the party's deeply-held faith in industrial democracy promoted schemes of worker participation. In short, LKP's action plan for 1984–6 represents perhaps the most radical and modern programme of any party in Finland. It was a wholly different matter whether it could be effectively projected at Liberal voters whilst the party was a member organisation of the Centre Party.

STRATEGY

At its eighth party conference in Joensuu on 19 June 1982, the Liberal People's Party decided by 141 votes to 26 with 25 abstentions to become a member organisation of the Centre Party.[17] Although this did not involve forfeiting its independence, it is apparent that over one-quarter of Liberal delegates did not vote in favour of the union of the two parties. Indeed, immediately after the decision to merge, Jukka Kilpi resigned from LKP and when this was submitted in writing, a further twenty signatures were appended to his. Significantly, too, the reports of the liberal youth and liberal students' organisations had not been communicated to the conference and their delegates were not present. The LKP's vice-chairman, Paavo Nikula, a former Minister of Justice, resigned from the party's executive committee.

There were, of course, precedents for federations of autonomous parties. In 1944 the newly-legalised Communist Party and People's Democrats came together under the umbrella of the Finnish People's Democratic League, whilst for more than a decade the UDF has harnessed the parties of the traditionally fragmented French centre. In Sweden there has been ephemeral talk of fusing the Centre and Liberal Parties. Underlining the subordinate position of the Finnish Liberals, however, was the fact that the Centre Party provided the name and the framework for the new federation. According to the

1982 agreement, LKP assumed a position within the Centre Party comparable to the latter's youth and women's organisations, although formally the Liberals continued as a registered party with their own organisation. They were allocated five seats on the Centre Party's central council, *puoluevaltuuskunta* (out of a total of 138), two seats on the Centre Party's executive committee, *puoluehallitus* (out of a total of about 30), and they could send a minimum of three delegates to the Centre Party's biannual party conference (normally there are about 4,000 delegates present). In addition, LKP was entitled to a representative for every Liberal association, provided it had availed itself of the provision for affiliating to a local or district branch of the Centre Party. The Liberal Party's four sitting MPs became members of a new Centre parliamentary group.

The public rationale for joining Liberal and Centre Parties was the need to consolidate the centre ground at a time when the principal governing party, the Social Democrats and the chief opposition group, the National Coalition, were running well ahead of the field. There had been talk of a nascent bipolarity in the party system. The Centre (formerly Agrarian) Party, under a new generation of leaders, had largely succeeded in arresting the decline which followed its change of name in the mid-1960s, but to bolster the urban base of the political centre and enhance its appeal as an electoral alternative, a formal arrangement between Liberals and the Centre Party was deemed timely. This could be presented as a logical progression of events since the two parties invariably entered into electoral alliances and worked closely together at the parliamentary and cabinet levels.

The electoral horse-trading had generally favoured the Liberals. In 1975, for example, LKP and the Centre Party had forged electoral alliances in thirteen of the fourteen mainland constituencies – that is excluding the single-member constituency of the Åland islands. Only in north Häme did the Liberal candidate, Olavi Borg, a Professor of Political Science, prove unacceptable to the Centre, and though LKP's vote dropped from 5.2 per cent in 1972 to 4.3 per cent in 1975, the party's parliamentary representation increased from seven to nine delegates. This is largely explained by tactical voting on the Liberal side. LKP supporters concentrated their ballots on the party's leading candidates because the Finnish variant of the d'Hondt list system permits personal votes to determine the distribution of seats on a party list.

As in Sweden, there had earlier been intermittent talk of a merger of centre groups. In 1976 for instance, LKP's Helsinki branch proposed at the party conference that a loose federation comprising the Centre, Liberals and Swedish People's Party be formed, but the reaction of the last mentioned was lukewarm.[18] The Swedish People's Party had in fact little to gain from it because they have traditionally concentrated their efforts on those four constituencies with a numerous Swedish-speaking population, making a national alliance of very limited value. By 1982 circumstances had changed. There was a new Centre Party chairman, Paavo Väyrynen, and a new LKP chairman, Jaakko Itälä, both favourably disposed to pooling their resources, and the union of the two parties went ahead in March of that year.

If the public justification for the merger focused on the need to consolidate the political centre, the Liberals in private had far less altruistic motives for making common cause with the Centre. First, there was the importance of buying time in which to revitalise themselves (generate new policies and a revised programme), whilst maintaining their precarious toehold in the assembly. The gradient of the Liberals' electoral decline was becoming ever steeper. At the 1979 general election, after a period of intense factionalisation within the parliamentary group, LKP had lost five delegates and the party's vote had subsided to a mere 3.7 per cent. The Liberals had presented themselves, against the wishes of many rank-and-file members, as a middle-class party and this brought LKP into head-on confrontation with the National Coalition. Moreover, they had sacrificed a clear voter identity after long years of participation in government. There was a strong feeling after the 1979 election that the liberals would profit from a period in opposition – 95 per cent of the party's central council favoured such a move and the case was strengthened by individual Liberal MPs who complained that in government the Centre and Social Democrats would decide something and the Centre then merely inform LKP as a matter of courtesy.[19]

In retrospect it is clear that the intended Liberal recuperation in opposition served only to aggravate the patient's condition. Mauno Koivisto proved an extremely popular prime minister between 1979 and 1982 and his centre–left coalition was notably stable. Furthermore, when the long-serving head of state, Urho Kekkonen, was forced to retire through ill-health in 1981, Koivisto was swept into the highest office on an avalanche of popular support. True, opinion polls had registered an astonishing 8–9 per cent level of Liberal support during the autumn 1981. But though LKP made history in being the first to nominate a female presidential candidate (Helvi Sipilä), she contrived only one seat in the 301-member electoral college in January 1982. The Liberal vote amounted to a mere 1.8 per cent, and against this backdrop the Liberal leadership sought an electoral lifeline in alliance with the Centre Party.

There was another extremely powerful reason for the alliance, namely LKP's grave financial predicament. LKP viewed the arrangement in part as a means of clearing off a long-standing legacy of debts inherited from its predecessor, the Finnish People's Party. In 1982 LKP was 2.2 million marks in the red[20] after various unsuccessful business ventures and ten elections (national and local) in the 1970s which had been financially catastrophic. Approximately four-fifths of LKP's resources during that decade derived from the state-funding of parliamentarians (a system introduced in 1968), but with only four MPs in 1982 this was proving hopelessly inadequate. The remainder of the party's income came from contributions from the small and medium-sized businesses and from subscriptions of individual members. In short, it was anticipated that the arrangement with the Centre Party would facilitate the contesting of elections and permit a savings drive designed to get LKP back 'into the black'.

On the last count, LKP's calculations were vindicated. During their three-year association with the Centre, the Liberals managed to halve their debts. They retained the same level of funding they had received in 1982 (a sum corresponding to four MPs which came out of the Centre Party's allocation) and saved money at the local elections in October 1984. LKP was not, however, thrown an electoral lifeline. It lost all four MPs in March 1983 and won less than one per cent of the active electorate. Moreover, although at a press conference on 24 March 1982 the Liberal chairman, Jaakko Itälä, claimed that his party would acquire an influential position within the Centre Party and greater opportunities to work for liberal ideas, the mathematics of LKP's representation on the decision-making organs of the Centre Party militated in practice against this.

The Liberals obviously had no voice in a vital forum – the (five-strong) group of Centre Party ministers which convened at least once weekly. They had only a minimal presence on the influential working groups of the Centre's executive committee. Attendance at the weekly meetings of these six working groups (*puoluehallituksen työvaliokunnat*) comprised, in addition to a basic membership (usually six persons), the party's ministers, the chairman of its parliamentary group and senior civil servants (highly party-politicised since the mid-1960s). In 1985, however, only the Liberal chairman, Kyösti Lallukka, sat on a working group of the Centre Party's executive committee – and then no more than one of them. The policy influence of the Liberals was likely to be marginal. The problem for LKP was compounded by the conflicting priorities of the two parties. The Centre Party was mainly concerned with agricultural and regional matters, whereas the

Liberals stressed the problems of the southern conurbations. In the area of industrial democracy the Centre Party did adopt much of the Liberal approach.

In view of LKP's meagre influence, there was growing discussion among its leaders about severing the connection with the Centre, and by mutual consent the union was ended in November 1985. The arrangement had afforded the Liberals varying degrees of discomfort. Shortly after the merger, in July 1982, the Liberals' student organisation left the party, insisting that in important respects the Centre was more conservative than the right-wing National Coalition. Many of these renegade students swelled the ranks of the Greens to whom the Liberals lost out in the southern towns at the local elections in October 1984. Indicative of the unease at the grass-roots was the fact that only about one-half of the Liberals' local organisations affiliated to the Centre Party, whilst many of the Liberal groups on the local councils – LKP has delegates on 101 of the 484 councils – maintained their separate identity and refused to join forces with the Centre Party's councillors. There was a residue of resentment among ordinary Liberals at the apparently precipitate manner in which LKP had thrown in its lot with the Centre. This resulted from the recommendation of a secretly-held joint meeting of the two central councils on 25 March 1982 and Liberal members first heard about it on radio and television. LKP's subsequent disappearance from the television party-political broadcasts undermined its identity and proved a major consideration in the Liberals' decision to break with the Centre. For the Liberal chairman, Kyösti Lallukka, projecting a distinct and radical image in a crowded multi-party market-place using the vehicle of the mass communications media was essential to resuscitating liberalism as a significant electoral factor. Väyrynen, the Centre Party chairman, was not himself averse to a revival in Liberal fortunes since this would be to the overall benefit of the political centre. The timing of the Liberal split with the Centre was strongly influenced by the staggering rise in Liberal support at the 1985 Swedish general election and the hope that by once again presenting itself as an independent option, the Finnish party might just attract a little of the star-dust of its successful Nordic neighbour.

There was overwhelming support at LKP's central council meeting for the decision to leave the Centre Party. The chairman of the Helsinki district Liberals, for example, observed that in the capital city, in particular, Liberals had never really come to terms with the merger. In contrast, the Mikkeli district delegate regretted the separation claiming that it had consolidated LKP's position in his part of central Finland.[21] LKP also proceeded to back a historic four-party declaration on 8 November 1985 in which all the centre-based parties committed themselves to work to achieve broad electoral alliances and after the polls to enter joint discussions on the shape of the forthcoming government. Some delegates at the central council meeting, to be sure, expressed concern at the inclusion of the Finnish Christian League in the proposed alliance dubbing it a reactionary right-wing party.[22] But there was strong backing for a policy of continuing to work closely with the Centre Party. Any increase in Liberal votes, it was argued, was not likely to be at the expense of the Centre, but rather the National Coalition or Social Democrats. Moreover, if the Liberals were to regain cabinet status and/or exercise an influential policy role it would be in close co-operation with the Centre Party.

CONCLUSION

In few West European states has a long liberal lineage appeared more fragmented than in Finland. No less than five liberal groups have gained parliamentary representation since 1917, culminating in the formation in 1965 of the Liberal People's Party – the only liberal party with a capital 'L' in the Nordic states. In many respects though, breaks in the liberal tradition have been more illusory than real: whilst punctuated by a series of redesignations and mergers between existing liberal groups, a basic ideological and partisan continuity has been maintained in the fact that liberals were elected to parliament throughout the period 1917–83. Equally, the numerical strength of liberalism has been reduced by its inability to embrace the two national cultures. Liberal parties in Finland, in short, have been supported exclusively by Finnish-speaking electors.

Few liberal parties in Western Europe have participated in ruling coalitions more frequently than the liberal parties in Finland – in the early independence period the National Progressive Party also performed a vital system-defence role – so that, together with the Agrarian–Centre, the liberals have functioned as a hinge group in Finnish governments. In this last context, there are obvious comparisons between the Finnish liberal parties and the pivotal role of the Free Democrats in the Federal German Republic since 1945. Both have played a strategic part in building majority coalitions – the Finnish liberals (in the absence of a qualifying threshold) from an even lower electoral base than the FDP. Both have enjoyed a tactical position at the political centre, though the Finnish liberals have constituted only one element in a highly disparate middle ground and they have preferred to exercise coalition options to the centre-left more than their German counterparts. Governmental co-operation with the parties of the centre-left in the late 1960s and 1970s brought the liberals into the mainstream of consensus politics (stable coalitions which included the radical left facilitated co-operation in the corporate channel and the development of a durable incomes policy system), whilst also undermining the party's basic identity along with its capacity to compete successfully with the National Coalition (Conservatives) for the middle-class vote. Indeed, the brazen targeting of the middle class has been a feature of the liberals' approach since the last war. Although claiming to be a party of the whole nation, the liberal parties in Finland have increasingly sought salvation in a sectional support base.

First among the Nordic parties, the National Progressive Party espoused the basics of social liberalism in the decade after independence. Yet, importantly, liberalism in Finland evolved an identity by reference to fundamental political issues rather than a socio-economic creed – its defence of constitutionalism against tsarism before independence, support for republicanism against the installation of an imported monarchy during the form of government crisis, and backing for the new bourgeois state against anti-system threats from communism, Swedish minority separatism and, by the late 1920s, Lapua-style neo-fascism. In any event, the ideological cohesion of liberal parties has long been limited by the existence of internal tensions and contradictions – the protection of individual liberties against the need for state intervention, the defence of minority rights against the interests of the majority; and the inherent conflict between the tenets of social and economic liberalism. In the 1950s and 1960s, in particular, the Finnish liberals appeared patently right of centre in their advocacy of free enterprise, individual initiative and the market. At no point, though, have liberal parties in Finland adopted the blatantly rightist posture of the German FDP in the early 1980s (prior to the split with the SPD) or the Liberals in Holland and Italy.

In few West European states has liberalism declined so dramatically as in Finland. Only in Norway has the Liberal Party suffered a similar loss of parliamentary status and, unlike the Finnish party, Venstre was racked by internal dissension over the EC. The Liberal People's Party's uneasy interlude as a party within the Centre Party did little to help its cause and significantly reduced its visibility in the eyes of the electorate.

A resurgence of liberalism in Finland on the scale of Folkpartiet in Sweden (over one-sixth of the electorate in 1985) is inconceivable in anything shorter than the middle term. The party's return to parliament and a modest increase in its vote is by no means inconceivable, however, especially in view of the continuing volatility of a section of the electorate. Plainly there is a premium on appealing to a younger generation of voters so that liberalism does not die with the older age cohorts. It is also essential to advocate policies and deploy a rhetoric appropriate to an increasingly technocratic, bureaucratic, post-industrial society in which the classical liberal appeal to individualism and the inviolability of the fundamental rights of citizens in the face of a vast and intrusive state remains as cogent as ever. Above all, the Liberals need an attractive leader capable of selling the party and convincing voters of its renewed credibility and sense of purpose. In both Finnish and Nordic politics, history has repeatedly demonstrated the considerable electoral impact of strong leaders – leaders with self-belief and the capacity to communicate this confidence to electors. If ever the Finnish Liberal People's Party was in need of a personality to profess its cause – a Westerberg,[23] Ståhlberg, 'anyberg' in the populist mould – that time is now.

NOTES

1 L.A. Puntila, *Ruotsalaisuus Suomessa* (Otava: Helsinki, 1944).
2 Kauko Kare (ed.), *Näin puhui Snellman* (Werner Söderström: Porvoo, 1960) 73.
3 Interview with Professor Osmo Jussila, University of Helsinki, 28.9.1984.
4 Olavi Borg, *Suomen puolueet ja puolueohjelmat 1880–1964* (WSOY: Porvoo/Helsinki, 1965) 9–12.
5 *Santeri Alkion päiväkirja* 7.9.1918, 26.9.1918.
6 In April 1987, however Harri Holkeri became the first National Coalition (Conservative) prime minister in Finland since the Second World War.
7 Klaus Törnudd, 'Ministeristöjen rakenne' in *Valtioneuvoston historia* 1917–1966, III (Valtion painatuskeskus: Helsinki, 1978) 410.
8 Pertti Pesonen, 'Dimensions of political cleavage in multi-party systems', *European Journal of Political Research* I (1973) 121.
9 Eino Jutikkala, 'Säätyvaltiopäivien valitsijakunta, vaalit ja koostumus', in *Suomen kansanedustuslaitoksen historia*, IV (Valtion painatuskeskus: Helsinki, 1974) 121.
10 Viljo Hytönen 'Talonpoikaissäädyn historia', *Suomen valtiopäivillä 1809–1906*, I (WSOY: Helsinki, 1923) 354.
11 Pertti Pesonen and Risto Sänkiaho, *Kansalaiset ja kansanvalta* (Söderström: Juva, 1979) 116.
12 Marjatta Astrén, 'Aika keskustella naisjärjestön tarpeellisuudesta', *Polttopiste* 16.1.1986.
13 Armi Mikkola, 'Vapaan opintokeskuksen alkutaipaleelta, *Polttopiste* 16.1.1986.
14 *Liberaalinen Kansanpuolue. Periaateohjelma. Hyväksytty varsinaisessa puoluekokouksessa Jyväskylässä 2–3.6.1984*, p. 2.
15 The NPP embraced the republicans in the Young Finns, Old Finns and People's Party. The People's Party (*kansanpuolue*) was founded in 1917 with the objective

of integrating the two wings of the Finnish movement. In October 1917 it gained five Eduskunta seats as part of the electoral alliance of the united Finnish parties.

16 A package of constitutional reforms approved by Eduskunta in summer 1982 made provision for consultative referenda and the direct election of the president, if one candidate receives an absolute majority of the popular poll. If no candidate gains over 50%, the electoral college (separately elected) comes into operation. This system was used at the 1988 presidential election.

17 *Pöytäkirja Liberaalinen Kansanpuolue rp:n sääntömääräisestä puoluekokouksesta, joka pidettiin kesäkuun 18–20 päivinä Joensuussa kauppaoppilaitoksella.*

18 Reima T.A. Luoto, *Liberalismi – johtava valtioaate* (Librum: Helsinki, 1983) 291.

19 Terhi Nieminen, 'Olen valmis vaikka mihin', *Suomen kuvalehti* 7, 17.2.1978, 53–7.

20 2.2 million marks in debt is the figure cited by the present party secretary Jari P. Havia; the sum mentioned at the 1982 party conference by the then secretary, Kalevi Viljanen, was 1.7 million.

21 'LKP:n valtuusto kannatti suorituksia', *Polttopiste* 14.11.1985.

22 '35 kysymystä Esko Almgrenille keskustayhteistyöstä', *Kristityn Vastuu* 9.1.1986, 5–6. In the event, the Swedish People's Party participated in the Holkeri government in April 1982 whereas the other centre-based parties remained in opposition.

23 Bengt Westerberg is the leader of Folkpartiet in Sweden.

REFERENCES

Borg, Olavi, *Suomen puolueet ja puolueohjelmat 1880–1964* (WSOY: Porvoo and Helsinki, 1965).

Hytönen, Viljo, 'Talonpoikaissäädyn historia' in *Suomen valtiopäivillä 1809–1906* I (WSOY: Helsinki 1923).

Jutikkala, Eino, 'Säätyvaltiopäivien valitsijakunta, vaalit ja koostumus' in *Suomen kansanedustuslaitoksen historia*, IV (Valtion painatuskeskus: Helsinki, 1974).

Kare, Kauko (ed.), *Näin puhui Snellman* (WSOY: Porvoo, 1960).

Luoto, Reima, T.A., *Liberalismi – johtava valtioaate* (Librum: Helsinki, 1983).

Merikoski, Veli, *Valtiotietoa paloittain* (Librum: Helsinki, 1980).

Pesonen, Pertti, and Sänkiaho, Risto, *Kansalaiset ja kansanvalta* (WSOY: Juva, 1979).

Puntila, L.A., *Ruotsalaisuus Suomessa* (Otava: Helsinki, 1944).

Törnudd, Klaus, 'Ministeristöjen rakenne' in *Valtioneuvoston historia* 1917–1966, 111 (Valtion painatuskeskus: Helsinki, 1978).

Virkkunen, Sakari, *Ståhlberg* (Otava: Helsinki, 1978).

14

Liberal parties in Switzerland

D.L. Seiler

To talk about parties belonging to liberalism in Switzerland is not an easy task. To the outsider the Swiss political system is quite a sophisticated one; so sophisticated that a political scientist following an approach based on economic rationality would give up the idea of studying such a country, since it is far too complicated given its political weight and influence in the world system.

As a federal country, Switzerland is divided into 26 states (cantons and half-cantons) with their own political culture, tradition, administration and party systems. The country is split into four languages and two religions; some cantons are bilingual and others are bi-denominational. Federal parties are rather vague and badly organised bodies, and the main parties are cantonal. Parliamentary parties and parliamentary groups do exist, but they are quite undisciplined. Even the social democrats are unable to achieve the political cohesion they show in other parliaments in the world. MPs do not sit either following the French hemicycle or the British 'face to face' opposition system. In the Senate – Conseil des Etats, Ständerat – they sit by cantonal delegation and in the House – Conseil national, Nationalrat – the MPs' desks are allocated according to a rather mysterious formula, combining language, party and canton, with decisions taken randomly. There is no majority rule, and the sole opposition is made up of small right-wing and left-wing parties – xenophobes, neo-fascists, communists and left socialists – even the ecologists accept the rules of amicable agreement. This means that the majority/opposition pattern varies depending on the issues involved. When an opposition party becomes electorally important, it receives a portfolio in either the federal or cantonal cabinets. But is it correct to talk about 'cabinet' in Switzerland? Both federal and cantonal executive bodies are collegial and fairly representative of the major political forces of either Switzerland or the cantons. For instance, the Federal Executive Board – Conseil Fédéral, Bundesrat – has, since 1959, been composed of: 2 Radical Democrats, 2 Socialists, 2 Christian Democrats and 1 Agrarian. Last but not least, any bill passed by parliament can be defeated in a referendum and citizens have the right of initiative, which means they can propose a bill directly to the voters. It is not very easy for a party to act in such a political and institutional context.

On the other hand, to define European liberalism is not an easy job. The word *liberal*, depending on the language of the country, can adjust to any point from left to right on the political spectrum. As Gordon Smith says in Ch. 2, p. 16, 'European liberalism is ambivalent.'

Thus, nobody will be surprised to discover that such an ambivalent political stream in such an ambivalent country will be ambivalent. Actually, Switzerland has known, and still knows, several brands of liberalism: democratic liberalism, national liberalism, secular liberalism, Catholic liberalism and social liberalism. Some of them are broadly and nationally based, others are regional parties. However, does the concept of 'regional party' mean something in a country like Switzerland? One of the three major parties of the Swiss system, the Christian Democratic Party (CVP–PDC) gets electoral returns ranging from 92.2 per cent of the votes in Nidwalden to 0 per cent (it did not even contest seats) in Glarus, Neuchâtel and Uri. Furthermore, it was not able to have a single MP elected in such important cantons as Berne and Vaud.

THE AMBIVALENCE OF SWISS LIBERALISM

In Switzerland, the importance of a party does not depend primarily on its size in national terms. How can we then select the liberal parties in Switzerland that are of greatest relevance and interest for this chapter?

First of all, it is accurate to eliminate Catholic liberalism from our analysis for both comparative and historical reasons. A comparison of Western European party systems shows that when Christian democracy does exist, Catholic liberalism has merged together with conservatism and Christian socialism in order to create Christian democracy. This is true for the Benelux countries and Italy, it has been true for Germany, and it is the case for Switzerland today. When one looks at the historical pattern of conflicts, cleavages and political parties, it immediately becomes apparent that Catholic liberalism does not belong to the same kinship as the other various 'brands' of liberalism (Diagram 14.1).

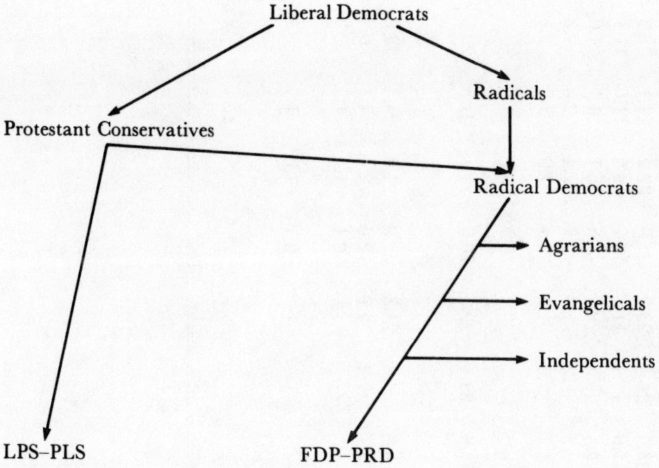

Diagram 14.1 The Protestant-secular tree and the genealogy of liberals in Switzerland

The decision to omit Catholic liberalism leaves us with the parties belonging to the Protestant–secular tree. This means that no less than five political parties are represented in the Federal Assembly: the Radical Democratic Party (FDP–PRD), the Liberal Party of Switzerland (LPS–PLS), the Union of the Democratic Centre – the former agrarians – (SVP-UDC), the Evangelical People's Party (EVP-PES) and the Alliance of Independents (LdU-AdI).

Table 14.1 shows clearly that Liberals and Evangelicals are small parties and the Independents a medium-size one on the basis of Swiss standards. However, the cantonal distribution gives another view of the situation. These three parties are essentially regional. The pattern of the LdU-AdI confirms the existence of a clear-cut, medium-size, German-speaking urban party, which did not contest seats in the French- or Italian-speaking parts of Switzerland, with the exception of Neuchâtel, or in the traditional and rural cantons of Uri, Schwyz, Unterwalden, Glarus, Zug, Appenzell or Grisons. The fact that the Independents are also absent from urban Lucerne reveals the fact that they still retain a Protestant image in the eyes of this leading canton of Catholic Germanic Switzerland.

The pattern for the Liberals is quite different: they exist only in four cantons, Basel-Stadt, Geneva, Neuchâtel and Vaud (see Table 14.2). The LPS-PLS is a small party in Basel-Stadt, which is the only non-Francophone canton where the party is present. In the other three cantons it is an important party. This is obvious when one looks at the results polled for the Senate (2 senators for each canton) and for the

Table 14.1 *Party strength since 1919 in the National Council,* %

Parties	1919	1922	1925	1928	1931	1935	1943	1947	1951	1955	1959	1963	1967	1971	1975	1979	1983
Protestant secular:																	
FDP-PRD	28.8	28.3	27.8	27.4	26.9	23.7	22.5	23	24	23.3	23.7	24	23.2	21.9	22.2	24.1	23.3
SVP-UDC	15.3	16.1	15.3	15.8	15.3	11	11.6	12.1	12.6	12.1	11.6	11.4	11	10.2	9.9	11.6	11.1
LdU-AdI	—	—	—	—	—	4.2	5.5	4.4	5.1	5.5	5.5	5.6	9.1	7.6	6.1	4.1	4.0
LPS-PLS	3.8	4.0	4.1	2.9	2.8	3.3	3.2	3.2	2.6	2.2	2.3	2.2	2.3	2.2	2.4	2.8	2.8
EVP-PES	0.8	0.9	0.9	0.8	1.0	0.7	0.4	0.9	1.0	1.1	1.4	1.6	1.6	2.1	2.0	2.2	2.1
Catholics																	
CVP-PDC CSP-PCS	21.0	20.9	20.9	21.4	21.4	20.3	20.8	21.2	22.5	23.2	23.3	23.4	22.1	20.6	21.1	21.5	20.6
Workers' parties:																	
SPS-PSS	23.5	23.3	25.8	27.4	28.7	28.0	28.6	26.2	26.0	27.0	26.4	26.6	23.5	22.9	24.9	24.4	22.8
PdA-PST	—	1.8	2.0	1.8	1.5	1.4	—	5.1	2.7	2.6	2.7	2.2	2.9	2.6	2.4	2.1	0.9
POCH	—	—	—	—	—	—	—	—	—	—	—	—	—	0.1	1.0	1.7	2.2
Extreme right:																	
NA-AN and REP	—	—	—	—	—	—	—	—	—	—	—	—	—	0.1	1.0	1.7	2.2
Ecologists:																	
Greens	—	—	—	—	—	—	—	—	—	—	—	—	—	—	—	—	1.7

Table 14.2 *Cantonal electoral performance (cantonal elections)*

			LdU-AdI		LPS-PLS	
Canton	Election year	Total seats	%	Seats	%	Seats
Zurich	1983	180	7.3	12	—	—
Berne	1982	200	1.7	2	—	—
Solothurn	1981	144	0.2	0	—	—
Basel–Stadt	1980	130	5.2	5	13.7	18
Basel–Land	1983	84	3.7	3	—	—
Schaffhausen	1980	80	5.9	5	—	—
St Gall	1980	180	5.1	6	—	—
Aargau	1981	200	3.8	7	—	—
Thurgau	1980	130	3.0	1	—	—
Vaud	1982	200	—	—	21.5	47
Neuchâtel	1981	115	3.8	3	27.3	33
Geneva	1981	100	—	—	23.9	25

(*Source:* Grüner (1977) 152).

cantonal executives (7 or 5 councillors of state), both of which are directly elected in a two-ballot majority system. For the Senate, this means 3 Liberals – elected in Geneva, Neuchâtel and Vaud, 2 Radicals and 1 Socialist. For the cantonal governments, the outcome is as follows: in Geneva – 2 Liberals, 2 Socialists, 2 Christian Democrats, 1 Radical; in Neuchâtel – 2 Liberals, 2 Socialists, 1 Radical; and in Vaud – 1 Liberal, 3 Radicals, 2 Socialists, 1 Agrarian. In contrast, the Evangelical People's Party is definitely an urban-based, small Protestant party. Furthermore, it claims to be a progressive party, based on Protestant principles, which does not fit at all into the general framework of liberalism.

It is also easy to drop the SVP-UDC out of our analysis. This party clearly belongs together with the Finnish, Norwegian, Swedish centre parties and the Icelandic progressives to the European family of agrarian parties.

The last problem to solve is what to do with the Radical Democratic Party – the FDP-PRD – which represents the strongest branch of the genealogical tree shown in Diagram 14.1. Historically, the Radicals are the Swiss variety of the national–liberal stream, which has also been active in both Germany and Austria. They split with the liberals over issues like egalitarianism, state centralisation, nationalism and religion. They led a set of revolutions, called regeneration, in a number of cantons, won the 1848 civil war against the Catholic cantons and organised modern Switzerland in 1848 and 1873. Swiss Radicals are nation-state builders rather than liberals.

Furthermore, they had a long flirt, if not an affair, with socialism. For instance, they were members of the first International together with Marx, Engels and the anarchists. Then, when they ran the country, they characterised themselves and their policies as belonging to socialism. Bismarck was not far away!

The crystallisation of the radical ideology owes a lot to political refugees who left Germany and Italy after the failure of their revolutionary attempts. 'Le fumet que dégage le radicalisme suisse alliera donc un zeste de mazzimisme à un solide parfum de national libéralisme, renforcé d'une bonne rasade de *Kulturkampf* bismarckien.'[1]

Nowadays, the Radical Democratic Party is, together with the SPS-PSS, the only truly national party, and it is active in each of the 26 cantons and half-cantons. It is a broadly based, unideological catch-all party, favouring consensus and proud of its pragmatic approach to politics. This party is really the father of modern Switzerland, as well as the designer of the constitution, as in matters like the amicable agreement-systems which control the political life of the country.

The Radical Party is a confederation of cantonal parties, which vary a lot in terms of platforms and electoral bases. Some are conservative and favour neo-liberal policies as advocated by the British Tories and by the Reagan administration. This is the case for some German-speaking cantons where Radicals and Protestant Conservatives joined their forces in a united party. This is, for instance, the case in Zurich with the FDP, which speaks for the business community. In those cantons, the Radicals are a strong party representing the opposite of socialism in a mildly bipolar system just like the British conservatives; the Alliance of Independents play the role which in Britain is performed by the Liberals. On the other hand, in most of the Catholic cantons there is a radical-secular party defending the state against the church. In Valais, where the Socialist Party is weak, the Radicals are the leading forces on the left.

The Radical Party of Switzerland is a political universe in itself. For this reason it is impossible to discuss it as a whole, and the only way to deal with it in detail is to employ the scope and methods of comparative politics. However, the FDP-PRD can certainly be classified as a centralist state-building party, like the French Gaullists from 1958 to 1974.

The two remaining parties – LdU-AdI and LPS-PLS – are similar in size to average Western European liberal parties today. Furthermore, they offer a contrasting picture of the two possible ways chosen by European liberalism. The LdU-AdI appears to be a renewed version of the old bourgeois left, and the Liberal Party of Switzerland shows a strong bias against the role of the state and in favour of the individual's and cantonal rights.

THE DEVELOPMENT OF LIBERAL PARTIES IN SWITZERLAND

As Diagram 14.1 shows clearly, the Liberal Party of Switzerland represents the oldest branch of the Protestant-secular tree, whereas the Alliance of Independents is the youngest to emerge.

With 12 parties represented in the National Council, Switzerland has a very sophisticated and intricate party system. Fortunately, a look through history allows us to clarify the situation. All those various parties belong to five mainstream genealogical trees: the Catholic, the Protestant-secular, the socialist, the nationalist-rightist and a recent newcomer, the ecologist. Together with the Radical Democrats, the Agrarians and the Evangelicals, our two liberal parties are on the Protestant-secular tree (Diagram 14.1).

From old left toward new right: the liberal party

If one compares the trees presented here with Rokkan's paradigm of the four basic cleavages, one can see that the Protestant-secular and the Catholic kinship originate in the centre versus periphery cleavage.

At the beginning of the nineteenth century the early cleavage line opposed *unitarists* – mainly Protestant or secularist – who wanted to build a republic – 'une et indivisible' on the French model, to *federalists* – mainly Catholics plus patrician Protestants in Berne and Zurich – who favoured the old confederation, or, if that was not possible, a weak federal system. Napoleon Bonaparte was convinced that Switzerland's destiny was written in her geography: *L'Acte de Mediation* (1803) imposed a compromise taking into account both federalism and democracy. In 1815, the collapse of the Napoleonic system restored the old system to Switzerland, as it did everywhere else in continental Europe.

In 1815 conservatives took over the government of both the confederation and the cantons. They were supported by the aristocracy, the urban upper class and the Catholic church. Between 1815 and 1830, the Liberal Party was created in several cantons, calling for political liberty and individual freedom. Constitutions – cantonal and federal – based on the people's sovereignty and guaranteeing civil rights, were, for the Liberals, the only ways to attain a political system which respected freedom. The Swiss have definitely not listed Jean-Jacques Rousseau among their prominent contributors to the history of ideas. Instead of this well-known Genevan, they preferred the typical Vaudois, Benjamin Constant. They were not in favour of either equality or direct democracy, and they believed that the individual had to be protected against the rule of the masses. The Liberal Party was essentially committed to liberal democracy. As Biaudet wrote: the liberals 'respectueux à la fois de la liberté et de la souveraineté populaire, voulurent associer les droits imprescriptibles de l'une avec l'idéal de l'autre; ils voulaient unir libéralisme et démocratie'.[2]

The reform movement led by the liberals was successful and in 1831 the *ancien régime* had been abolished in twelve cantons in favour of constitutional democracy. All the Protestant cantons were regenerated – the word used at the time – with the exception of Basel-Stadt, which diverged from the rest of the canton, now called Basel-Land, and Neuchâtel, which remained a county under the Prussian crown. If the liberals succeeded in the most developed part of Switzerland, they failed at national level. Respecting minority rights, they were not able to find a federal or democratic solution which would have accommodated the Catholic cantons. The radicals – the so-called left wing of the liberal movement, actually the nationalist sector – split and formed their own party. In the name of national unity, the radicals pushed the liberals out of the governments of the Protestant cantons. This political change was not always the result of democratic elections, and the new party never hesitated to organise coups and revolutions, as in Geneva and Vaud. The radicals even launched *Freikorps* against Lucerne because this Catholic canton, ruled by reactionaries, had allowed the Jesuits to set up the educational system.

The outcome of the radical take-over was the Sonderbund War against the Catholic cantons in 1847. The Catholics were defeated, but fortunately the radicals did not fully implement their policies, and Switzerland did not become a unitarist republic. A compromise was imposed on the minority, and the political system moved from confederation to a federal state.

The second half of the nineteenth century was a time of opposition. For the liberals, at the federal level, were located in the centre of the left–right political spectrum. They opposed both Catholic conservatives and radicals. They opposed conservatives and Catholic ultramontanes on the issue of civil rights. They fought against radicals in matters related to centralisation. In between nationalists, radicals and Catholics defending state rights, the liberals took a firm federalist stand, which they still maintain today. At state level, and in Protestant cantons, the Liberal Party was the 'loyal opposition'. They particularly defended religious freedom against the national churches

Table 14.3 *National electoral performance, 1918–43*

	LdU-AdI		LPS-PLS	
	%	Year	%	Year
Minimum	4.2	1935	2.8	1931
Maximum	5.5	1943	4.1	1925
Mean	4.5		3.2	

imposed by the radical cantonal governments, and they opposed the state-oriented economic policies implemented by the same governments.

The first half of the twentieth century was an era of decline for Swiss liberalism (see Table 14.3). With the rise of socialism and the Catholic response to this challenge in terms of a Christian social movement, the Liberal Party lost its centralist position, and became regarded as being on the right. At the same time, a lot of cantons like Zurich, Berne or Lucerne, where the radicals forgot their old quest for equality, moved towards conservative positions mixed with anti-clericalism in the Catholic cantons. Their great issue had been national unity and direct democracy, and having succeeded, they entered into a long period inside an ideological vacuum. The gap between liberalism and radicalism was closed in those cantons, and the two parties merged. Today, in some areas like Lucerne, Jura, Ticino or the French part of the canton of Berne, the FDP-PRD is still called the Liberal Radical Party.

Located in Basel-Stadt, Geneva, Vaud and Neuchâtel, rather entrenched in the milieu of the old Protestant, aristocratic families, the Liberal Party of the 1950s looked like a dinosaur and, of course, it seemed destined to perish. This bleak future did not come about and in the mid-sixties the party revived. If the old liberal stock remained, the party could attract the new middle classes and make solid inroads in the world of finance and business. However, the phenomenon was limited to the cantons of Geneva, Neuchâtel and Vaud. The image of the party has changed: it does not appear any more like the advocate of great families, Protestant ministers or lawyers, but as a dynamic broker for all those who want modernisation based on free enterprise.

Social liberalism from business and co-operation toward consumerism and moderate ecologism: the Alliance of Independents

Social liberalism in Switzerland means the Alliance of Independents: the LdU-AdI – and it is a difficult task to deal with this party. All comparisons made with other parties – the Dutch Democrats '66 or the Danish Justice Party, for example – throughout the industrialised part of the world seem unsatisfactory. As Clausewitz said 'war was diplomacy continued by other means', one can say that the Alliance of Independents is a commercial enterprise continued by other means. Actually, the LdU-AdI was launched by Gottlieb Duttweiler in the early 1970s in order to bring some political support to his network of general stores – the nowadays very popular Migros co-operatives. Even as a rather successful politician, Duttweiler remained a salesman all his life. However, he was also a businessman with faith and principles, who completely conformed to Weber's type of Protestant ethic and the spirit of capitalism.

Gottlieb Duttweiler's involvement was in business: he wanted to build up a strong system of sales distribution, narrowing the distance between producers and consumers. Starting with groceries, he opened stores in Zurich and the neighbouring cantons. Then he bought four lorries, transforming them into mobile shops which were sent all over the country. This was quite a success and Migros opened more stores and sent more lorries. The response of the competitors was tough, and Migros came under attack from both producers – especially multinational corporations – and small shopkeepers. Duttweiler, the outsider, became the enemy of the Zurich business community and establishment. Their lobbying was efficient. Several cantons, including Zurich and Berne, passed legislation against networks of general stores and they made sales by lorries difficult, if not impossible. Attacks even took place on Migros' lorries.

Rather than give in, Duttweiler and Migros decided to use the Swiss system of referenda and 'initiatives', and thus they attempted a mobilisation of consumers. While both big business and political establishments were strongly opposed to Migros, Duttweiler and his friends had to win enough backing to put their plans to referenda. From one referendum to another, the hero of consumerism and free enterprise took charge of permanent and efficient political organisation. In 1935, the pro-Migros movement decided to run in the federal elections and presented a so-called 'Independent List' of candidates in three cantons. However limited, the attempt was rather successful: the Independents scored an overall result of 4.2 per cent of the national vote (see Table 14.1). Seven MPs were elected to the National Council, five for Zurich, one for Berne and one in St Gall. After this success, Duttweiler decided that all profits made by Migros would be given to a foundation for a 'neutral' organisation dealing with science, culture and charity.

The name 'Independent' meant that the candidates were free from any links with party politics, big business or unions. Duttweiler himself had refused to join the Radical Party of Zurich. The new parliamentarians claimed that they were not politicians. However, one year later, in December 1936, a new political party, the Alliance of Independents, was created.

In Duttweiler's time, the party devoted to the idea of social capitalism, followed a rather ambiguous and erratic course: from compromises with fascism to another political party. After Duttweiler's death in the early sixties, the Alliance survived its founding father and became a 'parti comme les autres'. Some observers expected to see it decline, but this did not happen. The party actually benefited, in the late sixties, from a European trend favouring social liberalism: the moves of the German FDP to the left, the creation of the Dutch Democrats '66, etc. The words 'social liberalism' officially replaced those of 'social capitalism' in the creed of the party. In the eighties, the Alliance took a moderate but clear stand in favour of ecologism. Nowadays, the LdU-AdI is still regarded as the most important of the non-governmental parties.

ORGANISATION AND STRUCTURE

The general notion that the less organised a party, the more it must rely on interest groups seems certainly true in the Swiss case. Due to federalism and direct democracy, political parties are weakly organised and they rely greatly on interest groups, which are numerous, well-organised and efficient. Thus the linkage approach is one of the best ways to deal with the study of Swiss parties.

This fact is apparent and well known in the case of the Alliance of Independents. The party would not exist without the Migros. This national network of general stores based on co-operative principles is an institution of Swiss life and far broader and more important in economic and social life than its political counterpart is in the party system. As far as politics is concerned, Migros and the LdU-AdI are not linked, although they share the same values. The LdU-AdI is the political translation of Migros, and Migros is in business what the LdU-AdI is in politics.

This is a phenomenon which is very hard to understand for somebody living outside Switzerland, and it is quite unique in the western world. However, Migros is not just a successful commercial enterprise. It is more than a network of general stores ranging from large scale supermarkets to country stores, more than the symbol of good value for low prices, more than a lot of goods – from jeans, watches and shoes to petrol – labelled 'M', more than an insurance company, more than Migros Club, where you can learn anything you want. It is even more than green buses bringing the famous 'M' products up to isolated mountain valleys. Migros is morality, if not faith, combined with capitalist efficiency.

For instance, it sells neither tobacco nor any alcoholic beverages. Also, the corporation provides information to consumers and gives a part of its profits to the Duttweiler foundation, which sponsors culture. In fifty years, this prosperous Zurich co-operative has become as much a part of the Swiss dream as William Tell.

Migros and the Alliance had the same founding father: Gottlieb Duttweiler. Both are convinced that capitalism and free enterprise are not working against democracy and social welfare. Both trust the ability of *kleiner Menschen* to act as counterweights to the influence and actions of big corporations without the need for any state intervention. Duttweiler believed in what he called 'social capitalism' and he thought that the best way to attain this goal was through a co-operative system. He was not exactly a thinker and so he wanted to implement his ideas himself, first by founding Migros and then, in a process akin to economic diversification, a political party, the LdU-AdI.

Thus, the Alliance relies heavily on an interest group, but a very special one. The Liberal Party of Switzerland also has to rely on interest groups, but its pattern of linkage is far more complex. Liberals present themselves as the strongest political supporters of private enterprise. Most observers, friends or enemies of the LPS-PLS, define this party as closely linked to the industrial and business community. Traditionally, the party leaders call for money from private corporations in order to finance electoral campaigns, as well as the day-to-day running of the organisation. Furthermore, a party official told me that the sole advantage of the transformation of the former Union Libérale Démocratique Suisse – which was just a parliamentary party – into the Liberal Party of Switzerland was the improvement and modernisation in fund raising. With the label 'LPS-PLS', it is quite easy to collect money from industrialists and businessmen in cantons where the party is completely absent. Linkage is a two-way process, and the four cantonal Liberal Parties are members, together with some radicals and prominent representatives of the industrial and business community, of an informal but influential committee. This body, which changes name depending on the issue, has to defeat any kind of referenda on the people's initiatives that could be damaging for the interests of business and/or industry, i.e. proposals on social welfare, consumers, defence or ecology. Liberals greatly help the committee, bringing with them as they do considerable expertise in canvassing and campaigning.

The mutation of Liberal Democrats from a declining party into a dynamic force – wanting to challenge and become a viable alternative to the left and to socialism – had some influence over party structure. With the exception of Basel-Stadt, where liberalism is still declining and has not yet been restructured, one can see two main streams or strata in the LPS-PLS which can be termed 'old timers' and 'new wavers'. Historically, Swiss liberalism is a moderate, centrist and religion-oriented party, strongly committed to federalism and the defence of cantonal rights, (see Tables 14.4 and 14.5). It relied on a network of so-called 'great families'. These bourgeois dynasties were not greatly involved in business, although some were prominent in banking, especially in Geneva, but most of them belonged to what French historians call *bourgeoisie* or *noblesse de robe*. Most of them were lawyers, medical doctors or university professors. For these people, liberalism was first of all a kind of morality, the political translation of Calvinist Christian values. This aspect still exists within the Liberal Party and defines the group as 'old timers'. It would be highly misleading to talk about them as forming the right wing of the party. Of course, some are clearly conservatives, others are Protestant fundamentalists and reactionaries. However, most of them are open-minded and intend to give an ethical response to issues such as public liberties, viewed in a broader aspect, including the defence of the individual against private corporations, and ecology. Two of the three LPS-PLS senators are 'open-minded old timers' – Mrs Bauer-Lagier from Geneva and Professor Aubert from Neuchâtel – both count among the most prominent MPs in Berne. The third Liberal senator belongs to the farming lobby.

In the early seventies, a new wave invaded Swiss liberalism. It was made up of young urban professionals. They did not benefit from a fine liberal stock nor did they identify liberal ideology with a set of ethical or religious values. Some of them were even Catholics. The 'new wavers' were not liberals because of family traditions, but because they trusted in liberal capitalism and believed in a market economy. They first took over the party in Geneva where, for a while, they borrowed the LEM symbol from NASA. But LEM meant 'Libéral et moderne'. There was obviously a 'Giscardian' wind blowing over the LPS-PLS. The example was followed by Vaud's liberals and the new 'Lemarian' wave was helped by Giscard's victory in 1974 in France. In Neuchâtel the new liberalism had some problems finding its way in the party. Thus the 'new wave' were obliged to organise themselves outside, and they created the progressive national party, PPN, which had a solid touch of Gaullism about it.

Fortunately for the future of liberalism in this canton, the two rival

Table 14.4 *Electoral base of liberal parties,* %

	LdU-AdI	LPS-PLS
Class:		
Working class	28.4	12
White-collar workers	37.1	28
Upper and middle class	6.2	28
Farmers	—	12
Religion:		
Catholics[a]	17.7	45.8
Protestants[b]	61.7	45.8
Others (and no answer)	20.6	8.4
Age:		
Below 25	12.4	0
25 to 39	12.4	32
40 to 64	34.5	56
Over 65	40.7	12
Sex		
Males	69.1	60

[a] Percentage of total Swiss population: 41.6.
[b] Percentage of total Swiss population: 56.3.
(*Source:* Grüner (1977)).

Table 14.5 *The Radical Democratic Party (FDP-PRD),* %

Class:		
Working class	12	N 100
Civil servants	18	N 100
White-collar workers	28	N 100
Professionals	31	N 100
Farmers	10	N 100
Religion:		
Catholics	15	N 100
Protestants	25	

Source: D.L. Seiler (1980) 357.

factions decided to unite, then they presented joint lists of candidates and, at the end, the PPN went back to the Liberal Party.

Valéry Giscard d'Estaing was, for a while, the common reference and the ideal for young French-speaking liberal elites in Switzerland. They often identified liberalism with 'Giscardianism'. With the election of their hero to the presidency of the French Republic, disappointment set in. This occurred a short time before Giscard was beaten in the May 1981 French elections. The former president appeared to be far too much of a social democrat. Nowadays Giscard's image has been replaced by Thatcher's and Reagan's, although Vaud's liberals are still rather suspicious of imported political models.

LIBERAL PARTIES IN THE SWISS POLITICAL SYSTEM

Party manifestos are weak criteria for studying political parties, mainly because average voters do not read them and because voters have a very poor idea of what is going on in terms of their favourite party's platform. As Richard Rose wrote, a general election campaign is about a choice between organisations and not between ideas. This is definitely the case in Switzerland. There is no such thing as a national electoral campaign for the federal elections: there are 26 cantonal campaigns. Federal electoral manifestos do exist, but they are purely formal. Cantonal party organisations do exactly what they want with the national platform. Furthermore, the federal parliamentarians are not very keen to defend their parties' manifestos. So-called governmental parties sometimes negotiate, but they show a great ability to forget electoral promises which are, in any case, unknown to the public.

Electoral slogans are more interesting because they are better known to the voters. For the LdU-AdI, the theme of the last party conference was: 'Social liberalism and ecologism'. For the LPS-PLS it was: 'Moins d'Etat, plus les Libertés' ('Down with the state, more freedom').

There is a far better criterion than manifestos to judge the position of liberal parties in Switzerland – the pattern of coalitions and opposition. Once again, Switzerland is idiosyncratic in this matter. As we saw, governments are reasonably proportional, and ministers are 'condemned' to work together. Thus, one cannot apply the theory of coalitions and look for which party could have a pivotal position. Fortunately for political scientists, two elements are helpful: the electoral system and some differences in local government.

The proportional representation system of Hagenbach-Bischoff favoured electoral coalitions. As during the French Fourth Republic, parties were allowed to sign pre-electoral agreements called *apparentement*.

The analysis of the *apparentements* at both cantonal and federal levels reveals a clear-cut pattern. The Liberal Party – where it exists – is always *apparente* with the Radicals; this alliance also includes the

Table 14.6 *Electoral alliances ('related' lists) LPS-PLS, 1983*

Cantons	FDP-PRD	PDC-CVP	UDC
Basel-Stadt	+	+	–[a]
Vaud	+	–	+
Geneva	+	+	–[a]
Neuchâtel	+	–[a]	

[a] Do not present candidates.

Table 14.7 *Electoral alliances ('related' lists) LdU-AdI, 1983*

Cantons	EVP-PES	European Federalists	Greens
Zurich	+	+	
Berne		+	
Basel-Stadt	+		
Aargau	+	+	
Thurgau			+

Agrarians in Vaud (see Table 14.6). On the other side, the Independents remain – independent! When they conclude *apparentements*, it is with minor and insignificant splinter groups, but those belong to social liberalism (see Table 14.7). The Liberal–Radical electoral alliance is opposed to similar agreements often concluded between left-wing parties.

Like federal and cantonal governments, local government has a collegial executive. However, unlike federal and state executives, the local ones have a president, the mayor. The LdU-AdI was once able to get the job of mayor of the most important city in Switzerland – Zurich. The candidate for the Alliance, Sigmund Widmer, was elected against a candidate of the right and with the support of the left. When elected, he kept the balance of power between left and right, with a moderate trend towards the left. When the right took over again, the majority in Zurich, the Independents, gave back the mayorship to the Radicals.

Like the Netherlands, and to a lesser extent Italy, Switzerland is a show-piece of the ambiguity of liberalism and liberal parties today. One party with a real left-wing origin has moved to the right and can be located at the right of both Christian democracy and agrarianism. It understands liberalism as 'Reaganomics' and belongs to the French meaning of the word 'liberal'. It even has quite different historical roots, and as a member of the Liberal International, it is the Swiss counterpart of the British Conservative Party. A second party with a rather peculiar origin has kept a clear centre-left stand and can be located at the left of both Christian democracy and agriarianism. It understands liberalism as being social and protective of consumers and the environment. It belongs to the Anglo-Saxon meaning of the word 'liberal'.

It is this debate that the future of liberalism in Western Europe will continue to revolve around.

NOTES

1 D.L. Seiler, *Partis et familles politiques*, Paris: PUF, 1980 356.
2 J.C. Biaudet, 'Les partis politiques' in V. A., *La démocratie Suisse 1848–1948*, Morat: Ed. patriotiques, 1948, 141.

REFERENCES

Arlettaz, G. (1980) *Libéralisme et société dans le Canton de Vaud*, Lausanne: Bibliothèque historique vaudoise.

Codding, G.A. (1965) *The Federal Government of Switzerland*, Boston: Houghton Mifflin.

Gierisch, B. (1974) *Interest Groups in Swiss Politics*, Zurich: Soziologisches Institut.

Grüner, E. (1977) *Die Parteien in der Schweiz*, Berne: Francke.

Kerr, E. (1981) *Parlement et société en Suisse*, St Saphorin: Georgi.

Klöti, U. (ed.) (1984) *Handbuch: Politisches System der Schweiz*, Vol. 2, Berne and Stuttgart: Haup.

Lipson, L. (1956) 'Le système des partis politiques en Suisse', *Revue française de science politique*, 813–32.

Meynaud, J. (1963) *Les organisations professionnelles en Suisse*, Lausanne: Payot.

Meynaud, J. and A. Korff (1965) *La Migros et la politique: l'Alliance des Indépendants*, Lausanne: Etudes de science politique.

Reiss, C. (1958) *Gottlieb Duttweiler: Eine Biografie*, Zurich: Die Arche.

Schmid, G. (1981) *Politische Parteien, Verfassung und Gesetz*, Basel: Albing und Lichtenhahn.

Schumacher, J.-J. (1970) *Sociologie du Parti libéral*, Neuchâtel: Faculté des sciences économiques et sociales.

Seiler, D.L. (1977) 'Clivages, régions et science politique: application d'un schéma d'analyse aux cas de la Suisse et de la Belgique', *Canadian Journal of Political Science*, X, (3), 447–72.

Seiler, D.L. (1980), *Parties et familles politiques*, Paris: PUF.

Sidjanski, D. and D. Handley (1969) 'Note de recherche sur les partis politiques et le processus de décision', *Annuaire suisse de science politique*, IX, 75–95.

Steiner, J. (1973) *Amicable Agreement versus Majority Rule: Conflict Resolution in Switzerland*, Chapel Hill: University of North Carolina Press.

Tschani, H. (1983) *Wer regiert die Schweiz?* Zurich: Orell Füssli.

15

The Luxemburg Liberal Party

Derek Hearl

INTRODUCTION

In the same way as in neighbouring West Germany and Belgium, and for similar reasons, the identification of a liberal party in Luxemburg presents no difficulty, the Demokratesch Partei[1] qualifying by virtually any criterion. Of all the parties considered in this volume, the DP is by far the smallest in absolute terms but this has not prevented it from becoming one of the more important. In recent years especially, both domestically and internationally, it has become one of the most highly-influential liberal parties in Europe. For this reason alone, no study of present-day liberalism in Western Europe could be complete without reference to the Luxemburg *Demokratesch Partei*.

This influential position is due to a number of factors, of which the most important are probably the DP's almost uniquely high (for a European liberal party) vote percentage; its regular participation in government (and hence from time to time the presidency of the EC council of ministers); its rather strategic position virtually in the ideological centre of European liberalism; and, not the least important, the personality of several of its leaders since the Second World War, most notably Gaston Thorn.

Yet, as an organised party political force, liberalism was a distinctly late developer in the Grand Duchy, the country's first proper liberal party not emerging until as late as 1925 or so, even though both as a philosophy and as a political tradition, liberalism has had a long history in Luxemburg. However, in purely organisational terms, it remained weak until well after the Second World War, suffering from considerable vote fluctuations at successive elections, and it is really only since the late 1960s that a Luxemburg liberal party can be said to have acquired any measure of electoral stability and, hence, real governmental power.

THE DEVELOPMENT OF LIBERALISM IN THE GRAND DUCHY

The early years

In Luxemburg as elsewhere, it was the classic *laisser-faire* and anti-clerical liberals who fought and won the great constitutional struggles and the battle for parliamentarianism in the mid-nineteenth century; in 1848 they forced the king-grand duke to concede a more democratic constitution making the government responsible to parliament and proclaiming a wide variety of civil liberties. Although this constitution was later to be suspended and then arbitrarily amended in the so-called *coup d'état* of 1856, the radicals again won power some years later ensuring that the amendments were interpreted in a liberal spirit.[2] Finally, in 1868, they were successful in securing the enactment of the current constitution which, like its 1848 predecessor, was explicitly modelled upon the Belgian one, itself widely recognised at the time as one of the most liberal in the world.

Throughout this period there were two quite distinct factions among liberals in Luxemburg:

- the doctrinaire liberals, who were socially conservative, politically authoritarian, Orangist and anticlerical . . . [they were] a party of high functionaries, lacking deep roots among the population.
- the progressive liberals: [who] were partisans of constitutional reform in the more liberal sense (i.e. the extension of the prerogatives of the legislature, of individual liberties, the freedom of the press, etc.) [who] advocated social reform albeit without daring to go as far as universal suffrage.[3]

Nevertheless, a properly organised parliamentary liberal party did not emerge until the turn of the century. Even then it did so following the example set by the Catholics and socialists. This is in marked contradistinction to the pattern in other countries where it seems generally to have been the case that it was the liberals who organised themselves first.

There appear to have been two principal reasons for this rather different chain of events in Luxemburg. First, the very dominance of liberals from both traditions during the mid-nineteenth century meant that they faced no real threat and hence no real need to organise themselves. Secondly, their long tradition of being divided into two warring factions meant that it was difficult for them to co-operate with one another as long as their rivals remained unorganised and excluded from political power. This disorganised and divisive tradition was to have profound effects upon Luxemburg liberalism throughout the first half of the twentieth century.

The beginnings of organisation

An important step was taken in 1904 when Robert Brasseur founded the Ligue libérale and, indeed, many Luxemburgers today date the origins of the modern DP from this time, in spite of the fact that the Ligue was really not much more than a committee for the re-election of its members rather than a genuine political party in the modern sense.[4]

During this period, a number of attempts at Liberal–Socialist co-operation were made, particularly by the 'radical' Liberals, and in due course these led to the establishment of a 'Bloc de la Gauche' in the country's second city, Esch-sur-Alzette, to contest the legislative elections of 1908. The Bloc secured a notable victory obtaining an overall majority in the chamber and soon provoking a violent confrontation with the Catholic 'right', first over the establishment of a state-controlled girls' grammar school, and then over the wider issue of schools legislation in general. In contrast to the situation in neighbouring Belgium, however, where the 'schools war' was to persist on and off for some fifty years, the 1912 liberal–socialist schools legislation in Luxemburg was eventually to be widely accepted, albeit only after a great deal of initial opposition over the following decade.

In spite of the fact that the struggle surrounding the 1912 *Loi scolaire* was a very bitter one dividing the country into two quite distinct and mutually hostile camps, it was not to provide sufficient ideological cement to prevent liberals and socialists from falling out among themselves over other issues.

> One could see this during the debates in the Chamber on the subject of mining concessions in 1912. The socialists demanded universal suffrage and represented the interests of the workers. This was the very stuff of disagreement. The orientation of the catholics towards a social-christian policy widened the fissure. The 1914–18 war aggravated social tensions and in 1916/17 the Bloc de la Gauche disintegrated.[5]

The formation of the Parti Radical-Libéral

The years 1919 to 1926 were difficult ones for liberals in Luxemburg. As so often before, two ideological streams re-emerged, known this time as the 'old' liberals and the 'young' (or 'progressive') liberals

Table 15.1 *Pre-Second World War national electoral performance*

	Parti Radical-Libéral	
	%[a]	Year
Minimum	7.7	1931
Maximum	16.9	1919
Mean	11.2	

Source: Rose and Mackie, *International Almanac of Electoral History*, 2nd edn (London, 1982). (Results for 1922 and 1925 not available.)
[a] Unadjusted national vote, (see note 11).

Table 15.2 *Pre-Second World War national government participation*

	Number of times	Total length
Parti Radical-Libéral	3[a]	13 years

[a] i.e. under 3 different prime ministers. Due to the system of partial elections then in force, governments only resigned if they lost their majority, which happened only twice during this period.

respectively. The latter, led principally by Gaston Diderich, wanted to cut loose from Brasseur and his colleagues. The gulf widened as a result of dissensions in the socialist party, one of whose deputies defected to the progressive liberals to form a new 'radical socialist' grouping which openly opposed Brasseur and the 'old' liberals at elections until 1925 when the latter were practically wiped out and Diderich and his supporters founded the Parti Radical-Libéral which was to survive until the Nazi invasion of 1940. Nevertheless, the divisive character of Luxemburg liberalism remained, and the new party was in its turn to suffer a long series of splits and reconciliations. In spite of this it found itself in more or less permanent coalition with the Catholics for most of the period between the two World Wars. (See Tables 15.1 and 15.2 for elections and government participation during that period.)

Schaeffer sums up the history of Luxemburg liberalism in the nineteenth and early twentieth centuries as not the story of a party, but rather that of a movement which, right up to 1940, was sometimes divided into two or three parties and sometimes represented by only one.[6]

The liberal spirit, during the whole of the first half of the twentieth century, may be compared . . . to that of the radicals in France. On each side one finds anticlericalism, republicanism and the taste for ministerial portfolios.[7]

The post-Second World War era and the emergence of the Demokratesch Partei

Following the liberation in September 1944, domestic politics quickly reverted to something like their pre-war pattern. The two principal parties, the Catholic CSV and the Socialists, both re-emerged in more or less their previous forms, as did the Communists. The radical liberals, however, did not. Many of their former supporters, together with others who had never previously been associated with any of the major parties, but more importantly many of those who had been active in the Resistance, wanted to break away from what they saw as the outdated and corrupt pre-war style of politics. In due course, these elements formed an entirely new movement (D'Unio'n) which they hoped would transcend philosophical and political boundaries in the wider national interest in the same way as the Resistance had done during the war. Consequently a 'Groupement Patriotique et Démocratique', was established by members of D'Unio'n and others to fight the 1945 election in competition with the CSV and LSAP – although its leaders continued to insist that it was not a party in the traditional sense.

Nor, indeed, was it originally seen as liberal either:

It was more an association of all members of the Resistance except the Communists. Two of its principal components were D'Unio'n and the Ligue der Jongen, i.e. those young Luxemburgers who had been forcibly sent to work in Germany or who had gone into the *maquis* to escape.[8]

According to Schaeffer, the relaunching of Luxemburg politics in the post-war years was more difficult for the Liberals than for the three other parties since of the pre-war Liberal leaders only Gaston Diderich remained, and he effectively subordinated himself to the various Resistance interests in order not to lose out in the 1945 election.

The calculation succeeded . . . the 'Groupement Patriotique et Démocratique' won 9 seats at the 1945 elections, only three less than the Socialists, (who were the great losers of the campaign) and three more than the Parti Radical-Libéral had had in 1934 and in 1937. Two of its members entered the [all-party] Government of National Union.[9]

In due course, however, the Groupement (inevitably, given the revival of the other three parties in more or less their pre-war forms) soon came to be seen as the legitimate heir to the long Luxemburg radical-liberal tradition as it came first to be dominated, and then completely taken over, by its erstwhile liberal faction which in the meantime had acquired some significant new blood in the persons of Eugène Schaus and Emile Hamilius. Largely under their influence, by 1957 the Groupement had evolved into the genuinely liberal Demokratesch Partei.

Consolidation and growth

The new party scored its first real success at the 1959 election when it won 11 seats in the then 52-member *Châmber vun Députéirten*, three more than it had had at the dissolution. Eugène Schaus took over the leadership and under him the DP began to consolidate its position. In March 1959, for the first time in eleven years, Liberals entered the government in coalition with the CSV, with Schaus as Deputy Prime Minister and Minister of the Interior. They were to leave again in 1964 but returned once more in 1968.

Over the next five-and-a-half years, the party underwent a major transformation. Under the leadership of a trio consisting of Colette Flesch, Marcel Mart and Gaston Thorn, the DP was given a brand-new, young and dynamic image much more in tune with the aspirations of 'new middle-class' voters. Both Thorn and Mart (but especially Mart) seem to have realised that if the party could shed its rather right-wing 'classical' liberal image, it stood to gain the support of this new group which was at that time such a growing factor in the population. On top of this, with both Mart and Thorn heading prominent ministries and Colette Flesch in the City Burgomaster's office, the triumvirate was in a position to build up a reputation for competence and innovation in stark contrast to the rather staid image of their CSV partners in government.

The new style proved dramatically successful. At the 1974 election, in what must be seen as perhaps the most significant event in Luxemburg's post-war political history, the CSV was ousted from power and replaced by an LSAP–DP coalition effectively led by the latter. In fact, the LSAP was the larger of the two parties in the *Châmber* with 17 seats to the Liberals' 14, but this did not prevent Thorn and his colleagues from making all the running. Not only were they able to secure half the cabinet posts (and more than half the individual ministries – see below p. 386), but it was Gaston Thorn and not the Socialist leader who became prime minister. In government, the DP applied the same tactics to its new coalition partner that it had previously so successfully used against the CSV. Again it was the DP ministers who shone, especially Thorn himself who became ever more visible both at home and abroad. The LSAP ministers in contrast were made to appear dull and even reactionary.

In a very real sense, however, these tactics proved too successful

Table 15.3 *Post-Second World War national electoral performance*

Election year	Demokratesch Partei[c]	
	%[a]	seats
1945	18.0	9
1948 } [b]		
1951 }	16.4	5
1954	13.0	6
1959	20.3	11
1964	12.2	6
1968	18.0	11
1974	23.3	14
1979	22.5	15
1984	20.4	14

[a] Adjusted national vote, (see note 11).
[b] Partial elections only.
[c] Groupement patriotique et démocratique 1945 to 1951; Groupement démocratique in 1954.
Sources: Bulletin de STATEC (Luxemburg, various dates).

and the 1979 election was both a triumph and a disappointment. Inevitably, it turned into a gladiatorial contest between Thorn and Werner, the CSV leader and former prime minister, with the LSAP effectively condemned to fight on the sidelines in support of their Liberal ally. The result was perhaps predictable. Both the DP and the CSV increased their seat totals – the former to 15, the highest a liberal party in the Grand Duchy has ever achieved – but was forced to watch its LSAP partners fall back to third place with only 14. This meant that the outgoing government as a whole lost its majority and the CSV once more took over the leadership of a new coalition with the Liberals. Gaston Thorn left to become President of the European Commission and was replaced as DP leader and Foreign Minister by Colette Flesch. However, in 1984, the party suffered its first electoral setback for 20 years – albeit a slight one entailing the loss of only one seat – and returned to opposition. (See Table 15.3 for details on the electoral performance of the DP.)

Party structure and organisation

Although neither the old Parti Radical-Libéral nor the post-war Groupement could be described as anything but 'cadre' parties, this is now no longer true of the Demokratesch Partei which is today a 'mass' party by any standard. Most observers agree that its paid-up membership is between 3,500 and 4,000, representing some seven per cent of its voters.

Internally, the DP has a simple and straightforward three-tier structure, closely similar to those of its two principal rivals. At the bottom tier are the branches (or *sektiounen*), based on local government *communes*. These branches are in turn grouped into 'districts', one for each of the country's four parliamentary constituencies, and capping the whole structure is a national organisation with headquarters in Luxemburg City. Each of the three levels has a similar representative structure of a congress, a council and a committee; each tier is directly represented at the level above, and the powers and functions of the various bodies are generally those that would be expected and are much the same as their equivalents elsewhere.

Compared to its counterparts in other countries, the DP has little more than a skeletal organisation at national level comprising no more than one or two full-time staff occupying a small suite of offices in Luxemburg City and in this it is typical of Luxemburg parties in general. On the other hand, each of the parliamentary *fraktiounen* has its own premises and staff paid for out of public funds, and these obviously carry out many of the functions – particularly in the research field – which the various party headquarters proper would otherwise have to provide for themselves. This is as true for the DP as it is for the other parties.

The party has inherited a strong tradition of internal decentralisation of power. For example, writing of the old Groupement's pre-1959 statutes, Schaeffer points to

> a very great autonomy of decision-making at intermediate levels with a strong influence over the party's conduct granted to ordinary activists and lower-level officials [while] the power of the party's MPs and ministers was restricted . . . The party's governing national council and national committee, from which ministers were excluded, had complete sovereignty over decisions on the 'Groupement's' participation or non-participation in governmental coalitions. Ministers were required to conform to the injunctions which were given them . . .[10]

To some extent the DP's new statutes which it adopted in 1959 must be seen as a reaction against this decentralist tradition. Under the new rules, MPs and local councillors were given more important powers of decision and the position of party leader (still at that time held by the unchallenged Eugène Schaus) was formalised. Since then it has certainly been the case that the incumbent leader has wielded considerable informal power within the party. Delvaux claims, for example, that, at the DP's Echternach congress held prior to the 1974 election, Gaston Thorn personally drew up the party's electoral lists and successfully resisted demands for any coalition agreement to be subject to the approval of a full party congress (as is the case in both the other parties). In the DP, somewhat paradoxically, given its otherwise strong decentralist traditions, this power remains with the much smaller (and generally leadership-dominated) national committee. Nevertheless, the tradition of local autonomy and decentralised decision-making remains strong.

It is, of course, the four constituency-based district organisations which are responsible for drawing up lists of candidates for parliamentary elections to the *Châmber vun Députéirten*. Formally at least, these are subject to the approval of the party's national committee but, apart from the above example cited by Delvaux, there is no indication that this power is seriously exercised, and if it were it would probably be strongly resisted. Great care is taken by the districts to 'balance' the lists in terms of such criteria as age, sex, occupation and place of residence as well as in terms of political factors such as seniority, party faction and incumbency. However, an examination of DP parliamentary lists for the past few elections clearly shows that the most important considerations are incumbency and place of residence. It seems that virtually any sitting *députéirt* can expect to be reselected if he or she so wishes while, particularly in the more rural constituencies, candidates are very evenly spread in geographical terms. Nevertheless, the opportunities for doing this depend heavily upon the size of the district concerned: for example, the south constituency, the largest, elects 24 *députéirten* while the smallest, the east, has only six. Obviously, there is far more scope for a 'balanced ticket' in the former than in the latter.

The DP also owns a mass circulation daily newspaper, *De Lëtzeburger Journal*, born in the early post-Second World War years of a merger between the organ of the ex-resistance Union movement already referred to, and a regional newspaper from the east of the country, the *Obermoselzeitung*. At first, the new paper was something of a disppointment since, according to Schaeffer, many of the latter's readers felt that their paper had lost both its political independence and its specifically regional character and defected in large numbers to the country's principal daily, the Catholic *Luxemburger Wort*. However, following the launch of the Demokratesch Partei at the end of the 1950s, the *Journal* was considerably revamped and its circulation has grown steadily, roughly in line with the party's own post-war electoral success. Today it is the country's second-largest newspaper selling some 27,500 copies per day.

The DP has a number of affiliated (or, more strictly, closely

Table 15.4 *Post-Second World War national government participation*

	Number of times	Total length
Demokratesch Partei[a]	7	27 years 5 months

[a]Groupement patriotique et démocratique and Groupement démocratique prior to 1957.

associated) 'daughter' organisations of which by far the most important is its youth movement, the *Jeunesse Démocratique*, although there are those for women, trade unionists and so on, as well. The party has had least success in the latter field, however, where at any rate formally there has never really been an explicitly liberal orientated trade union federation (as there have been socialist and Catholic ones). On the other hand, a number of so-called 'neutral' unions, mostly in the professional and white-collar sectors, remain unaffiliated to either of the main federations, and not unnaturally these tend to be more sympathetic to the Demokratesch Partei.

It is difficult to be precise about the social composition of DP members and activists since no published surveys exist. However, it is clear that in addition to such groups as the liberal professions, public-sector workers such as civil servants, teachers, etc. also support the party in large numbers and may be presumed to be disproportionately represented among its activists.

THE DP'S PARTICIPATION IN GOVERNMENT

The DP has a record in government which many of its larger sister parties from other countries might well envy. It (or its predecessor, the Groupement) has served in seven of the country's twelve post-World War II cabinets and for 57 per cent of the period (see Table 15.4). Over time the party has seen its influence in government steadily increase, whether measured in terms of cabinet ministers or of ministries (the two are not synonymous in Luxemburg where individual members of the government typically head two, three, or even four separate departments simultaneously). Eventually, of course, the party actually gained the premiership itself, in the person of Gaston Thorn, and in effect led the 1974–9 government in coalition with the Socialists.

This high point in the party's post-war history came about following the general election of June 1974 when it increased its parliamentary representation to 14 while the Catholic CSV which had dominated every government since the introduction of universal suffrage in 1919, fell back to 18 seats, thereby losing its pivotal position in the chamber and opening up the possibility of a coalition from which it might be excluded altogether.

Negotiations to this effect were swiftly opened between the socialist LSAP and the DP, and they were rapidly concluded. To many people's surprise, it appeared to be the smaller party which got the better deal. Not only did the Liberals obtain parity with the Socialists in the government as a whole with four ministers each, but one of them was the presidency of the government itself. If this were not enough, of the four principal Ministries of Economics, Finance, Foreign Affairs and Interior only Finance was conceded to the LSAP. In terms of actual departments, too, it was the DP which secured the lion's share with 13 out of 24.

Subsequently, too, it was Thorn and his DP colleagues who dominated the new government, almost completely eclipsing their Socialist partners in the process. So much so, indeed, that at the ensuing election in 1979 the DP actually out-polled the LSAP, gaining 22.5 per cent of the adjusted national vote[11] compared to the latter's 20.4 per cent and increasing its total of seats to 15 compared to the Socialists' 14. In spite of this, the principal beneficiary of the election was the Catholic CSV which, after five years in opposition, saw its fortunes recover very dramatically. Consequently, in spite of the DP's own increased share of vote and seats, it had to cede leadership of the government once more to the veteran CSV leader and former prime minister, Pierre Werner.

Featherstone concludes:

> [The LSAP] appears to have suffered [in the 1979 elections] because of its lack of a national personality to intervene in the clash between Thorn and Werner – both very experienced leaders – a contest which received much publicity.[12]

Following the election, coalition negotiations were delayed pending Gaston Thorn's confirmation as president of the EC Commission, the first time a Luxemburger had held that office, and it seems clear that he would otherwise have remained as Foreign Minister. In the event, however, he did leave for Brussels and was replaced as party leader by Colette Flesch, the then Burgomaster of Luxemburg City and former DP *fraktioun* leader in the *Châmber*. At the 1984 election the 'pendulum' of Luxemburg politics finally swung against the DP to the benefit of the Socialists who once again went into government with the CSV relegating the DP to the opposition benches for the first time since 1969.

An examination of the list of ministries held by the DP when it has been in office shows a marked concentration upon Energy, Econ-

Table 15.5 *Ten leading issue categories for Luxemburg governments (overall and by coalition type)*

	All governments	CSV–DP governments	CSV–LSAP governments	Thorn government
1. Social services expansion	7.2	5.9	6.6	21.2
2. Government efficiency	6.5	7.3	7.7	3.3
3. Farmers and agriculture	6.1	6.8	6.8	5.1
4. Labour groups	5.1	4.2	7.8	7.4
5. Technology/infrastructure	4.9	6.1	3.1	7.1
6. Education	4.9	6.6	4.4	3.3
7. Economic orthodoxy	4.4	6.6	3.6	0.8
8. Constitutionalism	3.7	2.5	2.6	2.3
9. National effort	3.6	5.3	1.4	0.8
10. Social justice	2.8	2.4	3.8	0.5

Note: Scores are percentage references to each topic in relevant government declarations. (See Laver, M. and Budge, I. and Hearl, D. (eds.), *Party Policy and Coalition Government* (forthcoming).)

omics, Foreign Affairs, Justice, Public Works, Transport, and Sport and Recreation, and to a lesser extent Armed Forces/Defence, Civil Service, Interior, Middle Classes and Public Health. In contrast, the party has never held the important posts of Education, Finance, Labour or Social Services, even though the last of these at least is regularly given high priority in its policy documents. It has held the Agriculture portfolio only once (during the Thorn government), otherwise this particular ministry has been the CSV's exclusive preserve.

An estimate of the influence which the DP has had in government can be made from the various government declarations which Luxemburg prime ministers make to the *Châmber* at the start of each government and this is done in Table 15.5. (The coding categories are the same as those used in the ECPR manifestos project described in Ch. 17 of this volume.) The table shows the mean scores for all twelve post-war government policy statements taken together, as well as the scores for the five CSV–DP coalitions, the five CSV–LSAP coalitions and the DP–LSAP Thorn government of 1974–9.

Generally speaking, the patterns shown in the table are plausible. The 'top ten' issues themselves compare pretty favourably with those found in party manifestos, while differences between the scores for all twelve governments and those for each of the three coalition types are in the expected directions. So that, for example, CSV–DP governments have laid more stress than have CSV–LSAP ones on the issues of technology, education, economic orthodoxy and national effort (reflecting traditional liberal concerns in particular), while the CSV–LSAP coalitions have shifted the policy balance more towards social services (albeit only slightly), labour groups and social justice. The Thorn government, for its part, put unusually high emphasis on social services, labour groups and technology/infrastructure and put unusually low emphasis on government efficiency, economic orthodoxy, national effort and social justice. This accords nicely with that government's reputation as a high spender to which the maze of new motorways and other prestige infrastructure works now to be found throughout the Grand Duchy eloquently testify. Certainly the extent to which the Thorn government was 'different' in this as well as in other respects is clearly shown in the table.

THE ELECTORAL BASE OF THE DP

Luxemburg is a highly industrialised country whose economy has in the past been overwhelmingly dependent on its massive coal and steel industry. During the latter half of the post-Second World War era, however, there have been dramatic changes in the economic structure. The coal industry has been practically eliminated and the steel industry cut back as a result of ECSC rationalisation, while there has been a spectacular growth of new industries, especially around Luxemburg City itself. Of even greater importance has been the explosion of the services sector, particularly banking, again in and around the capital resulting in its emergence as a European financial centre second only to the City of London. In addition, Luxemburg City has become a major administrative centre, not only of the European Community, but of a host of other international institutions as well.

These changes have had a profound effect on the country's socio-economic make up. For example, the proportion of the work-force employed in the services sector in 1960 was 38.6 per cent; less than 20 years later in 1978, it had risen to 51.2 per cent. This was almost entirely at the expense of the agricultural sector where the percentage employed fell from 16.6 per cent to only 5.7 per cent over the same period.

Most experts agree that the DP was the party to benefit most from this evolution. For example, Michel Delvaux writes:

> [Formerly] the liberal party was primarily the expression of the 'non-monopolistic classes' (i.e. the liberal professions, artisans, small landowners, shopkeepers, the old 'in between' or 'middle' classes). The 'second industrial revolution' [and the growth of] American multinational companies, big

Table 15.6 *Electoral base of Demokratesch Partei*, %

		National mean	1984	1979
Class				
Working class		34.5	6.9	21.6
Middle class		59.9	82.8	73.7
Farmers		5.6	10.3	4.8
Religiosity				
Religious	(1984)[a]	80.1	94.6	
	(1979)[a]	93.9		93.7
Age				
Under 25		17.8	11.1	17.6
25 to 39		26.3	22.2	40.5
40 to 59		34.3	38.9	20.3
Over 60		21.7	27.8	21.9
Sex				
Male		54.0	52.8	48.5
Urban/rural				
Urban		52.7	44.4	55.5

[a] *Note:* Religiosity question differently worded in 1979 and 1984.
Sources: Eurobaromètres 11, 12 (1979) and 20 (1984).

banks, [and the] extension of the services sector has produced a new liberal party, in which the 'new middle classes' [*petite bourgeoisie*, executives etc. in both the public and the commercial sectors] feel themselves more easily at home but which the older middle classes have not deserted.[13]

Certainly, all available evidence supports the hypothesis that the DP is a middle-class party. Election results, for example, show its vote nowadays firmly entrenched in those areas with high concentrations of the so-called 'Californians' (i.e. 'new middle-class' white-collar workers, executives etc.), particularly associated with the new service industries. Not only is the party's greatest electoral strength in the better class suburbs and the commuter belt around Luxemburg City where the 'Californians' tend to live, but these have also been the areas of its greatest percentage growth. Nevertheless, it still retains a significant following in the rural east and north constituencies as well. On the other hand, the DP has as yet to make significant inroads into the traditional working-class vote, especially in the heavily industrialised South, which still largely goes to the LSAP and CSV, (see Table 15.6).

Such impressions are confirmed by the limited survey evidence which is available, in particular the *Eurobaromètre* series of surveys

Table 15.7 *Distribution of Liberal vote by parliamentary constituency at post-Second World War elections*

	Under 10%	11–15%	16–20%	21–25%	26–30%	Over 30%
South	1 2 3 4	5 6 7				
East			1	2 4 6	3 5 7	
Centre			2		1 3 4 6 7	5
North		2	1 4 6	3 5	7	

Key: Constituencies:
South = Capellen and Esch/Alzette;
East = Echternach, Grevenmacher and Remich;
Centre = Luxemburg and Mersch;
North = Clervaux, Diekirch, Redange, Vianden and Wiltz.
Elections:
1 = 1945; 2 = 1954; 3 = 1959; 4 = 1968; 5 = 1974; 6 = 1979; 7 = 1984.
(NB: the partial elections of 1948 and 1951 are not shown).

sponsored by the European Commission upon which Table 15.6 is based. Although these figures have necessarily to be treated with some caution due to the fact that only some 300 or so respondents are surveyed in Luxemburg, it is quite clear that, compared to the national average, the DP is highly distinctive in its class profile, albeit slightly less so in 1979 when it attracted a higher than usual proportion of working-class support. In the same way its much remarked-upon appeal to younger voters in that year is clearly shown in the table. With these two exceptions, however, the party's voter profile is generally very representative of the electorate as a whole, even somewhat unexpectedly in religious terms (although this last may partly be explained by the fact that *Eurobaromètre* only asks whether respondents think of themselves as 'religious' and not about the more generally recognised operational definition of 'religiosity', frequency of church attendance). Nevertheless it is somewhat surprising that DP voters should appear not only to have been at least as 'religious' as the average voter in 1979 but actually *more* so in 1984.

THE POLICIES OF THE DP

Originally Luxemburg liberalism drew much of its inspiration from its counterparts in Belgium and France and, like them, was very firmly rooted in the classic anti-clerical tradition. However, the rather different nature of Luxemburg society and its different style and pace of economic development led in due course to a system in which the left–right socio-economic and clerical–anti-clerical cleavages came to coincide much more than in these other countries. The result of this was a marriage between right-wing economic interests and conservative clerical ones, first in the pre-Second World War Partei der Rechten and then, more importantly, in its post-war successor, the CSV, which – particularly under Pierre Werner's leadership during the 1960s and 1970s – came to resemble more closely its West German, rather than, say, its Dutch or Belgian, cousins.

Under these conditions it is not surprising that it was the 'progressive' or 'radical' liberal tradition – always, of course, very strong in Luxemburg politics – which came to dominate the post-1960s DP in a way which it could not do in such countries as Belgium or the Netherlands where right-wing forces, estranged as they were from clerical ones, remained in (and in control of) the old Liberal Parties. It is for this reason as much as for any other that today's DP must be seen as a party of the centre-left more akin to its British and German counterparts than to its Dutch or Belgian ones.

According to Trausch, for example:

> The new liberals dropped the anticlericalism of the old doctrinaires. Adopting a position in the centre they presented themselves as men of reconciliation and adversaries of extremism . . . [They] took up liberal ideas adapted to the new [social] evolution.[14]

There is a wealth of evidence to support this conclusion. First, the party is in any case generally seen both by its own activists and supporters as well as by its opponents as being to the left of the CSV. For example, the famous ten-point 'left–right' scale pioneered by *Eurobaromètre* and reported, for example, by Inglehart and Klingemann, regularly shows DP supporters lying between those of the other two parties in terms of their self-placement on this scale.

Secondly, the ease with which the DP was able to agree upon a coalition programme with the LSAP clearly indicates that by that time the two parties were no longer really very far apart on the political spectrum. According to Delvaux:

> The two parties . . . represent the most dynamic forces in the social field [and] have allied themselves on a reformist platform. The [1974] government programme [stated]: 'Stability and democracy can only be found and assured by change. It is this which some people still do not understand.'[15]

Finally, of course, there are the party's own policy pronouncements, in particular its election programmes. A full set of the latter, dating from the DP's formal constitution in 1959, has been collected in the context of the ECPR manifestos project (reported more fully in ch. 18). These documents show very clearly not only how DP policy has evolved over the years but also how it relates to that of the other parties in the system. Consequently it is a very valuable data source.

In common with its principal rivals, the CSV and LSAP, and in contradistinction to the communists, the DP has very clearly changed its orientation over the period away from inward-looking policies concerned with the material issues of a mixed industrial and agricultural economy, towards those of the post-materialist society which the Grand Duchy has undoubtedly become. More often than not, it has been the DP which has taken the lead in this. The party has constantly laid more stress than any of its rivals upon such issues as the interests of the 'middle classes' (i.e. as opposed to employers and organised labour), technology, the European Community, environmental protection and, above all, the traditional liberal concern with freedom and human rights. Over the years it has put a much less marked emphasis upon such right-wing economic concerns as free enterprise, incentives and economic orthodoxy than have the liberal parties in a number of other countries, such as Belgium, Denmark, the Netherlands or Italy, for example. At the same time, it has vied with its opponents at home to be the party most stressing social justice, social services and democracy, all issues which in Luxemburg as elsewhere tend to be more associated with parties of the left than of the right.

In terms of its economic policies, however, the DP must be classified as a party of the moderate centre or even centre-right. It strongly supports the principle of individual property rights, the free market economy and free trade as opposed to protectionism. However, it is also in favour of increased public investment (as has already been noted, the Thorn government was a very high spender) both in the interest of creating employment and of improving public services. It has tended to lay considerable emphasis upon agrarian interests in general (and upon those of the wine producing sector in particular, although how far this last is a matter of principle and how far one of partisan self-interest is unclear. Much of the party's traditional rural vote comes from the east constituency which is where the country's small but important wine growing region is situated.)

In social terms, however, there is no ambiguity. Apart from its traditional anti-clerical stance (now to all intents and purposes a dead issue in Luxemburg), the party has been an unswerving exponent of civil rights and liberties of all kinds, both at home and abroad; it has sought to improve and extend education to all classes of society; and it has taken a very progressive view of the problems of various minority groups such as unmarried mothers, homosexuals and, in particular, the Grand Duchy's very large migrant worker community.

Internationally, too, the Demokratesch Partei has taken a progressive view towards such issues as decolonisation, overseas aid, support for international organisations in general (but particularly the UN of whose general assembly Gaston Thorn was at one time president). It has taken a rather centrist view towards defence issues, strongly supporting the Grand Duchy's continued membership of NATO on the one hand and helping to bring about the abolition of conscription on the other, and – as already mentioned above – it is the strongest supporter of European integration in what is in any case one of the Community's most enthusiastic member states.

THE STRATEGY OF THE DP

Delvaux has argued that the electoral tactics both of the former Groupement and of its direct descendant, the DP, at any rate during their early years, consisted merely of gathering together isolated individuals and unclearly defined pressure groups. However, not only did such groups have no real identity of interest anyway, but, as Delvaux somewhat cynically maintains, the Liberals did nothing to keep such electoral promises as they were able to make. He seems to imply that it was for these reasons as much as any others that the party's fortunes went up and down so much from one election to another.

> Today the Democratic Party has many more means of resistance. Its electoral base is assured by the numerous adhesions of salaried workers in the tertiary sector, above all those young white-collar workers who are attracted by the impression of social success, of prosperity, of competence and dynamism which the party's leaders give. The accession of Gaston Thorn, Marcel Mart, Colette Flesch and Jean Hamilius to posts of great responsibility has changed the party's image.[16]

Certainly since the early 1970s, the DP leadership deliberately concentrated upon catering to the needs of the new middle-class voters, and in the rather prosperous circumstances of today's Grand Duchy this obviously meant the adoption of socially progressive policies which at the same time did not threaten the economic interests of this highly significant new group.

At about the same time and in similar vein the party also made an overt bid for the environmentalist vote, initially to some effect. However, the emergence (and electoral success) of an explicitly 'green' party in the 1979 and 1984 elections may now have somewhat attenuated this source of support.

> The party permits the middle classes and the bourgeoisie to acquit themselves of a good conscience at a low price. In voting liberal, they may

pass for progressives in regard to everything which concerns culture, education and justice, without having to suffer any damage to their class privileges.[17]

Apart from targeting new voters in this way, the DP has also made good use of the preferential voting features of the electoral system under which any elector may give up to two votes to particular candidates regardless of party. By deliberately putting forward colourful and charismatic candidates and emphasising their individual as opposed to purely party virtues, the DP has been able to attract many more votes than it might otherwise have expected on a purely partisan basis.

In concentrating attention upon its political 'stars' in this way, the party became adept during the 1970s and early 1980s at showing its opponents' leaders in a comparatively unfavourable light. The leaders of both the CSV and the LSAP were effectively portrayed as dull, pompous and boring as well as unimaginative and incompetent, in stark contrast to the young, modern and dynamic leadership of the DP itself. For many years this strategy was markedly successful. Now, however, the fact that first Marcel Mart and then, much more seriously, Gaston Thorn have both left domestic politics, coupled with the advent of a new generation of leaders in both the other main parties, almost certainly means that the party can no longer play this particular card as effectively as before.

The DP seems always to have put most emphasis upon *Châmber* elections rather than on local ones which are in any case only fought along political lines in the larger *communes*, although not unnaturally Luxemburg City is the exception to this rule. Something like a quarter of the entire population lives in the capital which has traditionally been a Liberal 'fief', the party having supplied four of the City's five post-war Burgomasters. Elections here are very definitely taken seriously by the DP at national level. Nor has the advent of European elections changed this pattern, although this must partly be due to the fact that they have so far been held on the same day as national elections, with the inevitable result that they have to all intents and purposes been completely eclipsed as separate political events in their own right.

NOTES

1 This is its Luxemburgish name which is increasingly used domestically although the party is perhaps better known internationally by its French name, Parti démocratique.
2 Trausch, *Le Luxembourg à l'époque contemporaine*, p. 63.
3 Trausch, p. 54.

4 Trausch, p. 81.
5 Trausch, p. 82.
6 Schaeffer, *Les forces politiques au Grand-Duché de Luxembourg*, p. 98.
7 Schaeffer, p. 108.
8 Schaeffer, p. 132.
9 Schaeffer, p. 131.
10 Schaeffer, p. 147.
11 In Luxemburg the number of votes cast by each elector varies according to constituency, so votes cannot simply be added up nationally. The 'adjusted' vote is calculated by dividing the total vote for each party in each constituency by the mean number of votes cast by each elector in that constituency; the resulting quotients are then summed.
12 Featherstone, Kevin, 'The Luxembourg Socialist Party' (unpublished manuscript, University of Stirling, 1986).
13 Delvaux, Michel, *Structures socio-politiques du Luxembourg*, p. 7.
14 Trausch, p. 197.
15 Delvaux, p. 8.
16 Delvaux, p. 159.
17 Hirsch, Mario, 'Et si Dieu était à gauche?' *Lëtzeburger Land*, No. 35 (Luxemburg, 30 August 1974).

REFERENCES

Essential reading

Becker, Pitt and Joseph Anen, 'Parti démocratique, 1945–1970 – Demokratesch Partei: Chronik einer Partei', in *Lëtzeburger Journal*, 30 September 1970 to 21 January 1971 inclusive, (Vol. 90, nos. 221ff. and Vol. 91, nos. 1–16).

Delvaux, Michel, *Structures socio-politiques du Luxembourg* (Luxemburg, 1977).

Hearl, Derek, 'Luxembourg' in Budge, Ian and D. Robertson and D. Hearl (eds.), *Party Strategy*, etc. (Cambridge, 1986).

Majérus, Pierre, *The Institutions of the Grand Duchy of Luxemburg* (Luxemburg, 1976).

Schaeffer, Nico(las), *Les forces politiques au Grand-Duché de Luxembourg (1919–1960)*, Mémoire présenté à l'Institut d'Etudes politiques (de l'université) de Paris (Paris, mars 1961).

Trausch, Gilbert, *Le Luxembourg à l'époque contemporaine: du partage de 1839 à nos jours* (Luxemburg, 1981).

Further reading

CRISP, *Les Elections législatives du 26 mai 1974 au Grand-Duché de Luxembourg: Analyse des résultats et des comportements électoraux* (Brussels, no date).

Hearl, Derek, 'The Grand Duchy of Luxembourg: a political study' (unpublished paper, University of Essex, 1973).

Hirsch, Mario, 'Luxembourg' in Reif, K.-H. (ed.), *Ten European Elections: Campaigns and Results of the 1979/81 First Direct Elections to the European Parliament* (Aldershot, Gower, 1985).

Nicolas, Jean, *Le parti démocratique tel que je l'ai vu* (Walferdange, 1981).

Parti radical-libéral luxembourgeois, 'Un siècle de politique libéral' in *Annuaire du parti radical-libéral luxembourgeois 1939–1940* (Luxemburg, 1940).

16

Identifying liberal parties

Michael Steed and Peter Humphreys[1]

INTRODUCTION

When the president of the European Parliament was elected in January 1987, the Liberal group voted for the left-wing Radical Marco Panella on the first ballot and for Sir Henry Plumb, a Conservative, on the second. The group claimed that 'by shifting en bloc from Panella to Plumb' [it] 'thereby illustrated the deep unity which exists – in their diversity – between the European Liberals'.[2] Others might consider that this behaviour illustrated the lack of political coherence amongst the European parties which claim to be liberal. Liberal parties thus confront us with a major problem of classification and of analysis. In simple terms, the problem arises because the Liberal family itself asserts that it exists; yet even the most superficial glance at the Liberal group in the European Parliament or at the Liberal International finds it to be a most heterogeneous collection, embracing elements that on close inspection strike the political scientist as being surprising candidates for inclusion. This problem is exacerbated by the fact that political scientists have, until now, tended to focus only on the major party families and have not yet given much attention to the smaller party families. The problem is, in fact, very complex and can be approached at several different levels.

At the intellectual level, attempting to identify liberal parties should produce important lessons for the study of parties and party systems. In this respect, the important questions are: is there a group or family of parties that we can meaningfully classify as liberal; if so, what are the distinguishing features of such parties; and what are the conditions that we might expect to produce them? Whilst there have been attempts to classify parties as liberal, there has been no associated attempt to address these important questions in a comparative, systematic and comprehensive manner. The result of this omission has been that the study of liberal parties exists in a theoretical vacuum. Investigating the Liberal family and trying to explain why it exists for some purposes, and yet in other respects it remains rather heterogeneous, may provide a key to a better understanding of cleavages and the classification of party systems more generally.

The question has been faced in a different manner by the transnational organisations of liberal parties, which have approached the question of identification as a purely political matter, balancing what was to be gained by adding this or that party to itself (principally numbers and therefore weight) against what might be lost (usually offence to one or more existing members). Since liberal parties, of their nature, admit no pope or twenty-one conditions, the various transnational parliamentary groups and party federations have grown incrementally in this fashion, with each fresh adhesion implicitly redefining the character of this self-identified family of parties. The transnational party organisations are rather shadowy bodies, which, unlike national parties, have no chance of exercising actual power. But in one respect, they are certainly real: they constitute mutual recognition systems which decide what national parties themselves see as their equivalents across frontiers, thereby maintaining, if not indeed creating, the collective self-image of a family of parties. It is not by chance that the transnational bodies formed between liberal parties have had to grapple hard with this question.

The purpose of this chapter is to compare and, so far as possible, combine the answers produced by the questions asked at these levels. It thus seeks to bring together evidence from two contrasted sources, the relatively objective judgements of experts and the totally subjective decisions of the parties involved; and two contrasted sorts of evidence, the actual lists that both sources provide and the broader categorisations produced by the study of West European party systems. We start with the historical development of liberal parties since this leads most clearly to a systematic definition of what a liberal party is. We then look at how both the liberal parties have defined themselves and have been defined by political scientists, putting together the evidence in Table 16.1 on pp. 408–9. Having done this we are able to examine what position in party systems these liberal parties occupy, drawing some tentative conclusions about the study of the broad character of West European party systems. Finally, we look at the fringe of West European countries in which liberal parties are, more or less, missing. In comparative politics the missing case is an important test of generalisations.

In this wide-ranging exercise, two types of information about parties are left out. The first is their policies. This has only recently come under systematic scrutiny, through the ECPR manifestos project; Hearl (ch. 17) reports on that, and his findings should be regarded as complementary to this chapter.

The other is the electoral support of liberal parties, on which there is now an abundance of both ecological and survey data, summarised in the country chapters of this book. One reason for this omission is the amount of such data; to cover it effectively would enlarge this chapter unduly. The other is a judgement: that liberal parties, as a group, are uniquely not defined by those who characteristically vote for them. Other types of parties are by their nature linked with the groups they arose to defend or to emancipate. Liberal parties did not arise in this fashion because of the nature of liberalism, though in practice they only flourished and survived because they found particular supportive groups. But the fact that their opponents were more sectionally defined meant that these particular areas of support tended to be determined by who those opponents were. Hence while the comparative study of liberal electorates most certainly merits attention, it would be a mistake to make it a starting point for defining liberal parties.

THE ROOTS OF LIBERAL PARTIES

Liberal parties originated in the political conflicts of mid-nineteenth century Europe. Liberal factions, clubs and local organisations appeared, as well as the usage 'party', but no nationwide organisation linking elected members of a parliament with local organisations designed to secure their election under a collective ideological label was formed until the Belgian Liberal Party in 1846. Other countries followed suit, but slowly. Although liberalism was frequently the first challenging political movement, such nationwide liberal organisations were sometimes only formed in response to challenges from social democratic and Christian democratic organisations. For decades liberal was more a label for an intellectual movement than for party organisations in the sense in which we know them today; as a term for parties it has always been somewhat imprecise.

Nevertheless, there was important common ground between European liberals in the mid-nineteenth century. All were concerned with constitutional issues, challenging aristocratic and autocratic forms of government and demanding progress towards responsible parliamentary government and guarantees of such freedoms as that of the press, the principle of rule of law (*Rechtsstaat*) and most generally the concept that obligation to government should derive from citizenship rather than from duty to a monarch. Usually, but not invariably, they were also the movement demanding extension of the franchise; in some countries a distinction between liberalism and radicalism revolves around the extent of this support. Invariably, they also challenged any religious basis of government, whether from a rationalist viewpoint or that of dissenting minority churches. Secularism, therefore, sometimes allied with non-conformism, was another common hallmark of liberal parties.

Liberalism was also the creed of the newly emerging bourgeoisie of the early nineteenth century, and therefore widely associated with the new capitalism. But although economic liberalism was a major component in the character of many liberal parties, it was not so clearly a distinguishing hallmark. In some countries liberal constitutional demands received more support in the countryside and among the peasantry, and liberalism became allied to agrarian interests, as in Scandinavia. Generally liberalism went with free trade but where national interests dictated otherwise liberals were capable of being protectionists, as for instance the French radicals (on behalf of agrarian interests) and some German liberals (reflecting German industrial needs). In contrast, 'free trade' remained the rallying cry of the British Liberal Party up to the mid-twentieth century. Defining parties by their economic attitudes during their formative period reflects, therefore, differing national contexts.

The significance for the analysis of contemporary political parties of this historic common ground has generally received little attention from political scientists. Von Beyme (1985) is the first analyst of political parties to use historic ideology as the basis of his classification. He points out the significant fact that liberal and radical parties were the first of the main *familles spirituelles* amongst political parties, conservative parties being formed in reaction to them (p. 31). His discussion of political parties distinguishes a series of families which arose in sequence – liberal and radical parties (acknowledging a distinction between the two, but arguing that it was clearer in some countries than others), conservative parties, socialist and social democratic parties, Christian democratic parties and communist parties – along with some smaller, more recent groups.

Historians of liberalism offer a broader view. Salvadori (1977), or a classic work such as de Ruggiero (1927), by concentrating on the constitutional ideas of liberalism tend to see all modern democratic parties as inheritors of nineteenth-century liberalism. In that sense all social democratic, liberal and Christian democratic parties today are liberal; only a few such as extreme right-wing, communist and perhaps the French Gaullist parties are not covered by the term. Clearly this is not a useful way of categorising contemporary political parties. Von Beyme's approach is much more useful for our purpose. He provides a table of electoral support over long periods for groups of political parties, thus acknowledging that whilst his categorisation is based on ideology, continuity in electoral terms is the link between contemporary parties and their historic roots.

A very different approach is to be found in Seiler (1980). This has significantly only been published in French, and one of the problems of comparing his highly distinctive contribution to the classification of political parties with others is that political terms such as liberal, conservative and radical carry different connotations in English and French. Seiler attacks the practice of taking at face value the labels that parties use and is particularly scathing about treating political parties called 'liberal' as a group. He argues for a classification of parties based on the cleavage system proposed by Lipset and Rokkan (1967) and with rigorous logic derives from their four cleavages seven types of party (one theoretically possible type, the urban opponents of agrarian parties, does not occur):

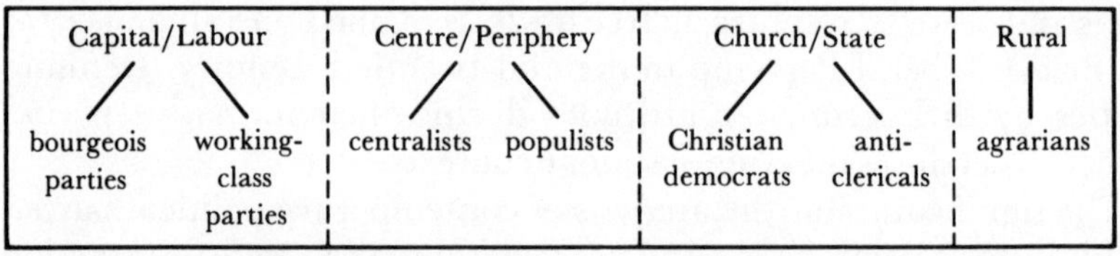

Diagram 16.1 Seiler's cleavage-based party families

A major weakness in his approach is that his cleavage-derived categories are exclusive, so that for instance a bourgeois anti-clerical party has to be either bourgeois or anti-clerical, often an impossible judgement. The consequence is that what others have seen as liberal parties are scattered over six out of the seven categories. Seiler does not, therefore, provide a list – or a definition – of liberal parties comparable with other political scientists. He does, however, offer an alternative approach to the classification of those parties derived, like von Beyme, systematically from their origins but based on cleavage analysis rather than ideology.

Over the last two decades the Lipset and Rokkan cleavage-system approach to understanding the pattern of political parties in Western Europe has proved fruitful and provocative. It is particularly challenging for the study of liberal parties since it is not clear how such parties occur within the Lipset and Rokkan model and the assertion, whether by themselves or by political scientists, that liberal parties are a meaningful group appears to run counter to the cleavage approach.

This is clearly evident if we look at how Seiler has classified liberal parties. They appear most frequently under his 'bourgeois' heading – including those in Belgium, Denmark (both Venstre and the Radicals), Finland, Germany, Great Britain, Greece (the Centre Union), Italy (PLI only), the Netherlands and Sweden. In a few cases (Greece and the Netherlands) they are identified as the main bourgeois party; in most cases (e.g. Germany, Great Britain and Sweden) there are other, usually stronger, bourgeois parties. One liberal party (the French MRG) is identified as a working-class party, although it used to refer to itself as being the bourgeois salt in the Union of the Left. Other liberal parties are placed in terms of the centre – periphery cleavage of politics. The Austrian FPÖ and the Swiss Radicals are identified as centralists; the Norwegian Liberals as populists. The Italian Republicans and Luxemburg Democrats appear as anti-clericals and the Icelandic Progressives as an agrarian party. One could debate very much the details of this classification (e.g., why is Danish Venstre not agrarian?); the point in quoting it in detail, however, is to illustrate the immense problems of applying this approach to liberal parties rather than discussing Seiler's precise solution.

The Lipset and Rokkan scheme is one of the alliances and opposition that could be formed by the choices made by nation-building elites. They do not allow for a cleavage around issues of participation and constitutional reform and so do not allow for a choice on the constitutional front. But just as nation-building elites had to make choices on other fronts, so they had to on the constitutional question. In some countries liberalism became the creed of the nation-building elite; in others, liberalism was the creed of an opposition to it. Thus, it is natural that liberal parties should appear either side of the Lipset and Rokkan nation-builder versus peripheral protest cleavage. Similarly, just as nation-building elites made choices between urban and rural alliances, so did liberal elites. The one early alliance ruled out by the nature of liberalism was with the Catholic church, hence wherever the secular–clerical cleavage arose liberals were on the side of secularism. In due course, as the capital – labour cleavage arose liberals were on the side of capital, opposed by the new working-class, socialist parties.

As they set it out, Lipset and Rokkan do not predict the existence or occurrence of liberal parties. But once it is acknowledged that an additional conflict at the period of party formation was that represented by the liberal thrust for constitutional reform, one can readily see how liberal parties fit into their scheme. Two conclusions derive from this. First that one defining characteristic of a liberal party today is essentially a negative one of being neither socialist nor clerical. Secondly, that otherwise liberal parties can have acquired from their origins a variety of other alliances and hence have always had a degree of heterogeneity.

THE MUTUAL RECOGNITION SYSTEMS

Nineteenth-century liberal parties did not find the need for any transnational organisations. There was a weak *entente* between liberal, radical and similar parties in the period between the two World Wars but co-operation between liberal parties only acquired an enduring framework with the establishment in 1947 of the Liberal International (LI). This, in the words of the opening clause of its constitution 'is an association of parties, groups and individuals throughout the world', though it has been in practice largely confined to Western Europe. The World Federation of Liberal and Radical Youth (WFLRY) was established at the same time in parallel, but with complete autonomy as to decisions on membership. Similarly in practice a Europe-wide rather than a world-wide body, its title now commences with 'International' (hence IFLRY). There used to be a distinct Liberal Students International which broke up in 1960 with its members joining WFLRY. Henceforward WFLRY/IFLRY has consisted of political youth and student organisations, usually but not necessarily those recognised by and attached to a political party.

Unlike the exclusive principle of the Socialist International, LI always recognised the possibility of having more than one member party in a country, and WFLRY/IFLRY followed suit. LI statutes, however, used to allow an existing member organisation to veto a new application (clause 9); this right of veto was removed at the 1986 LI congress in Hamburg. IFLRY simply recognises the right of every national youth and student organisation which agrees with the 'Liberal and Radical Manifesto' drawn up by IFLRY to apply for membership. LI was founded around such a manifesto (the Liberal Manifesto of Oxford, 1947) to which it has subsequently added and which is also regarded as a test for potential adherents. There are thus several sources of possible difference between LI and IFLRY – LI's groups of individuals; political youth or student organisations without a party; a different decision over whether to seek membership as between a national party and its youth or student organisations; a different attitude towards prospective members on the part of the international organisation, whether reflecting a collective view or a national veto; or a different collective view as to what is liberalism (or liberalism and radicalism). Any of these may register uncertainties as to what a liberal party has been considered to be over the last forty years.

LI's system of groups was a particularly interesting form of handling such problems. At its formation LI sought to cover as many Western democracies as possible, and wherever it did not find a liberal party ready to join immediately, it sought to identify individuals who would form a special group, whether the more internationally-minded members of a liberal party, the more liberal members within a dubious party, or members of more than one party or of none. As it developed, LI became more an organisation of parties, preferring to involve party leaderships directly instead of self-selected clubs of internationalists within parties. In some countries, groups survive alongside a member party as just such clubs. But where LI continued to have only a group it has tended to reflect a question mark over a party.

Thus, although LI was formed at a meeting in Britain, at Oxford, and located its headquarters in London, the British Liberal Party was not a founder-member. In 1947 there had been not only the Liberal Party to consider but the Liberal Nationals, a parliamentary scission from the Liberal Party, most of whom were to end up in the Conservative Party. A few, however, did return to their original political home (the Liberal leader from 1945 to 1956 was one who had done so a few years earlier) and more to the point in the 1940s, there were mainstream British Liberals who hoped that others would do so. The British group conveniently opened its door to both Liberals and Liberal Nationals, though the latter (renamed National Liberals and formally allied with the Conservative Party in the same year that LI was founded) rapidly dwindled into insignificance. The British Liberal Party formally joined LI in 1955 and the British group became simply a club (to which one leading ex-Liberal Conservative cabinet minister continued to pay his subscription until his death).

The German Liberal Party, the FDP, did not join formally until 1975, by which time the fact that such a leading liberal party was only officially involved in LI through a group of individuals was highly anomalous. Earlier, however, it reflected the strong doubts about the presence within the FDP of former Nazis, and of the liberal credentials of the party itself, doubts which were stirred in the mid-fifties by the attachment to the FDP of the German nationalist campaign in the Saar and a decade after that by the attitude it took towards the statute of limitations on war crimes. The German group of LI, initially led by a pre-World War II liberal of impeccable anti-Nazi credentials (he fled Germany in 1936 and spent the war in Britain) who did not get involved in national politics again, was for a period a means of involving leading figures from the FDP without their party (see MacCallum Scott (1967) for an account of these difficulties).

Today, LI prefers to operate through parties wherever it can and is able to do so throughout Western Europe except in Catalonia and, until 1986, in France; the continued role of groups in these two cases has been a good indicator of the problematic nature of the classification of any party there as liberal, as it was earlier elsewhere.

Though LI's and WFLRY/IFLRY's identification of liberal parties largely coincides, their collective character has diverged. There has always been a tendency for youth and student organisations to be somewhat to the left of parent liberal parties, a not unusual phenomenon in politics. But for the first two decades of the two bodies' life, LI and WFLRY were not markedly out of political step. In both there was a clear difference between the more conservative continental liberal parties and the more progressive Anglo-Scandinavian ones, with the former predominant but not overwhelmingly so. In the late sixties the balance in WFLRY began to tilt leftwards, encouraged initially by the radicalisation of the German member organisations (which partly reflected the switch of coalition partners made by the FDP, and partly the general radicalisation of German youth), and confirmed later by new member organisations from southern Europe. Today IFLRY has a distinctly different internal political balance to that of LI and provides therefore an independent test of liberal credentials.

Another transnational liberal body which had diverged a little from LI's definition was the Liberal and Allies group in the nominated European Parliament where the allies even included at one time the French Gaullists and the neo-fascist MSI. Unlike the Socialist and Christian Democrat groups in the parliament, this group did not develop an extraparliamentary structure to link the parties which participated in it, an absence which avoided the problem of whether some of the parties concerned would have accepted some of the others. As direct elections approached, the initiative to forming a European Community-wide organisation of liberal parties was taken at the 1972 Liberal International congress and in due course the Federation of Liberal and Democratic Parties of the European Community (usually known more briefly as European

Liberals and Democrats, ELD) was formed in 1976. As this federation was intended to be a more integrated body, designed to produce an effective common effort at European parliamentary elections, it could not afford a casual or incremental approach to determining its membership. In January 1976, a meeting of the leaders of the LI member parties in the Community, together with the leader of the group in the European Parliament, decided on a list of parties to be invited to a launching meeting in Stuttgart in March, and these potential founder-parties were accorded the right, by the terms of the invitation, to take up membership at any stage up to the first congress of ELD, held at The Hague in November 1976. The addition of the 'democratic' epithet at Stuttgart was intended to open the federation up to parties with misgivings about the word 'liberal', and the discussion about the federation's name was the most lively debate at the launching meeting. In the end all the invited parties decided to take up membership, but as there were clear political incompatibilities between the three French parties, one of them withdrew dramatically at the congress (Steed (1982) 178–9). This meant that the French membership of ELD diverged from LI's, reflecting instead the composition of the European parliamentary group.

For ten years ELD and LI offered strikingly different views as to which were liberal parties in France. The modern embodiment of the French conservative tradition, the Parti Républicain, had been the strongest element within the European Parliament's Liberal group since the Gaullists left in 1963. They became the largest party within ELD, along with one of the two small splinters formed out of the declining French Radical Party. The PR tentatively applied to join LI but was vetoed by the existing member organisation, a group which after the split in the Radical Party continued to combine its two wings. In 1986, LI moved to resolve the situation and encouraged interested political parties in France to apply for direct membership. With the support of the French member group, the two radical parties applied for membership; but shortly before the opening of the Hamburg LI congress in October, they learnt that the PR had also applied, with the support of the LI executive committee. The veto being abolished at the same congress, the MRG withdrew its application and the French member group withdrew from LI in December 1986.

With the enlargement of the Community to include the new Mediterranean democracies, ELD faced the need to find new partners in countries where identification of liberal parties was problematic. The outcome was a very uneven expansion, with tiny parties in Greece and Spain joining readily and after some hesitation a large party in Portugal (larger in terms of its share of the national vote than any existing member party) which requested some changes in ELD to accommodate itself. One was an even clumsier title, with 'reformist' added; the new name, European Liberals, Democrats and Reformists, was adopted at the 1986 congress, held significantly in the Mediterranean, at Catania. Thus ELDR now defines a family of liberal parties within the twelve countries of the European Community whose composition reflects a further set of influences particular to its own history and only indirectly derived from the LI family.

There is also a youth organisation for liberal parties within the European Community, the Liberal and Radical Youth Movement of the European Community (LYMEC). Since membership of LYMEC is confined to member organisations of IFLRY (unlike the LI–ELDR relationship), it does not provide a fully independent test.

THE LIST OF LIBERAL PARTIES

Not all books on West European politics or on political parties offer a listing of liberal, or other, parties. The first to do so seems to have been Henig ((1969) 516) which classified the parties in the fifteen parliamentary democracies under ten ideological or functional labels. Henig seems to have constructed his table on the basis that each country could have only one party of each type. He did not define his liberal category precisely, but implied that it comprises parties either with the word 'liberal' in their title, or claiming a liberal tradition; he noted that the category appears almost universal in Europe (save Iceland and Ireland).

Three years afterwards the first edition of Smith appeared. This has held its own as the leading comprehensive textbook on West European politics through four editions, each thoroughly revised. Smith (1972) covered the full fifteen countries, with Greece, Spain and Portugal added later as their parties were able to participate in parliamentary elections. He started with ten headings, which became eleven in Smith (1983) with the addition of a 'new politics' (post-materialist) category. The most significant difference between his labels and Henig's is that Smith divided the liberal parties into two, 'liberal-radical' and 'liberal-conservative'; the main difference in method is that Smith tried hard to cover all parties in each system, and to fit them into his headings, with no compunction about recognising that more than one party may fit in a cell. He was particularly prone to move some of the more difficult parties around, and this, plus the availability of two liberal categories, means that several parties made a fleeting appearance as liberal in one edition. In the first three editions he also placed some difficult parties under two adjoining headings and thus created a special transitional category of parties which could be considered as conservative or as liberal-conservative or as both at once. Because the liberal-conservative and liberal-radical columns were not adjacent, his layout did not permit that solution to the evident problem he had in placing some liberal parties.

The virtue of Smith's approach is that it is essentially pragmatic, making sense of the parties of Western Europe in terms of a mixture of observations of their names, their social bases, their traditions and their behaviour, with no overriding criterion. However, he saw the critical distinction between liberal-radical and liberal-conservative as best gauged from the alliances made by a liberal party (a view modified in ch. 2 of this book). This meant that the placing of a party could reflect that party's own inclinations, as revealed through its preferences for coalition partners – or it could be a misleading product of the relative sizes of competing parties and their willingness to ally with it. Thus, the coalition between the Austrian FPÖ and Austrian Socialist Party should not be held to determine that the FPÖ is more radical than the Norwegian Venstre, which has only formed a recent coalition with the Norwegian Conservatives; on almost every other test Venstre is a much more radical liberal party than the FPÖ.

Lane and Ersson (1987) adopt a rather different approach. Their analysis of cleavages and social structure offers a more systematic basis for classification of political parties and they claim (p. 101) that liberal parties can be identified by ideology, label and international co-operation. They provide an undifferentiated list of liberal parties, which appears in reality to be as pragmatic as Smith's – and includes two curiosities (the Danish Centre Democrats and Irish Fianna Fáil) neither of which are liberal by label, ideology or international co-operation.

We now bring together the evidence that we have so far considered. Table 16.1 (see pp. 408–9) sets out the evidence for the thirteen countries which are covered by individual chapters in this book. It is no coincidence that these comprise the countries of Western Europe with continuous existence of political parties since the very beginning of the twentieth century and more usually since the latter part of the nineteenth century. As the table shows, the various sources concur to a high degree as to which are the liberal parties. Nineteen parties (marked **) are clearly liberal on every, or all but one, test. There have long been some doubts about the Austrian FPÖ and the Danish Venstre, due respectively to the FPÖ's hybrid origin (see p. 408) and

Table 16.1 *Liberal parties in Western Europe*

Country	Party	Historic roots	Membership of: LI	ELDR	IFLRY	Classified by: Smith (1972–83)[f]	Henig (1969)[j]	von Beyme (1985)[k]	Lane and Ersson (1987)[m]
Austria	FPÖ**	Liberal/ nationalist	Yes	n.a.	Yes	Conservative (I)[g] Liberal-Conservative (II, III, IV)	Liberal	Liberal	Liberal
Belgium (Flemish)	PVV**	Liberal	Yes	Yes	Yes[d]	Liberal-Conservative	Liberal	Liberal	Liberal
Belgium (Francophone)	PRL**	Liberal/ regionalist	Yes	Yes	Yes(?)[d]	Liberal-Conservative	Liberal	Liberal	Liberal
Denmark	Venstre**	Liberal	Yes	Yes	Yes	Liberal-Conservative	Agrarian	Liberal	Rural
	RV**	Liberal	Yes	No[b]	Yes	Liberal-Radical	Liberal	Liberal	Liberal
Finland	Liberal People's**	Liberal	Yes	n.a.	Yes	Liberal-Conservative (I, II) Liberal-Radical (III, IV)	Liberal	Liberal	Liberal
	Swedish People's	Nationalist	Yes	n.a.	No	Ethnic/regional	Ethnic	Not listed	Ethnic
	Centre	Agrarian	Observer	n.a.	No	Centre/agrarian	Agrarian	Not listed	Rural
France	UDF, combining since 1978:		No	No	No	Conservative/Liberal-Conservative (III)[h] Liberal-Conservative (IV)	n.a.	see note [l] (France, all UDF rows)	Not listed
	PR*	Conservative	Yes[a]	Yes	No	Conservative (I, II)	Conservative		Conservative
	CDS	Christian democratic	No	No	No	Christian (I) Centre/agrarian (II)[i] (CDS and PRS)	Christian		Religious
	PRS**	Liberal	Yes[a]	Yes	No	Liberal-Radical (I) Liberal-Radical (II, III, IV) (PRS and MRG)	Liberal (PRS and MRG)		Liberal
	MRG**	Liberal	No[a]	No[c]	Yes				Liberal

Germany	FDP**	Liberal	Yes	Yes	Yes	Liberal-Conservative (I, IV) Liberal-Radical (II, III)	Liberal	Liberal	Liberal
Great Britain	Liberal**	Liberal	Yes	Yes	Yes	Liberal-Radical	Liberal	Liberal	Liberal
Italy	PLI**	Liberal	Yes	Yes	Yes	Liberal-Conservative	Liberal	Liberal	Liberal
	PRI**	Liberal	No	Yes	Yes	Liberal-Radical	Not listed	Liberal	Liberal
	Radical*	Liberal	No	No	Indirect[e]	Liberal-Radical (III) New Politics (IV)	Not listed	Not listed	Environ-mental
Luxemburg	Democratic**	Liberal	Yes	Yes	Yes	Liberal-Conservative (I, II) Liberal-Radical (III, IV)	Liberal	Not listed	Not listed
Netherlands	VVD**	Liberal	Yes	Yes	Yes	Liberal-Conservative	Liberal	Liberal	Liberal
	D'66*	Modern	Observer	No	Yes	Liberal-Radical	Protest	Liberal	Liberal
Norway	Venstre**	Liberal	Yes	n.a.	Yes	Liberal-Conservative	Liberal	Liberal	Liberal
	People's**	Liberal	Yes	n.a.	Yes	Liberal-Conservative (II) Liberal-Radical (III)	Liberal	Liberal	Liberal
Sweden	Fp**	Liberal	Yes	n.a.	Yes	Liberal-Conservative	Liberal	Liberal	Liberal
Switzerland	FDP**	Liberal	Yes	n.a.	Yes	Liberal-Conservative	Liberal	Liberal	Liberal
	LPS**	Liberal	Yes	n.a.	?	Liberal-Conservative	Not listed	Not listed	Liberal

[a] The French member of LI until 1986, 'Liberté et Démocratie', was based on the group in the French senate, Gauche démocratique, which has continued to combine senators from PRS and MRG since the 1972 split in the Radical Party. In 1986 the PR and PRS joined the Liberal International directly; the MRG which had applied withdrew its application, and the French 'Liberté et Démocratie' group withdrew from membership.'

[b] RV was a founder-member of ELD, present at both the launching meeting (Stuttgart, March 1976) and the first congress (The Hague, November 1976); in his statement of adherence, subject to confirmation, its leader, Hilmar Baunsgaard, explained at Stuttgart that his party saw membership of ELD as a continuation of its long involvement with LI. Membership was confirmed, on a contested vote, and the party attended the first congress (The Hague, November 1976) but it did not participate in the drafting of a common electoral programme for the European parliamentary elections and at its next national congress in September 1977, RV decided to withdraw from ELD; opponents of membership argued that the draft ELD

programme involved an unacceptable commitment to political integration which the party, always lukewarm about Danish membership of the European Community, had consistently opposed.

[c] MRG was a founder-member of ELD but its delegation walked out of the first congress; it regarded itself as an observer for a further year before formally withdrawing from membership.

[d] Of the four Belgian student and youth organisations only the Flemish students are full members of IFLRY. The Flemish and Francophone youth organisations are observer members but the Francophone youth has not participated in the congress since 1981. The Francophone students have no link with IFLRY but are linked to the international conservative student organisation.

[e] Centro Italiano di Critica Liberale is a member of IFLRY. This is a left-liberal political club, several of whose members are active in the Partito Radicale.

[f] The four editions of Smith are referred to by Roman numerals – I (1972), II (1976), III (1980) and IV (1983). Where no numerals are indicated, the classification is consistent across the four editions; no mention indicates that Smith does not include the party – e.g. the Norwegian People's Party had not been formed by 1972, and was presumably considered too insignificant by 1983.

In addition to the parties listed Smith also classifies the following parties in the countries covered in this table under the liberal heading: Denmark: Retsforbundet liberal-radical in Smith (I) only; Italy: PSDI liberal-radical in Smith (II) and (IV); liberal-conservative in (III); Great Britain: SDP liberal-radical (IV); Netherlands: PPR liberal-radical in all editions.

[g] Smith (I) places the FPÖ across two columns, ultra-right and conservative.

[h] Smith (III) placed both the UDF and the Gaullist RPR across two columns, conservative and liberal-conservative.

[i] Mouvement réformateur, which temporarily united the CDS and PRS.

[j] Derived from Table II (p. 516) of Henig (1969).

[k] Derived mainly from Table 2.1 in von Beyme (1985), which lists votes cast for liberal parties. Von Beyme also lists conservative (Table 2.2) and Christian democrat parties (Table 2.4) but does not list agrarian or regional/ethnic parties.

[l] Von Beyme's listings in France are unclear and incomplete. Up to 1962 the CDS's predecessor is listed as Christian and the PRS as liberal, but the PR's predecessor is not listed. From 1962 to 1973 the PR's predecessor's vote is included in the conservative listing, and no party is listed as liberal or Christian. In 1978 the UDF and MRG are both listed as liberal, while the 1981 entry is not clear.

[m] Derived from Table 3.7 (p. 102). In addition to the parties listed, Lane and Ersson also classify the following parties in the countries covered in this table under the liberal heading: Denmark: Retsforbundet and Centre Democrats; Switzerland: the Alliance of Independents.

to the Venstre's strong agrarian base, which makes it in electoral, but no other, terms more like a Scandinavian centre party (see p. 408). More recently, the merger of the conservative wing of the Walloon Rally with the French-speaking wing of the classic Belgian Liberal Party has produced another hybrid party which has shown more than one sign of putting one foot into the conservative family of political parties whilst keeping the other still in the liberal family (see p. 408); the behaviour of this party's youth and student movement is perhaps the firmest indicator.

There are three parties in the list which are clearly not liberal parties. The French CDS is only present because of its link with two other parties in the UDF and, despite Frears's treatment of the UDF as liberal in ch. 6, every other authority treats this party as Christian democratic – which is where its members sit in the European Parliament. The entry of the Finnish Centre Party into observer status in the Liberal International in 1983 may be a forerunner of the expansion of LI to include the Scandinavian agrarian parties; the presence of the Danish Venstre and of the Icelandic Progressives (see p. 401) make this entry all the easier. The Swedish People's Party is a more difficult case since it is a full member of LI; but it is not liberal upon any other test. The party is in reality a composite party with distinct agrarian, conservative and liberal elements within it, and its adhesion to the Liberal International may be a reflection of the fact that neither the agrarian nor the conservative parties have set up as useful an international forum for it to join. It is interestingly similar to the Catalonian nationalist group, the CiU, which is discussed on p. 427. In addition, there are half a dozen parties which either Smith or Lane and Ersson list as liberal (see notes *f* and *m*); significantly only one of these, the tiny Retsforbundet, appears in both their lists. Mention should also be made of the Alliance Party of Northern Ireland, newly formed in 1970 without historic roots, which has deliberately avoided ideological identification in its attempt to build a non-sectarian force in Northern Irish politics. The Alliance Party joined ELD in 1983, with a view to the European parliamentary elections, but has not joined LI and is nowhere classified as liberal.

Thus, there are quite a number of mainly small parties which can for only one purpose be considered liberal but are ruled out by the other tests. There remain only three genuinely marginal cases (marked *), where changes in the contemporary character and international alliances of a political party raise more difficult questions. If the French right can be divided into three traditions – legitimist, Orleanist, and Bonapartist (Rémond (1968)) – then clearly the Giscardian PR should be considered to be in the Orleanist line of descendancy (Bourricaud (1977)). At any rate, most observers today assign the Parti Républicain to the conservative camp, including the most recent (Lane and Ersson). The matter is complicated by the French use of the word 'liberal' which was used by a clerical party – Action Libérale Populaire – at the beginning of this century, since the secular forces were grouped under the 'radical' title; 'liberal' in France has subsequently never carried quite the same meaning as it does in English, Dutch, German or Italian, or even in French-speaking Belgium. The PR's controversial entry into ELD (Steed (1982) 178–9) and in 1986 into LI does not, therefore, mean that it considers itself liberal in the sense in which other parties do, although it does now undeniably accept that label. The PR is probably best seen as a conservative party which has one foot, only firmly placed in 1986, in the right wing of the liberal camp and whose future identity is still open to question – but whose size is such that the more it comes into the liberal camp, the more the liberal camp will be moved to the right.

The other two marginal parties are both small and on the radical or the left wing of the liberal camp. D'66 initially regarded itself as closer to the socialist parties and its first appointed MEPs sat in the Socialist group, though in the 1979 directly-elected parliament they sat as *non-inscrits*, with both seats lost in 1984. A D'66 youth movement was formed in 1983 and took the first steps into the Liberal family through observer membership of IFLRY in 1985. By acquiring observer status in the LI in 1986, D'66 appears to be accepting the classification which most political scientists now give it. The Italian Partito Radicale, which undeniably sprang from a liberal tradition, has been moving in the opposite direction and the change between Smith (1980) and Smith (1983) is a reasonable reflection of that movement. Pridham (see p. 30) gives good reasons for no longer considering it as liberal; yet the indirect link it retains with the Liberal camp through IFLRY is evidence that its identity is yet to be firmly established.

LIBERAL PARTIES IN POLITICAL SPACE

We have established that the historical, ideological and empirical approaches produce a list of liberal parties very close to that established by the test of mutual recognition and fitting, though less neatly, into the cleavage approach to party systems. We now turn to see how far that list of liberal parties makes sense in terms of current research into the character of party systems. The left–right dimension has long been seen as a useful analytical tool in political science. Even

Downs (1957), the arch-exponent of a de-ideologised 'economic' view of democracy, suggested that the voting decisions of the electorate are conditioned, on the one hand, by their own self-placement and, on the other hand, by their placement of the parties on a left–right continuum. Several approaches to the empirical measurement of ideology have been attempted by political scientists (Barnes (1966)), but the fact remains that the most widely-used approach has long remained based upon the familiar left–right continuum (Converse (1964)). Coalition theorists have also used a left–right categorisation of parties (de Swaan (1973) 132–43); so, too, research on voting behaviour has employed the left–right dimension as an adjunct to the more traditional party identification approach (Inglehart and Klingemann (1976)). Whilst remaining suspicious of the left–right dimension – calling it the 'layman's index of politics' and pointing out that in reality it is a 'hopelessly multidimensional dimension' – Sartori ((1976) 78–9) has admitted that 'it appears to be the most detectable and constant way in which not only mass publics but also elites perceive politics'.

In fact, a good case could be made for arguing that political elites are more likely to perceive politics in such ideological terms. There would seem to be two distinctly different elite perceptions of left–right placings of parties which we might explore: the self-placement (whether of themselves or their parties) of those involved actively in parties, and the placement of parties as seen by those, like political scientists and political journalists, who perform a key role in communicating views about political parties to the wider public.

It is therefore surprising, and disappointing, that there is so little systematic data available for the classification of political parties in these terms. Nevertheless, we are able to refer to one very useful study, namely the survey of party activists known as the 'middle-level elites survey', organised by the European Elections Study team directed from the University of Mannheim in 1978–9 (unfortunately this survey was restricted to the nine states that were members of the European Community at that time). Most liberal parties were covered by this survey but it is unfortunate that three more left-wing liberal parties, the MRG, the PRI and the RV, were not. For most liberal parties in the nine community countries, therefore, this survey provides a measure of how party activists perceived their position.

Another entirely different approach has been adopted by two political scientists, Castles and Mair (1984), who conducted a survey of leading political scientists' classifications of parties on the left–right scale. This survey omitted some smaller countries, and in some other cases the number of respondents was suspiciously small. It has the

Table 16.2 *Left–right placings (1): Liberal, Christian democratic, conservative and social democratic/labour parties covered by* both *surveys*

	Activists	Experts	Adjusted figures for experts	Difference
Liberal (GB)	4.1	5.0	5.6	+1.5
FDP (FRG)	4.9	5.1	5.6	+0.7
PRL (Belgium)	6.0	7.6	7.8	+1.8
PVV (Belgium)	6.4	7.8	8.0	+1.6
VVD (Netherlands)	6.5	7.4	7.7	+1.2
Venstre (Denmark)	6.9	6.7	7.0	+0.1
Liberal average	5.7	6.5	6.9	+1.2
DC (Italy)	4.1	5.4	5.9	+1.8
CVP (Belgium)	6.0	5.8	6.2	+0.2
PSC (Belgium)	6.1	6.3	6.7	+0.6
CDU (FRG)	6.2	6.7	7.0	+0.8
CSU (Bavaria)	6.6	7.9	8.1	+1.5
CD average	5.8	6.4	6.8	+1.0
Conservative (GB)	7.6	7.8	8.0	+0.4
Conservative (Denmark)	7.9	7.3	7.6	−0.3
Conservative average	7.8	7.6	7.8	0.0
PSB (Belgium)	2.2	2.5	3.2	+1.0
BSP (Belgium)	2.4	2.9	3.6	+1.2
DSI (Italy)	2.7	3.1	3.8	+1.1
PvdA (Netherlands)	2.8	2.6	3.3	+0.5
Labour (Ireland)	2.9	3.6	4.2	+1.3
PS (France)	3.0	2.6	3.3	+0.3
Labour (GB)	3.6	2.3	3.1	−0.5
SPD (FRG)	3.6	3.3	4.0	+0.4
SD (Denmark)	3.8	3.8	4.4	+0.6
Social democratic/Labour average	3.0	3.0	3.7	+0.7
D'66 (Netherlands)	4.0	4.4	5.0	+1.0

advantages, however, of opposing experts' perceptions of party positions to activists' perceptions and of covering certain non-EC countries (Austria, Norway, Sweden, Finland, but not Switzerland).

Attention has also to be drawn to an important technical difference in the measurements incorporated in data from these two surveys. The middle-level elites survey adopted the ten-point scale (from 1 to 10), in common with the *Eurobaromètres* and much of the other research into the left–right dimension of politics. The mid-point on

Table 16.3 *Left–right placings (2): Countries covered by only* one *survey*

	Social democratic	Liberal	Christian democratic	Conservative
Austria[a]	3.7 (SPÖ)	7.1 (FPÖ)	6.2 (ÖVP)	—
Finland[a]	3.7 (SDP)	6.0 (LKP)	—	7.5 (KOK)
Norway[a]	3.7 (DNA)	4.6 (V)	—	7.9 (H)
Sweden[a]	3.6 (SD)	6.0 (FP)	—	7.9 (M)
Luxemburg[b]	2.4 (LSAP)	5.4 (DP)	7.4 (CSV)	—

[a] Derived from the Castles and Mair experts survey and adjusted, as above, to match the figure of the middle-level elites survey.
[b] Middle-level elites survey.

this scale, therefore, falls half-way between 5 and 6. However, Castles and Mair chose to adopt an eleven-point scale (from 0 to 10), with a corresponding mid-point exactly at 5. There is, therefore, a discrepancy between the two scales which requires mathematical adjustment to make them strictly comparable. In this case, the Castles and Mair findings have been adjusted to accord with the more widely used ten-point scale of the middle-level elites survey.

Table 16.2 compares the findings of these two surveys in the eight countries covered by both, looking only at parties in the main social democrat/labour, Christian democrat, conservative or liberal families together with one party on the fringe of the Liberal family (D'66). There is a systematic difference between activists' and experts' placements, except for the two conservative parties, which suggests that political activists in liberal and Christian democrat parties tend to share with their socialist or social democrat counterparts a tendency to see themselves as more progressive than their parties appear in practice to the cold eye of the political scientist. It is striking, indeed, how similar this discrepancy is. Its consistency provides, curiously, confirmation that the two different elites are perceiving, although from slightly different angles, essentially the same phenomenon. It confirms that the distances between groups of parties and the variations within each group are picking up something real in the shape of party systems. We conclude that the data is useful for analysis, providing that it is treated more as a measure of distance between neighbouring parties rather than as some absolute measure of position.

This finding gives us the confidence to introduce the data from the five countries covered by only one of these two surveys, which is shown in Table 16.3. Together, these two tables provide us with data from fourteen out of the fifteen countries in which liberal parties were listed in Table 16.1 above and provide us with a measurement of the distances between those liberal parties and the main competing parties in their national party systems, as well as – as we have laid out the tables – some measures of average positions for groups of parties.

It is also possible, from these tables, to compare the cross-national consistency between the placings of parties of the same political family. It is clear that social democrat/labour and conservative parties (of whom, admittedly, there are fewer) appear to be more similar across national boundaries than do either liberal or Christian democratic parties. However, the diversity amongst liberal parties is not so great as to undermine a view that they have something in common, whilst the closeness of positions between liberal parties and Christian democratic parties and their tendency to be sometimes to the right and sometimes to the left of one another in different countries raises a major question: why does left–right placing distinguish other families of parties so clearly but fail to distinguish these two families?

We conclude that there is a clear pattern, namely a difference between the Anglo-Scandinavian party systems, on the one hand, and the continental party systems, on the other. In the British and Scandinavian systems the liberal parties occupy a clear ideological space between the social democratic parties to the left and the conservative parties to the right. By contrast, in continental party systems, the overlapping positions of liberal and Christian democratic parties suggest that they are competing for much the same ideological space and that whatever divides them is not easily assimilable into the left–right dimension of politics. The positioning of continental liberal and of Christian democratic parties appears to lie somewhere in between that of Anglo-Scandinavian liberal and conservative parties, suggesting that the space for which they are competing effectively envelops the space covered in a different manner by Anglo-Scandinavian liberals and conservatives. We have attempted to indicate this difference diagramatically below. The asterisks indicate what would be the average placement in left–right terms if parties indeed occupied the space shown:

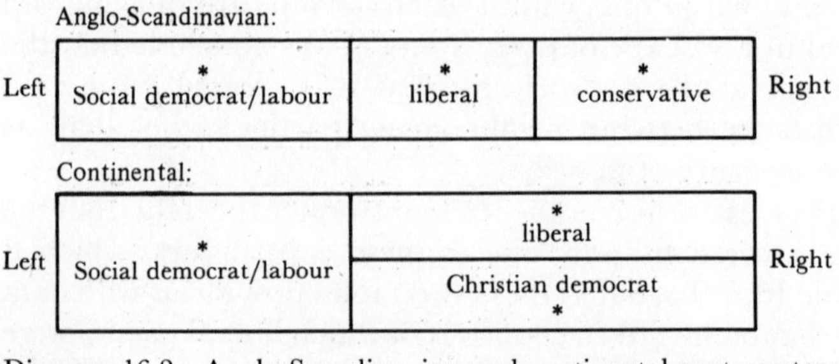

Diagram 16.2 Anglo-Scandinavian and continental party systems

We are not suggesting that this diagram works exactly in each country, rather that the distinction between the two alternative models explains a great deal of the variation in placement of parties on the centre and right of politics. In specific detail, it is clear that the liberal space in some countries is subdivided between competing more left-inclined and more right-inclined parties – e.g. Denmark and Italy. Both France and Germany have in the past had competing conservative, Christian democratic and liberal forces, making them perhaps hybrids between these two models: the re-formed party systems of the Federal Republic of Germany and Fifth Republic France, therefore, do not necessarily fit into either model.

In so far as this contrast between Anglo-Scandinavian and continental models of how parties compete within their systems for space in left–right terms is valid, it suggests that the crucial variable between the two systems is the line, drawn at a right angle to the left–right dimension, which separates off liberal and Christian democratic parties – in other words the secular–clerical cleavage in politics. We believe this to be so, and our conclusion for the study of liberal parties is that this fascinating group of parties cannot be comprehended other than in terms of the presence or absence of this cleavage. The classification of liberal parties into liberal-radical and liberal-conservative parties, which Smith made originally on a purely empirical basis, fits closely to this more theoretical distinction (but see also Smith's modified approach in ch. 2 of this book). It is complicated by the cases of competing liberal parties which do tend to differ from each other on a left–right basis. But where there are only single liberal parties, and where the party systems fit clearly into one of these two models, we suggest as a more meaningful distinction the one between those liberal parties which compete on their right with conservative parties and those which are in competition on both the centre and the right with Christian democratic parties.

The middle-level elites survey also asked opinions on fifteen issues (covering 49 parties this time), allowing us to compare party activists' views on a range of issues. Using a sophisticated statistical technique (stochastic unfolding), van Schuur (1984) came close to confirming (although not exactly) a simple left–right structure to political beliefs. His analysis found the best 'fit' to the pattern of individual responses was provided by introducing a pair of scales. One scale, which he called the 'progressive scale', represented responses in favour of issues supported on the left (e.g. fighting unemployment, reducing income differentials). The other scale, which he called the 'conservative scale', represented responses in favour of right-leaning issues (e.g. stiffer penalties for terrorism, increasing defence expenditure). How each activist scored on these two scales was found to correlate highly with their self-placement on the left–right scale. However, the two scales did not correlate nearly so well with each other, indicating a degree of independence between activists' views on progressive issues and those they hold on conservative ones. Significantly, van Schuur's findings suggest that views in the centre ground of politics may be those most misleadingly portrayed by the use of a single left–right scale.

Unfortunately, van Schuur's work – based on the middle-level elites survey – was also limited to EC countries (in 1978–9). The Scandinavian countries are therefore missing, with the exception of Denmark, which has competing liberal parties, one of which, RV, is also missing. This we have only the British Liberal Party as an example of a party clearly in the Anglo-Scandinavian mould. Van Schuur confirms the pattern shown in the diagram: namely the different patterns of ideological space in the British and continental party system. Moreover, van Schuur's findings suggest that the 'leftness' of the British Liberals is only half of the explanation: the British Conservatives shared the distinction with the Danish Konservative Folksparti (their partner in the European Parliament) of being more right-wing than their continental 'equivalents' (the British Labour Party, on the other hand, is highly comparable to the continental social democratic/socialist parties).

Van Schuur's scores can be used to compare parties across frontiers; this is potentially a more objective comparison than left–right placing since it reflects activists' responses to identical questions about political issues, and the collapsing of these twelve responses into two scales is on the basis of an analysis of the structure common to these responses. It is here that comparing the British Liberal position with others is most striking; in Table 16.4 we show both the party in each country whose activists' score comes closest to the British Liberals' score and the response in that country of the liberal party.

The pictures presented by the two parts of this table are strikingly different. On the conservative scale, the British Liberals, broadly speaking, 'belong' amongst continental social democratic parties – just as they are close to the British Labour Party. Apart from the FDP (and D'66) all continental liberal parties are well to the right of the British position (roughly half-way between British Liberal and Conservative positions). On the progressive scale, however, the British Liberal score is most similar to a variety of parties which are, broadly, just to the right of centre on the simple scale. Continental liberal parties are all slightly less progressive than the British Liberal Party, but only in one case (the VVD) is the difference really significant.

Table 16.4 *Conservative and progressive placings*

Scores on the conservative scale	Nearest to UK Liberal (1.4)		Liberal party score	
Belgium (Flanders)	Social Democratic	1.2	PVV	2.6
Belgium (Wallonia)	Nationalist	1.4	PRL	2.9
Denmark	Social Democratic (PS)	1.3	Venstre	2.8
France	Social Democratic	1.8	(UDF	3.2)
Germany	FDP	1.1	FDP	1.1
Ireland	Social Democratic	1.3	—	—
Italy	Social Democratic (PSI)	1.4	PLI	2.7
Luxemburg	Social Democratic	1.3	DP	2.2
Netherlands	Christian Democratic	1.2	(D'66	0.6)
			VVD	2.1
Scores on the progressive scale	**Nearest to UK Liberal (3.3)**		**Liberal party score**	
Belgium (Flanders)	Christian Democratic	2.8	PVV	2.6
Belgium (Wallonia)	PRL	2.7	PRL	2.7
Denmark	Christian People's	3.2	Venstre	2.4
France	UDF	2.9	—	—
Germany	FDP	2.2	FDP	2.2
Ireland	Fianna Fáil	3.2	—	—
Italy	Christian Democratic	3.5	PLI	2.5
Luxemburg	Christian Democratic	3.5	DP	2.5
Netherlands	D'66	2.9	VVD	1.8

This exercise seems to us to have independently confirmed the problem of comparing Anglo-Scandinavian and continental liberal parties. Britain (and also Scandinavian countries) have a clearly right-wing party; and a liberal party in the centre which is clearly to the left of that party. In the rest of the European Community, Christian democratic, liberal and nationalist parties (e.g. Fianna Fáil, Gaullists) divide on issues and split up both the centre group and the right of politics in ways clearly different to the Anglo-Scandinavian case. Interestingly, the West German Free Democrats are the exception to this dichotomy. The FDP is clearly close to the British Liberal Party, although perhaps significantly to the right of it on some issues (which on closer analysis, not surprisingly, turn out to be economic ones).

This exercise suggests both that there is common ground amongst liberal parties and some important differences between them. They all share some part of the centre space in politics, therefore all have a left wing within themselves which is to the left-of-centre. Some, however, stretch well to the right; others do not. A few lie complicatedly between these two simple cases. We suggest that this distinction, rather than a simple categorisation into more radical and more conservative liberal parties, helps to explain the variety of parties within the Liberal family. Similarly, the existence of some portion of the political space that all liberal parties share helps to explain the way in which they recognise each other as part of the same family. We could think of that space in terms of issues such as human rights or education that tend to bring otherwise different liberal parties together.

THE MISSING CASES

We observed above that the list of countries covered in Table 16.1 comprised those in Western Europe with a long continuous development of political parties. We now turn to a group whose critical common feature is that of relatively late development of their parties, associated with either relatively late state formation or with recent restoration of liberal democratic institutions. Iceland and Ireland only attained independence following the First World War, and their party systems essentially date from that time. Greece, Spain and Portugal have party systems newly developed in the 1970s, although there are some links – especially in Greece – with earlier parties.

It is no coincidence that in none of these countries is there an unequivocal liberal party of any significance. These five missing cases confirm emphatically an interpretation that the presence of liberal parties everywhere in the remainder of Western Europe has to be seen in terms of the historic roots of party systems. However, these five countries are in Western Europe, four of them in the European Community and one in the Nordic Council, and their parties have, particularly in recent years, had to face up to the question of an alignment with parties in the rest of Western Europe in order to take an effective part in transnational parliamentary forums, the European Parliament and the Nordic Council. In consequence, either ELDR or LI now has a member party in four of these countries; only in Ireland has any political party yet to identify itself as part of the liberal family.

That has not prevented some political scientists identifying a liberal party in Ireland, although there is no agreement as to which of the two contending parties is the appropriate case. Fianna Fáil was identified as 'agrarian (?)' by Henig; Smith (1972) and (1976) followed Henig's view but Smith (1980) put the party straddling the conservative and liberal-conservative categories, while Smith (1983) shifted it to conservative. Lane and Ersson have decided to call it a liberal party; in the European parliament it sits with neither Christian democrat nor conservative nor liberal parties but with the similarly nationalist French Gaullists. However, the Fianna Fáil members of the Council of Europe's Parliamentary Assembly switched in 1985 from the Conservative to the Liberal group. As for Fine Gael, Henig and Smith (1972) saw it as conservative; Lane and Ersson place it where it sits in the European Parliament with the Christian democrats, but Smith (1976), (1980) and (1983) decided to call it liberal, though inconsistently as to which sort of liberal party. We consider that no useful purpose is served by a procrustean effort to force either party into the liberal mould. Doing so obscures the significant point about the Irish party system, the complete absence of anything resembling a liberal party in a country where the existence of church–state issues and the nineteenth-century influence of British liberalism might have been expected to produce one of either the continental or the Anglo-Scandinavian type.

The most obvious explanation is the lack of a secular–clerical cleavage in Irish politics in the late nineteenth century. The coincidence of interest between a non-established Catholic church and the modernising nation-builders, who would otherwise have been likely to espouse liberalism, in opposing British, Protestant rule produced – uniquely for Western Europe (but similarly to Poland) – an alliance of Catholicism and nationalism which left no place for a secular liberal nationalism. In so far as this interpretation is correct, the Irish case very specifically confirms the importance of the historic cleavages at the critical period for the development of liberal parties. When the Irish party system developed in the 1920s, it was too late for a liberal party to emerge. This does not imply that the issue-space for a secularising, non-socialist party does not exist in Irish politics; the emergence of the Progressive Democrats at the 1987 election could be interpreted in these terms. What it does imply is that where a historic liberal party did not emerge, typically liberal issues will be handled within other parties, thereby causing confusion to comparative political scientists.

Iceland

Like Ireland, Iceland has two substantial non-socialist parties, each of which can be classified in comparative terms under another heading but either of which might be considered liberal. Historically, the best candidate is the Icelandic Independence Party, formed in 1929 as a merger between a significant conservative party and a tiny liberal one (Elder *et al.* (1982) 48–9 and Kristjánsson (1979) 32–8), but although Smith (1972) placed this party in the straddling conservative/liberal-conservative category, he subsequently, along with most other authorities, including Elder *et al.* (p. 31), sees the party simply as conservative. The alternative, the Icelandic Progressive Party (Framsoknarfokkur) is unanimously classified in political science as an agrarian or rural party, yet by joining the Liberal International in 1983 it consciously gave itself a liberal identity.

Founded in 1916, the Progressive Party is a classic case of a Scandinavian farmers' party, strongest in small rural districts and very weak in the large urban areas. During the period after the Second World War it has averaged around 23.5 per cent of the vote in (thirteen) general elections, polling 19 per cent in April 1987. Because of the peculiarities of Iceland's electoral system (unequally-sized constituencies), the Progressive Party has obtained many more seats per vote than the national average. Due to this and the party's pivotal role in coalition formation, the Progressives have shared long periods of governmental responsibility. It is inclined to neutralism in international affairs, which puts it to the left of liberal parties elsewhere, but like any other farmers' party is somewhat conservative in economic and social matters, and typically Scandinavian in an emphasis on co-operative enterprise. It thus fits into the diverse Liberal family, but so could the other Scandinavian centre parties. Because it has the capacity, rare amongst liberal parties, to send a prime minister to international meetings, the significance of the enlargement of the Liberal family by its adhesion may be greater than the small size of Iceland might otherwise imply.

Greece

The military regime in Greece, which fell in July 1974 after a seven-year period, marked a profound and remarkable break in Greek party-political development: it introduced the spectacular disappearance of a historically strong and proud Greek liberal party, largely to the benefit of PASOK.

The Greek Liberal Party, originally called Komma Fileletheron, was founded in 1910 by Eleftherios Venizelos. Greek politics between the two World Wars was largely dominated by the cleavage between the liberal republican constitutionalists and the monarchist conservative right. In addition, the whole of this inter-war period was marked by active military intervention and attempted military coups. From 1936 until 1941 Greece succumbed to the dictatorial rule of General Metaxas. The development of political parties was further interrupted by the Second World War and the subsequent Greek civil war. This latter disjuncture ushered in a long period (1946–63) of uninterrupted rule by the right, first in the form of the Greek Rally (Hellinikos Synagermos) led by the victor of the civil war, Field

Marshal Alexander Papagos, subsequently in the form of the National Radical Union (Ethniki Rizopastiki Enossis – ERE) of Constantine Karamanlis. This long time of periodically interrupted democracy, bitter political violence and right-wing dominance naturally took its toll on Greek liberalism. Nevertheless, in 1961 liberalism revived powerfully in the shape of the Centre Union (Enossis Kendrou) under the leadership of George Papandreou.

The Centre Union experienced a brief period of astounding electoral success – winning elections in 1963 and 1964, even gaining an absolute majority (52.7 per cent) in 1964, and looking set to win the 1967 elections, too. However, the momentum of this success was rudely interrupted by the 1967 military coup. After the fall of the military regime, the Centre Union reappeared briefly under a new name, Centre Union–New Forces (Enossis Kendrou–Nees Dynamis, EK–ND) under the leadership of George Mavros.

In the 1974 elections, which were won by Karamanlis' reformed conservative party, New Democracy, with 54.4 per cent of the vote, the Centre Union–New Forces polled a respectable 20.4 per cent, while the new left-of-centre party, the Pan-Hellenic Socialist Movement (PASOK) polled 13.6 per cent. At first sight, it hardly seemed to present real cause for concern to Centre Union–New Forces. Nevertheless, PASOK was actually founded by Andreas Papandreou, son of the pre-dictatorship Centre Union leader and, for a brief period before the junta, leader of its radical wing. In the late 1960s Andreas Papandreou's centre-left faction of the Centre Union appeared to be successfully mobilising considerable new support for social and political reforms among both middle and working classes of a country in the thralls of belated modernisation (indeed this was the 'hidden agenda' for the intervention of the military) (Lyrintzis (1984)). Another cause for concern was that after 1974 the Centre Union–New Forces seemed to differ little in ideological terms from New Democracy. Veremis ((1981) p. 91) notes that 'with the death of George Papandreou in 1968 and the departure of Andreas to PASOK, the party had lost its comprehensive appeal for both old and new supporters.' Finally, the abolition of the Greek monarchy in 1974 deprived the Liberals of a historical popular cause and buried the constitutional cleavage around which Greek liberalism had been defined.

In the 1977 general elections the Centre Union–New Forces, with 11.9 per cent of the vote, fell critically behind that of PASOK, with 25.3 per cent, as the main alternative to New Democracy. Following this disappointment, the Centre Union distintegrated with astonishing rapidity. Its successor parties could barely muster 1 per cent of the vote between them in 1981. This must be one of the most striking cases of rapid disappearance by a major political party. Only twenty years earlier, in 1964, it had polled an absolute majority of the votes!

It is clear from an empirical election study by Featherstone and Katsoudas (1985) that PASOK has drawn its support from the same sources as the old Centre Union. However, they also demonstrate how 'the long-term shift in the Greek party-system has been the collapse of the Centre, and the polarisation of the vote between Left and Right, though skewed more to the former.' PASOK's ideological principles are not those of the old Centre Union. Nevertheless, almost symbolically, George Mavros, George Papandreou's successor as the Centre Union's leader until 1977, transferred to PASOK in 1981. Clearly, in the post-dictatorship period, PASOK has inherited the political space formerly occupied by the Centre Union and the mantle of the principal force for progressive but moderate change in Greece.

The Centre Union–New Forces left two very small successor parties in its wake. In 1979, the Party for Democratic Socialism (Komma tou Dimokratikou Socialismou, KODISO) was established by several former centrist parliamentarians. In 1981 this party demonstrated that it was capable of drawing support in the European elections, where it gained 4.1 per cent of the vote. However, in the general elections on the same date, it mustered only 0.7 per cent of the vote. John Pesmazoglu, who headed its list of candidates for the European elections, subsequently served as its only MEP from 1981 until 1985. Pesmazoglu was at the heart of attempts to reconstruct the old Centre. However, he did not identify himself as a liberal but rather as a social democrat; in the European Parliament he joined with two D'66 MEPs and one Francophone nationalist from Brussels to form an unofficial centre-left quartet. In the 1985 European elections, even his modest level of support collapsed, and the KODISO has since been dissolved.

The other attempt to salvage something of the old Centre does perceive itself both as the inheritor of the Greek liberal tradition and as the equivalent in Greece of European liberalism. The 'Liberal Party of Greece' is led by a grandson, Nikitas, of the founder of the original Liberal Party, Eleftherios Venizelos, and is a member party of both the ELDR and the LI. It claims in the documentation supplied to LI to have five thousand members; but its claim of electoral support (a more verifiable figure) is of 0.01 per cent of the votes in 1985. In the 1984 European elections it polled a little more (0.35 per cent), with a small pocket of more significant support in Crete, the former great Venizelos Liberal stronghold. That apart, the

Liberal Party of Greece is no more really than a personal club of Nikitas Venizelos, and its membership of the international organisations is a platform for him to propagandise the Greek case against Turkey, in line with his grandfather's nationalism.

Spain

A superficially similar 'collapse of the centre' seems to have occurred in Spain. Prior to the 1982 election, when the PSOE first swept to power with the remarkable level of support of almost half the votes cast, politics in Spain was marked by instability of the party system. Caciagli (1984) speaks of the Spanish case as being characterised by the 'insufficient penetration of the parties in society and the vagueness of their images'. The collapse of the Union de Centro Democratico (UCD), after a five-year period in office, was undoubtedly the major casualty of this instability and lack of penetration.

The UCD had been formally constituted as a 'party' following the electoral victory in 1977, but it was in reality a coalition of at least twelve small parties – including liberal, Christian democratic and social democratic elements – around the strong, semi-authoritarian leadership figure of Spain's first post-Franco prime minister, Adolfo Suarez. The principles elaborated in its programme attempted to produce a synthesis of Christian democratic, social democratic and liberal thought. However, its ideological positions remained very vague and vacuous: stressing 'humanism', 'equality' and 'freedom'. Yet, this very openness was not conducive to pragmatism, since the party was too prone to internal dissension.

There had been attempts of liberal groups to turn themselves into an independent federation of parties. The best known attempt was made by Enrique Larroque who founded the Liberal Democratic Union as the prototype for a single great Spanish liberal party. Another was represented by the Liberal Federation led by J. Garrigues Walker; Kohler ((1982) 17) regards this group as representing a distinctly liberal/conservative position in both economic and social affairs. J. Camunas' Democratic People's Party stood to the left of these two. However, all were 'absorbed' into the UCD.

For a while, it appeared that the UCD presented the possibility of a powerful centrist force in Spanish politics as the counterweight to the left. Instead, however, the PSOE and the conservative AP despoiled the centre. In addition, the UCD helped to seal its own fate by its internal divisions. In fact, the UCD never became a coherent party organisation. Its crisis-riven and factionalised nature could be traced back to its original polymorphism (Almodia (1983)).

Significantly, the party split between its liberals and its Christian and conservative elements over divorce-law reform and abortion. The liberal elements in the 'party' were also critical of the 'personalism' surrounding the leadership of Suarez and of the 'presidentialism' which he personified. Less significantly, the UCD split over economic issues as well. Its second party congress of February 1981 was overshadowed by the resignation of Suarez. Subsequently, the UCD collapsed in the elections of October 1982 (its vote sliding from 35.5 per cent in 1979 to a mere 7.2 per cent). As in the Greek case, the UCD failed in the competition with a dynamic new left force, the PSOE, for the moderate reformist vote. Yet, unlike the Greek Centre Union–New Forces, the UCD collapsed in both directions; a large proportion of its electorate went to the conservative AP, who emerged from the elections along with the PSOE (with 46.5 per cent) as 'winners' (with 25.6 per cent). In February 1983, the UCD ceased operations as a 'party'.

The UCD's international links were to conservative and Christian rather than to liberal parties; it had enjoyed observer status in the European Democratic Union and subsequently developed strong links with the European Union of Christian Democrats and the European People's Party. Significantly, the West German Friedrich Naumann Foundation failed to negotiate allied party status for the West German Liberals, the FDP (Kohler (1982) 33–4). However, one Spanish senator, elected as UCD and sitting in the mixed group in the senate, joined the Liberal group in the European parliament when Spain nominated MEPs on entering the EC in 1986.

Following the collapse of the UCD in the 1982 elections, liberal elements from it founded a small right-wing Liberal Party (PL) which subsequently joined Christian democratic remnants in the Popular Coalition with the Popular Alliance (AP). Suarez himself had meanwhile founded the Centro Democratico y Social (CDS) in an attempt to salvage the kind of 'personalised' centrist party that he had sought in the UCD. Whilst the CDS only achieved 2.0 per cent of the vote in 1982 in competition with the UCD, it appears since then to have established itself as the third force of the Spanish party system. It polled 9.1 per cent (19 seats) in the 1986 national elections and in the first election of Spanish MEPs in June 1987, it won seven out of the sixty seats (10.2 per cent of the vote). The seven new MEPs decided not to join any of the European Parliament's eight existing groups and briefly in September 1987 they formed with the three Italian Radicals and two other MEPs a new, ninth group for the 'Technical Co-ordination of Independents'. This highly 'personalised' party is not a convincing candidate for inclusion in the liberal party family; or any other for that matter.

An older liberal tradition in Catalonia has surfaced in a variety of organisations and under several party labels. In 1974 the Liberal International recognised a group of republicans in Catalonia, called 'Liberty and Social Democracy' (Llibertat i Democracia Social). This group tapped the historic republican left of Catalonia, individual adherents of which had, throughout the Franco period, maintained links with the Radicals in the South-West of France. It subsequently gave issue to the 'Democratic Convergence of Catalonia' (CDC) in 1978. In turn, the CDC formed a major part of the Convergence and Union of Catalonia (Convergencia i Unio, CiU). The CiU is a centrist bourgeois nationalist coalition which clearly has absorbed an element of liberal tradition. When the UCD had been in power it had stood close to it (except on the autonomy issue), favouring the UCD's conservative neo-liberal economic programme and its liberal social policies. The CiU won 2.7 per cent of the vote in 1979 and 4.9 per cent of the vote (and therefore as many as 18 seats) at the general elections of 1986. One nominated MEP from the CiU joined the Liberal group in the European Parliament in January 1986, as did two out of the three CiU MEPs elected in June 1987 (the third went into the Christian Democratic group). While the CiU has no official link as such with the ELDR, Catalonian radical liberalism is linked with international liberal youth. A Barcelona group (Moviment de Critica Radical) is a leading member of IFLRY and LYMEC and supplied the president of LYMEC, Joan F. Pont Clemente in 1985/6.

The one Spanish party which is a member of both LI and ELDR is the Democratic Reformist Party (Partido Reformista Democratica, PRD). This party was formed in 1984 by Antonio Garrigues Walker, the president of the former tiny Liberal Democratic Party (PDL) and Miquel Roca, deputy leader of the Democratic Convergence of Catalonia. One of its central aims was to surmount Spain's traditional centralism and to give the regions (and especially Catalans) a stronger voice in national affairs. It attempted to practise what it preached by deliberately giving itself a federalist structure. It also pledged itself both to 'progressive liberalism' and to a more limited role for the state in the sphere of the economy and individual liberties. However, the PRD only won an ignominious 1 per cent in the 1986 elections and no seats (though an allied group won a seat in Galicia). Robinson ((1987) 124) views the PRD as a 'complex, opportunistic and essentially schizophrenic attempt to coalesce moderate regionalism with Spanish centrism' and considers its disastrous result as inevitable. The PRD did not even contest the 1987 election of Spanish MEPs.

Interestingly, there may be a rather simple explanation for the absence of a significant liberal party in Spain. The rapid secularisation of post-Franco Spanish society, facilitated by the break-up of pre-civil war social structures, has eroded religion as the basis of primary cleavage. Anti-clericalism is low on the political agenda. This might explain why neither a Christian democratic party nor a liberal party was able to mobilise (see Caciagli (1984)).

Portugal

In common with the other two Mediterranean countries discussed here, Portugal has a long history of political instability. Between 1910 and 1926, there were 18 governments. Indeed, it was this instability that prompted the military coup that closed down Portugal's limited democracy for the next fifty years. In the case of Portugal, no party has links with the pre-dictatorship period of democracy. Moreover, no party calls itself 'liberal'. This can be explained, at least partially, by the eclipse of the distinctly 'compromised' (i.e. monarchist and conservative) brand of Portuguese liberalism by a clear republican tradition during the last quarter of the nineteenth century and the early decades of this century (Opello (1985) 87–90).

Four major parties emerged from the rebirth of democracy in Portugal in 1974. One, initially called the 'Popular Democratic Party' (Partido Popular Democrata, PPD), subsequently – in October 1976 – renamed the 'Social Democratic Party' (Partido Social Democrata, PSD) was established by a small group of 'liberal' deputies who had sat in the Portuguese parliament under the authoritarian regime and formed a focus of 'loyal opposition' (Kohler (1982) 203). Shortly before the coup they became 'disloyal' and registered their 'principled opposition' by leaving the parliament. Thus, the origins of the PPD have something in common with the origins of some nineteenth-century liberal parties, namely that of an opposition to autocratic government on constitutional grounds, clearly distinguishable from the origins of the PPD's competitor on the right, the Centre Social Democratic Party (CDS) which was founded by those who had tried to operate within the authoritarian regime.

From the start the newly-formed party seems to suffer a profound identity crisis: its intra-party life was highly volatile, with numerous congresses and scissions. Initially, the party seemed to be much closer to the socialists than to the CDS. Its 1974 programme even proclaimed that its goal was 'the establishment of a socialist society in conditions of freedom, and by exclusively democratic means' (Kohler (1982) 206). Subsequently it unsuccessfully sought entry into the

Socialist International and into the Socialist group in the Council of Europe.

However, its electoral following was never characteristic of a socialist party. Overall it attracted mainly professional people, the self-employed, businessmen and intellectuals. Later this expanded to take in farmers, small traders and the lower grades of the civil service (Kohler (1982) 205). Opello's analysis ((1985) 121–8) indicates that voters for the PSD and CDS had a very similar regional, religious and rural profile, in contrast to the wider social base of the Socialist Party. The party veered towards the right, emphasising the need for a market economy and private enterprise, calling for the revision of the Portuguese constitution to remove its socialist objectives and fighting the 1979 and 1980 elections jointly with the CDS.

Following the break-up of the PSD–CDS coalition which won these two elections, it fought the 1983 election on its own, winning 27.0 per cent of the vote (76 out of the 250 seats) and then formed a post-election coalition with the Socialist Party. That coalition collapsed after two years, following the victory at a PSD party congress of the faction led by Anibal Cavaco Silva in favour of supporting a CDS presidential candidate. Cavaco became the party's seventh leader and fresh parliamentary elections ensued in October 1985.

These brought a small advance to the PSD (29.9 per cent of the vote: 88 seats) but with it a clear lead over the Socialist Party (20.8 per cent: 55 seats) which hitherto had been Portugal's largest party. Cavaco formed the first PSD minority government and began to build up a personalised grip on the party. Under his premiership, Portugal's economy expanded fast, and investor confidence in him and his government grew. But the three parties of the left had a majority and combined to bring the government down in March 1987; another premature election followed in July 1987. This time the PSD achieved a spectacular triumph, winning just over 50 per cent of the votes cast and, with 148 seats, a large overall majority in the new parliament.

This was an earthquake in a system characterised up to 1983 by a very stable pattern of voting. In February 1986, the PSD-supported presidential candidate had been defeated by a Socialist who polled 51.3 per cent. Yet in July 1987, the three parties of the left, who had never at five previous parliamentary elections polled less than 44.6 per cent, could together only muster 39.4 per cent. The CDS was all but annihilated, winning only four seats. The new majority PSD government could look forward to an assured four-year term of office, an entirely new experience for Portuguese democracy.

It was difficult enough to categorise the PSD before this massive upset; it may be even more difficult, and indeed premature, to assess it now before Portugal has adjusted to the effects of one-party majority government. Yet, since the PSD has begun to identify itself with the family of European liberal parties, we must attempt some evaluation of it in comparative terms.

Before 1985 the party was riven by competing factions, led by what were termed *baronatos*. Now, under Cavaco it can clearly be seen as a leader-dominated party. Earlier, it experienced the personalised and autocratic style of its founder-leader, Francisco Sa Carneiro, until his sudden death in 1980. Such leadership is hardly an expression of liberal or social democratic principles, and invites comparison with parties formed around charismatic leadership such as the French Gaullists or the Irish Fianna Fáil. Yet the role in its internal life of its well-articulated mass-membership structure, with frequent congresses and national committee meetings to resolve disputes (and even a referendum amongst the membership to try to resolve the presidential candidature issue in 1985) is more characteristic of some liberal parties, or indeed those of the left. Bruneau and Macleod ((1986) 89–94) regard the PSD's defining characteristic as 'personalities, and the conflicts among them' and conclude that, because of its propensity to swing between left and right, the PSD makes for instability in the whole system.

During the period before he captured the leadership in 1985, Cavaco's faction had contested the party's strategy from a right-wing position. With his triumph in 1987 and the eclipse of the CDS the key to the character of the PSD now may become its success in aggregating the anti-socialist forces in Portugal and creating a mass party of the right, comparable to the German CDU or British Conservatives. A party in search of a role may now have found its opportunity. Moreover, Cavaco is a strong champion of free enterprise, and there are many parallels between his arguments and those of Mrs Thatcher's government. Yet perhaps this should not be stressed too much; the swing towards market economics within the PSD can also be paralleled by switches in policy of socialist governments in Greece and Spain, and may better be seen as a reflection of the vulnerable position of these countries in the world economy.

Indeed it is significant that the Portuguese context differs from that of more developed West European economies. Data on the membership of the party (Bruneau and Macleod (1986) 83) indicates a preponderance of civil servants and the professions, with a scattering of skilled workers and students, but with fewer entrepreneurs than the CDS has. The PSD is perhaps best seen as the party of internationally-minded technocrats more concerned to modernise their country than with an ideological model, and a party within which the strong presence of lawyers and academics guarantees vigorous debate.

The PSD has continued to see itself as more centrist, and despite scissions it has retained a distinct left wing. Furthermore, it is involved in the Portuguese trade-union movement, something not characteristic of parties of the right. The General Union of Workers (UGT), founded in 1979 jointly by the Socialist Party and the PSD to contest the primacy of the communist-dominated CFTP, represents about a third of organised labour in Portugal and is particularly strong in the tertiary sector and in the textile and chemical industries. Until the UGT's third congress in March 1984, its leadership was based on parity between PSD and Socialist members. But as from that congress (where the PSD had 36 per cent of the delegates), the UGT's leadership has reflected the Socialist Party's majority within it (Bruneau and Macleod (1986) 103–6).

Its voters (at any rate prior to 1987) tend to identify themselves as lying between the CDS and the Socialist Party, but closer to the CDS. In 1978 the average left–right self-placement of Socialist voters was 4.6, of PSD voters 6.9 and of CDS voters 7.9 (Condomines and Barroso (1984) 409–10). A 1984 survey showed remarkably similar figures: 4.7, 7.1 and 8.5 respectively (Bruneau and Macleod (1986) 88).

Indeed, as a party which is on the right in the role of the main opponent to a socialist party, but which has demonstrable left-of-centre emotional tugs within it, as well as an organised trade-union base, and which has a smaller rival seen as a bit further to its right, the PSD has a clear resemblance to the Italian and Benelux Christian democratic parties. Paradoxically on that test, the Portuguese party which joined the Christian democratic camp at the European level, the CDS, is also out of place. Its position in the Portuguese party system has a closer resemblance to the position of the liberal parties in the Italian and Benelux systems.

We argued above, however, that rather than defining the differences between such parties in left–right terms they were better seen as occupying parallel space in their systems, separated by the secular–clerical cleavage. But in Portugal – as in Spain – anti-clericalism, once so strong, hardly figures on the current political agenda. A divorce law was legalised during the Portuguese revolution without much opposition from the church. The church did oppose, ferociously but unsuccessfully, the very limited abortion law enacted in 1984; the PSD and CDS voted together against this reform (Bruneau and Macleod (1986) 114). We can find no evidence that a secular–clerical cleavage separates the PSD from the CDS. The one clear historic difference between them lies in attitudes to the previous regime and in the constitutional debates of the mid-1970s. That recalls the classic difference between conservative and liberal parties.

It also makes for a different parallel – with Spain and Greece – where more conservative parties (AP and ND) have been, like the CDS, distanced from the centre by their attitude to an earlier regime but unlike it have succeeded in becoming electorally the main party of the right. It may be that personalities, the context of the Portuguese revolution and the pragmatism of most voters on the centre-right rather than the nature of such a constitutional cleavage explains why this has not happened in Portugal. But the fact remains that it has not happened and that the main non-socialist party there has liberal and centrist, or even left-of-centre, ideological roots rather than conservative ones. It is important for the systematic comparative study of parties and may be important for the future role of the PSD both in Portuguese politics and in transnational party alignments.

When Portugal joined the European Community, the PSD decided to join the European Parliament's Liberal group, but required a name change to incorporate reform (see above, p. 406) so as not to identify itself too much with the word 'liberal'. The PSD is now playing an active role in ELDR and invited ELDR to hold its congress in Lisbon in 1987 but has not even become an observer of the Liberal International. Nevertheless, as the second largest group within the ELDR in the European Parliament, the PSD has the potential to play a major role in any future realignment within the Liberal family.

CONCLUSION

Our findings have interesting implications for the study of party systems. The fact that the key defining characteristic of liberal parties proves to be their historical ideological development, illustrates and supports von Beyme's approach. Nevertheless, we do not hold that this undermines the Lipset and Rokkan cleavage approach. On the one hand, the persistence of a historically determined occurrence of liberal parties fits remarkably with the freezing hypothesis which Lipset and Rokkan argued. On the other hand, the variety among liberal parties can be well explained by alliance choices made in their formative stage, along Lipset and Rokkan lines. We do suggest, however, that the Lipset and Rokkan model could be enriched, and made more applicable to the actual map of political parties in Western Europe, if allowance were made within it for a constitutional cleavage at the time of the democratic revolution.

Lipset and Rokkan, of course, had much wider concerns than our narrow focus on explaining the group of liberal parties. So, too, had Smith, yet our findings lend empirical weight to his 'intuitive' view that liberal parties have to be divided into two types in order to be fitted within an overall classification of West European parties. We offer a more theoretical explanation of this distinction than Smith did in his *Politics in Western Europe*, though he has provided an equally interesting theoretical explanation in this volume; see ch. 2. Our suggestion that Smith's liberal-radical parties are to be explained in terms of Anglo-Scandinavian party systems in which they compete with a clearly right-wing conservative force whilst his liberal-conservative parties are to be explained by the fact that they compete in continental party systems with rival centre-right Christian democratic parties, is not an all-encompassing explanatory model, just as not all liberal parties can be easily fitted into such a simple dichotomy. Nonetheless, we suggest that this 'political space' approach produces a more satisfying and workable explanatory model. Moreover, it suggests that fitting parties into two-dimensional political space, albeit with a dominant left–right dimension, is preferable to placing them on a simple left–right scale; in so far as this is valid, it has important repercussions for the broader study of party systems and particularly of coalition formation. Furthermore, we suggest that an underlying dichotomy between Anglo-Scandinavian and continental party systems, with the French and German fitting clearly into neither, makes a crucial distinction which has hitherto been overlooked. The most important factor in this distinction is the effect of a secular–clerical cleavage on the overall shape of the party system. There we rejoin the Lipset and Rokkan approach, suggesting a fundamental importance for this cleavage in any typology of West European party systems.

As for liberal parties themselves, we have found that, their diversity notwithstanding, they do amount to a meaningful group, and not only by label or by mutual self-recognition. However, the fact that their common character is so grounded in the past indicates doubt as to how far they can continue to develop as a single group. The variation in their electoral success, which has been very marked in the last two decades, is one indication of this. The differing responses of liberal parties to the economic recession and to the re-ideologisation of the debate over the size of the public sector is another. The international organisations themselves give further indication of future problems. During the first forty years after the Second World War, LI and ELD maintained a remarkably stable grouping of parties, broken only by the admission of the Parti Républicain into ELD in 1976. In the 1980s the emphasis has been on the enlargement and diversification of the transnational organisations. LI has enlarged to the right with the PR and to the centre with the partial movement into it of the Scandinavian agrarian parties. The initial effect of the entry of the PSD into ELDR, given its weight, should tend to pull ELDR towards the centre, illustrated by the move of ELDR MEPs from the far right towards the centre in seating arrangements of the European Parliament. Predicting its future effect is more problematic. Enlargement and diversification may assist these international groupings to survive and develop and bring a political payoff to the political parties within them of belonging to a growing group. But it may also raise tensions and open up the problems of historic diversity, which may one day prove to be irreconcilable.

NOTES

1 Michael Steed is primarily responsible for the sections of the chapter on the roots of liberal parties, the mutual recognition systems, and the list of liberal parties; the two authors are jointly responsible for the remainder of the chapter, including the introduction and conclusion.

2 Statement in *Liberal Flash, Information Bulletin of the Liberal, Democratic and Reformist Group*, 5th year, No. 1.

REFERENCES

Almodia, J. (1983) 'Union of the Democratic Centre' in Bell, D. (ed.), *Democratic Politics in Spain* (London: Frances Pinter).

Barnes, S.H. (1966) 'Ideology and the organisation of conflict: on the relationship between political thought and behaviour', *Journal of Politics*, 28, 513–30.

Beyme, K. von (1985) *Political Parties in Western Democracies* (Aldershot: Gower).

Bourricaud, F. (1977) 'The right in France since 1945', *Comparative Politics* (October, 1977).

Bruneau, T.C. and Macleod, A. (1986) *Politics in Contemporary Portugal* (Boulder, Colorado: Lynne Riener).

Caciagli, M. (1984) 'Spain: parties and the party system in the transition' in Pridham, G. (ed.), *The New Mediterranean Democracies: Regime Transition in Spain, Greece and Portugal* (London: Frank Cass).

Castles, F. and Mair, P. (1984) 'Left–right political scales: some "expert" judgements', *European Journal of Political Research*, 12, 73–88.

Condomines, J. and Barroso, J.D. (1984) 'La dimension gauche–droite et la compétition entre les partis politiques en Europe du Sud (Portugal, Espagne, Grèce)', *Il Politico, Rivista Italiana Di Scienze Politiche*, 3, 405–38.

Converse, P.E.P. (1964) 'The nature of belief systems in mass publics' in Apter, D. *Ideology and Discontent* (Free Press of Glencoe: Collier-MacMillan).

Davis, M. (1963) *Iceland Extends its Fisheries Limits* (Copenhagen: Universitetsforlaget).
Downs, A. (1957) *An Economic Theory of Democracy* (New York: Harper & Bros.).
Elder, N., Thomas, A.H. and Arter, D. (1982) *The Consensual Democracies* (Oxford: Martin Robertson).
Featherstone, K. and Katsoudas, D. (1985) 'Change and continuity in Greek voting behaviour', *European Journal of Political Research*, 13, 27–40.
Henig, S. (1969) 'Conclusion', in Henig, S. and Pinder, J. (eds.), *Political Parties in the European Community* (London: Allen & Unwin).
Inglehart, R. and Klingemann, H.D. (1976) 'Party identification, ideological preference and the left–right dimension among Western publics' in Budge, I. et al. (eds.), *Party Identification and Beyond. Representatives of Voting and Party Competition* (London: Wiley).
Kohler, B. (1982) *Political Forces in Spain, Greece and Portugal* (London: Butterworth Scientific).
Kristjánsson, S. (1975) 'The electoral basis of the Icelandic Independent Party, 1929–1944', *Scandinavian Political Studies*, vol. 2, n.s. 1.
Lane, J.-E. and Ersson, S.O. (1987) *Politics and Society in Western Europe* (London: SAGE Publications).
Lipset, S.M. and Rokkan, S. (1967) 'Cleavage structures, party systems, and voter alignments: an introduction' in Lipset, S.M. and Rokkan, S. (eds.), *Party Systems and Voter Alignments: Cross-national Perspectives* (New York: Free Press).
Lyrintzis, C. (1984) 'Political parties in post-junta Greece: a case of bureaucratic clientalism' in Pridham, G. (ed.), *The New Mediterranean Democracies: Regime Transition in Spain, Greece and Portugal* (London: Frank Cass).
MacCallum Scott, J.H. (1967) *Experiment in Internationalism* (London: Allen & Unwin).
Opello, W.C. Jnr. (1985) *Portugal's Political Development. A Comparative Approach* (Boulder and London: Westview Press).
Rémond, R. (1968) *La Droite en France*, 2 vols. (Paris: PUF).
Robinson, R. (1987) 'From change to continuity: the 1986 Spanish election', *West European Politics*, vol. 10, no. 1, 120–4.
Ruggiero, G. de (1927) *The History of European Liberalism* (London: Milford).
Salvadori, M. (1977) *The Liberal Heresy. Origins and Historical Development* (London: MacMillan).
Sartori, G. (1976) *Parties and Party Systems* (Cambridge: CUP).
Schuur, H. van (1984) *Structure in Political Beliefs – A New Model for Stochastic Unfolding with Application to European Party Activists* (Amsterdam: CT Press).
Seiler, D.L. (1980) *Partis et Familles Politiques* (Paris: PUF).
Smith, G. (1972) *Politics in Western Europe* (London: Heinemann Educational) (subsequent edns: 1976, 1980, 1983).
Steed, M. (1982) 'The Liberal Parties in Italy, France, Germany and the United Kingdom' in Morgan, R. and Silvestri, S. (1982) *Moderates and Conservatives in Western Europe* (London: Heinemann Educational).
Swaan, A. de (1973) *Coalition Theories and Cabinet Formations: A Study of Formal Theories of Coalition Formation Applied to Nine European Parliaments after 1918* (Amsterdam: Elsevier).
Veremis, T. (1981) 'The Union of the Democratic Center' in Penniman, H. (ed.), *Greece at the Polls* (Washington and London: American Enterprise).

17

Ambivalence revisited: an analysis of liberal party manifestos since 1945

Derek Hearl

INTRODUCTION

The question as to what is and what is not a liberal party has continually been raised throughout this volume, both explicitly and implicitly, while Gordon Smith addresses it directly in ch. 2, pointing out that answers depend fundamentally upon the analyst's perspective. Smith identifies two such perspectives, the historical and the contemporary, and correctly goes on to show that these are not necessarily entirely divorced from one another since contemporary liberalism is inevitably rooted in its own past in any case. Nevertheless, virtually all the country chapters in this volume have tended to concentrate upon the first of Smith's perspectives for the simple reason that the 'contemporary' mode of analysis is obviously a much more difficult one to conduct in a purely national context than it is in a comparative one. This chapter will attempt to correct this balance by concentrating upon a comparative analysis that in Smith's terms might be also be thought of as 'contemporary'.

It is able to do so because of the recent availability of the data-set compiled by the ECPR manifestos project which, virtually for the first time ever, provides strictly comparable cross-national scores taken from the electoral programmes published by almost all significant parties from some 20 countries since the Second World War and on the basis of which a range of different political and ideological measures can be constructed.[1]

Originally, eleven European countries were covered, while a twelfth, Norway, was added later. However, these are not the same as those dealt with in this book since neither Finland, Switzerland, nor any part of the Iberian peninsula has (yet) been included in the ECPR project, and consequently these countries cannot be covered in this chapter. On the other hand, Ireland, which did form part of the ECPR project, has no liberal party and does for that reason not appear in this volume. In the Belgian case, where the main parties 'split' along linguistic lines during the late 1960s and 1970s, the data has been reaggregated into political 'families' to facilitate both international and diachronic comparison so that we continue to have scores for a single, united 'PRL–PVV'.[2] Finally, there is a major difficulty for our present purposes in that the French manifestos data was collected on the basis of party *tendances* rather than individual parties as such. In practice, this means that the parties of the centre and the centre-right (i.e. precisely those with which we are concerned here) are grouped into a rather amorphous 'other' *tendance* that cannot easily be disentangled. Consequently, the French case is left out of the first part of the following analysis altogether, although an attempt will be made to reintroduce it later in the chapter. With this proviso, therefore, the analyses which follow are based upon the ten countries and fourteen parties shown in Table 17.1.

In all the countries studied, political parties publish detailed policy statements in advance of each election. Although the names given to these documents – most usually 'election programme', 'election platform' or 'manifesto' – vary by country (and sometimes even by party within country), they all have a number of important features in common. That is to say, they are drawn up on behalf of the whole party by, or with the backing of, its leadership and can be singled out as being uniquely representative and authoritative statements of party policy at a given point in time. Precisely because they are election documents which all a party's candidates will have to defend, they almost always express the official point of view of the whole party – or the current balance of forces within it – rather than merely those of the leadership. (Indeed, to the extent that this is not so, it can be safely assumed that the party is under leadership control to such an extent as to render such distinctions superfluous.)

Party programmes concentrate, of course, upon the particular issues of the day and, it may be assumed, especially upon those which the party feels are likely to be advantageous to it in electoral terms. However, it is clear that in practice this does not preclude the inclusion of other elements of a more enduring nature, thereby giving a party a link with its traditional past. At least in principle it should be possible to detect both these influences and to distinguish between them, thereby permitting the analyst both to assess a party's current position in terms of the issues of the day and to measure its political and ideological continuity and consistency (or lack of it) over time.

In the course of the ECPR project, nearly 1,000 different documents were collected and content-analysed using an agreed 'coding frame' designed as far as possible to be internationally comparable. Each sentence (strictly speaking, each 'quasi-sentence' or other group of words expressing a *single* policy position) was classified into one – and only one – of 54 different coding categories. These covered such relatively broad concepts as 'peace', 'freedom and human rights', 'free enterprise', 'farmers' and so on that could be presumed to be relatively invariant both between countries and over time (which the detailed promises themselves obviously could not). So that, for example, a sentence promising to spend more on sheltered housing for the elderly, one undertaking to oppose a rival party's cuts in unemployment pay, or one pledging support for improved sickness benefit would all be coded under the same 'social services' rubric. The researchers went to considerable lengths to ensure that not only were these categories given the same meanings in different national contexts but also that, as far as possible, the coding operation itself was consistent between the various coders in different countries. The resultant 'raw' scores are standardised as percentages of each programme's total length in order to control for varying lengths of document.

This method of coding is explicitly based upon 'saliency theory' which holds that competing parties actually 'talk past each other' rather than arguing directly over opposing policies. In other words, the different parties are all associated with generally desirable goals, but these tend to be in different policy areas. So that in Britain, for example, it is difficult for the Conservatives to argue that they will do better than Labour in the field of social services, while the reverse holds true for the Labour Party on, say, law and order questions. Even to mention an opponent's topic runs the risk of bringing it into prominence and thus benefiting that opponent. Rather than mentioning it, the best strategy is not to refer to it all or to deal with it cursorily. Such empirical evidence as the ECPR group was able to obtain, at least from the election programmes, strongly supports this argument.[3]

'FREQUENCIES' ANALYSIS

One of the simplest, and yet most useful, ways of analysing data of the kind collected by the ECPR group is through the use of straightforward frequency counts of the various coding categories. If, say, the ten highest scores for each party are then ranked, one has a simple and easily interpretable 'profile' for that party, either over time or for a particular election. Table 17.1 shows such 'profiles' for each of the 14 liberal parties in the data set averaged over the post-war period, and it is worthy of some consideration.

Overall, a number of things stand out. First, there are quite a large number of issues which all or nearly all the fourteen party profiles have in common; secondly, there are some which appear to relate to the liberal-conservative and liberal-radical distinction, and thirdly, some issues are given very high placing by one or two parties but are completely ignored by all the others.

Among the first group is freedom and human rights which we would in any case expect to see among the chief concerns of virtually any liberal party and it is gratifying, therefore, that it occurs in all but three of the 14 profiles. Others are perhaps less obvious, such as agriculture and farmers, which occurs in half the profiles (and not necessarily the ones that we might expect, such as Danish Venstre), but these are easily understandable when we take into account the peripheral, and hence substantially rural, nature of several of the parties' electoral support. It is presumably this fact which accounts for the prominence which such otherwise rather differently leaning parties like the Belgian and British give to the interests of this group of voters.

The very high placings given to what is almost the defining characteristic of classical economic liberalism, a belief in the merits of free enterprise, by such classic liberal-conservative parties as the Belgian PRL–PVV, the Italian PLI and the Dutch VVD is very encouraging, as are the equally high but contrasting emphases given to social services by their more liberal-radical cousins in Luxemburg, Norway, Sweden, Britain and by the D'66 in the Netherlands. There is clear evidence here at least of the expected left–right division between the two branches of the Liberal family.

The more idiosyncratic issues emphasised by particular parties are also of some interest. Among these are the patriotic, if not necessarily jingoistic, national way of life on which the Austrian FPÖ lays such stress, the anti-militaristic views expressed by Radikale Venstre, and the concern for economic planning shown by the Italian Republicans. Nevertheless, given what we know of these particular parties' origins and development, these are not especially surprising attitudes for them to take, in spite of the fact that they are things for which other liberal parties have little sympathy.

In short, these profiles are already rather instructive. First, the extent to which the same issues occur in different party profiles is

Table 17.1 *Liberal party policy 'profiles'*

Austria

FPÖ	(N=9)	%
202	Democracy	13.56
107	Internationalism	7.49
503	Social justice	5.92
201	Freedom and human rights	5.25
504	Social services	5.17
401	Free enterprise	4.38
606	National effort	4.22
703	Agriculture/farmers	4.20
601	National way of life	4.10
706	Non-economic groups	3.93

Belgium

PRL/PVV	(N=13)	%
401	Free enterprise	10.56
706	Non-economic groups	7.94
704	Middle-class groups	6.85
414	Economic orthodoxy	3.99
703	Agriculture/farmers	3.69
301	Decentralisation	3.54
303	Government efficiency	3.47
606	National effort/social harmony	3.27
201	Freedom and human rights	3.21
411	Technology and infrastructure	2.97

Denmark

Radikale Venstre	(N=16)	%
410	Productivity	5.95
503	Social justice	5.06
105	Military: negative	4.88
606	National effort/social harmony	4.69
706	Non-economic groups	4.34
408	Specific economic goals	3.23
402	Incentives	2.97
107	Internationalism	2.41
504	Social services	2.31
506	Education	2.22
403	Regulation of capitalism	2.22

Denmark

Venstre	(N=16)	%
414	Economic orthodoxy	8.78
410	Productivity	4.77
402	Incentives	4.27
401	Free enterprise	3.86
503	Social justice	3.44
408	Specific economic goals	2.53
506	Education	2.25
301	Decentralisation	1.88
201	Freedom and human rights	1.83
703	Agriculture/farmers	1.83

Germany

FDP	(N=8)	%
503	Social justice	6.54
201	Freedom and human rights	4.20
411	Technology and infrastructure	4.15
706	Non-economic groups	3.77
703	Agriculture/farmers	3.68
506	Education	3.41
504	Social services	3.18
101	Foreign special relations	3.00
202	Democracy	2.55
108	European Community	2.54

Italy

PLI	(N=8)	%
401	Free enterprise	7.58
503	Social justice	4.51
201	Freedom and human rights	4.39
202	Democracy	3.46
403	Regulation of capitalism	3.01
414	Economic orthodoxy	3.00
108	European Community	2.51
303	Government efficiency	1.88
701	Labour groups	1.78
706	Non-economic groups	1.77

Italy

PRI	(N=6)	%
303	Government efficiency	6.68
202	Democracy	4.67
503	Social justice	4.18
201	Freedom and human rights	3.71
404	Economic planning	2.37
301	Decentralisation	2.20
706	Non-economic groups	2.10
408	Specific economic goals	1.60
410	Productivity	1.49
604	Traditional morality(negative)	1.33

Luxemburg

DP	(N=7)	%
704	Middle-class groups	12.40
504	Social services	8.97
703	Agriculture/farmers	6.70
503	Social justice	6.67
706	Non-economic groups	5.88
201	Freedom and human rights	4.42
202	Democracy	4.26
506	Education	4.02
411	Technology/infrastructure	3.72
502	Art, sport, leasure, media	3.72

Netherlands

VVD	(N=11)	%
401	Free enterprise	10.75
503	Social justice	5.88
414	Economic orthodoxy	5.65
504	Social services	4.28
706	Non-economic groups	3.89
506	Education	3.83
201	Freedom and human rights	3.67
402	Incentives	3.46
107	Internationalism	3.04

Netherlands

D'66	(N=4)	%
504	Social services	9.40
202	Democracy	9.19
501	Environment	7.79
503	Social justice	6.39
107	Internationalism	4.97
201	Freedom and human rights	4.86
411	Technology/infrastructure	4.72
506	Education	4.31
303	Government efficiency	3.40

Table 17.1 (*cont.*)

Norway Norges Venstrelag (N = 11)		%	*Norway* Det Nye Folkepartiet (N = 1)		%
504	Social Services	7.96	411	Technology/infrastructure	7.68
506	Education	7.40	501	Environment	7.68
411	Technology/infrastructure	6.81	107	Internationalism	7.09
703	Agriculture/farmers	6.46	706	Non-economic groups	6.30
503	Social justice	6.10	703	Agriculture/farmers	6.10
410	Productivity	5.19	202	Democracy	5.41
502	Art, sport, leisure, media	4.87	301	Decentralisation	5.41
501	Environment	4.77	504	Social services	5.41
704	Middle-class groups	4.50	506	Education	4.82
301	Decentralisation	4.44	503	Social justice	4.43

Sweden Folkpartiet (N = 13)		%	*United Kingdom* Liberal Party (N = 11)		%
504	Social services	13.48	201	Democracy	5.10
503	Social justice	5.59	107	Internationalism	4.77
201	Freedom and human rights	5.39	504	Social services	4.48
202	Democracy	5.13	301	Decentralisation	4.15
107	Internationalism	4.97	503	Social justice	3.56
506	Education	4.40	408	Full employment	3.43
401	Free enterprise	4.37	606	National effort/social harmony	3.24
402	Incentives	4.12	703	Agriculture/farmers	3.19
414	Economic orthodoxy	3.95	706	Non-economic groups	3.08
501	Environment	3.68	201	Freedom and human rights	3.08

'N' = Number of manifestos in each case.

obviously an indicator of agreement between them in the same way that the occurrence of an issue in only one or two profiles is a measure of that party's or those parties' idiosyncracy. However, there are two quite different reasons why all or nearly all of the parties in Table 17.1 might emphasise the same issue. Either it is because that issue is particularly distinctive of liberal parties as such, or instead, it may simply be because it is an issue which *all* (or nearly all) parties emphasise, whether they are liberal or not. Clearly this point needs to be checked before too much can be read into similarities of this kind. Table 17.2, therefore, shows the same set of issue categories that appears in Table 17.1 – that is those that are empirically important for liberal parties whether distinctively so or not – but this time it gives certain other information as well.

The first two columns in the table give a) the overall scores for all those parties in the ten countries for which we have manifestos data[4] and b) those for the fourteen liberal parties taken together. The issue categories themselves are ranked according to their scores in this second column, thereby giving an indication of their relative importance to liberal parties as such. Secondly, in Table 17.2 the parties are grouped according to Gordon Smith's classification as either 'liberal-conservative' or 'liberal-radical',[5] while the five lead-

Table 17.2 *Comparison of issue emphases for liberal parties in Western Europe since 1945*

			Liberal-conservative						Liberal-radical									
			A	B	D	DK	I	NL	DK	I	L	N	N	NL	S	UK	All Liberal cons. parties	All Liberal radical parties[a]
Categories	All parties	Liberal parties	FPÖ	PVV PRL	FDP	DK Ven	PLI	VVD	RV	PRI	DP	N Ven	NF	D'66	Fp	Lib		
Social justice	5.23	4.89	**5.92**	2.72	**6.54**	**3.44**	**4.51**	**5.88**	**5.06**	**4.18**	**6.67**	**6.10**	4.43	**6.39**	**5.59**	**3.56**	4.84	5.36
Social services	5.71	4.67	**5.17**	2.06	3.18	1.21	1.34	4.28	2.31	0.70	**8.97**	**7.96**	5.41	**9.40**	**13.48**	**4.48**	2.87	6.76
Free enterprise	2.75	3.99	4.38	**10.26**	1.95	**3.86**	**7.58**	**10.75**	0.95	0.52	2.61	1.39	0.79	0.36	4.37	1.64	6.46	1.69
Democracy	3.61	3.98	**13.56**	1.99	2.55	1.17	**3.46**	2.22	2.11	**4.67**	4.26	3.79	5.41	**9.19**	**5.13**	**5.10**	4.16	4.89
Non-economic groups	4.14	3.83	3.92	**8.15**	**3.77**	1.22	1.77	**3.89**	**4.34**	2.10	**5.88**	4.18	**6.20**	4.60	3.66	3.08	3.79	3.98
Freedom and human rights	2.91	3.54	**5.25**	2.99	**4.20**	1.83	**4.39**	3.67	2.18	**3.71**	4.42	2.95	1.77	4.86	**5.39**	3.08	3.72	3.80
Economic orthodoxy	2.97	3.41	2.19	**4.43**	1.92	**8.78**	3.00	**5.65**	2.16	0.52	1.09	1.00	1.18	2.22	3.95	2.65	4.33	1.94
Education	3.36	3.08	2.80	2.24	3.41	2.25	1.00	**3.83**	2.22	0.52	4.02	**7.40**	4.82	4.31	4.40	1.57	2.59	3.49
Agriculture and farmers	2.93	2.85	4.21	**3.80**	**3.68**	1.83	0.16	2.54	1.47	0.41	**6.70**	**6.46**	**6.10**	1.04	1.27	3.19	2.70	2.93
Internationalism	2.32	2.76	**7.49**	1.11	2.03	0.25	0.36	3.04	2.41	0.46	0.60	4.08	**7.09**	**4.97**	**4.97**	**4.77**	2.39	3.18
Productivity	2.56	2.59	0.17	1.11	0.69	**4.77**	1.54	1.18	**5.99**	1.49	1.09	5.19	3.35	1.27	1.50	2.79	1.58	2.76
Incentives	1.98	2.49	2.00	2.14	1.62	**4.27**	0.54	3.46	2.97	0.18	1.32	0.89	2.66	1.08	4.12	2.76	2.34	1.90
Middle-class groups	1.93	2.49	1.44	**7.26**	0.00	1.12	1.60	1.27	1.16	0.87	**12.40**	4.50	3.94	0.20	0.05	1.30	2.11	2.93
Full employment	2.55	2.40	1.29	3.37	2.21	2.53	0.36	1.74	3.23	1.60	2.06	1.59	1.57	2.55	2.45	3.43	1.92	2.42

Technology and infrastructure	2.97	2.34	2.95	3.44	**4.15**	0.56	0.00	2.08	0.37	0.35	3.72	**6.81**	**7.68**	4.72	0.99	1.55	2.20	2.64
Government efficiency	1.84	2.24	2.60	3.42	1.75	1.58	1.88	2.60	2.00	**6.68**	1.24	1.74	0.49	3.40	1.16	2.43	2.31	2.66
Decentral-isation	2.63	2.18	0.37	3.29	0.91	1.88	1.51	1.74	0.85	2.20	1.06	4.44	5.41	1.05	1.95	**4.15**	1.61	2.24
Environment	1.85	1.88	2.14	1.36	1.89	0.70	0.00	1.46	0.59	0.00	2.39	4.77	**7.68**	**7.79**	3.68	1.55	1.26	2.97
National effort/social harmony	1.29	1.80	4.22	3.09	1.51	1.19	0.00	0.84	**4.69**	0.41	0.93	0.10	0.00	0.20	0.63	3.24	1.81	1.46
Arts, sport, leisure, media	1.89	1.56	2.76	1.95	1.42	0.24	0.00	3.61	0.26	0.00	3.72	4.87	3.25	2.65	0.92	0.12	1.66	1.79
European Community (positive)	1.20	1.50	1.20	1.72	2.54	0.84	2.51	1.64	0.31	0.26	1.90	0.26	1.38	1.72	0.56	2.80	1.74	1.12
Regulation of capitalism	1.97	1.66	1.19	1.15	2.24	1.31	**3.01**	1.61	2.22	0.00	0.95	2.17	1.77	1.84	1.95	1.83	1.75	1.57
Foreign special relationships	1.27	1.50	1.88	1.56	3.00	1.33	1.13	1.89	2.09	0.26	1.73	0.58	0.89	0.17	0.56	1.52	1.80	0.99
Labour groups	2.08	1.14	1.54	1.69	1.89	0.29	1.78	0.54	0.78	1.05	2.59	1.67	1.67	0.37	0.28	1.43	1.29	1.17
Economic planning	1.22	1.01	2.56	0.21	0.00	0.26	0.53	0.25	1.27	**2.37**	0.68	1.54	0.98	0.96	0.92	2.04	0.64	1.40
Military (negative)	1.17	0.86	0.00	0.43	0.48	0.00	0.00	0.05	**4.88**	0.00	0.75	0.11	0.00	0.64	0.40	1.28	0.19	1.15
National way of life	0.81	0.85	4.10	0.98	0.05	1.61	0.00	0.11	0.26	0.00	0.93	0.43	0.20	0.00	0.00	0.85	1.14	0.35
Traditional morality (negative)	0.21	0.29	0.00	0.30	0.00	0.00	0.93	0.91	0.07	1.33	0.39	0.06	0.00	1.57	0.00	0.00	0.36	0.49

[a]Liberal radical mean scores do not include Norwegian NF (see text).

ing issues for each party are printed in bold type so that one can see at a glance how closely any of them approaches the consensus of the group as a whole. Finally, in the last two columns the table shows the mean scores for each of the two groups of parties separately. (However, it should be noted that in calculating the liberal-radical scores in the last column, the Nye Folkeparti from Norway was not included owing to the fact that the scores for this party are based on only one document.)

The single most striking feature of the table is perhaps the fact that the patterns shown in the first two columns, i.e. those for all parties and those for liberal parties, actually differ so very little. Not only is the rank ordering of the different categories virtually identical, but the actual percentage scores themselves are quite remarkably similar. This is a telling demonstration of the fact that liberal parties, at any rate as a bloc, are really very representative of European party 'space' in general. Nevertheless, there are some differences, most notably in the slight right-of-centre bias indicated by the liberals' rather higher than average placings of such issues as free enterprise, incentives, economic orthodoxy (which stands for such old-fashioned virtues as a balanced budget, stable currency and so on) and the interests of middle-class groups on the one hand, and the rather lower emphasis they give to social services in particular, on the other.

The table also shows that the explanation for the appearance of 'social justice' in thirteen of the parties' 'top ten' (i.e. all except the Belgian) is precisely due to the fact that this is one of the issues most commonly stressed by parties of all ideological persuasions. Its high placing among liberal parties' concerns is simply a reflection of this and in no way distinguishes them either as a political tradition or 'family' in their own right or from each other within that tradition. However, there are grounds for supposing that this category at least (it is one covering demands for 'fair' or 'equal' treatment for all groups in the population) means different things to different parties – almost all of which are likely to claim that their 'own' particular client groups are unfairly or unequally treated in some respect.

The next most commonly stressed issue among liberal parties is social services, perhaps, to use Stokes' term, *the* 'valence' issue *par excellence*. Indeed, it is the single most emphasised category across all parties in all ten countries. Nevertheless, unlike social justice, emphasis on social services provision does distinguish very clearly between the two separate liberal traditions – the parties of a liberal-radical persuasion giving it a high priority, higher indeed than the average for all parties, and those of the liberal-conservative tendency giving it a lower one.

In contrast, the latter put considerably more emphasis than do either their liberal-radical partners, or indeed Western European parties as a whole, upon the more right-wing categories of free enterprise, incentives, economic orthodoxy and so on. Indeed, the Liberal family's overall, slight centre-right flavour already remarked upon is entirely due to the influence of its liberal-conservative members.

However, Table 17.2 also identifies a number of issues which liberal parties, on average, not only stress more frequently than other political families but which also tend to unite them. Paramount among these, as is really only to be expected, is freedom and human rights, a classic liberal concern which appropriately appears in the top ten for all fifteen parties except Radikale Venstre and the two Norwegian ones. (And it must be pointed out that the latter still give this category more emphasis than do other parties in Norway, although this is not true for Radikale Venstre in Denmark.)

All but three parties, (the exceptions this time are the two Venstre Parties and Folkpartiet in Sweden), give considerable attention to the interests of 'non-economic groups' (which mostly means women, old people, the young, etc.). Again, this issue is typical of liberal parties not only in Europe, but world-wide. Democracy, however, which – as the table shows – tends also to be a distinctively 'liberal' issue in most countries, is actually left out of their 'top ten' altogether by the PRL–PVV, Radikale Venstre, the VVD and both the Danish and Norwegian Venstre.

In short, a clear cross-national pattern emerges, in which liberal-conservative parties tend in the main to be more concerned with right-wing economic policy issues than are their liberal-radical cousins who, for their part, are more prone to stress such things as 'social services', 'internationalism' and 'environment'. On the other hand, it remains the case that more or less all liberal parties continue to lay greater stress than do most others on such classic liberal values as 'democracy' and 'freedom'. In other words, not only are there clear indications of 'ambivalence' in European liberal manifestos, but there are also good grounds for suspecting that the bi-dimensionality to which Gordon Smith also points in ch. 2 is present as well.

FACTOR ANALYSIS

Another very obvious technique (or rather set of techniques) to use with data of the kind collected by the ECPR research group is factor analysis, since this permits us to look for any underlying structure in the data which might be interpreted in dimensional terms. Accordingly, by way of initial exploration, the data for some manifestos representing 77 different political parties of all ideological persuasions and from eleven countries (i.e. this time also including France), was submitted to a straightforward principal components analysis.[6] Given that all 54 issue categories were included in the analysis it was not to be expected that any very simple structure would emerge and, in one sense, it did not. Nineteen factors with eigenvalues greater than unity were produced accounting for 62.4 per cent of the common variance. However, application of the 'scree test' to the eigenvalues isolated only the two leading factors and these are, therefore, the only ones considered here.

The two factors accounted for 7.6 per cent and 7.2 per cent of the total common variance, figures which – considering there are so many variables, and consequently so many factors – are not at all low. Indeed, they compare well with those from the ECPR group's own analyses.[7] Certainly, both proved readily interpretable, particularly in their rotated form, and are described below and in Table 17.3, which shows all those issue categories that achieved factor loadings in excess of 0.3 on either side of a standardised mean of zero.

It is clear beyond dispute that factor one is a left–right one, concerned primarily with economic policy although there are elements of foreign relations in it as well. It is so clear, in fact, as to call for little or no discussion – certainly one would expect that the various liberal parties in the eleven countries would take up clearly different positions on such a dimension in accordance with their known leanings. For our present purposes, however, it is factor two which is more interesting. This second dimension combines the (essentially material) interests of farmers, middle-class and non-economic groups with the somewhat more intellectual and altruistic 'bourgeois progressive' concerns of culture, education and environment. To all intents and purposes, too, the dimension is 'unipolar', that is to say, apart from economic orthodoxy and the (very weak) loading for anti-EC attitudes, there is no significant opposition to the values it expresses.

In other words, once we have identified the left–right issues in Western European manifestos and controlled for their effect (for this, in essence, is what principal components analysis does), what is left is an essentially 'valence' or 'salience' dimension of issues no party is likely actually to oppose but which it may stress to a greater or lesser degree, regardless of its position on the left–right dimension itself. As such, it is obviously one which very largely (although probably not exclusively) expresses the particular concerns of liberal parties as revealed in the previous stage of the analysis.

Table 17.3 *Issue dimension emerging from factor analyses of Western European party manifestos*

Original categories	Factor loadings	Interpretation
Positive loadings		
Economic orthodoxy	0.53	'right'
Free enterprise	0.51	
Incentives	0.43	
Social service (negative)	0.38	
Military	0.38	
Law and order	0.31	
Negative Loadings		
Anti-military	−0.53	'left'
Nationalisation	−0.50	
Labour groups	−0.46	
Social justice	−0.38	
Regulation of capitalism	−0.37	
Controlled economy	−0.34	
Eurpean Community (negative)	−0.33	
Peace	−0.31	

a) First dimension rotated factor (Eigenvalue before rotation: 4.1; % of variance: 7.6)

Original categories	Factor loadings	Interpretation
Positive loadings		
Art, sport, leisure, media	0.65	'progressive'
Technology and infrastructure	0.54	
Education	0.53	
Agriculture and farmers	0.43	
Non-economic groups	0.42	
Social segmentation (*Verzuiling*, etc.)	0.42	
Internationalism	0.41	
Underprivileged minorities	0.39	
Environment	0.39	
Middle-class groups	0.36	
Negative loadings		
Economic orthodoxy	−0.39	'conservative'
European Community (negative)	−0.31	

b) Second dimension rotated factor (Eigenvalue before rotation: 3.9; % of variance: 7.2)

Because economic orthodoxy loads at the negative end of the factor, it has been labelled – for convenience as much as anything else – 'progressive versus conservative' although, of course, this is not to imply that the factor represents anything other than a linear combination of the various categories already mentioned and shown in Table 17.3.

One of the advantages of the principal components method, producing as it does factors which are orthogonal to one another, is that the factors can be plotted in two-dimensional graphs or scattergrammes. Diagram 17.1 shows the mean post-war positions in terms of the two factors for most of the parties of the analysis, including all fourteen liberal parties together with estimated positions for the French 'radical' and UDF *tendances*. The liberal-conservative and liberal-radical parties are indicated separately, as are those of the four other main political families. For the sake of clarity, not all these other parties are shown but the missing ones do all lie within the areas indicated.

Generally speaking, the discrimination both between and within political families is very satisfactory. There is even an area of the diagram, bounded by the Belgian PRL/PVV, the German FDP, the Dutch D'66 and the Austrian FPÖ, which is almost exclusive to the Liberal family and which significantly overlaps only into the Christian democratic area.

As expected, this territory is more wide-ranging in left–right terms than that of any other political family stretching from D'66's position near the more moderate socialist parties to the PRL/PVV which appears almost as right-wing as the Danish and Norwegian conservatives. Gordon Smith's 'liberal-conservative' and 'liberal-radical' classification, too, seems to work rather well, although there are one or two doubtful cases, most notably the two Norwegian parties, both of which appear well inside the area bounded by parties of the liberal-conservative type, and the Austrian FPÖ, which Smith identifies as liberal-conservative but which not only appears in the dead centre of the left–right dimension, but is also the single most 'progressive' of all liberal parties. On this evidence at least, the FPÖ appears to have more in common with the liberal-radical camp which, given the party's origins, might be thought of as somewhat surprising.

For its part, the 'conservative-progressive' dimension distinguishes fairly well between the liberal-conservative parties on the one hand and the genuinely conservative ones on the other, as well as between the former and virtually all Christian democratic parties. However, there is a considerable overlap between latter group and several of the liberal-radical parties in the centre of the space, although this particular finding may be more apparent than real. Liberal-radical and Christian democratic parties rarely coexist in most West European countries, so such an overlap probably does not really occur in practice.

Indeed, the picture shown in Diagram 17.1 can easily be inter-

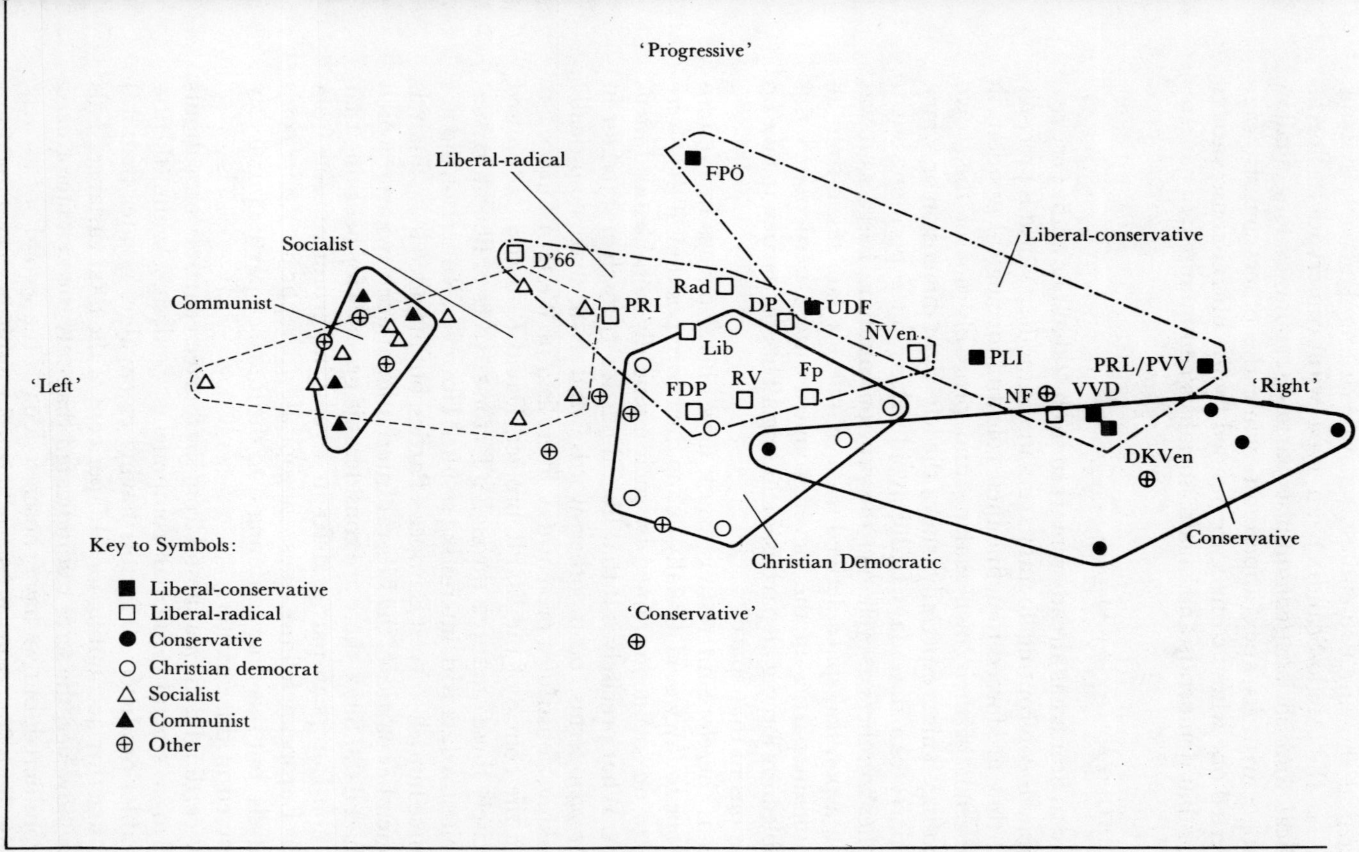

Diagram 17.1 Party systems

Note: for clarity not all non-liberal parties are shown

preted as showing two entirely separate 'triangular' party systems. One is the Anglo-Scandinavian type with conservative, liberal-radical and socialist/communist parties forming a long shallow triangle with its apex uppermost, while the other consists of an inverted one whose corners are defined by the liberal-conservatives, Christian democrats and, again, socialists/communists.

WITHIN-FAMILY ANALYSIS

Gordon Smith has already remarked in ch. 2 that one of the very real problems confronting liberal parties in the modern world is precisely that they are forced to define their role and ideological positions in terms not of their own making and probably not of their own choosing. This is especially true of the left–right dimension on which no party can nowadays really avoid taking up a position, but it applies to others as well. Yet the previous analysis, based as it was upon a political space derived from manifestos data taken from all significant parties in the eleven countries, itself perpetuated this problem by forcing all parties, including all liberal parties, to take up positions in that space.

It is therefore interesting to ask how liberal parties in Western Europe today would actually define their own positions if they were free to do so unconstrained by such essentially non-liberal dimensions. What precisely is it that liberal parties themselves stand for in their *own* terms, or in other words what is it that, empirically speaking, constitutes present-day liberalism in Western Europe?

In the course of the ECPR project, David Robertson addressed precisely these questions through a factor-analysis of liberal parties' manifestos data with interesting results.[8] However, Robertson did not confine himself to West European Parties, but included in his analysis all member parties of the Liberal International world-wide for which he had data. Since there are considerable grounds for believing that the non-European parties differ in several important respects from their European fellows, it is appropriate to replicate Robertson's analysis, but this time confining it to the fourteen parties previously analysed in this chapter.

Accordingly, the manifestos from the fourteen parties were submitted to a second principal components analysis. Again, the 54 variables produced 19 factors having eigenvalues greater than 1.0 and together accounting for 74.0 per cent of the total variance. This time, however, the scree test indicated that only the first factor need be considered, but we have chosen to look at the second one as well. Again, both factors are more easily interpretable in the rotated form shown in Table 17.4.

Table 17.4 *Issue dimension emerging from factor analyses of Western European liberal party manifestos*

Original categories	Factor loadings	Interpretation
Positive loadings		
Peace	0.49	'new liberalism'
Internationalism	0.49	
Art, sport, leisure, media	0.44	
Environment	0.44	
Democracy	0.42	
Technology and infrastructure	0.38	
Education	0.38	
Social segmentation (*Verzuiling*, etc.)	0.34	
Foreign special relationships	0.31	
Regulation of capitalism	0.31	
Negative loadings		
Social services (negative)	−0.52	'old liberalism'
National effort/social harmony	−0.45	
Government effectiveness and authority	−0.42	
Full employment	−0.36	
Incentives	−0.34	

a) First dimension rotated factor (Eigenvalue before rotation: 4.5; % of variance: 8.4)

Original categories	Factor loadings	Interpretation
Positive loadings		
Underprivileged minorities	0.63	'groups'
Non-economic groups	0.60	
Environment	0.42	
Middle-class groups	0.40	
Decentralisation	0.37	
Social segmentation (negative)	0.36	
Agriculture and farmers	0.36	
Law and order	0.35	
Labour groups	0.34	
National way of life (negative)	0.34	

b) Second dimension rotated factor (Eigenvalue before rotation: 3.7; % of variance: 6.9)

Not surprisingly, although inevitably there are some differences, there are major similarities between this structure and that found by Robertson in his world-wide analysis. So much so, in fact, that his interpretation of his first factor seems almost as valid for the purely European one and could not be bettered here.

Liberals [unlike Conservatives] incorporate the traditional concerns for democracy and for civil liberties into their ideal. Distrust of strong governments . . . and controlled economies, along with a concern for

> economic necessities like productivity, characterise what we . . . call the 'hard' end of the Liberal spectrum. Along with democracy/civil liberties (including decentralisation) go, for example, a *laisser-faire* economic theory. The only associated economic variable is the classic 'holding the ring' notion of Regulation of Capitalism. All the 'green' issues – environmentalism, art, sport, etc. (but not, let it be noted, traditional welfarism or educational concern) – go at this end. The same emphases on groups (non-economic and underprivileged minorities) occur. The only surprises, perhaps, are the essentially 'un-soft' categories of 'Law and Order' and 'Traditional Morality', but these two fit the classic Liberal idea of holding in order the structure of society but interfering as little as possible. The dimension . . . represents what any theorist would see as degrees of orthodox Liberalism.[9]

Perhaps the only caveats that need to be made about this description are that in the European case freedom and human rights does not load significantly in either direction on the factor as it does in the world-wide analysis, presumably precisely because it is an issue which does not divide European liberals from one another, and that, in Europe at least, education does indeed load with the 'soft' end of liberalism, as Robertson implies it should.

If this interpretation is correct, then – although factor one can be seen as representing alternative foci for liberal parties – it does so in terms which are not constrained by the essentially economic thinking imposed by the non-liberal right and left. Rather, as Robertson says, it is a dimension of liberalism *per se*. However, it is noteworthy that the particular mix of categories loading positively on factor one, including as it does such things as peace, internationalism, art, sport and environment, typifies precisely that set of attitudes which we earlier christened 'bourgeois progressivism', in short, the issues of the 1970s and 1980s rather than those of the 1940s and 1950s. For this reason, we prefer to see the factor as one differentiating between what we might call the 'new liberalism' at one end and the rather more materialistic 'old liberalism' at the other.

Factor two also, of course, must be seen as a dimension of pure liberalism, albeit orthogonal to the first, and not one imposed by an alternative non-liberal view of the world. And so it proves, the factor needing little, if any, interpretation. It is a simple unipolar one concerned with the varied interests of particular sectional groups, whether economically-defined or not, as opposed perhaps to those of society as a whole.

These interpretations are lent considerable weight when the individual parties themselves are plotted in the two-dimensional space defined by the two factors, as is done in Diagram 17.2.

This time, the liberal-conservative and liberal-radical distinction breaks down completely, clearly underlining the fact that this is an

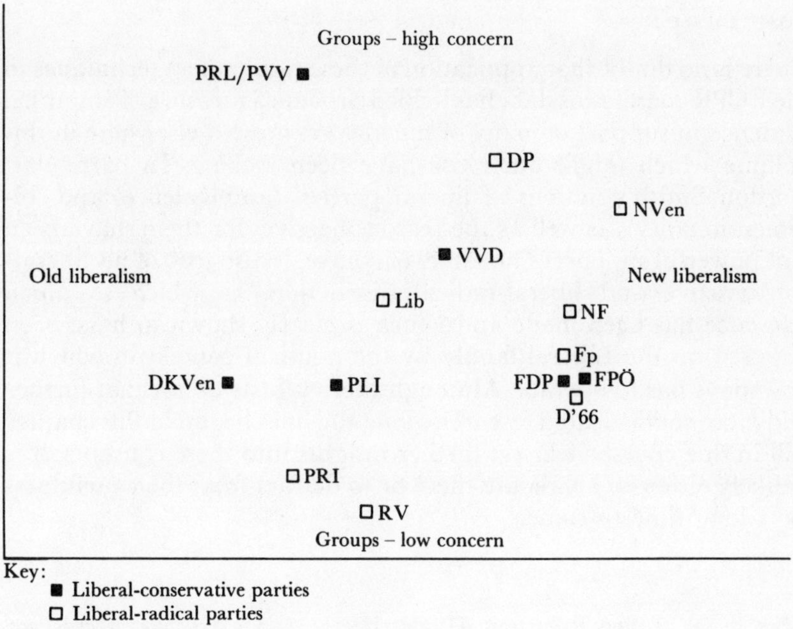

Diagram 17.2 Inter-party relationships

essentially left–right distinction in terms of economic policy imposed by the pervasive but non-liberal *Weltanschauung* of politicians and political observers alike. When left to speak for themselves, as it were, it seems that liberal parties differentiate themselves from one another on quite different grounds. Nevertheless, Diagram 17.2 does show a perfectly intelligible set of inter-party relationships if the above interpretations given to the two factors are borne in mind. The cluster of parties from Austria, Germany, Sweden and the Netherlands in the lower right-hand quadrant of the diagram for example, together with the single manifesto published by the Norwegian Nye Folkeparti, exhibit the twin characteristics of low levels of concern for purely sectional interests and for the 'new liberalism', a combination which seems perfectly sensible in these relatively successful and culturally homogeneous economies. On the other hand, the positions of such parties as Norwegian Venstre, the Luxemburg DP and, above all, the Belgian PRL/PVV clearly show the great importance given by these parties to more particularist interests in their respective countries. (The exaggeratedly high Belgian score on this dimension, of course, is a function of the overriding necessity for all parties in that country to pay particular attention to the different regions and linguistic communities there.)

CONCLUSION

There is no doubt that application of these (and other) techniques to the ECPR manifestos data has helped provide a measure of empirical evidence in support of many of the ideas expressed elsewhere in this volume which might otherwise have been lacking. In particular, Gordon Smith's notions of liberal parties' 'ambivalence' and 'bi-dimensionality', as well as the reasons he gives for them, have been lent powerful support. The same, of course, is also true of his liberal-conservative and liberal-radical distinction, to which so much reference has been made and which is clearly shown to have been imposed on the Liberal family by the political context in which it nowadays has to operate. Although there is little doubt that further and more sophisticated research along the lines begun in this chapter will in due course yield yet further insights into these concepts, it is unlikely either to invalidate them or to detract from their usefulness for a long time to come.

NOTES

1 See Budge, I. and Robertson, D. and Hearl, D., *Ideology, Strategy and Party Movement: A Comparative Analysis of Election Programmes in Nineteen Democracies* (Cambridge: CUP, 1987). Note that, since this book was written, at least one other country has been added to the data set which may be obtained from the ESRC Data Archive at the University of Essex. I am grateful to my fellow contributors for permission to make use of it here.

2 In point of fact this procedure makes very little difference. The separate PVV and the PRL 'profiles' differ from one another hardly at all except over the finer points of decentralisation policy and even here there is probably a greater degree of agreement between the two parties than there is within their rival Christian-social and socialist 'families'. (See Budge et al. (1987) ch. 11.)

3 See Budge, I. and Farlie, D., *Explaining and Predicting Elections, Issue Effects and Party Strategies in Twenty-Three Democracies* (London: George Allen and Unwin, 1983) ch. 2, for an extended version of this argument.

4 The ECPR project used a modified form of Sartori's criteria of 'relevance', which means that, in practice, all major parties in the countries concerned are included.

5 See Smith, G., *Politics in Western Europe*, 4th edn (London: Heinemann Educational Books, 1984).

6 This was done using the 'FACTOR' routine in SPSS (Version 9) with all default switches in force. The effect of this is to perform a 'PA2'-type principal components analysis with (orthogonal) varimax rotation. See Nie, N. et al., *A Statistical Package for the Social Sciences – SPSS*, 2nd edn (New York: McGraw–Hill, 1975).

7 See Budge et al. (1987).

8 See Budge et al. (1987), ch. 18.

9 See Budge et al. (1987).

18

Transnational links: the ELD and Liberal Party Group in the European Parliament

Rudolf Hrbek

BACKGROUND AND HISTORICAL DEVELOPMENT

International co-operation of political parties belonging to the same political-ideological 'family' in the framework of 'Internationals' is a well-known phenomenon. Parties understand such organisations primarily as round tables for exchanging views and discussing ideas in a rather general manner. In 1947, liberals established the Liberal World Union, now renamed as the 'Liberal International', as such a forum for mutual information and communication. It has to be regarded as a loose grouping, since the participating parties did represent the whole broad spectrum of liberal positions. The Liberal Manifesto of Oxford, adopted at the founding convention in 1947 – amended in 1967 with the Liberal Declaration of Oxford – did reflect the political heterogeneity of the member parties; it was too general to serve as a basis and programmatic guideline for common activities. The members regarded the organisation as a loose but useful forum.[1]

In 1952 the 'Mouvement Libéral pour l'Europe Unie' (MLEU) was founded as an organisation which should concentrate its activities on issues of European unification; the MLEU was independent from the Liberal International. In 1961 membership in this specialised organisation was restricted to parties and politicians from EC countries only. In 1972 the MLEU was incorporated as a regional organisation into the Liberal International, which since 1969 had started to promote the establishment of closer links and more intense co-operation amongst liberal parties from EC countries, adding to the consolidation of the community. This trend culminated in the decision to establish an EC-wide federation of liberal parties, adopted during the 1972 Convention of the International in Paris.[2]

Founding a party federation is a much more ambitious enterprise compared to the traditional party co-operation in the framework of the Internationals: it has as its perspective and aim the development of a party organisation at transnational level which would and should function as a political actor with respect to EC affairs. An EC-wide party federation would represent a new type of transnational party links and co-operation.

The reasons for the efforts amongst liberals to establish a transnational party federation were more or less the same as for the other two party families – socialists and Christian democrats – who started identical moves in the early seventies. They can be summarised as follows:

Responding to the challenge of direct elections to the European Parliament. When it became obvious in the early seventies that the governments of the EC member states would agree on having the EP directly elected, political parties had to prepare for this event. The existence and activities of transnational party federations would contribute to give such elections a 'European' character by presenting to the electorate a common programme agreed upon by all member parties, by campaigning in a transnational framework, and perhaps by co-operating in the selection of candidates.

Supplying the political groups in the European Parliament with a party political basis and thereby strengthening their political weight and impact on EC decision-making. There were expectations that a party federation would provide political guidelines for the parliamentary group.

Adapting to the new period of Community development into which the EC had entered and which had been labelled as 'positive integration'.[3] The term has been used to give the Community a framework where crucial problems can be discussed and decided (cf. projects towards an economic and monetary union, a social union and a European union). Perceiving these trends, political parties were eager to be present at Community level and have a better chance of influencing developments affecting their particular concerns.

Following other socio-economic associations which had already established Euro-organisations (cf. COPA and UNICE, created as early as 1958, and the ETUC, founded in 1973).

Contributing to reduce the 'deficit' in the EC's democratic legitimacy. In national political systems, parties have the function of transmission belts between the electorate and the political institutions; they do articulate what people think and explain to them what the political elites do. An active communication process of that kind is essential for a political system's legitimacy. Most observers of European integration agreed that the EC was lacking legitimacy and active support; they used instead the label 'permissive consensus'[4] to characterise the overall attitude of the general public. If one sees the EC as a multi-level system, following Puchala's notion of a 'Concordance System',[5] and if one understands integration as a process during which mutual links between these levels grow, then the existence and activities of transnational party organisations are important for the integration progress. They help to establish and maintain links between different levels; they are a component of the socio-political infrastructure of the EC system which can be regarded as an emerging political system.

This list of major motives indicates at the same time the goals expected from the establishment of transnational party organisations and their development towards efficient political actors in the Community's decision-making system. Given the fact that the European liberals cover a broad spectrum, their efforts towards more intense transnational links could be regarded as both difficult and ambitious.

Liberal party leaders who used to meet regularly after 1964 on an informal basis played a dominant role in these efforts; they became the driving force towards the establishment of a transnational party organisation by 1973. For example, they arranged for the constituent convention in 1976 and contributed to its steady development. The Liberal Party Group in the European Parliament, on the contrary, played only a marginal role in this preparatory period, due to the group's heterogeneity. The group had the Gaullists as members until 1963 when this particular national group decided to leave the liberals and form a group themselves; in addition, the Italian monarchists and neofascists did belong to the group and were only expelled in 1973. In the consolidation period of the liberal party federation, however, the party group of the EP was of great help in terms of financial and organisational support.

The founding convention took place in March 1976 in Stuttgart; 14 parties from 8 EC countries (without Ireland) were present and 9 joined the federation immediately, 5 others joined before the first congress at the end of the same year in The Hague. The Stuttgart

Declaration agreed upon at the founding convention contains the basic concept of the European Liberal Democrats (ELD) for establishing a European Union and the future integration process. It served at the same time as the starting point for the debate on the political platform of the ELD, and contained the following five points: the guarantee of political, human and civil rights; a democratic constitution based on the principles of separation of powers, majority decision and protection of minorities; continuous and balanced economic growth; a common foreign policy; individual freedom, equality of opportunity and free competition of ideas and parties as indispensable components of a democratic society.

COMPOSITION AND ORGANISATIONAL STRUCTURE OF ELD

Membership

In 1979, the year of the first direct elections to the European Parliament, the ELD had 11 members: 2 parties from Belgium (one from Flanders, one from Wallonie; the latter was the result of a fusion of 2 separate parties), 2 from France (Republicans and Radical Socialists), 2 from Italy (Liberals and Republicans); and one from the other 6 countries with the exception of Ireland. Another Danish party, the Radicals Venstre, had left the ELD in 1977 for political reasons: the party did not agree to an increase in power for Community institutions and also – due to its pacifist tradition – to the involvement of the EC in security affairs.

The French MRG (Mouvement des Radicaux de Gauche) left after the general elections in 1978 since the party was in opposition to the Republican Party of President Giscard.

The left-wing Liberals in the Dutch D'66 decided not to join the federation, since they were in opposition domestically to the more right-wing Liberals in the VVD, and they also criticised the French Republicans whom they declared to be openly conservative. This latter aspect has been a permanent problem for the British Liberal Party which usually feels uneasy belonging to the ELD together with the French Republicans.

From the very beginning the ELD made efforts to establish links with parties from Greece, Portugal and Spain. Parties from these countries applying for EC-membership were admitted as 'observers' to the congress meetings. In 1983 the Liberal Party of Greece under N. Venizelos (only a splinter group in Greek politics) became a member; in 1984 the Alliance Party of Northern Ireland; and, in connection with the accession of Portugal and Spain to the EC, the Portuguese PSD (Social Democrat Party) and the Spanish PRD

(Democratic Reform Party) were admitted as full members. As a result of this enlargement in membership, the party federation changed its name to the 'Federation of European Liberal, Democratic and Reform Parties' (ELDR).

LYMEC (Liberal and Radical Youth Movement of the EC) is represented in the institutions of the party federation and the same is true for the Liberal group in the European Parliament. There is no individual membership in ELD.

Organisational structure

The statutes of the federation had been adopted in Stuttgart in 1976 and revised in Venice in May 1982. The congress and the executive committee are the two organs of the federation; they are assisted by the secretariat general.

The composition of the congress is as follows (Art. 28):

Six representatives from each country. If there is more than one party, these representatives shall be allocated to each party according to the proportional strength they achieved at the last general election.

For each member party, a number of representatives based on the following relationship to the number of votes: one representative for each 100,000 votes or a major part thereof up to three million votes; one representative for each 250,000 votes or a major part thereof between three and five million votes; one representative for each 500,000 votes or a major part thereof exceeding five million votes.

All members of the Liberal and Democratic Group in the EP and all members of the EC Commission belonging to a member party.

10 representatives from LYMEC.

The congress meets annually. It elects the president of the federation for a two-year term (he may be re-elected twice) and those 6 members of the executive committee who are not appointed by their parties. The congress is the supreme organ of the federation and it has the power to decide on all matters within the competence of the treaties on the EC and on EPC affairs. The statutes provide for majority decisions: a two-thirds majority of members present and voting is needed for a valid decision. The following amendment to the statute adopted in 1982 was to strengthen the transnational character of the federation at the expense of national parties: the right to submit proposals as resolutions and their amendment, originally reserved for the executive committee or one member party, was extended to 25 delegates.

The executive committee consists of the president, the chairman of the Liberal and Democratic Group in the EP, EC Commission members who belong to a member party, one LYMEC representative; each party has 2 members, but a party entitled to more than 10 per cent of the delegates of the congress has a third member. The additional clause ('However, there may be no more than 4 members from any single member state as party representatives') is directed against the 2 French member parties, especially the Republicans. Finally, there are 6 members elected by the congress to be nominated by 25 delegates; and this is another provision which is to accentuate the federation's transnational character by breaking the monopoly of national parties to make proposals. The executive committee appoints 2 vice-presidents – with 15 member parties there will be a third one from 1986 – the secretary general and the treasurer. The executive committee meets at least four times a year; between meetings of the congress, it has the power to speak and act on behalf of the federation. Decisions are taken by majority vote.

In principle, the possibility to take majority decisions tends to reduce the autonomy of each member party. In practice, however, there is no excessive use of this provision; the member parties try to reach a consensus. But there are often cases where a party finds itself in a minority position and outvoted.

The first president of ELD was Gaston Thorn from Luxemburg. After being appointed president of the EC Commission, Willy de Clercq (Belgium) became his successor and held this position until he entered the EC Commission in 1985. Now Colette Flesch (Luxemburg) is president. There is a high degree of continuity in the executive committee's membership. The secretariat general (with Mechthild von Alemann, Federal Republic of Germany, as secretary general) has its seat in Brussels; it is dependent on the ELD parliamentary group's financial and organisational support.

POLITICAL PROFILE AND PROGRAMME OF THE ELD

The Stuttgart Declaration of March 1976 served as the basis for the elaboration of an election platform to be used for the first direct elections in 1979. Seven working groups set up by the Stuttgart convention prepared a draft which was discussed at the first congress in The Hague at the end of 1976. This congress set up a programme committee (the chairman was Martin Bangemann, Federal Republic of Germany) which was given the function of co-ordinating the preparatory work. The executive committee agreed to a new draft and passed it on to the member parties; within these parties an intense discussion amongst party members took place. The second congress in November 1977 in Brussels reviewed the draft, including many proposals for amendments, and agreed upon a final version (the LYMEC delegates abstained).

The programme not only contains statements concerning actual EC issues but also the basic positions of Western European liberalism which are the guidelines for ELD activities in the EC context. As such the document goes way beyond an election platform.[6] There are propositions in the programme which are mandatory for all member parties; additional clauses offer the freedom to be interpretated by each party in turn. The concept of a liberal society – in favour of human and civilian rights and rejecting dogmatism and intolerance – forms the core of the programme. A liberal approach to politics is focused on the value of individual freedom, combined with solidarity as the main principle for society as well as international relations. Other points made in the programme include:

The EC will develop towards an economic and monetary union; its institutions – primarily the Commission and the EP – shall be given increased powers; majority decisions in the council are regarded as a condition for greater efficiency. Regarding the electoral system for the EP elections, the ELD parties demand a uniform system and are in favour of proportional representation which would open the way for the British Liberals to gain entry to the European Parliament.

The EC will play an active role in international relations: strengthening the Atlantic Alliance and improving co-operation between Western Europe and the USA; co-ordinating their foreign and security policies including defence; further developing *détente*. The programme welcomes the EC's southern enlargement but stresses at the same time that enlargement must not negatively affect the process of Community development. International economic relations shall be managed in accordance with the principles of a free market system; this should apply to policies towards underdeveloped nations with an emphasis on private initiative.

The relatively broad political spectrum of ELD member parties can be seen in the paragraphs dealing with economic and social affairs. The statements are not precise enough to serve as elements of an action programme: e.g. the common agricultural policy shall be further developed – farmers belong to the electorate of some member parties – but deficiencies of the system should be reduced; additionally, the issue of using nuclear energy has been left open.

The organisation and management of the economy has to follow, in principle, the free market system. In practice, however, the dynamism of private enterprise should be combined with methods of flexible planning, the participation of the two sides of industry in decision-making in economic and social affairs and some form of fixing guidelines for wages and prices. This means a certain ambiguity, but on the whole the function of the state should be restricted to maintaining the general framework for a market system: state intervention should strengthen free competition, small and medium enterprises (they represent a guarantee for a real market, a pluralist society and the existence of independent economic forces) should be supported. The programme is rather vague concerning the issue of economic democracy by mentioning the right of the employed to participate in the management of enterprises without recommending any particular scheme.

The ELD concentrated its activities after the first direct elections to the European Parliament in 1979 on the following fields:

Human rights. Following liberal principles, the ELD has been demanding a European charter for civilian and political rights; among these, for example, access to information from state authorities in cases affecting the interests and concerns of the citizen; and the right to be consulted by local and national authorities in such cases.

Development of the EC towards a European union. Again and again there are resolutions supporting initiatives in this direction; e.g. the Genscher and Colombo plan or the initiative of the European Parliament (Spinelli). The ELD favours a treaty on European union which would include an increase in the EC's functional scope (including environmental/ecological and security issues) as well as strengthening the institutions. The EP should be given greater powers and the council should take majority decisions more frequently.

Introduction of a uniform electoral system. Elections to the EP should be based on a uniform system in all member countries. The ELD has been very strongly in favour of proportional representation which would require a change in the traditional British system which results, at present, in discrimination against the Liberal Party.

From the very beginning the ELD as a transnational party federation aimed at achieving political cohesion as a basis for common activities. No doubt, the member parties could reach consensus on major questions, but they are still far from having achieved the cohesion of a tightly-knit group of political actors.

The discussion of the electoral platform for the second direct elections of the EP in 1984 at the ELD congress in Munich in December 1983 is an illustration of the divergent outlooks and positions within the party federation. There were two major issues in which the British Liberals found themselves in a minority position. They voted against a clause demanding strict stability in economic policy; their attitude has to be understood in terms of domestic political reasons: they had entered an alliance with the Social Democratic Party and, within this partnership, they opposed the course of Margaret Thatcher's government. It was for the same domestic political reasons that the representatives of the Liberal Party were not ready to welcome the dual-track decision of NATO and the deployment of cruise missiles in Britain. They criticised particularly the German Liberals (the FDP) for taking a new stance after changing coalition partners in Bonn; in October 1982 the FDP helped to replace the Social Democrat Chancellor Schmidt by the Christian Democrat Kohl, and the general election in West Germany in March 1983 confirmed this new coalition. On both issues – economic policy and the dual-track decision – however, the German Liberals stuck to their traditional position.

The congress in Groningen in June 1985 was another example of the group lacking political homogeneity. In the field of external relations, the British Liberals favoured unilateral disarmament whereas the Italian Republicans submitted a draft motion with a very 'Atlantic' tendency. The result was a compromise. In the field of internal security, the congress was not even capable of passing a motion due to unbridgeable divergencies on competences and functions attributed to police forces and the nature of democratic control mechanisms *vis-à-vis* the police. Here, British and German Liberals, together with Italian Republicans, opposed a 'law and order' statement which they regarded as being incompatible with liberal thinking.

A strong indicator of the still absent homogeneity in the political outlook and profile is the way the member parties carried through their campaign for the second direct elections in 1984. They had formulated a common electoral platform but the parties used the elections primarily as a national contest; the 'European' dimension played only a minor role, if any at all.[7]

THE ELD GROUP IN THE EUROPEAN PARLIAMENT

The party federation ELD represents only one element of the transnational party links and co-operative work of the liberal parties within the EC framework. The liberal group in the EP ('Liberal and Democratic Group' and, since December 1985, renamed as 'Liberal, Democratic and Reformist Group') forms the other one. This coexistence raises the question of the nature of the relationships between these two components. When the party federation had been founded, it was expected to take the lead and give the parliamentary group political guidelines.

In practice, however, things developed differently. It was the parliamentary group of the European Liberals and Democrats which played the major role and which became associated with the label 'liberal' in dealings with EC affairs, primarily with the EP group and its activities.

The organisational and financial structure of the parliamentary group is superior to that of the party federation; the latter is, in this respect, dependent on the parliamentary group's support. Here is a first factor which does explain the latter's superiority and which must not be underestimated.

A second, more important factor has to be seen in the rhythm of EP work: as an institution in search of a more powerful role in EC decision-making, the EP and most of its members started large-scale activities with the result that all party groups had to deal with a large number of EC issues. The rhythm generated by a continuous sequence of plenary sessions, group and committee meetings and detailed agendas forced the groups, including the ELD Group, to formulate their answers and points of view. As a consequence, it was the ELD Group in the EP which shaped the 'liberal' profile in the EC context. In general, there is no possibility of postponing issues, since the parliamentary agenda demands a quick decision. The political composition of the EP is characterised by a plurality of different groups and this makes it necessary to form alliances which require that the groups accept compromises. One can easily imagine that conflicts between party federation and parliamentary group will arise, a pattern with which the analyst of politics in a national political system is familiar.

In the first directly elected European Parliament, the Liberal group had 38 members. 15 French members formed the biggest section, followed by 5 Italians (from 2 parties), 4 Belgians (2 parties), 4 Dutch and 4 Germans, 3 Danes, 2 members from Luxemburg and one independent Irish deputy who joined the group as an 'ally'.

There were no members from Greece and the United Kingdom.

The weight of the French component representing a more conservative, right-wing position was therefore relatively great. Together with the Dutch and the Danish members – both parties can be placed at a centre-right position in their domestic party spectrum – the Liberal group could not be expected to be a potential ally for the Socialists. The chairman of the group, the German Martin Bangemann, who held the office for the whole period from 1979 to 1984, was known to represent the right-wing elements in his party, which from 1969 until October 1982 formed a federal coalition with the Social Democrats in Bonn.

Whenever economic and social issues were on the EP's agenda, the Liberals could be expected to be on the right, together with the Christian Democrats (European People's Party), the Conservatives (European Democrats) and the Gaullists. The Socialists used to complain about this 'bloc' of the right. But there is not only the right–left cleavage in the EP. The other potential cleavages are: small versus big countries; northern versus southern European countries; old versus new member countries; pro-integrationist versus anti-integrationist attitudes. There are also many issues where these additional categories play a role. As a consequence, there are no permanent coalition/alliance patterns in the EP. It would require very careful investigations – including the analysis of committee work and intra-group discussions – to give a full picture of all the different relationships and issues.

After the second direct elections, the profile of the Liberal group changed slightly. Its numerical strength was reduced to 31 members. There were losses (one each) for the Danish and the Luxemburg member parties; the Italians maintained their number of seats; the Belgians and the Dutch won one seat each; and the French were reduced to 12 members (a loss of three). The independent Irish member again joined the group. Again there were, as in the first directly elected European Parliament, no Greek or British representatives but also no German Liberals since their party had failed to surmount the 5 per cent clause and was thus excluded.

The political profile of the group became even more right-wing, something which reflected coalition patterns in the domestic political settings of most member parties – in the majority of cases they opposed the socialists. The admission of Portugal and Spain had the effect of a numerical increase for the group: 9 Portuguese and 2 Spanish members joined the Liberal group. The Portuguese represent the governing party; the general election in October 1985 saw the Social Democrat Party – a member in ELD – win 29.9 per cent of the votes; its chairman, Anibal Cavaco Silva became prime minister. It is impossible to make a forecast concerning the effects of the group's enlargement on its activities. The French politician, Simone Veil, president of the EP for the first 2½ years (1979–81), is now chairwoman of the Liberal group.

MAJOR PROBLEMS FOR THE TRANSNATIONAL PARTY LINKS OF THE LIBERALS

The ELD has been established with the perspective and aim of developing a party organisation as a political actor at EC level, one which should play a role in EC decision-making and be more than a loose round table for mutual information and discussion. The following three aspects can be regarded as decisive for the quality of the party federation as a transnational actor as well as its ability to meet the expectations associated with its activities and development:

Its internal cohesion: Has it been able to reach consensus on principal questions and achieve the organisational and political strength necessary to fulfil the main functions attributed to a transnational party organisation? Would it develop towards a party organisation or only a slightly improved round table?

Its relationship with the Liberal and Democratic Group in the EP: Has it been able to achieve the position of a powerful party political base and give the parliamentary group political guidelines?

Its relationship with the member parties in the nation states: Has it been able to exert some influence on national member parties on EC-related issues and has it been accepted and respected as a party unit at European level?

Internal cohesion within the ELD suffers from a variety of factors. Liberal parties do represent a broad political spectrum – there are different profiles of political liberalism. Liberal parties are small parties which makes them search for coalitions within their national political systems. Differences in coalition patterns at national level affect the efforts of the parties at transnational (ELD) level to reach consensus and to formulate a cohesive programme as the basis for common action. Another factor in this context is the difference in the structure of the electorate of the parties. Some have their basis and strongholds in the agrarian sectors of society, others are oriented more towards white-collar employees, or to groups in industry and finance.

Such structural divergencies are aggravated by the organisational and financial weaknesses of the ELD. The budget is too small to allow the establishment of a larger and more efficient secretariat or regular editions of a newsletter. The lack of resources is a restriction which affects the routine work considerably. Another weakness lies in the fact that representatives of national parties in the institutions of the ELD do not belong to the top leadership. One can observe the emergence of a Euro-elite within the parties but these people have often no firm roots and no standing and prestige in their national party organisations.

The party federation tried to concentrate its activities by using an additional institution: the Bureau. According to the statute this institution consists of the president, the vice-presidents, the treasurer, the secretary-general and the chairman of the EP group.

With respect to the second major aspect – relations between the party federation ELD and the parliamentary group – it became obvious that the Liberal and Democratic Group in the EP has become the predominant force. There is a whole network of organisational and personal links: representatives of the parliamentary group are members in ELD institutions and the general secretary of ELD used regularly to attend meetings of the parliamentary group. But the latter is, no doubt, superior with respect to organisational capacity and financial resources.

A crucial problem for this relationship results from the fact that two major parties – the British Liberal Party and the German FDP – are not represented in the EP; on the other hand, French deputies have more than twice the strength within the parliamentary group compared to the French element at ELD congresses. We have mentioned the perception of the French component by other member parties, especially the British, who deny the French the label 'liberal'. Such a relationship means a heavy potential burden affecting relations between the party federation and the parliamentary group. One cannot expect that, under the circumstances, the latter will recognise the claim of the federation to take the political lead. On the other hand, it is primarily the parliamentary group with their intense activity within the EP which observers will associate with 'liberal' positions; this might in turn cause some irritation and perhaps criticism within the federation with its differing composition and distribution of party strength.

Concerning the third major aspect – relations between party federation and national parties – there are some assets. For one, the fact that the draft electoral platform had been transmitted to all national parties for intense discussion before the congress adopted the final version. Moreover, we have already mentioned that the individual member parties try to maintain their autonomy and this can be demonstrated in connection with their behaviour in the EP election campaigns. Despite the existence of majority voting in the institutions of ELD, each member party continues to insist on its own autonomy.

On the whole, however, transnational links are a fact; they have developed in the EC system and will continue to develop. The existence and performance of the party federation ELD and the Liberal and Democratic and Reformist Group in the European Parliament have become an integral part of the Community's decision-making system. They have contributed to the integration progress and have given the EC its specific character distinct from other international organisations. Such transnational links and organisations form one component in the socio-political infrastructure of the EC.[8] This is a remarkable asset for the Community and EC integration, irrespective of the list of weaknesses and restrictions mentioned above. The parliamentary group in the EP seems to represent the most efficient and important element of the party political dimension at transnational level. Difficulties in achieving cohesion and consensus which can and will be found in the parliamentary group as well as in the transnational party federation only reflect the inevitable problems which arise in any process of integration.

NOTES

This contribution is based on a series of articles of the author on transnational party federations in a yearbook (Rudolf Hrbek 'Die europäischen Parteienzusammenschlüsse' in: Werner Weidenfeld and Wolfgang Wessels (eds.), *Jahrbuch der europäischen Integration 1980, 1981, 1982, 1983, 1984, 1985*, Bonn 1981, 1982, 1983, 1984, 1985, 1986); on two articles of the author in *Pipers Wörterbuch zur Politik*, vol. 3: 'Europäische Gemeinschaft. Problemfelder – Institutionen – Politik', ed. by Wichard Woyke, Munich 1984 (Europäische Liberale Demokraten, pp. 201–7; Europäische Parteienföderationen, pp. 221–6); and on a paper prepared for and presented at the IPSA World Congress Paris, July 1985, Research Committee on European Unification ('Transnational party federations: towards the emergence of European political parties').

1 See the brief description by Rudolf Hrbek, 'Liberale International/LI' in Uwe Andersen and Wichard Woyke (eds.), *Handwörterbuch Internationale Organisationen*, Opladen 1985, pp. 318–19.

2 Basic works for the early period of the party federations are: Institut für Europäische Politik (ed.), *Zusammenarbeit der Parteien in Westeuropa. Auf dem Weg zu einer neuen politischen Infrastruktur*, Bonn 1976; Norbert Gresch, *Transnationale Parteienzusammenarbeit in der EG*, Baden-Baden 1978; Geoffrey and Pippa Pridham, 'Transnational parties in the European Community' in Stanley Henig (ed.), *Political Parties in the European Community*, London 1979.

3 John Pinder, 'Positive integration and negative integration: some problems of economic union in the EEC' in *The World Today*, vol. 24 (1968) 88–110.

4 Cf. Leon N. Lindberg and Stuart A. Scheingold, *Europe's Would-Be Polity. Patterns of Change in the European Community*, Englewood Cliffs 1970, pp. 249ff.; and Thomas A. Herz, *Europa in der öffentlichen Meinung. Zur politischen Mobilisierung in Deutschland und Frankreich zwischen 1962 und 1977*, Bonn 1978, pp. 159ff.

5 Donald J. Puchala, 'Of blind men, elephants and international integration' in *Journal of Common Market Studies*, vol. 10, no. 3 (March 1972) 267–84, and 'Trends in the study of European integration: recent efforts by American scholars', paper prepared for and presented at the IPSA World Congress Moscow, August 1979, Research Committee on European Unification.

6 Cf. Eva-Rose Karnofsky, *Parteienbünde vor der Europawahl 1979. Integration durch gemeinsame Wahlaussagen?* Bonn 1982.

7 Cf. Oskar Niedermayer, 'The transnational dimension of the election' in *Electoral Studies*, vol. 3, no. 3 (Dec. 1984), special issue on European Elections 1984, pp. 235–43; and Rudolf Hrbek, 'Direktwahl '84: Nationale Testwahlen oder "europäisches" Referendum?' in *Integration* 3/1984, pp. 158–66. Karlheinz Reif and Hermann Schmidt, 'Nine second order National elections: a conceptual framework for the analysis of European election results' in *European Journal of Political Research*, vol. 8, no. 1 (March 1980) 3–44) have stressed this aspect in analysing the first direct elections in 1979.

8 For the actual discussion on transnational party co-operation and organisation, cf. Oskar Niedermayer, *Europäische Parteien? Zur grenzüberschreitenden Interaktion politischer Parteien im Rahmen der Europäischen Gemeinschaft*, Frankfurt 1983; D.L. Seiler, 'Les fédérations des partis au niveau communautaires' in R. Hrbek and J. Jamar and W. Wessels (eds.), *The European Parliament on the Eve of the Second Direct Elections. Balance-Sheet and Prospects*, Bruges 1984, pp. 459–504; and Geoffrey and Pippa Pridham, *Transnational party cooperation and European integration. The process towards direct elections*, London 1981.

19

Western European liberal parties: developments since 1945 and prospects for the future

Emil J. Kirchner

INTRODUCTION

By June 1986, liberal parties were represented in the governments of ten of the thirteen Western European countries examined in this book. This was a better record than, for example, social democratic, socialist or labour parties could boast at that time. Yet, in the post-Second World War period, liberal parties have generally been counted far more in electoral terms than with regard to their role in coalitions and governments. They have consequently been regarded as 'small' or 'minor' parties and their influence has been neglected or concealed.[1] Influence over government policy can be exercised both from within a governing coalition and from without. The latter prevailed, for example, in Italy in the mid to late seventies when the Communist Party became a 'silent partner' in government by often abstaining in votes on bills the ruling Christian Democratic Party introduced in parliament – undoubtedly at a bargaining cost over policy content. On the other hand, participation within a governing coalition is no guarantee for wielding influence, if either no cabinet posts are held (as, for example, in the British Lib–Lab Pact in the seventies) or only a few and relatively unimportant portfolios are held by a particular party. In other words, the number and importance of portfolios held, the length of time parties have been either in government or in certain ministries, and similarities and differences in policy content *vis-à-vis* other coalition partners become important factors over whether or not influence can be wielded by particular parties.

On the surface, the length of time liberal parties have been in government during the post-war period, the number of cabinet posts held and the regularity with which certain ministries have been occupied appear to be impressive and would seem to be important factors for influencing coalition formation and maintenance as well as government policy.

Why do liberal parties have such a favourable record in government participation, in spite of the fact that in many cases they score low in electoral terms? How important are the policies they hold for encouraging or discouraging government participation by liberal parties? Are there conditions or mechanisms inherent in Western European political systems which promote the role of liberal parties in government disproportionately to their electoral size and largely irrespective of their policies? Consideration of Riker's (1962) 'size principle' and of Downs's (1957) notion of 'voters' rationality' help to underscore the theoretical significance of these questions. Furthermore, an answer to these questions will help to determine future prospects of liberal parties. The rise of protest parties or environmentalist parties since the mid-seventies is as relevant here as the current debate regarding electoral dealignment (see Kavanagh (1986)). In several instances the rise of protest parties has not only been challenging liberal parties in electoral terms, but also in their capacity for exercising 'pivotal' roles for alternative coalition arrangements. On the other hand, there are indications that liberal parties will (if they have not done so already) benefit favourably from an apparent weakening of the relationship between partisanship and voting in several Western European countries.

The following steps will be taken in the course of this chapter. First, an examination will be made of the electoral performance of liberal parties over the post-war period in order to determine overall trends, to classify parties according to electoral strength and to assess similarities and differences in electoral strength. Secondly, the extent and degree to which liberal parties have participated in government during the post-war period will be determined and correlated with electoral performance. Thirdly, the policy content of liberal parties will be analysed together with an assessment of conditions or mechanisms fostering the extent and degree of government participation. Fourthly, the future of liberal parties will be considered in the light of current debates in electoral studies about partisan volatility (Crewe and Denver (1985)).

LIBERAL PARTIES IN PARLIAMENTS AND GOVERNMENTS

The following analysis covers the seventeen parties examined in the country chapters of this book plus the Swedish-speaking People's Party of Finland (SFP), and the Swiss Free Democratic Party (FDP). The latter two parties were either not treated, or not treated extensively, in the respective country chapters, for reasons provided by the respective country authors, but since both belong to the Liberal International, they are included for analysis in this chapter.

Table 19.1 attempts to provide a picture of the electoral performance of liberal parties, broken down into two time periods: 1945 to 1965 and 1966 to 1986. The figures provided in Table 19.1 should be viewed with some care, given the complexity in establishing election results for single parties in some countries (because of, for example, electoral pacts or two ballots). In most cases, data are listed both for individual parties and for the combined total of liberal parties in those countries where there is more than one.

When comparing both twenty-year periods, a number of observations can be made. An upward trend for the last twenty years is only recorded for seven of the eighteen parties which had existed prior to 1966. (The Dutch D'66 was established in 1966.) Ten parties – the majority of liberal parties – show a declining trend, half of which are marked by a 'small' decline, while the other half manifests quite a significant decline. Parties with a significant decline include the French group of liberal parties (under the heading of the UDF), the Swedish FP, the Danish Venstre, the Norwegian LP, and the Austrian FPÖ. These findings correspond with those of Strom and Svåsand (1985) who found liberal parties, out of a group of different parties, to have suffered most. However, reversals are possible, as the threefold vote increase between 1982 and 1985 indicates for the Swedish FP. Whether, in those cases where a long-term decline is recognisable, as in Finland and Norway, the trend will continue and result in extinction, or whether a threshold exists below which liberal parties will not fall, is still an open question. As Strom and Svåsand (1985) point out, the decline of political parties necessitates consideration of 'party innovation'. It also requires assessment of contextual factors, such as changes in the party or electoral systems, or in voting habits. We will return to these considerations later on.

In the meantime, it appears that the generalisation of liberal parties as 'small' or 'minor' parties needs re-examination even in electoral terms. As Table 19.2 shows, one can talk of some liberal parties as being either medium-sized or as constituting 'main' political parties. In other words, the electoral strength of the Belgian,

French (grouping of UDF), Luxemburg, and the Swiss (FDP) liberal parties is close to the electoral strength of other major parties in their respective party systems. They can thus be considered as potential governing parties. It is therefore not surprising to find, as Table 19.3 indicates, that these parties have been in government for considerable periods since 1945.

Still more revealing, moreover, is the fact that relatively low electoral results can sometimes be inversely connected with high levels of government participation. For example, the Finnish SFP and the German FDP have shared governing responsibilities for four-fifths of the entire post-war period, and the Dutch VVD and the Italian PRI did so for half of that period. Overall, the extent of government participation by liberal parties is far in excess of what their electoral performance would imply.

The latter factor can be further exemplified by the number of portfolios held by liberal parties when in government. As can be seen from Table 19.4, the number of portfolios obtained, as a percentage of total cabinet posts in relation to electoral strength, is often disproportionately in favour of liberal parties. The data presented in this table should not be seen as a simple equation of percentages, but as a rough indicator of relative strength of liberal parties *vis-à-vis* other, mostly senior, coalition partners. For example, the German FDP with around 9 per cent of the votes gets more than twice that percentage when it comes to cabinet posts. Neither the CDU nor the SPD, which have around 40 per cent of the vote each, have been able to obtain more than 75 per cent of total cabinet posts when in coalition with the FDP.

Thus, whilst liberal parties, with the exception of the Swiss FDP, are no longer in such strong positions as to be considered one of the 'natural' governing parties – as the Norwegian Liberal Party was prior to the Second World War – or as 'indispensable' for coalition formation – as the Austrian GdFP was in the inter-war period – they have a record of extensive involvement in government coalitions. In a few instances, liberal parties have even been the sole occupiers of government, though as 'minority' governments (Danish Venstre from 1945 to 1947 and in 1973/4; and the Swedish FP in 1978/9). In the Italian case, the PRI with an average electoral mean of 2.74 per cent has twice managed to obtain the prime ministership. The reference to 'minor' or 'small' party status is, therefore, for a considerable number of liberal parties, largely inappropriate in terms of the scope of influence wielded in government. This fact can be underlined further when types of portfolios held by liberal parties are considered.

Which portfolios do liberal parties seek and which portfolios do

Table 19.1 *Electoral performance of liberal parties, 1945–86*

	Average mean 1945–65 %	Average mean 1966–86 %	Trend %	Highest score 1945–86 %	Lowest score 1945–86 %	Average mean 1945–86 %
Austria						
VdU→FPÖ	8.76	5.48	−3.28	11.7 (1949)	5.0 (1983)	6.97
Belgium[a]						
PVV/PLP	13.2	17.83	+4.63	21.6 (1965)	8.9 (1946)	15.51
Denmark						
Venstre	23.08	15.22	−7.86	27.6 (1947)	11.3 (1981)	18.92
RV	7.31	8.27	+0.96	15.0 (1968)	3.6 (1977)	7.83
Together (V, RV)	30.39	23.51	−6.88	34.5 (1947)	15.6 (1977)	26.75
Finland						
NPP→FPP→LKP	5.82	4.57	−1.25	7.9 (1954)	0.8 (1983)	5.19
SFP	7.36	5.15	−2.21	8.8 (1945)	4.2 (1979)	6.25
Together (LKP, SFP)	13.18	9.72	−3.46	14.88 (1954)	5.4 (1983)	11.44
France[b]						
Moderate conservative	15.31					
Radicals	11.66 UDF	20.18				
MRP	17.41					
Together (MC, R, MRP, UDF)	44.39	20.18	−24.21			33.22
Germany						
FDP	10.28	7.94	−2.34	12.8 (1961)	5.8 (1969)	9.11
Italy						
PRI	2.26	3.22	+0.96	5.1 (1983)	1.4 (1958)	2.74
PLI	4.82	3.16	−1.66	7.0 (1963)	1.3 (1976)	3.99
Together (PRI, PLI)	7.08	6.38	−0.70	11.2 (1946)	4.4 (1976)	6.73

Luxemburg								
GPD→DP	15.98	21.05	+5.07	23.3	(1974)	12.2	(1964)	18.23
Netherlands								
PV→VVD	9.08	15.89	+6.81	23.1	(1982)	6.4	(1946)	12.75
D'66	—	6.06		11.1	(1981)	4.2	(1972)	6.06
Together (VVD, D'66)	9.08	21.95	+12.87	28.4	(1981)	15.2	(1967)	18.81
Norway								
LP	10.97	4.60	−6.37	13.8	(1945)	3.0	(1985)	8.4
Sweden								
FP	20.63	11.67	−8.96	24.4	(1952)	5.9	(1982)	15.81
Switzerland								
AdI	5.18	6.18	+1.00	9.1	(1967)	4.0	(1983)	5.68
LPS	2.50	2.50		3.2	(1947)	2.2	(1955, 1963, 1971)	2.50
FDP	24.16	22.68	−1.48	24.8	(1959)	21.7	(1971)	23.42
Together (AdI, LPS, FDP)	31.84	31.36	−0.48	33.4	(1967)	23.4	(1983)	31.60
UK[c]								
LP	6.75	13.52	+6.82	19.3	(1974)	2.5	(1951)	10.13

[a] The three linguistics wings, in existence since the late seventies, are treated as one party.

[b] The breakdown into moderate conservative, Radicals, and MRP was taken from the chapter by John Frears, who presented an election analysis along these lines in his Table 6.2. For the period 1966–86, election results of liberal parties predating the establishment of the UDF were treated like UDF results. In the 1986 general election some joint RPR/UDF lists and some separate UDF lists were used. Only the separate UDF lists results of 20.3 per cent were used for the statistical analysis here.

[c] The Liberal Party share of the 1983 British general election, when the Liberal and Social Democratic Parties fought the election as an alliance, was taken from a calculation provided by John Curtice (1984) in 'The United Kingdom election of 1983'.

Source: Election results provided in country chapters of this book.

Table 19.2 *Classification of liberal parties by electoral strength (average means in the post-Second World War period)*

Minor parties: below 6%	*Medium-sized parties: between 12 and 18%*
Switzerland: LSP	Netherlands: VVD
Italy:PRI	Belgium: PVV/PLP
Italy: PLI	Sweden: FP
Finland: LKP	
Switzerland: AdI	
Small parties: between 6 and 12%	*Main parties: between 18 and 24%*
Netherlands: D66	Luxemburg: DP
Finland: SFP	Denmark: Venstre
Austria: FPÖ	France: UDF
Denmark: RV	Switzerland: FDP
Norway: LP	
Germany: FDP	
UK: LP	

they normally obtain when in government? First and foremost, they seek those portfolios relating to the protection of individual rights (Interior or Justice) and free market principles (Economics, Finance or Trade). Evidence indicates that they have held office extensively not only in these fields but in nearly every capacity, except for limited engagement in the Ministries of Social Affairs, Labour Policy and related subjects.

As Table 19.5 illustrates, liberal parties, even in cases where they obtained below 6 per cent of the votes, have had their claims for leading offices fulfilled, such as Foreign Ministry, Defence, Interior, Economic or Finance. In situations where either one of two large parties is able to become the main coalition partner, there is a tendency to grant disproportionate pay-offs to small parties both in quantity and quality of cabinet posts. This phenomenon is not unknown to coalition theorists (Browne (1982)) and can be described as analogous to an exploitation or 'black-mailing' by the small of the big. It can, therefore, also result in situations whereby liberal parties heavily monopolise certain leading cabinet positions. For example, the German FDP has held the post of Foreign Minister uninterruptedly for over 17 years (since 1969). This would appear to provide great opportunities for influencing such offices with liberal principles and values. The extent of the actual influence is, of course, subject to general trade-offs in policy programmes between coalition partners, as well as to the extent to which a general consensus prevails in societies regarding, for example, foreign and economic policy.

In some countries liberal parties play important roles in the

Table 19.3 *Liberal parties in government in the post-Second World War period*

	Total length of government period	Proportion of liberal parties in government[a] (in months and days)	%
Austria: FPÖ	18.12.45–30.6.86	37m/6d	7.65
Belgium: PVV/PLP	11.2.45–30.6.86	211m/17d	42.62
Denmark: Venstre	31.10.45–30.6.86	178m/26d	36.65
RV		133m/15d	27.36
Cumulative[b]		267m/29d	54.91
Finland: NPP→FPP→LKP	17.4.45–30.6.86	218m/23d	44.24
SFP		367m/21d	78.01
Cumulative		404m/29d	81.96
France: Various[c]→UDF	21.11.45–30.6.86	430m/11d	86.17
Germany: FDP	15.9.49–30.6.86	337m/16d	79.17
Italy: PRI	10.7.46–30.6.86	240m/11d	50.11
PLI		181m/24d	37.90
Cumulative		324m/23d	65.62
Luxemburg: GdP→DP	14.11.45–30.6.86	317m/25d	65.19
Netherlands: PV-VVD	3.7.46–30.6.86	265m/15d	55.31
D'66		60m/3d	12.52
Cumulative		325m/18d	67.83
Norway: LP	1.11.45–30.6.86	77m/6d	15.82
Sweden: FP	11.10.46–30.6.86	73m/10d	15.38
Switzerland: AdI		—	—
LPS		—	—
FDP	1.11.45–30.6.86	498m/	100.0
UK: LP		—	—

[a] Not counted in this analysis are situations where liberal parties have supported the government in parliament whilst not being in the cabinet.
[b] *Cumulative* signifies the total period in which either one of the two liberal parties, or both liberal parties, were in government, i.e. combining both single and multiple liberal party representations in government.
[c] Space would not allow to list the various parties and/or complexities of the French party system both in the Fourth and Fifth Republics, which have been used to constitute the respective figures. The term *various* is therefore to be seen as a shorthand expression of the several liberal parties in existence between 1945 and 1986.
Sources: Compiled from Vernon Bogdanor (ed.) (1983) *Coalition Government in Western Europe*; Eric Browne and John Dreijmanis (eds.) (1982) *Government Coalitions in Western Democracies*; *Keesing's Contemporary Archives*. Data supplied in country chapters of this book.

formation of coalitions. For example, the Swedish FP is usually entrusted with the task of sorting out a coalition arrangement within the non-socialist block. The UDF in France and the Luxemburg DP also exercise influential roles in coalition formation. The latter, for example, acted as the senior partner in the 1974 to 1979 coalition with the Socialist Party, by taking the prime ministership, in spite of the

Table 19.4 *Comparison between liberal parties' share of cabinet posts and electoral votes, 1945–86*

	Number of prime m'ships.	Average share of total ministerial posts held when in cabinet, %	Average electoral strength during periods in which cabinet posts were held, %
Austria: FPÖ	—	20.00	5.00
Belgium: PVV/PLP	—	26.51	15.64
Denmark: Venstre	4	57.53	15.22
RV	1	28.76	8.48
Finland: SFP	1	11.24	6.25
LKP	1	11.00	5.78
France: All liberal parties	23[a]	55.80	34.39
Germany: FDP	—	23.04	9.27
Italy: PRI	2	11.74	2.84
PLI	—	14.59	4.19
Luxemburg: DP	1	39.64	20.42
Netherlands: VVD	—	22.39	14.53
D'66	—	19.90	7.65
Norway: LP	—	23.33	9.53
Sweden: FP	1	47.48	10.95
Switzerland: AdI	—	—	—
LPS	—	—	—
FDP[b]	12	?	?
UK: LP	—	—	—

[a] It is also worth while mentioning that the UDF group held the presidency – with Giscard – in the period from 1974 to 1981.
[b] Because of the peculiar structure of the Swiss government, no exact data could be obtained concerning cabinet posts.
Sources: Compiled from Vernon Bogdanor (ed.) (1983) *Coalition Government in Western Europe*; Eric Browne and John Dreijmanis (eds.) (1982) *Government Coalitions in Western Democracies*; *Keesing's Contemporary Archives*. Data supplied in country chapters of this book.

fact that it had fewer votes than the Socialists. Potentially, such a role over coalition formation could be exercised by the British Liberal Party. Because of size, however, liberal parties are more likely to be led into coalitions than to be leading the formation process, and often they exact a relatively high price for their participation, especially in situations where they effectively play a 'pivotal' role in determining a given coalition.

PARTY ORGANISATION AND LINKS

Liberal parties not only often operate from a small electoral base, they are also generally unable to boast large organisational resources. As

Table 19.5 *Extent to which liberal parties held the five top ministries in the post-Second World War period, %*

	Foreign (%)	Interior (%)	Defence (%)	Finance (%)	Economics (%)
Austria: FPÖ			7.65		
Belgium: PVV/PLP		20.40	13.61	30.19	22.53
Denmark: Venstre	24.03	19.90	15.40	21.39	29.00
RV				6.31	18.28
Together				27.70	47.28
Finland: SFP	18.03		11.68	7.18	1.87
LKP	11.08	13.11	.51		6.87
Together	29.11		12.19		8.74
France: MRP	21.05		12.29	17.82	7.71
RSP/RAD	1.74	26.96	9.62	12.26	7.51
IND/RI/DPR/CDP	2.26	21.37		30.12	0.20
Together	25.05	48.33	21.91	60.20	15.42
Germany: FDP	40.99	30.83		13.54	35.03
Italy: PRI	3.71	1.40	27.76	11.31	9.42
PLI	4.59				2.32
Together	8.30				11.74
Luxemburg: GdP→DP	51.25	39.34	25.84	12.34	28.36
Netherlands: PV→VVD	18.15	35.65	13.94	12.56	13.12
D'66		0.64	2.56		2.56
Together		36.29	16.50		15.68
Norway: LP			2.39	15.66	0.16
Sweden: FP	7.73	2.51	2.51	11.63	6.20
Switzerland: AdI					
LPS					
FDP	?	?	?	?	?
UK: LP	—	—	—	—	—

Sources: Compiled from Vernon Bogdanor (ed.) (1983), *Coalition Government in Western Europe*; Eric Browne and John Dreijmanis (eds.) (1982), *Government Coalitions in Western Democracies*; *Keesing's Contemporary Archives*. Data supplied in country chapters of this book.

Table 19.6 shows, they do not have a sizeable membership. Membership density (the percentage of voters who are members of a party) is traditionally regarded as higher in ideological, tightly-organised parties than in pragmatic patronage (K. von Beyme (1985) 171). Exceptions are the Danish Venstre, with its large farming membership, and the Austrian FPÖ, which also has a substantial rural membership. Membership is particularly low within the French UDF, the German FDP and the Dutch D'66. This is why many liberal parties are referred to as 'voters'' rather than 'members'' parties.

The absence of well-developed ties with particular interest group associations is another general characteristic of liberal parties. Formerly, some liberal parties have had close links with trade-union

Table 19.6 *Membership of liberal parties*

Country	Party	Year	Total membership	Membership density, %
Austria	FPÖ	1985	31,057	15.4
Belgium	PVV/PLP	1984	134,537	10.6
Denmark	RV	1983/4	10,000	5.0
	Venstre	1983/4	89,500	22.0
Finland	LKP	1985	8,500	
France	UDF	1986	60,000	1.2
Germany	FDP	1984	70,000	2.6
Italy	PLI	1983	39,200	3.4
	PRI	1983	108,201	5.4
Luxemburg	DP	1986	3,800	7.0
Netherlands	D'66	1986	8,500	1.5
	VVD	1986	89,570	5.6
Norway	LP	1986	11,000	14.0
Sweden	FP	1985	42,000	5.3
UK	LP	1985	100,000	4.2

Source: Data supplied by country chapters.

organisations, such as the Belgian PVV/PLP with the liberal trade union organisation, the Italian PRI with the republican/social democratic trade-union organisation (UIL) and member parties of the UDF with the CFDT, but these links have weakened rather than strengthened. Several liberal parties have links with white-collar trade unions, but they are, with the exception of the British and Scandinavian cases, not well developed. A similar situation applies with regard to liberal party links with employers' associations. However, some liberal parties, like the Danish Venstre and RV, the Austrian FPÖ, the French UDF and the German FDP, liaise often with their respective farmers' associations. Many also have links to education (teachers') associations. Some, like the Norwegian LP, also retain close links with ecological groups.

Liberal parties have, with few exceptions (Dutch VVD, Danish Venstre, British LP, the Swiss FDP and the German FDP), retained the character of 'cadre' or elite parties, i.e. parties of notables and leading personalities, which is often reflected in the nature of members elected to parliament.

Two interrelated questions might be posed. How can parties with relatively low organisational bases and electoral results assume such powerful positions? And, if their participatory performance in government has been so impressive why has this not, in turn, stimulated more favourable electoral results or membership? An examination of the nature of the Western European party systems, constitutional requirements relating to the formation and maintenance of governments, and the way policies and issues have been presented to the electorate in the past, might help to find some answers to these questions and provide some indication about the prospects of liberal parties.

DETERMINANTS OF PARTY COMPETITION AND STRENGTH

By competing for voters, political parties affect each other through policy stances, organisational innovation, leadership qualities, election campaign styles, and declared or practised coalition strategies. Reference by Lipset and Rokkan (1967) to a 'freezing' of the political party landscape in Europe since the 1920s implied that parties of the left and right of the political spectrum were dominating the agenda for policy stances and that the electorate identified with this ideological breakdown (Smith, ch. 2 above). This phenomenon seemed, by and large, to hold up into the late 1960s in spite of the occurrence of two significant changes after the Second World War. One was the arrival of mass parties, in the shape of Christian democratic parties (as well as the Gaullist Party) and the other was the transformation of some social democratic parties from ideological purity/rigidity to a more pragmatic outlook.[2]

The arrival of mass parties on the right and centre coincided with, or was precipitated by, the expansion of the new middle class (white-collar workers), and hence the expansion of the centre of the political spectrum. This second significant change appeared to have direct implications for the size of the working class and the support base of parties on the left. As portrayed by the 'embourgeoisie thesis',[3] economic growth and prosperity would become a prime mover for the expansion of the middle class which would absorb large sections of the working class.

Whilst for the latter, changes in class structure were seen as the essential factor for affecting party alignment, another school, known as the post-materialists,[4] argued that important changes in political values and socialisation were occurring in Western Europe (as well as the United States) in the post-war period, affecting particularly those born after 1945. Unlike the school emphasising changes in the class structure, the post-materialists did not concentrate on the working class in their analysis but focused on the white-collar workers who are well educated, secular, and predominantly urban. Both schools, however, agreed in their predictions of a growing middle class.

Developments in the 1950s and 1960s thus seemed to provide both favourable and unfavourable circumstances for the electoral fortunes of liberal parties. On the one hand, the 'centre appeal' of liberal parties seemed to find increasing recognition by the electorate. In the case of some liberal parties this appeal was reinforced by changes in policy, image and organisation. This was true for the Belgian Liberal Party, which modified its stance on anti-clericalism and undertook organisational changes in 1961. The term 'liberal' was explicitly added to its name by the Finnish Liberals (LKP) in 1966, and the liberal component/image was strengthened through organisational reforms by the Austrian Liberals (FPÖ) in 1956, the Luxemburg Liberals (DP) in 1957 and the Danish Venstre in 1970. In addition, the appeal of the Dutch VVD as a centre party was aided by the weakening of the Dutch religious alignment in the early 1960s (Daalder, ch. 7 above), which, however, also meant the arrival of a second liberal party in Holland, in the shape of D'66. Election results (see Table 19.1) confirmed the electorate's support for those parties mentioned, as well as for the British Liberals and the German FDP.[5]

On the other hand, the 'centre leaning' of parties on the right and on the left of the political spectrum, described by Kirchheimer (1966) as manifesting 'catch-all' parties, meant that the electoral impact for liberal parties was either counterbalanced or resulted in smaller increments.[6] Moreover, initial predictions about the 'embourgeoisie thesis' turned out to be either overstated with regard to the declining support for parties on the left or had neglected a number of important intervening variables. As argued by Sainsbury ((1985) 3) affluence *per se* has a negligible effect on the socialist allegiance of workers. More significant in determining their partisanship is the presence or absence of 'class reinforcing factors such as class origin and trade union membership'. Most revealing and important for liberal parties is Sainsbury's claim ((1985) 12) that 'non-socialist parties could not attract as many working-class votes as socialist parties were able to attract middle-class voters.'

Thus, whilst class changes, political value changes, as well as changes within political parties did not, to any great extent, alter the share of votes held by political parties, they increased the number of voters who were uncertain about their party identification and resulted in frequent switches between parties. The increasing phenomenon of electoral volatility seemed to affect liberal parties in particular. Empirical studies show that the electorate of many liberal parties in Western Europe is heavily made up (ranging from 40 to 65 per cent) of transient voters.[7] This phenomenon is invariably known as 'negative', 'protest' or 'fickle' votes, implying that voters are not necessarily attracted to what liberal parties stand for, but support them because of disenchantment with previous allegiances or uncertainties over party identification (Heath and Jowell and Curtice (1986) 151; and Curtice (1983) 103).

Why do liberal parties attract more fickle voters, relatively speaking, than other parties? Is it because they are seen as 'centre' parties and thus a convenient stop for voters on their way between left and right or vice versa? Whilst this might hold some truth, there are a number of factors which are important, two of which in particular need highlighting: government office and the ambivalence of policy programmes.

GOVERNMENT OFFICE

Government incumbency has provided some liberal parties, like the Dutch VVD, with the opportunity to project themselves into the limelight, to claim some of the credit for sustained economic success and to use the mass media to good effect in terms of stressing the achievements of the government in which the parties have participated. Of course, the reverse can also happen whereby the unpopularity of the coalition partner contaminates or negatively affects the standing of a liberal party.

In a few cases contextual factors allow liberal parties to act as a 'pivot' between different coalitions. This is most marked in the German case where – although the constitution stipulates majority government – it is usually the case that neither of the two big parties (CDU/CSU or SPD) can achieve this on their own and 'grand coalitions' are the exception rather than the rule. In principle, a similar role could be played by the Austrian FPÖ, the Belgian PVV/PLP and the Luxemburg DP, except that in those countries 'grand coalitions' involving the two respective major parties are much more common. The role of a 'pivot' is also diminished in cases where 'minority' governments prevail (Scandinavia) or where several parties participate in coalition (Italy).

AMBIVALENCE OF POLICY PROGRAMMES

Paradoxically, government office has helped many liberal parties to conceal or to promote an inherent ambivalence between left- and right-wing policy orientations within their own ranks. Coalition agreements require trade-offs and compromises on policies, and in some cases where alternative coalition arrangements can be made, allow one or the other wing of the involved liberal parties to emphasise its policies more prominently. Coalition strategies lead liberal parties to express general rather than specific policies and thereby hide latent tensions between their two prevailing wings, i.e. between those who would like to put emphasis on individual rights/freedoms and those who stress the need for collective/state action. On the other hand, general policy expressions often have an element of ambiguity attached and thus might attract some uncertain voters or those with weak partisan ties.

However, in spite of a tendency by liberal parties to pay more attention to coalition prospects than to ideological principles, it would be inappropriate to characterise liberal parties as opportunistic in policy aims.[8] It is probably true to say that liberal parties have been less eager than parties on the right and left to develop comprehensive programmes, and have preferred sectoral programmes and pragmatic election platforms to the basic and long-term programmes of their larger competitors (K. von Beyme (1985) 38), but they have expressed distinct views from other parties and have pursued distinct policies when in coalition. The distinction of liberal policy can be seen primarily on: (a) the stress on individual rights/freedoms and (b) on the free market. Liberal parties consider these to be central aims, though the degree to which they are emphasised might vary among them at any given time. Anticlericalism is still strongly apparent among liberal parties, though the stress now takes more the form of favouring 'weak' religious ties, and in a few instances, as within the French UDF, there is actual support for religious views. Many liberal parties stress the small and medium-sized business sector, free trade, decentralisation, support for European unification, more efficiency in economic production and participation in decision-making, and disarmament. The latter needs to be explained. Most liberal parties are pro-NATO, but some strongly oppose certain aspects of NATO's strategy on nuclear arms such as deployment of cruise or medium-range missiles in Western Europe.

There are also particular policy aims. Examples include the Belgian PVV/PRL emphasis on law and order, defence and tough immigration laws; the stress by the Swiss FDP on centralisation; the British Liberal Party's urge for constitutional reforms (primarily electoral reforms); and the stringent measures favoured by the Italian PRI on terrorism.

Liberal parties are generally in favour of limiting/reducing the state's role in the economy but there are instances when state intervention is tolerated or encouraged, such as in the social or environmental field. A revival of the nineteenth-century concern over the role of the state when the 'night-watchman state' was stressed can, however, be observed not only with liberal parties, but also within the economic policies of the British Conservatives under Thatcher and of the USA under Reagan. These administrations, like liberal parties generally, take a neo-liberal approach and are critical of the corporate state, i.e. the overextended role of both government and economic interest groups in economic management (Bertsch and Clark and Wood (1986) 129). Derek Hearl (ch. 16 above), in the analysis of party platforms, reveals similarities between the policies of liberal parties and Christian democrats/conservatives, but argues that liberals (unlike conservatives) feature concerns for democracy and civil liberties more prominently.

Both the aspect of policy similarities and differences, and the development of class/value changes mentioned above, influence party allegiance and raise the crucial question as to who supports or votes for liberal parties.

ELECTORAL SUPPORT

Like other political parties, liberal parties have a group of core or stalwart supporters. The rest are either 'floating' voters or voters who vote for the first time. Thus, most liberal parties are not able to rely on strong loyalties and affective ties of a large segment of their votes.

Liberal support is not clearly organised on class lines, though it tends to concentrate among those with no religious affiliations, those of middle-class origin, those from higher levels of education and those with an above average income. Unlike many other liberal parties, the British Liberals draw their support only a little more from the middle class rather than from the working class. Other liberal parties with working-class support, mostly skilled workers, of between one-quarter to one-third can be found in the Swedish FP, the Norwegian LP, the Danish RV, the Swiss AdI, and the Austrian FPÖ. Most liberal parties appear to draw more heavily from the urban electorate than the rural, although the British Liberals, the Austrian FPÖ, the Danish Venstre and RV, and the Swiss AdI attract proportionately more from rural areas. Whilst in the latter cases the urban electoral component is also growing, it should be recognised that there are specific party circumstances which will prolong the rural influence. For example, the social/economic structure of the AdI (the Migros co-operative system) is primarily rural. Similarly, Venstre has retained farming support from the days when it became the political spokesman of the farmers and for the British Liberals the 'Celtic fringe' represented the main electoral base throughout the 1950s and 1960s.

Whilst the notion of class, and particularly the differentiation between classes, is subject to an ongoing debate in the study of electoral behaviour (Heath (1986); Kavanagh (1986)), there is an increasing tendency to speak of two segments of the middle class. For convenience, they will be referred to as the 'bourgeoisie' and the 'white collar'. The former, a traditional recruitment base for all liberal parties, consists of those variously known as small entrepreneurs, the self-employed, the independent professions and, to some extent, farmers, especially those with higher incomes. The second category, representing the greatest potential for liberal support, is made up of salaried workers in professions and management, both in the private and the public sectors, and comprises people who are well educated and earn high income. Civil servants, including teachers, seem to account for a significant proportion of this group.

These two segments appear to differ with regard to value orientation, with the more materialist bourgeoisie segment particularly emphasising the notion of private property and the white-collar segment tending to hold more social liberal attitudes in line with post-materialist values on such issues as environment, disarmament and foreign aid. Another characteristic of the white-collar group can also be trade-union membership, at least in the British and Scandinavian contexts (Curtice, ch. 4 above; Sainsbury (1985)). As can be gleaned from Table 19.7, some liberal parties have more of one segment than the other, but for many liberal parties the white-collar segment is becoming the target group.

DEALIGNMENT DEBATE AND IMPLICATIONS

Since the mid-1970s two main arguments have been advanced with regard to voting behaviour. The first maintains that class has become a less important predictor of individual voting behaviour. The second suggests that an individual's issue stance does play a significant role in determining the choice of vote. The first argument has become known as the dealignment debate.[9] It describes a process of weakening or erosion of an existing party alignment (LeDuc (1985) 379). The second argument can be seen as being inversely related to the first, in that a decline in class voting is associated with an increase in the importance of issues (Franklin (1985) 52). Because of these developments Kavanagh ((1986) 19) argues that the 'source of electoral change may increasingly have to be sought in the arena of politics – in the events, personalities and policies of parties, rather than in partisan loyalties or social class'. The lessening of class as a determinant of voting behaviour has been attributed to structural

Table 19.7 *Proportion of electoral support from white-collar and bourgeoisie middle-class groups*

Country	Substantial bourgeoisie segment	Strong white-collar segment	Half and half
Austria	FPÖ		
Belgium	PVV/PLP		
Denmark	Venstre[a]		RV[a]
Finland	LKP		SFP
France	UDF[a]		
Germany			FDP
Italy	PLI		PRI
Luxemburg		DP	
Netherlands		D'66	VVD
Norway		LP	
Sweden			FP
Switzerland	LSP	AdI	FDP
UK		LP	

[a]These parties have also a significant proportion of farmers.
Source: Data supplied by country chapters.

changes associated with the transition to a post-industrial society (signifying an expansion of the service sector and a decline of industrial employment).

Whether liberal parties will benefit and, if so, to what extent, from the development of post-industrial society, is difficult to predict. There are simultaneously positive and negative indications.

PARTY CHALLENGES AND ADJUSTMENTS

On the one hand, there are indications that the decline of industrial employment will lead to a decline of those with working-class origin and thus result in a decline of the working-class vote for parties on the left (see Sainsbury (1985)). Against these indications, or the full impact of such developments, must be held the developments of two countervailing factors. One is the possibility that the conflict between labour and capital will continue rather than decrease. The other is the possibility that parties on the left will readjust or fight back to recapture voters.

With regard to the former, as social classes become more complex, intertwined with one another, and more divided internally, the class struggle, rather than declining, has taken on new forms (Duverger (1972) 61). The impact of introducing new technologies in the service sector, as in banking, fosters this conflict by affecting the composition of the white-collar labour force (Kirchner and Hewlett and Sobirey (1984)). As the ranks of white-collar workers have grown, the work of many of these employees has been reduced to routine or menial tasks. Moreover, the economic recession confronts the white-collar sector as well as the blue-collar one and, together with the impact of introducing new technologies, results in underemployment and redundancies in this sector. The gulf between the secure, the contented, and the high-income earners on the one hand, and the insecure, the poor, the marginal, and the impatient, on the other, might therefore widen (Steel and Tsurutani (1986) 239).

If, as Sainsbury (1985) argues, white-collar workers with a working-class background are more likely than those of a middle-class origin (the downwardly mobile) to retain allegiance to parties on the left, how many of those white-collar workers with menial tasks, underemployed or unemployed have either a working-class origin or a middle-class one? If the former is larger, the likelihood of parties on the left benefiting is greater than if the latter category is larger, in which case non-socialist parties seem likely to benefit more. However, site of employment (private or public) for white-collar workers, as well as trade-union membership, might act as an intervening variable and affect how certain voters determine their choice of party.

Of course not all white-collar workers with working-class origin will retain allegiance to parties of the left, and there are also some cases where origin at the working-class level is associated with allegiance to non-socialist parties. Moreover, lower taxes and less government bureaucracy, as advocated by many liberal parties, attract the affluent blue-collar workers. Thus, it is likely that as the segment of white-collar workers with working-class origin shrinks, the electoral base of parties on the left will erode. This leads to further questions:

(a) How effectively can parties on the left readjust, as they did in the 1950s and 1960s, and what methods (leadership qualities, campaign styles) can they employ to fight back?
(b) Will liberal parties be able to integrate successfully the two components of 'bourgeoisie' and white-collar liberals or will they lose members/voters from the 'bourgeoisie' segment to the conservatives, or members/voters of the white-collar segment to green or protest parties?

With regard to the latter, as Duverger ((1972) 61) points out, 'there is a fundamental difference between salaried middle class and the capitalist (bourgeoisie) middle class'. The latter 'although very fond of political freedom is even more devoted to private property'.

Different prevailing values are not new to liberal parties and it might even be argued that they are inherent in their ideological roots, i.e. tensions between individual interests and collective action. However, there have been periods when these differences have resulted in splits, as , e.g., around the turn of the century when many countries introduced universal franchise. Furthermore, as K. von Beyme (1985) 163 points out, primarily with regard to Germany:

> The reorientation of many young Liberals towards a more social Liberalism, which suggested a coalition with Social Democrats, loosened the ties with the remaining interest groups in the middle class who had once been the Liberals' staunchest supporters.

The Norwegian case might also be an indication of things to come. As the Liberal Party turned more towards ecology and environmental concerns in the late seventies, its white-collar voters increased, but this increase was less than what it lost in support from traditional (bourgeoisie liberals) supporters.

In the 1970s and early 1980s it appeared that liberal parties had become vulnerable to the manoeuvres of the green and 'anti-tax' parties. The green parties, particularly in Germany, Austria and Finland were able to attract electors who had previously formed key 'target' groups for liberal parties, namely, the young, well-educated voters, mostly living in urban areas, whose partisan ties were less deeply embedded and more fickle than older people's with less formal education in a rural milieu.

In the meantime, it appears that some liberal parties have either recaptured or invented more effective methods for recapturing young voters. These include the Finnish LKP, the Norwegian LP, the German FDP, and the Dutch VVD. Moreover, 'the phenomenon of sustained youth unemployment may suggest a conservative trend among young voters back to the traditional parties' (Chandler and Saroff (1986) 322).

Thus, the prospects for liberal parties of net gains in votes, whereby the increase in the youth and especially in the white-collar component can outweigh potential losses in the 'bourgeoisie' segment, look brighter for some than for others. Some liberal parties have, over the past two decades, appealed to and attracted an increasing pool of white-collar workers, as well as younger people, and thus increased votes without seemingly losing too many of their traditional supporters. This trend, prevailing primarily in the British LP, the

Luxemburg DP, the Swiss AdI and the Radicals of the French UDF, is likely to continue. The Dutch D'66, right from their start, have drawn heavily from the youth and white-collar sector. A loosening of dominant subcultures (the break-up of 'Verzuiling' in the Netherlands and the impact of the Italian divorce referendum) have also presented new opportunities for the Dutch VVD and the Italian PRI and PLI. These parties, except for the VVD, have been classified by Smith (ch. 2 above) as 'liberal-radical' parties, i.e. parties in which the social and collective aspects are emphasised.

On the other hand, the likelihood of transfers from liberal to conservative parties is greatest in those cases where there are tensions between 'bourgeoisie liberals' and white-collar liberals and, at the same time, a coalition with Christian democrats or conservatives prevails. This seemingly was already a factor in the 1986 Dutch general election and potentially exists with the current Danish, French and German coalition arrangements. Moreover, the British Conservatives have been conducting a policy which resembles nineteenth-century liberalism and could thus attract liberal supporters of the bourgeois type. The opposite might be expected in the Belgian case, where the Liberal Party is reviving traits of nineteenth-century liberalism, together with a tough stand on law and order and defence. Here it is likely that the Liberals could attract voters from the Christian Social Party. In addition, both the Belgian and the British Liberals appear capable of making significant inroads into the blue-collar/working-class vote.

There are also cases where the gains of white-collar votes do not appear to compensate for the loss of traditional supporters, such as for the Norwegian and Finnish (LKP) Liberal Parties. Both parties seem beset by chronic decline and both tried, unsuccessfully, to better their chances through 'electoral pacts' (LKP with the Finnish Centre Party) or alternative coalition arrangements (the Norwegian LP's attempt to coalesce with the Labour Party). Having committed itself strongly towards ecological concerns in the last few years, it is likely that the Norwegian LP could transform itself into an environmentalist party. Survival is therefore of uppermost concern to these two parties, together with the Finnish SFP which suffers from the gradual shrinkage of the Swedish-speaking population in Finland.

Thus, social changes affecting the size and composition of both the working and middle classes appear to create greater electoral gains than losses for liberal parties. Moreover, in countries where environmentalist or anti-tax parties exist, liberal parties have, so far, been able to adjust successfully to their challenges. To keep up with these challenges, to pursue policies suitable to both the 'old' and 'new' middle-class supporters, as well as to meet the anticipated reaction of traditional parties on the left and right to either recapture lost voters or to attract new ones will be among the main tasks facing liberal parties in the future. Whether these tasks can be met successfully will depend, in part, on the ability of liberal parties to adopt and relate to the phenomenon of opinion or issue voting.

ISSUES

The notion of issue voting needs qualification. Do issues *per se* become more prominent in voting patterns? This kind of consideration would be different from that of new issues or new politics noted under the rubric of post-materialism. If we deal primarily with the latter category, the prospects appear to be mixed for liberal parties. On the one hand, liberal parties seem prepared to support issues about ecology or social liberalism. On the other hand, many liberal parties are torn between a constituency which favours bourgeois values and one which aspires to post-materialism. How ambivalent in policy terms can liberal parties be under these circumstances and how flexible must they be to retain their coalition options?

Many liberal parties are, and several others could become, coalition partners. Coalition arrangements normally entail a willingness to compromise over policy stances. The tendency of liberal parties to advocate general rather than specific policy programmes has not only the advantage of concealing an inherent ambivalence over ideology but also of introducing flexibility over coalition arrangements and of offering opportunities to relate or feature specific issues if and when needed. In addition, there is a tendency for routine behaviour. As postulated by Steel and Tsurutani ((1986) 240) 'the more practical experience one has had in the arena of electoral politics and that of policy negotiation, bargaining, and compromise, the more pragmatic and instrumental one becomes'. Power and policy thus become closely intertwined and interdependent. There is consequently an emphasis on general programmes, stability, continuity and proven competence.[10] This is particularly enhanced in situations where contextual factors, like the need for majority government or a 5 per cent threshold representation, promote strategic voting in favour of a liberal party (Pappi and Tanvey (1982) 183).

On the whole liberal parties have neither the membership, the financial resources nor the ties to interest-group associations and subcultures to count on a large supportive and loyal electoral base. However, as politics become personalised and television comes to play an ever more important role in election campaigns, the personal qualities of political leaders become increasingly crucial (Strom and Svåsand (1985) 20). Thus, government offices are seen as important forums for presenting the qualities of liberal leaders. Generally, liberal parties have good links with the mass media.

However, the absence of large membership or interest-group ties allows liberal parties, through efficient and effective leadership qualities, to relate more easily than large parties – or parties with strong ties – to a given political situation/issue. Their 'small' base, it appears, lends itself particularly well to such a purpose. This would seem to indicate that as 'small' parties, liberal parties have more to gain than if they were larger. If larger, they would not only have to take account of a larger group of voters when shifting policies or pressing for specific issues, but could also undermine their chances of becoming coalition partners. Rather than being seen as 'junior' coalition partners, enlargement in size and strength might be perceived as a greater threat by the other coalition partner and might either provoke a more orchestrated counter-attack than would otherwise be the case or it might promote prospects for 'grand coalitions' in countries where two large parties exist.

This is probably of less concern to the Swiss FDP – given the peculiar circumstances of the Swiss political system – or the British Liberals who either play a major role in the present 'Alliance' or have the potential to become the major component in a future merger with the Social Democratic Party, or the Luxemburg DP and the French UDF, who can be considered as 'equal' coalition partners. These parties have to force issues much more and take more precise stands during election campaigns than other liberal parties are able, or willing, to do. Nonetheless, both the British Liberals and the French UDF are constrained through electoral co-operative arrangements, i.e. with the SDP and Gaullists, respectively.

Whilst coalition strategies are greatly influenced by each partner's priorities and the extent to which each government is 'open' or 'closed' in terms of policy distance on key issues (Browne (1982)), new coalition arrangements will not appear to be greatly different from existing ones in which liberal parties are engaged, since other parties, like liberal parties, will also seek to support post-materialist issues. Therefore, the 'openness' or 'distance' between liberal parties and coalition partners will remain somewhat the same. Moreover, as before, in cases where liberal parties benefit from a pivotal role, they have to be careful not to alternate coalition arrangements too often, or too quickly, if they want to be seen as credible, reliable or responsible coalition partners. But government office can be a two-edged sword for liberal parties, as they are mostly the junior partner in coalitions. Through it, if successful, they can help to maintain or enhance electoral results as well as enhance credibility for further office-holding. If unsuccessful, or if they have been negatively affected by unpopular coalition partners, credibility can be undermined for government office-holding and particularly for election prospects.

Green and 'protest' parties are on the increase, challenging not only the electoral base of liberal parties but, in part, also the roles, including 'pivotal' ones, liberal parties play in governing coalitions. Whether their record of 'good' and responsible government will help them avoid being replaced, is at this stage an open question.

CONCLUSION

One of the significant features of many Western European liberal parties in the post-war period is the difference between extensive government participation and mediocre electoral results. Whilst contextual factors help to promote the former, the nature of party competition (dominance of parties on the right and left), at least until the 1970s, is a factor influencing the latter. The need to form majority governments, peculiarities in the electoral system, or the ineligibility of certain parties in the party system, often become helpful contextual factors for liberal parties in entering coalitions. Indirectly, however, the relatively small size of many liberal parties (organisationally and electorally) might also help to make them attractive for coalition consideration. As small parties they can be tolerated or accepted, whereas if they were larger they could be seen as more of a threat by (larger) coalition partners.

Whether the implications of dealignment (a weakening of partisanship and increases in electoral volatility and issue voting) will entail a reversal of this trend, whereby electoral increases will be inversely related to lower levels of government participation, is difficult to predict. As Curtice ((1983) 104) points out, liberal supporters 'are a constantly shifting group who, in a sense, represent a much larger number of people who at some point in their voting lives have actually voted liberal or seriously considered doing so'.

Lacking comparative organisational resources or effective ties with interest associations, and relying on a small partisan support base, liberal parties are heavily affected by activities of other parties.

On the other hand, by presenting their policy programmes in broad terms, they achieve flexibility in coalition negotiations, conceal an inherent ambivalence about different streams of liberal ideology and are able to relate to new issues more quickly than larger parties are able to do. Moreover, as Smith (ch. 2 above) argues

> It is also true that the liberal values, especially those relating to the freedom of the individual, will become more relevant, and that is particularly so for voters who have lost their party loyalties and who no longer see voting as an expression of group identity.

The increasing pool of fickle voters provides more equal opportunities for parties to compete but it also signifies an electorate which by its very nature is unstable and unpredictable. Since liberal parties draw disproportionately large numbers from this pool there are opportunities to be had as well as challenges to be met. They have the opportunity to project themselves more strongly than in the past as classless parties who are to govern in the interests of the nation as a whole. The benefits of this projection will depend on the outcome of a number of developments.

The transition of working-class people into white-collar positions, the proportion of those who become downwardly mobile and, importantly, changes within the middle-class group, are of great significance in the struggle for votes. The latter group is facing a clash of values between bourgeois and post-materialist (white-collar workers') liberalism, exacerbated by the impact of economic and technological factors which can prolong the conflict between labour and capital and may suppress post-materialist values for a certain proportion of the white-collar group, as well as increase the potential for protest votes and/or left-wing party support. Eventual losses of bourgeoisie voters, however, might be replaced by gains of the more affluent blue-collar workers. These workers may feel attracted to parties, whether liberal or Christian democrat/conservative, which emphasise tax cuts.

Leadership qualities, effective use of election campaigns, especially via television, a good rapport with the mass media and the tactical exploitation of issues as they arise, become significant future criteria in the party competition and in the battle over voters. Liberal parties can take nothing for granted, whether in electoral terms or in coalition strategies, but many appear to stand a good chance of profiting from increased electoral volatility. Whether they indeed come through on that chance and find adequate competitive space in the party spectrum, depends in part on how well they have learned from the past. Perhaps the painful lessons learned from the confrontation at the beginning of this century between middle-class and working-class interests can this time be used more advantageously.

NOTES

1 A number of studies and scholars refer to liberal parties as 'minor' or 'small' parties. See, for example, K. Strom and L. Svåsand (1985) 6; M. Duverger (1972) 65–6 and J. Steiner (1986) 28.

2 One of the outstanding examples was the transformation by the German Social Democratic Party in 1959.

3 For further details see J. Goldthorpe, K. Lockwood and F. Bechhofer and J. Platt (1969); K. Roberts, F.G. Cook, S.C. Clark and E. Semeonoff (1977) ch. 3.

4 For a review of the literature on post-materialism see, for example, R. Inglehart (1977 and 1981); S. Barnes and M. Kaase (1979) and W.M. Chandler and A. Siaroff (1986).

5 The FDP had its best result ever in 1961, but the CDU's slogan 'no experiments' (either on education or on relations with East Germany) as well as the growing unpopularity of an ageing Adenauer (chancellor) helped to contribute to this result.

6 A well-argued case by parties of the left and right manoeuvring for centre positions is provided by Steel and Tsurutani (1986) 236–7.

7 This statement is based on data provided in the country chapters of this book.

8 For example Duverger (1972) 65–6 states that the 'marginal role' of liberal parties 'leads them to take demagogic stands . . . and sometimes they tend to abuse their freedom by pursuing revolutionary currents close to those of the far right'.

9 For one of the first and outstanding studies on the subject see I. Crewe, B. Sarlvik and J. Alt (1977).

10 There is evidence also to suggest that, for example, the German FDP is not perceived by the wider electorate in term of specific policies but more for its contribution to the party system.

REFERENCES

Barnes, S. and M. Kaase (eds.) (1979) *Political Action: Mass Participation in Five Western Democracies* (Beverly Hills: Sage).

Bell, D. (1973) *The Coming of Post-Industrial Society* (New York: Basic Books).

Bertsch, G.K., R.P. Clark and D.M. Wood (1986) *Comparing Political Systems: Power and Policy in Three Worlds* (3rd edn) (New York: John Wiley and Sons).

Beyme, K.v. (1985) *Political Parties in Western Democracies* (Aldershot: Gower).

Bogdanor, V. (ed.) (1983) *Coalition Government in Western Europe* (London: Heinemann).

Browne, E. (1982) 'Introduction' in *Government Coalitions in Western Democracies* ed. by E.C. Browne and J. Dreijmanis (New York: Longman).

Chandler, W.M. and A. Siaroff (1986) 'Postindustrial politics in Germany and the origins of the Greens', *Comparative Politics* 18, 303–25.

Crewe, I. and D. Denver (eds.) (1985) *Electoral Change in Western Democracies* (New York: St Martin's Press).

Crewe, I., B. Sarlvik and J. Alt (1977) 'Partisan dealignment in Britain 1964–1974', *British Journal of Political Science* 7, 129–90.

Curtice, J. (1983) 'Liberal voters and the Alliance: realignment and protest' in *Liberal Party Politics*, ed. by V Bogdanor (Oxford: Clarendon Press).

Dalton, R.J., S.C. Flanagan and P.A. Beck (eds.) (1984) *Electoral Change in Advanced Industrial Democracies* (Princeton: Princeton University Press).
Downs, A. (1957) *An Economic Theory of Democracy* (New York: Harper and Row).
Duverger, M. (1972) *Party Politics and Pressure Groups: A Comparative Introduction* (New York: Thomas Crowell Co.).
Franklin, M. (1985) 'Elections since 1964', *Electoral Studies*, 37–56.
Goldthorpe, J., D. Lockwood, F. Bechhofer and J. Platt (1969) *The Affluent Worker in the Class Structure* (Cambridge: Cambridge University Press).
Heath, A. (1986) 'Comment on Dennis Kavanagh's "How we vote now"', *Electoral Studies* 5, 29–30.
Heath, A., R. Jowell and J. Curtice (1986) 'Understanding electoral change in Britain', *Parliamentary Affairs* 39, 150–64.
Himmelstrand, U., G. Ahrne, Leif Lundberg and Lars Lundberg (1981) *Beyond Welfare Capitalism* (London: Heinemann).
Huntington, S. (1974), 'Postindustrial politics: how benign will it be?', *Comparative Politics* 6, 163–92.
Inglehart, R. (1977) *The Silent Revolution: Changing Values and Political Styles among Western Publics* (Princeton: Princeton University Press).
Inglehart, R. (1981) 'Post-materialism in an environment of insecurity', *American Political Science Review* 75, 887–90.
Kavanagh, D. (1986) 'How we vote now', Review Article, *Electoral Studies* 5, 19–28. *Class Structure* (Cambridge: Cambridge University Press).
Keesing's Contemporary Archives: Record of World Events (Harlow: Longman Group).
Kirchheimer, O. (1966) 'The transformation of the Western European party systems' in *Political Parties and Political Development*, ed. by J. LaPalombara and M. Weiner (Princeton: Princeton University Press).
Kirchner, E.J., N. Hewlett and F. Sobirey (1984) *The Social Implications of Introducing New Technology in the Banking Sector* (Luxemburg: Office for Official Publications of the European Communities).
Korpi, W. (1978) *The Working Class in Welfare Capitalism* (London: Routledge and Kegan Paul).
LeDuc, L. (1985) 'Partisan change and dealignment in Canada, Great Britain and the United States', *Comparative Politics* 17, 379–98.
Lipset, S.M. and S. Rokkan (eds.) (1967) *Party Systems, and Voter Alignments* (New York: Free Press).
Pappi, F.U. and M. Tanvey (1982) 'The German electorate: old cleavages and new political conflicts' in *Party Government and Political Culture in Western Germany*, ed. by H. Döring and G. Smith (London: Macmillan).
Riker, W. (1962) *The Theory of Political Coalition* (New Haven: Yale University Press).
Roberts, K., F.G. Cook, S.C. Clark and E. Semeonoff (1977) *The Fragmentary Class Structure* (London: Heinemann).
Sainsbury, D. (1985) 'The electoral difficulties of the Scandinavian social democrats in the 1970s: the social bases of the parties and structural explanations of party decline', *Comparative Politics* 18, 1–19.
Smith, G. (1984) *Politics in Western Europe* (4th edn) (London: Heinemann).
Steel, B. and T. Tsurutani (1986) 'From consensus to dissensus: a note on postindustrial political parties', *Comparative Politics* 18, 235–48.
Steiner, J. (1986) *European Democracies* (New York: Longman).
Stephens, J.D. (1979) *The Transition from Capitalism to Socialism* (London: Macmillan).
Strom, K. and L. Svåsand (1985) 'Political parties in decline: dilemmas and strategies', paper presented at the Fifth International Conference of Europeanists, Washington, DC, October 18–20, 1985.

Index of political parties

General index